Old Testament Theology

Paul R. House

InterVarsity Press
Downers Grove, Illinois

InterVarsity Press
P.O. Box 1400, Downers Grove, IL 60515
World Wide Web: www.ivpress.com
E-mail: mail@ivpress.com

InterVarsity Press® is the book-publishing division of InterVarsity Christian Fellowship/USA®, a student movement active on campus at hundreds of universities, colleges and schools of nursing in the United States of America, and a member movement of the International Fellowship of Evangelical Students. For information about local and regional activities, write Public Relations Dept., InterVarsity Christian Fellowship/USA, 6400 Schroeder Rd., P.O. Box 7895, Madison, WI 53707-7895.

Cover photograph: Kathleen Campbell/Tony Stone Images

ISBN 0-8308-1523-6

Printed in the United States of America ♾

Library of Congress Cataloging-in-Publication Data

House, Paul R., 1958-
  Old Testament theology / Paul R. House.
    p. cm.
  Includes bibliographical references and index.
    ISBN 0-8308-1523-6 (cloth: alk. paper)
    1. Bible.   O.T.—Theology.   I. Title.
  BS1192.5.H68 1998
    230'.0411—dc21
                                                                                      98-8087
                                                                                         CIP

20	19	18	17	16	15	14	13	12	11	10	9	8	7	6	5	4	3	2	1
15	14	13	12	11	10	09	08	07	06	05	04	03	02	01	00	99	98		

Preface

Anyone picking up a volume on Old Testament theology has a right to know what sort of book he or she is holding. Therefore I offer the following explanations, some of which are intended to state what the volume consciously intends to do, while others are given so that the book will not be read with false expectations.

First, this book is written primarily for college and seminary students, though I hope that it will be of use to scholars and teachers of Old Testament theology. Given this audience, I have tried to produce an analytical study of the Old Testament and the theology that can be derived from its pages. Thus there is more description, even summary, of texts than would be the case if I could have assumed that the audience had been the academic guild. After years of teaching undergraduates and seminarians I have learned that one cannot take for granted a shared knowledge of the Bible's contents. The good news is that I have learned that both types of students are eager, intelligent learners. They simply need the chance to absorb the biblical text and its theological emphases. I have also spent a good bit of time with the text because I think theology should come from the Bible itself, not from the system I bring to the Scriptures.

Second, research for this volume, with a few exceptions, stops at the end of 1993. Scholarship in any biblical field continues unabated while one is writing and then editing for final publication a manuscript. Therefore I found it necessary to state where the scholarly material for the book ends. Sadly, certain works that would have informed and challenged my own were not available to me until it was too late in the writing process to use them. Several of these volumes are discussed in the appendix.

Third, I have emphasized the importance of historical context for theological analysis. To try to be consistent with this assertion I have included some discussion of authorship, date and setting issues. Of course such matters are usually reserved for Old Testament introduction, but I felt it necessary to suggest historical settings for the biblical books if I was going to argue for the value of historical study for Old Testament theology. Most of this type of material was cut from the final manuscript, but I trust that my views will be clear enough to be serviceable.

Fourth, I have utilized a canonical approach that attempts to demonstrate the Old Testament's coherence through discussions of intertextual connections. In this way I have tried to keep faith with the theological contribution of each section of the Old Testament, yet without losing a sense of the canon's wholeness. Some linkages with the New Testament have been made in hopes that future research might show how both parts of the Scriptures cohere.

Fifth, I have sought to incorporate the findings of scholars of various theological persuasions. I am an evangelical Old Testament scholar, but I see value in the works of writers with whom I disagree on a number of issues related to authorship, date and specific details of Old Testament theology. Thus I have utilized a wide variety of scholarly writings. I have attempted to make my own views plain. No doubt at times I have not been as irenic as I ought, yet my respect for those with whom I disagree should not be doubted. I am under no illusion that I am always correct, and I sincerely hope that I have been fair to the authors I have cited.

Sixth, this book has been written with the help of a number of persons. Each one made a significant contribution, and each one deserves more than the thanks I can give for their support.

Most of the manuscript was written while I was teaching at Taylor University in Upland, Indiana. During my ten years in the Department of Biblical Studies, Christian Education and Philosophy I had the privilege of working with as congenial and close-knit group of colleagues as I believe exists in academe. The encouragement of Herb Nygren, Bob Pitts, Win Corduan, Larry Helyer, Gary Newton, Bill Heth, Ted Dorman, Faye Chechowich, Doug Geivett, Ron Collymore, Mike Harbin, Jim Spiegel, Bob Lay and Ed Meadors was as kind as it was constant. Other Taylor friends such as Tom Jones, Carol Mott and Daryl Yost were helpful to me as I worked on the project. I am thankful that Dean Dwight Jessup, Associate Dean Steve Bedi and the Faculty Policies Committee made it possible for me to have a sabbatical and two-month-long study leaves during the research and writing process. Joanne Giger and Kari Manganello typed the long text, and Kari even completed the task after I had left Taylor University. June Corduan edited the footnotes and seemed to enjoy herself while doing so. These friends know that I owe them a debt I cannot pay.

The writing was completed after I moved to the Southern Baptist Theological Seminary in Louisville, Kentucky. I am grateful for the affirmation I have received while teaching classes and seminars on Old Testament theology. Friends such as Ben Mitchell and Greg Thornbury offered specific encouragement. Bev Tillman helped produce the manuscript. Heather Oldfield, a great editor, aided in the honing of the final copy, and Kyle McClellan helped proofread the page proofs. Each of these persons made the least exciting part of writing a book much more than bearable. My daughter, Molly, was excited about this project. Scott Hafemann, who is as close as family, was as enthusiastic as I was about the book. You do not make friends like Scott; God sends them to you.

I appreciate all the aid I received from Jim Hoover and the staff of InterVarsity Press. Jim was especially helpful in making the final draft of the book better than its predecessors. He also secured excellent comments from readers that honed weak portions of the text.

Finally, this volume is dedicated to my father, Roy D. House. He taught me to know God, to know what I believe and to stay connected to the Bible. For the past twenty-seven years he has supported my preaching, teaching and writing ministries. With the death of my mother in 1982, no one else survives from my beginnings, so no one person has been more steadfast in his encouragement and counsel.

For these and other kindnesses I am extremely grateful.

1

Old Testament Theology

History & Methodology

· · · · · · · · · · · · · · · · · · ·

WITHOUT QUESTION THE OLD TESTAMENT DESERVES CAREFUL STUDY AND accurate interpretation. After all, this body of sacred Scripture chronicles such diverse and important events as the creation of the world, the origins of Israel, the ongoing relationship between God and Israel and God and the nations, the destruction of world powers and the rise and fall of mighty rulers. It stresses vital themes like the sinfulness of the human race, the certain judgment of that sinfulness, God's willingness to save and forgive sinners and the ultimate renewal of all God has created. The Old Testament promises that a descendant of David will someday lead Israel and the rest of the nations into an era of salvation, peace and purity. Without forfeiting this sense of hope, the Old Testament refuses to live only in the future. Rather it boldly presents the pain and suffering inherent in human life. Incredibly, the Old Testament teaches that God is able to sustain the weary, heal the hurting, judge the wicked, empower the oppressed and do anything else necessary to be a loving Creator. Thus the Old Testament tells a vital story. It speaks of major issues to real people. It portrays a magnificent and all-sufficient God who constantly surprises his followers with a perfect blend of power and goodness. No wonder these texts have captivated readers through the centuries.

At the same time, any reader of the Old Testament understands there are certain difficulties in approaching this material. First, there are historical barriers. One does not have to be an expert in ancient history to read the

Old Testament intelligently, but some historical context is necessary. Such knowledge is particularly important if for no other reason than that the books of the Old Testament are not in chronological order. Unfortunately few readers are knowledgeable in even basic background matters. Second, there are literary barriers as well. Most readers can easily comprehend narrative books like Genesis, Joshua and Esther. Poetic works and prophecies, though, are more difficult to manage. Protoapocalyptic writings like Daniel 7—12 are even harder.

Third, theological barriers exist. How does one reconcile the love of God and the wrath of God? How does God effect salvation in the era before Jesus? How does the Old Testament relate to the New Testament? What does the Old Testament have to say to current readers? Is the Old Testament relevant for worship today? These and other theological questions cause readers to pause, reflect and seek difficult answers. Fourth, the barrier of general unfamiliarity with the Old Testament hampers many readers. If there ever was a time when the Old Testament's contents and emphases were well known, then that time has passed. Many if not most undergraduate and seminary students have never read the entire Old Testament. Fifth, there are scholarly barriers. Old Testament experts do not agree on how to approach the Old Testament's history, contents and theology. Again, if such agreement ever existed; it no longer does so. The diversity of opinion can be quite confusing.

Clearly, then, Old Testament students and teachers are left with a dilemma. On the one hand is the opportunity to analyze and enjoy enriching, inspired literature that makes up three-fourths of the Bible. Yet on the other hand lie the problems of understanding, interpreting and unifying the material being studied. Any attempt to discuss Old Testament theology must therefore strive to bridge these gaps while remaining faithful to the Old Testament's message.

Though it can only partially succeed, this book seeks to face this challenge. It will do so by first sketching the history of the academic discipline known as Old Testament theology. A complete survey of this subject is impossible, since that topic itself can only be treated in book-length form.[1] Next, a methodology for analyzing Old Testament theology will be suggested. Then a book-by-book analysis of the Old Testament's unfolding theology will be offered. The Hebrew order of books will be followed because of that sequence's clarity and ancient roots. Finally, some suggestions about how the Old and New Testaments are linked will be noted. One of the questions students ask most often is how the Bible holds together, so some response is necessary. Throughout the discussion, a single unifying theme will be used to keep the various topics together, and Israel's historical context will be duly recognized at strategic points. By the end of this work readers will grasp the basic details of Old Testament theology, will know how those details unfold in Israel's history and will understand how the details unify the Old Testament and the whole of Scripture. Even partial fulfillment of these goals may prove helpful to many students.

A Survey of the Study of Old Testament Theology

It is quite difficult to choose a starting point for a description of the study of Old Testament theology. One could begin with the Old Testament itself, for there are many places where a text is influenced by a previous passage or refers to what "is written" in another part of Scripture.[2] Certainly how the Old Testament's theology grows and develops within its own pages must be part of a serious analysis of the subject. Still, attempting to chart how ideas originated and grew to maturity has the potential to leave interpreters seeking the history of theological processes rather than the conclusions of theology proper. Such analyses are legitimate forms of scholarship, but pursuing them in detail does not fit this book's purpose.

One could also start the description with the New Testament's treatment of the Old Testament. This approach also has validity, because the New Testament writers make extensive use of the Old Testament. After all, it was their Bible! To start here, however, is to run ahead of one's self. The New Testament authors knew the Hebrew Scriptures thoroughly and expected their readers to possess a similar familiarity. Most current readers need to examine the whole of the Old Testament and digest its theological contents before undertaking a study of the relationship between the testaments. Some knowledge and expertise are needed to proceed further.

Another potential entry point is to examine how the early church fathers, medieval interpreters and leaders of the Reformation viewed Old Testament theology. Brevard Childs's clear, concise description of these approaches demonstrates the richness and variety that has always attended biblical theology.[3] John Calvin and Martin Luther are particularly notable examples of figures from church history who interpret the Old Testament as a theological document closely linked to the New Testament.[4] The problem with this approach is that none of these individuals ever produced a single volume specifically devoted to Old Testament theology. Their ideas must be gleaned from literally dozens of sermons, commentaries and other works. Though this is an enriching task, once again an entire work or series of works would be required to complete the assignment.

One other beginning place must be mentioned. Rabbinic scholars have been commenting on the Hebrew Scriptures since the Old Testament was completed. Thus some modern writers argue that the synagogue tradition is the place to start when assessing Old Testament theology.[5] This approach is certainly legitimate and enlightening, yet it has the same constraints as trying to gather the various comments from church history. There are precious few concise works in the rabbinic tradition on the theology of the whole of Hebrew Scriptures. Much valuable linguistic, historical and inspirational data can be gained from rabbinic studies. But Judaism and Christianity disagree over the value of a two-Testament Bible and over the nature and work of Jesus Christ. Therefore common concerns of both religions can and should be addressed, yet without glossing over real differences.[6] Only those who are open about their disagreements can truly relate their commonalities. Future dialogue between Judaism and Christianity can surely proceed only with complete candor.[7] Honesty and kindness should, of course, characterize such discussions.

Thus despite the importance of these four possibilities, another starting place is preferable. Over the past two centuries a number of works that deal specifically with Old Testament theology have been written. These efforts vary in style, substance and length, of course, yet they also share certain characteristics. First, the purpose of the book or books is to discuss *Old Testament* theology. Before this era the Old Testament's theological statements were systematized with New Testament statements to describe Christian doctrine. Sometimes the biblical texts were part of an extensive biblical-theological system, such as in Calvin's *Institutes*. At other times they were part of a philosophical and biblical system, as in Thomas Aquinas's *Summa Theologiae*. In Calvin and Aquinas the Old Testament contributes to a larger theological scheme but does not appear as a separate theological voice. The pioneers of Old Testament theology attempted to analyze and explain what the Old Testament itself taught. They then sought to incorporate those teachings into a larger biblical or systematic theology. Scholars who have followed them have continued this pattern.

Second, specifically Old Testament theologians pay close attention to historical data. That is, they strive to determine what each biblical author's statements meant in their ancient context. They view this commitment as fundamental to accurate application of texts for today, since they believe strongly that "a text cannot mean what it never meant."[8] This emphasis breaks with the allegorical method of interpretation, whose best-known practitioner was St. Augustine. Of course, Old Testament experts hardly agree on the background of every biblical book, paragraph or sentence. Indeed Old Testament theologians have been participants in these disputes. At times they have proposed such radical historical reconstructions that a passage's statements have largely been lost.[9] Still, the effort to establish historical context must continue. Authors of Scripture wrote in concrete historical settings to real people. The ongoing value of the Bible stems in part from its ability to continue to speak to real people in the midst of everyday life.

Third, though there are notable exceptions to this generalization,[10] most Old Testament theologians seek to relate the Old Testament's message to the church. Some do so by showing how the Old Testament leads naturally into the New Testament. Others state where the Old Testament no longer applies in Christian doctrine but maintain as valuable for the church as much of the Hebrew Scriptures as possible. Still others treat the Old Testament as a document that describes part of the history of Israel's religion. These writers tend to exclude elements of the Old Testament such as animal sacrifice and holy war from any segment of Christian doctrine, yet they assert that universal truths such as the Ten Commandments are still valid for the Christian faith. Regardless of their approach, these authors believe that the Old Testament has always been the church's Scripture and must therefore be incorporated into the church's doctrine and practice. How to do so is the challenge they face.

As has already been indicated, even these basic agreements cannot hide the differences that divide Old Testament theologians. They agree that the Old Testament deserves to be heard as an individual theological voice, yet they do not listen the same way, for the formats of their works are not all alike. They do not hear the same voice, and their conclusions differ. Though they think historical analysis is vital to their task they cannot always agree on a text's actual historical background or what that background tells them. Despite their belief that the Old Testament belongs in the Christian Bible they are not unanimous on what the Old Testament teaches the church.

Simply put, the history of this discipline is rather untidy. It does not reflect perfect agreement or unfailingly harmonious Christian unity. In other words, it is a bit like worldwide Christianity itself: imperfect, struggling, yet moving toward a worthy goal. The brief history sketched below will demonstrate the discipline's agreement, disagreement and potential. Four periods are highlighted, each of which moves Old Testament theology studies onto new and challenging ground. Not every stage improves the discipline, but each one shapes it.

Beginnings: From Gabler to Wellhausen (1787-1878)

The beginnings of the discipline of biblical theology are commonly traced to March 30, 1787, when Johann P. Gabler delivered an address entitled "An Oration on the Proper Distinction Between Biblical and Dogmatic Theology and the Specific Objectives of Each" at the University of Altdorf, Germany. Before this time biblical theology had been subsumed under systematic theology (dogmatics). Gabler declared that biblical theology differs from dogmatics in origin and purpose. He writes that there is truly a biblical theology, of historical origins, conveying what the holy writers felt about divine matters; on the other hand there is a dogmatic theology of didactic origin, teaching what each theologian philosophizes rationally about divine things, according to the measure of his ability or of the times, age, place, sect, school, and other similar factors.[11]

According to Gabler, the origin of biblical theology lies in the Bible itself, while dogmatic theology stems from individual theologians with prior philosophical and ecclesiological commitments. Biblical theology's purpose is to set forth what the biblical writers actually believed. Dogmatic theology's goal is to perpetuate a preestablished point of view. As a rationalist, Gabler particularly wanted to eliminate all precommitted approaches to theology.[12]

Gabler suggested a three-stage approach to examining biblical theology. First, interpreters must gather data on "each of the periods in the Old and New Testaments, each of the authors, and each of the manners of speaking which each used as a reflection of time and place."[13] Second, having gathered this historical material theologians must undertake "a careful and sober comparison of the various parts attributed to each testament."[14] Biblical authors' ideas should be compared until "it is clearly revealed wherein the separate authors agree in a friendly fashion, or differ among themselves."[15] Third, the agreements and disagreements must be duly noted and analyzed in order to determine what "universal notions" emerge.[16] Gabler offers no specific criteria for determining what constitutes universal notions except to cite "Mosaic law" as one example of what no longer applies to Christians.[17] He simply distinguished between that which applied to the authors' times alone and that which has more long-term value.[18]

Underlying Gabler's approach was a rationalistic view of the inspiration and reliability of Scripture. For him, only eliminating the temporary, human, nonuniversal elements of Scripture's teachings can produce ideas that are truly inspired and valuable for church dogmatics. Even an appeal to passages on the Bible's inspiration does not help determine the extent of the Bible's inspiration, since "these individual passages are very obscure and ambiguous."[19] Therefore those who "wish to deal with these things with reason and not with fear or bias" must not "press those meanings of the Apostles beyond their just limits, especially since only the effects of their inspiration and not their causes, are perceived by the senses."[20] Only through careful exegesis and adherence to what Christ has spoken on inspiration can it finally be determined "whether all the opinions of the Apostles, of every type and sort together, are truly divine, or rather whether some of them, which have no bearing on salvation, were left to their own ingenuity."[21] Only then can the Bible's pure doctrinal essence emerge ready for dogmatic collation.

Obviously Gabler's methodology has strengths and weaknesses. Its chief strength is the insistence on the value of biblical theology. Surely systematic theology benefits from careful, accurate analysis of what Scripture itself says. Church doctrine can become infinitely sterile if it decides what the text must say before it says it. Another strength is the call to historical analysis. Scripture speaks to all eras because it first spoke to a specific era. It embeds itself in human experience by having a concrete point of entry. Allegory agrees with the first part of that statement yet errs because it forgets the second part. History does matter in interpretation.

Gabler's scheme also has serious flaws. First, his insistence on rationalism and its refusal to discuss what lies beyond the human senses eliminates much of Scripture from serious theological consideration. None of the Bible's miracles, very little of authorial inspiration and only a limited number of the apostles' statements remain. One wonders how Gabler can speak of a Savior or of salvation[22] and stand by his convictions. After all, salvation hardly seems a sense-oriented category. Clearly Gabler had his own governing ideology, just as those he criticized did. Second, despite his program for incorporating biblical and systematic theology, Gabler's theories open the door for a negative separation of Old and New Testament theology. So little of the Old Testament would presumably have non-time-bound principles that it would be rendered fairly insignificant for biblical theology. This fact leads to the conclusion that Old Testament theology may be worthy of historical study but that it is not overwhelmingly pertinent to the church. As will be discussed later, many scholars adopted this approach after Gabler's time. Third, a cleavage is created between the academic study of theology and the church's teaching of doctrine. The idea emerges that "truth" is learned in the library and expounded in the lecture hall but the church teaches its same biases from one generation to the next. This division between church and academy exists in too many instances.

This analysis of Gabler's oration is longer than the treatment given most other authors because of its seminal nature and long-term impact. Without question Gabler helped chart the course for a new discipline. Also without question this course led in positive and negative directions that are still apparent in Old Testament studies.

Many of the strengths and weaknesses of Gabler's proposals appear in the first work devoted to Old Testament theology, which was published by Georg Lorenz Bauer in 1796. As the first to separate Old and New Testament theology, Bauer agreed with Gabler's conviction that biblical theology should precede and inform systematic theology. He also sought to apply a historical methodology in his research and attempted to discover the universal ideas found in the Old Testament, which the volume's very subtitle (*A Biblical Sketch of the Religious Opinions of the Ancient Hebrews*) indicates.[23]

Bauer's work is also unstintingly rationalistic. R. C. Dentan notes that to Bauer

> any idea of supernatural revelations of God through theophanies, miracles, or prophecies is to be rejected, since such things are contrary to sound reason and can easily be paralleled amongst other peoples. Thus Bauer regarded Moses as a brave, intelligent man, well instructed in the wisdom of Egypt, whose high purposes were strengthened when he saw a bush which had been kindled by lightning in a thunderstorm.[24]

He interprets the Old Testament miracles as myths and indeed authors another volume that discusses both Old and New Testament "myths."[25] This antisupernaturalist commitment affects Bauer's view of history. For Bauer, history is that which conforms to historical methods in use at the end of the eighteenth century.

Since he was the first author of a distinctly Old Testament theology, it is interesting to note Bauer's format for presenting his work. Though he determines to break away from dogmatics he still chooses to divide his work into the three traditionally dogmatic categories: theology, anthropology and christology.[26] Perhaps he hoped to be able to influence dogmatic theology more readily by adopting common categories. Whatever his reasons, Bauer's mode of presentation introduces an ongoing dilemma for Old Testament theologians: How does one incorporate all the biblical data into workable categories that fit the author's purpose in writing? In Bauer's case these categories are appropriate, because he wants to collect universal ideas that apply to Christians regardless of when they live.

Given the long-term impact of Gabler's and Bauer's ideas and the fact that the discipline takes a different turn after 1800, it may be helpful to summarize their contribution to Old Testament theology.

1. Gabler and Bauer basically create the discipline of Old Testament theology. They argue that the Old and New Testaments deserve to be heard on their own terms before their ideas are incorporated into dogmatic theology.

2. Both Gabler and Bauer believe Old Testament theology must have a strongly historical component. Unfortunately this historical component is based on a rationalism that leaves little room for the supernatural. It also questions a great deal of material that is suspect only to keen rationalists.

3. Gabler and Bauer argue that the Old Testament teaches some universal truths applicable to Christians in all eras. To find these concepts, however, both men eliminate much of the Old Testament as being due to the authors' "own ingenuity."[27] This approach questions the general value of the Old Testament and leaves it with little to say that the New Testament does not repeat.

4. Gabler never writes an Old Testament theology, but in his work Bauer divides the biblical material into the study of God, humankind and Christ. These are certainly topics of concern for any theologian, but they fit the whole of the Old Testament only imperfectly, as Bauer himself no doubt knew.

Even though these notions are two centuries old, they continue to be debated to this day.

Following Gabler's and Bauer's seminal efforts, Old Testament theologians began to respond to their findings. In his *Die biblische Theologie,* published in 1813, G. P. C. Kaiser pushed Gabler's and Bauer's rationalistic theories still further. Given its similarities with other ancient religions and its tendencies towards mythical writing, Kaiser argued, Old Testament religion is really just one religion among many. As Dentan concludes,

> With all their rationalism, previous writers had at least paid lip service to the doctrine of the finality of the Christian religion. With Kaiser the pretense disappears. For him, the idea of particular revelation seemed irrational and impious. The Bible was chiefly of interest as giving concrete instances of the application of universal laws.[28]

Given his position on the relative value of the Old Testament, it is understandable that Kaiser became the first scholar to view the study of Old Testament theology as essentially a history of religion rather than a history of God's revelation. This emphasis on Old Testament theology as a strictly historical exploration was to become the dominant methodology in biblical studies later in the century.

Wilhelm M. L. de Wette attempted to chart a path between traditional orthodoxy and committed rationalism in his *Lehrbuch der christlichen Dogmatik* (1813; third edition 1831). Though he shared the rationalists' conclusion about the Bible's depictions of miracles, prophecies and so forth, he thought the rationalists' dismissal of such accounts wrongheaded. Rather, de Wette argues, myths are poetic means of expressing feelings about God and all sacred things.29 Many ancient peoples thought and wrote in such terms, so it is not unusual that Israel did so as well. Thus Old Testament theologians must seek to understand the feelings and universal truths behind the myths, not simply discard them as fantasies penned by irrational or primitive people. Obviously readers who take the miracle stories literally also miss the point, since they, too, focus on the reliability of the account rather than the account's deeper expression of religious feeling.

Clearly de Wette takes a strongly philosophical approach to theology. Tutored by his friend J. F. Fries, who was strongly influenced by Immanuel Kant,[30] de Wette believed that God inspires human reason and religious feeling. It is this divine inspiration that balances reason and feeling and gives both meaning.[31] By making this assertion de Wette attempts to avoid Kant's separation of the two impulses. He also tries to give meaning to historical analysis. Historical research does not exist solely for its own sake but rather to help reproduce the feelings and ideas of Old Testament faith.[32] When it reveals these feelings and ideas it serves the church, which needs to feel and think in a similar manner.

De Wette's approach provided a bridge between the past and immediate future of Old Testament theology. Like his predecessors, he employed a historical methodology based on rationalistic principles. These principles helped him decide what is myth and what is history. He also searched for the universal in the Old Testament, which he thought begins with the notion of a holy God who rules the earth.[33] Further, he believed parts of the Old Testament are simply human notions not inspired by God's holy will.[34] Such impure ideas must be separated from those of universal value. Thus he shares the strengths and weaknesses of Gabler and Bauer.

However, de Wette leads the way for future researchers. His emphasis on myth as meaningful religious writing instead of useless fabrication inspired similar analyses. His concept of inspiration as a middle ground between reason and feeling gave many scholars who accepted rationalistic views of history a way to maintain contact with biblical piety. Finally, de Wette's emphasis on the development within Old Testament religion encouraged movement toward studies of the text as a history of religion, though de Wette himself had no such inclination.

Wilhelm Vatke's *Biblische Theologie, wissenschaftlich dargestellt, Die Religion des Alten Testaments* (1835) also nudged Old Testament theology away from pure rationalism through philosophical means. This time it was Vatke's teacher and colleague Georg W. Hegel, not Kant, who provided the stimulus.[35] Vatke agreed with Hegel's belief that history is a series of developments from lower to higher stages of thought and action. These stages occur when an action or thought (thesis) produces a reaction (antithesis), which afterward finds a higher stage of thought or action (synthesis). History's continual creation of syntheses creates progress in whatever area of life that produces them. Hegel's theory applied to Old Testament theology means that Old Testament religion grew progressively more complex as it evolved. This complexity may be good or bad, depending on one's viewpoint. Since Hegel found meaning in these historical collisions, Vatke rejected the rationalist's division between the purely historical and the Old Testament's universally valid principles.[36] Rather the two work together to advance Old Testament religion.

Despite this affirmation of history, however, Vatke made some harsh observations about the Old Testament's historical statements. He asserted that the first four books of the Pentateuch were not products of Moses' time but were rather documents produced by a nation whose religion had evolved to a quite involved stage.[37] Further, Deuteronomy was written during Josiah's reformation of about 622-621 B.C., not by Moses, a position already forwarded by de Wette.[38] Finally, the prophets must therefore be seen as the founders of specifically monotheistic Israelite religion.[39] As R. K. Harrison notes, according to Vatke, over the centuries "the religion of the Hebrews evolved from comparatively primitive and unhistorical beginnings into the monotheistic faith that characterized the religion of Judaism."[40] In Israel's history, then, the final synthesis was the sort of religion found in Ezra's time (c. 450-425 B.C.) and beyond. Virtually all historical references that predate the prophets are later writings that project then-current ideas into the past.

Vatke's opinions took historical methodology in Old Testament theology to a new stage. Rationalists had simply declared certain parts of the Old Testament unhistorical. De Wette argued that even if these accounts are unhistorical they still express religious feeling through myth, which was a common ancient form of writing. Vatke believed that many accounts were simply not from the time period or authors stated in the text and that the events Scripture depicts did not occur as the Bible portrays them. Because he was committed to a specific interpretation of Hegel's theory of history, Vatke found it impossible to accept that Israelite religion began with a monotheistic Mosaic covenant. It must have developed from nature religion to monotheism in an evolutionary manner. Once Old Testament history was reconfigured according to these principles, theologians could then interpret the Old Testament's theology against this "correct" historical background. Very few readers utilized Vatke's viewpoints until years after *Biblische Theologie* was published. One who did, however, was Julius Wellhausen, and that one disciple made Vatke's ideas more prominent than Vatke ever did himself.

By the time Vatke's work was published and read, a perceptible dogmaticism had settled into the liberal ranks of Old Testament theology. First, the Old Testament's historical statements were clearly suspect. Stated authorship of books, accounts of the miraculous and description of historical events were all challenged and often denied. Second, the Old Testament was at worst a slight contributor to legitimate biblical theology and was at best a legitimate source of universal ideas and inspired religious feelings. Third, it was unlikely, then, that the unity of the Bible could be maintained. Evolutionary views of history made it much more likely that the Old Testament was a lower religious state that had to be completed for the New Testament to emerge. Challenges to these assertions were soon to come, but they were not to have the lasting force their authors desired.

Conservative responses to the liberal tendencies in the new discipline started in 1829, when E. W. Hengstenberg began to publish his *Christologie des Alten Testaments,* which was completed in 1835 as a four-volume work.[41] Before this time conservatives resisted Old Testament theology, most likely because of its adherents' opposition to traditional views of the Bible's unity and historicity. They also rejected any differences between biblical and systematic theology.

In time conservatives decided that Old Testament theology offered them a means of expounding sound doctrine, disputing views with which they disagreed and explaining ancient truth effectively to contemporary audiences.[42]

Hengstenberg's christological studies were not a complete Old Testament theology. Nonetheless, in this work he struck at some of the cardinal opinions of his colleague Vatke and other nontraditional scholars. In the first place, by choosing to expound the Old Testament's messianic prophecies he disagreed with the notion that the Old Testament's potential contribution to dogmatic theology was limited in any significant way. Further, if the messianic prophecies are so prevalent and such a part of the Old Testament's overall structure and method, then the Hebrew Scriptures are distinctly valuable in biblical theology. Too, if the Old and New Testaments both give extensive witness to Jesus Christ, then surely there are grounds for claiming that there is great unity in Scripture.

Second, in his subsequent *History of the Kingdom of God in the Old Testament* (ET 1871) Hengstenberg critiqued the historical conclusions reached by liberal historians. His chief means of attack was to defend Mosaic authorship of the Pentateuch.[43] He correctly sensed that this topic would be a determining factor in the success or failure of either his views or his opponents'. If Mosaic authorship could be sustained, then Vatke's historical reconstruction and the theology built upon it could not be accepted.

Hengstenberg's conclusions have more than apologetic implications. His insistence on the importance of the Old Testament's messianic prophecies sets up a close relationship between the Testaments based on the Old Testament's promises and their fulfillment in the New Testament. His adherence to Mosaic authorship maintains a traditional attitude toward the historical claims of Scripture and of biblical inspiration and divine revelation. Emphasizing the accuracy of the Old Testament's historical descriptions allows his promise-fulfillment scheme to unfold gradually over time, yet in a linear, not evolutionary, manner. Because of his role as first respondent to the new ideas in theological studies, Hengstenberg has influenced heavily the course of conservative Old Testament scholarship.[44]

Despite his defense of traditional attitudes toward the Old Testament's historicity, Hengstenberg did not explain clearly the relationship between historical analysis and theological reflection. This task was assumed by a group of scholars who stressed salvation history as a way to connect these two vital aspects of Old Testament theology. In a posthumous volume published in 1848,[45] H. A. C. Havernick, a student of Hengstenberg, insisted that the ideas of Scripture could not be separated from the history in which they were born and declared. He also claimed that history slowly unfolded until it reached its ultimate climax in Jesus Christ.[46] Thus history serves as God's vehicle for salvation through the centuries.

Havernick's vision of history and salvation was shared by J. C. K. von Hofmann. In his *Weissagung und Erfüllung* (1841-1844),[47] where the phrase "salvation history" first appeared,[48] Hofmann stated that the Old Testament records God's efforts to redeem the human race. Within the text are stages of this process. Each succeeding stage describes God's redemptive methods in that era. Finally, God's people find salvation in Jesus Christ, God's perfect means of redemption. Clearly, then, history and theology are not the same thing, but they are inseparable in the sense that one cannot exist without the other.

The most famous and popular proponent of salvation history in this era was Gustav Oehler, whose *Prolegomena zur Theologie des Alten Testaments* (1845) and *Theologie des Alten Testaments* (1873-1874) were highly influential. Like Havernick and Hofmann, Oehler believed that history and theology must remain carefully linked. In fact, he defines Old Testament theology in the following manner:

> As a historical science, it rests on the results of grammatico-historical exegesis, the business of which is to reproduce the contents of the biblical books according to the rules of the language, with due regard to the historical circumstances under which the books originated, and the individual circumstances of the sacred authors.[49]

Besides carefully determining a text's historical-grammatical background, interpreters must also chart the "process of development" in Old Testament faith. How does one discover this process? Oehler says,

> Since every such process can be comprehended only from its climax, biblical theology will have to understand the Old Testament in the light of the completed revelation of God in Christ for which it formed the preparation—will have to show how God's saving purpose, fulfilled in Christ, moved through the preliminary stages of this history of revelation.[50]

When these two emphases are combined, exactly how and under what circumstances the Old Testament writers produced their messages will become clear, as will the overall progress of the history of salvation. Again history operates as a vehicle of salvation. Salvation unfolds in history.

Scripture is God's revelation of how this process manifests itself in the lives of God's people.

Oehler used an interesting format to discuss his views. He presents the biblical material in the Hebrew Bible's three-part scheme of Law, Prophets and Writings, though he called this third section Wisdom.[51] In each of the first two sections he offers a historical summary of Mosaism and prophetism and then follows that analysis with systematic comments. His historical findings are conservative, in contrast to those of de Wette and Vatke. The third section has only systematic conclusions. This manner of presentation allows Oehler to demonstrate how the biblical books follow a sequential historical and thematic path. It also gives Oehler the opportunity to show how historical interpretation of Scripture can lead to doctrinal statements. The major problem with this format is that the Writings are not fully incorporated into the salvation-history scheme.

These early conservative Old Testament theologians shared specific strengths and weaknesses. The first strength is their commitment to the inspiration of Scripture. To them, the Bible is God's Word in its entirety. Not all of them believed the Scriptures inerrant, but each rejected the rationalists' claims that the Bible is basically a human composition with few truly divine elements. A second strength is their insistence on the Old Testament's historical accuracy. Part of this emphasis grows out of their position on inspiration, just as the opinions of Gabler, Bauer, de Wette and others grow out of their ideas on the matter. Still, they present serious historical and literary evidence that defends the Mosaic authorship of the Pentateuch and the historical statements in the Old Testament.

A third strength is their belief in the possibility of miracles and supernatural occurrences on earth. This issue is often the dividing point between the liberal and conservative camps. Once scholars conclude that miracles may occur within human history, many of their views on other details of biblical history take their course. The fourth strength is their attempt to link history and theology. By struggling with how theology becomes real in human life they broke away from cold, sterile, unnecessarily transcendent views of how Scripture relates to people. Emphasizing salvation history also helped them relate the Old Testament to the New Testament, thus offering some possibilities for understanding biblical unity. Two testaments still exist, yet not as strangers.

Certain weaknesses also emerge in their writings. First, they overemphasize their views of Hegelian thought as much as their rivals. They correctly see value in how history occurs over time, but they stress historical development to the point of leaving the Old Testament with few distinctly important ideas of its own. The Old Testament's promises of a coming messiah are of great importance. But what of the Old Testament's unique contributions to issues not specifically connected to redemption? For instance, what about the Hebrew Scriptures' teachings on holy living, wisdom or social justice? These are vital matters the New Testament does not cover as extensively as does the Old Testament.

Second, they do not always present their material in an accessible fashion. They do write a great deal about methodology, especially a methodology of uniting historical research and theological reflection. Still, they are unable to find a way to explain the whole range of theological ideas in the Old Testament. Oehler's *Theologie des Alten Testaments* comes closest to what is needed, but the following of the Hebrew order of books and historical exposition breaks down in the section on Wisdom. This format may also try to do too much. In a way this weakness of format could be claimed against every Old Testament theology, given the vastness of the task, but it is still important to find effective ways to put methodology into readable form.

By the time Oehler's work became the first work of Old Testament theology to be translated into English (1875), a stalemate obviously existed. Liberal and conservative scholars agreed that there should be a strong historical component in Old Testament theology. Given their differing views on inspiration, the supernatural and historical theory, though, they seldom concurred on historical details. They agreed that biblical theology should inform systematic theology, but one side sought universal truths, common religious feelings and how the Old Testament served as a stage on the way to the New Testament, while the other made fewer distinctions between the Testaments and focused on salvation history. One group shied away from church authority and leaned toward academic historicism, while the other made close links with the church and struggled to use an appropriate philosophy of history. This stalemate was soon broken in a way that neither side would probably have suspected.

The Dominance of Historicism: 1878-1920

It is rare indeed for a single volume to change and set the course of all studies related to Scripture. In fact, such a feat may no longer be possible. It is not an exaggeration to say, however, that Julius Wellhausen's *Prolegomena to the History of Ancient Israel* (1878; ET 1885) did just that.[52] No segment of biblical studies, not even those related to the New Testament, was unaffected by its influence. In many ways this volume dictates a large portion of the agenda in Old Testament research to this day.

Wellhausen's genius lay in his ability to synthesize the findings of earlier scholars into a readable and unified whole. Dentan describes Wellhausen's style as "lucid, persuasive, and gently humorous,"[53] rare qualities in academic writing. Wellhausen accepted de Wette's conclusion that Deuteronomy was written in the seventh century B.C. instead of by Moses. He agreed with Vatke's assertion that Israel's religion evolved over time, which meant to him that complex priestly material like that found in Leviticus was written at the end of Israel's history and that the Pentateuch was completed after the Prophets. Likewise, he agreed with Karl F. Graf, Abraham Kuenen and other scholars who thought the first four books of the Pentateuch consisted of written documents, or sources, that used different names for God and proclaimed differing theological views. He agreed that Vatke's views about Hegelian historical theories and de Wette's conceptions about myth were correct. To these notions Wellhausen added his own thoughts on the prophets as the founders of ethical monotheistic faith and on the origins of Israel's religion in nature cults.

The synthesis of all these beliefs began with the assumption that Israelite religion evolved from roots in nature religion similar to other ancient Canaanite religions, to ethical monotheism in the prophets and the early stages of the Pentateuch, to a stronger monotheism and insistence on a central sanctuary in Deuteronomy and books it influences (Joshua, Judges, 1-2 Samuel, 1-2 Kings, Jeremiah), to the detailed, priest-guided religion like that found in Ezra, Leviticus, Ezekiel and 1-2 Chronicles. Unlike Vatke, who saw this evolution as positive, Wellhausen mourned the loss of the earlier, simpler religion. Like Vatke, Wellhausen considered much of the stated historical contexts in the Old Testament to be reflections of later generations transposed upon the past. To Wellhausen, Moses was at best a shadowy historical figure, and the patriarchs could not have been as advanced culturally as the Old Testament indicates. Prophetic monotheism eventually led to the Law, not the reverse as the Old Testament says.

Simply put, Wellhausen's views swept the theological field. By the end of the century his ideas were opposed by only a handful of scholars in Germany. After the publication of *Prolegomena* in English (1885) Wellhausen's theories quickly came to dominate Old Testament studies in England. Even in the United States, which accepted European theology more slowly, Wellhausen made a large impact by 1900. As early as 1879 C. H. Toy was dismissed from his teaching position at the Southern Baptist Theological Seminary in Louisville, Kentucky, for espousing views similar to Wellhausen's.[54]

What this development meant for Old Testament theology was that a strictly historical approach to the subject dominated the scene. With sequential coherence gone in the Old Testament text itself, scholars began to reconstruct "coherent" histories of Israelite religion of their own. The Old Testament's ideas were used to get at the "real" events and progressions of the history of an ancient religion. Concerning this era Walther Eichrodt writes that there was no longer any unity to be found in the OT, only a collection of detached periods which were simply the reflections of as many different religions. In such circumstances it was only a logical development that the designation "OT Theology," which had formerly had quite a different connotation, should frequently be abandoned and the title "the History of Israelite Religion" substituted for it. Even where scholars still clung to the old name, they were neither desirous nor capable of offering anything more than an exposition of the historical process.[55]

Neither the old liberal nor the old conservative camp triumphed. The historical studies both groups emphasized overran the various Old Testament theological principles they deemed valuable. Little if any of the unity of the Testaments remained—not the universal ideas of the rationalists, not the salvation history of the conservatives. Even de Wette and Vatke, whose historical ideas Wellhausen used extensively, could hardly have been pleased at the fate of their theological reflections.

As Eichrodt suggests, several books that were actually studies of the history of Israel's religion appeared under the title "Old Testament theology" during this era. Though A. B. Davidson's *The Theology of the Old Testament* (1904)[56] is an exception, Bernhard Stade's *Biblische Theologie des Alten Testaments* (1905)[57] and E. Kautzsch's *Biblische Theologie des Alten Testaments* (1911),[58] to name a few, are examples of such works. Despite retaining this title, however, they actually had more in common with those who chose to use "history of religion" in their titles than with the founders and early developers of Old Testament theology.

Despite the clear dominance of historicism, some writers attempted to continue the tradition of theological reflection grounded in historical analysis. W. L. Alexander did so without grappling with Wellhausen and his followers' ideas.[59] Hermann Schultz and August Dillmann, however, dialogued with the prevailing theories. Schultz's *Alttestamentliche Theologie* went through five editions between 1869 and 1896, which means the author worked before and during the period of historicism's dominance. Though he adopted many of Wellhausen's conclusions about the composition of the Old Testament, Schultz maintained contact with older traditions. He asserts that the Old Testament is the result of God's revelation and claims that the one who studies it must be "able to bring himself into a living sympathy with the spirit of that religion."[60]

Further, he believed that there is unity between the Old and New Testament and traced this coherence by focusing on the single theme of "the kingdom of God on earth."[61] He argues that "no one can expound New Testament theology without a thorough knowledge of Old Testament theology. But it is no less true that one who does not thoroughly understand

New Testament theology cannot have anything but a one-sided view of Old Testament theology."[62] The results of these biblical studies are the data that should inform an accurate biblical theology.[63]

To demonstrate the validity of this claim, Schultz divides his work into two parts that describe the evolution of Israel's religious worldview and a concluding section that deals with systematic topics such as God and the world, the human race and sin.[64] His emphasis on a single theme that unifies Israel's history and theology parallels the earlier conservatives' stressing salvation history as a unifying factor in Scripture. It also set a precedent for the future. Just as many historicists followed Kaiser's suggestions about Old Testament theology from a history of religions viewpoint, later Old Testament theologians chose to adopt a single-theme approach to unifying the Hebrew Scripture.

Dillmann agreed with Schultz's conclusions about the revelational nature of the Old Testament, the need for theologians to have a sympathetic approach to their task and the value of Old Testament theology for forming systematic theology.[65] He disagreed, though, with Schultz's acceptance of Wellhausen's theories of the evolution of Israel's religion. Dillmann did not believe that the Israelites developed involved religious practices and writings about these practices at the end of Old Testament times. Such views did not, in his opinion, match what occurred in the religions of Israel's neighbors, who shared Israel's general cultural environment.[66] If Dillmann's conclusions about the Pentateuchal materials are correct, then most of Wellhausen's reconstruction of Israel's history dissolves, and with it many of the theological theories carefully constructed on it fall as well. A few conservative biblical scholars attempted to prove the fallacies of Wellhausen's hypotheses, most notably J. Orr,[67] and German scholars began to alter his findings.[68] Still, variations of Wellhausen's ideas were forwarded, not repudiations of it, and arguments such as Dillmann's were not accepted by many academicians.

The Reemergence of Old Testament Theology: 1920-1960

By 1920 the atmosphere was much more congenial to Old Testament theology. A number of factors contributed to this reversal. World War I demonstrated the moral depths to which human beings can sink. Hundreds of thousands of soldiers died, and virtually no nation on earth was unaffected by the carnage created by new weapons of destruction and governments that ordered their use. Many individuals realized that it was not enough to study Scripture historically, for the world cried out for meaning that created obedience to a Governor holier than any earthly governor. Pastors wrestled with how to make ancient texts relevant to congregations suffering in the modern world.

The most famous pastor to struggle with these issues was Karl Barth, a Swiss minister serving in Safenwil. Barth was convinced that theology must once again stress God's revelation in Scripture and turn away from focusing on historicism and notions such as the inevitable progress of the human race. His commentary on Romans, first published in 1919 and subsequently thoroughly revised, helped turn the theological world back to Scripture and the church.[69] To write the sort of theology he envisioned, Barth looked not to authors from the previous several decades for models but to Calvin, Luther and Søren Kierkegaard. He also applied his own approach to Hegel's historical and philosophical theories, focusing on a dialectical approach to theology in his monumental *Church Dogmatics*.[70] Barth did not return to Calvin's and Luther's views on Pentateuchal authorship, nor did he champion other conservative viewpoints. But he did help move all theological studies back toward Scripture, which was no small achievement in his era.

Besides these cultural and ecclesiastical influences, Dentan notes two other major factors that also led Old Testament theology to regained prominence. First was the general loss of faith in evolutionary naturalism, which resulted in a steadily increasing dissatisfaction with the *religions-geschichtlich* attempt to explain Israel's religion as but one example of a universal law by which humans inevitably progress from animism to ethical monotheism. Second, there was a reaction against the mid-nineteenth-century conviction that historical truth can be attained by pure scientific objectivity or indeed that such objectivity is itself attainable. Stated in positive terms, there was a growing feeling that the inner truth of history, in contrast to mere external facts, is accessible only to those who in some way "feel themselves into" the situation that they are attempting to describe so that they in some sense become participants, not mere observers.[71]

In other words, the claims of the earlier conservatives and Dillmann that the evolutionary scheme was flawed became more widespread, though these individuals did not necessarily impact this change at this particular point in time. Too, de Wette's ideas about the truth behind not-necessarily-historically-accurate events gained acceptance. No concerted effort was made to return to prerationalist views of history, then, but the biblical texts were no longer deemed "false" just because they were "not accurate."

The first Old Testament theology written in this period reflects the struggle to modify existing notions of history and thus balance history and theology. Like several of its predecessors, Eduard König's *Theologie des Alten Testaments* (1922) endeavored to show how historical analysis informs theological reflection.[72] Despite having distinct reservations about this volume, Eichrodt notes that König's effort, coming when it did, "was a real act of courage which deserves to be recorded."[73] König's insistence on the revelatory nature of Scripture and value of Old Testament theology for dogmatic theology was not new. It had just been some time since these ideas had been given a fair hearing.

Though König's work opened the door for a renewed theological emphasis in Old Testament theology, the history-versus-theology debate continued for some time. Otto Eissfeldt argued in 1926 that historical and theological analyses of Scripture must be kept separate. After all, he says, "the historical or the scientific study of religion, requires that the religion of the Old Testament be investigated by the same means with which historical scholarship otherwise works," while the theological "discloses itself only to faith, and that is something different from empathetic reliving; it consists, namely, in being overwhelmed and humbled in inner obedience to that which has taken hold of oneself."[74]

Eichrodt disagreed with Eissfeldt's clean break between history and theology in an article that appeared in 1929. He admitted that historical analysis cannot "command assent" to the Bible claims.[75] But he also forcefully states that

> it is an impermissible restriction of the concept "historical" to relate it, as if self-evidently, only to observation of the growth process, to the genetic method; rather, "historical" may be understood as the opposite of anything normative. Thus, the systematic consideration is to be comprehended completely within the historical.[76]

So, to be truly historical, interpreters must be willing to describe theological claims made within history and their initial backgrounds. Further, Eichrodt denies that theological studies are less objective than historical analyses. Even in historical research there is subjectivity in the selection of the object of study, the historian's principles for choosing what data to include and the work's purposes and guiding conceptions.[77] It is untenable, then, to separate history and theology on qualitative grounds. Neither is inherently objective or subjective. Only historians and theologians make them so. Finally, given these theoretical observations, Eichrodt called for cooperation between historians and theologians. He asks that history help "lay a cross section through the developed whole in order to demonstrate the inner structure of a religion in the mutual relation of its various contents."[78] This "inner structure" will then aid in uniting the Old Testament's various theological contents. Even if history makes this data available, history cannot make the data normative, for each person must make that theological decision themselves.[79]

It soon became apparent that König's and Eichrodt's vision for Old Testament theology would supersede Eissfeldt's. Eichrodt himself was the major factor in this development. Beginning with the first volume in 1933 and continuing through the next two volumes published in 1935 and 1939, Eichrodt's landmark *Theologie des Alten Testaments* once again marked Old Testament theology as more than a historically based discipline.[80] Without question this project is one of the most important works of its kind in the twentieth century.

Building on the methodological conclusions in his earlier essay, Eichrodt says that the "cross section" that demonstrated "the inner structure of a religion in the mutual relation of its various contents"[81] could be found. One concept unites the various aspects of Old Testament theology, and that concept is God's covenant with Israel. Though many scholars disagree, Eichrodt claims that certainly from post-Mosaic times Israel did not conceive of its relationship with God outside of covenant terminology.[82] God's dealings with Israel, the world as a whole and the human race all flow from a covenantal perspective. Eichrodt finds that this emphasis on covenant fits the historical and theological details described in the Old Testament. The covenant model also offers a bridge between the Testaments, a linkage "which must be taken into account if the OT is to be understood."[83] When taken into account, interpreters will realize that what "binds together indivisibly the two realms of the Old and New Testaments—different in externals though they may be—is the irruption of the Kingship of God into this world and its establishment here."[84] This irruption occurs in God's self-revelation in the covenant with Israel in the Old Testament and then is completed through God's new covenantal self-revelation in Christ in the New Testament.[85]

Eichrodt chose not to present a reconstruction of Israel's history before making his theological statements, as Oehler and Schultz had done. Instead he presents his material within the broad systematic categories of God and covenant people (volume one), God and the world (volume two) and God and humankind (volume three). Within each section he offers comments on how Israel's institutions, leaders and worship practices operate inside the covenant framework. No attempt is made to follow the canonical order of the Old Testament books. Rather Eichrodt cuts across the grain of the Old Testament, matching his covenant emphasis as he goes, linking the contents to his systematic categories.

There is no question that Eichrodt was the major force in changing the direction of Old Testament theology. Like Wellhausen, he was able to synthesize his own ideas with those of earlier writers in a powerful way. His choice of a single theme mirrored Schultz's emphasis on the kingdom of God and linked him at least thematically with the best of the salvation history proponents. By selecting covenant as his own focal point, Eichrodt was able to unite the Old Testament using a distinctly biblical notion. Though he did not break with Wellhausen's theories of Pentateuchal authorship, Eichrodt took biblical accounts seriously and accepted the Bible's revelatory nature.

Thus he was able to return Old Testament theology to where Schultz left it.

Other scholars soon followed Eichrodt's lead. Ludwig Köhler's *Old Testament Theology* (1935; ET 1957) also chooses a single theme, which is God the ruling Lord. Köhler declares, "God is the ruling Lord: that is the one fundamental statement in the theology of the Old Testament. . . . Everything else derives from it. Everything else leans upon it. Everything else can be understood with reference to it and only to it."[86] Like Eichrodt, Köhler divides his study into basic systematic categories, such as God, humanity and judgment and salvation, and he subdivides these sections according to key theological concepts. Köhler's historical conclusions do not vary from the now-critical norm of placing much of the Pentateuch's composition after the time of the writing prophets.[87]

World War II interrupted the flow of work on Old Testament theology. Just as Eichrodt's third volume and the Roman Catholic scholar Paul Heinisch's *Theologie des Alten Testaments* (1940; ET 1950)[88] appeared the war began. Toward the end of the war, British and American authors ventured to publish some works related to Old Testament theology, though not complete treatments of the subject. Included among these efforts were H. H. Rowley's *The Relevance of the Bible* (1942),[89] N. H. Snaith's *The Distinctive Ideas of the Old Testament* (1944),[90] which stressed Israel's unique theological witness in the ancient world, and G. E. Wright's *The Challenge of Israel's Faith* (1944).[91] These works foreshadowed similar efforts in the future. Each author claimed that the Old Testament has relevance for modern believers, that the Old Testament was not just another ancient religion without revelatory elements and that the Old Testament contributes heavily to any legitimate biblical theology.

After the war a number of Old Testament theologies were published along lines begun by Eichrodt. More monographs like those described in the preceding paragraph were also produced, which gave birth to what is known as the biblical theology movement. T. C. Vriezen's 1949 work *An Outline of Old Testament Theology* echoed Eichrodt's and Köhler's methodologies. Vriezen's single theme is God's communion with the human race, which he believes is the underlying factor in God's self-revelation, the making of the covenants, the creation of a covenant community and the worship of God.[92] In his tracing of this theme, though, Vriezen displays a freshness in his approach.

First, he begins the volume with a major (c. 150 pages) discussion of the Old Testament's relationship to the church. Certainly most if not all Old Testament theologians note the necessity of understanding the Hebrew Scriptures for grasping the New Testament, but few take the subject as seriously as does Vriezen. Second, he keeps the continuing relationship between God and the human race constantly before readers, which illustrates how the Old Testament relates to the church. Third, Vriezen spends the last one-third of his book discussing the "community of God." This emphasis illustrates how having a relationship with God affects ethics. Clearly Vriezen presents a theology that he believes can and must impact the church.

Most of his historical conclusions were identical to those of the critical school, however, which raises a fundamental question of the Old Testament's authority and truthfulness. Vriezen answers this question by stating that

the Bible does not derive its authority from its historical correctness or infallibility, but from its theological truth, from the reliability, the trueness to life of its message. The authority of the Bible rests on the spiritual force of the Biblical testimony on God and man, on sin and grace, life and death, world and re-creation.[93]

Though different in many respects, this explanation sounds a great deal like the old search for universal truths and significant religious feelings or needs. If Old Testament and biblical theology are to be historically based, it is inadequate to retreat to these old categories when faced with convictions about a text's historical setting that seemingly contradict what the text says about itself. If history matters for theology, then accuracy matters. Vriezen was not alone in this struggle to determine the Bible's authority in light of historical-critical conclusions. This issue emerged again and again, as will be seen.

Two other significant works appeared in 1949, both of which fit the then-current concerns of single themes and the Old Testament's relevance for the church. Otto Baab's *The Theology of the Old Testament* was the first complete Old Testament theology published in English since Davidson's 1904 volume.[94] This work was thoroughly historical-critical in its historical conclusions, yet it also attempted to find ways to link Israel's religious consciousness with the modern world. Otto Procksch's *Theologie des Alten Testaments* appeared two years after the author's death, though Procksch "himself prepared the manuscript for the press and its appearance was delayed only by the advent of the War."[95] Procksch believed, like Hofmann, that theology is really a theology of history, since history is the vehicle for theology.[96] He also divided his study into the same three categories as did Eichrodt, who acknowledges that it was from Proksch that he got his own scheme.[97] The publication of Procksch's theology, then, served to continue Eichrodt's influence on the discipline.

In the early 1950s the biblical theology movement and the writing of complete works of Old Testament theology intersected at certain key points. Both groups also continued to some extent Eichrodt's agenda. Wright sought to focus on the uniqueness of Israel's religion in *The Old Testament Against*

Its Environment (1950) and then suggested that the single theme "God who acts" summarizes Old Testament theology in *God Who Acts: Biblical Theology as Recital* (1952). Both these efforts were part of the Studies in Biblical Theology series that produced dozens of titles on biblical theology from 1950 to 1976.

Wright's first work challenged some fundamental principles of developmental historicism. He first asserts that "it is increasingly realized to-day that the attempt to make the Old Testament a source book for the evolution of religion from very primitive to highly advanced concepts has been made possible only by means of a radical misinterpretation of the literature."[98] Next, he claims that "we cannot assume that a mere description of an evolutionary process provides the explanation for matters which belong to the realm of religious faith."[99] Finally, Wright notes that something made Israel's faith radically different than their neighbors' cults.[100] He agrees with Eichrodt that this "something" is God's redemption of Israel from Egypt and making of the Sinai covenant.[101] God's self-revelation and mighty acts on Israel's behalf, then, led Israel to reject polytheism and embrace monotheism.[102] God's clear activity in history caused this belief, not a slow, steady evolution over time.

In *God Who Acts,* Wright discussed some of the implications of his theories stated in *Israel Against Its Environment.* First, since decisive divine acts sparked Israel's monotheistic beliefs, Israel's theology is not so much a history of ideas as

> a theology of recital, in which Biblical man confesses his faith by reciting the formative events of his history as the redemptive handiwork of God. The realism of the Bible consists in its close attention to the facts of history and of tradition because these facts are the facts of God.[103]

Again, Wright agrees with Eichrodt that the exodus and Sinai covenant are at the center of Israel's recital.[104] Second, the historical narratives, the Prophets and the psalms reflect on God's actions and what they mean for their audiences.[105] Third, the church must present God's acts in both Testaments as part of God's redemptive plan leading to the end of the world.[106] Fourth, it is not enough to find certain universal truths in the Old Testament nor to fall back on discussions about myth when discussing the Old Testament's authority. Indeed, "now in Biblical faith everything depends upon whether the central events actually occurred."[107] Still, and here Wright illustrates the authority dilemma again, "it must be admitted that the Bible . . . continually pushes beyond what is factually known. . . . Consequently, one cannot maintain the historical value of all parts evenly."[108]

Edmond Jacob seconds Wright's insistence on God's acts in his *Theology of the Old Testament* (1955; ET 1958). While discussing the permanent value of the Old Testament for Christianity, Jacob says, "Two closely connected themes have come to our notice more forcibly than others, the themes of the presence and the action of God."[109] The first idea serves as the basis for the initial part of the work, which describes the character of God. The second idea undergirds the book's other two parts, both of which stress the work of God in history. Once again central themes (the Old Testament and the church) and historical details emerge as the major elements of theological reflection.

Though other Old Testament theologies were written in the late 1950s,[110] one two-volume effort made the most significant impact. Gerhard von Rad's *Old Testament Theology* (1957, 1960; ET 1962, 1965) attempted to turn Old Testament theology in an entirely new direction. Like Procksch and Wright, von Rad believed strongly that the Old Testament speaks repeatedly of God's saving acts in history. He took a much more critical approach to Israel's history than did Wright, though, claiming that it is impossible to determine the Hexateuch's basic historical features.[111] Von Rad concludes that

> in the last 150 years critical historical scholarship has constructed an impressively complete picture of the history of the people of Israel. As this process took shape, the old picture of Israel's history which the Church had derived and accepted from the Old Testament was bit by bit destroyed. Upon this process there is no going back, nor has it yet to come to an end. Critical historical scholarship regards it as impossible that the whole of Israel was present at Sinai, or that Israel crossed the Red Sea and achieved the Conquest en bloc—it holds the picture of Moses and his leadership drawn in the traditions of the Book of Exodus to be as unhistorical as the function which the Deuternomistic book of Judges ascribes to the "judges."[112]

How then can a theologian assemble a historically based theology? Von Rad's answer is that interpreters must take Israel's confessions about God as preaching, not specifically as history. This preaching *(kerygma)* is summarized in Deuteronomy 6:20-24; 26:5-9; Joshua 24:2-13; and 1 Samuel 12:7-8. In particular von Rad thinks Deuteronomy 26:5-9 "bears all the marks of great antiquity," manages to "recapitulate the main events in the saving history" and does so "with close concentration on the objective historical facts."[113] Given his historical convictions, how can von Rad speak so confidently of historical fact? Chiefly because the elements of this confession occur repeatedly in Scripture.[114]

With his underlying historical confessions in place, von Rad then traces the elements of these traditions and their offshoots through the Old Testament. He basically follows the Hebrew order of books in his analysis, though at times he diverges to fit a critically reconstructed historical scheme. At many points he emphasizes textual unity and the Old Testament's connectedness to the New Testament. Because of his modified book-by-book approach, many of von Rad's best reflections are accessible. The real strength of von Rad's work is his emphasis on the Old Testament's message that God has acted graciously on Israel's behalf. This conviction helps von Rad argue for the Old Testament's validity for the church in every generation. The most painful weakness is his failure to link reliable history and reliable historical theology, but his rich statements on the value of Israel's preaching and their enduring traditions made it virtually impossible for later writers to ignore these aspects of Old Testament theology.

A summary of the years 1920 to 1960 reads somewhat like the one for 1787 to 1878. Theologians insisted that Old Testament theology be historically based, be allowed to express its own discreet witness apart from systematic theology yet also be able to inform biblical and systematic theology. As before, there was disagreement among scholars over just how these goals were to be reached. New forms of salvation history were the preferred means of linking history and theology. Eichrodt's emphasis on covenant, Vriezen's on communion, Wright's on God's acts and von Rad's on Israel's confessions were variations on this time-tested idea. Overcoming the domination of historicism, Old Testament theologians began once more to attempt to link the Testaments. Biblical theology did not seem as impossible as it did during 1878 to 1920. Finding a historical foothold and authentic base of authority, though, troubled the discipline. While rejecting many of Wellhausen's historical reconstructions, most writers continued to accept to some extent his views on the Pentateuch and the late nature of priestly writing. This tendency left theologians trying to overcome the limitations Wellhausen's views represent while still embracing Wellhausen's presuppositions.

Several possible formats for presenting Old Testament theology had also emerged. Some writers continued to use systematic theology categories. Some utilized a single theme that united the various parts of Old Testament theology. Von Rad traced thematic threads as they became traditions within Israel's history. On the one hand this diversity was positive, since it allowed freedom of expression and appropriate creativity. On the other hand this situation demonstrated that a methodological crisis was approaching that, coupled with the crisis of authority, would eventually result in new paths for the discipline. The question remained whether these new paths would be like the one taken from 1878 to 1920 or whether the basic goals of Old Testament theology would actually be realized.

The Growth of Diversity: 1960-1993

The 1960s represented something of a lull between the scholarly storms of the postwar years and the 1970s and 1980s. Some single Old Testament theologies were written, monographs continued to appear, and articles were published, but they came at a reduced rate of volume. Conservative scholarship, which had not been a serious partner in the discipline's dialogue for many years, once again entered the picture. Overall Old Testament theology seemed a bit weary, its methodologies worn, its giants getting older. As is often the case in such situations, new ideas and new authors stepped forward to suggest how the discipline might move ahead. This shifting of purpose led to a diversity of opinions and methodologies never seen before in Old Testament theology. The same sort of ferment was also occurring in Old Testament studies as a whole.

Conservative scholarship rejoined the discussions in 1958, when E. J. Young published a short survey of trends in the discipline entitled *The Study of Old Testament Theology Today.*[115] This analysis stressed the lack of works based on conservative views of Scripture, biblical history and the unity of scriptural doctrine. J. Barton Payne certainly addresses these issues in *The Theology of the Older Testament* (1962). In the preface to this volume, Payne notes the lack of textbooks that correspond "to the historical sequence and redemptive character of Biblical Theology."[116] This gap caused him to write a work whose thesis is that

> God actively directs human history for the purpose of redeeming men to Himself. Objectively, He has accomplished our redemption once and for all by sending His Son Jesus Christ to die on the cross for man's sin. Subjectively, however, he mediates this salvation to mankind through the instrument of His covenant, or to use a more accurate term, His testament.[117]

So far this approach sounds much like other salvation history efforts. Payne quickly places himself in the Hengstenberg and Hofmann camps of salvation history, though, by stating that

> in approaching the Old Testament, the writer has made two assumptions: 1) that this book is the equivalent of God's words; and 2) that its teachings are binding upon Christian faith and practice. The only exceptions to this latter assumption might relate to certain of the Old Testament ceremonies and to a few of the specific applications of its moral principles that concern ancient Near Eastern society (e.g. inheritance laws). The former assumption marks it as evangelical and distinguishes it from theological legalism; the latter marks it as traditionally orthodox and distinguishes it from modern dispensationalism.[118]

These quotations indicate that Payne believes conservative Old Testament theology ought to offer a clear alternative to critical scholarship. Conservative theologians should stress the unity of God's word and God's revelation. They should also seek the redemptive connections between the Testaments and trace these saving elements in history. His comments also reveal the division between conservatives who are covenant theologians, as Payne himself is, and dispensational theologians, whom Payne thinks draw too many distinctions between the Testaments. Certainly conservative scholarship after Payne took many forms, but at least the emphases on infallible revelation and on redemptive history remained. A tone was set for future studies.

Payne's format for presenting his conclusions has seven parts, each of which leads readers progressively through the stages of redemption. This systematic study does not reproduce the canonical flow of Old Testament history, nor does it follow a set order of biblical books. Thus the volume is an exceptionally thorough treatment of redemption. It is not, however, structured to allow careful analysis of many secondary doctrines.

Three volumes from other authors reflected the emerging diversity in Old Testament theology. Werner Schmidt attempted to stand between the history of religion and theology of the Old Testament approaches in *The Faith of the Old Testament: A History* (1968; ET 1983).[119] Schmidt traces both the faith of Israel as it develops in history and its relationship to and divergences from other ancient religions. He manages to do so concisely. This book demonstrates the ongoing problem critical scholars felt in drawing together history and faith.

Like his earlier monographs, G. E. Wright's *The Old Testament and Theology* (1969) sought to draw conclusions about biblical theology without offering a full-length study of Old Testament theology. At the outset of the book, Wright states that he wants "to say what consequences follow for theology when one takes the Old Testament seriously: not seriously as solely a historical document of importance only as background for later movements, but vitally as canonical and of serious moment for present life and faith."[120] He repeats this concern from his earlier books because he believes "it runs counter to much that is being done as theology by 'younger' theologians at the present time."[121] While reaffirming his earlier works, Wright hopes the current one will break new ground in such areas as revelation and theology, the nature of God as Creator, Lord and warrior, and hermeneutics. Certainly Wright offers extensive explanations of concepts he introduces earlier. Still, the issue of authority remains unresolved, the unity of Scripture is still a goal rather than a reality, and the parts of Scripture that are not narrative history remain mostly outside the patterns he suggests.

Given these and other methodological stalemates in the biblical theology movement, in *Biblical Theology in Crisis* (1970) Brevard Childs claimed that the time had come to move in new directions.[122] Childs remained committed to uniting Scripture in a truly biblical theology. Likewise, he maintained the biblical theology movement's emphasis on historical revelation, the uniqueness of Israel's religion and the Old Testament's value for the church.[123] He no longer believed, however, that these goals could be reached outside of a new approach. Thus he proposed to make the canon, the Hebrew order of books, the context for Old Testament theology. From these fixed, authoritative, revealed Scriptures one can find the necessary data for biblical theology. Childs's ideas are discussed extensively later, so they will not be dealt with in detail here. It is sufficient to note at this point his belief that the biblical theology movement was exhausted and that the canon, not history, preaching or a single theme, must become the focal point of Old Testament theology.

Though not a specific study of Old Testament theology, R. K. Harrison's *Introduction to the Old Testament* (1969) offered conservative Old Testament theologians a tremendous opportunity.[124] Probably the most impressive book of its genre to appear to date in conservative circles, this massive volume critiques in great detail the assumptions and conclusions of critical scholarship. After copious references to ancient sources, to philosophers of history and to archaeological findings, Harrison rejects all evolutionary views of Israel's history and de Wette's, Vatke's and Wellhausen's theories of Pentateuchal authorship. He specifically argues that priestly writings were not written last in ancient cultures, a point Dillmann made earlier. Harrison presents the plausibility of biblical history and of Mosaic authorship of the Pentateuch. He also divides his study of the Old Testament books themselves into the traditional Hebrew categories of Law, Prophets and Writings.

The opportunity Harrison's magisterial work gives conservatives is a solid historical basis for writing Old Testament theology. If his conclusions are sound, then conservatives can approach the text without having to choose nonhistorical categories for their work. Once again conservative biblical and Old Testament theology can be grounded in a legitimate historical context. Harrison's volume also shows the value of following the Hebrew order of books when describing the Old Testament's message.

The 1970s saw a number of Old Testament theologies published that either reflected older methodologies or suggested new ones. Diversity continued to flourish. Walther Zimmerli's *Old Testament Theology in Outline* (ET 1978) and Georg Fohrer's *Theologische Grundstrukturen des Alten Testaments,* both originally published in 1972, sought centers for their studies from which they could expand their discussions. In this way they echoed the efforts of Schultz, Eichrodt and others. Zimmerli explains that the need for a uniting principle grows out of Old Testament theology's obligation to "lead readers to bring together in their own minds the diverse statements the Old Testament makes about God, who wishes to be known not as a manifold God but as the one Yahweh."[125] To accomplish this task, Zimmerli chooses the first of the Ten

Commandments as his foundational principle. He says, "Obedience to Yahweh, the one God, who delivered Israel out of slavery and is jealous of his own uniqueness, defines the fundamental nature of the Old Testament."[126] Zimmerli's conclusion is basically correct, as will be argued later. All of Israel's faith and actions rise or fall on this conviction that there is only one God, whose name is Yahweh.

Fohrer's volume revolves around the twin themes of God's sovereignty and God's communion with human beings.[127] These two ideas help hold God's nature, human history and individual and human community in their proper balance. Elmer Martens observes that Fohrer's work also breaks away from the many purely descriptive theologies of the past. Unlike Eichrodt, to cite one example, Fohrer has no problem stating the normative nature of Old Testament theology and offering lengthy applications for the modern world.[128] Thus he urges the importance of the Old Testament for the church, much as the biblical theology movement had done for twenty years.

Most of the theologies written since Gabler's oration at least stated in passing the Old Testament's value for understanding the New Testament. John McKenzie broke with this tradition in *A Theology of the Old Testament* (1974). Indeed he claims that he wants to write as if the New Testament did not exist,[129] since "the Old Testament is not a Christian book."[130] Instead McKenzie places a study of Israel's cultic life first, and then he examines such topics as revelation, history, nature, wisdom and institutions. Expressing his feeling of closeness to Adolf von Harnack and Rudolf Bultmann, McKenzie appreciates the Old Testament's existential roots yet does not extend those roots into Christianity.[131] This reversion to the 1878-1920 opinion of the Old Testament does not benefit biblical theology, as McKenzie would probably admit. If the Old Testament is Christian Scripture, is part of the Bible, then its relationship to the whole must be taken into account, unless one wants to remove the Old Testament from the canon, as Harnack seemed to wish to do.

Four significant Old Testament theologies were published in 1978. Two of them, Walter Kaiser's *Toward an Old Testament Theology* and Samuel Terrien's *The Elusive Presence,* used older methodologies to present their own creative ideas. The other two, Ronald Clements's *Old Testament Theology: A Fresh Approach* and Claus Westermann's *Theologie des Alten Testaments in Grundzügen* (ET 1982), charted newer paths in both methodology and commentary.

Kaiser's work is thoroughly conservative in its opinions on revelation, history and the unity of Scripture. After a brief analysis of the crisis in biblical theology at that time, Kaiser declares that "biblical theology has not been able to restate and reapply the authority of the Bible. In fact, the Bible's authority has, if anything, diminished during this period rather than increased."[132] Why does Kaiser think so? Because biblical theology

> has not fully avoided the sterility of source criticism on the one hand or the historicism of the history of religions on the other. Nor has the force of philosophical theology been exchanged in every case for a methodology that refused to lay any a priori grids of any sort over the text.[133]

To break this stalemate, Kaiser proposes to listen "to the canon as a canonical witness to itself."[134] When one does, Kaiser says, it will become apparent that the Old Testament's "canonical theological center" lies in its ongoing system of promises and the fulfillment of those promises.[135] He chooses this central theme despite many scholars' reluctance about this methodology[136] and argues that history itself carries promise and fulfillment through the Scriptures.[137] Kaiser traces God's promises from Abraham's era (see Gen 12:1-3) through the Old Testament, focusing on the messianic promise. Almost as an appendix, he offers some suggestions on linking the Testaments, but many linkages have already been made clear.[138]

Without question, Kaiser wrote in the conservative salvation history tradition of Hofmann and Hengstenberg. He also utilized a single-theme approach as did Schultz and Eichrodt. His tracing of the messianic theme in Scripture is as convincing as his conservative counterpart J. Barton Payne's was of redemption in Scripture. Both share the same difficulty, however, for neither work has the breadth needed to cover Old Testament theology as a whole. No doubt this difficulty is part of the reason for the "toward" in Kaiser's title. Kaiser's emphasis on canon is also significant, since he joins Childs and others in a growing interest in the canon's role in Old Testament theology.

Terrien also used a single theme to give his volume focus and unity. He says, "The reality of the presence of God stands at the center of biblical faith. This presence, however, is always elusive."[139] Terrien's emphasis on presence is similar to Vriezen's and Fohrer's stressing of communion with God, but Terrien places more weight on the elusiveness of God's presence than do those writers. Like Kaiser, Terrien thinks "that the crisis of contemporary theology is related to the problem of authority in all domains, and that the perennial authority of Scripture requires new tools of semantic interpretation."[140] Terrien believes centering on God's presence helps rebuild this authority because the Old Testament's "theology of presence leads to the Christian theology of the eucharistic presence," which indicates a unity of cult and faith, of belief and action.[141]

Much of Terrien's charting of this pattern follows the general flow of the Old Testament canon. Whether discussing the patriarchs, prophets or kings, Terrien always highlights these persons' perception of their relationship with God. Probably his best achievement is his chapter on Wisdom, where he links a relationship with Wisdom's teaching and one's relationship to God.[142] Terrien must also be commended for his desire to create possible ways to unite the Old and New Testaments. Perhaps the book's greatest flaw is its overemphasis on the elusiveness of God's presence without explaining that human sin and life's circumstances, not God's nature, make God seem elusive.[143] A truly biblical theology must take the human sin problem more fully into account.

Clements promised a fresh approach in his short volume and to a real extent delivered on the pledge. Like most recent writers of Old Testament theologies, Clements seeks a way to break the impasse he finds in the discipline. He welcomes Childs's and J. A. Sanders's[144] insistence on the value of the canon for theological reflection and then concludes that

> at a very basic level we can see that it is because the Old Testament forms a canon, and is not simply a collection of ancient Near Eastern documents, that we can expect to find in it a "theology," and not just a report of ancient religious ideas. There is a real connection between the ideas of "canon" and "theology," for it is the status of these writings as a canon of sacred scripture that marks them out as containing a word of God that is still believed to be authoritative.[145]

Clements then chooses the Hebrew canon as the object of his studies because he determines "that this Palestinian form of the canon represents the oldest, and most basic, form of the Old Testament."[146] Thus he finds it appropriate to analyze the three traditional Hebrew sections, Law, Prophets and Writings, in an Old Testament theology, though he does not examine the Writings in this volume.[147] He hopes using the canon as theological document may help explain the Old Testament's authority.[148]

In his treatment of the biblical material, Clements argues that the Law, or Torah, "presents those demands which God has set before Israel as a consequence of his election of them, and as the condition of the covenant by which this election has been constituted. The Pentateuch therefore is a covenant literature."[149] Whether narratives, poetry or sermon, all of the Pentateuch's contents help make up this unified "covenant literature." While the Pentateuch presents instruction in covenant living, the Prophets highlight promise, both of hope and of woe.[150] Because the prophets gain their ideas about judgment and blessing from the Torah, especially as it is declared in Deuteronomy, there exists real unity between the Law and Prophets.[151] Because the Prophets section of the canon looks both backward and forward in human and Israelite history, these books serve as a bridge to the Writings and to the New Testament.[152]

Like Terrien's and Kaiser's efforts, Clements's book has a "toward" feeling about it. The author does not seek to present a methodology and an analysis of the Old Testament, just the former. At times Clements leaves excellent ideas without fully explaining them, and he suffers the same difficulty with authority that most historical critics share. Still, this monograph represents a real step forward in using the canon as a means of illustrating the Old Testament's relationship to history, authority and unity.

Westermann's *Theologie* also effectively utilizes underlying themes and an emphasis on canon. For Westermann, "a Theology of the Old Testament has the task of summarizing and viewing together what the Old Testament as a whole, in all its sections, says about God."[153] He does not believe any single theme can achieve this goal, so he claims it is best to focus on "events rather than concepts."[154] Emphasizing events to the exclusion of ideas leaves Wisdom Literature no real place in Old Testament theology, which Westermann admits. Rather he sees God's work as creator as the spark that ignited Wisdom Literature.[155] Thus, though Westermann follows the canonical categories of Law, Prophets and Writings, a significant portion of the canon is neglected. This problem with the Writings is not new, for it goes back at least as far as Oehler's theology.

When Westermann analyzes God's acts traditional themes emerge. God's deliverance of Israel from Egypt indicates that the Lord saves. Creating the world indicates that God blesses. God also judges and demonstrates compassion for the weak and hurting. God also acts in and through Jesus Christ. Therefore Westermann departs from the single-theme approach to some extent, both by using God's acts as a starting point, as Wright had done earlier, and by adopting a canonical structure. Even though his theological observations are not startlingly different from those of his predecessors, he still helped Old Testament theology try to break loose from its then-current gridlock.

The 1980s did not produce as many theologies as did the preceding decade, but scholars applied the principles suggested in the 1970s quite decisively. It should come as no surprise that Childs, who critiqued the biblical theology movement in 1970, led the way in finding new directions for Old Testament theology. His first work in the 1980s was not a theology but instead an *Introduction to the Old Testament as Scripture* (1980). This effort was but the latest installment of Childs's determined effort to write a biblical theology that took the Old Testament's and New Testament's historical backgrounds, separate theological witnesses and canonical unity seriously. This effort was to culminate twelve years later.

Like Harrison's *Introduction,* Childs's book offers possibilities for Old Testament theology. First, it suggests a fixed starting point for reflection: the final form of the Hebrew canon.[156] The fixed canon's shaping in history informs one's grasp of the text, but that history is not the goal of the study. The canon's message has that position. Second, it suggests an order of study for theology. Childs's careful analysis of each book in its place in the Hebrew canon gives his analysis focus. Third, it attempts to solve the history-faith dilemma by noting the canon's status as faith document written in a historical context. Fourth, it tries to locate authority in the whole canon, not just in selected universal ideas or in selected portions of the Old Testament. Childs's *Introduction* sparked heated debate among scholars committed to primarily historical background approaches to the Old Testament. In due time it provided Childs with a way to analyze Old Testament theology itself.

Elmer Martens did not reflect the movement toward canon in his *God's Design: A Focus on Old Testament Theology* (1981). Instead he chose a key passage from which he was able to trace four significant themes that illustrate God's design for Israel and the human race in history. In his preface Martens admits that writing an Old Testament theology is a daunting task and then says, "A theology of the Old Testament should lay bare, I believe, the essence of the Old Testament message, a message that centres in Yahweh, the God of Israel and the world."[157] At this point Martens's concern sounds very much like Zimmerli's, but he takes a different approach to fulfilling this goal.

Martens's volume distinguishes itself in its methodology and its evangelical theological and congregational commitments. On the former, he states that

> my claim is that the overarching theme of the Old Testament is God's design, a design that incorporates four components: deliverance, community, knowledge of God, and the abundant life. This design is articulated at the exodus, implemented and tested in the monarchy, reaffirmed in the post-monarchy period, and continued into the New Testament.[158]

As he implies, Martens chooses these themes as a result of his analysis of Exodus 5:22—6:8, not from systematic or topical categories.[159] On the latter issue Martens writes, "It is my conviction that, since the Old Testament is God's Word, a theology of the Old Testament should point beyond the description of the message to an indication of its importance for today's believer."[160] Though based on different grounds, Martens's conviction here mirrors that of Fohrer.

There is much to praise in Martens's work. He writes plainly and follows his program in an understandable way. His linking of history, text and revelation moves beyond the much-discussed authority impasse. Also, his choice of four themes offers a broader slice of Old Testament theology than is offered by Kaiser or Payne. Though weakest in its treatment of the Writings, overall this book sets high standards for later conservative theologians.

During the 1970s and 1980s, Hartmut Gese wrote a series of articles and monographs on biblical theology that culminated in the second edition of *Zur biblischen Theologie* in 1983. Gese, a student of von Rad, argued for a renewed emphasis on traditions in Scripture. Gese thinks the multiplicity of traditions made it impossible for a single theme to "be torn out of its context and absolutized."[161] Gese believes that it is essential to treat the Old and New Testaments together, since

a unity of the Bible is not to be established artificially through exegetical cross-references between the Old and New Testaments. A unity exists already because of tradition history. The gulf supposedly between the Old and New Testaments does not exist traditio-historically at all, and no dubious bridges are needed to span it. There is a difference between the Old and New Testaments insofar as the New Testament represents the goal and end, the *telos* of the path of biblical tradition. With the death and resurrection of Jesus, that event takes place toward which the earthly *Heilsgeschichte* [salvation history] of biblical revelation is moving.[162]

Many authors at least loosely affiliated with salvation history theologians would agree with this conclusion. Many would not agree, though, with the methodology Gese uses to reach this decision. Besides disagreeing with scholars who focus on single themes, Gese argues with critics like Kaiser, Childs and Clements who think the final form of the Hebrew canon is normative.[163] For one thing, Gese says, the Old Testament canon was formed over time only after thorough revising and cannot therefore be interpreted as a set document if one wants to recapture Israelite theology.[164] For another, the Apocrypha must be included if one wants to trace the flow of tradition from the Old to the New Testament.[165] Gese also locates biblical authority in Israel's "life processes" as God identifies with them,[166] a viewpoint that scholars who locate revelation and authority in the text itself could not hold.

Thus those committed to biblical theology must applaud Gese's emphasis on biblical unity.[167] They must also appreciate his insistence on the breadth of Old Testament theology. Still, Gese's placement of authority in the process of tradition forming rather than in some final text leaves interpreters with no fixed point of entry in their work. Jesper Høgenhaven rightly determines that Gese's methods could lead to methodological chaos.[168] Indeed it seems Gese himself analyzes the final, canonical text when claiming the resurrection as the ultimate goal of salvation history. Regardless of one's opinions about Gese's methodology and theological observations, his writings demonstrated once again the diversity that had arisen in Old Testament theology and biblical theology by the mid-1980s.

Childs continued in his determination to write a biblical theology by publishing two significant works in mid-decade. The first, *The New Testament as Canon: An Introduction* (1984),[169] supplemented his earlier similar work on the Old Testament and created a context for future observations on the New Testament's role in biblical theology. The second, *Old Testament Theology in a Canonical Context* (1985), presented in concrete form ideas

Childs had mentioned in earlier articles and books.

As he indicated in *Introduction to the Old Testament as Scripture*, Childs believes the starting point for examining Old Testament theology is the final form of the canon itself.[170] This initial conviction means that the "materials for theological reflection are not the events or experiences behind the text, or apart from the construal in scripture by a community of faith and practice."[171] Rather such historical events inform interpreters about how theological conclusions were reached. Childs does not ignore history; he moves it to a role in theological studies subordinate to the theology itself. Second, the canon is "the scope of the authoritative literature."[172] Within the text the church finds its authority. Third, Childs claims that Old Testament theology is essentially a Christian discipline "because the church assumes a relationship between the testaments."[173] In this assumption biblical theology finds its starting place. Childs cautions against christianizing the Old Testament unduly and encourages efforts to hear the Old Testament's "own theological testimony to the God of Israel whom the church confesses also to worship."[174] Underlying these main principles is Childs's desire "to free the Old Testament for a more powerful theological role within the life of the Christian church."[175]

Childs separates his canonical approach from other methodologies. His approach does not utilize a single theme, nor does he choose between systematic or tradition-based categories. Instead Childs states that a canonical approach recognizes that both types of features appear in the Old Testament, as do "innumerable other options."[176] Again the canon shapes the discussion, not a system attempting to explain the canon's contents. Similarly Childs refuses to distinguish sharply between salvation history and "real" history, preferring "to follow the biblical text in its theological use of historical referentiality."[177] Finally, Childs disagrees with attempts to place revelation outside the canonical Scriptures.[178]

Despite his strong convictions about the ultimate value of biblical theology, Childs still affirms the importance of Old Testament theology for four reasons. First, he finds it wise to come to grips with the enormous and complex Old Testament materials before coordinating them with New Testament data. Second, Childs hopes studying the Old Testament from within a theological discipline "provides a major check against the widespread modern practice of treating it solely from a philological, historical, or literary perspective."[179] Third, he thinks such studies will help highlight the Old Testament's valuable unique theological contributions, and fourth, he believes his approach will aid correct interpretations of the New Testament.[180]

When he actually comments on the Old Testament, it is somewhat surprising that Childs does not work through the books of the Hebrew canon, as he does in *Introduction* and in his later complete *Biblical Theology*. Instead he uses the systematic category "revelation" to begin the work, then offers analyses of the major canonical categories (e.g., Law, Prophets, Covenant) and concludes with thematic studies such as "Male and Female as a Theological Problem," "Life Under Threat" and "Life Under Promise."

This volume has definite strengths and certain weaknesses. Childs's conviction that the finished canon is the authoritative, historically produced, normative object for theological reflection is correct. All pretextual matters, however valuable for understanding the text, are servants to the text that has influenced readers for centuries. Childs's reasons for writing an Old Testament theology as a prelude to biblical theology are also true to the best traditions in the discipline. Further, attempting to examine and explain Old Testament theology by interpreting each book and section in its sequence offers both beginning and advanced theologians a focused way to discover and present their findings. Finally, the canonical approach gives history a viable place within the theological process without allowing it to become the chief goal of that process.

Despite these advantages, some problems exist in the book. First, though Childs rejects any equation of revelation and history, he also is careful not to equate revelation and the text. He observes that

in sum, the use of the term revelation within the context of the canon reflects the concern to be open to the theological dimensions of the biblical tradition which can never be either separated from or identified with the life of empirical Israel.[181]

Placing any more weight on the text than "openness to theological dimensions" may lead to "misconstruals of interpretation which derive from over-emphasizing the cognitive, experiential, or historical elements."[182] But can Childs have it both ways? Can he deny source, form and tradition critics their insistence on pretextual authority and not equate text and authority? Is it possible to separate canon, text and authority in this manner?

Second, Childs's approach works best when he follows a book-by-book format. This departure from one of his strongest earlier details hampers his efforts to explain the inner structure and vital facets of the canon as it unfolds. Third, at one very key point Childs exits the canonical approach in favor of source criticism. He places his material on priests and the cult after the prophetic segments instead of with his statements on the Law. It is appropriate to wonder why Childs appears to want both late priestly writing and a methodology that stresses the final, received form of the canon. Not allowing the canon to speak on its own terms undercuts the canonical approach. Fourth, as is the case with many theologies, this volume does not deal extensively with the Writings, though it does devote a solid chapter entitled "The Shape of the Obedient Life" to this literature.

Since 1985, the stressing of canon has continued, older emphases have been revived, and still more new approaches have been suggested. Paul Hanson offered the first of the new methodologies in *The People Called: The Growth of Community in the Bible* (1986).[183] This volume treads a path somewhere between an Old Testament theology and a monograph devoted to a single major topic. Hanson's thesis is that tracing the birth, growth and changes within the Old Testament community of faith reveals the best of Israelite faith. This analysis, in Hanson's view, links Israel's history and theology and helps demonstrate continuity between Old and New Testament believing communities.

Hanson reconstructs Israel's history along source-critical lines[184] and determines that within this history the people of God at times transcended their surroundings and obeyed such covenant ideals as mercy, justice, liberation and equality.[185] Rejecting most traditional definitions of revelation (conservative or liberal), Hanson finds authority in Israel's continual process of doing God's will. He says the Old Testament community "did not offer a finished program; it inaugurated a process. It did not commend to its members static answers; it offered the perspective of those who had experienced deliverance to others who suffered under various kinds of oppression."[186] When the church follows this heritage it recaptures the Scriptures' revelation and authority.[187]

Hanson's study observes the value of life in community in Old Testament times and strives for a means of linking the Testaments. His methodology leaves one groping for fundamental principles, however, in much the way Gese's does. For Hanson, authority exists only in the reenactment of commitments held by his reconstructed community. Central themes tend to sound as much like mainline Protestant theology as they do Old Testament theology.[188] Ideology, both historical-critical and political, enter the picture too often.

Christoph Barth's posthumous *God with Us* (1991) turned to older ideas for its methodology.[189] Barth's emphasis on God's presence reminds readers of the writings of Vriezen, Fohrer, Terrien and others. The book's outline charts nine great acts of God that Barth believes unifies Old Testament theology, a strategy akin to Wright's convictions. This volume shows that earlier methodologies continue to be valid and useful in the hands of resourceful authors.

Like Hanson, Walter Brueggemann sought to cast Old Testament theology in a different mold. His collected articles entitled *Old Testament Theology: Essays on Structure, Theme and Text* (1992) asserted the need for a new dialectical, or bipolar, approach to the material. After noting with approval the earlier bipolar proposals of Westermann, Terrien, Hanson and others,[190]

Brueggemann declares, "The bipolar construct I suggest is that Old Testament faith serves both to legitimate structure and to embrace pain."[191] Much of Brueggemann's discussion flows from ideas found in sociological theory and political science.[192]

By "structure legitimation" he means that much of the Old Testament's theology exists to keep society under control. Such theology "allows no slippage," "is easily supportive of the *status quo* and readily becomes available for ideology," "is the working of the nonreflective, . . . is the useful theology of dominant interest" and is too often the theology today's church adopts.[193] Much of the Sinai covenant and royal texts fall into this category.

Theology that embraces pain, which Brueggemann defines as dysfunction in human beings' relationship to God or one another,[194] rocks the theological boat. It forces structure to have compassion, to put its power to better use.[195] It laments, demands answers and cares for the oppressed. As a minority voice, it causes continual tension between itself and keepers of societal and theological structure.[196] Though Brueggemann believes both types of theology are needed to balance church life correctly, it is clear that he thinks the pain expressed by the prophets and Wisdom writers has the most important word for modern Christianity.

Brueggemann writes powerfully in all of his books, and this volume is no exception. He is challenging and thought-provoking. His concern for theology and church has been proven over his long and productive career. In this work his interests do not change. What does seem to change a bit from his earlier writings is his shift toward a sociopolitical approach that yields a program similar to Hanson's. It is questionable whether the Old Testament was written against the backdrop of class struggles and ideological battles, however diverse the material may be. Indeed many laments are the result of problems between the rich, not between the rich and the oppressed. Pain and structure both exist in the Old Testament, then, but it is not clear that they oppose one another in the manner Brueggemann describes.

In 1992 Childs published his *Biblical Theology of the Old and New Testaments: Theological Reflection on the Christian Bible*. As has been discussed, this book was the culmination of at least two decades of reflection and writing on the Old and New Testaments. By now Childs's methodological categories were hardly a surprise, nor were his theological conclusions startling. His commitments to church, canon and biblical theology remained intact. Still, the quality of his comments and the fact that he wrote a biblical theology received attention.

Childs first surveys the history of biblical theology, then defends his approach against certain critics, next notes hermeneutical issues involved in the discipline and finally discusses a canonical methodology. Two basic conclusions inform his study. First, he asserts that the canonical structuring of theology reflects the fact that the Old Testament was written within Israel's historical context. This fact does not mean the Old Testament only records historical events, for this history is selected according to its importance. Further, these historical events are told in various literary types and are not all applied to the community of faith the same way. Thus the canonical approach embraces the Old Testament's diversity and unity.[197] Second, though different in many respects, the New Testament plays a similar role in the life of the church. It is also significant that the New Testament "bears its witness to the radically new in terms of the old."[198] It continually uses the Old Testament as its authoritative point of reference.

The analysis of Scripture unfolds in three basic parts. First, Childs describes the "discrete" witness of the Old and New Testaments. In the Old Testament section he follows the canon closely and even places a small section on priesthood and the tabernacle in the material on Mosaic traditions.[199] Second, he analyzes Genesis 22:1-19 and Matthew 21:33-46 to help relate the two Testaments to one another. Third, Childs examines themes such as God, God the Creator and Christ the Lord that he believes unite the Old and New Testaments. This approach allows Childs to move from methodology, to summary and description, and finally to theological reflection, which is a sound hermeneutical procedure.

All but one of the strengths and weaknesses noted above for Childs's *Old Testament Theology in a Canonical Context* apply here except one. Though he still places the actual writings of priestly material late in Israel's history, Childs does at least place the priesthood and tabernacle back in its canonical place. Even those who disagree with Childs must admire the persistence and consistency with which he has forwarded the canonical approach.

One other significant scholar seconded many of Clements's, Childs's and Sanders's comments on canon. Rolf Rendtorff, a student of von Rad, challenged the conclusions of source criticism and used canonical analysis as a new paradigm for exegesis and theological reflection. In *The Problem of the Process of the Transmission of the Pentateuch* (1977; ET 1990), Rendtorff critiqued Wellhausen's JEDP theory of Pentateuchal authorship and its reconstruction of Israel's history. He observes that despite the alterations in the theory suggested by the work of Hermann Gunkel, Martin Noth, von Rad and others,

> the overwhelming majority of scholars in almost all countries where scholarly study of the Old Testament is pursued, take the documentary hypothesis as the virtually uncontested point of departure for their work; and their interest in the most precise understanding of the nature and theological purposes of the individual written sources seems undisturbed.[200]

Theology continues to be formulated against this historical backdrop.

Rendtorff then examines certain criteria commonly used for dividing sources. He finds that linguistic evidence for the J or P sources "is reduced to a tiny crumb."[201] Likewise, careful analysis of the Pentateuch's theology leads to "but one explanation: a 'Yahwist,' who shaped and handed on the patriarchal stories and the complexes of tradition that follow them, does not exist."[202] Also, he concludes, "it is clear that a coherent P-narrative in the patriarchal story cannot be demonstrated."[203] Rendtorff does not believe source criticism asks illegitimate questions, nor does he turn to Mosaic authorship; he simply believes such questions cannot be answered using source-critical methodology. Instead new approaches must be sought that focus on larger literary units and their theology.[204]

At least partly due to such historical conclusions, Rendtorff features canonical analysis in his *Canon and Theology: Overtures to an Old Testament Theology* (ET 1993). Here Rendtorff suggests an Old Testament theology that sounds a great deal like Childs's scheme:

> Consequently my own proposed outline is to consist of two main parts: a first section which will follow the "canonical" plan of the Old Testament books or collections . . . and a second which will consider individual themes and concepts—perhaps also individual theological outlines, and so on, within the Old Testament.[205]

He also registers his distrust of traditional source criticism and declares, "The subject of any interpretation has to be first and foremost the given text of the Hebrew Bible."[206] Rendtorff notes that canonical criticism's greatest strength is its dealing with the received text's "larger units, such as biblical books, and even with the canon as a whole."[207]

To illustrate his methodology's ability to aid interpretation of large sections of biblical material, Rendtorff offers studies of covenant as structuring device in Genesis and Exodus, the literary framework of 1 Samuel 1—2, three separate articles on the unity of Isaiah and an analysis of Ezekiel's structure. Each of these essays follows a canonical approach in that it works from the received text and quotes biblical texts related to the study without positioning them along source-critical lines.

Without question Rendtorff's observations further the cause of canonical analysis. His exegetical work shows its value for unlocking keys to the unity of whole books. His historical studies of the Pentateuch make it essential that a historically based Old Testament theology move away from Wellhausen's opinions, which in turn makes the canon an attractive place to begin anew. Certainly he shares some of Childs's problems as well, such as the appropriate role of authority and revelation. Together with Childs's efforts, Rendtorff's writings make canonical analysis a likely major force in the future of Old Testament theology.

One final theology concluded this era. Ralph Smith's *Old Testament Theology* (1993) proceeded basically along systematic lines. He includes solid scholarly commentary on such issues as knowing God, election, God's nature, sin and redemption, and judgment. The book's most impressive feature is Smith's excellent introduction to the discipline and methodology of Old Testament theology.[208] It is instructive about the diverse nature of the discipline to read Smith's purpose for writing, which is "to explore, not to argue or debate. It [the book] does not set out any radically new method of doing theology or of interpreting the Old Testament."[209] Rather he seeks to describe, analyze and promote the Old Testament's great doctrines. He succeeds in his descriptive purpose.

Conclusion

More than two hundred years have passed since Gabler's formative essay. Hundreds of volumes and articles related to the discipline have been published. Rationalism has given way to historicism, which has in turn given way to the diverse situation that now exists. What has been gained? Where is the discipline at this point? Perhaps these two questions can guide a brief summary of the situation.

Certain overriding principles have been gained over the years. Virtually every Old Testament theologian agrees that the discipline must maintain ties to the ancient world's historical context. Also, most Old Testament theologians believe that their conclusions ought to aid biblical theology, though some writers are now stressing the Old Testament by itself or as it relates to Jewish thought. This conviction is held without any effort to neglect the Old Testament's own unique message or its own special unity. Finally, there is a growing conviction that theology must address the world in some normative fashion. Totally descriptive theology is waning at the moment.

The current state of Old Testament theology is that little agreement exists about how to achieve these common goals. Does one adopt a methodology that embraces a single theme or bipolar distinctives? Does one examine the Old Testament canonically or according to a reconstructed history of Israel? How does one deal with the role of revelation and authority in Scripture? How does one relate the Old and New Testaments? These questions are being asked by all scholars whether liberal or conservative, Catholic or Protestant, pastor or academician.

No single volume will solve these matters. Still, progress can be made if recent trends away from Wellhausen's program and toward the fixed biblical text can be utilized. If the authoritative text as it now stands can be explained in a way that highlights God's nature, person and actions, then this book may be part of a return to truly Old Testament and biblical theology. Only then can it have anything of value to say to the church.

A Methodology for Examining Old Testament Theology: Basic Principles

This survey of literature makes it quite clear that several methodologies for composing Old Testament theology exist. Every serious analysis of the discipline makes this point. The question arises, then, of how to proceed in a manner true to the Old Testament itself.

Certain definitions and convictions undergird this volume's approach to Old Testament theology. No doubt the most important definition is of *theology* itself. This Greek word means "the study of God" and implies that those who undertake to study God will learn a great deal about God's nature, actions and attitudes. From learning about God they will in turn discover how God relates to the created world, including the human race. All analyses begin with God and flow to other vital subjects. Thus Old Testament theology itself can be defined as "the task of presenting what the Old Testament says about God as a coherent whole."[210] Only by keeping God at the forefront of research can one compose a viable and balanced theological work.

As has been stated, a few basic convictions have generally characterized Old Testament theology. First, it must have a historical base. Second, it must explain what the Old Testament itself claims, not what preconceived historical or theological systems impose upon the biblical material. Third, when part of Christian theology, as this book attempts to be, Old Testament theology must in some way address its relationship to the New Testament. Fourth, by joining with the New Testament to form biblical theology, Old Testament theology offers material that systematic theologians can divide into categories and topics for discussion. Fifth, by stating what the Old Testament says about God's nature and will, Old Testament theology moves beyond description of truth into prescription of action. After all, if interpreters agree that the Old Testament teaches that God commands certain behavior, it seems evident that a description has discovered a norm. One may obey the normative command or not, but the fact that a norm has been uncovered remains unchanged.

Beyond these shared convictions lie some concepts this volume holds in common with many, though not all, other similar works. First, Old Testament theology must be presented in a clear, coherent pattern so its readers can incorporate its findings into their lives and ministries. Second, Old Testament theology must try to display the Old Testament's theological unity within diversity. Difficult ideas must not be hidden, but the text's wholeness should have priority for the preceding objective to be reached. Third, authors must be honest about their established mindset. These mindsets are developed over time and after careful consideration. This volume is written by an evangelical Christian who has come to this position only after serious study, reflection and struggle. Certainly those of a different mindset also went through a similar process.

Because of these definitions and convictions, Old Testament theology should not include certain tasks. For instance, though historical studies undergird Old Testament theology, it is not the discipline's role to write a history of all Israelite religious beliefs. Old Testament theology should focus on what the Bible's authors believed, while historians of Israelite religious beliefs must, among other things, take into serious consideration what Israelites who did not agree with the Bible's authors believed. Such data informs Old Testament theologians, but is not their main priority when they present their findings. These disciplines intersect at key points, but they are not identical.

To cite another example, though Old Testament theology has a close relationship to the New Testament the two have discrete witnesses of their own.[211] Therefore Old Testament theology must state the Old Testament's unique message before incorporating the New Testament perspective. The ultimate goal is still to produce biblical theology yet to unite the testaments at the proper moment. This procedure is sound on historical, canonical and exegetical grounds and will make scriptural unity plainer than starting from the opposite end of the canon. It will also help the Old Testament's unique value for theology clearer.

Finally, if the text is allowed to dictate theological reflection, then it is not Old Testament theology's task to incorporate its results into a formal system. Old Testament theology must not be written in order to justify Calvinism, Arminianism or some other time-honored system of belief. If the results are congenial to a system, then proponents of that system may use the data. The goal is to avoid forcing the text into a mold before the text is studied. Scholars of all faiths and ideological convictions have committed this error, and to some extent this failing is universal, so it is necessary to attempt to be careful in this area.

A Methodology for Examining Old Testament Theology: Specific Principles of a Canonical Approach

With all these considerations in mind, it is possible to move toward stating this book's methodology. Gerhard Hasel claims that there have been ten different methodologies used in the history of Old Testament theology. These include

1. the dogmatic-didactic method, which organizes Old Testament theology along the lines of systematic theology (Bauer, Köhler, Jacob)

2. the genetic-progressive method, which traces the growth of Israel's faith in history (Clements)

3. the cross-section method, which utilizes a single theme to explain the

Old Testament's contents (Eichrodt, Vriezen, Kaiser)

4. the topical method, which focuses on major ideas regardless of their historical emergence or ability to unify the Old Testament (McKenzie, Fohrer, Zimmerli)

5. the diachronic method, which charts the use of basic traditions in the Old Testament (von Rad)

6. the "formation of tradition" method, which goes beyond von Rad's arguments to claim that a series of traditions unify both testaments (Gese)

7. the thematic-dialectic method, which arranges its studies around "opposing" ideas such as presence/absence (Terrien), deliverance/blessing (Westermann) and structure legitimation/embracing of pain (Brueggemann)

8. recent "critical" methods, which is Hasel's category for scholars who question whether Old Testament theology can be done at all (e.g., James Barr and John J. Collins)

9. the new biblical theology method, which attempts to relate the Testaments to one another; the chief proponent of this method is Childs, who utilizes a canonical approach to biblical theology (Hasel also places Vriezen and Clements in this group and notes Terrien's, Westermann's and Gese's interest in the discussion as well)

10. the multiplex canonical Old Testament theology method, which is Hasel's own program for the discipline (it consists of four main points: a study of the canonical Scriptures rather than a history-of-religions approach, a summary of the canon's concepts and themes, a utilization of more than one methodological scheme and an analysis of blocks of material without following the specific order of Hebrew canon)[212]

Hasel's excellent list makes the methodological possibilities and difficulties in Old Testament theology evident. He is correct in stating that a combination of methodologies must be used but incorrect in which combination works best.

First of all, Old Testament theology that seeks to contribute to biblical theology should indeed analyze the Hebrew canon, for it is this canon that the New Testament mentions (see Lk 24:44) and quotes as divine revelation. Since it is the three-part (Law, Prophets, Writings) scheme that the New Testament mentions, the general order of the canon ought to be followed as well. Because it is an unfolding canon, intertextual connections between the books must be duly noted. Since the apocryphal books are not so quoted and described, they should not be included in Old Testament theology.[213] Analyzing the canon offers the best chance for the Old Testament to speak for itself.

Second, following the canonical order keeps the Old Testament's historical context before the reader. This principle is generally true for any reader who thinks Vatke's and Wellhausen's reconstruction of Israelite history and biblical composition faulty. Also, many scholars who agree broadly with Wellhausen and his successors believe that the Pentateuch and Prophets at least contain many materials that are quite ancient, so they also appreciate the canonical text's stated historical sequence. Other experts hold to Mosaic authorship of the Pentateuch and that the stated authors of biblical books are indeed those books' authors. They, too, find historical progression in the canon. This volume adopts a conservative approach to Israelite history and biblical composition yet hopes its comments on the canon can at least aid those who disagree at many points.

Third, despite the current reluctance among some scholars to adopt a single centering theme,[214] Old Testament theology needs focal points. The key here is to argue for *a* main focal point, not necessarily for *the* central theme of the Old Testament. A focal point is valuable as long as it is true to Scripture and actually helps the theologian's analysis hold together. Attempting to argue a certain theme as the only major uniting idea can succeed only if all other motifs are proven secondary, and this volume makes no such exclusive claims for its centering theme. Surely such an argument would require an extended discussion before the theologian could begin. This book uses the Old Testament's insistence on the existence and worship of one God as a major, normative, theological and historical emphasis. Several theologians mention this theme's centrality (see below), though none uses it to the extent employed here. This fundamental concept helps explain the Old Testament's ideas about God, Israel and the human race. It also provides an extremely important theological link between the Old and New Testament communities of faith.

Fourth, this wedding of canonical and thematic approaches also has a practical goal. One of the drawbacks of a noncanonical, or non-book-by-book, approach is that many current students do not have extensive biblical knowledge. Therefore it is quite difficult for these students to use a systematic or dialectic approach that assumes they have already mastered the theological details in individual Bible books. Such students are not intellectually weak; they lack exposure to and experience with the material for a systematic analysis of Scripture. I hope, then, this book's approach will be both accurate and appropriate for a majority of theological students.

Given these assertions, this volume adopts a canonical approach to Old Testament theology that can be summarized by the following principles. First, the Old Testament canon accepted by the first-century Palestinian Jewish/ Christian and Jewish/non-Christian communities will be examined. The canon will be treated in the general order accepted by those groups: Law, Prophets and Writings. Analysis of specific groupings within these three parts will follow the Masoretic text found in *Biblia Hebraica Stuttgartensia,* an imperfect but reasonable procedure that keeps faith with the contours of each section as they have been handed down through the centuries. Second, each book of the canon will be examined to show its unique theological contribution to the Old Testament. Then intertextual connections between the individual book and the rest of the canon will be noted. The thematic wholeness of Hebrew Scripture will thereby be illuminated.[215]

Third, the treatments of single books will at times include brief comments about historical details such as authorship, date and audience. The canon's contents did not emerge in a vacuum, nor is their historical context irrelevant to their message. Choosing the Law, Prophets, Writings sequence allows the basic outlines of Israelite history to be followed without a history of religion approach taking over the study. Fourth, the Old Testament's insistence on monotheism will be used as a historically attested centering theme to give focus to the text's many emphases.[216] This emphasis will also aid the volume's attempt to focus on God's character and acts more than on other matters. Fifth, the canon will be treated as Scripture, as divinely inspired texts that claim and are accepted as having authoritative status. Neglecting this principle in effect leads to approaching the Old Testament in a manner foreign to the history of its interpretation and foreign to its own subject matter.

Thus by "canonical" this volume means analysis that is God-centered, intertextually oriented, authority-conscious, historically sensitive and devoted to the pursuit of the wholeness of the Old Testament message. It means theological reflection that intends to deal carefully with the uniqueness of the Old Testament so that its influence on the New Testament and systematic theology can be better understood. Of course such goals may not be attainable by any author, much less by this one. Still, this sort of canonical analysis may make a small contribution to the practice of Old Testament theology during an era in which the discipline seems to be seeking an identity. It may also help remove a few of the barriers that keep biblical and systematic theology unnecessarily apart from one another.

No methodology for writing Old Testament theology is flawless, and the one proposed here is no exception. Still, the suggested format is valid on historical, canonical and literary grounds. It offers a chance to read the Old Testament as communities of faith have done for centuries: as authoritative Scripture born in history, intended for the ages. It also attempts to keep theological reflection focused through the use of a theme recognized by large numbers of scholars as central to the Old Testament's message. In short, then, it may be one way to break through the common problems with the Old Testament's historicity, authority and unity. If so, it may also be an approach that bridges gaps between the testaments and thereby contributes to an informed and valid biblical theology.

2

The God
Who Creates

Genesis

. . . .

GENESIS STANDS AT THE HEAD OF THE CANON AND OF THE PENTATEUCH. AS the first book of the Bible it introduces the Lord, Israel and its importance and the way God's covenant binds the Lord and Israel to one another. It also establishes God as the sole creator, sustainer and judge of all persons regardless of their race or nationality. As the first book of the Pentateuch Genesis acts as foundational prelude to Israel's greatest leader (Moses), Israel's most crucial event (the exodus), Israel's defining moment (Sinai) and Israel's immediate future (the conquest of Canaan). It expresses the roots and results of worldwide rebellion against God and Israel's place in the remedy for that rebellion. Standing serenely above all these vital, defining ideas, though, is the book's portrayal of one God who alone creates and rules all that has been created. Thus Genesis has its own discrete theological witness that contributes to the Pentateuch and the Old Testament's theological unity.

As virtually any student of Scripture knows, Genesis has sparked heated debate for centuries. Rather than cooling over time, the arguments seem to have increased in volume and vehemence in the past several decades. Standing juxtaposed to one another have been Darwinists and creationists, scientists and theologians, professional theologians and laypersons, believers and skeptics. It is not the goal of this chapter to revisit or attempt to solve all these disputes. Rather this chapter intends to chart the theological message of Genesis as it relates to the whole of the Old Testament canon. To do so it focuses on the book's major thematic divisions; yet it also tries to incorporate important ideas that emerge within these divisions.

The book of Genesis has several separate sections, each of which testifies to the one God of Scripture. First, Genesis 1—2 provides the essential idea upon which the rest of the Scriptures are based: One God is the creator. This belief separates Old Testament faith from its ancient Near Eastern counterparts. Second, Genesis 3:1—6:4 presents the God who judges and protects. Human sin must be punished, yet God protects people from themselves and from one another. Third, Genesis 6:5—11:9 depicts the Lord as the one who punishes and renews. Worldwide punishment occurs here, yet God begins afresh with those made in his image.

Fourth, Genesis 11:10—25:18 describes the God who calls and promises. Abraham becomes the focal point of God's redemptive work. It is Abraham to whom the Lord pledges heir, relationship and land, themes David Clines identifies as central to the whole Pentateuch.[1] Fifth, in the life of Isaac the Lord is revealed as the God who provides covenantal continuity (25:19—28:9). The Abrahamic promises do not expire when he dies. They continue on through his son. Sixth, Genesis 28:10—36:43 portrays God as the one who elects and protects. No clearer case of divine election exists in Scripture than God's choice of Jacob. This painfully human man becomes the bearer of God's most precious promises. Seventh, Genesis 37—50 sets forth the God who preserves the covenant people. No threat, however severe, can thwart the Lord's plans for Abraham's family. The Creator's purposes for creation will be upheld through the lives of these particular creatures.

The God Who Creates: Genesis 1—2

From the very first verse of the canon God's uniqueness and sovereignty emerge. "In the beginning" only one God creates the heavens and earth. No other deity challenges God's right to create; no other deity helps God create; no other deity opposes God's creative activity. From the beginning, or from the origin of time and history, only God exists or acts. Only God's spirit hovers over the chaos of watery darkness. Whatever else Genesis 1:1-2 implies, it certainly portrays God as self-existent, unmade by anyone else, as timeless, since he exists whenever "the beginning" begins, and as able to generate the heavens and earth without aid.

This depiction of a self-existent, solitary, self-sufficient Creator differs sharply from other ancient creation accounts. Since 1876, when George Smith first published *The Chaldean Account of Genesis*,[2] scholars have discussed the relationship between how Genesis portrays origins and how texts from Babylon and Egypt describe those events. Soon after their publication some authors, such as Hermann Gunkel, analyzed the texts and concluded that Genesis and the Babylonian account share some common mythic elements.[3]

Other writers admitted certain similarities in the stories yet stressed their fundamental differences.[4] More recently commentators have stopped debating the relationship between the differing accounts and have tried to explain Israel's distinctive witness in the midst of the ancient world.[5] This approach is the most productive for theological inquiry and also offers the best way for the unique message of Genesis to be understood.

All scholars note that the chief difference between Genesis and other creation texts is the Israelite insistence on monotheism. Babylonian stories state that a dispute among the gods resulted in a dead god's body being thrown from heaven. This body becomes planet earth, and the drops of blood from other injured deities become individual persons. Egyptian stories are more sedate, but they too include several gods. Israel stands alone in claiming that a single God created all that exists. Monotheism in creation means that God is limited neither in nature nor by region to a particular place. God has no rivals. God has jurisdiction over all created persons and things.

In what appears in the text as swift succession, the Lord creates night and day, land and water, animals and people. Generally speaking, Genesis 1:3—2:3 presents the natural results of the preceding two verses. If only one God exists, then that God must be responsible for every creative act. Every created entity derives its existence, its name, its function, its basic "good" nature, its limitations and its sustenance from the one Creator. Clearly these verses stress God's sovereignty over creation. They state that this sovereignty begins with the ability to speak things into existence. Further, they imply that God's power and ownership extend to a sure knowledge of all that occurs. God has the authority to create and an awareness of how creation coheres.

These verses affirm the order and dignity of creation. While other creation stories tend to treat the human race as an aggravation to the pantheon and the created world as an afterthought of the gods, Genesis 1:1—2:3 presents the created order as the result of purposeful activity on the one God's part. Thus the natural world functions smoothly on a day-to-day basis under God's supervision. Each creature has its place in this world, and that place has inherent dignity because God insures that everything made is "good," whole and appropriate, for its purpose. God's sovereignty, knowledge, personal goodness and resolve produce an orderly world that removes the chaos and void mentioned in Genesis 1:2.

Human beings occupy a unique place among the creatures. They alone are made in the "image and likeness" of God. They alone are told to "rule and subdue" the earth, a command that seems to explain at least in part what "God's image" means. Like God, human beings have the capacity to make decisions that affect the earth and its inhabitants positively or negatively. The whole earth is given to sustain them (1:29-30), rather than vice versa, yet obviously wise rulership will be necessary for humans to draw sustenance from the land. At this point in Genesis there is no reason to expect anything but wise rulership. Simply put, humans are God's representatives on earth.[6]

Several other possible interpretations of "God's image" have been suggested, most of which can be drawn from Genesis 1—2. For example, God's image may include the ability to relate to the Lord (1:28-30; 2:15-25). At no point in Scripture does the text imply God has this sort of relationship with animals or plants. Only people converse with God; only people are held responsible by God for their actions; only people are given standards by which they must choose to live. Each of these elements implies a relationship between thinking, responsible, communicative personalities. Unless such a relationship exists it is impossible for people to act as God's representatives, or stewards, on earth.

Augustine believed the phrase "image and likeness" refers to "the powers of the soul, in memory, intellect, and love."[7] Certainly God has these capacities, and Adam's ability to work, name animals and "cleave" to Eve indicates both the man and the woman possess memory, intellect and the ability to love. Again, such qualities are necessary for relationship with God and for stewardship of the animals and the earth. Augustine's ideas complement a broader notion more than they stand alone.

The option that is unlikely is that the verse means that humans beings physically resemble the Lord. Gunkel thinks the text means just that and claims that this interpretation shows how Genesis reworked and adapted mythic ideas.[8] Gerhard von Rad believes that the passage at least implies this meaning.[9] This reading of the text neglects the obvious noncorporeal nature of the God who functions in Genesis 1—2. God can oversee the earth before, after and during the creative process and is evidently able to assess what occurs on earth from a "higher" vantage point. God can choose to speak elements such as light into existence, view the elements and assess the elements. God can also decide to relate closely to Adam in the garden without being confined to that space-time limitation. God is able to go between earth and nonearth. Thus the humans can do some things God can do; yet there are many things the Lord can do people cannot. The main difference lies in the humans' physical limitations, which God does not share. Physical resemblance, then, does not explain "image and likeness." It is much more likely that the human race's duties and relationship to God mentioned earlier fits the context.

One other issue in Genesis 1:26 deserves mention. The Lord says, "Let us make man in our image," a potentially odd comment in a monotheistic creation account. Since the next verse emphasizes "God created man in his own image" and stresses "he created" male and female, it is improbable that any other deity is invoked in Genesis 1:26. It is more likely that a plurality of personality is meant,[10] since both God and the Spirit of God appear in Genesis 1. It is not likely that the Lord addresses angels and other celestial beings.[11] To interpret the phrase in this manner implies that these beings share creator status with the Lord.

After creating the heavens, the earth and the human race, God establishes the seventh day as a time of ceasing of activity. This ceasing, or *shabbat* (sabbath), sets the seventh day apart from the other days of activity. Thus constant activity does not consume or define God and must not consume or define the rest of creation either. A time of ceasing is as valid as the times of making and doing in these seven days of creation.

Genesis 2:4-25 deals specifically with concepts introduced in the previous thirty-four verses. Most especially it focuses on God's initial relationship to the newly created human race. The self-existent, self-sufficient, transcendent yet present and involved Creator personally creates the first male (2:4-7). His life comes from God, not through a random coalescence of cells and tissue. When "Adam" receives life he awakes to an earth already prepared to sustain him, just as Genesis 1:3-26 has indicated. On this earth the man begins to work in and care for the garden in which he has been placed (2:15, 19-20), an activity that fulfills God's commands in Genesis 1:28. God allows the man total freedom in his pursuits with one exception: he may "not eat from the tree of the knowledge of good and evil" and is promised death if he breaks this command (2:17). It becomes clear, then, that God's favor is not unconditional in the sense that Adam may do as he pleases and still enjoy God's blessing. Rather he must abide by this simple law code to continue as he has begun. To do so he must trust God's word and believe God's warning. Faith is required.

Without a mate, though, the man's life is "not good," not complete (2:18). Such a conclusion cannot be final for a God whose character and creation are both "good" (e.g., 1:10, 12, 18). Thus God completes the human race by forming a woman from the man's body (2:21-22). Adam confesses his closeness to her, and Moses adds the comment that this union is the basis for the man's forsaking all previous familial relationships for a sole commitment to his wife (2:24).

A happier scene could hardly be imagined. The first couple is perfectly at ease with one another, for they are "naked and not ashamed" (2:25). There is no division, no emotional pain, no contention between them. Presumably they will fulfill the Lord's command to multiply on the earth (1:28), which indicates that sexuality has an important role in human relationships. No problems exist in this realm either.

The Creator God has completed the creative task. Earth, human beings and plant and animal life are all "good," all appropriate for their function. Humans exercise their "imaging" of God by relating to their Creator and by ruling the animals and the earth according to the Lord's command. Flawless in its design, perfect in its purpose, the creation reflects the Creator's genius and self-unity. Nothing more and nothing less could be expected. Time and human history have begun from the uncaused decision of God to speak them into existence.

Canonical Synthesis: Creation

Besides setting the stage for what immediately follows in Genesis itself, the creation account is used for a variety of canonical purposes in the rest of the Old Testament. Though these texts will be examined in due course, it is proper to note their existence now to demonstrate how creation influences other books. First, in the Prophets creation serves as evidence of God's concern for Israel and the rest of the human race and as proof that the Lord has every right to judge every living creature. For example, Isaiah claims that the fact that Yahweh creates the heavens and earth means that the Lord never grows weary and is ever willing to comfort a hurting people grown weary of Assyrian oppression (Is 40:12-31). Further, Isaiah links the notion that God alone made the earth with Yahweh's sovereignty over and redemption of Israel (Is 44:24). Finally, Isaiah says that since God is Creator, it is possible, no, necessary, that the Lord dictate history, even to the point of issuing a predictive prophecy about a future Persian leader, Cyrus (Is 45:1-8). Isaiah also states that a once-good earth can spring forth salvation and righteousness (Is 45:8). Amos, however, uses three creation hymns to punctuate denunciations and threats of certain punishment for sin (Amos 4:13; 5:8-9; 9:5-6). The Lord who created the earth and its people can certainly assess what occurs in human history. Turning in repentance to the Creator is the only way to avoid the coming devastation (Amos 5:8-9).

Second, several psalms celebrate Yahweh's status as Creator with the intent of stressing God's incomparability, the dignity of the human race made in Yahweh's image, the redemption of Israel and the constancy of God's commitment to David and his lineage. These latter two themes appear prominently in Psalms 136 and 89 respectively and will be treated later in light of the exodus and the Davidic covenant. It is significant to observe, however, that without God's status as solitary Creator these events become less significant, indeed no greater than claims about other gods made by polytheistic nations. Psalms 8, 47, 91 and 93—99 proclaim that God's greatness transcends yet permeates the earth and that the Lord also entrusts people with great, challenging tasks that prove the dignity in being God's creatures. In all these passages God stands supreme as the only God of record.

Third, Job 28 and Proverbs 8 argue that God's skills as Creator prove the Lord's unsurpassed wisdom. According to Job, God alone possesses an understanding of wisdom's depths because only the Lord has created mysterious elements like wind, water, lightning and thunder (Job 28:25-26). Since God's wisdom surpasses any human's, the author counsels readers to develop a healthy respect or fear of the Lord (Job 28:28). Similarly Proverbs 8:22-36 traces wisdom back to the creation of all things, for Yahweh created by using infinite wisdom. Thus for the writers of these wisdom-oriented texts the creation accounts testify to the majesty of God's applied intellect. This emphasis completes a biblical picture of God that includes images of God as maker, judge, master and sage. These ideas imply the Lord has creative, decisive, supervisory and intellectual capabilities no other single being possesses.

The God Who Judges and Protects: Genesis 3:1—6:4

When readers finish Genesis 2 it is with a sense of well-being bordering on euphoria. After all, the incomparable, solitary God has made an ideal world for a fully rational, relational, functional human race that in turn enjoys work, sex and spiritual pursuits. God's only rule, the prohibition against eating from "the tree of the knowledge of good and evil," has been kept so far.

What occurs next shatters this serenity. The woman encounters another created being, a serpent, that is subtle, crafty and verbally combative. It is important to emphasize the serpent's "creatureliness,"[12] because otherwise readers may conclude that this tempter has power equal to that of God. Later Scriptures discuss how the serpent became one who attempts to get people to turn against God (cf. Is 14:12-17; Ezek 28:2-5), but no such explanation appears here. Clearly, though, the serpent represents interests diametrically opposed to those stated by God in Genesis 2:16-17. Thus at least one created being resists Yahweh's commands. Since Genesis 1—2 reports that everything created is "good," it seems likely that the serpent represents a being that has corrupted its own good purpose, not one that God created corrupt from the start.

The conversation between the woman and the serpent begins with a thinly veiled challenge to God's single, simple command, proceeds to an outright denial of the consequences of disobedience announced in Genesis 2:17 and concludes with an overt temptation based on an attack on the Creator's character (3:1-6). After considering the serpent's arguments, the woman eats, as does her husband (3:6). This breaking of the Lord's command constitutes sin. The command was not too difficult to understand, nor was the consequence of this action. Rather eating the fruit amounts to a trusting of the tempter over the Creator and a desire for knowledge that destroys. Sin begins with mistrust of God, includes a craving for what harms one's self, neglects revelation of truth and ultimately concludes in destruction. Believing lies based on a lack of faith cannot produce obedience to the Creator.

Subsequent to their sin the humans experience the penalty for their disobedience. Their ease with one another is shattered, for they cover their nakedness (3:7). Their communion with God is broken, and they hide from the One who created them in his image (3:8-9). Their grasp of truth is weakened as they blame others for what they each have done (3:10-13). Fractures in friendship, fellowship and integrity are all casualties of sin.

Other consequences follow that are imposed by God. First, God condemns the serpent to eat dust and to a certain knowledge that he will duel with humans only to be crushed eventually (3:14-15). This text has rightly been deemed the *protoevangelion,* or first statement of good news, since it reassures readers that evil will not always dominate human beings. As the canon unfolds, this promise grows to include messianic concepts. Even at this seminal stage, however, the notion comes as a relief. The Creator remains in control of even the rebellious segments of the creation.

Second, the woman receives two basic penalties for her actions. One is physical, and the other is relational. Pain will accompany childbirth (3:16), which indicates that the effects of sin cannot be localized to some spiritual portion of human life. Rather sin impacts the woman's physical being as well, forcing her to remember her failure during what should be a joyous moment in her life. As hard as this punishment is, it is less pervasive than the second. Her sin also bears the penalty of frustration in her relationship with her husband (3:16).

Martin Luther argues that this punishment means that women are now placed under the man's authority in all matters but procreation and the nurturing of children, tasks he considers eminently honorable. This subjection would not have occurred without sin.[13] G. C. Aalders offers the fairly common idea that though the woman knows the pain associated with childbirth she will still desire sex with her husband, which in turn leads her back to her pain. He agrees in principle with Luther's opinions on the woman's subjection to her husband.[14] Victor Hamilton modifies this viewpoint somewhat, stating that this punishment means that instead of "being a reign of co-equals over the remainder of God's creation, the relationship now becomes a fierce dispute, with each party trying to rule the other."[15]

None of these interpretations has the universal implications the account seems to intend. Again the issue appears to be chiefly relational. Her desires will not be fulfilled in the manner she wishes. Never again will she enjoy flawless communion like that in Genesis 2:25. Claus Westermann captures the force of the passage by writing that

what he [the author of Genesis 3:16] really wants to say is much more
sober: just where the woman finds her fulfillment in life, her honor and
her joy, namely in her relationship to her husband and as mother of her
children, there too she finds that it is not pure bliss, but pain, burden,
humiliation and subordination.[16]

Emotional pain has been added to spiritual and physical pain. The pressures
caused by sin keep expanding.

Adam fares no better. Besides the problems he will encounter through the
punishment given to the serpent and the woman, he learns that his work
will not always be successful. He will sweat and strain yet encounter struggles
and setbacks in his efforts to make the ground produce. Work is not the
punishment, since God tells humans to work in Genesis 1:28. Sin results in
no ease for Adam, then, for he must battle the serpent, deal with the
frustrations he and his family produce and also face the certainty that no
certain success in labor will ever exist.

With the consequences of sin clearly stated and with a long-term promise
of the serpent's defeat in place, God acts in mercy to sustain the fallen couple.
God clothes them (3:21). The Lord also removes them from the garden to
protect them from eating of the tree of life, which had not been forbidden
previously, so that they will not live forever in a sinful condition (3:22-24).
Not even their sin can separate them from God's concern for and commitment
to the well-being of the people he has created.

Rapidly, inexorably, sin spreads. Eve gives birth to two sons, Cain and
Abel, who grow up to become a planter and a herdsman respectively (4:1-2).
Though the text does not explain how they know to do so, both men bring
offerings appropriate to their professions. Again without saying exactly why,
the text reports the Lord accepts Abel's sacrifice but not Cain's.[17] Though God
warns a pouting Cain that he must master sin, Cain not only ignores the
Lord's caution but also kills his brother (4:5-8). Sin shows itself here as
violence, as cruel, cold-blooded murder, as injustice. Obviously, too, one of
the results of sin is that an innocent party may suffer for the sins of others.

Like his parents, Cain responds to his own standards rather than to God's.
Therefore like his parents he suffers punishment, in his case the necessity of
living a nomadic, unsettled life (4:9-14). Still, God responds to Cain in mercy,
just as the Lord responds in mercy to Cain's parents (4:15-16). Cain has his
own family, which eventually produces Lamech, a man as violent as Cain
himself (4:17-24). Human technology improves (4:17, 21-22), but this ingenuity in no way diminishes the effects of sin. God graciously replaces the
dead with new life (4:25), and people learn to call on the Lord (4:26), yet
there is no return to the "goodness" of Genesis 1—2, nor can there be.

The genealogy in Genesis 5 and the strange account in Genesis 6:1-4 conclude the text's initial description of human sin and lead to the book's next major segment. From Adam to Lamech the human race begins, begets and dies (5:1-31). Humans fill the earth with their offspring in fulfillment of God's command (1:26-31), and they share the curse of death and painful toil on the earth (5:29). Despite the seeming monotony and sameness of procreation, life and death, under the surface of the text lies a sad fact: sin continues to increase as well, and sin never dies. This fact is evident in Genesis 6:1-4, where the world seems completely out of control. Interpretations of this text range from the idea that the verses are basically mythological[18] to the notion that they mean humans "involved themselves in unholy marriages, and sin soon became the dominant characteristic of the race."[19] All scholars agree that the passage demonstrates pervasive human sinfulness, the consequences of which emerge in Genesis 6:5 and the following text.

Canonical Synthesis: Pervasive Sin

Who is responsible for all this sin? It is vital to conclude that each individual is responsible for his or her actions. Though God created the serpent, the serpent was not commanded to tempt the humans. God warned the people against eating the fruit of one tree, but Eve and Adam lacked the faith necessary to believe the Lord instead of the serpent. When faced with believing God enough to keep one law, the humans fail. Their failure is their own, though, since they had been warned and since the serpent possessed no physically coercive powers.

How continuous is this sin? How ongoing is it? Jewish and Christian scholars have stated for centuries that humans are born in sin after Adam and Eve's fall. Many thinkers have also disputed this interpretation. Though the Genesis texts make no explicit statement one way or the other, no human avoids sin after Genesis 3. No one is sinless; everyone is affected by living in a sinful world. By birth, by choice or by both, the result remains that every human sins and that every human suffers for that sin spiritually, physically, emotionally, relationally and vocationally.

How important is the prevalence of sin in the rest of the Old Testament canon? In a very real sense, the rest of Scripture deals with the solution to the sin problem. Moses mediates a covenant in the Pentateuch that includes sacrifices for sins offered in faith by penitent sinners. The Former Prophets sketch how long-term, habitual sin, left unchecked, gradually pulls Israel into destruction. Prophets like Isaiah and Jeremiah lament being among an unclean people (Is 6:5) and being a person with a wicked, diseased heart (Jer 17:9). Isaiah 13—27, Jeremiah 46—51, Ezekiel 25—32, Amos 1:2—2:3, and other passages proclaim the sinfulness of all nations. The psalmists declare there are no righteous persons (e.g., Ps 14:1-3; 53:1-3; 140:3). Job and Proverbs counsel wisdom in light of human error and foolishness, while the remainder of the Writings depict the effects of sin on Israel's exiles (see Esther and Daniel) and the nation's attempt to overcome its own sin (see Ecclesiastes, Ezekiel, Nehemiah, 1-2 Chronicles).

Thus sin never skips a generation, nor does it skip a single individual. Perhaps these particular stories are not retold as the reason for relentless human sin, but the canon certainly wrestles with the results of these accounts from this passage forward.[20] The starting point, the place where sin enters the human race, is Genesis 3, a fact Paul highlights in Romans 5:12 as a contrast to Christ's work.

The God Who Punishes and Renews: Genesis 6:5—11:9

This section of Genesis provides significant insight into God's interior and exterior character. That is, these verses explain how God's motives lead to God's actions. While doing so, they also indicate what the Lord plans to do in the long and short term about runaway human sin. So far God's major attributes have been creativeness, power, mercy and a commitment to high ethical standards. God's concerns have included sustaining and relating to people. Now sustenance and relationship will occur in a way that will force human beings to take full responsibility for their reprehensible actions.

Genesis 6:5-8 is probably the most negative statement in Genesis about the human race as a whole. Whereas Genesis 1:31 and Genesis 2:25 speak of goodness and a lack of shame, this passage states that sin pervades every pore of the human being. At the same time, few texts in all of Scripture speak more clearly about God's motives for action. The fact that God's motives remain good when the human race's have become so impure highlights sin's inappropriateness and God's correctness in doing something about it.

As in previous texts, God sees what occurs on earth. This time the Lord sees how the human race has grown progressively more violent and wicked. The Lord knows the inclinations of human hearts, a sure sign that God knows everything. Sadly, every inclination is always toward evil. Every plan made tends toward wickedness. Having seen (6:5), God now feels grief and pain over what people are doing. God's power and all-inclusive seeing lead to proper emotion, not to callousness or cynicism or brutality. Based on this seeing and feeling, the Lord determines to change the policy of allowing the human race to live in this condition. God's regret means action must be taken, not that a great cosmic mistake has been made.[21] Therefore the Lord determines to punish the wicked but to spare Noah, a man who acts differently than others and who thereby avoids their punishment (6:8).

Noah becomes the catalyst for God's mercy and judgment. God decides to punish worldwide sin by eliminating the sinful through a comprehensive flood (6:13). Noah will be spared by building a boat and will save his family and the animals by leading them into the ship (6:14-22). Through this process God's intentions of punishing sin and sparing a righteous minority, or remnant, are realized. Noah's family thus becomes the means by which a merciful God preserves the human race as well as a visible symbol of how a just and good God distinguishes between faithful and disobedient persons.

The major theological force of this section is magnified by the differences between the Genesis flood account and certain Babylonian parallel stories.[22] As is well known, the Babylonian flood story has elements in common with the biblical account, such as the presence of a hero who builds a boat, a devastating flood, a bird sent to survey earth's terrain and a sacrifice made when the humans emerge from the ship.[23] Though these framing devices serve both stories, the reason for the flood, the reason a human is spared, the purpose for sacrifice and the very number of existing gods differ in the accounts. Clearly this last difference takes precedence over the others, for it ultimately explains the other variations, as will be noted.

Once the flood recedes and Noah emerges from his ship he worships God through offering sacrifices (8:20). God responds favorably and graciously to Noah's devotion. Despite the sinfulness of the human race the Lord promises never again to destroy sinful persons as in the flood (8:21-22). Further, God renews the original commands made to people in Genesis 1:26-31. Humans are to multiply, rule the creatures and receive sustenance from the earth (9:1-3). Only two requirements are expected from humans: they must not eat animals whose blood has not been drained, and they must not take human life (9:4-6).

Based on God's promises and Noah's commitments, these two parties make a covenant, or binding agreement that includes pledges, responsibilities and blessings. This word *(covenant)* will occur in several future key contexts in the canon, so it is important to make some preliminary observations about the concept now. By Moses' time (c. 1450 B.C.) the covenant was an established part of ancient society, but what does the concept mean in Genesis 6:17-18 and Genesis 9:8-17?

In the first text the covenant is based on God's prior knowledge of and relationship with Noah.[24] The Lord already knows the quality of Noah's character and offers the covenant based on this awareness. Besides stating the quality of the relationship between God and Noah, the covenant separates Noah from the sinful humanity of that era. He becomes the sole focus of God's work with creation. Finally, the covenant includes responsibilities that go with the privileges connected with the offer.[25] Noah must believe God's word, build the ark, collect the animals and his family and actually survive the flood. God saves Noah by explaining the future to him.

After the flood the covenant is explained, expanded and formalized. Though their hearts remain wicked (8:21), human beings are expected to care for the animals and stop brutalizing one another (9:1-6). In other words, they are to treat one another the way they want to be treated instead of acting like Cain and Lamech. They are also to fulfill God's original commands (1:26-31). In return the Lord will sustain them (9:1-4) and protect them from watery cataclysmic judgment (9:11). These conditions and promises in place, God establishes the rainbow as a sign that the covenant benefits are unceasing. This whole process highlights God's gracious and saving personal self-revelation and foreshadows virtually every subsequent occurrence of covenant making in the Old Testament.

Two striking incidents follow the covenant text. First, Noah makes wine, gets drunk and lies naked in his tent (9:20-21). Ham sees his father yet does nothing but tell his brothers Shem and Japheth about their father's condition. The brothers cover Noah without looking at him (9:23). Clearly the human race will not stop sinning, as Genesis 8:21 has already indicated. Second, upon awaking, Noah curses Ham, the father of the Canaanites, but blesses Shem and Japheth, especially Shem (9:25-27).

Noah's blessing is unusual in that it really blesses Shem's God instead of Shem himself.[26] Of course if Shem's God flourishes, then Shem will prosper as well. This blessing subsumes the human under the divine[27] and also implies God will aid Israel, the descendants of Shem.[28] From this point forward God's specific electing work will go through Shem's family.[29] The impact will be that God will be blessed, glorified and exalted in some manner through the particular lineage of this respectful son of Noah. Just how will unfold later in the text.

Despite all that the Lord has done to create, sustain, correct and renew the earth and the human race, sin continues. New ways to sin are devised. As the people multiply and spread, they center their population in "a plain in Shinar" (11:1). There they use their technological expertise to build a city and a tower for the express purpose of honoring themselves and avoiding God's command to fill and rule the earth (11:2-4; cf. 1:28; 9:7).[30] Human pride is certainly not new, but the corruption of technology to tempt them to act proudly has not been mentioned to this point in the text.

Once more God "sees" what occurs on earth, and once more God acts to counter what people are doing (11:5-9; cf. 6:5). Since the humans use their common language to undergird their work the Lord confuses their speech patterns. The project thus interrupted, God scatters the people, which forces them to fulfill the Lord's purpose for them. This punishment reemphasizes God's sovereignty, God's determination to fulfill the stated purpose for creation and God's merciful nature. Rather than destroy the culprits, the Lord chooses to force them to do what is best for them. Still, sin continues unabated. No real long-term solution to this menace has appeared.

Clearly polytheists must accept limited confidence in the gods' character, limited security under the gods' "ordering" of the earth and limited knowledge of how or why they may be judged. Moses' account, however, urges readers to know that God grieves over sin, controls injustice, never perpetuates tyranny of any sort and empowers those who are obedient. Monotheists therefore have the freedom to live confidently even in the midst of a chaotic world.

The God Who Calls and Promises: Genesis 11:10—25:18

If Genesis 1—11 highlights the creation of earth and humanity, then in a very real sense Genesis 12—50 emphasizes God's creation of a special clan, or nation. This group of chosen people plays several strategic roles. First, their election is the key to solving the sin problem related so unrelentingly in Genesis 3—11. Second, they provide a visible symbol to the world of God's forgiving grace to sinful human beings. Third, they demonstrate the necessity of commitment and adherence to the one Creator God. Fourth, they illustrate the necessity of exercising faith in their relationship to the Lord.

These chapters mark the beginning of canonical texts that can be dated with some historical precision and illuminated with details from extrabiblical sources. Most scholars agree that, broadly speaking, the patriarchs (Abraham, Isaac and Jacob) lived about 2100-1700 B.C. Some experts argue for later dates,[31] but these claims are unlikely given the preponderance of contrary evidence.[32] This ability to link text and history not only expands interpreters' knowledge of biblical backgrounds but also shows how theology was hammered out in the midst of both everyday life and earth-shattering events. Theology marked human lives then as well as now.

Genesis 12—50 can be divided by the appearance of its major characters. Abraham dominates the scene from the first mention of his name in Genesis 11:26 until his death in Genesis 25:11. Traveler, warrior, thinker and all-too-human struggler for faith, this father of the Israelite people begins the process of initiating a single nation and salvation for all people. Though Isaac, Abraham's son, is also a vital character, it is Isaac's son Jacob who dictates the story line in Genesis 25:19—36:43. This enigmatic man fathers twelve sons who become the twelve tribes, or clans, of Israel. One of these sons, Joseph, acts as central figure in Genesis 37:1—50:26, though the tenacious Jacob remains in view until 50:14! Each of these individuals, their wives, their children, their friends and their enemies provide a panoramic yet personal view of how faith, work, comedy and tragedy interact in history and theology.

By the close of the tower of Babel account, human sin's scope and depth ought to concern even the most dispassionate reader. After all, sin is indeed universal and corrupts even the human race's technological achievements. It seems logical for another universal solution, such as the flood, to emerge, but God opts for a different approach. God works through Shem's line until Abram appears, then elects him to bear the hope humans need to find relief from their guilt. This telescopic approach to a problem will appear again and again in the Scriptures as the canon unfolds.

At first Abram seems as ordinary as any of the other persons named in a genealogical table (11:10-32). In Genesis 12:1-9, however, he becomes the focal point of God's dealings with the human race. Through an act of direct, personal revelation the Lord commands Abram to leave his homeland and his father's house (cf. Gen 2:24) and go to an unspecified location he will be shown (12:1). In response to Abram's act of faith, God promises certain blessings: Abram will become a great nation (12:2), which is quite a pledge to a man whose wife has already been identified as barren (cf. 11:30); Abram will be blessed with a great reputation (12:2); Abram will be blessed with protection (12:3); Abram will bless all nations (12:3). The blessing of a homeland implicit in 12:1 becomes explicit in 12:7, where God tells Abram that Canaan will belong to his "seed," or descendants. Clines summarizes these blessings as heir/nation, covenant/relationship and land.[33] Each of these blessings deserves brief treatment.

First, Abram will receive a replacement for the homeland he leaves in response to God's summons. Obviously he must act in faith to gain this particular blessing. Thus both divine promise and human obedience make the blessing occur. Since all subsequent blessings are dependent on this initial faithful response, none of the promises are unconditional in the sense that Abram need do nothing to inherit them. Though the realization of this promise requires several centuries, as will be seen, from this point forward Abram and his progeny believe the land is theirs by divine right. Emphasizing the land here indicates that the earth, or land, may finally be inhabited by people willing to obey Genesis 1:26-31.

Second, the pledge of a great nation means that God may begin redeeming sinful humanity by calling a single individual but fully intends for that number to grow. Thus not only will a childless, barren couple birth a nation, but also the morally barren world will flourish again. As is the case with the land promise, Abram must wait what will seem to him an interminably long time. Perhaps more than with any other single promise, Abram struggles to believe this blessing will ever materialize or to allow God to deliver on the pledge in a timely fashion.

Third, the mention of a great name, or reputation, highlights the spread of Abram's influence to a world that needs to imitate his faithfulness. God's name will be honored as Abram's is honored, so the blessings of his fame will enhance God's reputation as well.

Fourth, God's protection insures the new nation's future. Abram himself need not fear those who wish him harm, for God will protect the chosen man and his family. The Lord's guardianship guarantees that only those who can overthrow the Creator can destroy Abram. More immediately, as Abram journeys toward the land God will show him, he will pass safely. Just as in Genesis 1:26—2:17 and Genesis 3:21-24, the Lord pledges to sustain those whom he has created, called and made promises to.

Fifth, the notion of all nations being blessed by Abram seals God's plan for worldwide renewal of human beings. All persons are infected with and affected by sin. The results of this fact have been catastrophic. Now God identifies an individual through whom the Lord's plan can be revealed. Abram's faith can replace Adam and Eve's doubts about God's commands, can offer further insight into how evil's head will be crushed (cf. Gen 3:15), can begin the process of magnifying Shem's God (cf. Gen 9:26) and can reverse the international pride and chaos surrounding the Babel episode. What remains to be seen is how this promise comes true, which places it on the same footing as the other four.

God's choice of Abram also initiates the ongoing practice of divine election. Perhaps God elects Noah, too, but the text at least hints that in Noah's era the Lord has no one else to choose. Here God selects Abram from people like himself, though Abram may indeed have possessed special qualities for the task given him. Still, the Lord chooses Abram the same way God determines to create the heavens and earth, out of the sheer freedom that comes from being the unique, all-sufficient, self-contained God. The Lord also chooses that which is good, that which benefits creation. Election here does not exclude or condemn anyone. Rather it works exclusively as a benefit to a world that has no intention of doing what is right. Election in this case proves God's merciful kindness to the world, not just to Abram.

Though he sets out from Haran in response to God's commands, Abram does not exercise faith in every situation he faces. For example, after encountering famine in Canaan, the land God promises him, Abram keeps journeying south until he arrives in Egypt. Once there he forgets the Lord's promise of protection and seeks to protect himself by calling Sarai his sister. For placing his wife's and the Egyptians' virtue in jeopardy he receives a tongue lashing from the pharaoh, who nonetheless sends him away with gifts that add to Abram's wealth (12:10-20). Similar lapses in faith occur when he has a child with Hagar and then allows her to be mistreated (16:1-16), when he repeats the "sister" deception a second time (20:1-18) and when he questions whether he will ever have a child with his wife (17:17-18). He may be the key to the solution of the sin problem, but he is far from sinless himself.

However, Abram definitely displays faith in God at strategic points. He allows his nephew Lot first choice when they divide land (13:1-18), he rescues Lot from kidnappers and refuses reward from Sodom's king (14:1-24), he adopts the practice of circumcision as a sign of his family's commitment to the Lord (17:1-27), and he prays for Sodom and Lot to be spared God's judgment (18:16-33). Each of these episodes indicates Abram's potential for permanently embedded trust in the God who has elected and called him. Two other incidents, however, act as final proof of his moral fiber and as examples for future people of faith. One takes place relatively early in Abram's journey and the second later in his life when he has become Abraham, the father of nations.

In Genesis 15, Abram's early mistakes and initial victories lie in the past. Once again Yahweh's revelation comes to Abram, but this time he questions whether God's promise of a son, which is in turn the key to the promise of land, will ever be fulfilled (15:1-3). In response to the chosen's agony, God reiterates the promise. Solely in response to the Lord's reassurance Abram believes God, and God counts that belief as righteousness on his part (15:6). Certainly his earlier acts of faith help him believe now,[34] yet this instance is all the more impressive because it occurs years after the original promise is tendered and because it continues to have no evidential basis other than God's word and God's character. As Walter Brueggemann says, this renewed faith "is not grounded in the old flesh of Sarah nor the tired bones of Abraham, but in the disclosing word of God."[35] This faith resides in God's reliability, which is inseparable from the Lord's personhood. Faith here amounts to one friend's trust of another friend's promises.

Because of his faith, God considers him righteous, or rightly related to God, and thus secure in the Lord,[36] even though Abram has not technically done anything. Abram's faith is not a work, but it does require a willingness to set aside clear physical evidence (no child) in favor of the unadorned promise of God. In other words, faith may not be physical work, but it is not easy nonetheless. God realizes its value and strenuous nature and recognizes that faith is the first step to obedient action. Faith leads Abram to demonstrate his righteousness by offering a sacrifice in 15:7-21, faith sustains Abram when he learns his descendants will not inherit Canaan for over four centuries (15:13-14), and faith therefore provides the basis for the covenant between God and Abram that is implicit in Genesis 12—14 but made explicit in Genesis 15. Without faith there can be no righteousness. Where faith exists, however, more and more righteous action will follow as the human-divine relationship unfolds.[37]

Years after the formalization of this faith-based covenant, Abram, now called Abraham ("father of nations"), faces the most significant "test" (22:1) of his belief in God. Having adopted circumcision as a sign of the covenant (17) and having received his heir after twenty-five years of waiting (21:1-8), Abraham is tested when God commands him to sacrifice Isaac, the son of promise (22:1-2). Without hesitating, Abraham takes the boy to a place of offering and then prepares to kill him (22:3-10). God stops him, stating that this action proves Abraham "fears" God, which is another way of saying that he bases his life on God. Here "faith" and "fear" amount to the same thing, obedience. Once again faith works itself out in actions that have their basis in trust in God alone. Abraham trusts God even when the Lord commands the unthinkable, indeed when God commands what seems to be the irreparable removal of the key to the promises in Genesis 12:1-9. The Lord honors this faith by offering renewed reassurances of blessing (22:15-19). With the test over and Abraham's faith proven, the chosen servant of God, the key to the sin problem's solution, concludes his life by paving the way for Isaac to continue to build the nation (23:1—25:18).

The very nature of Abraham's faith invites reflection on the character of the God in whom he trusts. First, it is clear that only one deity appears in this story. Though he believes the term *monotheism* can be properly applied only when the text chooses Yahweh over "a possible worship of several gods," Westermann writes, "What is decisive is the following. In the individual patriarchal narratives people always stand face to face with only one God; it is always only one God who deals with and speaks to people."[38] This God is identical to the deity in Genesis 1—11, so the Lord who creates, sustains, judges and renews also elects, calls, sustains, promises, tests and blesses. The same deity concerned about the creation's sin calls and relates to the one chosen to mediate eventual victory over sin.

Second, this one God relates to people on a personal basis, communicating commands, promises and guidance through each successive decade. It is impossible to know so many years after such revelations exactly how they occurred, but it is important to note that these encounters come at God's initiative and that they convey actual concrete communication concerning Abraham's past, present and future. The Lord never stops guiding human beings who listen to the Lord.

Third, the promises of heir, land, nation and international blessing require faith on Abraham's part. Abraham must find his security in God rather in shifting circumstances.[39] He must believe that to possess a relationship with God is the same thing as possessing the fulfillment of the Lord's promises.[40] Just as God counts Abraham's faith as righteousness, so also does Abraham count God's promise as righteousness. Abraham believes that the Lord's plan for history is real and therefore bound to occur.[41] No lesser faith could possibly lead him to accept signs such as circumcision or endure commands such as to leave his homeland or, more particularly, to sacrifice his son.

Fourth, God's promises to Abraham provide a framework for the rest of the Old Testament, indeed for the rest of the Bible. No doubt many routes to the unity of Scripture exist, but none dare neglect Abraham's role in that unity. Israel emerges as his descendants. David is an Israelite, and the messiah comes from his lineage. Israel becomes the people of God that are called to glorify the Lord in all the earth, a role the combined Israelite and non-Israelite church says in the New Testament that it assumes. The desire to conquer, to possess and to keep the land promised to Abraham consumes many pages of the Old Testament, though these concerns recede in the New Testament. Simply stated, then, it is hard to overstate this section's importance in biblical literature and thus biblical theology.

Canonical Synthesis: Abraham and the New Testament

Canonically speaking, Genesis 12:1-9, 15:6 and 22:1-19 receive significant treatment in the New Testament. Paul concludes that Jesus fulfills the promise of international blessing, for Jesus is the offspring of Abraham who mediates salvation to all persons (Gal 3:16). As E. J. Carnell states, "Abraham is a blessing to all nations because Jesus Christ is the true offspring of Abraham. There is one covenant; it unites both economies in the Bible."[42] Further, Paul argues that in Abraham's life faith produced righteousness that led to the patriarch's acceptance of circumcision, which means that salvation occurs without works of righteousness (Rom 4:1-15). The only way for God's promises to come true, therefore, is for faith to be exercised, not for works to occur (Rom 4:16-25).

In his discussion of Abraham's life, James declares that the faith mentioned in Genesis 15:6 is proven by the willingness to sacrifice in Genesis 22:1 (Jas 2:18-24). Paul's ministry requires a focus on the fact that works without faith are dead, while James's requires the emphatic comment that faith without works is dead. Both men placed priority on faith, for both knew which text comes first in the canon (cf. Rom 4:10; Jas 2:23). Both recognized the foundational nature of faith. Both realized the logical, essential, historical, practical emergence of obedience from this faith. Without faith, promises are just words. Without obedience, "faith" is mere mental, emotional or verbal assent and thus has no real substance. Abraham's faith had substance. The New Testament writers tried to insure that no one claiming Abraham's lineage lacked the substantive faith of their father.

The God Who Provides Continuity: Genesis 25:19—28:9

Upon Abraham's death his son Isaac becomes the story's central character, though just for a few pages. This Isaac is the chosen heir of faith (17:15-21), the son for whom Abraham waited twenty-five years (21:1-4), the son Abraham loved but refused to love more than God (22:1-11). Isaac witnessed, indeed experienced, his father's greatest test of faith and therefore knew that faith required obedience. He also knew that God provides for the faithful (22:13-14).

Isaac's life quietly proclaims the necessary truth that the faith required for blessing has been passed to the next generation. Continuity has been assured, and continuity of faithful persons is clearly and sorely lacking in Genesis 1—11. God acts directly to effect this continuity, for in Genesis 26:1-5 the Lord appears to Isaac in an unspecified manner and commands him to stay in the promised land (12:7) instead of fleeing to Egypt. God pledges three things in return. First, the Lord "will be with" Isaac, a phrase that indicates continual presence. This benefit grows in importance as the canon continues to the point that it becomes the only absolute, constant detail in the call stories related to Moses, Jeremiah and others. Second, God will bless Isaac as Abraham was blessed. In other words he will be protected and will enjoy material prosperity. Third, the Lord will multiply his descendants. In fact God must do so to keep previous pledges to Abraham.

His lifestyle demonstrates that Isaac acts in faith on God's promises. He knows that God's assurances provide the necessary theological link between himself and Abraham. Like his father, he is far from flawless, yet like his father he refuses to shrink from the arduous process of living in an unpossessed promised land. His patience and durability give witness to God's presence with him in every area of his life (26:28-29). Also like his father he experiences pain in his family, in his case pain due to his twin sons' rivalry (25:19-34; 27:1-40). He also suffers physically more than any person in Genesis.

In the midst of his worst pain, Isaac attempts to bless his oldest and favorite son, Esau, with the Lord's covenant (27:1-4). His attempt runs contrary to the Lord's prediction when the twins are born (25:23) and eventually fails through Jacob and his mother's deceitfulness (27:5-31). This loss is a great blow to Esau, who earlier despised his birthright and sold it to Jacob (25:29-34). The faith passes to the next generation, but to what sort of man? How can continuity continue when Jacob seems to possess little if any of the character Abraham and Isaac exhibit? Theologically speaking the issue is whether sin will consume the earth again as it did after the flood.

Ultimately the answer to these questions lies in the nature of the God who created Adam, Noah, Abraham, Isaac and Jacob. Either the Creator can handle the creation or not. In this monotheistic account there is no other option. But in this account God has already shown that two generations of faith and obedience are possible. Therefore the possibility definitely exists that God's plan is effective and will lead to future glory. At this point the plan seems imperiled or at least in doubt from a human perspective. The most comforting fact is that God has not swerved in purpose, promise or power. God's character remains intact in a way that increases the reader's respect and anticipation for the future.

Though Genesis 27 states that Isaac believes his death is imminent, he in fact lives for another two decades, not succumbing to his afflictions until Genesis 36:27-29. His prolonged illness causes Jacob to surpass him as the story's main character before his death. This situation will occur again, since Joseph dominates Genesis 37—50 even though Jacob lives until Genesis 49:29-33 and since Joseph dies in Genesis 50:26 yet remains a factor in the account in Exodus 1:1-18 and Exodus 13:19. Not until Moses dies does the text produce a clean break between major characters, and even Moses is followed by the by then quite familiar Joshua. Again the inclusion of this type of historical fact makes the theological point that the Lord provides linkages between each successive generation.

The One God Who Elects and Protects: Genesis 28:10—36:43

Few Old Testament texts highlight the biblical concepts of election and grace more than the Jacob accounts. As has already been noted, God says that Jacob will rule over Esau while the twin boys jostle each other in their mother's womb (25:23). God's prediction comes true in part when Jacob gains the birthright Esau considers unimportant (25:34) and steals the blessing Esau wants desperately to possess (27:1-40). Because of Esau's hatred of Jacob, their parents send the "blessed one" to Laban, his uncle (27:42—28:2; cf. Laban's role in Gen 24). Before he leaves, however, his father states clearly that Jacob must carry on the Abrahamic faith and receive the Abrahamic blessings (28:3-4). Certainly Jacob has demonstrated no godly character to this point. Rather God chooses before such actions could possibly occur, a point Paul makes in Romans 9:10-18. God blesses Jacob above Esau out of love for Jacob, an idea Malachi 1:2-3 highlights. God's grace selects this terribly imperfect man and not because of merit on his part.[43] Love dictates the decision, and this love is as much for Abraham and Isaac as it is for Jacob, since God's earlier promises remain in effect.

What is left unstated at this point in Genesis is whether God's choice of Jacob precludes faith and obedience on the chosen one's part. Slowly, perceptibly, even inexorably the Lord makes the elected one a person of faith, but the task is neither quick nor easy.[44] God begins the work in the same manner as with Abraham and Isaac—through revelation and promise (28:10-22). Every promise made to Abraham and Isaac is offered to Jacob:

land (28:13), descendants (28:14), being a blessing to all peoples of the earth (28:14) and God's abiding presence (28:15). Jacob learns beyond a shadow of a doubt what it means to possess the birthright and blessing in Abraham's family.[45] He seems impressed that he has received such promises, but he offers an equivocal response that pales in comparison with his grandfather's and father's reactions to their own initial divine encounters. As if he were trading with Esau or a tribal leader, he promises to make the Lord his God only if he returns home safely at some point in the future. God's love for Jacob has not been conditioned by works, but Jacob seems determined not to offer *his* love quite so cheaply.

The circumstances of Jacob's life magnify the consequences of wanting blessings without offering unreserved obedient faith. At the same time they reveal that God's purposes and promises will be realized no matter how difficult their fulfillment. For example, Jacob eventually fathers twelve sons and one daughter. The twelve sons become the beginnings of the twelve tribes of Israel and thus the catalyst for the completion of God's promises to Abraham, Isaac and Jacob of a great nation developing from their progeny.

To have these children, however, Jacob endures marrying two women, one he loves and one he does not love (29:15-30), because of a deception played on him by the women and Laban their father (29:1-14). He suffers division in his household brought about by the women vying for his attention (cf. Gen 30:8) and labors under the watchful eye of Laban, his self-serving father-in-law (30:25-43). Eventually he gets rich, just as his father and grandfather before him did, but only after two decades of hard labor for Laban, whose sons interpret Jacob's prosperity as detrimental to their family (30:1-2). In his father-in-law Jacob finds a man as willing to deceive, as willing to pursue his own ends, as willing to make deals as himself. As G. J. Wenham summarizes these episodes,

> Yet through these experiences God's purposes were advanced. Jacob had been promised he would have a multitude of descendants, and it was through the unloved Leah and her maid Zilpah that eight of the twelve tribes traced their descent. Thus even the deceitfulness of Laban and Jacob can be overruled to bring the divine plan to fulfillment (cf. Hos 12:2). Human sins may have delayed Jacob's return to his homeland, but all other aspects of the promises made to him were advanced by his unhappy sojourn in Mesopotamia.[46]

God has kept every significant promise to Abraham, Isaac and Jacob to this point in the story. Still, Jacob remains a less than faithful individual. When the Lord promises to "be with" Jacob if he will return home, however, even this problem finds its solution. Jacob fears going home because of Esau's hatred, so he divides his family into units and sends Esau presents (32:1-21).

At the same time he fervently prays that God, who promised to be with him, will protect him from his brother (32:9-12).

In countering Jacob's fears the Lord takes extraordinary measures to secure, to elect, Jacob's character in faith. Late at night, near the river Jabbok, Jacob is attacked by a person whose identity is slowly divulged in the account. First the one who wrestles with him is called "a man" (32:24) but is no typical man, for he merely "touches"[47] Jacob's thigh and yet cripples him for life (32:25, 31-32). Next, the crippler asks the tenacious Jacob to release him, noting that daybreak approaches. Is this attacker a river demon that fears light, as Westermann suggests,[48] or simply one ready to bring the encounter to a climax? The situation clarifies when the attacker changes Jacob's name to Israel, or from "heel grabber/supplanter" to "he struggles with God," and promises him he has "overcome." In blessing Jacob and changing his name the attacker proves superior to the newly crippled, newly named man. When the episode ends, the text says Jacob believes himself lucky to be alive, for he thinks he has seen God and survived (32:30). He has not encountered a river demon in his opinion. He has encountered one who knows his past, present and future. Only God fits this description in the book of Genesis.

But does God really act in such a manner? Does the Lord insist on obedience in such a determined fashion? Does God use physical coercion for spiritual ends? Does election extend so far? These pertinent theological questions have been answered negatively by many scholars who believe mythical or legendary elements have crept into Genesis here. They believe the text's theological thrust is that it explains that God's selection of Israel goes back to Jacob's experiences in ancient times and places. In their view, then, election remains the passage's major emphasis, even though the details are not totally accurate.[49]

Certainly God works in a reasonably similar way in other canonical texts. For example, Jeremiah believes his own ministry occurs under a compulsion he likens to rape (Jer 20:7-12). Ezekiel's work may have included a period of divinely induced dumbness (Ezek 3:26), and Job's testing included physical suffering (Job 1—2). In the New Testament, Paul's entrance into the church and the ministry begins with blindness caused by a bright light sent by God (Acts 9:1-19). Clearly, canonically speaking at least, Jacob's experiences are unusual to be sure, yet not totally unique. Election and service sometimes entail physical as well as emotional and spiritual pressure. God is not limited to any one aspect of human existence when calling, preparing and disciplining the chosen.

Beyond the oddness of this account lie two vital theological points that characterize Jacob's entire experience with the Lord. First, God wrestles with Jacob because Jacob is a major key to the fulfillment of the promises to

Abraham, which in turn is the Lord's response to the human race's sin problem. Thus his election amounts to the latest step in a redemptive process. Second, God wrestles with Jacob and changes his name to reassure him that he has indeed "overcome." He will return home. He will be blessed. Esau will not kill him. All God's promises made in Genesis 28:10-22 will be fulfilled, and his prayer for help in Genesis 32:9-12 has been answered. Therefore the scene has the theological impact of demonstrating God's mercy for both Jacob and the human race, since it is the pledges from Genesis 12:1-9 that come true.

God indeed does protect Jacob from his brother (33:1-17) and also keeps the clan safe from those who abuse them and even from their own vengefulness (34:1-31). In response Jacob sets up an altar near Shechem (33:20), but is he willing to make a commitment to singular devotion to the Lord as he himself promised in Genesis 28:21-22? The answer comes in Genesis 35:1-5. Here Jacob receives another divine command to travel, this time to Bethel, the site of the Genesis 28 vision. There the family will settle and build an altar to the God who speaks and protects (35:1).

Jacob senses the importance of the command, for he orders his family to rid themselves of all idols and to purify themselves for worship (35:2). Jacob intends to keep his earlier vow (35:3), so the family hands over earrings and idols (35:4). As Derek Kidner observes, "Any impression that patriarchal worship was free and easy is dispelled by these demands, which already have the makings of the Sinai law in their call for a single loyalty, ceremonial purity and the renunciation of magic (the earrings were evidently charms; cf, perhaps Ho. 2:13)."[50] The fact that Jacob buries the idols illustrates these images' lack of value and vitality. These idols are stolen in the first place by Rachel under somewhat humorous circumstances (cf. Gen 31:22-35), only to be buried like the nonentities they are. Certainly Moses has no respect for these images and thereby strips them of any sense of dignity or worth.[51] It is impossible to imagine treating the God who creates, calls, chooses and protects as these images have been.

Once again God encounters Jacob at Bethel to reaffirm the promises made to Abraham and Isaac, yet also to Jacob. First, God repeats the name change initially mentioned in Genesis 32:28 as a way of reminding Jacob of the divine election and protection that are his (35:9-10). Second, God repeats the promise of nationhood (35:11). Third, God reemphasizes the gift of land (35:12). At long last Jacob's commitments have become more worthy. He has ceased making deals. Instead he recognizes God's faithfulness as a spur to his own. This one who wrestles to become a person of faith has at last chosen to serve the only God who cannot be stolen, sat upon and buried, the God of his fathers and mothers.

Canonical Synthesis: Jacob and Election

Three texts highlight Jacob's importance in the canon outside Genesis. Hosea 12:1-6 charts the major events in his life as a means of imploring eighth-century B.C. Israelites to turn from sin as their ancestors did. In life Jacob grabbed Esau's heel and struggled with God, yet he overcame and committed himself at Bethel (Hos 12:3-4). Likewise Israel must return to the Lord in humility, love, justice and patience (Hos 12:6). Hosea's interpretation of Jacob's life highlights the patriarch's journey toward faith in the one God, a journey the people of Hosea's era needed to make.

As mentioned earlier, Malachi 1:2-3 and Romans 9:10-18 stress the Lord's love for Jacob and freedom in election respectively. In the Malachi text, the Lord reassures a fifth-century B.C. audience that their current harsh situation in no way proves God does not love them. Rather the love shown for Jacob in Genesis 25:23 continues unabated yet is hidden by the people's own sinfulness and complaining spirit. Paul adopts a similar trajectory in Romans. That is, he stresses God's compassion in choosing Jacob (Rom 9:15) and then asserts that the Lord's electing love occurs "to make the riches of his glory known" (Rom 9:23). Finally, he states that it was Israel's lack of faith, not God's lack of love, that caused the break between the two. Israel responded by pursuing righteousness "as if it were by works" rather than believing that only by faith could a relationship with God occur (Rom 9:30-33).

In all three texts election is used as an encouragement to repent and relate to God, yet in each text the authors sadly relate how Jacob's descendants failed to realize what their father learned through many hard experiences: the one God wants singular devotion, faith and obedience. Blessings and protection come from God's grace and kindness, not as a reward for good deeds or as a tribal entitlement.

The One God Who Preserves the Covenant People: Genesis 37—50

Life was many things for Abraham, Isaac, Jacob and their families in Genesis 12—36, but "safe" would hardly describe their situation. Their travels alone put them in constant danger and thus in constant need of God's promise of protection (12:3; 26:2-3; 31:3; 35:5). Their own family squabbles added to their difficulties. Most of the time, however, their foes were people and circumstances they could see and assess. But in this section Jacob's family faces an unsparing famine they can neither predict nor conquer, which means they need the help of a God who knows the future, prepares for disaster and manages people, events and nature. That such a God exists is the major emphasis in the rest of Genesis.

Family fights and famine provide the unlikely framework for the Lord's preserving acts in these chapters. Revelatory dreams once again (cf. Gen

28:10-15) act as means of guidance for the story's chief character, and persons outside the chosen clan serve as helpers and hindrances in the account. Jacob retains his role as bearer of the Abrahamic covenant, yet it is his son Joseph who dominates these chapters and eventually saves his family from disaster. This concluding segment of Genesis continues the text's emphasis on election, introduces the Scriptures' ongoing concern with unjust suffering, begins the motif of God delivering Israel and conclusively shows that the Lord has kept all promises made to Abraham, Isaac and Jacob.

Election and oppression collide in Genesis 37—45. Jacob loves Joseph more than his other sons because the boy was born in his old age and because Joseph was Rachel's son (37:3; 42:38). Thus he puts Joseph in charge of his brothers, many of whom are older, a decision that the brothers resent so much they hate Joseph (37:4). To make matters worse, Joseph relates dreams that indicate his brothers and the cosmos will bow down to him (37:5-11). Jealousy and hatred cause the ten oldest brothers to sell Joseph into slavery and allow Jacob to believe his son has been killed (37:12-36). Subsequently the text reveals that Judah, one of the more prominent brothers, indeed the one who suggested selling Joseph (37:26-27), has a habit of mistreating others even while fulfilling his own sexual appetite (38).

In contrast Joseph avoids sexual misconduct but initially to no avail. His reward for not sleeping with his master's wife is time in jail, where even kindly interpreting others' dreams seemingly does him no good (39—40). It appears that wickedness triumphs, since abusers and oppressors like Judah, the other brothers and the seductive wife of Potiphar walk free while the victimized Joseph remains imprisoned. Nothing in the story seems fair, just or good, and the God who intervenes against evil in the fall narrative, flood story and tower of Babel episodes does nothing the text cares to mention about these outrages.

Despite his difficulties, Joseph professes a faith in God that has certain key facets. First, he senses the presence of God regardless of where he goes. Joseph obviously rejects any notion of the Lord as a local or regional deity, for he acknowledges God in every episode.[52] Second, he believes God's presence "is the ultimate sanction of morality."[53] He refuses his master's wife's advances because he views such actions as sin against God (39:9). Third, he credits God with his ability to interpret dreams as a matter of habit (40:8; 41:16, 51-52).[54] Like his ancestors, Joseph learns that

> God can be with him in a foreign land, in the territory which is in the preserve of foreign gods; he can affect the people of this land through him. There is no thought of competition or polemic in this action of God through Joseph, just as there was not in the case of the God of Abraham, Isaac, and Jacob. . . . The religion of the God of the fathers is not confined

to an isolated area; God acts and speaks directly and immediately within the whole realm of reality.[55]

Eventually Joseph's God-given interpretative powers take him out of prison and into Egypt's halls of power as prime minister. He has endured and overcome and sets out to help Pharaoh, his benefactor, guide Egypt through the seven-year famine Joseph predicts based on Pharaoh's dreams (41). Though he has emerged from oppression, no real reason for his suffering has been given. The Egyptians seem to receive more attention in these accounts than do Abraham's descendants.

When the text finally divulges the reason for Joseph's suffering he demonstrates other characteristics of his monotheistic faith. The most prominent feature of this mature faith is forgiveness. His brothers come to buy grain from him and do not recognize him. After a series of tests that help him know his father and full brother (Benjamin) are alive and that his brothers regret selling him (42—44), he reveals his identity and forgives his brothers' guilt without punishing them (45:1-5).[56] This action parallels Esau's pardoning of Jacob (33:4-5) yet surpasses it because of the more desperate situation from which Joseph has come. Another characteristic explains Joseph's motive for forgiveness: he fears God (42:18). From this first mention of reverent "fear" a great biblical theme will grow, eventually reaching its apex in the Writings. At this point it is enough to say that his fear means obedience to what he believes God requires of him.[57] His relationship with God dictates his relationship with human beings.

Finally, his realization that God has placed him in power to save his family from extinction reveals a willingness to suffer redemptively. The fact that his troubles result in deliverance for others eases his pain (45:5). Now he understands why he has suffered, and he wastes no time rescuing the entire clan (45:21-24). Endurance of pain, then, acts as God's mode of deliverance here. What the brothers have done is not good, but as in the cases of Abraham's, Isaac's and Jacob's mistakes, fears and outright sins, God makes good out of the bad that has been done.

Two Abrahamic promises collide in Genesis 46—50. For the clan to endure and become the great nation promised to Abraham, Jacob, the resident patriarch, must lead the family/nation out of the promised land, Israel's true homeland. Just as God had earlier assured Jacob it was time to go home (31:3), so now God reveals to Jacob that it is time to leave home, to go to Egypt (46:1-7). This journey in no way jeopardizes the land promise, since the move has been anticipated since Genesis 15:13. The time has come for the four-hundred-year sojourn God revealed to Abraham. As always, God pledges to be with Jacob (46:4), and the aging bearer of faith must act solely on his belief in this renewed promise and on his past experiences with the Lord. To his credit, he does go to Egypt, accompanied by every member of his clan (46:8-27). Once there he is reunited with Joseph, who secures the best of Egypt's pasture land for his people (46:28-34).

Blessing and a determination to return to the promised land frame the remaining episodes in Genesis. Jacob blesses Pharaoh, an ironic scene, since Pharaoh exceeds Jacob in every earthly manner except age (47:7). Next, Jacob blesses Manasseh and Ephraim, Joseph's sons, putting the younger Ephraim above his brother (48:12-20), a not too unlikely action given Jacob's own experience. Finally, based on his knowledge of their character and on his insight into the future, Jacob blesses his sons before he dies (49:1-28). Certainly Joseph receives high praise for his faithful endurance (49:22-26), yet it is Judah, the leader of his siblings, who is promised "the scepter," "the ruler's staff" (49:10). Leadership will continue to come from Judah, and eventually Judah's authority will extend until other nations obey him. Whatever international power the clan will possess must come from Judah's family, and how Abraham's lineage will bless all nations must therefore begin there, though Joseph's activities certainly fit that category as well.

With the appropriate blessings made, Jacob and Joseph turn their thoughts to the land. Jacob promises Joseph that the land promise will come true, for God will be with the people and take them there (48:21-22). Because of this conviction, Jacob instructs his sons to bury him with his fathers and mothers in the promised land (49:29-32), a task they perform in due time (50:1-14). Similarly Joseph tells his brothers to carry his bones from Egypt when God gives them the land (50:25-26). Thus to his faith in God's presence, his obedience to divine standards, his willingness to suffer on behalf of others, his ability to aid his own family and a foreign nation and a gracious power to forgive, Joseph adds an unshakable hope that exile will end and the chosen people will reside in their God-given home.[58] The man who interprets dreams by God-given insight also possesses a God-given dream for the future. Still, just how this dream will come true has not yet been revealed.[59]

Conclusion

When Genesis ends many theological themes are firmly fixed into a pattern, while others remain outside the pattern, not yet connected to the whole. Certainly a definite portrait of God has emerged. God is the sole deity who acts in these accounts. God alone creates, so God alone judges sin, calls, guides and blesses Abraham and his descendants, and protects and delivers the people now called Israel in all circumstances. This God communicates with people, alternately expressing commands, promises and guidance, and this God works to remove the sin that hounds the whole human race. This

God has no beginning, no rival, no time or space boundaries, no moral flaw, no hidden agenda.[60]

A picture of the human race has also emerged. People are made in God's image yet are not satisfied with this lofty position. They desire to be God in the sense that they disobey God's word, thus attempting to seize divine authority for themselves. Humans eat the fruit of pride, violence and immorality, and therefore they learn to fear, hate, lust and disobey. Yet they also have the capacity to hear God's promises and act in faith, and however halting and short-sighted that faith may be, it is still faith, not in images that can be stolen and buried but in the one God who creates, communicates and redeems. The human race is clearly at its best when its members believe in God and by faith obey God's communicated standards.

With these pictures in place it is possible to note what has yet to occur that has been foreshadowed thus far. The one God has yet to eradicate human sin. The groundwork for this eradication has been laid, since Abraham has been chosen and the promise of nationhood has been in large part fulfilled. But the promised land remains in the hands of "foreigners," no specific moral law exists, all nations have yet to be blessed through Abraham's lineage, and Israel lives in Egypt. Clearly, then, some important details need to be clarified. It seems appropriate, though, to assume that resolution of these items will come from the twin themes of God's uniqueness and the human race's faith. The Creator God stands alone as the single hope for the created human race to fulfill their potential as rulers of the created earth.

3

The One God
Who Delivers
& Instructs

Exodus

· ·

C ANONICALLY AND THEOLOGICALLY SPEAKING, EXODUS PROVIDES CONTINU-
ity with the accounts and emphases in Genesis yet also creates a whole new
framework for what follows. Issues such as God's uniqueness as creator and
sustainer of all that exists, the fulfillment of God's promises to Abraham,
God's ability to deliver the chosen people from danger, the human race's sin
against one another, and the human race's need for direction and for divinely
stated boundaries continue to be stressed. Characters such as Abraham, Isaac,
Jacob and Joseph are used as reminders of what has already occurred and
of what must yet happen. At the same time, God uses new persons such as
Moses, Aaron, Miriam, Pharaoh and others to move history and revelation
forward. New theological matters also emerge, such as the role of God's
instruction, or law, in Israel's and other nations' lives, the nature of God's
choice of Israel as special people and the means of securing forgiveness for
sin.

Some of these concepts still cause serious debate, for who are truly God's
people, who should possess Palestine (Canaan) and who has a God-given
religion makes a great deal of difference in the Middle East to this day. The
role of Exodus's divine laws in Christianity can cause furious discussions
among Christians even now, two thousand years after Jesus died. Clearly this
book deserves serious theological and canonical reflection, and just as clearly

such reflection makes a great deal of difference if theologians want to link biblical theology to the church's current mission.

Though Exodus offers several major themes and subthemes one idea dominates and makes all others possible, even necessary: there is only one God. This one God is the same God who led Joseph, Jacob and the rest of the chosen family into Egypt. Thus this is the same God who created the earth and human race. By the midpoint of Exodus this one God demonstrates an ongoing commitment to promises made hundreds of years earlier, an ability to deliver a numerous but weak and enslaved people from a powerful and oppressive ruler, a willingness to work with a fearsome yet fearful leader (Moses), the foolishness of worshiping humanly manufactured gods and a desire to communicate beneficial standards to the newly freed nation. At this midpoint God declares all other deities invalid and commands exclusive worship of himself (Ex 20:1-11). Perhaps no other declaration was as revolutionary in the ancient world or is in today's postmodern, pluralistic world. This statement of uniqueness explains how it is that God can choose Israel, deliver Israel, make covenant with Israel and call Israel to teach God's ways to other nations. Simply stated, there is no other deity to stop, rebuke or oppose God, and it is this "simple" theological issue that Moses attempts to teach the ancient audience and that constitutes the foundation for the Bible's enduring message for today.

This volume's outline of Exodus integrates major characters, events, places and themes. Thus it continues the emphases begun in Genesis, particularly those that trace the continuation of the Abrahamic promises,[1] and also demonstrates Exodus's unique contribution to Old Testament and biblical theology. It also highlights the ongoing importance of monotheism in the Old Testament. Five basic headings reveal that the book's primary purpose is to explain God's uniqueness and presence among his people.[2]

First, Exodus 1—18 focuses on Israel's deliverance from Egypt. Within this overall concern with salvation the text stresses that God sees and remembers (Ex 1—2), reveals, calls and promises (Ex 3—4), sets people free (Ex 5:1—15:21) and provides for the chosen people (Ex 15:22—18:27). These ideas grow naturally out of the book's historical setting, as well as out of Israel's distant past. Second, Exodus 19—24 explains how God makes a covenant with Israel. No other event affects the Old Testament's historical or theological framework as much as this one.[3] Embedded in this inaugural statement of God's law are notions such as God's transcendence (Ex 19), God's total authority (Ex 20) and God's wisdom for daily living (Ex 21—23). Third, Exodus 25—31 focuses on the tabernacle and the priesthood's role in worship. Here the Lord is the One who dwells among the people (Ex 25—27), employs mediators (Ex 28—29) and meets with mediators (Ex 30—31). Each of these truths is necessary for a theology of worship.

Fourth, Exodus 32—34 tells of the golden calf incident, an occurrence that reveals how quickly Israel can depart from God's standards. In this section God is depicted as justifiably jealous (Ex 32) yet constantly present (Ex 33) and ready to forgive and renew (Ex 34). Fifth, in a second segment on the tabernacle and priesthood, Exodus 35—40 is the natural result of God's unmerited forgiveness. God empowers and gifts individuals to build the tabernacle (Ex 35—39), and God abides with and guides the covenant people (Ex 40). Only one God manages all these achievements, and only one God remains present with the people no matter what they do or what takes place around them. Therefore only one God deserves worship, honor and praise.

Part One: The Exodus (Exodus 1—18)

Probably no event in Israel's history rivals the exodus for its theological importance. This historical deliverance of God's chosen people acts as a chief paradigm for salvation, as evidence of God's love for Israel and as a spur toward loving obedience on the part of God's people in the rest of Scripture. The event's magnitude is heightened by the struggle that precedes it and the challenges that follow it. Thus its value best emerges through a careful theological analysis that links Genesis and Exodus and offers commentary on how Exodus moves the biblical history forward.

The God Who Sees and Remembers: Exodus 1—2

Exodus begins auspiciously. Though Israel remains in Egypt, the people prosper and grow into a large group in their adopted country (Ex 1:1-7).[4] This numerical expansion of Jacob's twelve sons' clans fulfills God's promise to Abraham to multiply his descendants until they can scarcely be counted (cf. Gen 12:1-9; 15:1-6).[5] Thus the book's opening verses are to be read as a theological affirmation of God's ongoing faithfulness, kindness and provision for Abraham, Isaac and Jacob. The promise-keeping God continues to act across centuries, keeping pledges to men and women now long dead. Certainly these verses also vindicate the suffering and life work of Joseph, the human instrument of divine deliverance for Israel in Genesis 37—50.

Unfortunately suffering soon enters the story again, and this time it includes all Israel in its grip. This turn of events begins with the rise of a new pharaoh who has no ties to Joseph (1:8), who probably comes from a different ethnic background and espouses different political and economic goals than did Joseph's pharaoh[6] and who views the Israelites as a threat to national security (1:9-10). He first attempts to limit their multiplication by enslaving them, but he manages only to increase their progeny.[7] Since he in fact attempts to reverse God's promise to Abraham, his efforts prove futile.

Next, he orders all male Israelite babies killed at birth, a plan foiled by midwives who fear God (1:17) and are blessed by God for protecting the Israelite children (1:20-21). Even in the midst of terrible days the people have not been deserted by their God. As in the Joseph narratives, suffering is real and threatening here yet does not mean the Creator, the promising, guiding, delivering God, has lost power or run into an undefeatable natural, human or divine foe. Suffering has its own role here, though, as subsequent accounts demonstrate. Undeterred, Pharaoh orders every male Israelite infant thrown in the Nile River (1:22).

Despite this horrible situation's seemingly insoluble nature, the canon has already offered clues that this dilemma will be resolved. According to Genesis 15:13-16, after Abram believes God and has that belief counted as righteousness (15:6) and after Abram asks how he may know Canaan will be given to his descendants (15:8), God unfolds the future for Abram, telling him his "seed" will live in a foreign land four hundred years, suffering some of that time (15:13). But afterward they will come out of that land (15:14). Given this information, the people's pain has purpose. Their suffering is definitely terrible yet serves as the birth pains of a nation. God's promises of land must be about to come to fruition. This canonical realization does not minimize the problem of unjust suffering any more than Joseph's belief that his pain was for a redemptive reason did (cf. Gen 50:20), but it does demonstrate that God is still with the covenant people. Without this canonical realization God's absence from Exodus 1—2 seems much more palpable than it needs to be if one reads these chapters in isolation.[8]

Two theological issues, Israel's eventual deliverance and resettlement in Canaan and Israel's suffering, now frame the account. In the midst of these issues emerges an individual who will prove vital to the solving of both matters. An unnamed Levite couple[9] has a son that they refuse to throw into the Nile. Perhaps they "fear God" as the midwives in Exodus 1:15-22 did. When they can no longer hide the child, the mother prepares a basket boat for the child, places him in the boat, puts the basket in the Nile and posts his sister to watch what will occur (2:1-4). There is little doubt that the mother somehow hopes to save the child by taking these precautions.[10] She succeeds. Ironically, the pharaoh's daughter discovers and takes pity on the baby (2:5-6), a turnabout as startling as Abram's experience with another pharaoh in Genesis 12:10-20 and Joseph's change of fortune in Genesis 41. Once again Egypt provides unexpected help for the chosen ones. The princess names the child Moses, provides for his upbringing and thereby makes it possible for an Israelite to gain, presumably, an education and other royal privileges. One has to wonder why this man has survived the pharaoh's genocidal wrath.

When he comes of age, Moses apparently decides that he has been spared so that he can help his fellow Israelites. He kills an Egyptian who oppresses an Israelite but soon discovers that not all Israelites value his protection or covet his advice (2:11-14). The murder discovered, he flees to Midian, where he meets and marries a priest's daughter and settles down in what he considers a foreign land, a fact highlighted by the naming of his first son Gershom ("stranger").[11] Whatever role Moses is destined to play remains delayed for now.

Meanwhile, Israel suffers. They cry out to their God, who hears their groaning, remembers the patriarchal covenant and determines to act on their behalf (2:23-25). The fact that God hears means that God will act. The fact that God remembers underscores God's faithfulness, since remembering does not of necessity take place after an extended period of forgetting. God knew how long the suffering would last before it occurred (cf. Gen 15:13-16), so it seems unlikely that God stood by, oblivious to what the people felt. The work of deliverance must now commence, and it will be enacted by the God who has been faithful to Abraham for four centuries and who will prove just as faithful to those who suffer, cry out, hope and dream of freedom in this new era.

The God Who Reveals, Calls and Promises: Exodus 3—4

Exodus 3—4 is a theologically densely layered account. Nearly every verse reveals the nature of the God the canon has been describing and the role of the human race within God's plans for eradicating evil and keeping promises already made to Abraham, Isaac and Jacob. At the heart of God's self-revelation lies God's continuing twin aims of calling individuals to extraordinary tasks and empowering those individuals for these tasks by divine presence and divinely guaranteed promises. In this way the canon links the life experiences and personal commitments of Abraham, Isaac and Jacob with those of Moses.

Moses has apparently been living a normal life in Midian, for Exodus 3:1 finds him keeping his father-in-law's flocks. Though Moses surely expects a typical day, the text alerts readers that unusual events are about to occur because Moses has come near to "God's mountain," a designation given for the first time here. He himself soon learns the day is not typical when he observes a bush burning yet not being consumed (3:2-3). From the bush a voice instructs Moses to remove his shoes because he is on "holy ground" (3:5).

This reference to holiness begins the Law's extensive emphasis on God's holiness, the people's holiness and the nature of holiness in worship. In its simplest usage the word *holy* means "set apart for a specific purpose," "different" or "unique." Here these basic definitions apply, since the place itself is "unique" or "set apart" by the very existence of the extraordinary bush. Other places, particularly those "set aside" as worship sites, will be called holy later in the book (cf. Ex 25—31; 35—40).

What truly makes the place holy, though, is the fact that God is present there, addressing Moses, claiming to be the God of Abraham, Isaac and Jacob. Just as God "was with" those persons, so now God "is with" Moses, making the divine presence known and felt by both visual and auditory means (3:6). Moses feels free to look at the burning bush, but encountering God frightens him, leaving him awestruck before the revealed deity. As Donald Gowan observes, "God's appearance on the mountain is thus described as both frightening and attractive, daunting and fascinating."[12]

The God of continuity, the God who keeps faith with covenant people, quickly explains that the time of the Israelite sojourn has come to an end, and Moses must lead them to a new place (3:5-10). The date fixed in Genesis 15:13-16 has arrived. Certainly the end of the oppression era comes as no great surprise, given the Genesis text and given the notice of God's compassion in Exodus 2:23-25, but the calling of Moses is a bit surprising because of his past failures. Still, surely the God who transformed Jacob can determine to call and equip nearly anyone. The God who began the Israelite nation by calling one person can deliver the people by the same method.

Certainly God's call surprises Moses. He asks two questions that amount to reasons why he thinks God should not have chosen him. First, he asks, "Who am I, that I should go?" (3:11). God's response provides canonical links among Abraham, Isaac, Jacob and Moses. As in Genesis 17:4 (Abraham), 26:3 (Isaac) and 28:15 (Jacob), the Lord pledges to "be with" Moses, which means his mission cannot fail any more than the patriarchs' mission could fail. God's presence guarantees sustenance and success. If this promise of presence is not enough for Moses, he also is given a sign: after Israel's deliverance the people will worship at this same mountain of revelation, promise and calling (3:12). Such promises require faith on Moses' part, just as the promises offered to the patriarchs required them to believe. Promise and faith are inextricably joined. Clearly the issue is not who Moses is but who will be with Moses.[13] He correctly believes he will fail if left to his own devices yet must believe that with God's help he will succeed.

Second, since God has become the focal point of the discussion, Moses asks God's name so that he may explain the identity of the God of their fathers to the Israelite people (3:13). God's answer has sparked enthusiastic discussion for centuries. God says, "I AM WHO I AM," and offers the name Yahweh, which is a play on the first phrase. Both statements are derived from the Hebrew word for "to be," so the name at least "marks the certainty of Yahweh's existence."[14] Surely this revelation does more, however, since God's existence does not seem to be disputed. Rather Moses apparently desires assurances that encompass the past ("the God of your fathers"), the present ("I will be with you") and the future ("they [will] ask me"). Thus God's answer must cover all time possibilities to relieve fully the burden of Moses' question.

The scholarly discussions of this verse help highlight the importance of its claims. Edmond Jacob stresses that this text means the name "Yahweh expresses life in its continuance and its actuality."[15] In other words, the reference to the patriarch and the derivation of Yahweh from the verb "to be" indicates that God's abiding and relational presence is emphasized in this verse.[16] The revelation of this name also implies that the ever-present, promise-keeping God wants to be approached by persons like Abraham, Isaac, Jacob and Moses. Walther Zimmerli observes that

the "name of Yahweh" has been revealed to the faith of the Old Testament believer. He may—indeed must—call upon him without hesitation. How totally different is the mystery surrounding the secret name of the sun god Re in the Egyptian myth of Isis and Re (ANET, pp. 12-14)! But there is also another difference: the name never becomes a technical device by which the supplicant tries to coerce the God of Israel.[17]

Thus God's revelation of abiding presence and personal approachability in no way invites magical incantation, manipulation of God or a belief that God has no higher moral or ethical standards than does the human race. It separates God from human beings and from other so-called deities yet does so without compromising the possibility of humans having close relationships with God.

Besides constant presence and relational openness, it is possible, though not proven, that the revealed name may embody creation theology. W. F. Albright states that the phrase "I AM WHO I AM" derives from the third-person singular of the Hebrew language's causative stem *(hiphil)* and therefore should be translated "He Causes to be what Comes into Existence."[18] Various scholars have disputed Albright's conclusions on linguistic grounds. Gowan summarizes these objections by noting that this theory "requires different vowels and one different consonant for the words in question, and introduces a causative stem for the verb *hayah,* which never occurs otherwise in the Old Testament."[19] Even if Albright's idea cannot be sustained, however, his point about creation theology should not be missed. If God's presence is an "active being" that truly means God "'Always Is,' or 'Am,'"[20] as John Durham argues, then canonically speaking the God who addresses Moses is the same God of Genesis 1—11, since the canon admits no other God. The reference to the patriarchs supports this assertion, since those accounts also reveal and discuss only one God. The reference to constantly active being, coupled with the notation of the patriarchal covenant, covers all the historical and canonical ground from Genesis 1:1 until Moses' era.

Finally, the revelation of God's name emphasizes God's active, creative, constant, approachable presence in actual human history. Just as God actually guided, blessed and corrected Abraham, Isaac and Jacob, so now God intends to work in the daily history of Moses and his contemporaries. Gustav Oehler claims that it is in "an historical relation to mankind, and in particular to the chosen people" that God reveals his true nature.[21] Walther Eichrodt concurs, noting that "this divine name has its particular significance for the historical mission of Moses. . . . The only thing which could provide the religious basis for a new national entity was the certainty, deeply impressed both on the founder of the religion and on his people, that the deity was demonstrably and immediately present and active."[22] Only through this activity in history can God demonstrate that promises actually are fulfilled and that God will be present with Israel now.[23] Only then can Moses believe that "Yahweh" will deliver Israel in his time.

Given these basic observations, it is clear that in Exodus 3 Moses learns that the God of all history has decided to shape immediate history as a means of determining the future. As Carl F. H. Henry says, "While the forward-looking manifestation of YAHWEH has in view the pledge of redemptive presence, the name YAHWEH accumulates to itself all that the patriarchs had already known about God."[24] In other words, all of history, past, present and future, merges in this passage. What unites this collective history is the living, ever-present, creative, promising God. What Moses discovers will sustain him and Israel if he fully believes what he has been told. Only a lack of faith in and obedience to the God called Yahweh can stop the promises made to Abraham, which in fact are intended to solve the human race's sin problem, from being realized partly through Moses' ministry. Moses has the chance to proceed with as much certainty as he really needs.[25]

After revealing the name, Yahweh instructs Moses to tell the desperate Israelites that all covenantal pledges will soon be actualized. God also proves master of history by predicting Pharaoh's opposition to Israelite independence, by pledging to visit plagues on the Egyptians and by promising that Israel will leave Egypt enriched by local bounty (3:15-22). Each successive revelation heightens Moses' reason to believe. Still, he must believe, which he is not yet ready to do, as his next comments reveal.

Far from believing God's promised scenario in the preceding verses, Moses questions that the Israelite elders will trust him (4:1). Still patient, God provides him with miraculous powers (4:2-9), only to hear Moses declare his inability to speak well in public (4:10). Now God reminds Moses who creates human beings, who gives people the ability to speak (4:11-12). Once again God's uniqueness and creative power take thematic precedence. Surely the

God who creates can sustain the called. Still Moses protests and asks God to send someone else (4:13). As the flood account has already demonstrated, God is patient but also knows when the time has come for decisive action. Moses is given his brother Aaron as a helper but must indeed go lead Israel. As in the case of Jacob, God's choice of Moses does not come as option. It comes as an imperative that cannot be spurned or even politely refused (4:14-17).

Moses bids his father-in-law goodbye only to learn two difficult lessons about the sovereignty of the God who has called him. First, he learns that, as Exodus 3:19-20 has already mentioned, Pharaoh will not let Israel go until miracles force him to do so. This knowledge yields both a good and a bad bit of news. The bad news is that God says, "'But I will harden his heart so that he will not let the people go'" (4:21), which indicates the extreme difficulty of Moses' task and makes readers wonder if Pharaoh has any real chance to do the right thing. It must be remembered, however, that Pharaoh has long had the chance to cease oppressing, enslaving and killing the Israelites. Further, as later texts reveal, Pharaoh also hardens his own heart, a fact that highlights his personal responsibility for his actions. In all, between Exodus 4:21 and Exodus 14:17 God hardens Pharaoh's heart ten times, and Pharaoh hardens his own heart the same number of times.[26] Each hardening comes after God warns Pharaoh to release Israel, so the hardening "is produced less by absence than by excess of revelation, a point which stresses man's responsibility."[27] The more Pharaoh does the wrong thing, the less likely it becomes that he will be able to do what is morally correct.

Moses also learns the good news that God will redeem Israel, for these people are God's "'firstborn son'" (4:22). They receive this designation not by inherent virtue but due to the fact that God remembers the covenant with Israel's ancestors (cf. Ex 2:23-25; 3:6). They are God's people (cf. Ex 3:7) and are thereby ultimately part of God's plan to deal with the human race's sin problem (cf. Gen 12:1-9). God's grace therefore insures Israel's deliverance, just as Pharaoh's obstinance guarantees the eventual death of Egypt's firstborn children (4:23). As firstborn Israel certainly bears the privileges of freedom and blessing yet also carries the responsibility of leading the world away from sin and toward God.[28] Thus Israel's election comes from the Lord of history and has practical impact on history.[29] Despite the difficulty of the victory, it will be won, and won in a way that will highlight who God's people truly are. Walter Kaiser observes that this information will surprise Pharaoh, since in Egyptian religious cults he was considered "the son of the gods."[30]

Second, Moses and his family encounter God's unchangeable decision to make Moses lead Israel properly. The strange account in Exodus 4:24-26 proves at least that God is determined to force Moses to enter fully into

Israelite life. His son has not been circumcised, which conflicts with God's will as revealed in Genesis 17:7-14. Only under pressure and only through his wife's wrath does Moses do what he should have done earlier. As in Genesis 32:22-32, God confronts in a physical manner the person chosen to lead God's people. In a much more placid way, Aaron, Moses' brother, learns he has a role in the unfolding drama (Ex 4:27-28). He becomes Moses' mouthpiece (cf. Ex 4:10-17) and companion. Together the brothers tell the hard-pressed Israelite elders what Yahweh has said and show them the signs they can perform (4:29-30). The elders believe and worship (4:31), responses that demonstrate their desire for God and their potential for spiritual greatness or that may reveal their simple and understandable craving to escape their desperate circumstances.

Canonical Synthesis: Moses' Call

Exodus 1—4 is used in the rest of the canon in a variety of ways. For example, though Moses' call is not mentioned explicitly in other call stories, Norman Habel and Ernst Kutsch observe that Exodus 3—4 may serve as a pattern for similar accounts in the Old Testament. Habel notes six distinctive elements in Moses' call that relate to other stories: divine confrontation (3:1-4a); introductory word (3:4b-9); commission (3:10); objection (3:11); reassurance (3:12a); sign (3:12).[31] Kutsch, however, lists four topics: commission (3:10); objection (3:11); rejoinder (3:12) and sign (3:12).[32] Both Habel and Kutsch argue that these same general details occur in the call stories of Gideon, Jeremiah, Saul and Isaiah.

Though it is possible to critique certain specific conclusions Habel and Kutsch reach, their general thesis is sound. Moses' call prefigures that of others. The same God reveals divine orders to other leaders. The same God appears as the only Lord, the only deity, to later prophets, judges and kings. Further, this same God pledges presence, protection and achievement at the hour of calling (cf. Judg 6:12-14; Jer 1:1-19). Also, the God who calls is obviously the God who chooses, who elects, specific persons. Isaiah feels no more worthy to serve than Moses does, yet God selects Isaiah and expects him to go preach, just as God insists that Moses obey the divine summons. Human messengers remain fallible, but God continues steadfastly committed to using them all the same. Thus the human scene and the human instrument change. History moves forward. As the God of continuity, however, Yahweh never changes, falters, fails or retreats. As each call story reminds readers of its predecessors the Lord's uniqueness and permanence and faithfulness shine forth.

Canonical Synthesis: "I AM"

The Old Testament also uses the name Yahweh and the phrases "I AM," "I am Yahweh" and "I, Yahweh, am he" in ways quite reminiscent of Exodus 3:14. For example, Deuteronomy 32:39 quotes God as saying, "See now that I myself am he! There is no god besides me." This declaration separates the Lord from so-called gods who have no power to save their worshipers (cf. Deut 32:39). These monotheistic claims come at the end of Moses' career and thus provide, with his call, brackets to Mosaic theology. Later authors leave no doubt that Yahweh is the only God Moses has in mind in any of his teachings. Hosea 13:4 and Joel 2:27 state that Yahweh is Israel's God because Yahweh has delivered the people and that indeed no other God exists to deliver anyone. Like Moses, Hosea and Joel emphasize and link God's name, God's action in history, God's relationship to Israel and God's uniqueness.

It is Isaiah, however, who forges the closest connections to the Mosaic texts. Eight passages in this prophecy state specific attributes of Yahweh in first-person language similar to that in Exodus 3:14. Two of these declarations include the terminology "I, Yahweh . . . I am he" (Is 41:4; 43:11-13), while one says "I am Yahweh" (45:18). The other five texts (43:25; 46:4; 48:12-13; 51:12; 52:6) simply have the Lord declaring "I am he," though the fact these verses quote Yahweh means that God's identity is understood. These passages portray Yahweh as Lord of history (41:4; 43:11; 45:18), as Creator and sustainer of the earth and the human race (41:4; 45:18; 46:4; 48:12-13), as Israel's savior (43:10-13, 25) and as Israel's comforter (51:12) and hope for the future (52:6). Clearly all these concepts fit the theological emphases in Exodus 1—4, and they each help build an argument that Yahweh alone is God.[33] They also encourage Isaiah's eighth-century audience to seek the Lord's comfort and salvation based on God's deeds in Moses' time.[34]

The New Testament uses the assertions from Exodus and Isaiah about Yahweh the "I AM" to stress Jesus' unity with the Father and Jesus' preexistent nature. When asked in Mark 14:61 if he is the promised Messiah, Jesus answers "I am," a direct verbal equivalent to Exodus 3:14. Jesus then proceeds to claim he will reign with God (Mk 14:62). The Jewish leaders thereupon charge him with blasphemy, a clear indication that they think such claims indicate that Jesus believes himself to be equal with God.

John's Gospel is even more specific on this point. In John 8:24, 28 Jesus twice says "I am he," which echoes Isaiah's usage of that phrase.[35] Here Jesus' statement "I am he" includes the claim that he will judge the world after his death, resurrection and ascension.[36] When pressed to declare his identity as Yahweh was in the Moses story, and when called upon to declare how Abraham could believe in him, Jesus asserts, "Truly, truly, I say to you, before Abraham was, I am" (Jn 8:58 modified from KJV). F. F. Bruce asks,

How can a man who is "not yet fifty years old" speak like that? Only if he speaks as the Word that had been with God in the beginning and was now incarnate on earth. Abraham looked forward to the time of his incarnation, but he himself existed before his incarnation, before Abraham was born *(genesthai),* before the worlds were made. The Word of the eternal God cannot be other than eternal. So much, in this context, is conveyed by *ego eimi.*[37]

As in Mark 14:63-64, Jesus' declaration convinces his audience that his equating of himself to the "I AM" of Exodus and Isaiah, to Yahweh, amounts to a self-declaration of deity. They wish to execute him based on the admonition found in Leviticus 24:16 to stone blasphemers.

One other text deserves mention. When the mob comes to arrest Jesus he says, "I am he" (Jn 18:5). At this admission the mob draws back and falls to the ground (Jn 18:6). Raymond Brown suggests that the people hear these words as a claim of divinity, which may explain their reaction.[38] Without examining the implications of this or the Gospel texts further it is at least accurate to say that Jesus' statements are based on Exodus and Isaiah and that hearers and readers of his claims could hardly miss this verbal and theological connection.

The God Who Sets Israel Free: Exodus 5:1—15:21

At this juncture in Exodus theologians are challenged not only to examine the text's ongoing emphases but also to deal with new matters as well. God's work on Israel's behalf accelerates. Promises to Abraham are kept. The sin problem is attacked vigorously. Monotheism remains the single most unique theme. Still, other issues demand attention. For example, miracles within the natural order are described, which necessitates some explanation of their role in history. Further, history itself becomes a topic of consideration. Until now most of the Bible's accounts have featured individuals and their clans, albeit with the intention of impacting readers' grasp of worldwide problems and possibilities. Now, however, the scope widens to include Israel as a nation dealing with other nations of the ancient world. Thus some sense of how international history and theology interact must be gained. Certainly the integration of faith and history has mattered so far yet not to the extent that it will from this segment to the end of the canon.

Exodus 5:2 sets the stage for everything that happens in Exodus 5—15. Here, having been presented with Yahweh's demand to let Israel go Pharaoh replies, "Who is the LORD, that I should obey him and let Israel go? I do not know the LORD and I will not let Israel go." Ray Clendenen notes, "The names of about forty gods and goddesses from ancient Egypt are known, many by more than one name."[39] Perhaps Pharaoh knew all of these, but he did not know Yahweh's name and could not see any reason, then, to release the Israelites. Indeed their request seems like a way to dodge work to him, so he increases the slaves' workload (5:4-18). Not even Moses' and Aaron's mention of plagues dissuades him (5:3). The next several episodes introduce Pharaoh to Yahweh and teach him that he will let Israel go. At the same time these episodes also teach Israel the nature of the one God who will deliver them as a result of pledges made to Abraham, Isaac and Jacob.

Both Moses and his audience are discouraged by Pharaoh's response. The people blame Moses, while Moses blames God (5:19-23). Therefore Yahweh reinforces the call, promising again to deliver Israel (6:1). As part of this reaffirmation, God says more about the name Yahweh. God says, "I am the LORD" (6:2), and then proceeds to declare, "I appeared to Abraham, to Isaac and to Jacob as God Almighty, but by my name the LORD I did not make myself known to them" (6:3). In two verses God (*Elohim* in Hebrew) has said both "I am Yahweh" and "I appeared to Abraham . . . as God Almighty" (*El Shaddai* in Hebrew). Scholars have long debated this verse's meaning, since on the surface it appears to contradict itself, Exodus 3:14 and the several times the name Yahweh appears in Genesis (e.g., Gen 2:4; 12:8). What does "Yahweh" mean here?

Critical scholars since Julius Wellhausen have argued that this verse proves that written sources that utilize different names for God have been edited together over a period of several centuries. Though sympathetic with the source-critical tradition, John Durham correctly observes that the text's "compiler" was aware of the verse's ambiguity. In fact this ambiguity is probably an intentional confession of God's authority.[40] He concludes that

> what is of greater import here is the identification of Yahweh with the God of the patriarchs, whatever the name or names by which they called him, and the connection of the covenant made with them in the rescue and resettlement of their descendants, which is about the take place.[41]

According to Durham, then, the passage equates the God of Abraham, Isaac and Jacob with the God who has called Moses. What the editor intends is a theological linkage that still expresses God's work in this new situation.

Writers from a variety of theological perspectives agree that the passage intends to depict the new situation rather than announce the origins of Yahweh's name in Hebrew religious history. John Sailhamer states that the distinction made in Exodus 6:3 between the El Shaddai of the patriarchs and the Yahweh of Moses is one of intimacy. He writes that

> in Genesis, when God "appeared" to Abraham, he addressed him as El Shaddai, but when Abraham saw God "in a vision," he spoke with him as Yahweh. Thus, the present text intends to tell us that, unlike the patriarchs, Moses "knew Yahweh," not by means of a vision but "face to face" (Dt 34:10).[42]

Similarly, Brevard Childs stresses that this verse focuses on a renewed emphasis on God's character.

He had made a covenant with the patriarchs as El Shaddai, but they had not experienced the fulfillment of that promise. Indeed Moses had complained that God had done nothing. Now God reveals himself through his name as the God who fulfills his promise and redeems Israel from Egypt.[43]

Oswald T. Allis agrees that God's redemptive character takes precedence in this passage, noting, "That the name Jehovah [Yahweh] was known and used long before the time of Moses, is clearly indicated. But the full redemptive significance of the name was not revealed until the exodus."[44]

These quotations demonstrate that Exodus 6:3 makes certain specific theological points by stating a historical detail. What Moses is about to experience and mediate to the Israelites is a deepened expression of God's character. God is more personally and intimately involved in Israel's future than ever. God's concern for Israel has reached the point where it will be proven by Israel's redemption from slavery. Historically speaking God has always cared for Israel, since God has had a special relationship with Abraham, Isaac and Jacob. In this new, crucial moment of this new generation's history that relationship will be broadened to include thousands of persons, deepened by the explanation of God's law and heightened by the dramatic events that will set the chosen people free. Yahweh's renewed promises, stated fresh for this generation, are intended to spark Moses' zeal for his task but have no short-term effect (cf. 6:9-12, 28-30). Moses remains discouraged.

So God repeats, emphatically, what Moses must do (7:1-5). Moses and Aaron must speak God's word to Pharaoh (7:1-2). They have no other task. Yahweh will do everything else. God will make Pharaoh stubborn (7:3), multiply signs and extraordinary deeds, or miracles (7:3), and eventually cause Egypt to release Israel (7:4). Why? To demonstrate God's identity, "to bring the Pharaoh to an experiential knowledge of his powerful Presence, not of Moses' truthfulness or Aaron's eloquence."[45] Moses fears his inability to convince Pharaoh; he fears failure. God lays no such burden on Moses. Rather Yahweh emphasizes the responsibility of the divine word to create a certain situation and the responsibility of the divine nature to sustain that situation. In other words, God intends to speak and act as he has since Genesis 1—2. Moses and Aaron are to believe and obey, the very qualities God has required of human beings since Genesis 1:26. Their burden of producing success lifted, Moses and Aaron obey God's orders (Ex 7:6-7). Faith in God's word results in appropriate action.

Once Moses regains his courage, God produces ten plagues that force Pharaoh to loosen his iron grip on the people. The plagues display God's saving power on Israel's behalf and also act as avenues for God's judgment on Pharaoh's stubborn refusal to let Israel leave Egypt.[46] At the same time, they are Yahweh's means for instructing Moses, Pharaoh and their respective peoples about God's identity and sole claim to deity (cf. Ex 7:4). Pharaoh admits in Exodus 5:2 that he does not know Yahweh, so Moses emphasizes in Exodus 7:17, 8:10, 8:22, 9:14 and 9:29 that Pharaoh should learn about the Lord's strength and glory from the plagues. Similarly the entire Egyptian nation must discover Yahweh's nature and power (7:5; 10:2; 14:4, 18), as must the Israelites, who grew up in Egypt's polytheistic culture (6:7; 10:2; 11:7). Finally, Moses himself must grasp God's identity if he is to lead Israel effectively and confidently (10:2; 11:7).[47] Thus God's revelatory impulses reach from a single individual (Moses) to two nations (Israel and Egypt). Also, it is clearly God who takes the initiative to reveal himself to human beings. Revelation from above will result in experiential knowledge on earth, of course, for God's loving nature causes Yahweh to reach out in sufficient and appropriate ways to those who are hurting physically, emotionally, intellectually and theologically.

Slowly yet inexorably Yahweh removes Pharaoh's lack of knowledge. As a prelude to the plagues, Aaron turns his staff into a snake and back again, only to learn Pharaoh's magicians can do the same. Clearly, though, Yahweh's power is great, for Aaron's staff swallow his opponents', but Pharaoh hardens his heart just as the all-knowing God has already predicted (7:8-13). Virtually the same thing occurs in the accounts of the first two plagues: Moses turns the Nile to blood and then brings enormous numbers of frogs on the land, and both plagues are duplicated by the magicians (7:14—8:7). Still, it is Moses who has the upper hand, since he declares when the terrors cease (cf. 7:25; 8:9-15). God's word is honored, just as the faithful Yahweh promised in Exodus 7:1-5.

When the third plague ensues, however, the magicians cannot copy it and declare that God is at work (8:19). Thus they conclude that Yahweh's power has defeated them and that what now happens transcends the normal course of events. The next seven plagues take on truly miraculous status because they bring pestilence and death that afflict Egyptian health, safety and property while bypassing the Israelites (8:20—11:10). Again, the purpose of these abnormal physical occurrences is to teach Israel, Egypt and especially Pharaoh Yahweh's identity as sole ruler of the earth and the human race. There is no Egyptian god who can stop Yahweh, nor is there any rival Israelite god who helps or hinders Yahweh. Only one God is in view, and that God, the same God the canon has presented since Genesis 1:1, demands to be recognized and demands that Israel go free.

Because of its canonical emphasis on one God, the text has no qualms about declaring that miracles took place in space and time. Moses writes emphatically that the God who creates now delivers Israel. If God created the earth out of nothing, then it is certainly not impossible that he could create situations from which the Egyptian magicians rightly conclude that God directs history. The God who created and sustains nature can certainly factor in and control any temporary changes in the normal course of events caused by a miracle. Several philosophers, evangelical and otherwise, have argued recently that this theological conclusion is philosophically sound unless one adopts naturalistic, nonsupernaturalist principles such as those surveyed in chapter one of this volume.[48] Indeed they argue coherently that the very definition of the concept of God must include the notion that God is powerful enough to create, sustain creation, enact miracles or do anything else God deems fit. Further, if this definition is correct, then what God deems fit will be in keeping with what is best for what God creates and sustains.

But does this emphasis on miracles eliminate the reliability of Exodus as history? Does the fact that the text declares a specific theological viewpoint make it salvation history but not objective history? Not if certain issues are kept in mind.

First, all histories have a particular viewpoint, since historians must select what events are most important to relate.[49] Thus the supernaturalist viewpoint in Exodus should not necessarily disqualify the accounts as nonhistorical. After all, Edwin Yamauchi observes, "Roman historians do not reject Livy because his writings were ideologically slanted to promote the reign of Augustus, or Tacitus because of his senatorial prejudices against the emperors."[50] Indeed modern historians also take specific positions,[51] so it is not fair to eliminate Exodus's historicity on these grounds.

Second, it must be remembered that miraculous events are the exception in biblical narratives, not the norm. The accounts are therefore not myths or legends in any consistent generic sense. They are instead presented as exceptions within the usual course of history, which indicates the text's general normalcy and reliability.

Third, like all good historical accounts the book of Exodus has a coherent view of cause and effect. Human interaction creates action here, just as it does in other historical writing. Divine action is also consistent with the canon's depiction of God. It seems reasonable, then, to acknowledge the consistency of Moses' depiction of divine and human interaction and its role in historical cause and effect. Interpreters may not agree with Exodus's viewpoint but cannot fairly dismiss it as mythic, legendary, primitive or inconsistent.

Fourth, the institution of Passover as an annual festival commemorates Israel's plight and flight in a way that highlights their historical reality. They are to observe Passover as a day that marks a particular point when

Israel was delivered from Egypt (12:7). They are to eat foods that remind them of the plainness and bitterness of their bondage (12:8-9, 17-20) and reenact their eagerness and readiness to leave Egypt (12:11). Quite significantly, they are also told to date all future events from this night of deliverance (12:2), which means this historical occurrence makes all others in Israel possible. Everything about this yearly observance, then, anchors future Israelites to real past history and therefore gives them hope that Yahweh will act on their behalf in their own real histories. As a symbol of their belief in this God of past, present and future history, the Israelites will redeem their firstborn to demonstrate their faith in the God who has elected Israel as Yahweh's firstborn (13:1-16).

Once the ten plagues effect Israel's release, miraculous signs guide the people's path as they head for the promised land (13:20-22). Carrying Joseph's bones with them, Moses and his followers depart, only to be followed by Pharaoh, whose heart grows hardened one last time (14:5-9). When the Egyptians draw closer Moses asks the people to believe, to have faith that God will deliver a final time (14:13-14). God intends to demonstrate conclusively his identity (14:18) and achieves this goal by parting the sea, thus allowing Israel to pass through unscathed, then drowning the pursuing Egyptians in the sea (14:19-30). Indeed this final miracle does instill fear, faith and obedience in the people (14:31). Seemingly everyone—readers, Egyptians and Israelites—now know that the God who hears (2:23-25) and calls (3:1—4:31) also saves from oppression. Thus faith in Yahweh, either prior to (4:31) or after deliverance (14:31), is never misplaced yet never simple or lacking in challenge.

Exodus 15 concludes this section of the book by demonstrating the best response to deliverance and by presenting the normal, ongoing barriers to faith in the one delivering God. Here Israel offers the first of many communitywide praises of Yahweh in Scripture. Because of their gratitude for what God has done on their behalf, the people sing a victory song[52] that praises Yahweh as more powerful than "Pharaoh (15:1-7), the sea (15:8-12), and the nations generally (15:13-18)."[53] Though it includes a host of metaphors and confident pronouncements, at the very heart of the song is an emphasis on God's uniqueness. Exodus 15:11, D. N. Freedman says, "stands at the center of the poem, and is an elaborate apostrophe on the incomparability of Yahweh."[54] It therefore serves as a summary of the text's other major metaphors.[55] The fact that God is a warrior is proven by Yahweh's use of the sea to crush Pharaoh's army (15:1-10). This incident sets Yahweh apart from other gods as holy, glorious and able to work miracles (15:11). No other god can act in this manner. Similarly, God's mastery over all nations sets Yahweh free to bless the chosen people by liberating them and giving them a homeland (15:13-17). Surely this God whose power is endless will enjoy a reign over creation that is endless (15:18). Such conclusions point once more to the rhetorical question in Exodus 15:11, "Who among the gods is like you, O LORD?"

Two clear theological points emerge in these stanzas, both of which are introduced earlier in the canon. First, Yahweh's uniqueness is underscored again. God can control the seas, Israel, the nations and Pharaoh because God has made them all. Thus Yahweh stands alone. Elmer Martens observes that

> for Israel to claim no god was even in a position to be compared with Yahweh was to set foot on the firm ground of monotheism, one god. It was also to distinguish him from angelic or divine beings, as well as from men such as the god-king Pharaoh. The claim, while not dogmatic, was not a claim without support. The conquest over Pharaoh and the Red Sea experience fully justified that claim.[56]

Second, the uniqueness of Israel resurfaces as well. God's love results in Israel's victory over Egypt and other nations who tremble at the greatness of their Lord (15:13-16) and in the eventual "planting" of the Israelites in the land, which was promised as long ago as Genesis 12:1-9 (15:17). Just how Israel will show themselves to be God's people will be developed later, but for now it simply suffices for them to be Abraham's heirs (Ex 2:24) and people of faith in their own right (Ex 4:31; 14:31; 15:1-18).

For people of faith, praise must stand alongside obedience as the proper response to the incomparable God who loves them. Praise begins with acknowledgment of God's character. In this song God's power is duly noted as evidence of God's love and incomparability. Praise does not stop here, however, for it leads to how Israel as the chosen people will relate to Yahweh. They must return God's "unfailing love" (15:13) in some manner beyond singing. The postvictory issue for Israel is whether or not they will continue to trust the Lord and continue to enjoy the Lord's blessings.

Canonical Synthesis: The Exodus and Divine Deliverance

It would be difficult to assess the canonical significance of Exodus 5—15 in a multivolumed work, much less in a work of this one's size and scope. After all, as Gerhard von Rad comments, "wherever it occurs, the phrase 'Jahweh delivered his people from Egypt' is confessional in character. Indeed, so frequent is it in the Old Testament, meeting us not only in every age (down to Dan. IX. 15), but also in the most varied contexts, that it has in fact been designated as Israel's original confession."[57] Besides the prevalence of exodus-inspired confessions of faith, interpreters must also contend with the fact that other major themes appear in these chapters and that New Testament writers cite Pharaoh and Moses in studies on God's grace and sovereignty (cf. Rom 9—11) and on individual faith commitments (cf. Heb 11:24-28). Still, certain comments must be offered at this point and then supplemented later when their appropriate passages occur in the canon.

First, in the Law and Former Prophets God's deliverance of Israel in Exodus 5—15 is cited in Exodus 20:2 as the experiential basis for the Ten Commandments and the case laws and ceremonial laws that follow. Thus the bulk of the Pentateuch depends on the relational solidarity established between God and Israel through the exodus. Even after the first generation of freed Israelites dies, Moses bases the nation's continuing relationship (as God's people) with Yahweh on these occurrences (cf. Deut 5:1-22). To the next generation Moses declares that God's electing love was proven by the covenant with Abraham, Isaac and Jacob as well as by the defeat of Pharaoh (Deut 7:7-9). Joshua makes the same point to these people at the end of his career (Josh 24:1-15), and Solomon begins his survey of Israel's history and relationship to God at the temple dedication (c. 966 B.C.) by mentioning the exodus (1 Kings 8:16). Clearly the exodus demonstrates God's love for and relationship with the patriarchs and their descendants. In this way the event provides a relational link between the past, present and future. The Israelites are God's people.

Second, in the Latter Prophets the relationship between Israel and Yahweh cemented by the exodus is used as the basis for prophetic calls for repentance. The most graphic statements along these lines are offered by Jeremiah, Ezekiel and Hosea. Jeremiah observes that despite Israel's deliverance from Egypt the people have forsaken the Lord to act like an adulterous woman (Jer 2:6—3:25), an image Ezekiel 16 develops extensively (Ezek 16:1-34). Hosea uses parent-child imagery to highlight how Israel has ignored the exodus heritage and gone after other gods (Hos 11:1-2). Each prophet counsels repentance and return to the God who saves the chosen people (Jer 4:1-4; Ezek 16:35-63; Hos 14:1-9). They believe that those who have been redeemed ought to relate in a positive way to their redeemer.

Third, Martens contends that four themes embedded in Exodus 5:22—6:8 permeate the rest of the Old Testament canon: salvation, the covenant community, knowledge of God and life and land.[58] Each of these ideas does appear repeatedly in the Old Testament, so Martens accurately gauges their value as centering themes. Obviously the four ideas are more prominent in some sections of the canon than in others, a fact Martens himself underscores, yet the general concept is sound. Martens highlights Hosea 2:14-23, for instance, as a preexilic prophetic text that emphasizes all four elements and demonstrates how Ezekiel 34:17-31 is a postexilic prophetic text that does the same.[59] These themes are also prevalent in Psalms, Job and Proverbs.[60] Again it is clear that the Old Testament writers saw Exodus as a theological starting point that could be applied to a host of historical settings with theological needs.

Fourth, both the Old and New Testaments cite texts in Exodus 5—15 as evidence of God's unique sovereignty.[61] Isaiah 51:9-10 states confidently that the exodus proves God's ability to save in any situation. Psalm 78:12-20 notes that Yahweh performed whatever miracles were necessary to free Israel, which made their subsequent rebellion all the more inexcusable and unfathomable.

In the New Testament, Paul uses Pharaoh as an example that Yahweh has "absolute freedom in carrying out his plan for Israel and the nations."[62] Reflecting on Exodus 9:16, Paul says that God demonstrated his power to and against Pharaoh to bestow mercy on the elect (Rom 9:14-18).[63] To Paul, it is impossible for anyone to have faith unless God graciously instills that faith. Donald Bloesch correctly summarizes Paul's position by writing, "It is the Holy Spirit who empowers man to lay hold of God's grace; such a transforming event cannot be attributed to the natural free will of man."[64] God's use of Pharaoh helped Israel believe and therefore was part of God's mercy toward Israel and toward anyone who believes and acts in faith based on the exodus accounts.

In other words, God's self-glorification as revealed in Pharaoh's learning God's identity (cf. Ex 5:2) helped save Israel from sin as well as from slavery. C. E. B. Cranfield observes:

> That Paul should understand the reference to God's power in an evangelical way should not be surprising. Moreover, in so doing he would not have been untrue to what is after all the general sense of the Exodus passage; for there too the thought is not of a mere show of unqualified power, of power for its own sake, but of power directed toward the deliverance of God's people.[65]

Paul declares that as God saves Israel the Lord's name is proclaimed to all nations as a result (Ex 9:16; Rom 9:17). Israel's salvation matters a great deal to Yahweh, of course, "but the showing of God's saving power and the publishing abroad of His name, of His self-revelation, of His truth—this is the very purpose of God's election of Israel."[66] Seen in this light, God uses a rebellious, oppressive, stubborn Pharaoh to help save elect from all nations, an achievement only a loving, sovereign God could produce.

Fifth, the exodus symbolizes assurance of future deliverance in the Scriptures. Certainly Exodus 15:13-18 indicates that in the short term the exodus means God will help Israel conquer the land promised to Abraham,[67] an expectation repeated in Joshua 1:1-9 directly prior to the start of the conquest. Isaiah 51:9-11 has a longer-term goal in mind, which is that the first exodus prefigures Israel's "second exodus," or return from its post-587

B.C. Babylonian exile. Ezekiel envisions a similar second exodus return from exile, one in which Israel comes back to the land purged from the propensity to sin that caused them to lose it in the first place (Ezek 20:32-38). How can these prophets be so sure that one exodus implies that another will occur? Because Yahweh remains the God who delivers and Israel remains God's chosen, beloved people. As long as Yahweh's nature remains intact the exodus principle does as well.

The God Who Sustains the Redeemed: Exodus 15:22—18:27

The matter of Israel's consistency emerges quickly, for in Exodus 15:22-24 the nation lacks pure water, grumbles and generally wonders if they will have enough to drink. Genesis 1—2 has already demonstrated that God sustains what he creates. Likewise, Exodus 3—14 has proven that Yahweh is quite capable of performing miraculous works that meet all Israel's current needs. Though the people have exercised faith before they must do so again in each new crisis. Moses solves the water crisis and then reminds the nation that obedience to Yahweh will stave off the sort of disasters that overwhelmed Egypt (15:26). God has not redeemed them to destroy them but to love them and build their faith in the incomparable Yahweh.

Seemingly unaffected by this giving of water, the people next complain about the lack of food. They glorify slavery to the point of wishing they had died in Egypt rather than growing hungry in the desert. They blame Moses for taking them there (16:1-3). Once again the issue is whether the God who calls and delivers can sustain the elect in this new situation. Once again Yahweh rises to the occasion, this time in a way that "will test them and see whether they will follow my [Yahweh's] instructions" (16:4). Ironically, they believe they can test Yahweh's worth, when actually only their faithfulness remains in question.

As in Moses' call story and the plague accounts, God meets Israel's needs through miraculous means. Yahweh informs Moses that bread and quail will be given from heaven to fill Israel's stomachs (16:5-12). The breadlike substance is named "manna," a play on the Hebrew for "what is it?" (16:1-16). Martin Noth says that flocks of quail often appear in the Sinai Peninsula where Israel was located at this time and that the manna may well have been "a sort of droplike formation on the leaves of the tree or shrub" still common in this region.[68] Noth observes correctly, however, that even if manna was a natural food it was miraculous for enough to fall to cover Israel's needs while they observed the sabbath (16:21-30).[69] The notation in Exodus 16:35 that the manna lasted forty years, or until Israel settled in Canaan, certainly highlights the longevity of Yahweh's miraculous provision yet also forces readers to consider that something may delay the nation's entry into the promised land.

After God provides water again (17:1-7), thus quieting the people's grumbling for a short time at least, the text focuses on another way that the delivering Lord sustains the elect. This time the problem resides in Yahweh's ability to defeat enemies in the desert, which in turn deals with whether Yahweh is limited to a special geographical location or by desert conditions as opposed to the watery conditions of Exodus 14. In other words, the question is how universal Yahweh's power may be and therefore in what fuller sense Yahweh is a "warrior" (15:3).

Yahweh proves decisively to be as vigorous in the desert as near the sea. A new character, Joshua, leads the people to victory yet succeeds in doing so only because Aaron and Hur (another new character) steady Moses' upstretched hands as they lift God's rod to the sky (17:8-13). Again the battle has been the Lord's. Subsequent to the battle Moses is told to write about the affair in a scroll, which inaugurates the Bible's references to Moses' composing parts or all of the Pentateuch. This event merits permanent record because it reveals in a specific historical occurrence how Yahweh directs human events by empowering the chosen people. While Israel must exert enough faith to enter the battle, it is Yahweh's allegiance to them that clinches the triumph. Put another way, God's sovereignty creates, strengthens and validates faith in this episode.

Exodus 18 closes this section by showing that God sustains Moses, the leader of the chosen people, and provides a context in which Israel may govern itself. These concepts are expressed within a narrative in which Moses' father-in-law (Jethro) brings Moses' wife and sons to join the Israelites in the desert (18:1-6). Jethro's contribution consists of statements made in the form of a confession and out of concern for Moses' burden of leadership.

First, upon seeing God's work on Israel's behalf, Jethro, like the Israelites in Exodus 15, praises Yahweh's saving power and incomparability (18:9-10). To him such deeds prove the Lord's uniqueness, at least in the sense that Yahweh "is greater than all other gods" (18:11). Perhaps Jethro simply thinks that Yahweh is the greatest of all the gods who exist.[70] If so, he has learned what Pharaoh discovered, though he is not privileged to know what the readers of the canon know: Yahweh is the only God. Other gods may exist linguistically, but they do not exist ontologically.

Second, Jethro notes that Moses judges disputes all day long; he advises his son-in-law to place capable, God-fearing, honest judges "over thousands, hundreds, fifties and tens" (18:21). That way Moses will deal personally only with difficult cases (18:22-23). Moses agrees and implements the plan (18:24-26). Thus Israel's leader receives the help he needs to be sustained in his work. Also, the fact that several judges now exist make general instruction in societal moral ordering quite desirable, if not absolutely necessary. It should come as no surprise that standards for Israel's conduct will soon appear in the text.

Part Two: The Covenant (Exodus 19—24)

These chapters depict one of the great defining moments of Israelite history and of Old Testament and biblical theology. Though perhaps he overstates the case a bit, W. J. Dumbrell is close to the mark when he comments, "A correct understanding of these verses which summon Israel, as a result of Sinai, to its vocation, is vital. The history of Israel from this point on is in reality merely a commentary upon the degree of fidelity with which Israel adhered to this Sinai-given vocation."[71] What God and Israel say here brings together the canon's previous redemptive threads and at the same time sets the chosen people's future direction. Underlying principles such as grace, faith and obedience remain in place yet are given a broader context in which to operate. As they unfold, the uniqueness of God's transcendence, authority and wisdom becomes apparent. Indeed God, revelation and authority[72] combine here in a manner calculated to produce a unique and holy people.

The Transcendent God: Exodus 19

During Moses' call story the Lord promises Moses that a sign of victory will be that Moses will lead Israel back to "the mountain of God" (cf. Ex 3:1, 12). Now this promise is kept (19:1-2). At this sacred location Yahweh explains Israel's future based on what has occurred since patriarchal times. God has chosen Israel, the whole house of Jacob, has sustained them and helped them multiply into a great people, has now freed them from Egypt and has brought them near to himself (19:4). In other words, God's grace has created a special relationship between Israel and Yahweh, which allows them to know and experience the Lord's power and presence. Clearly God's action and the divine-human relationship are intentional and inseparable.

After stating the basis of the Israel-Yahweh relationship in Exodus 19:4, the text proceeds to note the purpose and function of that relationship in Exodus 19:5-6.[73] First, God announces that the relationship's purpose is to establish a covenant with the entire nation (19:5). Earlier God made a covenant with Noah (cf. Gen 9:8-11) and with Abraham (cf. Gen 12:1-9; Ex 2:23-25). Now, without subtracting anything from the promises made to Abraham, Yahweh endeavors to have a special friendship not just with one person or a single clan but with an entire nation composed of Abraham's descendants. The covenant comes with certain obligations, just as Abraham's embracing of Yahweh's covenant required faith, action and commitment (cf. Gen 12:1-9; 15:6; 22:1-11). Therefore this covenant bears a strong resemblance to earlier faith-based, obedience-oriented covenants.

Second, Yahweh states that the covenant's function is to set aside Israel as a special nation that can mediate God's identity to the entire family of nations. Because all the earth belongs to Yahweh,[74] Israel will be "a kingdom of priests and a holy nation" (19:6). The three phrases "treasured possession," "kingdom of priests" and "holy nation" all refer to God's previous promises to Abraham. The Israelites are chosen in Abraham ("treasured possession"; cf. Gen 12:1-9). As a "kingdom of priests and holy nation," Kaiser says,

> the whole nation was to act as mediators of God's grace to the nations of the earth, even as Abraham had been promised that through him and his seed all the nations of the earth would be blessed (Gen 12:3). The last title designated Israel as a separate and distinct nation because her God was holy, separate, and distinct, as were his purposes and plans (Deut 7:6; 14:2; 21; 26:19; Isa 62:12; cf. 1 Peter 2:9).[75]

Israel as a group must play its part in the one God's determination to eliminate the worldwide sin problem through the ministry of Abraham and his family. Abraham was called out of all the earth to participate in human redemption; so is Israel. Abraham received a covenant based on revealed grace, faith and obedience. Israel as a whole will soon receive a similar opportunity. Abraham was called to be separate from his home, his father and his people. Israel will soon be separate, or holy, in a similar manner. Centuries of planning and timing now come together in a single moment. The sense of drama could hardly be higher. Will Israel accept this opportunity to fulfill their redemptive ministerial function by drawing strength from their unique relationship with the unique Yahweh? They agree to do so (19:7-8).

Upon this agreement, Yahweh proceeds to remind the entire nation what Abraham learned in Genesis 12:1-9, 15:1-21 and 22:1-12, what Moses learned in Exodus 3—4 and indeed what the people themselves ought to have learned in Exodus 5—15: Yahweh is sovereign, holy, transcendent and fully alive. This is no placid, peaceful, silent idol. Yahweh lives, speaks and acts in a way that terrifies yet also instructs, frees, redeems, challenges and reassures. God desires to be revealed to Israel yet knows that this revelation must overthrow any residual Egyptian notions of deity and must give the chosen people a clear picture of who they are in relationship to Yahweh. Thus the Lord determines to highlight Moses' role as mediator of Yahweh's self-revelation (19:9) to highlight God's mercy in revealing himself to human beings. Yahweh also limits Israel's access to the location of this revelation and commands the people to prepare themselves spiritually for this revelation of covenant (19:10-13). Even the chosen people do not attain to the power and excellence of the God who elects them. They must learn to respect and place themselves under Yahweh's loving authority.

The final scenes in Exodus 19 drive home the chapter's emphasis on God's holiness and transcendence. Yahweh's holiness, or separateness, is under-scored by Israel's need to consecrate themselves before encountering the Lord and by Yahweh's telling Moses to have the people keep a respectful distance between themselves and the mountain (19:16-25). God's transcendence, or other-than-humanness, is highlighted by the twofold mentioning of how God descended on the mountain and the succeeding descriptions of the physical manifestations of this descending (19:16-22). God does not share human size or time limitations. God does not meet with people as peers. God is other than human yet desires to forge a relationship with humans or would not "descend" at all. Throughout the canon two undergirding principles have appeared with regularity: God's uniqueness separates him from creation, and God's love leads him to reach out to creation. The transcendent God is about to revisit these principles again.

The God Who Makes Covenant with Israel: Exodus 20—24

Having reemphasized the nature of God's character and noted clearly the purpose and function of Israel within the proposed covenant, the text next states the initial contents of that covenant. Two types of laws are presented: commands (20:1-17) and case laws (20:22—23:19).[76] These instructions are framed by a narrative that separates the first two sections (20:18-21), a succeeding promise of success (23:20-33) and a concluding description of Israel's response to the revealed standards that leads to further revelation (24:1-18). These elements work together to produce a unified picture of basic laws, reception of the law, case studies built on the basic laws, and human and divine reaction to the offering of these laws. This whole section has staggering implications for ancient history, since no other nation believed their deity made a covenant with them. No other god was thought to make and keep specific promises without fail.

Yahweh begins the Ten Commandments by linking the revealed standards to the exodus. The God who redeemed Israel now offers the following foundational covenant instruction (20:1-2). Not surprisingly, the first four commands cover various aspects of Israel's relationship to their God. Their friendship with Yahweh must take precedence over every other relationship. The last six commands deal with human relationships, though, which indicate that the covenant will indeed have ramifications extending from the covenant people to the outside world.

The first commandment summarizes the distinctive contribution of Old Testament theology. It also makes every other command and case law authoritative for this and each successive generation of covenant people.[77] In fact von Rad does not overstate the matter when he writes, "Indeed, the whole history of Israel's cult is a struggle solely concerned with the validity of the first commandment."[78] This commandment bears two possible interpretations. One is that "for Israel there shall be no other gods."[79] Other gods may exist in some irrelevant fashion, yet Israel must give such "deities" no worship, no offerings, no obedience. Another possible interpretation is that "no other god exists." If no other god exists, then it makes no sense to pay any attention to any God but Yahweh.

Either interpretation makes Israel unique among nations. Even if Israel did not deny the existence of other gods in some realm of reality, these other deities, John Bright says, were

> allowed neither part in creation, nor function in the cosmos, nor power over events, nor cult, were robbed of all that made them gods and rendered nonentities, in short, were "undeified." Though the full implications of monotheism were centuries in being drawn, in this functional sense Israel believed in but one God from the beginning.[80]

Unlike other countries, who at least granted lesser gods retainer status, Israel eliminates such gods by giving them nothing to do. Still, the canon makes the radical point that no other gods exist at all. Moses describes no other god unless it is an idol to be buried (cf. Gen 35:1-15) and thus nonexistent. No other gods appear even in the plague passages, where it would be natural to satirize Egypt's gods. In the text

> Yahweh is, in a word, all that is divine for Israel. This principle underlies all biblical literature. Other deities are mentioned in the biblical narrative but are accorded no reality. Wherever divine words or divine acts are performed, it is this one God who speaks and acts. Only this one God is known in biblical tradition, and the tradition as a whole identifies the one to whom sole loyalty is due.[81]

It is correct to say, then, that the canon eliminates all gods from contention. There is no room in biblical theology for any god but Yahweh, the one who creates, sustains, redeems, judges and calls.

The second command reinforces the importance of the one-God concept. Israel must not make idols based on nature, bow down to them or worship them (20:4-5). This prohibition covers both the gods and Yahweh. Certainly making images of and worshiping other deities breaks the first commandment. Thus the second commandment in effect tells Israel, "It is forbidden to claim Yahweh is your supreme god yet bow down to others. Sole allegiance to Yahweh is required. Nothing less." At the same time the prohibition covers images of Yahweh as well. Other nations believed their "deity took possession of the image and could thereafter be approached in it."[82] In this way the god could be tamed, controlled, domesticated, even manipulated. The fire on the mountain above their heads told Israel that Yahweh was no such deity. Rather Yahweh is the living, relational God who loves the chosen people enough to be properly jealous when they worship either nongods or pale imitations of the real Lord (20:5). This God wants to bless those who believe and obey and to punish those who rebel, not be placed on a shelf like a child's toy and be prayed to by those who made the toy in the first place (20:6). Clearly this commandment both removes Yahweh's "competitors" and eliminates spiritual nonsense at the same time.

The third commandment acknowledges the validity of its two predecessors and regulates the use of the name of the only God who may be worshiped (20:7). Only Yahweh may receive prayers and worship. This fact being so, worshipers must not treat God's name, character, reputation or teaching[83] lightly. Walther Zimmerli states that this prohibition eliminates magical incantations based on Yahweh's name such as those chanted by other nations using their gods' names. The command also denies blasphemy, false testimony and "giving Yahweh a bad name" through inappropriate behavior.[84] Childs adds that false teaching presented as deriving from Yahweh also amounts to taking God's name in vain.[85] In other words, those who speak for or about Yahweh must adhere to the revealed canonical truth about Yahweh. They must also not use Yahweh's name for their own selfish purposes. Later generations of Jewish people interpreted this command to mean they could not speak the name Yahweh, but this application goes beyond the command in a way that tends to depersonalize the personal God of Exodus 20.

The fourth command draws on creation theology to lead Israel toward a proper worship of their God. Genesis 2:2-3 states that God set apart the seventh day as a time of rest. Now the text makes the sabbath a permanent part of Israel's life. Every man, woman, child and beast must be given rest (20:8-10), which must have been an extraordinary gift in a work-laden society such as theirs. God has already proven powerful enough to provide for Israel's needs in six days (cf. Ex 16:21-23), so they should not worry that such "sloth" will lead to want. Besides a gift of physical rest, the sabbath also allows Israel one full day of unfettered time in which to worship Yahweh and receive spiritual refreshment. Specific worship rites are detailed later, but here the stark principle is introduced. If Israel believes Yahweh can meet their needs in six workdays and if Israel truly has no other God, then the sabbath will be a blessing, not a burden, to them. The basic human needs of rest and worship are ingrained in the fabric of creation (20:11-12) and in this way are acknowledged and fulfilled.

With foundational principles for a positive relationship with Yahweh in place, the next six commands regulate human interaction. The fifth and tenth commandments govern motives and actions while the sixth through ninth focus on actions. Yahweh stresses honor of parents as the key to lengthy possession of the land promised Abraham in Genesis 12:1-9 (Ex 20:12). Dale Patrick writes, "The word translated 'honor' frequently has God as its object, in which case it is translated 'glorify.' To honor parents is to accord them a respect and importance reserved for the sacred."[86] Whenever such respect exists, surely obedience to and care for parents follow. The most important long-term benefit of this honor should be that children will follow their parents' teachings about Yahweh and the covenant.[87]

The next four commandments bar taking precious elements of life from one's neighbor. Starting with murder (20:13), the premeditated taking of life, the text moves on to the taking of another person's spouse (20:14), the taking of someone's property (20:15) and the taking of someone's reputation or freedom (20:16). According to Genesis 1—2, God gives life (Gen 1:26), life partners (Gen 2:20-25) and labor and property (Gen 1:26-28; 2:15). Only God can determine, through either direct revelation or sovereign act, how or when life, marriage and property rights cease. Certainly God gives each human being individual dignity as well (Gen 1:26), so the unjust marring of another's reputation also violates the very fabric of creation. Each person in the covenant nation deserves to enjoy respect for his or her life, marital relationship, property and name. Violations of this pattern are blunt rejections of the will of the God who created it.

Finally, the tenth commandment denounces the specific attitude that leads to the breaking of all commandments (20:17). The word *covet* means to earnestly desire the specific possessions or persons attached to one's neighbor. Those who covet do not want a house or a woman. They want their neighbor's specific home or wife. Thus the desire fully realized is stealing or adultery. Similarly, rejecting the first four commands amounts to coveting God's authority. Just as faith leads to obedience (Gen 15:6), so does coveting lead to defrauding God and neighbor. Sin begins with one's desires. As Kaiser observes, "This commandment deals with man's inner heart and shows that none of the previous nine commandments could be observed merely from an external or formal act. Every inner instinct that led up to the act itself was also included."[88] The covenant initiates in the heart and will.

Case laws built on the commands soon follow, and further elaborations of these revealed truths appear in the rest of the Law, but the natural procession toward these case laws is interrupted by the Israelites' response to God's revelation. Stated simply, the people are terrified at Yahweh's awesome display of power (20:18). They affirm Moses' God-given (cf. Ex 19:9) mediatorial role (20:19) and receive assurance that all these events intend to instill a fear of the Lord that restrains sin (20:20). Having performed this pastoral function, Moses plunges into "the thick darkness where God was" (20:21) to receive more revelation from the authoritative, instructing God.

Moses begins the process of applying the ten commands to daily situations in Exodus 20:22—23:19. Scholars of virtually every commitment consider these case laws, commonly known as the "Book of the Covenant," a unified whole.[89] The instructions found here vary in their subject matter and content and are bound together only by the fact that they derive from the Ten Commandments in some manner. Still, Patrick correctly concludes that four broad categories link the laws:

1. The Law of the Altar (Ex 20:23-26)
2. The Judgments (Ex 21:1—22:20)
3. Moral Commandments and Duties (Ex 22:21—23:9)
4. Sabbatical Times and the Festival Calendar (Ex 23:10-19)[90]

Apparently these initial cases are to govern the people's behavior and guide the judges appointed in Exodus 18:17-26.

Yahweh's instructions about building altars reinforce the first four commandments. Since God has been revealed in such a spectacular manner (20:22), Israel surely knows that idols are meaningless to humans and offensive to God (20:23). The mention of altars and sacrifices (20:24-26) reminds readers of offerings made by the patriarchs and others and also prefigures more information to come. For now it suffices that the people embrace monotheism and practice obedience to the authoritative Lord who has redeemed them.

Human relationships dominate the case laws in Exodus 21:1—23:9. The basic requirements for treatment of others are fairness (21:23-25), holiness (22:31), justice (23:6) and the sort of mercy they craved while living as slaves in Egypt (23:9). In every situation the victim and the weak are afforded protection. For instance, Hebrew men and women may be bought as servants (21:2, 7) but must be treated fairly and may choose to leave or stay after six years (21:1-11). Their status or gender does not allow their temporary owners to abuse them, for they are not their master's property. Further, acts against unsuspecting persons such as premeditated murder, kidnapping or beating parents deserve death (21:12-17). Similarly, violent acts that cause injury or premature birth must result in exact payment for the harm done (21:18-27). All life, born or yet in the womb, is included under these protections. Finally, if innocent persons are harmed or killed through an animal owner's negligence, that owner is held responsible for the cost of the negligence (21:28-36). God did not redeem Israel from slavery so that they could oppress one another! Likewise Yahweh did not promise Israel a homeland, or property, of their own so they could covet and steal what others possessed. Thus Yahweh sets forth judgments against stealing and poor handling of others' property (22:1-15).

Every law code must be judged by how it raises accepted standards. This law raises women above the status of sexual object (22:16-17). It raises the emotions and loyalties of Israel above sorcery (22:18), bestiality (22:19), idolatry (22:20) and mistreatment of the poor, the orphan, the alien, the widow or anyone else who has no advocate (22:21-27). It raises their talk above blasphemy and cursing (22:28), their generosity above what is merely expected (22:29-31), their motives above maliciousness (23:1), their sense of justice above the mob's (23:2-3), their sense of responsibility beyond their own interests (23:4-5) and their love for fairness above the desire for mere money (23:68). In other words, it pushes them to treat others as they have always wanted to be treated (23:9) and forces each person to engage his or her internal and external self in this process. Moral and civic responsibilities are in no way kept separate.

Rest and worship are to be ingrained into Israel's life on a periodic as well as weekly basis. The sabbath principle includes a seventh-year rest for the land, which indicates the necessity of allowing people, land and even the nation's economy to heal (23:10-12). Other gods give no such rest (23:13). Israel also needs to gather three times a year to rekindle their collective love for Yahweh and to remind each other to keep the covenant (23:14-19). Each festival receives more detailed treatment later in the Pentateuch, so the intent of this passage is to set these agriculturally timed feasts aside in a preliminary way, a strategy that describes much of the rest of the material in the Book of the Covenant. It is evident at this point, though, that the Feast of Unleavened Bread is linked to Passover because they occur near the same time (23:15; cf. 12:2).

God's covenant demands do not come without promises. In return for their faith and obedience Israel will receive the long-promised land (23:20-33). Once again the key element in the reception of the promise is adherence to Yahweh alone (23:24, 32-33), for Yahweh alone can work the miracles necessary to achieve success (23:20-23, 27). All other gods can be is a snare (23:33).

With these basic commands and case laws in place, Moses is ready to offer this much of the covenant to the people. At least in general terms the people know what God requires and what God offers. Indeed the foundational nature of what has been revealed means that future covenantal elements will be similar. So Moses tells the people all he has heard, and the nation agrees to the covenant (24:3). Therefore Moses writes "everything the LORD had said" (24:4). A written record was made to show the long-term value of the words. Such a sacred transaction was not entrusted to even the most accurate oral tradition. Once composed, the book is read, and once more the people accept the covenant stipulations (24:4-7). Undoubtedly encouraged and emboldened, Moses, Aaron, Nadab, Abihu and Israel's seventy elders commune with the incomparable God (24:9-11). Communion results from obedience. Leaving Joshua somewhere between the mountain top and the camp, a bouyant Moses returns to God, with whom he will stay with "forty days and forty nights" (24:12-18), for further instructions. God will give him stones that will symbolize the covenant (24:12). It is hard to imagine a more positive scene.

Canonical Synthesis: The Basic Covenant Standards

This covenant offer was both startling and conventional in the ancient context. God's overture was startling because no other nation in the ancient world is known to have claimed a covenant with its deity. Israel was elect indeed. Yahweh was sovereign enough to control the situation and loving enough to desire to be obligated in a friendship relationship with Abraham's descendants. This sovereignty and love combine to combat the sin problem. At the same time, the covenant format was common in its time. G. E. Mendenhall's claim that the Hittite treaty form that includes preamble (Ex 20:1), historical prologue (20:2), stipulations (20:3—23:19), provision for reading the covenant (24:4-7) and the noting of blessings and curses (23:20-23) exists here is basically accurate.[91] Specifics differ, but the overall outline is intact. Clearly, then, God's revelation comes in an understandable, recognizable form. It can be written down, read, grasped and obeyed.

There is no way to describe adequately the canonical implications of Exodus 19—24. Everyone from Moses (Deut 5:6-21), to Jeremiah (Jer 7:1-15), to Jesus (Mt 5—7), to Peter (1 Pet 2:9), and every other biblical writer who has anything to say about covenant, morality and relationship to God reflects directly or indirectly on this passage. The same is true about much of the rest of the Pentateuch, so foundational are these chapters to biblical theology. Given the enormity of the task, perhaps it is best to deal with core beliefs about these verses that combat misconceptions about them. Three issues are vital.

First, Jesus summarizes the law by quoting Leviticus 19:18 and Deuteronomy 6:4-9 (Mk 12:29-31; Mt 22:34-40). In fact, he asserts that "all the Law and the Prophets hang on these two commandments" (Mt 22:40). Leviticus 19:18 reads, "Do not seek revenge or bear a grudge against one of your people, but love your neighbor as yourself. I am the LORD." This first half of "all the Law and the Prophets" corresponds to the last six commandments and the case laws in Exodus 21:1—23:9. Though it is not stated so succinctly until Leviticus 19:18, the principle underlies every mention of helping the weak, protecting the rights of all Israelites and punishing appropriately all law breakers. Revenge and all other forms of self-interest are banned in favor of attitudes like mercy and fairness that lead to appropriate behavior.

Deuteronomy 6:4-9 stresses loving Yahweh with heart, soul and strength. Though this summary verse appears after Leviticus 19:18 in the canon, its driving principle really precedes its counterpart, since it encapsulates the first four commandments, Exodus 20:22-26 and Exodus 23:10-33. Indeed it captures the essence of every teaching on monotheism and human relationship with God. It refutes all notions that the Law simply creates dread. It highlights love as the reason for keeping covenant.

Second, Paul emphasizes that law points out human sin, thus revealing each person's need for God's salvation (Rom 7:7-25; Gal 3—4). Without question, Paul in particular captures the use the prophets make of the covenant. Jeremiah cites the covenant as he pounds home his messages on repentance (e.g., Jer 7:1—8:3). Isaiah uses covenant language to call Israel back to their Lord (cf. Is 1—5). Hosea, Ezekiel, Amos and others adopt the same strategy. Sin is defined as covenant breaking in the prophetic literature, and covenant infidelity is evidence enough that Israel stands needy and spiritually poverty stricken before God. Again, the law here is used to turn hearts back to God (cf. Mal 4:6). Only then can proper external action follow.

Third, several psalms, but most conspicuously Psalm 119, celebrate the law as a gift rather than mourn it as a burden. To the writer of Psalm 119 the law offers guidance, strength, purity and confidence. It corrects, yet it also gives joy and provides evidence of Yahweh's compassion (Ps 119:156). No doubt the law becomes a burden when one does not keep it from the heart (cf. Deut 6:4-9; Mic 6:6-8) or when one replaces it for faith as the foundation of relationship with God (cf. Rom 9:31-32), but understood properly it is God's grace to a human race afflicted by a millennia-old sin problem it cannot solve. The very genesis of the law is grace, for it is instituted by Yahweh, who led Israel out of Egypt based not on Israel's intrinsic merit but based rather on Yahweh's promises to Abraham (cf. Ex 2:23-25). Those who attempt to make the covenant sheer obligation miss the point the canon has made to this juncture in the account.

Part Three: The Tabernacle (Exodus 25—31)

Hints that a permanent worship center would eventually be established emerge in the altar laws in Exodus 20:22-26 and in the festival regulations in Exodus 23:14-19. The presence of altars, sacrifices and festivals also implies that priests will be expected to facilitate worship. This section of Exodus provides preliminary instructions about the worship center, the priests who will minister there and the reasons both will exist. It is these reasons that matter most for Old Testament theology. Chief among them is that God will dwell among, be present with, the chosen people. Every other detail about the worship center and the priesthood derive from this theme.[92] A second foundational idea is the holiness of the dwelling God and the holiness of the worshiping people. Finally, a third concept found here is the value of communion between the people and their God. These truths intersect the various major topics in these chapters. Other major topics such as the importance of sacrifice are foreshadowed here but are discussed in detail later in the Pentateuch.

The God Who Dwells with Israel: Exodus 25—27

Yahweh commands Moses to take an offering to build a "holy place" for the purpose of having a visible symbol that God dwells among them (25:1-8). This sanctuary must conform exactly to God's revealed pattern (25:9) so that God's presence will truly be understood and experienced. Without question, it is for Israel's benefit, not because of pride on Yahweh's part, that these instructions are given.

Three worship implements are to be placed in the sanctuary. A chest (ark) representing God's presence among Israel[93] will be constructed. It will house the covenant stones God will give Moses (25:16) and will have a cover that helps mediate forgiveness. At this place of mediation God promises to "meet with" (25:22) Israel and forgive sins. Again presence is foremost in the text. A table will hold, among other things, daily bread that represents Yahweh's continuous sustaining presence among the Israelites (25:30). Also, a lampstand will be placed in the sanctuary. Though the purpose of the lamp was no doubt functional (25:37), it is also possible that it may have represented the life God gives Israel.[94]

This sanctuary ("holy place") will be placed within a larger area called the tabernacle, or meeting area. Measuring fifteen feet wide by forty-five feet long by fifteen feet high, the tabernacle is to have "walls" of linen (26:1-6), goat hair (26:7-13) and leather (26:14). It will look like a large tent, enclosing the sanctuary and the area around it. Outside the sanctuary are an altar for sacrifice (27:1-8), a courtyard where people may gather (27:9-19) and oil for lamps to be kept burning continuously (27:20-21). Inside the two-roomed sanctuary the ark of presence is given a special room, which is called the holiest place (26:34), while the table of presence and the lamps are left in the remaining space, called the holy place (26:33).

Whenever the people saw this worship area they were reminded that God lives among the chosen people. Israel has seen enough of God's power on Sinai to know Yahweh does not only dwell there and does not have to dwell there. God cannot be contained. God can choose to dwell in a place because of a merciful desire to relate to people, but it is indeed Yahweh's prerogative to do so or not. Thus this place of presence was intended to reassure Israel of God's voluntary, ongoing commitment to them.

The God Who Calls and Meets with Mediators: Exodus 28—31

Obviously someone will have to operate the sanctuary and carry it from place to place as Israel travels. So Yahweh determines that Aaron and his sons will accept responsibility for this task (28:1). They will be given garments appropriate for their work and symbolic of their position (28:1-42), and they will be installed permanently as Yahweh's priests (29:1-9). As permanent priests, they must offer sacrifices for their own sins and the sins of the people (29:10—30:10). Just as Moses mediates God's presence by conveying Yahweh's revealed standards, so Aaron and his sons will mediate God's presence by removing the sin barrier between the unfailingly holy God and the unfailingly imperfect human race. The priests' preparation for mediation includes washing of self, anointing of the altar with special oil and offering of incense to God, all of which highlights the sacred nature of serving the one holy God and the chosen people (30:17-38). Their efforts will be supported financially by all Israel (30:11-16).

Why does God call priests? Why does God empower men to build the worship center and craft its implements (31:1-11)? The answer is, again, that Yahweh wants to meet and speak with the Israelites (29:42-43). Yahweh sets priests apart so that Israel can know their God and be sure that Yahweh has not left them alone (29:44-45). Yahweh wants the chosen people to know they were chosen, redeemed from Egypt and brought to this point in their history so that Yahweh, the I AM, "might dwell among them" (29:46). The Creator, sustainer and redeemer of all created, sustained and redeemed persons and things desires communion, friendship with Israel. Everything done from Genesis 12 to Exodus 31 has been done to restore the human-divine interaction forfeited in Genesis 3.

Worship needs to have a physical context, and the worship center and priests provide this necessary component. It also needs a temporal context, and the sabbath day gives it this important time element (31:12-18). The sabbath will remind Israel that God is holy, set apart and unique, as the nation sets apart one day a week (30:12-13). This day will remind them who created and redeemed them (31:17) and will offer them specific, focused time in which they can enjoy God's presence among them, unfettered by day-to-day work concerns. Therefore worship will have a specific place in Israel's life and will mediate God's presence. The importance of these details is underscored by the fact that having received them Moses prepares to descend the mountain, armed with tablets of stone that solidify the Yahweh-Israel covenant.[95]

Part Four: The Golden Calf Incident (Exodus 32—34)

Scripture is dotted with extremely exciting and hopeful situations that are dashed by persistent human failure. Exodus 32—34 marks another occurrence of this pattern. Having agreed to do whatever Yahweh requires of them in the divinely offered covenant relationship, the people lose sight of Moses, Yahweh and faith. Disobedience of the most basic kind results. Sin captures the stage in a way unparalleled since Genesis. God's reaction to this sin demonstrates the greatness of Yahweh's holiness, the consistency of Yahweh's willingness to be present among the Israelites and Yahweh's readiness to forgive repenting people.

The God Whose Jealousy Is Holy: Exodus 32

Israel takes Moses' forty-day absence on the mountain (Ex 24:18) to mean that he may not return (32:1). Thus they pressure Aaron to make "real" gods, gods they can see, that they can worship (32:1). Aaron complies (32:2-4), declares the resulting idol the god that brought Israel out of Egypt (32:4) and announces a festival that turns into sheer decadence (32:5-6). The chosen people have forgotten who redeemed them and have reneged on their promise to keep the covenant. They have broken at least the first three of the ten commandments. Worshiping idols leads to other sins as well (32:6). Spiritual amnesia and rebellion set in after only a few weeks pass. Such is the resilient nature of sin in human events.

Yahweh the omniscient God informs Moses of what has occurred and tells the mediator that Israel will be destroyed and a new nation forged through Moses (32:7-10). Though an extreme measure, this offer would still keep all promises made to Abraham, since Moses is Abraham's descendant. Moses declines this offer by pleading Israel's case (32:10-14). God has noted how quickly Israel has turned away (32:8) and has stated how stubborn the people are (32:9). Moses responds by saying they are still Yahweh's people (32:11) and that God's promises to the patriarchs precludes this destruction (32:13). Again Moses and readers of the canon know the weaknesses in Moses' arguments. God can multiply Abraham through Moses, destroy sinful persons as necessary (cf. Gen 6—9) and deal with whatever Egypt says (cf. Ex 5—12). God's relenting derives from Moses' declining Yahweh's offer, not from Moses' persuasive argumentation or from some divine cooling off. Moses' selflessness and dedication to the people are evident in his prayer. He will need these traits on this and many succeeding occasions.

Is Yahweh's anger justified? Is such jealousy (cf. Ex 20:4-6) appropriate for a holy God? The answer is yes for at least three basic reasons. First, Yahweh has redeemed Israel and deserves to be obeyed on divine terms, not human ones (cf. Ex 20:1-2). Second, jealousy is appropriate when it protects a proper relationship from harmful disintegration, which is the case here. Third, for Israel to worship any other god is to worship emptiness, void, nothingness. Therefore whatever measures Yahweh takes to help the Israelites or anyone else to worship the God described in the canon amount to mercy. Worshiping idols is a waste of time at best. At worst it is an insult to the one real God and a form of intellectual and spiritual self-abuse. Clearly Yahweh's jealousy operates on Israel's behalf, not on a petulant-person level.

When Moses surveys the scene he breaks the covenant stones (32:19), which acts "as a sign that Israel had broken the covenant."[96] What remains to be seen is how or if the covenant relationship can be repaired. Moses attempts to begin to rebuild what has been destroyed by punishing the offenders (32:21-29). Next he asks Yahweh to forgive them or blot him out of God's book (32:30-32). Yahweh sends Moses back with assurances that Israel can still have the land (32:33-34), yet he also unleashes a plague (32:35), which indicates that the relationship has not been fully mended.

The God Who Is Faithfully Present: Exodus 33

As in Exodus 32:7-10, God makes Israel an offer that adapts to the present situation without altering God's character or promises. The offer is that they can have the promised land yet have it without a personal relationship with Yahweh (33:1-3). What Yahweh promised Abraham can still be fulfilled. To their credit, the people do not want this scenario (33:4-6). To his credit, Moses uses this situation to strengthen his own already incredible relationship with God. He also impresses on Yahweh his desire not only to enjoy God's presence (33:7-11) but also to mediate that presence to Israel (32:12-13). In other words, Moses wants to repair the Yahweh-Israel covenant.

God agrees, promising to go with them (33:14) because of his relationship to Moses, with whom Yahweh is pleased (33:17). Moses understands that God's presence, not the simple possession of land, makes Israel unique (33:15-16). He also knows that his own uniqueness lies in experiencing God's presence, so he requests and receives an extraordinary revelation of God (32:18-23). Yahweh is faithfully present with those who are faithfully responsive yet also with those who repent. Moses has counted on this faithfulness while hoping to renew the covenant, and he has not been disappointed.

The God Who Readily Restores: Exodus 34

In many ways Exodus 34 reads like a composite of Exodus 20—23. Moses goes back up the mountain (34:1-3), hears God promise to give Israel the promised land (34:10-13) and receives an abbreviated book of the covenant (34:14-26). Again he spends forty days with Yahweh, writing the revealed word of God (34:27-28). Clearly monotheism remains the heart of the covenant (34:13-17). There are two obvious differences, however, between this episode and its predecessor.

First, to accentuate the covenant reconstruction, Yahweh makes a self-declaration of character (34:5-7). What is God's nature? God once more proves a revealing God, for again he states "his name," Yahweh (34:5). Yahweh proclaims himself patient, loving, faithful, forgiving and just (34:6-7). Sin is appropriately forgiven or punished. God is no relentlessly hard and unsparing taskmaster.[97] Rather Yahweh loves Israel enough to base the covenant "upon the unchangeability of the divine nature and not upon the indifferent quality of human performance."[98] Perhaps no better summation of Yahweh's true nature appears in the Old Testament. The God who redeems from slavery (20:1-2) has now also become for Israel the God who forgives repentant gross idolaters.

Second, Moses' role as mediator is highlighted even further. He returns with new covenant stones, his face glowing from God's glory (34:29-30). To calm the alarmed people he wears a veil after speaking with Yahweh (34:31-35). Though this veil conveys God's mercy to a frightened people, it also starkly demonstrates their dependency on Moses and their uneasiness with Yahweh. It emphasizes the glory of God's revelation yet shows Israel's difficulty in obeying what Yahweh reveals. It praises Moses' relationship with God but leaves unanswered questions about the people's closeness to their loving, kind Lord. Surely Moses' ability to restore the covenant deserves whatever honor the veil affords him.

Canonical Synthesis: The Golden Calf

At least six Old and New Testament passages allude to or speak specifically about the golden calf episode and its aftermath. Each text emphasizes the foolishness of Israel worshiping idols when the one living God has done so much for them. In Deuteronomy 9:11-21, for instance, Moses includes a description of the events in Exodus 32—34 as part of his encouragement of Israel's second generation to serve the Lord. Surely in retrospect such idolatry can be seen as the destructive force it truly is in the midst of a covenant people. This destructiveness is even clearer in 1 Kings 12:28, where Jeroboam makes calves for Israel to worship and says these gods brought Israel out of Egypt (cf. Ex 32:4). According to the author of 1-2 Kings, such behavior doomed Israel (cf. 2 Kings 17).

Ezekiel 20:8-9 and Psalm 106:19-23 also include the golden calf incident in historical surveys of God's dealings with Israel. Without mentioning the calf explicitly, Ezekiel says Israel would not get rid of their Egyptian idols, and only God's desire to keep his name holy saved Israel at this time (cf. Ex 32:7-10). The psalmist specifically cites the calf worship as folly, noting, "They exchanged their Glory for an image of a bull, which eats grass. They forgot the God who saved them, who did great things in Egypt" (Ps 106:20-21).

Such rebellion deserved punishment, but Moses' intercession spared the nation (Ps 106:23). Both Ezekiel 20 and Psalm 116 highlight the stupidity and harmfulness of idolatry. In Israel's case such activity is spiritual foolishness at best and national suicide at worst.

Acts 7:39-41 fits the spirit of these Old Testament references, as does Paul's use of the event in 2 Corinthians 3:7-18, though Paul also utilizes the incident in some new ways. Stephen cites Exodus 32 as he builds his speech before the Sanhedrin to a climax that calls his hearers "'stiff-necked people'" (Acts 7:51; cf. Ex 33:5). Paul certainly considers Israel deficient in faith, but he focuses on Exodus 34:29-35 to encourage his readers to be like Moses, not like Israel. Paul himself, like Moses, mediates a covenant faithfully.[99] Moses' covenant was great but fading in that it gave way to the glory of the new covenant in Christ (2 Cor 3:7-11). Moses wore a veil because of the fear and dullness of the people's minds (2 Cor 3:12-14),[100] but Paul shares a covenant in which all may experience what Moses enjoyed—an unveiled, face-to-face encounter with God (2 Cor 3:15-18). Paul enjoys such a Moses-like relationship with God (cf. 2 Cor 12:1-10) and invites the Corinthians to be bolder than the desert-era Israelites. Thus Paul hopes his readers can trade their self-imposed veils for a closer relationship with God.

Part Five: The Tabernacle's Construction (Exodus 35—40)

Exodus 35 begins where Exodus 32 should have begun, with the building of the worship center and its related implements described in Exodus 25—31. The fact that Israel moves forward and obeys God indicates their desire to worship the covenant as a result of their repentance from idolatry. This positive desire to obey merges with God's desire to empower the people to build the worship center. It also leads to the fulfillment of the purpose of the tabernacle, which is to mediate Yahweh's presence among the people.

The God Who Empowers the Obedient: Exodus 35—39

The similarities between Exodus 25—31 and this segment are quite evident. Coming after Exodus 32—34, however, these chapters do highlight new activity on Israel's part that underscores the restored covenant mediated by Moses. Now Israel gladly takes an offering to build the center where sabbath observances and God's presence can be enjoyed (35:1-29). Now God empowers Bezalel and Oholiab to make everything described in Exodus 25—31 (35:30-35). These are skilled craftsman, to be sure, but even such secular abilities as crafting and building are results of God's spirit filling these men (35:31). With Yahweh's spirit driving them, they are able to produce the items "just as the LORD had commanded" (39:42; cf. 36:1—39:41), so Moses approves of their efforts (39:43).

The God Who Dwells with the Obedient: Exodus 40

At last Yahweh's intention to dwell among the Israelites is fulfilled. Moses erects the edifice as he has been commanded (40:1-33). The result is stunning. God's "glory," literally "God's heaviness," fills the tabernacle (40:34). Such is the heaviness of the Lord's presence that not even Moses can enter (40:35). This glory eventually subsides, but not totally, since God does remain in the people's midst.[101] Evidence of this ongoing presence is the fact that a cloud of presence leads Israel to break camp and travel when necessary (40:36-38). Thus Yahweh not only dwells with the people; Yahweh also keeps the promise to go with Israel and eventually give them the promised land (cf. 33:14; 34:1-14). Israel's rediscovered covenant obedience will result in tremendous physical and spiritual dividends. As Exodus 33:1-3 demonstrates, though, God's presence is the greatest benefit of all (cf. 33:14-17).[102]

Canonical Synthesis: The Tabernacle

Few biblical texts discuss the significance of the tabernacle. Most that do in the Old Testament simply refer to its location or normal usage.[103] In the New Testament the writer of Hebrews discusses the priesthood (Heb 4:14—8:13), tabernacle (Heb 9:1-10) and sacrificial system (Heb 10:1-18) as part of his argument that Christ is superior to the great elements of Old Testament religion. The author welds Old and New Testament theology together by emphasizing that both covenants require faith to please God (cf. Heb 11). Like all other Old Testament worship elements, the tabernacle is surpassed, in this case by a God who allows permanent forgiveness and presence. Still, Hebrews emphasizes that without the earlier sanctuary the New Testament community of faith would have a less impressive knowledge of what Christ's work means.

4

The One God
Who Is Holy

Leviticus

· ·

T HE SHEER WEIGHT OF EXODUS'S IMPORTANCE IN CANONICAL THEOLOGY
can leave interpreters staggering as they approach Leviticus. Clearly a great
deal that affects correct thought on biblical theology has been covered. Rather
than encountering what is for current readers a comfortable resting place,
however, these weary people experience Leviticus, a literary world foreign
to even many trained biblical scholars. Thus perhaps as much or more than
any other Old Testament book, Leviticus needs to be examined in its
canonical context. In other words, it should be analyzed as it fits into the
Pentateuch and as it relates to the rest of Scripture. If a canonical procedure
is followed, then both Leviticus's uniformity to and uniqueness for Old
Testament theology may be better appreciated.

Though it is hard to envision at first because of its unfamiliar subject matter,
even simple reflection on Leviticus quickly demonstrates that this is one of
the most theologically oriented books in Scripture. After all, it covers in some
detail how the holy God defines sin, forgives sin and helps people avoid sin.
It discusses how God's will is revealed and how God's presence can be
assured. Leviticus also describes how God's people may be declared holy or
how they may be what God envisioned from their origin (cf. Ex 19:56). No
wonder, then, that Jacob Milgrom declares, "Theology is what Leviticus is all
about. It pervades every chapter and every verse. . . . Indeed, every act,
whether movement, manipulation, or gesticulation, is pregnant with meaning."[1]

Any substantive outline of Leviticus illuminates Milgrom's assertion, for each section highlights specific aspects of God's character and dealings with human beings. Five distinct blocks of material are clearly distinguishable, each connected to the other by a narrative framework and each held together separately by distinctive phrases, or catchwords. Leviticus 1—7 discusses the process by which worshipers offer sacrifices for their sin. Unquestionably this section stresses that God forgives those who by faith bring the sacrifices Yahweh requires.

Next, Leviticus 8—10 details the ordination and earliest activities of the first priests. Here God obviously consecrates, sets apart, those who serve at the sanctuary, which is itself a set-apart ("holy") place. Then Leviticus 11—15 stresses how God's people may be "clean," or ready to appear before the Lord. Now Yahweh acts as the God who explains lifestyles and habits appropriate for the chosen people. Further, Leviticus 16 provides a sacrifice that removes all the sins of all the faithful once a year. This ritual presents the Lord as the God who is thoroughly and gladly merciful. Finally, Leviticus 17—27 offers extensive regulations for those wanting to fulfill Israel's purpose of being a holy nation (cf. Ex 19:56). Repeatedly in this material Yahweh operates as a holy God who expects and commands holiness of Israel. Nothing less than deliberate holiness on the people's part is worthy of the holy God.

As this last segment suggests, God's holiness pervades Leviticus. From the holy sanctuary and its holy implements, to the holiness of obedient behavior, to the very essence of the Lord, the reality of holiness, as both ideal and actualized principle, never leaves the book. Related to this concept is another foundational idea, God's presence among the people, a matter that has gripped readers' attention since the exodus but has become more vital since the golden calf incident. Only as Israel meets Yahweh's expectations for holiness can the people expect to insure and enjoy the Lord's presence. These twin underlying theological principles flow logically from Exodus, since Exodus 25—31 introduces the sanctuary, the altar and the priests, while Exodus 32—40 discusses the initial grounds upon which Yahweh will be present in Israel's midst. Given these connections, it seems appropriate to conclude that the ceremonies in Leviticus are designed to foster communion between God and Israel[2] and that this communion is based on how well Israel's commitment to holiness matches Yahweh's inherent holiness.[3]

Other divine characteristics inform specific segments of Leviticus. For instance, the sacrifices in Leviticus 1—7 are based on God's mercy, grace and kindness. God willingly forgives those who do not have any intrinsic merit of their own.[4] Those bringing sacrifices admit that they are sinners in need of forgiveness that only a holy, willing-to-be-present God can give. Further, while God's holiness certainly determines the need for priestly purity (Lev 8—10), community cleanness (Lev 11—15) and personal holiness (Lev 17—26), it is also true that the existence of these standards testifies to the holy, present God's desire to reveal his will in understandable terms.[5] Part of Yahweh's graciousness is this continued willingness. Finally, God's holiness means that Yahweh is as separate from sin as Israel is separate from other nations. It means that every time God reveals holy standards the Lord also reveals "divine transcendence, exaltedness, and otherness."[6] Paradoxically, the near, revealing, holy God is also the separate, distinct, other-than-human deity as well. God may come near to Israel, but God never shares Israel's need to repent of sins committed against self or others.

One last characteristic remains. Leviticus takes great pains to present Yahweh as the only God who must be considered when a sacrifice, regardless of its type or scope, is offered. No other god exists to be offended. More specifically, none of the demonic deities that other nations of that era believed could only be controlled by magic exist at all to be controlled.[7] Indeed, Milgrom argues, only Yahweh and human beings create the earth's moral climate. Speaking of ancient beliefs about malevolent deities, Milgrom concludes that

> the priestly theology negates these premises. It posits the existence of one supreme God who contends neither with a higher realm nor with competing peers. The world of demons is abolished; there is no struggle with autonomous foes because there are none. With the demise of the demons, only one creature remains with "demonic" power—the human being. Endowed with free will, his power is greater than any attributed to him by pagan society. Not only can he defy God but, in Priestly imagery, he can drive God out of his sanctuary. In this respect, humans have replaced the demons.[8]

Though certain aspects of Milgrom's comments are debatable, his major points about monotheism and the seriousness of human sin are accurate. Leviticus presents forcefully and in detailed fashion the notion that one God exists and this God lays down specific and merciful standards for people to follow. Whether or not human beings obey these standards determines their status before this deity. Humans cannot blame a sinless God for their sin, nor can they shift culpability for their wickedness on demons or other gods. Thus they are held accountable for their actions. They are either condemned for their rebellion or graciously blessed for their obedience. Truly the decision is in their hands.

The God Who Forgives and the Sacrifices: Leviticus 1—7
Few sections of Scripture baffle normal modern readers more than this one.

Unfamiliar with such rituals, all some people glean from these chapters is revulsion over dead animals and the notion that Yahweh required such activities. What must be remembered, though, is that these sacrifices did not sound so strange to the original audience. Rather they seemed logical, orderly, even simple given some of the complicated cults that operated in ancient times.[9] It is also important to remember that Exodus 32—34 obviously indicates that human beings sin and that a just and holy God cannot tolerate sin. Thus it seems logical for the narrative to divulge how that sin can be forgiven. At the core of the sacrificial system lie such familiar principles as God's holiness, human depravity, the high cost of sin, the personal nature of sin and God's willingness to forgive. Though the means by which these common biblical truths are conveyed differ from those in the current era, readers can still recognize the significance of what the text says.

Leviticus 1—7 can be divided into three clear parts. Leviticus 1—3 discusses burnt offerings, Leviticus 4—5 describes guilt offerings and Leviticus 6—7 depicts how the priests are to receive and officiate over these sacrifices. Each type of offering has its own purpose, but as Milgrom observes, "their common denominator is that they arise in answer to an unpredictable religious or emotional need, and are thereby set off from the sacrifices of the public feasts and fasts that are fixed by the calendar (chaps. 9, 16, 23; cf. Num 28-29)."[10] They also share in common the seriousness of sin and the joy of pardon from guilt brought on by that sin. Each one is substitutionary in nature and instructive to the person offering it.

Milgrom observes that the antiquity of the burnt offering in the ancient world indicates that it may have originally been brought for a variety of reasons. In this context, though, the intention is to atone for sin.[11] But for what sort of sin? The text does not say. Apparently the bringing of this sacrifice approximates a general confession of sin not unlike the "forgive us our debts" of the Lord's Prayer (cf. Mt 6:9-13). The burnt offering expresses the sinner's total dependence on and acceptance of God's grace. It also amounts to full abandonment to obedience. As Ronald E. Clements summarizes, "What he gave was for God alone, and thus in offering it he acknowledged the total sovereignty of God over all living creatures and the divine claim to full obedience in his own life."[12] Atonement resulted for those who faithfully obeyed.

The priest's role in the ritual is as helper of the worshiper, not as divine power broker or indispensable magician. Indeed the priest conveys to the worshiper what God has taught through Moses.[13] In this way the priest "mediates" the presence of God.[14] He leads the people to encounter Yahweh in the manner prescribed by the Lord, which has the twin benefit of avoiding righteous divine anger and securing forgiveness.

Two similar offerings are described in Leviticus 2—3 and again in 6:14-23 and 7:11-36. Like the burnt offering, the grain and fellowship offerings are brought voluntarily by supplicants who desire to please God (2:2; 3:5). The chief difference between these sacrifices and the burnt offering is that part of the grain (2:3) and a portion of the fellowship offering meat may be eaten by the priests (7:28-36). These sacrifices highlight the communal nature of Israel's worship. Priests and supplicant enjoy together the blessings of forgiveness, and since the priests represent the Lord, by extension the people enjoy communion with God. Elmer Martens explains this principle by asserting that

> Israelite sacrifice is not a matter of serving God or procuring benefits. A more biblical understanding of sacrifice . . . is that by sacrifice communion with the deity is established. The burnt offering represented thanksgiving and was received by God as sweet savor expressive of thanksgiving. The peace offering, because of the priest as God's representative eating the sacrificial meal, along with the offerer's partaking of the sacrifice . . . especially signified communion and fellowship with the deity.[15]

Such communion leads to meaningful, peaceful relations with God.[16]

Not all sins are unknown to the sinner, and not all sacrifices are offered out of joyful obedience to God and concern for the priests' well-being. Rather some sins are specifically and obviously contrary to "the LORD's commands" (4:2). Often these sorts of transgressions defraud God and neighbor. Therefore the next two types of offerings atone for such incorrect behavior. Though the general steps taken in the presentation of burnt offerings apply to sin and guilt offerings, the purpose of these sacrifices differs from those of their canonical predecessors.

Sin offerings must be brought by individuals (4:1-2), priests (4:3-12), the whole community (4:13-21) and leaders (4:22-26). Any one of these has the potential to break Yahweh's commands and incur guilt (4:2, 13, 22). Once one is aware of this guilt each person or group brings the necessary animal or food, depending on financial status, which God accepts as an atonement that results in forgiveness (4:20, 26, 31, 35; 5:6, 10, 13). Just as no segment of the Israelite community may sin with impunity, so no segment lies outside of the realm of grace either. Covenant breaking can be forgiven when Israelites believe the revealed standards, obey that standard by bringing what God requires and act in humility as Yahweh desires.

Guilt offerings also atone for known sin against divinely revealed standards. The difference is that they deal with sins against God and neighbors that require restitution (5:16; 6:5). Forgiveness does not come without cost in any of these five sacrifices, but the guilt offering entails the most expense of all. Atonement here comes by means of the appropriate offering and payment to the wronged party, which indicates that the process of confession ought to be as broad in scope as the sin itself. Forgiveness may be essentially a matter between God and the supplicant, but the means of securing favor is not solely a private issue. The fact that the priest may eat some of this sacrifice also underscores this offering's communal nature and inclusive scope.

Canonical Synthesis: Sin and Sacrifice

These seven chapters provide clues to the nature of sin, sacrifice and forgiveness. First, sin is defined as doing what God's commands prohibit (cf. 4:2, 13, 22, 27). Israel may not determine what constitutes sin, since their recent past indicates their inability to do what is right. Only the holy and merciful God has the character to set appropriate standards. Sin is personal, and it is costly. If sin is left unattended the cost can only go higher. Sin also affects every category of human being. The rich, the poor, the priest, the layperson all transgress. Sin has a demonically democratic nature.

Second, sacrifices that God chooses are accepted in place of sin and do indeed provide atonement for sin, which in turn means the one bringing the sacrifice is forgiven (cf. Lev 4:26, 31, 35). Offerings brought voluntarily, in true humility, remove any hint of divine anger, for such sacrifices please the Lord (cf. Lev 1:9, 13; 2:2; 3:5). When God is pleased and Israel's sin is forgiven there is no chance that the precarious situation described in Exodus 32—34 will be repeated. Since God is merciful, compassionate, slow to anger and willing to forgive (Ex 34:6-7), the Lord gives Israel ample opportunity to recognize and account for sin. Only willful disobedience of these generous provisions angers Yahweh.

Third, forgiveness requires human faith and obedience and divine generosity. Human beings have only to believe God's word and obey God's commands to be pardoned. People need only accept the fact that God accepts their offerings in place of their sin. The Lord must merely keep his word for pardon to result, and the canon betrays no notion so far that Yahweh has any difficulty doing so. In fact, God's word has been powerful and accurate since Genesis 1.

Canonical references to these three concepts verify these conclusions. No one could seriously question that all of Scripture depicts sin as doing what God has prohibited. It is breaking covenant commands. Throughout both testaments, sin costs human beings precious time in God's presence and communion with one another. Sin costs sinners a great deal.

Passages in the Prophets, the Writings and the New Testament indicate the importance of correct sacrifices brought in proper humility for the effecting of forgiveness. The author of 1-2 Kings, for instance, summarizes his account of Israel's demise by noting that the people broke their covenant with God by worshiping at unauthorized sites in unauthorized ways, which in turn led to idolatry and even human sacrifice (2 Kings 17:7-23). Isaiah 1:10-17, Jeremiah 7:21-26 and Malachi 1:6-9 do not complain that offerings are not brought. Rather they note that the people are insincere in their repentance, for they never change their behavior. Sacrifices offered without faith, repentance and humility are not sacrifices offered in obedience. Forgiveness does not come because an animal has been slaughtered out of habit. Atonement is not a magic ritual. It is a means by which Israel is allowed to enjoy a relationship with the Lord.[17] Gerhard von Rad states "that in the sacrificial cult too he [Yahweh] had ordained an instrument which opened up to her [Israel] a continuous relationship with him. Here Yahweh was within reach of Israel's gratitude, here Israel was granted fellowship with him in the sacred meal. Above all, here Israel could be reached by his will for forgiveness."[18] Psalm 51:16-19 agrees that confession and a contrite heart must precede sacrifice for it to be effective, a sentiment Psalm 40:6-8 describes as a desire to do God's will. This desire marks the human integrity needed in sacrificial rites to meet the inherent divine integrity in offering forgiveness.

Isaiah 52:13—53:12, the last of Bernhard Duhm's Servant Songs,[19] provides an important link between the Old Testament sacrificial system and the New Testament's conviction that Jesus Christ's death atones for sin. As is well known, Isaiah 53 describes the suffering of one called the Servant whose death is on behalf of others. Indeed Isaiah 53:10 calls the sufferer a "guilt offering," using a word common in Leviticus 5—7. Diether Kellermann notes:

> Not only does this song compare the servant with a lamb that is led to the slaughter (53:7), but it also says that he makes his soul an 'asham "offering for sin." The vicarious suffering of the righteous is the guilt offering for the many. Like a guilt offering, the death of the Servant results in atonement, the salvation of sinners from death.[20]

Nowhere else does the Old Testament state that a human being may serve as a guilt offering, which leads other scholars to think it "unwise" to press the meaning of this text.[21]

The New Testament is not so cautious, nor are many commentators. Gordon Wenham writes that guilt offerings are not mentioned in the New Testament but observes that "Isaiah 53 is quoted several times and its ideas underlie many passages describing Christ's sufferings (v. 1//John 12:38; Rom. 10:16; v. 4//Matt. 8:17; vv. 5-6//I Pet. 2:24-25; v. 9//1 Pet. 2:22; v. 12//Luke 22:37)."[22] Hebrews 9:11-15 "simply" presents Jesus as the substitute for all sacrifices and all sins, an idea implied in Isaiah 53:10. Few scholars would deny that New Testament writers saw a connection between the sacrifices in Leviticus 1—7, the Servant/guilt offering in Isaiah 53 and the death of Jesus

Christ. The notion in Isaiah 53:10-11 that the Servant divides spoil after this self-giving death only adds to the New Testament's conviction that this passage speaks of Christ's atoning death and victorious resurrection. C. A. Briggs concludes that because the Servant acts as an atoning sacrifice and then "must rise from the dead" to receive the rewards mentioned in Isaiah 53:10-11, this prophecy "finds its only fulfillment in the death of Jesus Christ, and in his resurrection and exaltation to his heavenly throne."[23]

Of course, Hebrews comments on the sacrificial system more explicitly than does any other New Testament book. Though Hebrews presents many ideas about sacrifices and how they are surpassed by Jesus' better atonement, perhaps Hebrews 10:1-18 summarizes the author's argument. Stated simply, the fact that Jesus' death was a final, nonrepeatable and sufficient sacrifice makes it superior to the perpetual nature of Leviticus's offerings (Heb 10:1-4, 11). Christ settles the matter of atonement in one act, while the older system requires ongoing sacrificial acts. Thus though forgiveness is extended through animal sacrifice, the work of Christ replaces the Old Testament system by rendering it ineffective by comparison but, more importantly, by rendering it obsolete by divine decree and divine self-sacrifice (Heb 10:12-18). After Christ's death, the old system no longer applies to the people of faith.

The God Whose Ministers Are Holy: Leviticus 8—10

Moses continues to return to the divine agenda announced in Exodus 25—31 that was interrupted by the golden calf incident. Exodus 35—40 refocuses Israel's attention on building a sacred (or holy) place where God's presence could be enjoyed. Leviticus 1—7 explains the sacrifices Yahweh accepts in place of human sin, which counters the illegitimate cult of the golden calf. Now Moses follows the Lord's directions for the priests. First mentioned in Exodus 29:1-37, these instructions show that God's ministers must be set apart to serve a set-apart people (Lev 8), must serve as the set-apart God has ordered (Lev 9) and must, like the people, expect God's judgment when these commands are ignored, abused or taken lightly (Lev 10). Being a priest means accepting more responsibility for holiness than the average member of the holy nation but in no way gives the priests special license to sin or the right to oppress "common sinners" thorough manipulation of worship rites.

God explained the ceremony found in Leviticus 8 earlier in Exodus 29. There the Lord explicitly states that these rituals are done "to make holy" or "set apart"[24] Aaron and his family as the chosen priests for the chosen people (Ex 29:1). The details set forth in Exodus differ somewhat from their actual execution here. Milgrom explains, "The text is here concerned with the procedural order, whereas the comparable verses of Exodus 29 are a random inventory of the materials required without even describing their function."[25] He further notes that this strategy "is standard scribal style in the ancient Near East. Among the Hittites, for example, we find repeatedly that items in an inventory text are enumerated in an order that differs from that in the ritual text prescribing their use."[26] No great significance should be attached, then, to the divergences.

Leviticus 9—10 displays the joy, wonder and gravity involved in priestly activity. When the priests begin to lead the worship God has commanded, at first they obey perfectly (9:1-22). Their fidelity to God's word leads to the Lord's approval, which in this case is demonstrated by God's glory encountering the people. In Exodus 40:34-35 the Lord showed approval of the tabernacle's completion by filling the worship center with glory in the form of a cloud, while here fire "comes from the glory"[27] and consumes the sacrifices (9:23-24). The people rejoice at this demonstration of God's acceptance of these initial sacrifices and personal presence, perhaps in part because they recall the threat of divine absence in Exodus 32—34.

Joy turns to sorrow in Leviticus 10:13. Again fire is the instrument used to evoke emotion, and once more God's presence is a key ingredient in the narrative. Two of Aaron's sons, Nadab and Abihu, use "alien" or "unauthorized" fire on the altar that "he [Yahweh] had not commanded them" (10:1 NRSV). Because of their presumption the Lord's presence produces a second fire (cf. 9:23-24), but this blaze kills the two men (10:2). Baruch Levine comments, "The text does not specify the offense committed by the two young priests; it merely states that they brought an offering that had not been specifically ordained."[28] Indeed that is the point. The priests disobeyed God's word and thereby committed the root sin of the human race. Moses' understanding of the situation is that the priests have not demonstrated God's holiness by their actions, so Yahweh has shown himself holy in the people's eyes by striking down the offenders (10:3). Clearly it is the priest's duty to guard the people's perception of Yahweh's holiness. The deaths prove the gravity of the Levites' task for themselves and for the people. As Walter Kaiser says:

> The point is that those who by virtue of their office are called to draw near to God constantly place themselves in a perilous, as well as privileged, position. . . . Any act, or failure thereof, that may detract from the deity's absolute holiness, and thus tend to treat God in a light, trite, or unthinking manner, would immediately expose those who draw near to possible danger.[29]

Subsequent events in Leviticus 10 reinforce this point. The priests' appearance (10:47), sobriety (10:89) and eating of their portion of the sacrifices (10:12-15) all must be carefully and properly done.

Why must the priests be so scrupulous in their observance of God's directions (cf. 10:16-20)? Why is Yahweh so concerned about the presentation of divine holiness? Two reasons are given here that relate to the priesthood's theological significance. First, Leviticus 10:10-11 highlights the priests' role as teachers of God's revelation to the people.[30] They are not mere functionaries. They are, rather, revelatory bridges. Just as God revealed these standards to Moses and Moses in turn relayed them to the priests, so the priests are to teach the Israelites the divine commands and how to obey them. The rituals themselves illustrate this teaching principle, since it is the priest's job to assist the worshiper in sacrificing, not to do the sacrificing for the worshiper. Also, in Leviticus 11—15 the priest's job as instructor will be heightened. Second, not only do the priests share Yahweh's revelation, they also facilitate atonement for sins (10:17), a role whose importance can hardly be overstated. The priests' seriousness about their task should match Yahweh's seriousness about sin and atonement. Such gravity is mixed with the joy of forgiveness but remains vital all the same.

The God Who Requires Purity: Leviticus 11—15

Of all the laws in the Pentateuch, those in this section may baffle current readers most. As the Lord continues to reveal the standards and practices that will foster divine presence, a series of actions that make the Israelites "clean" or "unclean" emerge in the text. Leviticus 10:10-11 has already stated that the priests must "distinguish between the holy and the common, between the clean and the unclean," and must teach the people how to do the same. The four words *clean, unclean, holy* and *common* are the main emphases in Leviticus 11—27. Much has been said about holiness already. God is holy, separate and special in nature and character, and Israel has been called to be a holy nation, a kingdom of priests (Ex 19:5-6). More on this concept and its opposite, that which is common, appears in Leviticus 17—27. But now the Lord stresses "clean" and "unclean," terms that basically mean "pure" and "impure." The issue is, however, pure or impure in what way or for what purpose.

Various actions render human beings unclean. Eating certain animals (Lev 11), childbirth (Lev 12), some skin diseases (Lev 13—14) and discharges from sexual organs (Lev 15) all make persons unclean.[31] Being unclean is not a permanent condition, for each example of uncleanness can be removed, thus rendering the worshiper clean. It is clear in these texts that the unclean are unclean for common traffic among other Israelites and for worship at the sanctuary. New mothers (12:4), victims of disease (14:1-32) and those who have experienced discharges (15:31) must stay away from the sanctuary or other people for a day or more. Time and ritual can heal and restore the person to full community life.

Why does God require such careful living? John Hartley notes that six basic answers have been offered over the centuries:

1. These laws promote good health by banning unhealthy foods.

2. These laws have allegorical or symbolic significance.

3. These laws are not to be explained. They are simply God's will.

4. These laws intend to limit human violence against animals and thereby help instill a general reverence for life.

5. These laws protect the community and Yahweh from demonic forces.

6. These laws are part of ancient Israel's view of social unity and wholeness.[32]

R. K. Harrison advocates the first position.[33] Certainly God is concerned about Israel's health, but as true as this point is, this position does not go far enough, because it does not explain how observing such laws makes Israel holy in the sense Exodus 19:5-6 expects. Most adherents of the second position date from earlier times when allegorical interpretation was more popular, while many persons holding the third conviction have correctly stated that God's will is given here without lengthy explanation but have sought no further interpretation of the reason behind them.[34] These approaches surrender the task of grasping the canon's teachings on the subject too easily.

Milgrom suggests the fourth position. This notion ties the dietary laws to the earlier prohibition against needless slaughter in Genesis 9:5 and the later prohibition of drinking blood in Leviticus 17:10-14.[35] Milgrom accurately states that these laws restrain human excess, yet this solution does not deal sufficiently with how adherence to these commands relates to Yahweh's and Israel's holiness. The fifth option has been offered by various authors since the dawn of the history-of-religions approach to Old Testament theology. There are several problems with this suggestion, but the most urgent one is that no such demonic forces are mentioned explicitly or implicitly in the text itself. No magic rites are used to ward off illness. No attempt is made to urge Yahweh to drive off malevolent spirits. No other powers appear at all. Time and normal sacrifice cure uncleanness because the Lord declares it so.[36]

Several scholars have adopted some variation of the sixth possibility since Mary Douglas's groundbreaking work on this possibility.[37] Douglas argues that the purity laws helped Israel grasp the unity and perfection of God's creation, which in turn led to a shared worldview and common sense of purpose that set them apart from their neighbors. This sociological explanation begins to get at the heart of these laws' purpose. Leviticus 11:44-45, nestled at the close of the segment on unclean animals, explains that these laws are to be kept so that Israel may be holy (cf. Ex 19:5-6) as God is holy (cf. Ex 32—34). In other words, these laws are one more means by which

Israel and Yahweh cement their relationship. They are also one more way Israel can begin to stand out among other nations. Not eating certain foods will keep Israel from joining their neighbors' polytheistic rituals.[38]

Also, Leviticus 12:4 states that the new mother must wait several days before entering the sanctuary. Another way of putting the rule is that she does not have to resume her regular duties until she and the baby have recovered from the birthing process. Rest, as always, is a blessing here. Separating birth from the sanctuary also keeps Israel from linking fertility rites to their religious practice, a particularly common trait in Canaanite cults.[39]

Finally, Leviticus 15:31 warns that breaking the clean and unclean laws will lead to death. Such actions defile the sanctuary, the main symbol of God's presence among the Israelites, and must be covered by acknowledgment of sin accompanied by sacrifice. Surely Israel desires to avoid a repetition of the Exodus 32 debacle. Surely they are prepared to accept the fact that Yahweh determines what fosters or forsakes his presence and that Israel is totally dependent on God's mercy in the matters of sin, holiness, forgiveness and purity.

To summarize, then, these instructions set Israel apart as a nation that has special purity laws that relate them closely to their God. These rules benefit them in many ways, but the chief benefit is God's presence among them, a reality that in turn sets them apart from other nations. Observing these laws protects Israel from polytheistic cults. It also throws Israel on the mercy of their God, who is the only deity these texts recognize. Once again the text focuses on God's uniqueness, Israel's elect status, God's holiness and mercy and God's revelation. A holy God once more determines to create a people who will fulfill the promises made to Abraham by standing against the sin and personal dissolution that mark a sinful world and by modeling reverence for the Lord, who deserves reverence.

The God Who Forgives All Sin: Leviticus 16

Leviticus 16 presents the heart of the book's theology. Here God's holiness and mercy, Israel's election and need for forgiveness and the book's emphasis on purity and atonement merge. All these details come together in a single ceremony that occurs on "the Day of Atonement," or what is still commonly called Yom Kippur. On this day occurs "the sacrificial expiation for all sin, except blasphemy against God (see Numbers 15:30; there called the sin with 'a high hand'), as well as the consequent removal of the guilt and remembrance of sins against individuals."[40] Thus confession of sin, sacrifice, the work of the priests and cleanness all find fulfillment in a single event. No clearer picture of God's grace and human faith in and acceptance of that grace appears in the Old Testament.

The Day of Atonement impacts the priesthood before it benefits the people. Leviticus 16:12 links the troubles of 10:1-3, the cleanness of the tabernacle mentioned in 15:31 and the overall need by the people and priests for cleansing, forgiveness and renewal. If the priests are to avoid desecrating God's revealed pattern for worship (cf. 10:1-3), then they must follow certain rules for the special day. First, they must learn that the holiest room in the sanctuary may not be entered whenever the high priest chooses (16:1-2). Presuming to do so will lead to death, for God's presence dwells above the ark of the covenant in a particularly powerful way.

Second, the high priest must wear different clothes than he normally does (16:3-5). George Knight comments, "On this one day in the year, when he did the holiest thing of all, he was to wear the vestments of any ordinary priest."[41] Before God on this special day the high priest stands as a sinner ministering to sinners, stripped of pride or privilege. Third, the priest must "make atonement for himself and his household" (16:6). Again the point is that even priests, maybe especially priests, must be cleansed, for the priests' care in this matter is the difference between physical and spiritual life and death. Fourth, the priest is to choose two goats, one of which will be a sin offering for the people and the other for what the Hebrew calls *azazel,* which is defined initially here as a live offering sent into the desert as an atonement (16:7-10). A fuller definition emerges later in the chapter. Fifth, the priest must kill a bull for his own offering and then take incense and some of the bull's blood into the holiest room. The blood is to be sprinkled on the cover of the ark after smoke from the incense clouds the cover (16:11-14). This process removes his sin and shows a proper reverence for the Lord's presence, both of which preserve him from death (16:13).

Now the priest acts on behalf of the people. First, he slaughters one goat for the sins of the whole community and sprinkles some of the goat's blood on the ark's cover (16:15). This act cleanses the most holy place in particular and the entire sanctuary in general. Israel's sins, whether breaches of the cleanness laws or outright rebellion against God (16:16), "pollute the sanctuary to some measure."[42] Sin is pervasive, but this sacrifice removes the guilt of all types of transgression. Second, the priest shall make atonement for the altar outside the sanctuary by applying and sprinkling blood from the bull on it (16:18-19). Again the goal is to cleanse the altar from Israel's uncleanness, which in this case may be their possible insincerity in worship (16:19).

Third, and most important, the priest places his hands on the live goat's head, transfers the people's sins to the animal by doing so and sends the goat with a man who will take it to the desert (16:21). Thus the people's sins, whatever their nature, are removed (16:22). Total atonement has been achieved, no condemnation or guilt remains, and God's grace and mercy have overcome sin and its partner, guilt. Any fears about unacknowledged, unintentional or inadvertent sins are removed, and the joy of reconciliation and friendship emerge.[43] The offerings in this chapter are substitutionary, for each animal is accepted in place of the people's pervasive, penetrating sins. This principle is especially obvious in 16:21-22, since the sins of the people are placed on the goat that goes to its death (presumably) in the desert.

After the goat has been taken away, the priest bathes, puts on his regular garments and makes a burnt offering for himself and the people (16:23-25). In other words, the priest and the people begin anew, fresh from the cleansing of their sins. Similarly, those who handled the goat and the refuse from the day's sacrificing must bathe and wash their clothes (16:26-28). Then they, too, may begin their lives afresh.

Just as the priests had to prepare for the rigors and holiness of the day of atonement (16:4-5), so must the people mark the day's importance by preparing their hearts and minds for these events. This day is a sabbath for all the people (16:29), and as such it is a day set apart for rest and for God. Surely the fact that all sins are forgiven make the day special enough for the people to obey the sabbath requirement (16:30, 34). That is, if they really believe that such is the case. It is indeed a faith response to believe that simply because God says forgiveness is mediated this way, these ceremonies remove all sins, thus freeing the people from guilt and the threat of spiritual and physical death. Those who believe prepare and participate. Those who do not must turn to their own futile means of removing sin that is so penetrating that it fouls even the regularly cleansed implements of worship.

Canonical Synthesis: Reverence, Faith and Sacrifice

Now that the core of the Pentateuch's teaching on cleanness, uncleanness, the priesthood and the Day of Atonement are in place, it is appropriate to make some observations about the canonical role of Leviticus 8—16. There are few canonical connections between Leviticus 8—10 and the rest of Scripture except for the presence of certain shared principles such as the importance of obeying God's commands, the necessity of a committed priesthood and the danger of offering "strange fire" before the Lord (cf. Lev 22:12; 16:40; Deut 25:5).[44] Otherwise the laws and incidents depicted here are not mentioned explicitly elsewhere. Still, it is important to note that the ideas contained here help explain why, for instance, Uzzah could be killed for being irreverent enough to touch the ark of the covenant (2 Sam 6:1-7), Uzziah could be struck with leprosy for usurping the priest's role (2 Chron 26:16-23) or Saul could be denounced for offering a burnt offering without priestly supervision (1 Sam 13:1-15). They also help explain why Malachi criticizes his postexilic (c. 450 B.C.) audience for bringing improper sacrifices and profaning God-ordained worship (Mal 1:6-14). Malachi also condemns priests for failing to minister in a way that honors God and the covenant God made with the Levites (Mal 2:1-9).

Direct references to Leviticus 11—15 are also meager, but again principles evident there are used in other passages. For instance, in Numbers 12:1-15 Moses' sister, Miriam, is struck with leprosy for opposing Moses, and even when she is healed she must be unclean for seven days. Saul's son Jonathan eats prohibited food in 1 Samuel 14:24, and Bathsheba was purifying herself from her uncleanness when David first saw her (1 Sam 11:4). Concerning these events Brevard Childs comments, "In sum, the narratives do not address directly the subject, but indirectly focus attention on other areas of Israel's moral life and thus force the reader of the whole canon to set the cultic and legal stipulations within a larger interpretive context."[45]

Childs also notes that the Prophets and the Writings stress what motivations stir worshipers to bring sacrifices and keep the basic clean and unclean laws.[46] For example, Isaiah 1:10-17 complains that Israel brings plenty of sacrifices, yet their doing so amounts to defiling God's sanctuary because their corrupt behavior proves their hearts remain unrepentant. Jeremiah 7:1-29 states that temple attendance and animal sacrifice do not impress God when no amendment of behavior results. Further, Yahweh argues that obedience and relationship undergird true worship, not the mere bringing of sacrifices (Jer 7:21-26). Amos 4:4-5 agrees by commenting that offerings brought so that the "worshiper" may brag about his religiosity offend the Lord. Malachi's sentiments have already been noted.

Psalm 50 likewise discusses the nature of acceptable worship. God initiated sacrifice to bind Israel to the Creator of the heavens and earth in a covenant relationship (50:1-6), not because God needed food (50:7-13). God desires to answer Israel's prayers (50:14-15), give the people guidance (50:17) and bring them salvation (50:23). Those who bring sacrifices yet reject Yahweh's teachings (50:8, 17-20) miss the point of why the Lord reveals standards for worship. They seem to believe God is like them. They surmise that God focuses on external observances and selfish gain in cultic matters, but they misjudge the Creator (50:21-22).

New Testament texts take this emphasis on inner faith and outward obedience even further. Jesus declares all foods clean (Mk 7:14-23), a fact Peter's vision and subsequent ministry to Cornelius illustrate (Acts 10:11-28). Jesus also spends time with lepers, which indicates that persons could reach out to the unclean as long as those reaching out were willing to be unclean for a time. Jesus also tells lepers to observe the rules for reentering society

(Mt 8:4). Still, Christ's main conviction was that a person's character is more important than external observance (Mt 15:11). Those who adopt Jesus' teaching determine to focus more on motivations that lead to actions than on external rituals alone.[47] They also no longer need to observe dietary and cleanness laws.

Clearly the Prophets, the Writings and the New Testament interpret Leviticus 8—15 in a similar fashion. That is, they agree that religious rituals stripped of faith and obedience are fruitless and are considered offensive to the holy God. Such activity seeks forgiveness through works, a vain proposition Paul says is the fundamental misreading of the Old Testament (cf. Rom 9:31-32). As Childs observes:

> The chief theological point to be made is that the canon has contained within itself a major critique, not just of cultic religion, but of religion in general. The attack is grounded in a vision of God which renders totally inoperative all human response seeking to merit God's favor.[48]

Genesis 15:6 remains in effect. Faith is the key to obedience, so faith is the key to righteousness. No naked deeds, especially those unaccompanied by even the barest ethical conduct, can impress Yahweh or atone for sin.

The Day of Atonement is mentioned only rarely as Scripture unfolds. Related details about its observance appear in Leviticus 23:26-32 and Numbers 29:7-11. These texts are parts of separate lists of sacred events and shed no special light on the Day of Atonement. Leviticus 16:29-34 clearly commands this event occur annually, so at first glance "it is curious that no specific reference to the day of atonement occurs elsewhere in the Old Testament, despite the periodic occurrence of certain significant events in the seventh month (cf. I Ki. 8:2, 65-66; Ezr. 3:1-6; Ne. 8:17-18)."[49] This absence may not be so unusual, though, if one considers the fact that due to spiritual decline Passover was observed only occasionally (cf. 2 Kings 23:21-23) and that the Prophets complain constantly that Mosaic, covenantal worship hardly exists in their eras.

Hebrews 9:7-12 makes the most extensive use of the Day of Atonement in the Scriptures. There the author says that the problem with the Day of Atonement was that it had to occur annually, which meant that the consciences of the worshipers could not be cleared permanently (Heb 9:7-9). Therefore these rules applied only until Christ's death atoned for all sins committed by God's people (Heb 9:10-12). Before the permanent atonement unfolded the Leviticus system atoned for sins on an annual basis and presented a picture of a greater sacrifice to come (Heb 9:6-8). Presumably the Day of Atonement helped instill in faithful Israelites a strong desire for a permanent forgiveness of sin.[50] After the cross, however, the Day of Atonement, like the other sacrifices, is subsumed under Jesus' one comprehensive payment for sins on the cross.

The God Who Requires Holiness: Leviticus 17—26

Leviticus 17—27 emphasizes holiness as an undergirding principle. Israel is to be different from the Canaanite nations they will dispossess (18:1-5). The Israelites must be holy because their God is holy (19:2; 20:7, 26) and has set them apart as a holy, chosen people (20:26). God makes the rules here based on personal holiness (21:23), makes the rules themselves holy (22:16), makes the people holy (22:31-33) and makes specially chosen religious festivals holy (23:1—25:54). God's purposes in revealing this material go back at least as far as Exodus 19:5-6, for the commands in these chapters intend to make Israel the distinct and separate people God chose and delivered them to become.

How so? By extending their commitments to Yahweh beyond the realm of specialized worship to include human sexuality, relationships and business practices. No significant arena of life escapes the call to holiness. As Clements explains:

> The holiness which it calls for is no mere private piety, nor even simply a fervent participation in public worship, but a total way of life, involving every aspect of personal, family, and social commitment. God's holiness imposes a complete pattern of moral and social behavior upon the people whom he has chosen, so that his holiness makes their responsive holiness an inescapable demand.[51]

Israel can be holy only as it obeys the word of the Holy One who has chosen and delivered them. Their holiness will derive from their relationship with Yahweh and will thereby extend to their activities and relationship with other human beings.

It would be pointless for God to deliver Israel so that the chosen people could engage in the same practices that cause the world to sink into ever-greater depravity. One more nation like all the others hardly improves the moral climate on earth. Thus the commands in Leviticus 17—19 highlight the fact that Israel must be different from, holier than, the nations they will dispossess. Their worship (17:1-16) and sexual practices (18:1-30) must be of better quality than those of the Canaanites. Rather than adopting corrupt nations as their model, Israel must emulate their holy God's character and resultant behavior (19:1-37).

Leviticus 17 reiterates the Lord's choosing of the tabernacle as the proper place of worship.[52] There the people must slay their sacrifices (17:1-9) and dispose of animal blood properly (17:10-12). As they learn to do so they will also know how to eat animals that may but do not have to be used in sacrifice (17:13-16). Being scrupulous in these matters will keep Israel from venerating false gods (17:7) and from practicing rituals that use blood drinking as a means of gaining divine power.[53] Thus they will set themselves apart from neighboring peoples as clear witnesses to the holy and singular nature of their God. Keeping the first of the Ten Commandments leads naturally to obeying and worshiping the only God who exists.

Leviticus 18 moves ever deeper into the Israelites' personal lives. Living as God's holy people includes avoiding sexual practices done in worship and in daily life by the Egyptians and the Canaanites (18:1-3). When Israel enters their homeland they must adhere to the standards given them by their God rather than rules they will discover when they arrive (18:3-4). The people stand between the worldview they left behind in Egypt and the thought patterns they will encounter in Canaan. They are being offered in this interim period a way of life that will guarantee long life in the land (18:5). This life entails living a set-apart existence as a people different from those who worship other gods, which is another way of saying those who revere themselves and their appetites.

Five concerns related to human sexuality are mentioned in this chapter, and each one relates to the interaction between worship and ethics. First, Leviticus 18:6 states that Israelites must not have sexual relations with "close relatives," and then verses 7-19 define this term. In so doing the text defines "immediate and extended family," which will in turn be the basic units that will enable Israel to maintain possession of the promised land (cf. 18:24-28).[54] These prohibitions against incestuous sexual activities demonstrate God's opposition to sexual abuse, the misuse of authority for sexual gain, the wrecking of relational trust in families and the use of any person, male or female, as an object for the satisfying of any individual's uncontrolled desires.[55] Other nations may view sexuality as a thirst to be quenched as humans see fit, but Israel must have a different, a holy, approach to these issues. Sex is not a weapon to be wielded to gain familial or societal advantage.

Second, Yahweh reminds the people that adultery is forbidden (18:20). Among other things, adultery defiles its participants (18:20), blurs family lines, destroys or at least damages spousal and community trust and betrays the covenant made with Yahweh, whose faithfulness and fidelity to Israel are never in question. Third, Israel's children must not be sacrificed to Molech, an ancient god who often "was represented by a brazen statue, which was hollow and capable of being heated, and formed with a bull's head, and arms stretched out to receive the children to be sacrificed."[56] Israel's children are not fodder for the gods, nor are they to be disposed of when they are inconvenient to raise. Theological fidelity includes parental responsibility.

Fourth, homosexuality is prohibited (18:22). Marvin Pope states that cults utilizing homosexual sacred prostitutes were doubtless "long established in Syria-Palestine, and all over the ancient Near East, in preIsraelite times."[57]

Such activities are "detestable," or "an activity that God abhors."[58] Homosexuality, like the sins already mentioned, destroys the family unity that God institutes and is willing to bless with continuation in the promised land. Once again theology impacts sexual activity.

Fifth, God denounces bestiality (18:23). Wenham says that bestiality is mentioned in Egyptian, Canaanite and Hittite sources. In fact, "there was a cult in the Eastern delta that involved the cohabitation of women and goats. Indeed Ramses II, possibly the Pharaoh of the exodus, claimed to be the offspring of the god Ptah, who took the form of a goat."[59] Bestiality breaks the family bonds forged when God determined that Eve, not an animal, completed Adam (Gen 2:18-25).

Participating in these five forbidden sexual practices jeopardizes Israel's future in the promised land. Indeed God decides to displace the Canaanites because of their corrupt theology and ethics (18:24-28). Israelites who prefer detestable acts to holiness must be cut off from the chosen nation lest the sin spread (18:29-30). Vigilance will be needed for Israel to remain distinctly Yahweh's when the people enter a new land and are confronted with new worldviews and value systems that are more like those in Egypt than those revealed at Sinai.

Yahweh's commands continue to move outward, gradually impacting more life settings. So far the people have been told how to behave at the sanctuary and in their homes, and now they are instructed in how to conduct themselves in a variety of other situations. As in the Ten Commandments, respect for God and neighbor frame these laws (19:2, 18), as does the fact that Israel as a whole belongs to Yahweh (19:3-4, 10, 12).

In Leviticus 19 Yahweh restates the basis for divinely given laws and the expectation that these commands be kept. As Leviticus 11:44 has already said, Leviticus 19:2 claims Israel's striving after holiness is founded on the principle that God is holy. Carl Henry comments that

> holiness is not an intrinsic human quality. God is the Holy One of Israel
> not because he is attached to Israel but because he attached Israel to
> himself. Only in and through God's revelation of this fact does Israel
> become a holy nation, a holy people, a holy seed, a holy congregation,
> a holy kingdom of priests.[60]

The key to Israel's status as holy nation is the willingness to keep God's laws and decrees because Yahweh is their God (19:37). Thus relationship and faithfulness unite to create holiness.

Between the basis (19:2) and expectation of holiness (19:2, 37) lie challenges that characterize the behavior of the holy people. Virtually every one of the Ten Commandments is repeated and/or explained, which makes this chapter one of the great ethical statements in Scripture along with such texts as Amos 5, Micah 6, Ezekiel 18 and Job 31.[61] As usual, idolatry is prohibited and quality worship of Yahweh expected (19:48, 30). Commands to avoid divination, sorcery, mediums and spiritists are added as well (19:26, 31), no doubt because these occult activities and their purveyors amount to worshiping false gods and consulting their false prophets for guidance. Israel must trust God and God's revealed will, and, Wenham adds, "when God was silent, the people were expected to walk by faith and live in accordance with God's general will declared in the law."[62]

Beyond these laws about divine-human relationships lie specific commands about how people must treat others. One summary command stands out above all others: "Do not seek revenge or hold a grudge against any of your people, but instead love your neighbor as yourself. I am the LORD" (19:18). Keeping this admonition enables the people to avoid stealing, bearing false witness, oppressing the poor or perverting justice (19:9-16). It covers sins that begin in the heart, where motives that cause such unholy activity originate (19:17). It also covers sins against foreigners, family and business associates (19:20-36). No person lies outside the individual Israelite's definition of "neighbor." All human beings must be respected and loved for the holy nation to give a clear witness of their holy God.

God's holiness includes more than electing love (18:13), divine guidance and personal self-revelation (19:2). It also includes punishing whoever rebels against these qualities and the commands that result from them. Otherwise God's imperatives devolve into God's preferences. The canon has already presented God the creator and sustainer as God the judge (cf. Gen 19). The same God who called and delivered Israel also judged its infatuation with the golden calf (cf. Ex 1—34), and the same God who chose Aaron's family to lead Israelite worship struck down two members of that family for disobeying orders and defiling the sanctuary (cf. Lev 8—10). Thus it is hardly surprising to discover specific penalties for sin set by the God who "is personally active in history and whose majestic righteousness not even chosen objects of his love dare provoke."[63] In this segment of Leviticus the Lord orders punishments for those who break the commands set forth in Leviticus 18—19 (Lev 20), for priests who sacrifice improperly or approach the altar without proper sanction (21:1—22:16) and for priests and general worshipers who bring the wrong offerings to the altar (22:17-33).

Perhaps the worst punishment possible is implied in Leviticus 22:17-33. Here Yahweh explains that there is no purpose in bringing defective animals to the altar.[64] Such offerings do not please God.[65] They forfeit fellowship with God.[66] In other words, they do not atone for sin, which means Israel's disregard for Yahweh's instructions precludes forgiveness at this point. No severer punishment exists. One might consider such strictures unloving until one remembers that the God who loves Israel devotedly makes these claims on the people (22:31-33). God's love leads to Israel's holiness, not to mention the nation's very existence. It is reasonable to conclude that love defines boundaries and consequences here as much as it opens new levels of freedom in Exodus.

That God rules history has been evident since Genesis 1—3. Though self-existent before days and seasons began to mark time, Yahweh directs events that occur in space and time. In this way the Lord makes sure that time has meaning, that happenings are events, that moments become momentous. Nowhere does this principle emerge more clearly than in Leviticus 23—25, where the Lord sets aside certain times as holy days and weeks that mark ancient and contemporary history as more than the passing of hours. The existence of the sabbath introduced this idea as early as Genesis 2:2-3 and the necessity of festivals since Exodus 12:1-28, 23:14-77 and 34:18-25, yet the concept of sacred time grows clearer now as part of God's comprehensive plan for worship revealed in Leviticus.

Sabbath observance serves as the foundation for all Israelite festivals. Woven into the very fabric of creation (Gen 2:2-3) and included as part of the ten fundamental commands given in Exodus 20:1-17, the sabbath is the most consistent, indeed a week-by-week, reminder that the holy people serve a holy God (23:3). Ceasing labor each week indicates that Israelites are no longer slaves to the Egyptians or slaves to their own work. Resting also allows Israel to stay in communion with their God.[67]

Passover is as integrally connected to the exodus as the sabbath is to creation and the covenant's Ten Commandments. This observance marks the beginning of Israel's year (23:4), just as the exodus marked the beginning of Israel's nationhood (cf. Ex 12:1-28). Passover reminds Israel that God delivered the chosen people to be a holy people and that God judges those who emulate the rebellious, callous pharaoh.[68] Thus God's character is revealed during this festival and also in its corollary observances, the Feast of Unleavened Bread (23:6-8) and the giving of firstfruits (23:9-14). Passover and the Feast of Unleavened Bread declare that God gave Israel its life and freedom, while giving firstfruits states that Yahweh grants Israel a fruitful existence in their homeland. Israel must recall year by year that the exodus was not an accident or a coincidence and that Yahweh, the Creator, makes crops grow that sustain the people. These reminders will be especially important when Israel encounters Canaanite nature cults in the promised land.[69]

Seven weeks after Passover, Unleavened Bread and Firstfruits begin Israel's year, the Feast of Weeks occurs (23:15-22). This harvest festival, like the Firstfruits observance, demonstrates that Yahweh blesses Israel with grain.

The seasons belong to the Lord who made them. Israel must give witness to this fact as a way of thanking the Lord and as a reminder that the one God who creates also saves and blesses.[70] As they do so, they will also give witness of Yahweh's power to other nations.

Three weeks are set aside in the seventh month for the kindred Feast of Trumpets, Day of Atonement and Feast of Tabernacles. The first event gathers Israel in sacred assembly on the first day of the month (23:23-25), apparently to prepare the people for the all-important Day of Atonement (23:26-32), which has already been described in detail in Leviticus 16. Having received forgiveness for their sins, the people commemorate and reenact the exodus by observing the Feast of Tabernacles (23:33-44). Again Israel is reminded that God is present among them now as much as in the exodus.[71] History demonstrates an ongoing reality, for it declares Yahweh powerfully present in an exoduslike fashion in the midst of a holy people committed to being like the pioneers who left Egypt to follow the Lord. God calls, provides, forgives and protects, and the observing of these festivals and their attendant rituals demonstrates Israel's faith in their God.

The final two sacred time frames offer Yahweh's most radical proposals for rest, renewal and forgiveness in normal life. Every seventh year the land must be given rest. It must lie fallow (25:1-6). Whatever grows by itself may be consumed (25:6), but Israel must have faith that God will provide enough growth in the years preceding the sabbath year that the people can survive the year of rest (25:18-22).[72] The manna they have received since leaving Egypt (cf. Ex 16) has operated in a similar, albeit weekly, manner, so the principle is not new. Still, the scope of Israel's faith must broaden, and for it to do so the people must truly believe that life does not consist simply of work, money, power, success and appetite. Rather they must find their personal fulfillment in being God's holy people.

Further, every fiftieth year Israel must celebrate a jubilee year in which debts are forgiven, indentured servants are released and ancestral lands are returned to their original owners (25:8-28). This observance rests on four specific principles:

1. The people must fear God and refuse to take advantage of one another (25:17).

2. The people must trust Yahweh to sustain them. They must have faith (25:18-22).

3. The people must realize that the land belongs to God, who divides it by grace, not by merit or social standing (25:23-24).

4. The people must understand that they themselves, regardless of economic standing, belong to God. Therefore human beings are not human property in any permanent sense (25:35-55).

In other words, Israel should acknowledge that the God who created and redeemed them owns them and that the God who created the earth may determine what human beings temporarily possess the earth.

These standards indicate that the poor and helpless must be helped in a holy nation (25:35-38; cf. 23:22). Other countries offered release laws during this era, so surely Yahweh's people can as well.[73] If all persons are made in God's image (Gen 1:26) and if all Israelites are participants in the Sinai covenant, then surely each person is inherently equal before God's law and must be so in human events.

Truly, then, time belongs to God. Humans who accept this principle grasp that their own personal history matters as much to God as magnificent historical events like the exodus. As Israel adopts this notion the people gain rest, freedom from self-enslavement to success, release from greed and an appreciation for community. In other words, they become holy as their God is holy when they recognize that God orders time, directs events and guides his people through a history they themselves cannot control.

By now Israel must have a sense of how God's character and God's expectations of them intersect. Not every possible life issue has been covered, but such vital matters as worship, sexuality, societal structure, human equality and consequences for unholiness have been addressed at least briefly. So now, much as Exodus 24:4-8 does after the initial giving of the law, the text calls Israel to decide to serve Yahweh. Here it does so by presenting blessings for obedience, consequences for rebellion and standards for keeping vows made to the Lord. God's holiness is once again presented primarily as a desire to bless and only secondarily, yet just as relevantly, as a willingness to judge.

Leviticus 26 sets forth potential blessings and consequences in a manner quite common in second-millennium B.C. political covenants.[74] Since the literature on this subject is vast and this topic will be revisited in the chapter on Deuteronomy, it suffices to say at this point that most scholars admit some similarities exist between this passage and the blessings-and-curses segment of ancient treaties.[75] Therefore this passage draws its original audience to a familiar form of decision. They must ratify the covenant in its present form,[76] or they must face the consequences of not doing so.

Stated simply, Leviticus 26 offers Israel total success in the promised land if they will obey God's commands (26:3). The same gracious, delivering God who gave them dignity (26:13) will graciously bless them for their faithfulness. Fidelity to monotheism (26:1) and its companion, careful worship (26:2), will result in permanent rest in Canaan. Disobedience, on the other hand, will lead to trouble (26:14-17), exhaustion (26:18-20), affliction (26:21-22), invasion (26:23-26) and banishment from the land (26:27-35). Confession of sin can forestall punishment or even restore Israel to the land (26:40-45). But any such negative scenario will result from the chosen people's self-chosen punishment for unholy behavior, not from God failing to offer them a more attractive option.

The God Who Demands Fidelity: Leviticus 27

Finally, the book closes with a section on vows made to the Lord. Leviticus 26 consists of God's vow to Israel, while Leviticus 27 reflects the seriousness of keeping vows made to God. Just as one can assume God keeps vows, it is likewise assumed that Israel will either do exactly as promised or will pay a penalty for not doing so. Surely no less could be expected of the holy God, and nothing else could be expected from a holy nation chosen by and in close relation to that God.

Canonical Synthesis: Holiness and Love

Though much could be said about the canon's use of many of the ideas in Leviticus 17—27, perhaps four texts deserve special mention as particularly vital to canonical theology. First, Leviticus 18:1-5 introduces the rules for sexual purity by reminding Israel of Yahweh's authority over them (18:2), by declaring that Israel must not live and worship like the Egyptians and Canaanites (18:3), by commanding Israel to obey God's revealed standards (18:4) and by promising that those who obey God's stipulations will gain life (18:5). In Leviticus the word *life* may mean physical life (cf. 10:1-3) or abundant, blessing-filled living in the promised land (cf. 26:1-13). In this text's immediate context the latter definition seems especially plausible given the repeated warning about conditions for possessing the land found in Leviticus 18:24-28. Ezekiel reflects on Leviticus 18:1-5 in Ezekiel 20:11, 13 and 21. Each time the prophet uses the phrase "the man who obeys them will live by them" to indicate that Israel has broken every command in Leviticus 18:1-4, which means the nation has forfeited the life the text promises in 18:5.

Three New Testament texts cite Leviticus 18:1-5. Jesus alludes to the passage when proving the rich young ruler's true level of obedience to the law (Lk 10:28). Paul quotes the verse in Romans 10:5 and Galatians 3:12, both times as a contrast to other quoted Old Testament passages that highlight faith, and both times to correct the misconception that salvation and righteousness come by works. It is likely that Paul's opponents quoted Leviticus 18:5 without referring to verses like Leviticus 19:17, which deals with motives, or Leviticus 25:18-22, which orders Israel to believe that Yahweh will meet the necessary requirements for jubilee, or even Leviticus 19:18, where love serves as the source of Israelite faithfulness.[77] They certainly appear to neglect the many faith-based texts Paul cites.

At any rate Paul points out that national Israel never kept the law for any length of time and therefore never fully enjoyed the blessings outlined in Leviticus 26:1-13. Rather they felt the sting of the consequences detailed in Leviticus 18:24-28 and 26:14-45.[78] Thus Paul's readers ought to receive God's offer of salvation through faith in Christ gratefully and with the sort of faith and joy Israel lacked during most of its history. New life has been offered not because the law was sinful but because people were sinful (Gal 3:21-22), not because God is inconsistent but because people are. Faith in God precedes and undergirds obedience before Christ's death (Gal 3:6-9, citing Gen 15:6). After the cross that faith is specifically in Jesus, and obedience is to his comprehensive teachings about the Old Testament and to other concepts based on his life and work that he, Paul, and other biblical authors share.

Another text with particular canonical significance is Leviticus 19:2, which declares that Israel's need to be holy is based on God's inherent holiness. The Old Testament defines God as holy both by direct statement and by the fact that God makes people and objects holy. For example, Israel's song of deliverance at the Red Sea includes the specific comment that God is majestic in holiness (Ex 15:11). Clearly the people deduce this conclusion from Yahweh's ability to save. Leviticus 11:44 and 19:2 demand holiness from Israel because of God's intrinsic holiness, a claim Joshua also makes when asking Israel to renew their covenant commitment to Yahweh (Josh 24:19). Isaiah designates Yahweh as "the Holy One" twenty-eight times.[79] Isaiah's best-known declaration of God's inherent holiness occurs in Isaiah 6:3, where the prophet envisions seraphim saying, "Holy, holy, holy is the LORD Almighty; the whole earth is full of his glory." Ralph Smith observes that perhaps the clearest statement of divine holiness appears in Amos 4:2, for here God makes promises based on his holiness.[80] God's word is as holy as God's character. Ezekiel 36:20 calls God's name holy, which is the same as saying God's character is holy. Finally, Psalm 89:35 parallels Amos 4:2 by having God swear by his holiness, and Psalm 99:39 repeats Isaiah's threefold repetition of God's holiness.

God reveals this characteristic holiness in many ways, but the canon focuses on the fact that Yahweh's holiness is best demonstrated by the covenant with Israel. God's very choice and deliverance of Israel show that God's holiness includes love and grace.[81] Yahweh's willingness to restore Israel after the golden calf debacle and God's revelation of the sacrificial system as a means of atonement indicate that the Lord's holiness embraces patience and forgiveness. The prophets' emphasis on God's refusal to reject Israel for the people's repeated transgressions means God's holiness dictates a passionate, seemingly illogical faithfulness to the chosen people (cf. Hos 11:8-9).[82] Defining God's holiness requires combining all the character traits the canon ascribes to the Lord.

But what about Israel's holiness? Exodus 32—34 shows that Israel can fail miserably in the attempt to be a nation holy to the Lord (cf. Ex 19:5-6). The aborted attempt to enter Canaan in Numbers 13—14, the periodic lapses into idolatry in Judges, the slide toward loss of land in 2 Kings, the corruptions the Latter Prophets chronicle so graphically, the weakness the people exhibit in many psalms and the moral failures in Ezra and Nehemiah testify to Israel's propensity to avoid holiness. However, Joshua's army does conquer Canaan, David does establish a strong nation, and the prophets themselves are faithful Israelites, as are Ruth, Daniel, Ezra, Nehemiah and the Chronicler. Sin eventually costs Israel their homeland, yet it never robs God of a remnant of persons who are Abraham's faithful children. Holiness fades but never disappears; yet it never pervades Israel enough to make the blessings in Leviticus 26:1-13 a permanent reality.

Peter revisits Leviticus 19:2 as he exhorts his readers to maintain a vibrant witness in the midst of persecution (1 Pet 1:13-16). He considers holiness the church's best defense against conforming to the world's expectations and also claims that holiness is a particularly effective way of giving witness of God's grace in their lives (1 Pet 2:9-12). Such convictions match Paul's belief that God has redeemed Christians "to be holy and blameless in his sight" (Eph 1:4). These and related passages explain why Paul routinely calls believers "holy ones," or saints (e.g., Eph 1:1; Phil 1:1), and why Paul considers anyone who trusts Christ a "Jew" (Rom 2:28-29) and one "grafted into" the people of God (Rom 11:17).

Besides Leviticus 18:15 and 19:2, the principle of loving one's neighbor as one's self found in Leviticus 19:18 also provides specific canonical insight. Exodus 21:24 and Deuteronomy 19:21 state that the covenant standard for justice is "eye for eye, tooth for tooth," which means every punishment should fit the crime it addresses. Leviticus 19:15 offers a similar standard, stating that fairness, not partiality, must be shown to each person, regardless of economic standing. As a further explanation of this principle, Leviticus 19:18 commands Israel to love their neighbor as themselves. Fairness and justice are defined by this type of appropriate love, not by vengeance or a "love" that never opposes wrongdoing.

Without question, Isaiah (e.g., Is 10:14), Jeremiah (e.g., Jer 7:18) and Ezekiel (Ezek 18:10-13) use Leviticus 19:18 as a general standard for condemning oppression and violence in Israel. They are joined in their outrage by Amos, who chronicles Israel's sin yet who offers a summary statement of the sins of Gentile nations as well. Amos claims that Tyre breached a "treaty of brotherhood" (Amos 1:9), which is another way of saying they did to others what they did not want done to themselves or to their families.[83] Thus the Leviticus 19:18 principle stands as a universal means by which to judge human sin. Certainly Jesus agrees, for he calls this command and the command to love God (cf. Deut 6:49) the two laws that summarize the whole of divine legislation (cf. Mt 22:39; Mk 12:31; Lk 10:27).

Finally, Leviticus 26 and its companion text, Deuteronomy 27—28, set the standard for Israel's potential success and failure in the promised land. As has already been stated, Israel's obedience or disobedience to the covenant stipulations determined whether they "lived" (18:5), were holy (19:2), loved their neighbor (19:18) or were blessed (26:113) or cursed (26:14-45) in their homeland. Those who assessed Israel's history in the Former Prophets (e.g., 2 Kings 17), the Latter Prophets (e.g., Ezek 20) and the Writings (e.g., Ps 78—79) were convinced that Israel's sin, not God's unfaithfulness, cost the chosen people the promised land.

Conclusion

Throughout Leviticus the one God continues to command fidelity to himself. Israel must avoid idols at all cost and must reject the worship practicies of the Egyptians and Canaanites. Only one God can save. Only one God makes a covenant with human beings. Only one God reveals concrete, understandable, holy standards to the people. Only one God lifts Israel out of harmful and shameful activities to make them a holy people. Only one God forgives unreservedly and judges fairly. Only one God stands ready to give Israel a land of its own.

5

The God
Who Expects
Faithfulness

Numbers

. . . .

READERS BEGIN NUMBERS WITH A KEEN SENSE OF THEOLOGICAL ANTICIPATION. Hundreds of years have passed from the giving of the Abrahamic promises (c. 2000 B.C.) to the conclusion of Leviticus (c. 1440 or c. 1290 B.C.), and at long last the promised land looms before the freed children of Abraham. The third of the heir, covenant and land pledges (cf. Gen 12:1-9) seems to be attainable. Israel has strong leadership, a divinely revealed code by which to live, a new sense of national identity and purpose and God's promise to make them successful. Israel knows the basic character of their God. They know what leads their Lord to punish them and have learned how to secure forgiveness. The potential for greatness is well within their grasp.

All these hopeful possibilities are obliterated due to the most fundamental sin of all, which is the human refusal to believe God's word. In a crucial moment, faithlessness costs the exodus generation their opportunity to possess the physical embodiment of Yahweh's covenant with Abraham and with the nation as a whole. They lose their opportunity to live in Canaan, the promised land. Instead they conclude their earthly journey by journeying among hostile peoples in barren desert lands. God's promise of land remains intact, though, so the next generation will conquer Canaan. But this triumph is deferred for nearly forty years due to theological amnesia that results in national disaster.

Each stage of the journey reveals theological concepts that connect with truths in Genesis—Leviticus. The events in Numbers 1:1—10:11 present God as the one who guides and inspires Israel. One of Scripture's greatest moments, the giving of the divine law at Mt. Sinai, ends here, yet not before Yahweh reveals how Israel will march, who will care for the worship facilities and how Israel may remain holy before God.[1] Besides these vital spiritual instructions, Yahweh also guides Israel by providing a cloud that shows the nation when and where to travel (9:15-23). Israel's willingness to follow the cloud in the book's initial segment demonstrates "that at this point in their walk with the Lord, Israel was obedient and followed the Lord's guidance."[2] Such obedience includes observing the first Passover (9:1-14), which indicates that Yahweh's continual holiness, presence and grace inspire Israel to use the past to be faithful in the present.

Numbers 10:11—12:16 portrays Yahweh as the God who calls and corrects. Here the Lord calls Israel to move toward Canaan, and here Yahweh calls elders to assist Moses in the leading of the people (11:16-17). At the same time God corrects grumbling among the people (11:1-3) and also corrects Miriam and Aaron's assumption that they are justified in criticizing Moses on the grounds that they are as much Israel's leaders as he (12:1-16). God's gracious holiness continues, then, to include elements of election and judgment.

Numbers 13:1—20:13 constitutes the theological and historical core of the book. In these chapters the fulfillment of the Abrahamic promises collides with unbelief in a defining historical moment. When Israel refuses to believe that God can give them the land the Lord punishes the exodus generation by confining them in the desert (Num 13—14). Immediately, however, God renews the promises by revealing laws that will apply in the promised land (Num 15).[3] Not even subsequent rebellions, met as they are by divine correction, can repeal the Lord's promise of land (see Num 16:1—20:13).

Numbers 20:14—22:1 reinforces Yahweh's determination to renew, for it stresses that the Lord sustains and protects the very people who have rebelled. Israel remains fed, clothed, guided and shielded from military defeat. The new generation emerges, surrounded by God's indomitable power to preserve the elect nation.

Finally, Numbers 22:2—36:13 reveals once again that God prepares Israel to receive divine promises. False prophets and false religions are contrasted with monotheistic faithfulness and divine revelation. Joshua succeeds Moses (27:12-23). Moses divides Canaan into sections for the people before Israel even crosses its borders (Num 34—35), which once again highlights the promise's potential benefits.[4] When the book ends Israel's punishment ends. A second opportunity for victory lies ahead.

There is considerable scholarly consensus on the book's basic theological teachings and canonical role. Gordon Wenham's summary provides a good point of reference for this agreement. He writes that Numbers stresses the character of God as holy, present, gracious and constant. Further he states that the book focuses on the land as God-given, holy and Israel's permanent possession. Finally he observes Numbers's emphasis on the people of God as unified, holy, rebellious and blessed by Moses' leadership.[5] George Gray, Philip Budd and R. K. Harrison agree with these basic categories, as do other scholars from their respective schools of interpretation.[6] Each of these commentators agrees that the book makes little sense outside its current canonical placement between Leviticus and Deuteronomy and note that the entire Pentateuchal message depends on Numbers's depiction of Israel's time in the desert. Without question, then, a canonical reading of Numbers has considerable significance for biblical theology.

The God Who Guides and Inspires Israel: Numbers 1:1—10:11

The same God who has been revealing the contents of Leviticus to Moses continues to communicate with Israel's leader in Numbers 1:1. The text notes that a year has passed since the Israelites left Egypt (1:2). Now it is finally time to move ahead with the plan to conquer Canaan. Thus the Lord guides Israel's preparations to march and inspires them to obey commandments made earlier. More specifically Yahweh gives an order of march (Num 1—4) and states how Israel may remain pure while they march (5:1—10:11). Yahweh inspires Israel to keep Passover (9:1-14) and to begin the process of possessing the promised land (9:15—10:11).

Some Israelites are called to express their desire for personal and community holiness in formal, public ways. For instance, men or women may choose to separate themselves as Nazirites, people who abstain from fermented drinks, let their hair grow and avoid dead bodies (6:1-8). They may do so for a short or long period of time (6:9-21). Their commitments demonstrate the high value these persons place on serving Yahweh in a self-imposed rigorous manner. Ronald Allen comments that "the Nazirite vow was not a demand of God on his people; it was a provision for men or women who voluntarily desired an unusually demanding means of showing their devotion to him."[7] Similarly, Israel's leaders show their love for God by giving gifts to the sanctuary (7:1-89), and the Levites give witness to God's worthiness by being set apart for the work at the worship center (8:5-26). At this point in Numbers the people respond in God-honoring obedience to the Lord who guides their present in a way that fulfills the past and offers hope for the future.

Yahweh inspires Israel to keep Passover and to follow his guidance for where they will go in Numbers 9:1—10:11. Israel celebrates the Passover at the appointed time (9:1-5). This observance indicates that God's deliverance in Egypt has meaning in the desert as well. The God who created all the earth can do great things in any geographical location. God is not limited by time, since an annual festival celebrates the endless nature of Yahweh's ability to save and to judge.

God also desires to accommodate the needs of serious worshipers, persons who desire to obey God as fully as possible. In Numbers 9:6-14 a dilemma arises when some dedicated worshipers become ceremonially unclean just before time to observe Passover. Moses inquires of the Lord, and God adds to the general Passover requirements allowance of a second Passover to be celebrated a month after the normal time (9:6-13).[8] Non-Israelites who share Israel's faith may observe Passover as well, which means that Yahweh's purposes for Passover goes far beyond racial or nationalistic aims. Clearly God intends for faith and desire to obey to take precedence over legalism and racial separation.[9] Perhaps these new insights will inspire Israel to show a similar concern for fairness, inclusion and a correct sense of the relationship between holiness and worship.

Israel will know when to break camp in two ways, one miraculous and one quite human. God will provide a cloud to rest over the tabernacle. When it lifts the people must follow it where it leads (9:15-23). Aaron and the priests will add human help to the order to leave by blowing trumpets (10:1-7). Some scholars seek to provide a natural explanation for the cloud,[10] but the very existence of a cloud in all seasons and the timing involved in its lifting and moving in a specific direction point to its miraculous nature. The cloud symbolizes God's presence among the people.[11] Specifically, God is present to lead, guide and inspire awe.[12] Once again Yahweh's presence manifests itself among the people in a way that indicates that God loves Israel enough to guide them, that shows that God moves among human beings, that demonstrates that Israel is totally dependent on God's presence and that illustrates that God, though present, is not like human beings. Yahweh has the ability to be present yet separate at the same time. Both nearness and distance can be felt and seen simultaneously.

Canonical Synthesis: Israel's Desert Era

Several Old and New Testament texts make use of the accounts of Israel's time in the desert.[13] These passages refer to different stages of the forty-year period, however, so it is important to determine whether individual texts comment on the exodus and succeeding one-year stay at Sinai (1:1—10:11), the rebellious thirty-eight years (10:11—22:1) or the several-months-long journey to the borders of Canaan (22:2—36:13). Most canonical references focus on the latter two eras and therefore will be noted later.

Perhaps only Ezekiel 20:10-12 and possibly Jeremiah 2:1-3 speak of the initial year of Israel's journey. Both prophets cite the year as evidence of God's goodness to Israel in discussions of Israel's disobedience, infidelity and ingratitude. Yahweh has always shown love for Israel, yet the beloved people have consistently turned against the Lord. No fault for Israel's actions can be traced to Yahweh or the Sinai revelation. All responsibility rests on Israel.

The God Who Calls and Corrects: Numbers 10:11—12:16

As long as the nation remains stationary at Mt. Sinai, the people seem quite capable of obeying the Lord. Three days into the journey toward Canaan, however, finds them complaining about their circumstances, especially their food rations (10:11—11:1). God judges their complaining and calls helpers for Moses so the people will not be so difficult to handle (11:2-35). Complaining eventually reaches every societal level, for Miriam and Aaron question Moses' authority (12:1-2). Like the people, they learn that those who complain about God's ordering of society will be punished (12:3-16). All these problems remind readers of the difficulties in Exodus 16—17 and leave one wondering if past and present problems mean future problems are just a matter of time.

Every person in Israel receives a specific task, or calling, from God. Israelites as individuals are called to family units that obey parents (Ex 20:12), respect the sexual dignity of each family member (cf. Lev 18:6-30) and take their place in the camp. From individual families come the warriors who will conquer Canaan. Each family is part of a tribe that will collectively share in the division of the land. Aaron's family and the Levites are called to specific service at the sanctuary. As a whole Israel is called to be the holy people of God, the fulfillment of God's promises to Abraham. The exodus marks them as Yahweh's people, though as Brevard Childs notes, "Israel does not become a people because it was delivered, but rather it was delivered because it was the people of God."[14] The Sinai covenant sets them apart even more as a called people who share one God, one covenant, one commitment. Elmer Martens comments that

> whatever else these people held in common, and whatever else united them, the allegiance which they shared collectively to one God whose provision and direction they experienced collectively, and by whose covenant they were collectively bound to one another, was a high consideration, if not the uppermost consideration.[15]

Every Israelite, then, possesses a unique and important calling as a member of God's chosen people. The exodus, the covenant, the tabernacle, the cloud of presence and the sustaining manna all testify to the greatness of Yahweh and the importance God places on Israel.

Despite this calling, guidance and provision, Israel collectively and certain Israelites individually complain about their situation. The people get weary of manna and wail for the wonderful days of slavery in Egypt when they had better food (11:1-9). Moses complains about Israel's infantile complaints (11:10-15). Joshua, Moses' aide, complains when God calls elders to relieve Moses' leadership burden (11:28). Based on a undisclosed dispute with Moses' wife, Miriam and Aaron complain about Moses' authority (12:1-2). It is apparent that Israel doubts God, Moses doubts God, Joshua doubts God and Miriam and Aaron doubt God. What remains to be seen is whether doubt will degrade into disbelief or whether full faith can be restored.

God responds by continuing to call persons for specific tasks and by correcting misguided beliefs. God meets Moses' concerns by designating and empowering elders who will share the burdens of leadership (11:24-27). Yahweh answers Israel's dietary wishes by sending quail, then a plague, on all who rejected the ever-present Lord's provision (11:18-20; 11:31-34). The Lord's ability to produce such a quantity of meat silences Moses' doubts (11:21-23), and a humble statement from his master satisfies Joshua's concerns (11:28-30). Miriam and Aaron learn that their own special standing does not entitle them to rebel against Moses, the one called to lead Israel and receive God's revelation (11:4-8). Yahweh strikes Miriam with leprosy, healing her only when Moses intercedes on her behalf (12:10-16). Surely now each Israelite knows how obedience to authority alone allows each holy one in the holy nation to flourish in his or her specific calling.

The God Who Punishes and Renews: Numbers 13:1—20:13

Located in the heart of the book, this segment of Numbers recounts events that have tragic personal, historical and theological implications. In these chapters virtually every significant element of the called and corrected people rebels against God and suffers the consequences of their actions. Not even Moses transcends unbelief here, so not even this great leader and thinker avoids heart-rending punishment. Still, Yahweh proves faithful to the Abrahamic and Sinai covenants by starting afresh with Israel's next generation. Such are the design and prerogative of the holy and self-existent God.

Poised at the edge of Canaan, Israel sends spies at God's command to view the promised land (13:1-16). Twelve tribal leaders are chosen for the task, with Joshua being the best known of the group. They are told to prepare a full report on Canaan (13:17-20), and they do as they are charged (13:21-27). None of them has anything negative to say about the land's fruitfulness. God's initial pledge to Moses to give Israel a "good and spacious land" seems about to come true (cf. Ex 3:7-10). Yahweh has been faithful.

Israel's spies do not interpret the accuracy of God's description of the land, God's saving work in the exodus, God's offer of the covenant or God's guidance in the desert to mean that Israel can actually possess the land they have seen. They do not believe that the God who has guided their historical past can determine their immediate future. In this new situation they see only Canaan's fortified cities and seasoned armies, easily forgetting the God who drowned Pharaoh's chariots in the Red Sea. Thus, with the exception of Caleb and Joshua (13:30; 14:6), the leaders counsel the people to stay in the desert rather than assault the Canaanites (13:31-33).

Quite understandably the people are grieved, yet they believe the majority report instead of their theological heritage (14:1-4). They wish again they were still slaves, fear for their children's lives and determine to choose a new leader and return to Egypt. One last time Moses, Aaron, Joshua and Caleb exhort the people to embrace the promise of land (14:7), to accept Yahweh's leadership (14:8), to obey God (14:9) and to choose faith over fear (14:9). For their efforts the people threaten to stone them (14:10). An impasse has been reached. Faith and obedience have disappeared from the majority of the people. Only a small faithful remnant remains.

Yahweh settles the situation decisively. God states that Israel's problem is not lack of military strength or the power of their enemies. Their problem is contempt for God fuelled by unbelief despite all the Lord has done for them (14:10-12). Every other motivation is secondary. John Sailhamer comments that

the people certainly failed in many respects, but the writer points specifically to, and takes great care to draw out, their failure to believe God. Thus this passage intends to show that the people failed to inherit the Promised Land and hence died in the wilderness without inheriting the blessing, not so much for a specific act of disobedience or for fear of the battles that lay ahead, but rather for the simple fact of their unbelief. They failed to trust in God.[16]

Because of their unbelief, the Lord renews the promise first made during the golden calf incident to destroy Israel and make a great nation from Moses (14:12; cf. Ex 32:9-10). As in the earlier episode, Moses declines based on his love for Israel and concern for Yahweh's reputation (14:13-16; cf. Ex 32:11-14). Moses also repeats God's self-revelation from Exodus 34:6-7, stressing Yahweh's patience, love, forgiveness and justice, and he then asks that Israel be spared (14:17-19). Once again Yahweh relents, but this time God does choose to start over with a new generation, albeit not all of them Moses' descendants. Israel will not have Canaan until forty postexodus years have passed and until all persons except Joshua and Caleb twenty and over, or of fighting age (cf. Num 1:5-46), have died (14:20-34). They will learn the ominous lesson of what it means to have God for an enemy (14:34). Further, the ten spies who did not believe will die immediately, but Joshua and Caleb will live to inhabit the promised land (14:34-38). Israel belatedly goes to battle. It is too late to change their minds, and they suffer a humiliating defeat (14:39-45).

God's wrath strikes at the heart of all sin, which is unbelief. Over a thirty-eight-year period Yahweh removes every person responsible for this debacle. God starts over in Numbers 15 just as surely as at the moment of Abram's call to leave Ur, for here God offers laws related to possessing the land (cf. especially Num 15:2). Wenham asserts that these laws retrace the main themes of Leviticus and demonstrate that Israel's "unbelief that was focused in the spy story did not nullify these covenant promises. Whole-hearted repentance and the offering of sacrifice can restore them to a position where they can fully experience God's blessing."[17] Unbelief is not a genetically transferred disease. The next generation's faith can surpass that of their elders.

Remarkably Israel continues to rebel even after the Lord's wrath in Numbers 14 and renewed promises in Numbers 15. A coalition of Levites and secular community leaders oppose Moses and Aaron with the intent of gaining the high priest's position for Korah, who is not a son of Aaron (16:1-3). Apparently this faction views the high priest's role more as a position of status than as a theological ministry dedicated to the proclamation of God's holiness. God removes the rebels (16:4-40), which results in the community accusing Moses of killing God's people (16:41)! Yahweh answers this insolence by sending a plague (16:42-50), by dramatically emphasizing Aaron's call to be high priest (17:1-13), by restating the duties of the priest and Levites (18:1-32) and by stressing the value of ritual cleanness (19:1-22). Moses' calling, Aaron's calling and the permanence of the Sinai commandments are all thereby reaffirmed. Israel's rebellions do not alter God's plans, Yahweh's covenant or Yahweh's personal character. All Israel's rebellion achieves is to doom the people to misery and death.

Certainly the rebellions in Numbers 13—14 and Numbers 16 are tragic in their origins and horrible in their consequences. Israel's unbelief and resultant disobedience cost them dearly. Though they have been called to be God's people, they have suffered God's wrath. Not even the chosen people may neglect Yahweh's instruction and emerge unscathed. Numbers 20:1-13 proves that not even Moses himself can disobey God without paying a spiritual, physical and emotional price.

After opening with an announcement of Miriam's death (20:1), Numbers 20 relates a familiar situation. Israel needs water, wishes they were dead, hates the desert (20:2-5). Moses and Aaron receive specific directions from Yahweh to speak to a rock, from which will come water to meet Israel's needs. Instead Moses does two uncharacteristic things. First, rather than give Yahweh credit for the miracle he asks if he and Aaron must get them water (20:10). Second, he strikes the rock as opposed to speaking to it (20:11).[18] Water flows from the rock, but Moses has not honored God in his own heart by obeying the Lord, nor has he glorified God in the people's presence by ascribing all miraculous power to Yahweh. God says Moses has not trusted God and has not caused Israel to understand God's holiness.[19]

Because of his lack of faith Moses cannot share in the blessing of the promised land. The issue is not whether or not he kept the law.[20] The problem is that he did not trust God in this instance, which was the root cause of his disobedience.[21] Despite this long-term punishment, however, the Lord still expects Moses to lead Israel until his successor is in place. By fulfilling this role Moses demonstrates a willingness to serve without receiving much-treasured rewards, and thereby he distances himself from the average grumbling Israelite who rebels at nearly every opportunity.

Canonical Synthesis: Israel's Unbelief

The rebellion episodes in Numbers 13:1—20:13 are used repeatedly in the canon and generally fall into one of three specific interpretive strategies. First, these accounts are used to depict Israel's rank unbelief and subsequent rebellion against the Lord. For example, in Deuteronomy 1:26-40 Moses tells Israel's next generation that rebellion and wrath led to Israel's and his own unnecessary time in the desert. Ezekiel 20:13-16 lists the wilderness era as just one more time when the people angered God. Ezekiel interprets the events in Numbers 13—14 as occurring due to a love of idols that exceeds a love for Yahweh. Similarly, Psalm 78:17-19 and 40—55 denounce Israel's actions as foolish in light of all God had done. Each of these passages in effect laments the nation's past as a way of exhorting their readers to better behavior.

Second, some references use the accounts to stress Israel's ingratitude in light of Yahweh's marvelous provision for their needs. Jeremiah 2:6 implies that God's leadership in the desert should have bound the people to Yahweh permanently. The prophet hopes such history lessons will help seventh-century B.C. Israel repent (cf. Jer 3:12, 14). Ezekiel 20:17 notes that God gave the people a second chance by not destroying them, a sentiment Amos 2:10 echoes and adds to by stressing that Yahweh's mercy led Israel toward Canaan. Psalm 78:38 argues that God was kind during this era, Psalm 114:1-8 states that the Lord's provision proves this kindness, and Psalm 136:16 thinks this kindness is part of God's never-ending mercy and faithfulness. These texts seem to conclude that if God did not cease being merciful to Israel during this era, then surely God's grace and compassion never cease. They also highlight Yahweh's sovereignty, for, Gerhard von Rad says, "what characterises all these expressions, which originate from the sphere of the cult, is the exclusive concentration upon the action of God."[22]

Third, a few canonical texts use the events to warn against repeating such activities. Psalm 95:7-11, which is quoted in Hebrews 3:15—4:7, counsels readers not to harden their hearts as the Israelites did. Persons who harden their hearts never receive God's blessings; they never receive rest. Paul warns the Corinthians against all Israel's desert mistakes as he teaches his readers how to avoid temptations. The major difference between these passages and the first way the Numbers 13—20 accounts are used is they are more pointed and specific. All these texts should be read as warnings, but these last three command their audiences to avoid the Israelites' mistakes.

Israel's sins are clearly against the only God in the story. Their unbelief is directed at the creator, sustainer, redeemer and covenant maker who has revealed himself since the Old Testament began. It is fitting for the one God who has been rebuffed to set all punishments in these accounts. In sheer indomitable grace and faithfulness to Abraham, though, the Lord punishes in order to renew. Sin does not have the final word because it did not have the first word.

The God Who Sustains and Protects: Numbers 20:14—22:1

There are now two Israels traveling through the desert. One Israel is the older generation that must die in the wilderness, never possessing the promised land, because of unbelief. The other Israel is the second generation that is growing, maturing and preparing to possess Canaan. God provides for both groups, giving them manna and water. Moses continues to lead at Yahweh's command. God also protects the people from both military defeat and self-defeating, unclean attitudes and actions. Clearly the Lord's character remains intact regardless of the situation.

Three specific accounts highlight God's protection from enemies. First, since Israel has turned away from southern Canaan, they now attempt to enter Canaan from the east by going through Edom (20:14-21). Edom does not allow them to pass through, however, so Israel goes another direction. Since Edom was not part of the promised land, the Israelites felt no need to fight.[23] Second, Israel encounters and defeats the army of "the Canaanite king of Arad" (21:1) because God gives them the strength to do so (21:2-3). This victory is a foreshadowing of greater victories to come, but the conquest of the entire region must await Moses' death. When the people are threatened (21:1), God responds. Third, God empowers Israel to defeat the kings of the Amorites (21:21-35). These victories are engineered by the Lord, and they result in Israel possessing land. Again such episodes indicate that Israel could have been winning these victories sooner if they had only trusted Yahweh, and the victories also offer hope and instill confidence in the people that they will indeed inherit a homeland.

Three accounts also demonstrate how God sustains key ingredients in Israelite life. When Aaron dies the Lord sustains the people's spiritual leadership by providing a smooth transition from Aaron's high priesthood to that of his son Eleazar (20:22-29). The sanctuary will continue to operate, and Israel's most important ministry will continue as well, thus mediating forgiveness for all the people.[24] Further, after the Arad victory the people complain, so Yahweh sends a plague to chastise them (21:4-6). Moses helps relieve the people (21:8-9), which demonstrates his ongoing call to lead. God intends to teach the nation to believe and obey, thus protecting Israel from death-producing attitudes. Finally, Yahweh guarantees safe passage to Moab, giving them needed water as they journey (21:10-20). Thus God provides religious continuity, necessary discipline and safety. Such merciful provision allows the second Israel to grow in faith as it grows in number and maturity.

Canonical Synthesis: Israel's Initial Victories

Israel's God-given triumph over Og, king of Bashan (21:32-35), becomes evidence of God's determination to give Israel the promised land in the rest of the Old Testament. It stands as a monument of Yahweh's greatness. Moses recites the victory to exhort the next generation to possess Canaan in Deuteronomy 3:1-11, 29:7-8 and 31:1-4. Rahab and the Gibeonites cite Og's defeat as one reason they believe Israel's invasion of Canaan will succeed (cf. Josh 2:10; 9:10). Psalm 135:11, Psalm 136:20 and Nehemiah 9:22 refer to the event while emphasizing God's power, lovingkindness and election of Israel respectively. In other words, this account comes to be interpreted as meaning that all things are possible for Israel because Yahweh is their God. No one can withstand the people who stand with God. This canonical conviction is underscored in Numbers 22—24, where Moab's king learns this lesson from an unlikely source.

The God Who Renews His Promises: Numbers 22:2—36:13

One thing is clear in Numbers 20:14—22:1, and that is that Israel is regrouping under punishment, not dying of it. Nothing can ultimately stop God's promises to Abraham, made in Genesis 12:1-9 hundreds of years earlier, from coming true. God's word is as unerringly holy, faithful and inevitably loving and correct as the God who uttered the words. Nothing else could be true, since one's words flow from one's character. In Numbers 22:2—36:13 Yahweh's promises endure attack. They also provide the foundation for God's preparation of the new generation to conquer the land their parents were afraid to invade. Israel's sins can delay yet never frustrate totally God's plans.

Israel now comes to the third stage of their journey. After leaving Egypt, they spend time at Mt. Sinai (Ex 19:1—Num 10:12) and in the desert (Num 10:12—22:1), and now they will dwell "across from Jericho" (Num 22:1) and the plains of Moab until Joshua 3:1 finds them invading Canaan. As they anticipate receiving the land just beyond their reach, enemies attempt to sabotage their future.

First the Moabites attempt to hire a prophet they hope can turn God's word against Israel; then they go to a simpler method of ruining their potential foes, which is to assimilate them into their orgiastic religious cults. Both attempts strike at the heart of the chosen people's identity.

Numbers 22—24 has long presented commentators with a variety of challenges. The fact that the main character, Balaam, is a non-Israelite who receives oracles from Yahweh suggests many interesting possibilities, as does how God deals with him. It is also somewhat difficult to determine the exact nature of Balaam's character, and it is not easy to know why the canon depicts him as it does. Despite such matters, these chapters clearly concern themselves with the accuracy of God's word and the enduring quality of God's promises. Words that come from God here and elsewhere are as real as the events they predict.

Balaam speaks four oracles about Israel. Though he uses practices of divination denounced in Leviticus 19:26, God places a word in his mouth. The first oracle stresses Israel's election (23:7-8), holiness or separateness (23:9), numerical strength (23:10) and blessedness (23:10). In other words, he echoes promises made by God to Abraham (cf. Gen 12:1-9; 13:16) and God's purposes for Israel stated at Sinai (cf. Ex 19:5-6).[25] When confronted by Balak for not cursing Israel, Balaam replies that he has spoken God's words (23:11-12). Balaam's second oracle is also preceded by divination rites (23:13-14). By switching venues Balak hopes to change God's mind.[26] Instead he learns that Israel's God is unique, for Yahweh does not change his mind. God cannot be manipulated (23:18-19). He also learns that Israel's uniqueness "is found in her unique relationship to her Lord."[27] God brought Israel out of Egypt without sorcery and is oblivious to sorcery (23:21-23). God's will for Israel is fixed. Thus Israel has great strength because they worship the only God (23:24). Having stressed the Abrahamic covenant in 23:7-10, Balaam emphasizes God's work through Moses in 23:18-24.

Angry, yet as defiant as Pharaoh before him, Balak takes Balaam to one more vantage point. This time Balaam blesses all Israel (24:3-5), predicts they will one day have a great king and be a great kingdom (24:6-7) and links their power to Yahweh's work on their behalf (24:8-9). Balaam's final oracle predicts Israel will defeat all their foes (24:15-24). Therefore Balaam has spoken God's word, and God has said that the promises of heir, covenant and land will indeed be fulfilled. These are God's words, and they are infallible even when delivered by a foreign, on-the-market, unseeing, divining man like Balaam. His true character may be uncertain, but the power and truthfulness of what God forces him to say are not.

Balak now realizes that Israel can be stopped only if the people stop worshiping Yahweh. So the Moabite women invite the Israelite men to participate in the worship of Baal, whom Canaanites believed was the god of fertility. Baal worship in this instance includes offering sacrifices, eating a meal and coupling with Moabite women (25:1-8).[28] Harrison observes, "What they experienced was a foretaste of the same kind of depraved cultic practices they would encounter in the Promised Land."[29] Harrison adds that Baal and his "bloodthirsty wife, Anat, variously identified with Asherah and Astarte/Ashtoreth, was venerated by means of the most sensuous, orgiastic practices known to humanity."[30] So blatant is the sensual idolatry that an Israelite man brings a Midianite woman "to his family" in plain view of Moses (25:6). Ashley notes that the man does so for illicit sex, marriage or some cultic observance.[31] Any of these options should be abhorrent to a people committed to the Sinai covenant. Post-Sinai Israel has indulged in polytheism.

To stem the idolatrous outbreak and the plague Yahweh sends to punish it, Phineas, Eleazar's son, executes the Israelite man and Midianite woman (25:7-9, 14-15). God had warned against adopting Canaanite worship practices in Leviticus 18:1-5 and Leviticus 24—30 and had ordered those involved in polytheistic worship "cut off" from the people, so Phineas probably sees himself as cleansing Israel according to God's revealed word. Apparently so, for the Lord halts the plague and blesses Phineas with "a covenant of lasting priesthood" (25:13) for what he has done. He has been zealous for God and has made atonement for Israel, which are the two most important things for a priest to do. After blessing Phineas the Lord commands Moses to make war against Midian for tempting Israel in this manner.

Israel has endured, but Numbers 22—25 demonstrates that the people's future depends on a commitment to Yahweh alone. These chapters also prove that Israel's history includes base polytheism and its attendant excesses. Yet they also reflect the canonical writers' complete disgust with such activities. Old Testament theology must focus on the canon's report and interpretation of Israel's history (see chapter two).[32] In Numbers 25 the text depicts Israel's history accurately and then comments on that history. One could argue with the interpretation of the events, but one could hardly charge the text with hiding unsavory and unsettling events in Israel's history.

For Israel's second generation, victory can be defined only as possession of Canaan. Thus every divine command and human deed must contribute to fulfilling this goal.[33] To this end the Lord instructs Moses to instruct the people in specific details necessary to organize for triumph. These chapters consist of a census (Num 26), worship-related commands (27—30) and orders concerning dividing the land (31—36). The twin appearances of Zelophehad's daughters in Numbers 27 and Numbers 36 frame the section. Every word of God and every obedience on Israel's part in this segment proves Yahweh's promises to Abraham concerning Canaan will come true.

Preparation for conquest begins with a census, a question about inheritance and the commissioning of Moses' successor. The census in Numbers 26 has the same purpose as the one in Numbers 1, which is to count Israel's potential army. Thirty-eight years have passed between censuses, and only Joshua, Caleb and Moses remain from the original counting (26:63-65). The number of available fighters has declined by only 1,820 men, so the nation has virtually the same strike forces as before.[34] God has sustained significant numbers of people in the desert.

Five women, all Zelophehad's daughters, approach Moses with an inheritance question. Their inquiry highlights the promise of land and a commitment to their family's tribal heritage. They have no brothers and fear the loss of their father's name and property (27:1-4). Yahweh rules that daughters may indeed inherit land when they have no living brothers and that land is to stay in the clan's possession if at all possible (27:5-11). Again the very discussion of such problems expresses confidence in the future. There will be land to be possessed. The new generation believes in and anticipates this blessing before they ever take the land. Their faith response condemns their parents' unbelief.

Moses' ministry will not last much longer now, though his lengthy speeches in Deuteronomy make it seem, textually at least, that he lives a long time. He asks God to appoint a sound leader (27:12-17), so Yahweh responds by choosing Joshua. This man has experience, faith and God's spirit (27:18). He receives Moses' authority in the presence of Eleazar and all the Israelites (27:19-23). This transfer of leadership, like the one between Aaron and Eleazar in Numbers 20:22-29, reflects Yahweh's continuing commitment to Israel. Now several centuries old, this commitment transcends time, circumstances and human failure. For God, promises are as real as the one who promised. Joshua will soon become the human instrument that helps actualize these ineradicable pledges.

Just as the last generation received commands about purity and worship after their census (cf. Num 5:1—10:10), so the second generation hears commands concerning offerings, festivals and vows (28:1—30:16) after theirs.[35] Jacob Milgrom comments, "Hence, whether in the wilderness or in its land, Israel can be assured by God's presence only through His sanctioned cult and sanctuary."[36] Joshua and the new generation must understand that the land can be held only by adherence to God's chosen sacrifices and specified calendar. Though all the offerings and festivals in Numbers 28—30 are familiar the text is not a blank repetition of earlier passages, for Gray says, "As a systematic table of quantities of the public offerings required at regularly-recurring periods the present section has no parallel in the Hexateuch."[37] The expected regularity of these offerings serves as yet another reminder that Israel will indeed occupy the land and have abundant resources from which they can bring sacrifices to their Lord.[38] Yahweh now speaks as if the promises cannot fail in this generation's lifetime.

Moses hears about Zelophehad's daughters again. This second time, clan leaders secure a ruling that the women must marry within the tribe so that Manasseh's share in the promised land does not diminish (36:1-13). Land has become exceptionally precious in the people's sight. It must not be lost through negligence or by even the lack of males in a specific family. God-given land must be possessed, protected and treasured. People raised in the desert seem to know how important this physical blessing can be. To them, the promise of land becomes the driving issue of faith in their lives.

Canonical Synthesis: Balaam and God's Word

Much of the canonical usage of Numbers has already been outlined. The great tragedies in Numbers 13—14 and Numbers 20, as well as the positive events in Numbers 1—10, are used in several later contexts. Still, the canon also utilizes the Balaam and Baal-Peor accounts of Numbers 22—25 to warn subsequent readers against duplicating the actions of Balaam and the idolatrous Israelites.

Canonical opinions of Balaam are hardly flattering. Numbers 31:8-16 begins the criticism by revealing that he advised the Midianites to lure Israel into idolatry. Such advice does not remove the chosen people's responsibility for their actions, but it hardly commends Balaam as a faithful servant of Yahweh either. Deuteronomy 23:4-5 portrays Balaam as a prophet for hire that God molded for purposes other than Balaam originally intended. Moses clearly questions Balaam's motives. In the New Testament, 2 Peter 2:15, Jude 11 and Revelation 2:14 characterize him "as an opponent of Israel who would have cursed Israel had not God intervened, a man who preferred money to serving God."[39] Peter and Jude compare greedy false teachers of their day to Balaam, while Revelation chastises the church at Pergamum for indulging in Balaam's teaching, which is the worship of idols and sexual immorality. Given the canonical reading of Balaam, Allen's depiction of him as a man who thought he could manipulate Yahweh, not a believer in one God, seems fair.[40]

If Balaam is no role model, then how can he speak such accurate oracles? The answer is that God used him to deliver an accurate message, a not-unheard-of occurrence in the canon. After all, Saul prophesies even after having lost God's blessings on his reign (see 1 Sam 19:23-24).[41] God uses a lying old prophet to deliver an accurate prediction in 1 Kings 13. What matters most is that God's inspired word never fails, regardless of the fallibility of the human witness. Yahweh remains faithful no matter how faulty people become.

Canonical Synthesis: Baal-Peor and Idolatry

Beyond Balaam himself, the idolatry at "Baal-peor came to be etched in the collective memory as a nadir in Israel's history (Deut 4:3; Hos 9:10; Ps 106:28)."[42] Moses cites the event in Deuteronomy 4:3-4 to remind Israel that those who worshiped Baal died, while those who trusted Yahweh lived. Thus he reminds the people of the clear results of choosing polytheism over monotheism. Hosea uses the Baal-Peor debacle as a historical parallel to the depraved Baal worship in which the people of eighth-century northern Israel indulged (Hos 9:10). Sensuous idolatry was centuries old by Hosea's time, and he warns that Yahweh has grown weary of such activity. Psalm 106:28 lists the Numbers 25 incident as but one national sin among many that led to captivity. Because of their misery, the psalmist asks God to save Israel from their well-deserved exile (Ps 106:47). This event clearly has no redeeming value, so it is referred to solely in terms of Israel's sin and thereby stands as a negative example to all later generations.

Conclusion

Numbers has a bittersweet place in the Hebrew canon and in the flow of God's redemptive work. On the one hand there is hope in Numbers 1:1—10:11 and confidence in Numbers 22—36. God continues to stay the course in his plan to eliminate the sin problem by keeping all the Abrahamic promises. Faith and obedience remain the keys to the Israelite people's pleasing God, and neither characteristic is impossible for the elect nation to attain. These sections also highlight Yahweh's never-ending faithfulness. Israel enjoys the benefits of a providing, promising, saving God.

On the other hand, however, episodes in Numbers 13—25 dominate canonical usages of the book. Israel's first generation is particularly remembered more for squandering opportunities, for rebellion and for unbelief than for anything else. From Deuteronomy to Revelation, accounts in Numbers illustrate biblical writers' concern with greed, faithlessness and idolatry. Therefore Numbers stands as the canonical book of horrors for persons of faith.

Still, when Numbers 36 closes, hope springs anew. A second generation, raised in the desert, hungry for victory, camps outside Canaan waiting to receive the promised land. A second high priest and a replacement for Moses stand ready to serve. Surely God can complete these people's preparation and thereby complete the fundamental heir, covenant and land promises made in Genesis 12:1-9.

6

The God
Who Renews
the Covenant

Deuteronomy

. . . .

BY ANY STANDARD OF COMPARISON DEUTERONOMY IS ONE OF THE MOST important books in the canon. Its historical setting links the Sinai and wilderness experiences with the conquest of Canaan and provides a transition from Moses' leadership to Joshua's. Its canonical placement concludes the Pentateuch by effectively interpreting Exodus, Leviticus and Numbers; yet it also provides an interpretive framework for the Former and Latter Prophets (Joshua—Malachi). Its theological emphases set the tone for how Israel must live in the land they will inherit from the God who has chosen them. Its exhortative, instructional style offers rhetorical patterning for Old Testament historians, prophets, psalmists and sages. Beyond the Hebrew canon, Deuteronomy is, with Genesis, Psalms and Isaiah, one of the four most-quoted Old Testament books in the New Testament. Jesus himself uses passages from Deuteronomy to resist Satan's temptations in Matthew 4:1-11. Unquestionably this book, the Pentateuch's capstone, deserves careful theological analysis.

Deuteronomy's structure and theology are integrated in an extraordinary way. A simple, straightforward reading of Deuteronomy yields a framework based on addresses Moses makes to the Israelites. After a historical and geographical notation opens the book (1:1-5), Moses addresses the people concerning their history (1:6—4:49), concerning their covenant with God

(5—28) and concerning the renewal of their covenant with Yahweh (29—30). These three sermonic interpretations of history and covenant relationships are followed by the transfer of power from Moses to Joshua, the production of a book of the law, Moses' blessing of Israel and Moses' death (31—34). History, covenant and transition dominate the book in a way that teaches the new generation to expect God to act decisively on their behalf because of similar acts in the past. Current divine demands of obedience are anchored firmly in God's grace, God's revelation and God's promises.

Four basic approaches to Deuteronomy's origins have emerged. First, there are still some experts who believe Julius Wellhausen correctly assessed Israel's covenant beliefs as a pervasive theoretical concept that received specific status only when Deuteronomy was written to support Josiah's reform. E. W. Nicholson is the ablest proponent of this viewpoint.[1] Second, A. D. H. Mayes says that Deuteronomy was initially an ancient law code that later had covenant and treaty elements added to it.[2] He believes this approach explains how Deuteronomy can reflect all these traits but not be wholly devoted to any one of them. Third, numerous authors believe that despite their conclusion that Deuteronomy is post-Mosaic, the book contains ancient material and reflects either a Hittite or an Assyrian treaty format.[3] Fourth, many traditionally minded writers think that historical and canonical data reflect a second-millennium B.C. date for Deuteronomy based on its similarities to the Hittite vassal treaty.[4]

These opinions do share some common ground. Most stress that covenant ideals, whether actual or conceptual, impact Deuteronomy significantly. Most stress that Deuteronomy helps shape Israel's postconquest history. Most recognize Deuteronomy's major role in the canon. Most agree on the basic theological truths presented in the book. Scholars disagree about how Deuteronomy reached its present form, but they agree to a significant degree on the basic characteristics of the book's final canonical form.

One other notion about Deuteronomy's date and authorship deserves mention at this point. Martin Noth argued in 1943 that one author wrote Deuteronomy 1—4, edited the rest of Deuteronomy and then utilized source material to compose Joshua, Judges, Samuel and Kings by about 550 B.C.[5] Therefore he considered Deuteronomy the theological basis for the deuteronomistic history found in the Former Prophets. Noth's hypothesis has significant canonical implications, since it makes Deuteronomy the theological parent of four subsequent books. That Deuteronomy serves this function can be maintained and will guide this volume's analysis of those books. This approach can be pursued, however, without adopting Noth's views of Deuteronomy's authorship. Surely a Mosaic book could carry sufficient authoritative standing to be used as a guide for historical reflection. Surely it could influence the canon in the way Noth describes.

This volume accepts the arguments for Mosaic authorship of Deuteronomy forwarded by Meredith Kline, Peter C. Craigie, Eugene Merrill and others (chapter two),[6] as well as their assertions about Deuteronomy's basic similarity to the Hittite vassal treaty. This conclusion is tenable given the research noted. Still, it is extremely important to highlight the agreements that characterize Deuteronomy research. Covenant terminology pervades the book. Deuteronomy's structure does match its message. Its theology impacts all of Scripture. Therefore a canonical analysis must bring together the best theological conclusions that have emerged from scholarly analysis rather than reject all comments that do not fit a specific conviction about authorship and date. At the heart of all Deuteronomy research published in the past several decades is a strong emphasis on how the book details the covenant relationship between God and Israel and how that relationship becomes the catalyst for the giving and receiving of divine revelation that guides Israel's life in the promised land.

Given the broad consensus of scholarship on the covenantal, relational nature of Deuteronomy, it is appropriate for a canonical approach to the book's theology to link Moses' speeches and the Hittite treaty format. In this way Deuteronomy's status as completer of the Pentateuch and impetus for other canonical writings can be highlighted. Each discrete speech has direct parallels with the ancient treaty outline, and the examination of each parallel section reveals specific details about the God who makes covenant with the second generation of the elect people.

Moses' first speech reviews and interprets God's past dealings with Israel (1:6—4:43). It therefore basically matches the Hittite treaty's historical prologue segment. Here Moses describes a great God who creates and shapes history, and here Israel is reminded of the great King they serve. Next, Moses' second speech interprets the Sinai covenant for the people and exhorts them to love and obey God in their new homeland (5—28). The end of this sermon includes a recital of blessings and curses that remind readers of Leviticus 26 (cf. Deut 27—28). This section corresponds to the Hittite treaty's stating of general and specific stipulations and on its listing of blessings for treaty keeping and curses for treaty breaking. Scholars have noted that Deuteronomy adapts these emphases for its own purposes but that ancient treaties generally include these items. This large block of material stresses love for a God who creates a holy community. Yahweh creates the community through election, deliverance, guidance and revelation, all of which show that the Lord loves Israel.

Finally, Moses' third speech calls Israel to covenant renewal (Deut 29—30). The people's agreement to keep the covenant leads to the writing of a book that concretizes the covenant, to the transfer of leadership from Moses to Joshua, to Moses' final blessing of Israel, to Moses' death and to the completion of the Pentateuch (Deut 31—34). Covenant commitment thereby becomes the Law's closing act. Though the treaty parallels break down somewhat at this point, it is fair to compare these chapters to the Hittite practice of calling covenant witnesses and the placing of covenant requirements in the participants' sanctuaries. Now the text declares Yahweh to be a God who effects continuity and transition. It also presents Yahweh as the God who inspires written revelation, who orders a record of intelligent divine communication kept.

Several important concepts undergird these truths, and each is connected to Genesis—Numbers. Issues such as nation, covenant, relationship, community and land receive significant treatment. Foundational to all these ideas, however, is the principle that the only God of creation makes these standards plain to Israel. No other deity exists for Israel, or anyone else for that matter. Thus G. E. Wright accurately summarizes the driving theological principle in Deuteronomy when he writes, "The primary exhortation of Deuteronomy, as the complete book now rests before us, is the intense and all-absorbing loyalty which Israel owes to Yahweh, who alone is God."[7] This canonical thread has not been severed. The one God who creates and delivers remains the one God who reveals. If this principle is lost the uniqueness of Israel's existence disappears, and the canon's claims of a God who controls history, crossing all geographical, cultural and theological boundaries to do so, evaporates. As this claim remains the text maintains ultimate authority to command and ultimate hope that sin can be defeated.

The God Who Creates and Shapes History: Deuteronomy 1—4

History receives its starting point from the God who creates heaven, earth, people and nations. History has no autonomous power of its own. It has meaning because God gives it meaning by dealing with human beings in space and time. Therefore, when Moses recounts Israel's history in these chapters, he does so knowing that Yahweh has created and enlivened Israel's national life. He preaches that Israel's history has been determined from the start by God, who elects Israel, makes covenant with Israel and guides Israel. In other words, he demonstrates God's faithfulness and uniqueness by stressing the Lord's acts in history on Israel's behalf.

Deuteronomy begins with an explanation of its setting (1:1-5). Moses speaks to Israel at the end of their forty-year desert sentence (1:3), and he does so as they dwell just outside the land of promise (1:1-2). They have been there before, only to rebel (Num 13—14). He speaks about God's revealed commandments (1:3). He explains the law that has already been revealed (1:5) rather than delivering any new laws. Moses offers a commentary on God's will, an exposition intended to make plain what Yahweh has already said.[8] The message is directed "to all Israel," a phrase that reveals the unified covenant status of the entire nation.[9] What follows is covenant revelation that reflects God's freedom and sovereignty in choosing and relating to Israel.[10] This revelation proves to be the people's only avenue for freedom and grace.[11]

Moses' initial speech begins with a reminder that God called Israel to leave Sinai so that they might possess the land promised to the patriarchs (1:6-8). The mention of the patriarchs forces Israel "to relate the impending conquest of Canaan under Joshua to the promise of God and not to any feelings of national superiority."[12] It also reflects on the fact that the land belongs to Yahweh, its Creator (Lev 25:23), and is therefore a gift to Israel that is inextricably linked to its relationship with the Lord.[13] The book's subsequent sixty-eight references to the land as "possession" and "inheritance" further drive home this point.[14] Israel continues to face the challenge and opportunity of enjoying this blessing. What has become clear is that Israel has no power in itself to take the land.[15] Every victory they have enjoyed has been God's gift to them.[16]

With the Lord's faithfulness illustrated by the facts of history, Moses proceeds to call the people to faithfulness in Deuteronomy 4:1-43. This invitation begins with the book's first of several summonses to hear, which means to hear and thus obey (4:1). It commands the new generation to follow the laws already delivered that Moses will now explain (4:1). The law stands as a divine revelation that may be interpreted and explained but that cannot be altered (4:2). Refusal to obey will result in loss of their opportunity to possess Canaan (4:1-2). Their whole future depends on personal and national faithfulness.

Beginning at Deuteronomy 4:3 and continuing throughout the book, Moses places single-minded monotheism at the forefront of Israel's commitment to Yahweh. The people must not act as they did at Baal-Peor (Num 25:1-18) if they want to live happily (Deut 4:3-4). Remembering, reciting and teaching the truths revealed at Sinai by the one God will prosper Israel and gain for them a reputation as a wise nation (4:5-14). However, Moses warns, their recent history has proven the dangers of idolatry, and their future history will be bleak as well if they worship images when they reach Canaan (4:15-20). They will be driven from the land if they "forget the covenant" and turn from sole devotion to Yahweh (4:23). Though God is merciful and will always honor the covenant with the patriarchs (4:29-31), God is willing to allow Israel to suffer for venerating gods that are not God (4:27-28).

Certain questions that produce specific propositions help Israel understand Moses' point. First, God created the earth (4:32). Second, since the creation, history has not seen another nation receive direct revelation from the Creator (4:33). Third, only Yahweh has acted on a specific nation's behalf, redeeming and freeing them via miraculous deeds (4:34). Fourth, these historical events prove "the LORD is God; besides him there is no other" (4:35). A clearer monotheistic statement could hardly be made. Fifth, Yahweh has brought Israel to the brink of the land pledged in Genesis 12:7 (4:35-38). The very fact that the Lord can cross geographical boundaries marks Yahweh as different from other supposed gods, who are limited to "ruling" over specific locations. As Creator and only deity, Yahweh can exert power in any setting. Sixth, Israel should obey the Lord in order to enjoy prosperity (4:40). Once again Moses declares God's uniqueness by saying that Yahweh "is God in heaven above and on the earth below. There is no other" (4:39). Since Yahweh is the creator, any gods who supposedly exist would have to be made by him, and the canon offers no such possibility. God's acts in history remove any doubt that Israel owes their God absolute fidelity as the only living deity.[17] Nothing less than unshakable commitment to the only God constitutes covenant obedience.[18]

Canonical Synthesis: History and Corrective Theology

Two significant canonical details emerge from Deuteronomy 1—4. The first is that Moses' review of Israel's past begins the process of biblical books reflecting on previous material. Such reflection does more than catalog past events. It assesses, interprets and packages previous data in a way calculated to exhort, correct or instruct the new text's audience. It also assumes that readers have amassed a cumulative knowledge of events that allows them to benefit fully from the combined effect of absorbing data and then seeing it used and reused. Readers must now examine a text by noting how previous passages impact that text and how that text interprets previous passages.

The second is that Moses begins a canon-long practice of assessing Israel's history by covenant standards. That is, authors interpret events' causes and effects based on how faithful Israel is to God and how merciful God is to Israel. The most obvious example of this tendency is the Former Prophets' (Joshua, Judges, Samuel and Kings) constant claims that covenant renewal and covenant keeping lead to blessing (cf. Josh 24:15-27; 1 Kings 8) while covenant breaking, best illustrated by idolatry, brings inevitable divine judgment that effects national collapse (cf. Judg 1—2; 2 Kings 17). This insistence on explainable cause and effect mirrors modern interpretations of history, though the theological nature of deuteronomistic history has few recent secular proponents. Beginning with Isaiah's ironic portrayal of Israel's covenant breaking being akin to a donkey's forgetting its owner

(Is 1:2-9), to Jeremiah's scathing denouncing of breaking of the Ten Commandments at the temple (Jer 7:1—8:3), to Ezekiel's recital of Israel's history as one broken promise after another (Ezek 20:1-29), to Hosea's comparison of Israel's unfaithfulness to that of an adulterous spouse (Hos 1—3), concluding with Malachi's call for the elect people to live according to the law, prophetic texts constantly compare Israel's historical acts to what God expects in the Pentateuch, especially Deuteronomy.

The Writings reflect a similar approach to Israelite history. Psalms 78 and 106 read Israel's past through Moses' theoretical and theological grids. Confessions of sin, such as those in Daniel 9:1-19, Ezra 9:1—10:12 and Nehemiah 9:1-37, link covenant ideals to the nation's success or failure. Chronicles concludes the canon with a different historical approach from that of the Former Prophets, yet with the same conviction that historical cause and effect in Israelite affairs derive from covenantal principles and the unswerving belief that Yahweh rules heaven, earth and human events.

The God Who Creates a Holy Community: Deuteronomy 5—28

Moses' emphasis on the past highlights God's centuries-old relationship with Israel. The Lord's claims on the people derive from a past filled with loving election and guidance. Likewise Israel's willingness to serve Yahweh comes from this long history of trying and failing and trying again to love and obey the God of Abraham, Isaac, Jacob, Moses and Joshua. By now this friendship includes more than the patriarchs and the exodus, which served as the relational basis for the Sinai covenant (cf. Ex 2:23-25; 20:2), for it encompasses Sinai itself, the desert journeys and quite recent military victories. Now there is even more reason for Israel to know that ever so slowly, over time, Yahweh has been and is creating a holy community, one set apart for divine purposes. Now there is even more incentive for the current Israelites to reaffirm their covenant with the God who alone rules heaven and earth (Deut 4:39).

With the nation's history sketched, Moses proceeds to his second major speech, which outlines the general and specific stipulations Yahweh requires from Israel. Fundamental to the general stipulations in Deuteronomy 5—11 is the fact that Israel must display total allegiance to God.[19] Nothing less can truly create a holy covenantal community. This God who deserves absolute dedication is the Lord who transcends time to renew the covenant with each successive generation of Israelites (5:1-33). Yahweh expects allegiance based on love that permeates the people's whole being (6:1-25), not on dutiful resignation to a stronger power. God commands that sole allegiance continue in war as it has in peace (7:1-26) and warns the people never to forget the God who, when remembered, always brings new life through forgiveness (8:1—10:11). Finally Moses reminds Israel that their God merits fear, respect, love and obedience (10:12—11:32). This Lord can give them the land.

Given these general principles, Moses details more specific expectations in Deuteronomy 12—26 and then concludes by stating the consequences of covenant breaking and obedience in Deuteronomy 27—28. Like the exhortations in Deuteronomy 5—11, these teachings are not new, but they express urgency for the people who will conquer Canaan. Here Moses presents a God who requires serious and careful worship (12:1—16:17), who has specific standards for leaders (16:18—18:22), who sets guidelines for civil behavior in a holy society (19:1—25:19) and who offers Israel the choice between life and death (27:1—28:68). Each law demonstrates how total dedication to Yahweh becomes concrete behavior in practical daily life. Each standard becomes a foundation stone for the holy community God intends to build. Each command helps God explain how much he cares about every minute issue that affects the beloved chosen people. Each stipulation strengthens the covenant relationship between the Creator and the elect nation.

The God Whose Commands Remain Relevant: Deuteronomy 5

Since the Ten Commandments served as the basis for the Sinai covenant, it is hardly surprising that Moses restates and contextualizes them when explaining the covenant to the new generation. These commands are as relevant in Moab as they were in Sinai and will be equally relevant in the promised land. They are authoritative revelation for each generation who reads the canon, a point their repetition surely makes.

Before stating the actual commands, Moses carefully removes any doubt that the Sinai commitment to Yahweh and Yahweh's standards still apply to the people forty years later. He calls Israel to hear God's word, learn it and follow it (5:1). The people must understand that the Sinai covenant, which he now interprets, was made with them (5:2-3). It was a permanent, "once-for-all establishment of the covenant in history"[20] that links the audience with its ancestors. Every time covenant renewal takes place the people identify with the original revelation.[21] Those who respond to God's promises are always as blessed as those who originally received those promises.[22] This covenant mediation by Moses reminds Israel that these standards come directly from God and remain the basis for their future (5:4-5).

The Ten Commandments are stated almost exactly as in Exodus 20:2-17. God says that deliverance proves divine devotion to Israel (5:6). In return Yahweh requires no other gods be worshiped and no images be venerated (5:7-10). These first two commandments cannot be separated, Moshe Weinfeld explains, because in the ancient Near East having gods means having idols . . . and, according to the Israelite monotheistic concepts, just as fetishes made of stone, wood, or gold have no "life," neither do the gods represented by them (Jer 10:2-10). The pagans themselves could not conceive a deity without an image, and the deity was considered present in its image. . . . Therefore, "having no other gods" actually means "having no images," and the second commandment, in fact, continues the idea or concretizes the first one.[23]

Monotheism remains the basic principle for the covenant people.

Reverence for God's name and sabbath keeping are likewise continually relevant (5:11-15). It is interesting that the basis for the sabbath is the exodus rather than the creation, as in Exodus 20:11. Craigie points out that creation remains the chief theological reason for the sabbath, however, since the exodus itself creates the newly free nation of Israel. Both the world and Israel are totally dependent on Yahweh for their existence and sustenance.[24] Worship and rest demonstrate to the world Israel's commitment to the first two commandments.

All the standards related to human interaction are given unchanged from the Sinai revelation (5:16-21). These laws may mean even more now that they have been fleshed out in Exodus 20—Leviticus 27. The promise of long life in the land (5:16) and the admonition not to covet (5:21) take on added significance in a context where settled life is a realistic possibility. Each of these last six commands provides a solid basis for case laws that follow. Raymond Brown observes that these standards also show God to be truthful, life-giving, generous and loving. Thus he says, "All the demands of the Decalogue [Ten Commandments] are a reflection of the nature of God."[25] What God expects flows from who God is.

Israel must understand that these words constitute specific divine revelation. They are Yahweh's words (5:22). Moses mediates them, but they are God's words nonetheless (5:22-27). These words reveal God's desire, which is for Israel to obey and prosper (5:28-29). Just as God reveals personal principles and emotions by offering commands in concrete, understandable language, so must Israel reveal what love and commitment reside in their hearts by offering total allegiance to God (5:30-33). Such commitment requires careful adherence to and consistent walking in faith according to God's word (5:32-33).[26]

The God Who Merits Love and Service: Deuteronomy 6—11

The very soul of the covenant is not coerced or obligatory obedience but love. God's love is evident in his desire that all go well with Israel (6:1-3). All divine commands flow from this love, which itself flows from God's character. There is one God, one love, one law.[27] These principles have been implied since Exodus 20:2-17, yet now they are stated explicitly in Deuteronomy 6:4-9, a text that has significant canonical importance.

Three distinct truths shape the confession of faith found in 6:4-9. First, the text says, "The LORD our God, the LORD is one" (6:4). These words confess that Yahweh is unique and possesses a unified character. Craigie states that Israel learned in the exodus that there is no god like Yahweh (Ex 15:11), for no god other than Yahweh acted or spoke in that crucial historical situation. Since no other god did so, they also learn there is no god but Yahweh.[28] Because God possesses constant character, the people may be sure that Yahweh is consistent, truthful, revelatory and worthy of worship.[29] Someday Israel may pursue other gods (cf. Deut 6:13-15), but they will learn, Brown says, that "to love other gods is to pursue nothing. They do not exist. He is the one and only Lord."[30] Read contextually with the first two commandments, with Deuteronomy 4:39 and with texts like Deuteronomy 10:17, this verse is definitely monotheistic.[31]

Second, Deuteronomy 6:5 commands Israel to love Yahweh with their whole heart, soul and mind. By now the canon has left no doubt that Yahweh loves Israel with a tender, undeserved yet determined, almost fierce love that refuses to let them finally sink into idolatry and its attendant obscurity and depravity. Israel must show a similar love to Yahweh, who, unlike Israel, merits it. Such devotion requires emotional volition (heart), spiritual personality (soul) and mental and physical vigor (strength). Thus it includes the entire range of human essence. No division of loyalty or segmentation of life or personality will do. Nothing may be held in reserve. This love amounts to total dependence on Yahweh, a truth Israel has been taught since at least Exodus 2:23-25. It also amounts to an obligation to obey the truth.[32]

Third, Yahweh commands the people to internalize the covenant and teach their children to do the same (6:6-9). Each new member of the holy community must be taught God's ways. Faith does not occur automatically. It must be understood and owned (6:6), so each parent must teach his or her children, just as Moses has been teaching them. Instruction must be purposeful, even to the point of becoming public (6:9). The idea is to "impress, or inscribe" truth on the heart, not simply to suggest it.[33] Such careful teaching will help avoid forgetting Yahweh in prosperity (6:10-12), in new settings (6:13-19) or when new generations emerge, uncertain of what the old revelation means (6:20-25). Only scrupulous integenerational teaching can keep exclusive love of Yahweh alive in a polytheistic culture.

Having commanded love, Moses explains how love must operate once Israel reaches Canaan. In doing so he concludes the book's emphasis on the basic covenant stipulations. Deuteronomy 7:1-26 begins this explanation by stating how Israel and Yahweh's mutual love creates a program of conquest.[34]

The program itself sounds harsh in many ways, so it is necessary to examine its goals and results in their canonical context.

When Israel enters Canaan they must destroy all the people they find. There must be no intermarriage, no treaties, no adherence to other gods, because Israel is God's holy nation (7:1-6). These principles of holy war, or God-ordered conflict, are to be carried out for two basic reasons. The first is that the canon states clearly that God will use Israel to punish Canaan's sins. In Genesis 15:16-21 God tells Abraham that his descendants may possess the promised land only when Canaan's sin becomes unbearable. Exodus 34:11-16 offers the first order of total destruction of Israel's enemies, implying that Canaanite idolatry is the reason for this command. Leviticus 18:1-28 bluntly states that sexual perversion, human sacrifice and bestiality are some of the reasons the land will "vomit" the Canaanites. Deuteronomy 18:9-13 adds witchcraft to this list of horrors. The conquest is holy war in that it purges sin from a particular geographical location. Later in Scripture, Israel's own transgressions will cause them to be on the punishment side of a divinely initiated military invasion (see 2 Kings 17).

The second reason is that allowing idolatry to exist will tempt the people, especially in the polytheistic ancient context (7:4). The Baal-Peor episode in Numbers 25 confirms this assertion. Canaan was filled with idols, all of which had adherents and worldviews backing them.[35] Allowing any alternatives to or substitutes for Yahweh will compromise Israel's covenant distinctiveness.[36] So holy war also protects Israel's future in the land (7:4).

As always, God's love and promises precede any activity on Israel's part. God's choice of Israel was based on sheer electing love, not on numerical prominence (7:7), and the gift of land occurs so that Yahweh can keep promises made to the patriarchs (7:8). If Israel obeys the covenant, then they can expect God to keep all promises made to their ancestors and to them (7:9-16). They can expect Yahweh to fight for them as in the exodus experience, a prospect that should banish fear and idolatry from their hearts (7:17-26). In other words, Israel must act in faith based on God's word and past blessing. Such faith has been required of human beings since Genesis 1—2. Only as Israel trusts that God will be present, giving them victory, can they actually do what the Lord requires.[37] Belief based on love leads to covenant completion.

Love is also defined as remembering. Now Israel humbly accepts the fact that they are dependent on Yahweh for food and protection (8:1-5). They have learned this much from the desert. But they will soon enter the land, where they will be more prosperous and may be tempted to forget what God has done (8:6-9). Then remembering will keep their commitments current (8:10-18). Then remembering will save Israel from Canaan's fate

(8:19-20). It will teach them all over again that life consists of God's word, not bread alone (8:3), and that they have not saved themselves (8:17-18).

Presumption must disappear for the future to be bright.[38] Again, it is Canaan's overt wickedness, not Israel's inherent righteousness, that makes the land available (9:1-5). Moses knows Israel to be stubborn and sinful (9:6), an assertion he illustrates by recounting the golden calf incident (9:7-29). At that time Israel discovered that intercession, repentance and forgiveness constitute comprehensive covenant love (10:1-11). The people must remember their history's revealed meaning, not just its bare, unadorned and uninterpreted details.

Moses completes the book's second major section by defining love as total respect (fear) and careful obedience. Respect and love lead to service (10:12). Wholehearted love leads to complete obedience (10:12-13). Acceptance of God's ownership of all creation (10:14), a claim that excludes all other gods from power on earth or in heaven, means that God may choose whomever he wishes,[39] and Yahweh has chosen Israel (10:15). God's character is flawless, uncontaminated by greed or prejudice, filled with kindness for the weak (10:17-18). This knowledge should move Israel to internal faith (10:16), external kindness to non-Israelites (10:19) and open worship of the Lord who created and protected their nation (10:21-22). Covenant faith operates from the soul to the world, not the opposite. Faith that is not internalized will not result in God-pleasing works.

As he has already done in Leviticus 26 and as he will do again in Deuteronomy 27—28, Moses tells Israel they have a choice to make. They may either obey God and be blessed or reject the covenant and be cursed (11:1-32). This call to decision indicates a distinct portion of the covenant text concludes here. God's love means the Lord wishes to bless, not judge. The people's love will determine which they receive. Having had love portrayed as the key to their future with Yahweh, the people should only ask what must be obeyed for the covenant blessings to unfold.

Canonical Synthesis: God's Oneness and Human Response

Canonical reflection on this section properly begins with Moses' treatment of God's oneness. Claus Westermann believes that Exodus 20:3-6, Deuteronomy 5:6-10, Deuteronomy 6:4-9, and Isaiah 40:28-31, 43:10 and 44:6 represent three stages in the Old Testament's conception of monotheism. The first stage states that the exodus means Israel must serve Yahweh but does not comment on the existence of other gods (cf. Ex 20:2-6; Deut 5:6-10). In the second stage Israel conceived of God as one, as unique (Deut 6:4-9), while in the third stage "divinity is denied for any other God."[40] Though Westermann's historical reasoning may be questioned, he does trace a legitimate canonical trajectory. From Sinai on the canon increasingly demands a singular devotion to the only God who exists, who is the only God who created what exists. By New Testament times serious Jewish thinkers almost uniformly believed that failure to adhere to one God doomed Israel to foreign subjection.

Christoph Barth suggests another canonically significant implication found in Deuteronomy 6:4-9. Moses clearly argues that there is one God and then explains in Deuteronomy 12 that Yahweh will choose one place where worship may occur, a choice that will limit polytheism's advance among the people. Ultimately Israel grasped the importance of a unified worship of a unique God. Barth suggests, "The uniqueness of God was the driving force behind the ultimate abandonment of the fatal pluralism. By the end of the royal period, especially with the destruction of Israel, it was being increasingly accepted that worship must be at the one house of God at Jerusalem, the one place that God had chosen to let his name dwell (Deut. 12)."[41] Barth's comment captures the spirit of the Former Prophets, all of which ascribe Israel's demise to idolatry and tolerance of pluralistic paganism.

Another canonical consideration has already been raised in the comments on Deuteronomy 1:6—4:43. As in that segment, in Deuteronomy 5—11 Moses freely draws upon experiences related in Exodus, Leviticus and Numbers to illustrate principles he teaches the people. He is steadfastly contextual in his approach. For example, he uses God's provision after Numbers 14 to remind Israel not to forget Yahweh's love (Deut 8:1-20). He also uses the golden calf incident to illustrate Israel's lack of intrinsic merit for election (Deut 9:7—10:11). Later texts such as Ezekiel 20 and Psalm 78 strive to mirror serious contextual illustration of how history and current issues intersect.

References to holy war in Deuteronomy 7 set the stage for comments about how Israel actually waged war during the conquest of Canaan. Joshua destroys the people of Jericho (Josh 6:20-27), Ai (Josh 8:20:27) and other cities according to Moses' command in Deuteronomy 7:1-26 and Deuteronomy 20:1-20. But failure to take Moses seriously results in the existence of nations who test Israel's commitment to Yahweh in the Judges era (Judg 2:20-23). Eventually Israel chooses Canaanite gods, according to 1-2 Kings and Hosea, which in turn leads to disaster (see 2 Kings 17). Israel failed to understand why holy war was to be fought, failed to see why culture wars were necessary, but then learned to bow to foreign gods in exile. By failing to obey Deuteronomy 7:1-26 the people embraced the consequences outlined in Deuteronomy 11:16-21.

Some of the canonical significance of Deuteronomy 6:4-9 for Jesus' teaching was noted in the comments on Leviticus 19:18. Jesus states that the whole law and prophets are based on loving God and loving neighbor (Mk

12:29-31; Mt 22:34-40), and it is evident that the Ten Commandments may be divided into these two basic categories.

Brevard Childs also observes that Jesus claims the Father's oneness includes himself, without jeopardizing God's character. Like the Old Testament, the New Testament affirms that "God's oneness also demands his uniqueness. He is one of a kind for God alone is God, who will tolerate no rival."[42] At the same time, Childs writes, "a central affirmation of the New Testament is that God's oneness (1 Cor. 8:4; Gal. 3:20) is not threatened, but rather confirmed by Jesus Christ. God does not cease to be one. According to John's Gospel, Jesus testifies: 'I and the Father are one' (10:30; cf. I Tim. 2:5)."[43] Jesus' claim is to be by nature part of the uniqueness and unity of God's personhood.

Finally, Moses' admonition to fear the Lord as a motive for service sets the stage for wisdom teaching such as that found in Psalms 1 and 37, in Job and in Proverbs. In both Deuteronomy and Proverbs, Christopher Wright comments, "there is emphasis on the virtues of faithfulness, kindness, work, compassion, social justice, especially for the poor and oppressed, generosity, impartiality, and incorruptibility."[44] Both books also offer readers life or death as a result of their actions, focus on community life and stress adherence to divine principles as the key to life. These similarities do not mean that Deuteronomy was compiled by court sages during Israel's monarchial period, as Weinfeld suggests,[45] but it does mean that the canon's later emphasis on wisdom has many parallels with the Law's stressing of covenant fidelity.

The God Who Deserves and Defines Worship: Deuteronomy 12:1—16:17

Specific covenant stipulations emerge in Deuteronomy 12—26 that actualize the love emphasized in Deuteronomy 6—11. Having discussed interior matters, Moses now outlines the covenant's outward forms and institutions.[46] He thereby provides a framework for Israel's religious and governmental realms in the land and sets forth standards by which subsequent generations may judge their own activities and those of their ancestors. The Former and Latter Prophets use this material to evaluate Israelite history.

Exodus 25—31, Exodus 35—40 and Leviticus 1—27 have already highlighted the primacy of worship in the covenant community. Worship includes sacrifices for sin but also encourages offerings of joy and gratitude that benefit the priests and express how highly Israel esteems Yahweh. Worship requires order so that the people will not make their own destructive rules or follow the practices of the Canaanites. In other words, disasters like Exodus 32 and Numbers 25 must not be repeated if Israel is to flourish spiritually and materially. Deuteronomy 12:1—16:17 addresses these concerns and not surprisingly does so from a monotheistic perspective.

All biblical law begins with God's absolute uniqueness and Israel's absolute commitment to this principle. Thus the first specific covenantal stipulation that governs worship tells Israel to destroy Canaanite gods and their worship sites (12:1-3). The whole land must be claimed for Yahweh, since the Lord created the land and gave it to Israel. God does not want Israel to replace worship of Yahweh in Canaanite shrines either. Rather Israel must "seek the place the LORD your God will choose . . . to put his Name there for his dwelling" (12:5) and bring their sacrifices there (12:5-14). Having a special place of worship will guard against "everyone [doing] as he sees fit" (12:8), a particularly risky lifestyle for a nation in covenantal partnership with the Lord. It will also facilitate the positive institutionalization of covenant worship, which will in turn guard against the acceptance of deplorable idolatrous practices such as child sacrifice (12:29-32; cf. Lev 18:21-30).

Deuteronomy 12 depicts the end of a journeying Israel that has the ark and tabernacle in their midst.[47] Once in Canaan the ark will obviously reside in one place, while the people will scatter throughout the land (see Num 34). J. A. Thompson notes that after the conquest the ark "rested at Gilgal (Jos. 4:19; 5:9; 7:6), Shechem (Jos. 8:33; cf. 24:1) and Bethel (Jdg. 20:18, 26-28; 21:2) at various times."[48] When Israel had been in the land for some time Shiloh had probably become a central sanctuary (cf. Josh 18:1; Judg 18:31; 1 Sam 1—2; Jer 7:12-15).[49] Then David brought the ark to Jerusalem during his reign (c. 1010-970 B.C.) to centralize worship in his capital city, an act that God clearly blesses (2 Sam 6—7). Solomon transferred the ark to the newly built temple (c. 960 B.C.; 1 Kings 8:1-13), whereupon Yahweh placed his name there forever (1 Kings 9:3). Canonically speaking, Moses' comment about a single place God will fix permanently does not reach fruition until God's statement in 1 Kings 9:3. Still, wherever the ark goes is the place where sacrifice and festival ought to occur. Forgiveness and national solidarity must be secured as God dictates, not as human ingenuity imagines, to ward off the encroachment of idolatrous practices (Deut 12:29-32).

Deuteronomy 13 continues Moses' emphasis on sole allegiance to Yahweh and on potential dangers in the promised land. Moses suggests three scenarios in which idolatry could emerge. First, he states that talented and persuasive prophets might steer Israel toward other deities (13:1-5). Perhaps he has Balaam in mind. Second, he observes that family members may want to serve gods that did not deliver Israel from Egypt (13:6-11). The golden calf incident certainly fits this description. Third, a specific town may secede from correct worship (13:12-18). In each case death is required (13:5, 10, 15; cf. Lev 20:1-27). Idolatry poses the clearest threat to national health and security (13:17-18).

By now Moses' comments have linked his current situation to Israel's history in Egypt, at Sinai and in the desert. They have also reminded readers of Exodus 20, Leviticus 1—7 and Leviticus 18—20 and have always kept the first commandment in the foreground. In Deuteronomy 14:1—16:17 he speaks of religious observances mentioned in Exodus, Leviticus and Numbers. Each topic, whether clean and unclean food (14:1-21; cf. Lev 11:1-23), tithes (14:22-29; cf. Num 18:21-29), debt cancellation (15:1-11; cf. Lev 25:8-38), freeing indentured servants (15:12-18; cf. Lev 25:38-55), redeeming the firstborn (15:19-23; cf. Ex 13:1-16) or celebrating national festivals (16:1-17; cf. Lev 23:4-8; Num 28:16—29:40), is addressed to highlight Israel's status as God's people (14:1-3; cf. Ex 19:5-6). Yahweh has chosen Israel to honor God among the nations by being different than other peoples. The goal is for them to stand out from, not be absorbed by, the cultural setting to which they are going. Historically speaking, their relationship to Yahweh sets them apart, and it will be this covenantal agreement that does so in the distant future.

The God Who Defines Effective Leadership: Deuteronomy 16:18—18:22

If it proves nothing else, Moses' career highlights the value of effective, God-called leadership. Once Moses dies the nation will face the ongoing difficulty of determining what leaders have God's approval. This section's depiction of a theology of leadership has far-reaching practical value for Israel's future. Over time, as the people applied these principles for judges, kings and priests they were able to draw conclusions that informed assessments such as those found in the Prophets and the Writings. Standards presented here differ from common ancient thought, which creates the Bible's unique perspective on public service that continues to influence moral governing.

Theology and public life are inseparable in Moses' opinion. Judges must be fair and immune to bribes (16:18-20). In other words, they must mirror Yahweh's immunity to injustice, manipulation and self-serving hypocrisy. They must also be willing to carry out even capital punishment, especially if the offense relates to idolatry (16:21—17:7), and must seek assistance from the Levites in determining especially difficult cases (17:8-13). Even in civil cases, monotheism and cooperation with Yahweh's priests take priority. Israel's status as a kingdom of priests (Ex 19:5-6) depends on such God-directed interaction.

God's definition of successful kings is especially startling by ancient standards. Israelite kings are given no special standing above ordinary citizens in God's eyes. Unlike Egyptian pharaohs, the Israelite king is not considered a god, and unlike Mesopotamian kings, he is not the mediator between Yahweh and the people.[50] He must not use the office to gain wealth, wives or foreign prestige (17:16-17). Kings must be native Israelites to guard against a departure from covenant faith (17:15).[51] Since kingship is acceptable yet not commanded, God must choose the king (17:15), and the king must keep a copy of the law as his guide for leadership (17:18-20). Reverence for God will "keep the king mindful of his true relationship to his fellow Israelites," which is as an equal, not a lord.[52]

Seen this way, kings are public servants, not masters of the masses. They are accountable to the covenant and are responsible for embodying and enforcing its principles. Thus, though kingship has secular duties, it is truly a religious institution that touches the heart and soul of the nation.[53] Israelite history rarely produced such a king, as 1-2 Samuel, 1-2 Kings, 1-2 Chronicles and the prophets testify, but when such persons emerged (e.g., Hezekiah and Josiah; cf. 2 Kings 18—23) they proved the value of high standards. Godly kings reflected the nature of the God who gave them their authority.

Priestly rights and responsibilities have already been stated in great detail in Leviticus 1—10. Here Moses simply reminds Israel of these items but does so in a way that ties priests to this section's other functionaries. Since they have no landed inheritance, the priests may live on offerings (18:1-2), sacrifices (18:3-5) and collective ministry earnings (18:6-8). Like the judge and king, the priest pleases Yahweh through service, not through seizing what is not his or by claiming societal status. The priests possess authority and prestige,[54] yet such standing comes because God chooses them, not because of any inherent or inherited merit.

Finally, Moses differentiates between true, God-sent prophets and prophets who are to be ignored. Once again the goal is to separate the covenant people from the surrounding nations and their religious worldviews. Canaanites seek mediums and spiritists to determine the future, but Israel must not do so (18:9-13). For God will call, equip and instruct one(s) like Moses to guide them (18:14-20). Prophets who presume to speak when they are not called or who speak on behalf of other gods must be put to death (18:20; cf. 13:1-5). Yahweh's prophets' predictions come true every time, without fail (18:21-22). Any other standard is not from God. Prophets thus have two basic rules: to preach the covenant (18:17-20) and to be perfectly accurate (18:21-22). By implication Moses claims these attributes as his own. Therefore, the prophets' consistency, fidelity and accuracy mirror the truthfulness God displays, just as the judge's honesty, the king's humility and the priest's helpfulness match God's.

Canonical Synthesis: God's Standards for Leaders

Few sections of the Pentateuch have the practical canonical value of this segment. Every succeeding biblical text that features a judge, king, priest or prophet now has revealed standards for these characters. Readers also have the privilege of assessing such persons, even when Old Testament authors do not do so overtly. Put another way, even if the author of 1-2 Kings did not judge monarchs readers could apply these standards themselves. Thus from now on authors will not always tell readers what to think about crucial characters and events, since these principles have been stated. Also, readers may determine that by revealed standards the writer of 1 Kings 16—22 is not too critical of Ahab, or that Jeremiah does not judge Jehoiakim too harshly (Jer 22:13-23), or that Isaiah is properly pleased with Hezekiah (Isa 36—39) or that Jeremiah correctly unmasks Hananiah as a false prophet (Jer 28). The fact that leaders can now be assessed by divine rules of conduct affects the theology of a vast portion of the rest of the Old Testament canon.

The God Who Defines an Orderly Society: Deuteronomy 19—26

So far in Deuteronomy Yahweh has been systematically defining a community in his image. Israel's past, Israel's interior and exterior love for God, Israel's worship and Israel's leaders all mark this chosen nation as a unusual, chosen, covenant people. In other words, Yahweh is creating a holy nation, a nation of priests, people who are holy as he is holy (Ex 19:5-6; Lev 11:44). At this point the specific covenant stipulations extend beyond worship and leadership categories to specific elements of daily life. Holiness must permeate polite society if Israel is to reflect Yahweh's character in the promised land.

Mercy, fairness, fidelity and justice, all clearly established divine character traits, undergird the commands found in Deuteronomy 19—26. These attitudes allow Israel to convey to one another in the land the sort of grace that God extends to the people in giving them the land. The establishment of cities of refuge certainly displays these principles. Mercy must be shown to the person who has killed someone unintentionally (19:1-7), yet justice, already defined as the punishment fitting the crime in Exodus 21:23-25 and stated the same way again in Deuteronomy 19:21, must be meted out on those who commit premeditated murder (19:11-13). Fairness and a desire to purge evil from the holy land demand capital punishment in such cases (19:13), just as mercy and justice demand that innocent blood not be shed in the land God gives them (19:8-10).

The existence of cities of refuge will be evidence that God has kept the land promise. Having any place of refuge fulfills the confident lawmaking Moses undertakes in Numbers 35:9-28 and Deuteronomy 4:41-43. Calling for three more safe areas when God enlarges their territory (19:8) magnifies and multiplies the expectation of possessing Canaan. God obviously shows strong fidelity to his promises, so Israel must show a similar fidelity by applying these principles, which will allow them to gain control over violence in their midst.[55] God's people must take a religious view of life and death, not just a functional one.[56] As they embrace God's approach to the loss of life they can more readily become a community committed to holiness among the nations.

As a further safeguard to justice, Moses regulates testimony in civil cases (19:15-21). To combat malicious charges and wrongful convictions, two or more witnesses are required to convict someone of a crime (19:15-16). Further, individuals who prove to be false accusers must be given the sentence they tried to secure for their enemy (19:18-21). Again the goal is to purge sin from the land (19:13, 19). Moses also intends for the law to restrain anyone thinking of committing perjury. God has never lied to Israel and has already prohibited bearing false witness against a neighbor (Ex 20:16). Israel must imitate Yahweh and obey Yahweh's word for a truly unique community to emerge.

Mercy, justice, fairness and fidelity are to remain constant impulses even during war. No aspect of life lies outside Yahweh's realm of authority or realm of concern. Every war Israel fights must be fought only at God's command, with God's presence and empowerment and with God's assistance (20:1-4). Because of Yahweh's role, it is unnecessary to conscript unwilling soldiers (20:5-9). It is also possible to show mercy to cities that Israel's armies will engage after the conquest (20:10-15) and to preserve the invaded land (20:19-20). At the same time, fidelity to the Lord's word means destroying the Canaanites, whom God has decided to punish (20:16-18). All wars, especially the holy war necessary to conquer Canaan, transpire when and how God commands.[57] Israel is not a rogue nation with a divine license to kill whenever and whomever they wish. Even the way Israel fights battles must set them apart from other nations.[58]

Institutional matters now give way to community and personal issues, but covenant principles continue to guide Moses' exhortation. God's authority still governs each situation discussed,[59] particularly cases that are hopefully rare ones, such as those found in Deuteronomy 21. Even life in Canaan will produce certain odd situations, such as unsolved murders (21:1-9), the desire to marry a captive woman rather than an Israelite (21:10-14), the temptation in a polygamous marriage to reward children of a favorite wife instead of the actual firstborn (21:15-17), the punishment of an incorrigible son (21:18-21) or the disposal of recipients of capital offense (21:22-23).

God's instructions in these cases are calculated to purge guilt from the land (21:9, 21, 23). In other words, they stress the power of justice, fairness and grace to overcome iniquity. Elders and priests must work together to offer sacrifices that remove taint from citizens of towns where unsolved murders occur (21:1-9). Covering of crime is thereby eradicated. Captive women and unpopular children are given rights uncommon in the ancient world. Conversely, those who dishonor parents are not allowed to set a negative example for others (21:21), and dead bodies, apparently an equivalent of unclean food,[60] must not defile the land (21:23). Personal rights and societal protection from injustice keep oppression and abuse in check.

It is difficult to categorize the series of laws found in Deuteronomy 22:1—23:14. Broadly speaking, they deal with loving one's neighbor in the holy community (cf. Lev 19:18), though some laws relate to stewardship of the land itself (e.g., 22:6-7, 9), which may reflect back to God's command that the human race care for the earth in Genesis 1:26-31. Once again Moses' major concern is for Israel to avoid defiling the land by acting like the Canaanites.

Israel must make a special effort to protect private property by returning lost animals to their proper owners (22:1-4). They must protect the land and workers from senseless danger (22:6-8). Also, they must protect sexuality, agriculture and fashion from mixtures that parallel pagan worship practices in Canaan and Egypt (22:5, 9-12).[61] Finally, they must protect the role of marriage in the holy community. Sexual activity has boundaries. Women are not objects of pleasure, as Leviticus 18—20 has already demonstrated. Men must keep wedding vows as scrupulously as women do. A man may not lie about his wife's virtue (22:13-19). Adultery, rape, premarital sex and incest jeopardize the family (22:20-30). These examples help the people know how to obey God's prohibitions against adultery, bearing false witness and coveting (cf. Ex 20:14, 16-17).

Israel's assembly and camp constitute the physical context for Israel's community. As such the assembly in particular defines "neighbor" within the covenant setting. Persons emasculated according to Canaanite worship practices or born as children dedicated to foreign gods may not be part of Israel's religious and legislative assembly (23:1-2).[62] Nor may persons committed to altering Israel's worship to include pagan elements enter the assembly (23:3-6). Foreigners are not excluded forever (23:7-8), but they must wait at least three generations before qualifying. Such laws approximate modern statutes about foreign-born persons serving in government. As Leviticus 15 has already indicated, Israel must be careful to keep clean before the Lord (23:9-14). The very camp itself mediates God's presence (23:14), so the holy community must take care to preserve the camp as a witness to God's glory.

No fewer than twenty-two case laws appear in Deuteronomy 23:15—

25:19. Each one continues Moses' application of the Ten Commandments[63] and his exhortation to keep the laws delivered in Exodus, Leviticus and Numbers. Every solution depicted leads Israel back to the concept of being a holy community in a holy land under the leadership of a holy God. Yahweh especially insists on behavior that clearly establishes Israel as a unique people in a grindingly sinful world.

Moses concludes this section of the book with comments about firstfruits and tithes and with a final exhortation. The commands about the firstfruits convey a simple elegance that makes the Yahweh-Israel relationship sound loving yet powerful. Once safely in the land, the Israelites must take the first fruit the land yields to the central sanctuary God will choose, give the produce to the priest and then confess that Yahweh chose and freed Israel from Egypt (26:1-11). Gerhard von Rad considers this confession one of Israel's oldest,[64] and the statement summarizes the basis of God's reason for making a covenant with Israel, as well as Israel's motivation for making a covenant with Yahweh. Yet it is not possible to use the confession for dating Deuteronomy, as von Rad attempted to do, a fact several scholars have asserted.[65] The issue is not whether the lack of any mention of Sinai means there were separate Sinai and Deuteronomy traditions either,[66] since the basis for all covenant making is relationship, not the contents of the covenant itself.

After confessing God's grace in giving the land, the people are to offer a prayer for Yahweh's continued blessing (26:12-15). This prayer, like the confession of faith, recognizes Israel's total dependence on the loving covenant God. Israel has no autonomous existence. Without Yahweh they would remain sojourners, strangers, captives to their own moral standards.

The oration ends with a statement of the covenant's mutuality. God commands Israel to observe the law with all their heart and soul (26:16) as they have declared with their mouths they will do (26:17). Because of their verbal pledge they are Yahweh's "treasured possession" (26:18), set to receive fame and glory given by the creator of all nations who has called them to be a holy nation (26:19). Deuteronomy 26:1-19 therefore offers a summary of major canonical events. God has created all nations (26:19), has called and redeemed Israel from slavery (26:5-9), has given Israel divinely revealed standards (26:16-19) and has promised to give the people a homeland (26:1-4). The covenant's general and specific stipulations are based on "objective historical facts"[67] encased in the canon.

Canonical Synthesis: Social Consciousness
Because many of the laws in Deuteronomy 19—26 are reminders of laws previously stated in the Pentateuch, their general canonical significance has already been mentioned. For example, Deuteronomy 20:1-20 and Deuteron-

omy 21:10-14 cover matters related to holy war in Canaan, a topic that observations on Deuteronomy 7:1-26 have addressed. Similarly, laws on distinctions between clean and unclean persons and objects such as those found in Deuteronomy 23:1-14 have received treatment in the discussion of Leviticus 11—15. The same may be said for the repetition in Deuteronomy 22:13-30 of principles of sexual purity in Leviticus 18—20. What occurs in such passages is not mere blank repetition, however, but rather the application of revealed principles in a new setting. Laws are not used in novel ways in successive Old Testament books. They are used contextually to speak to another generation of Scripture hearers and readers.

One of the most evident canonical usages of this section is the Prophets' utilization of the foundational principles undergirding Deuteronomy 23:15—24:22. Virtually every Latter Prophet of any length demands that justice, fairness and mercy be extended to even the poorest Israelite. The fact that God created all persons in his image makes this command reasonable. Amos particularly focuses on the theme of justice. The prophets decry oppression of all kinds, including that created by false oaths (Deut 19:15-18; Hos 10:4) and dishonest scales (Deut 25:13-16; Mic 6:11). They use covenant standards to call the people back to their God (e.g., Jer 3:11-20; Amos 4:6-11).

Certain later texts make use of or reflect specific passages in Deuteronomy 19—26. For instance, the book of Ruth is built on 25:7-10. Boaz becomes the one who restores his deceased relative's family by marrying Ruth and acting as kinsman redeemer (Ruth 3—4). Thus he becomes the human agent of God's mercy. Paul uses Deuteronomy 25:4 in two places (1 Cor 9:9; 1 Tim 5:18) to illustrate his contention that pastors and apostles deserve financial support. He also cites Deuteronomy 21:22-23 in Galatians 3:13 to argue that on the cross Christ bore believers' culpability for not obeying the law. Jesus' means of death was singled out as wretched and unclean by the law itself, Paul reasons, and this death thereby removes the wretchedness and uncleanness of those who by faith trust in Christ and receive the promise of the Spirit (Gal 3:13-14). Each of these usages attempts to do with Deuteronomy in their settings what Moses does with earlier laws in his setting in Deuteronomy: use previous Scripture to exhort a community of faith to do God's will in a new situation.

Finally, Deuteronomy 24:1-4 is cited in Matthew 19:1-12 by some Pharisees as evidence for the acceptability of divorce for any reason. Jesus isolates one reason for divorce in Matthew 19:9—sexual misconduct, which corresponds to the phrase "he finds something indecent about her" in Deuteronomy 24:1. Due to this reduction from "any reason" to a specific reason, Jesus' disciples, shocked, wonder if it is good to marry. Jesus' comments reflect Moses' concern for fidelity and strong marriages as the foundation for a holy community. Jesus' quoting of Genesis 2:24 in Matthew 19:4-6 reflects canonical reasoning. That is, Genesis 2:24 serves as a foundation for Deuteronomy 24:1, which in turn undergirds Jesus' teachings that are inscripturated in Matthew's Gospel. Jesus offers what he considers the proper application of Mosaic writings to the question at hand. By doing so he reaffirms the importance of marital permanence in the covenant community.[68]

The God Who Offers Blessings or Consequences: Deuteronomy 27—28

Moses calls the people to decision now that the covenant requirements have been described. He explains the benefits of covenant keeping and the dangers of covenant breaking in Deuteronomy 27—28 and then asks Israel to commit themselves in covenant renewal in Deuteronomy 29—30. This procedure basically parallels the fourth segment of the Hittite vassal treaty.[69] It also parallels Leviticus 26, which concludes the Sinai revelation with a similar choice between life and death. Thus this material fits the canonical and cultural requirements for the final stages of a covenant. Israel surely understood what was at stake.

The blessings and curses are preceded by regulations for a covenant monument. When Israel enters the land they are to erect on Mt. Ebal stones inscribed with "the words of this law" to remind them of their commitments and to set aside a place where future renewal ceremonies may take place. John Sailhamer notes that this procedure was common in the ancient world.[70] Besides serving as a prominent site for a covenant memorial, the choice of Ebal establishes it as a place where a future extensive renewal ceremony may unfold.

With a location chosen, Moses next relates a scenario for renewal. Half the tribes will stand on the barren Ebal to represent cursing, while the other half will stand on the more fertile, adjacent Mt. Gerizim to represent God's blessings. Once in place, the people shall pronounce curses on those who violate the laws related to monotheism, love of neighbor, sexual purity and social justice (27:9-26). No blessings are stated, but the people will be standing on the chief physical blessing for obedience, which is the land itself. Covenant renewal of their relationship with God must be considered the most important spiritual blessing.

Other blessings are noted in Deuteronomy 28:1-14. Covenant obedience will mean that God will give them prominence (28:1), prosperity (28:3-6), peace (28:7) and continual provision (28:8-13). Monotheism remains the key to God's favor (28:14). God desires to bless, not to curse, so the covenant is a positive offer of grace to an unlanded people.

Though they are given in great detail, there are only two basic consequences mentioned. First, financial collapse will result due to crop failure and infertility (28:15-24). Second, and more significant for the rest of the canon, Israel will suffer military defeat. That will result in exile, the loss of the promised land (28:25-68). Terror and suffering will mark their days in exile. Having become idolaters, they will have only "gods of wood and stone" (28:36) to help them, which means they will be helpless indeed. Just as Israel once punished the Canaanites by conquering their lands, so Israel itself will be judged through the invasion of a foreign power. The mirror reflection of holy war will be an ugly image to them.

Canonical Synthesis: Blessings and Consequences in Israelite History
Coupled with the threats in Leviticus 26, the warnings and predictions found here provide fertile ground for subsequent biblical authors who link Israel's covenant fidelity or lack thereof to Israelite history. Joshua 1:1-9 declares that Joshua's ability to lead Israel into the promised land will be directly related to his adherence to Moses' teaching. Likewise Israel's breaking of the laws about holy war yields defeat in the battle of Ai (Jos 7:1-12), and idolatry leads to God's allowing Israel's enemies to oppress them in Judges 2:20-23. Historical cause and effect occurs according to divine rules in these texts. Second Kings 17:7-23 interprets Israel's history from Solomon's era (c. 970-930 B.C.) to the destruction of Jerusalem (c. 587 B.C.) in terms of covenantal cause and effect. None of the other books in the Prophets and the Writings dispute this claim. The entire canonical witness is that Israel's prosperity, security and tenure in the land depended on Yahweh's blessing, which could be guaranteed only by faithfulness to the covenant Yahweh revealed.

Deuteronomy 27—28 amounts to an honest offer of divine grace or divine judgment. The fact that God reveals the offer of relationship at all constitutes grace, since human beings have no means of discerning Yahweh's will without Yahweh's communicated guidance. So Israel's opportunity to receive blessings for doing what they should do as God's creatures represents an extended, unexpected graciousness. Rejecting grace brings certain disaster. Yahweh's judgment always follows spurned grace. Israel can only merit punishment by rejecting Mosaic law and, in future years, the prophetic and wisdom writings based on that law. Each new generation must learn the results of responding to Deuteronomy 27—28, just as the Israelites discovered in Numbers 13—14 the implications of not responding properly to Leviticus 26.

The God Who Renews the Covenant: Deuteronomy 29—30
God's standards have now been explained, but Moses' work is not completed. He has linked Sinai to Moab, the first generation to the second and the grace of God to Israel's life (29:1). Now, in his third message he must summon the

people to embrace the covenant that determines their future. Moses considers this call one that mediates life to Israel through the revealed word of God (30:15). It is also a call that approximates the ancient treaty form's calling of witnesses to ratify the covenant.[71]

God's word enlivens in several ways here. First, it explains Israel's future life by interpreting their past (29:1-18). Walther Eichrodt observes that it is equally true that the covenant has been established permanently at Sinai and in Deuteronomy and yet is a living relationship that must constantly be renewed.[72] Second, the covenant they have received is personal, understandable and accessible (29:9-15; 30:11-14). Moses' constant use of "you" accentuates this point. The law challenges Israel to achieve difficult moral and military tasks, but attaining these goals is not beyond their capabilities.[73] Third, the covenant awakens Israel to service of the living God, who bears no resemblance to the idols the nations worship (29:16-18). Because Yahweh lives Israel lives and may relate to and obey the one creator, Yahweh.

Fourth, because God is a living, relational being, the Lord expresses wrath at covenant infidelity (29:19-29). Wrath is part of God's revelation (29:27-28), for it serves to educate Israel that God's judgment lasts only until the people repent, until they circumcise their hearts and love and serve Yahweh again (30:1-10).[74] Fifth, God's revelation is based on grace, and Israel's response to this grace should be based on gratitude fuelled by love. Von Rad argues that the grace expounded here negates any sense of salvation by merit or works:

Rather all the commandments are simply a grand explanation of the command to love Yahweh and to cling to him alone (Deut. vi. 4f.). And this love is Israel's return of the divine love bestowed upon her. The many imperatives in Deuteronomy are therefore appeals, sometimes implicit and sometimes explicit, for gratitude to be shown in action, and Deuteronomy regards them as easy to fulfil.[75]

Obligation results from love; obligation does not cause love.

Sixth, God's gift of land is a physical symbol of divine grace, just as the promise of presence is the main spiritual blessing God offers (30:17-18).[76] Lack of loving obedience on Israel's part is the only way the physical and spiritual blessings may be forfeited. Otherwise love and life are inseparable (30:19-20).

The God Whose Word Gives Life: Deuteronomy 31—32

Deuteronomy places extreme importance on words. Moses speaks to the Israelites words that are God's words. Since Genesis 1:3 God's words produce activity. God's spoken word initiates creation. It also initiates judgment (e.g., Gen 6:7), calling (Gen 12:1), law (Ex 20:1) and community (Ex 19:3-6). Life consists of God's word (Deut 8:3). Written down, God's word is a testimony to how persons and nations may enjoy God-given life (Ex 17:14; 24:4; 31:27). All these principles are repeated in Deuteronomy 31—32 to demonstrate to Israel that obeying God by obeying God's word holds the key to future life in the holy land.

God's word directs Israel's present. Moses knows when to turn the nation over to Joshua by divine guidance (31:1-8). Though Israel's leadership has changed, the Lord's unremitting purpose to give the chosen people the land promised to the patriarchs has never altered. Joshua becomes the current human means by which a timeless God-given promise reaches fulfillment.

God's written word directs Israel's future. Moses writes down the law (31:9) so that it can be read to the people during the sabbatical year (31:10-13). The intention is that God's word be reverenced as authoritative and sufficient for life in the land.[77] The written word replaces Moses, the covenant's mediator, as God's recorder of deeds and commands. Thus it has the timeless standing as God's permanent declaration of holy standards to the holy people. Future hearers must learn to respect Yahweh and follow the written word (31:13).

God's written word predicts Israel's future. God reveals to Moses that the people will incur the consequences depicted in Deuteronomy 28:15-68 by turning to idols (31:14-20). The word's authority comes from its ability to anticipate what will occur as well as from its ability to interpret what has already happened and its ability to direct lives through instruction. The written word is timeless in the sense that it makes sense of the past, the present and the future.

God's written word provides a testimony that witnesses on behalf of the righteousness and against the wicked (31:21-30). Moses' song (32:1-43) provides a poetic theological summary that separates persons of faith from rebellious covenant breakers. The faithful confess with Moses that God alone created and sustains nations (32:6-8), that God alone called and redeemed Israel (32:8-14) and that God alone judges and forgives Israel (32:15-36). Their testimony, as timeless as the written word itself, agrees that there is no god but Yahweh (32:39). All other so-called gods are demons or less (32:15-18, 21). They confess that God's character is marked by justice, faithfulness and goodness (32:4). They understand that their confession brings them life (32:47).

Canonical Synthesis: God's Word and Moses

Text after text in the Old Testament testifies to the value of Moses' written works (see chapter two). No scholar seriously questions that the Pentateuch was considered Scripture before the Prophets or the Writings. Joshua, Judges,

Samuel and Kings state that Israel's political and economic fortunes rested on their adherence to God's words delivered through Moses (cf. Josh 1:1-9; 8:34-35; 13:8; 24:6; Judg 2:1-15; 1 Sam 12:6-15; 1 Kings 2:3; 8:56; 2 Kings 18—25). Isaiah recognizes Moses' ability to mediate divine miracles (Is 63:11-12), Jeremiah notes his work as intercessor (Jer 15:1), Micah credits him with effecting the exodus (Mic 6:4), and Malachi recognizes him as the great lawgiver (Mal 4:4). Ezra and Chronicles link Moses directly to specific written laws (Ezra 6:8; 2 Chron 8:13; 23:18; 25:4). The New Testament treats the law as divinely revealed Scripture (Jn 5:45-47; 2 Tim 3:16-17). Every subsequent canonical segment accepts the authority and value of the foundational truths forwarded in the Pentateuch. All theology flows from the notion that one God created the earth and human beings, called Abraham and his family to solve the sin problem caused by humans after the creation and inspired Moses to mediate a specific covenant to Abraham's family at a certain point in history.

The God Who Blesses Israel: Deuteronomy 33—34

The Pentateuch concludes its discussion of God's relationship to Israel the same way it began its description of God's relationship to the human race: it speaks of God blessing them (Gen 1:26-31). At the same time it continues to stress the written word's ability to interpret the past, to guide the present and to predict the future. It also presents Moses himself as a unique blessing to God's people.

Before his death, Jacob, the father of Israel, blessed his twelve sons (Gen 49:1-28). He mentioned past offenses (49:4), current character (49:22) and future roles such as Judah's ruling over the rest (49:10). Now Moses, Israel's spiritual father since Sinai (Deut 33:1-2), blesses in a similar manner. It is evident that Moses loves Yahweh (33:26-27) and wants Israel to know that God loves them (33:3). Love remains the impetus for God's work, Moses' work and the work Israel does for God. Due to this love, both Yahweh and Moses desire to bless Israel, not curse them. Leviticus 26, Deuteronomy 27—28 and Deuteronomy 32—33 all agree on this point.

Finally, Moses himself has been a blessing to Israel. He has led them to the brink of Canaan even while realizing that he would not share it with them (34:1-8). Moses is unique in Israel's history as a prophet who knew God face to face, as a miracle worker and as the deliverer of God's people (34:9-12). His ministry proves God's love for the people who hold the key to solving the sin problem recounted so meticulously from Genesis 3 to Deuteronomy 34.

Certain canonical linkages between the Law, the Prophets and the Writings emerge from Deuteronomy 33—34. The first is that Moses' conveying of wisdom and leadership to Joshua links the Law and the Prophets. In Deuteronomy 31:1-8 Moses orders Joshua to "be strong and courageous," Deuteronomy 34:9 marks Joshua as a man of wisdom, and Joshua 1:1-18 confirms that Joshua fulfills expectations by trusting Yahweh and obeying Moses' law. The second is that Joshua 1:8 focuses on meditation on the law as the key to Joshua's success, while Psalm 1:1-6, which opens the Writings, likewise stresses meditation on the word as the key to wisdom and blessing. The third is that the search for a prophet like Moses (cf. Deut 18:15-22; 34:9) leads to waiting for a prophet like Elijah at the end of the prophets (cf. Mal 4:1-6) and then to waiting for persons willing to rebuild the temple at the end of the Writings (cf. 2 Chron 36:13). Moses and Elijah serve as symbols of someone important who has not yet appeared.

Conclusion: The Pentateuch's Self-Revealing God

It is impossible to express appropriately the Pentateuch's theological significance, for without the Law the rest of Scripture has no foundation. Without the Pentateuch the history of God's work with human beings has no interpretative framework. Without the Pentateuch what Elmer Martens calls "God's design" could not be determined adequately from the rest of Scripture, if indeed without the Pentateuch those texts would have been written.

What the Law offers is an opening yet comprehensive comment about God. The Pentateuch portrays God as unique in being, essence, character and action. One God creates and sustains the entire human race, every nation, every person. Because there is only one Creator, that creator's standards apply to every creature. There is no other god to give them some other set of laws. Israel must bless all nations (Gen 12:1-9) by being a kingdom of priests to the other nations (Ex 19:5-6). No other revelation appears as an alternative to these truths. These standards must be obeyed, or judgment may be exercised against the whole earth (cf. Gen 6—9), against a specific non-Israelite nation (cf. Ex 5—15), against a region (cf. Gen 15:13-16; Lev 18:24-30) or against Israel (cf. Deut 28:15-68). God rules the earth. Therefore God rules history.

But God does not rule history silently, daring humans to guess how to relate to him. The Pentateuch's existence indicates that God desires a relationship with people enough to reveal to Moses history's meaning and the covenant's standards. Revelation comes to sinful people through one who speaks directly with God. It is understandable whether read or heard. Yahweh's grace creates the written word, then, as much as it permeates it. Revelation does not cease with Deuteronomy, however, so canonical interpreters are called to press forward, applying the Law to every subsequent written revelation.

7

The God
Who Gives Rest
in the Land

Joshua

. . . .

O NE OF THE CHIEF DIFFERENCES BETWEEN THE ENGLISH AND HEBREW
Bibles is that the former welds together Joshua, Judges, Ruth, 1-2 Samuel,
1-2 Kings, 1-2 Chronicles, Ezra, Nehemiah and Esther to form a section of
historical books, while the latter lists Joshua, Judges, Samuel and Kings
together as the Former Prophets (see chapter one). The English Bible thereby
depicts the events of Israel's history from conquest (c. 1400 or 1200 B.C.) to
the return to Jerusalem during the Persian era (c. 425 B.C.) and then proceeds
to Job. The Hebrew Bible describes events that span the conquest to a few
decades after the Babylonian captivity (c. 550) and then presents the
prophetic books. These canonical distinctions allow a subtle but important
interpretive shift in thinking.

By distinguishing Joshua to Kings as prophetic literature the Hebrew canon
emphasizes the common ground shared by the prophetic books (Isaiah,
Jeremiah, Ezekiel and the Twelve) and their more heavily historical predecessors.
This grouping treats the Former Prophets as both proclamation and history, as
history written from a specific perspective. It also allows readers to discover that
the prophets were neglected throughout Israel's past and that they influenced
books that they did not write. The Hebrew order helps readers absorb the events
from a prophetic viewpoint and then encounter the words the prophets
themselves used to interpret the times in which they lived.

In the Prophets segment of the canon, it becomes evident that the members of the prophetic movement united narrative history and a deep concern for theological commitment in their written works. They did so to make sense of their nation's history. Here prophets and those who agree with them preach and write God's word. Prophets explain and predict the past. Prophets anoint and denounce kings. The existence of the prophetic books indicates that long after the prophets died the people of God determined that these men and women indeed spoke for the Lord.

As they tell Israel's history, the Former Prophets display at least five distinct characteristics.[1] First, they assess the past based on God's covenant with Israel. Second, whenever predictions occur they are formed by noting how God has blessed or punished Israel in the past and by stating what specific promises the Lord makes to individuals such as David. Third, they create plot by selecting events and persons for inclusion that fit the prophetic view of the past, present and future. Fourth, they assess characters in the history based on whether they help gain or lose the promised land. Fifth, they encourage readers to turn to the Lord so they can experience blessing instead of punishment, as stated in Deuteronomy 27—28. The book of Deuteronomy heavily influences many of the prophetic writers.

Who wrote Joshua, Judges, Samuel and Kings and in what manner has sparked lively debate during the past half-century. This debate has been divided between scholars who think the books were written by a single author who carefully crafted a consecutive history using accurate sources and those who believe the texts were composed by two, three or more careful editors writing at different stages of Israel's history. These commentators include a variety of data in their discussions but usually focus on evidence from the books themselves.

Though it is impossible to be certain on this point, this volume assumes that a single anonymous individual carefully collected relevant source data and shaped this material into a consecutive account that spans Joshua—Kings. This person finished the work by about 550 B.C. The narrative itself is a sweeping account of Israel's tragic loss of the land it was promised in the Pentateuch.[2] This tragedy occurred because the nation failed to live up to covenant standards, particularly those found in Deuteronomy. Despite this correlation with Deuteronomy, it is unnecessary to conclude that the historian wrote any part of that book. Deuteronomy's influence is sufficient to explain the emphases in Joshua—Kings. Though the loss of the promised land was quite a negative event, the Deuteronomist did not view the situation as permanent. Living after the nation's defeat, this great writer looked to God's eternal covenant with David as proof that Israel was not finished.

With this portrait in place, some tentative conclusions about the author's methodology can be suggested. First, the author decided to compose a history of Israel based on the theological principles found in Deuteronomy. Second, this individual collected and collated the written sources the books mention, perhaps other materials not specified in the texts and unique information the author possessed. Third, the author wove an account that stressed a continuity of leadership and mission from Moses to Joshua, the growth of the monarchy, the promises to David and the prophets' role in predicting the nation's demise. Throughout the process the Deuteronomist stressed that God was the one who determined history. Thus theology and detail were combined in a way that created a history, an assertion that is discussed below.

Joshua continues the theological emphases detailed in Deuteronomy yet at the same time reaches as far back as Genesis 12:7 and Genesis 15:6-16 to keep promises made to Abraham. The book also looks ahead to when Israel will be at home in Canaan, at rest from enemies but surrounded by new challenges to their faith. Its message therefore is grounded in Mosaic principles and at the same time exemplifies the prophetic beliefs that will permeate the Latter Prophets. The book provides a theological, historical and canonical base for reviewing the Pentateuch's teachings and for preparing readers for the convictions that will dominate the next several books of the Old Testament.

There is wide agreement on Joshua's basic theological convictions, and there are also certain questions that the book brings to the minds of most interpreters. No one seriously disputes the fact that Joshua continues the theological themes begun in Deuteronomy. Joshua believes that Israel is only as strong as their commitment to the covenant that Moses describes in his final speeches to the people. War must be conducted according to the standards found in Deuteronomy 7 and Deuteronomy 20. The land must be distributed as Moses declared in Numbers 32 and Numbers 34—35. Passover and covenant renewal services are to be observed. Because of this obedience, God can be expected to fight for Israel in a manner similar to the exodus miracles (cf. Deut 27—28).

Even with these principles in place, though, difficulties remain. The chief one for most writers is the whole concept of holy war, a practice that seems contradictory to the biblical passages, many of them in Deuteronomy itself, that speak of God's love and kindness. This issue will be dealt with when it arises in the text, but it is appropriate to address it briefly now. If Joshua is read in isolation from the rest of the Old Testament this problem is more acute than if it is considered in canonical perspective. The canon does not deal with the death of the Canaanites in an arbitrary or a flippant manner. Rather it prepares the reader from Genesis 15:16 onward for this difficult material. There the text gives Israel four hundred years in Egypt for the

Amorites to change their ways. Leviticus 18:24-30 takes pains to state that the people of Canaan are involved in repulsively immoral practices that force Yahweh to judge them. What occurs is not a God-ordained hate mission. Rather it is divine judgment for sin similar to that which God has reluctantly meted out since the Garden of Eden. Deuteronomy 27—28 has made it abundantly clear that if Israel sins in a similar manner, they will also feel the effects of the wrath of the Lord. Israel has no moral free pass in these accounts. They are simply the human instruments of divine intervention in human affairs and are on this mission based on a once-in-history revelation from God through Moses.

Joshua unfolds in a fairly simple way. In Joshua 1—12 Israel conquers the bulk of Canaan according to the promises of God. Here God is portrayed as Israel's God, the God of all the earth (2:11) and the God who fights for Israel. The Lord prepares Joshua to take Moses' place (1:1-18), then prepares the people to fight for the land that will be their inheritance from their God (2:1—5:15) and then leads the people to victory (6:1—12:24). As in Exodus 15, the Lord is depicted as a warrior who gives Israel the victory over nations seemingly more numerous and powerful. Second, Joshua 13—21 describes the dividing of the land. God is seen here as the God who gives the people a place of rest. Ironically they must fight to possess the outer reaches of the land of rest, which indicates the divine expectation of faithfulness and obedience has not changed. Third, Joshua 22—24 describes covenant renewal ceremonies that present the key to long-term possession of the land. Here Yahweh is the God who expects real commitment in victory, in times of suffering, in times of plenty. These ceremonies prove that the Lord is still the same God who asked Abraham to sacrifice Isaac, who asked Jacob to give up the household idols, who called Moses, who renewed the covenant in the plains of Moab.

Each of these sections clings to the theology propounded in the Law. There is no deviation from monotheism. There is no wavering from the written word that Moses gave the people. There is no doubt that the land they are invading is from God, a gift that they in no way merit. Still, mistakes are made. The people are as human as their parents. But they confess their mistakes, unlike their parents, and learn to avoid the harsh penalties that come from ignoring God's explicit word. Because they do, the book of Joshua depicts what is in effect as great a theological and historical triumph as the nation ever experienced.

The God Who Fights for Israel: Joshua 1—12

It should come as no surprise to readers of the canon that the Lord is prepared to fight on Israel's behalf.[3] Yahweh delivered the people from Egyptian bondage through miraculous means. The victory song after the Red Sea covered Pharaoh's forces focuses on the notion that Yahweh is "warrior" (Ex 15:3) who gives Israel the upper hand over their foes. God also led the chosen nation by the fire and the cloud, gave them manna to eat and dwelled in their midst via the worship center. Exodus 17:8-16, Numbers 21:1-4 and Numbers 21:21-35 depict battles in which Yahweh directs Moses to wage war against enemies the Lord has destined for defeat. It was Yahweh who ordered the people to come to the land in the first place and who punished them for not invading earlier (see Num 13—14). The issue as the book begins is not whether the Lord intends to fight on Israel's side but on what terms and in what way this divine aid will happen. The terms become apparent as God prepares the nation to attack the promised land.

Just as Moses was the key to Israel's trek to the edge of victory, so Joshua will be the most important human element in their future success. He has already been designated as Moses' successor (Num 27:15-23; Deut 3:21-22; 31:1-8), and he must come to accept the fact that his efforts toward "the establishment or renewal of God's kingdom society must be a continuation of the work of Moses."[4] To this end God encounters Joshua, reminding him that he has been called to lead Israel at this time as surely as Moses was called to lead Israel at the burning bush and as surely as Jacob was called to be the bearer of the Abrahamic covenantal promises at Bethel.

God's leaders are not self-selecting. They are the chosen heads of the chosen nation. Like Moses before him, Joshua experiences a call that gathers themes from the past in order to explain the nation's future. He must take the people forward so that the promises to the "fathers," to the patriarchs, will come true (1:1-6). He must meditate on the received word of God mediated through Moses if he is to be successful and courageous in his efforts (1:7-9). At the same time he will have all the divine resources given his predecessor, most particularly the presence of God, an item that was vital to Moses' calling (cf. Ex 3:12; 4:12) and to Israel's ability to move forward in the desert (cf. Ex 34:5-9). Because of the Lord's presence he will succeed in his endeavor to do what Moses was not able to do due to the events of Numbers 20. Israel has no doubt that he is the man for the job (1:10-18).

This call story not only prepares Joshua for what follows but also prepares readers for the themes that will come in the rest of the book. First, the call account expresses the canonical basis for Israel's foray into Canaan. God promised the patriarchs that the land would belong to their descendants, and the patriarchs believed the Lord, thus making the promises apply directly to themselves (Gen 12:7; 15:1-6). For Joshua, as much as for Abraham, Isaac, Jacob and by extension Moses, the promises must be believed and pursued in faith. Lacking faith, the people will never accept an abstract notion such as Yahweh fighting for them. The attitude of the previous generation bitterly proved this point. Second, the call story provides the standard by which the nation must operate as they live by faith. They have the covenantal principles expressed in the Mosaic law to guide them. This law will restrain sin, reward obedience, direct their worship, govern their private affairs and demonstrate their distinctiveness as God's holy people. Without it they have no life (see Deut 8:3; 32:47).

Third, the story stresses the physical goal to which the nation is headed. Israel wants to possess the land their ancestors believed would belong to their descendants. Walter Kaiser links the patriarchs' faith and the land by noting that the promised land was the place where the promise of Israel being a blessing to all nations could come true. This place is Israel's inheritance, a fact Deuteronomy stresses twenty-five times, but if the chosen people live as God intends the holy land will also be the place of blessing for all nations.[5] Fourth, the account also highlights the spiritual goal for the people, which is to "rest" in the land after the long travels and travails they have endured (1:15; cf. Deut 3:20; 12:9-10; 25:19). Trent Butler comments, "It [rest] represents freedom from enemy oppression and deadly war. It represents life lived with God by the gift of God."[6] Ironically, though, he continues, the people must wage war so that the rest may come to them.[7]

Fifth, the means by which the goals will be achieved are also explained. There is one God who reveals himself to Joshua, and this is the same God whose self-revelation as the self-existent God of the patriarchs spurred Moses to confront Pharaoh. This God is the Lord of the whole earth, since Yahweh pledges to be with Joshua wherever he goes, a unique promise in a theological milieu that believed individual gods of the nations were land-locked to their adherents' geographical boundaries. God created the heavens and earth and thus is able to accompany the chosen people to any location necessary to give them victory. This is the God who promises to fight for Israel. God gives the land because the land belongs to God (cf. Lev 25:23).

Having prepared the leader for what will follow, Yahweh proceeds to prepare the people as well. The chief lesson for the people to absorb is that they must apply the old principles they have learned in the past to their new situation. They have what they need to succeed. No novel theologies or battle plans are necessary.

As they did in Numbers 13, the Israelites send spies to determine the nature of their objective (2:1). Almost captured, the spies are delivered by a prostitute named Rahab (2:2-7). This Canaanite woman bargains for her life, yet does so based on theological convictions. She says that Israel's earlier victories over the Egyptians and the Amorites have become known and that this knowledge has led to terror in Jericho (2:8-10).

Why? Because the Canaanites realize God's role in these events and reason that Yahweh is Lord of heaven and of earth (2:11). In other words, there is no place where an enemy of Yahweh would be safe. Yahweh is not containable in Egypt, the desert or in Canaan. This God crosses all boundaries and shatters limited conceptions of deity. In the mouth of a non-Israelite, this speech is all the more impressive. Her foreignness also emphasizes the theme that Israel's relationship with God blesses peoples beyond their ethnic group (cf. Gen 12:1-9). When the men conclude their agreement to spare Rahab and her family, they return to Joshua, certain Israel will triumph because God has prepared the way (2:15-24). Their optimism puts the fear expressed in Numbers 13—14 to shame.

Thus emboldened, Joshua leads Israel across the Jordan River, a barrier that has come to transcend mere physical boundary (3:1). God has brought them to the promised land. They are no longer beyond the Jordan (Deut 1:1), no longer in the place of punishment. John Gray writes, "Theologically and in its present context the crossing of the Jordan marks a decisive juncture, heralding the consummation of God's gracious acts in the fulfillment of the promise of settlement, or 'rest' in the Deuteronomistic idiom."[8] As in the miracle at the Red Sea, the people are privileged to pass over on dry ground, a miracle that links the exodus to the current historical situation. God's work continues in a similar way in a new and distinct setting. J. Alberto Soggin states that the similarities between the Red Sea miracle and this situation "takes nothing away from the miracle itself, which is reduced neither to a normal phenomenon nor to a 'routine,' but on the contrary is effectively given a setting in history, outside the whole mythical sphere."[9] Yahweh is with the people as powerfully as in the past in real strategic historical moments.

Israel marks the event by the piling of twelve stones at Gilgal, where they set up their headquarters (4:9, 20). Beyond the miraculous nature of this event, there are two practical theological reasons for its memorializing. One is that the people might remember to follow Joshua (4:14). The other is that Israel and the people of Canaan might know and fear the Lord (4:24). As with Rahab's confession of faith, the text emphasizes God's reputation. No issue in the conquest matters more than the glorification of the Creator before the peoples of the earth, so once again Israel's obligation to bless others rises to the surface.

Israel's enemies are terrified of news of the miraculous crossing of the Jordan (5:1), yet the Lord does not send the army into battle immediately. Instead two more preparatory events are ordered, both of which, like the dry-shod crossing into the land, tie the nation to the best days of its relationship with Yahweh. First, God commands that the men be circumcised, a tradition begun by Abraham in Genesis 17:9-14 that highlights Israel's covenant with the Lord. This specific ritual occasion also signals that the men who disobeyed in Numbers 13—14 have all died and the army may now move forward with the conquest (5:2-5; cf. Deut 2:16).[10] God has renewed the nation and readied them for the new task in the new land.

Second, the people celebrate Passover (5:10), which links them to their deliverance from Egypt. Moses carefully explained in Deuteronomy that every event in Israel's past has the impact of things that happened to them and that the covenant made at Sinai was truly made with this generation of Israelites (cf. Deut 5:3). This observance of Passover affirms such teaching. What God did for them in Egypt God does for them in Canaan. Their sense of history thereby informs their activities in the present. After Passover the manna ceases (5:10-12). Yahweh's provision now switches from the miraculous manna to the miracle of living off the bounty of the promised land. They receive the fruit of the land as a prelude to receiving the cities of the land.[11] God's people surely know now that they have experienced a new beginning, a fresh opportunity to be the Lord's holy nation.[12]

As if all the previous preparatory events were not sufficient to express God's intention to give Joshua the land, a final revelatory meeting occurs. Joshua has already been called to replace Moses in a Moses-like call experience. Now the leader of God's armies meets with the head of Yahweh's army, an encounter that the text says requires Joshua to remove his sandals due to it occurring on "holy ground" (5:15), an unmistakable reference to Exodus 3:1-6. God is truly with him as he was with Moses (cf. Josh 1:1-9). Having led his charges in every covenantal observance relevant to their situation, Joshua receives God's full approval and affirmation of his obedience. The holy nation is ready for holy war.

Scenes and situations change from account to account in Joshua 6—12, but one principle remains constant: God fights for Israel as long as the people are obedient to the covenant. Jericho falls because of faith in divine power, not because of a long and successful siege against a fortified city.[13] Because of her faith, Rahab and her family are spared death, a privilege no one else in the city receives, due to the command of God (6:17). Canaan's judgment, predicted in Genesis 15:16, now begins. Israel's role as instrument of divine punishment is accentuated by its commitment to take no spoil but rather to place all captured wealth in the treasury of the Lord (6:18-19). This is not an excursion meant to enhance Israel's financial standing.

This unifying principle is illustrated when Israel fails to take its next objective, Ai, a relatively easy target. One family has kept spoil from Jericho, an offense that violates the concept of holy war, and it is not until they are executed that the nation can once again expect victory (7:1-26). If Yahweh does not fight for the people they have no chance for success. This war is about glory for the Lord, about promise keeping and about covenantal fidelity, not about whose army is particularly large or effective. Just as clearly the entire nation stands or falls together because the covenant was made with the whole nation. They are a community of faith as much as a collection of individuals who believe in and follow the Lord. Selfishness, disregard for Yahweh's commands and covering up sin therefore harms the entire group.[14] The fact that the whole community punishes the offenders demonstrates the solidarity of their repentance and desire for renewed relationship with the Lord.[15] Once the covenant relationship is restored, Ai falls (8:1-29).

Joshua freely acknowledges Israel's dependence on God by observing the ritual on Mt. Ebal and Mt. Gerizim that Moses commands in Deuteronomy 27 (8:30-35). The memorial stones are put in place and the covenant blessings and curses read. Israel is living the covenant. They have experienced both its promises and its consequences by now, particularly in the episode at Ai. By recognizing Yahweh's sovereignty in battle, Joshua's obedience is complete (8:35). The Lord's faithfulness is likewise complete.

Israel missteps by making a treaty with the Gibeonites, a Canaanite country they mistake for foreigners, but even that mishap leads to a great victory (9:1—10:14). God fights for the people to the extent of making the sun stand still so that victory over the enemy could be achieved (10:14). Eventually Yahweh wages war effectively enough to give Israel the southern sector of the land (10:42). The text gives Yahweh credit for triumphs in the north as well (11:1-9; cf. 11:8) and praises Joshua for carrying out everything that the Lord commanded through Moses (11:15). As was the case with Pharaoh, God hardens the heart of the enemy kings to wage futile wars against Israel so that their punishment might be complete (11:20). Again the conquest does more than reward Israel, for it fulfills all the promises of judgment the canon has unveiled over time.

God's fighting is completed. Canaan has been subdued, giving Israel a place in the promised land (11:23—12:24). Israel has work to do to possess the land, but God has done as promised. The fact that Israel will have to expend some effort to control their inheritance has been evident since Deuteronomy 7:22, where Moses says the conquest will not occur all at once so that the land will not become a vast haunt for thistles and beasts. Israel's periodic returns to a set camp at Gilgal also point to this eventuality (cf. Josh 10:15).

Joshua's life goal, and in a very real way Moses' as well, has also been achieved. Every promise offered in Joshua 1:1-18 has been kept, and the people are no longer a nation without a homeland.[16] Moses' longing look at the land in Deuteronomy 34 has become more than a look. It has developed into a promise kept by the God who made it. Joshua's and Moses' commitment to God's word has been vindicated as well, as has Joshua's and Caleb's belief that the land could have been theirs forty years sooner. Also, the second generation's determination to keep covenant and follow Joshua's leadership has also been rewarded. They have set a high standard for future generations in faith as well as in warfare. All this is true because the Lord has fought for the chosen people.

Canonical Synthesis: God-Given Rest in the Land

Canonical references to the conquest of Canaan focus on the fulfillment of promises to Abraham, the grace of God, the power of God, the law as the word of God and the concept of rest as a future blessing for God's faithful. After the long canonical buildup to the fulfillment of the promise of land, the conquest texts are almost an anticlimax. Readers have known since Genesis 12:1-9 that the Lord intended Abraham's descendants to have the land. The promise was repeated to Isaac (Gen 26:3) and Jacob (Gen 28:4, 13) and held a prominent place in the exodus accounts (cf. Ex 3:8; 6:4; 13:5). Much of the legislation in Exodus, Leviticus and Deuteronomy anticipates a settled culture dwelling permanently in Canaan. Still, the wonder of this event must be clung to, cherished as a remarkable monument to the fact that the Lord keeps all promises. This promise asked for faith yet also generated faith, for it was based on Yahweh's trustworthy character.[17] This promise's fulfillment gives hope that all God's pledges are kept, regardless of how long it takes.

It must be noted, though, that the fulfillment of the promise of land does not cease with the conquest. The power of God's word must guide the people's actions. Deuteronomy 28:15-68 has graphically illustrated the truth that the land may be forfeited by hardened covenant breaking, at least until the nation turns from its sin. Judges, Samuel and Kings state convincingly that when Israel breaks the Mosaic covenant they suffer the consequences. Second Kings 17 says that the exiles of 722 B.C. and 587 B.C. occurred due to covenant unfaithfulness. Isaiah, Jeremiah, Ezekiel and the Twelve call Israel to repent and return to the Lord, with Jeremiah leading the way with 111 usages of the word *repent*. Only a nation that understands that they cannot live by bread alone but must draw sustenance from God's word (Deut 8:3) can survive. Only a people that believes the word is their life (Deut 32:47) will continue on in the holy place.

Both the land and God's covenant are evidences of God's grace. Moses takes great care to tell the people that God's love (Deut 4:37-38), not Israel's power (Deut 8:17) or righteousness (Deut 9:6), secures the inheritance. As Creator, Yahweh owns the world and gives Canaan to Israel as a sacred trust (Lev 25:23). As God's stewards, they are under the Creator's protection, safe from their enemies.[18] Only a lack of covenant fidelity can sever this security, so several psalms celebrate the blessing of possessing the Law. Psalm 19:7-14 stresses the Law's perfection and consequent ability to help human beings identify and remove hidden sins that jeopardize the precious relationship with the Lord. Psalm 119 heightens these twin benefits of the Law and conveys a strong sense of joy in obeying standards that keep one close to the Creator. Nehemiah 8:1-18 portrays a scene in which a postexilic Jerusalem community uses the Law to rejuvenate its commitment to the Lord.[19] God's grace extends to every area of life necessary to keep the people safe in the land.

Besides Yahweh's grace, the conquest demonstrates God's undeniable power. Particularly as the Lord fights for Israel in ways human beings can only consider miraculous, this strength becomes as inherent as the loving grace already described. Jeremiah 2:7 states near the beginning of a long (2:1—6:30) treatise on Israel's covenant infidelity that God brought the people to a good land, only to see them defile it through idolatry. Ezekiel claims that Yahweh took Israel out of Egypt, gave them the covenant and gave them the land, only to have them serve idols (Ezek 20:12-17). Once again it is God's powerful hand that made the conquest possible. Amos 2:10 agrees that Israel's possession of Canaan was God's work, not the nation's.

Some of the psalms are even more explicit on the subject.[20] For example, Psalm 44:1-3 states that God's might, not Israel's, won the victory. In Psalm 78, one of Scripture's most God-centered psalms, the poet claims God "brought" Israel to "his holy land" and "drove out nations" (78:54-55). Psalms 104—106 present a theological summary of Yahweh's work from creation to the exile. Included in the Lord's mighty acts is the giving of the land as an inheritance (105:11, 44). Again God's power achieves the victory, and Israel has only to accept the blessing and live by the covenant.

In both the Prophets and in Psalms, the power of God evidenced in the conquest is juxtaposed to Israel's unfaithfulness. God's power has worked for their good, but they reject the gift and the One who gave it. Such ingratitude seems especially foolish in light of the Lord's ability to cause the sinful great pain. In forgetting God's grace Israel has also forgotten God's power.

Over time, "rest in the land" takes on significance far beyond nationhood or geography. Resting from enemies and wilderness journeying can hardly be overestimated.[21] Still, as time went on and their messages went unheeded, the prophets looked to an era when the exiled peoples would return to the land.[22] Isaiah 44:24-28 predicts a return to the land in Cyrus's time (c. 539 B.C.), and Isaiah 49:14-21 says the return will prove God's love for Israel. Jeremiah 31 views a return to the land as a prelude to a new covenant with

Israel that will mark all covenant persons as faithful followers of God (Jer 31:1-34). As in Isaiah, security in the land will demonstrate divine love (Jer 31:35-40). Ezekiel 28:25-26 claims this new security will make God's greatness evident to the nations. In these texts the restored rest will result in a new chance in the land, in new experiences of God's love, in a new covenant and in a new opportunity to bless all nations by exalting Yahweh before them. The prophets expect these events to occur sometime in the future, so these visions give the faithful hope in dark times.

The God Who Divides the Inheritance: Joshua 13—21
Israel's mere presence in the land does not complete God's plans for the nation. Moses' detailed plans for settling the people in specific areas, for setting aside Levitical cities and for establishing cities of refuge have been outlined in Deuteronomy 1:38 and Deuteronomy 3:28 as well as in Numbers 27:18-23, 32:17 and 34:17.[23] Dividing the land remains the one part of Joshua's calling that has not been accomplished (cf. Josh 1:6; Deut 31:7).[24] Thus, it is necessary for God's, Moses' and Joshua's purposes that the inheritance Yahweh gives Israel be divided among the heirs. Completion of the conquest will also mean the holy people have done their part in fulfilling the covenant. These chapters depict this completion process by describing general tribal divisions of land, special allotments of land and instances where the people are or are not anxious to do their part in finishing the military task. As the book unfolds significant themes emerge, such as the importance of obedience to God's plans, courage in fighting the Canaanites, the equality of each tribe, the concept of the land as inheritance and the grounding of canonical theology in history.

God assigns Joshua the task of dividing the promised land (13:1-8), so obedience is an issue from the start. Commentators have long puzzled over 13:1, which seems to contradict 11:23. The former passage speaks of the whole land having been taken, while the latter indicates land remains unconquered. Many possible source-critical solutions to this problem have been offered, but the issue is also a theological one. God fights for Israel in Joshua 1—12 and then exhorts the people to fight in Joshua 13—21. Joshua leads Israel into battle in the first section, taking every objective he attacks, and then exhorts them to finish the work themselves in the second section. The major cities have been taken and serious alliances broken, but individual places are left for each tribe to win. Just as Israel's obedience to God's revelation completes the covenant, so Israel's response to Yahweh's victories completes the conquest. The human effort must cooperate with the divine initiative. Obedience must accompany miracle.

Inserted between the land lists are three accounts that demonstrate that in this setting obedience can be displayed only by showing of courage in battle. Caleb, Joshua's contemporary in age and faith, demands the opportunity to fight for the most hard-to-take territory (14:6-15). All the people need his spirit. Joseph's tribe complains about not having enough space, only to be told by Joshua to attack difficult enemy positions (17:14-18). Again determination and courage are expected. Similarly Joshua tells seven tribes they have waited long enough to secure their inheritance (18:1-10). God gives the people the land (18:10), but they must grasp the inheritance in a Caleb-like manner.

Special allotments made to Joshua (19:49-51), for cities of refuge (20:1-9) and to the Levites (21:1-8) highlight the nature of the land as divine inheritance. God owns the land (Lev 25:23) and thus may divide it. The division of holy ground calls Israel to respect the land, neither selling it at will nor acting however they wish in it. Having a portion in God's land requires reverence for its purpose and value.[25] Giving specific allotments shows respect for the covenant's explicit statements regarding cities of refuge and the Levites (cf. Num 35:6-34; Deut 4:41-43; 19:1-14; Num 35:1-5). Allowing Joshua a particular piece of ground recognizes his position as God's chosen leader. Even the casting of lots to determine where each tribe will live (e.g., Josh 18:10-11) reflects a belief that God may be trusted to put each family in its appropriate place.

How the land is divided tribe by tribe indicates an inherent equality in the nation as a whole. This belief in the right to equality grows out of the conviction that God created the entire earth and elected Israel to be the holy nation that would receive an inheritance of holy land. Paul Hanson explains that

> this was a right based not merely upon a social ideal, but on the Yahwistic confession that every Israelite was the child of the same parents, a heavenly Parent to whom belonged the whole earth, who had chosen Israel as an inheritance out of all the families of the earth (Deut. 32:8-9; 9:26, 29; Ps. 28:9, 79:1; Jer. 10:16), and who now distributed, with evenhanded fairness, the land among the people.[26]

Israel's system precludes the sort of oppression seen in other ancient lands where royalty or large landowners could control most of a country's property.[27] In other words, it negated the slavery system the people had experienced in Egypt.

Finally, the conquest and division grounds Israel's theology in historical reality. Elmer Martens asserts, "Land is real. Earth is spatially definable. Life with Yahweh takes place here and now. The quality of that life is all-embracing—it relates to Yahweh, to neighbor, to environment."[28] It is also true that war is real, Canaanites are real and cities are real. Israel's theology does not occur in mythological realms but in life-and-death struggles, in mundane affairs, in the real events of history. Even the miracles are set in specific occurrences at specific times. They do not happen in a vacuum or in a mythological world. Still, it is difficult to express adequately how miracles and the normal course of human events intersect. T. S. Eliot captures the truth in this dilemma when writing about the incarnation in "Choruses from 'The Rock.'"

> Then came, at a predetermined moment, a moment in time and of time,
> A moment not out of time, but in time, what we call history:
> transecting, bisecting the world of time, a moment in time but not like a moment of time,
> A moment in time but time was made through that moment: for without the meaning there is no time, and that moment of time gave meaning.[29]

The conquest happens in moments of time whose meaning transcends normal happenings, yet it does happen, and in ways that make readers consider and believe, then wonder at their magnificence.

Canonical Synthesis: Faithfulness in the Land

Three canonical usages of Joshua 13—21 deserve mention. First, the author of Hebrews 4:1-3 links sabbath rest (Gen 2:2), Israel's failure to enter Canaan the first time (Num 13—14; cf. Ps 95:11) and Joshua's work in an effort to exhort God's people to strive to receive God's offer of final rest. He warns that rest takes faith, obedience and diligence, all of which he clearly believes the Israelites lacked. No diligence means no rest in his view, and Joshua says the same thing to the tribes who tarry in taking their inheritance (cf. Josh 17:14—18:10). Second, Israel's full possession of Canaan does not occur until David's victories in 2 Samuel 8:1-14. Israel does not do its share of the work until centuries after God places them in the land. The promise has both a fixed and continuous nature.

Third, the prophets chastise Israel for abuses of the principle of equality. Slavery, oppression and using the land to gain unfair financial advantage are inherently wrong based on the covenantal concept of inheritance. Hanson claims, "When Amos, Micah, and Isaiah inveighed against those who bought and sold property and amassed real estate at the expense of the impoverished, they were appealing to the early Yahwistic notion of equal distribution to which the right of the *nahala* [inheritance] gave social form."[30] The same may be said for Elijah's denouncing of Ahab for Jezebel's killing Naboth for not selling his land, his "inheritance" (1 Kings 21:3), to Ahab.[31] Before God, kings and paupers have the same status as they dwell together in the land Yahweh gives both as a gift (cf. Deut 17:14-20). Both live on inherited property, and neither merits the gift, so one oppressing the other is condemned.

The God Who Requires Ongoing Commitment: Joshua 22—24

This section reveals that Joshua and the generation he leads understand that conquering Canaan hardly concludes the covenant. Rather the God who has had a relationship with them since Abraham is a living God who loves and relates to successive generations (cf. Ex 3:13-15). Therefore it is necessary that they serve Yahweh according to Mosaic principles regardless of whether their inheritance is east or west of the Jordan River. It is necessary for each generation to embrace the covenant as its own, for their God transcends geographical and tribal boundaries (22:1-34), physical obstacles (23:1-16) and generational passage of time (24:1-33). Only covenant renewal on Israel's part allows them to keep up with a deity without physical or temporal limits. Only ongoing commitment to an exclusive relationship with Yahweh allows them to avoid mixing their faith with Canaanite fertility-dominated polytheism or rejecting the Lord altogether.[32]

Once he deems the land suitably at rest, Joshua releases the Reubenites, Gadites and Manassehites who were given an inheritance east of the Jordan by Moses in Numbers 32:1-43 yet who were charged with helping their fellow tribes conquer the land (Josh 22:1-4). Joshua commends these warriors, charges them with keeping the Mosaic covenant, blesses them and sends them to their homes (22:5-6). On the way home, however, they erect an altar, thus causing the other Israelite tribes to fear another incident like that involving Achan (22:13-20; cf. 7:1-26).

Theological reflection settles the problem. On the one hand the troubled tribes fear a breach of the law about one altar (22:16; cf. Deut 12:13-32), which would in turn incite a judgment from God like that at Baal-Peor or with Achan (22:17-20; cf. Num 25:1-18; Josh 7:1-26). Without question their concerns are covenantally based and canonically ordered. The tribes east of the Jordan counter with covenantal issues of their own. This altar, like the stones gathered by Jacob and Laban in Genesis 31:48, is "a witness" in this case of their unity with the other tribes and is not a place of sacrifice. They are in full agreement with Deuteronomy 12:13-32 (22:29). Their concern is to preserve the covenantal oneness among themselves, their children, their God and their nation (22:28-29). They want to give a witness to future generations of their faith so that it can never be said they have "no share" (22:27), no inheritance in the land.

Their explanation satisfies those concerned (22:30-34). It also indicates that God's covenant people may relate to Yahweh and to one another regardless of geographical separation. If God could take Israel from Egypt to Canaan, then God can dwell among all the people at all times wherever they may be. This fact becomes crucial when Israel actually suffers exile and has to deal with exercising faith outside the promised land.

The book's final chapters depict Joshua's last two speeches to the people. His initial oration reminds his audience of truths derived from Deuteronomy 4:25-26 and Deuteronomy 6:13-15, Joshua 1 and Joshua 2—12. Thus, like its predecessor, this chapter contains serious theological thought. Because God has fought for Israel (23:1-5; cf. Josh 1—12), which has brought to pass all Yahweh's promises (23:14; cf. 1:1-18), the people must obey "the Book of the Law of Moses" (23:6; cf. 1:1-9) by rejecting other gods and eschewing marriage to their adherents (23:7-13; cf. Deut 6:13-15). Failure to obey will result in loss of land (23:16; cf. Deut 4:25-26; 28:15-68). This speech asserts that God has overcome all military obstacles to Israel's life in the land. Israel has "only" to overcome covenantal obstacles to continue to enjoy the benefits of God's victories.

Joshua's concluding speech presents a canonical and theological summary that summons the tribes to covenant renewal. Beginning in 24:2, he charts the past, noting Abraham's polytheistic beginnings (Gen 11:26-32), the patriarchs' journeys (24:3-4; cf. Gen 12:1—50:26), the victory at the Red Sea (24:5-7a; cf. Ex 15) and the desert period (24:7b; cf. Num 13—14). He concludes by mentioning the early military victories (24:8; cf. Num 21:21-35), the incident with Balaam (24:9-10; cf. Num 22—24) and finally the conquest itself (24:11-13; cf. Josh 1—12). Only the covenant is not mentioned, but he has already mentioned it in Joshua 23:6, 16. All these events constitute the basis for Israel's relationship with and obedience to Yahweh. Theologically interpreted events should create the impetus for the nation's future.

Three responses are expected to flow from this relationship: fear of the Lord, service to the Lord and rejection of all other gods (24:14). These impulses were evident in Exodus 19:1—20:17, for the people respected the Lord's awesome presence on the mountain (Ex 19:7-25), agreed to do God's will (Ex 19:8) and received the monotheistic ten commands (Ex 20:3-17). God's work on their behalf stood behind these elements (Ex 20:1-2). Israel agrees to the covenant in Exodus 24:1-4. Joshua asks for a similar response now yet warns the people that God cannot be fooled. Monotheism alone pleases Yahweh (24:15-20). Gerhard von Rad observes, "As far as we can see, this cultic intolerance is something unique in the history of religion."[33] Israel agrees to the covenant renewal, and Joshua writes their pledge in the book of God's law (24:27).

Joshua's warnings are part exhortation and part suspicion. Moses predicted in Deuteronomy 31:16, 29 that the people would break the covenant some-day, so Joshua knows each generation must renew its love for Yahweh. As Christoph Barth says,

> Human beings cannot keep a vow of this kind faithfully for generation after generation. What happened at Shechem was only a beginning. Time and again Israel would in fact forget, violate, and deny the Shechem oath. Israel had to be reminded and rebuked by divine judgments. God would not himself forget. He would keep, lead, call and teach Israel, repeatedly reminding it of its commitment.[34]

Another way of stating Barth's comment is that faith is not genetic. It must be exercised by each new person and generation. For this reason Moses commands intergenerational teaching (Deut 6:1-9), and Joshua's last act as Israel's leader is to insure faithfulness in his time, even though he knows Moses' words will come true in the future. For now, however, it is pleasant to read that Israel served God during Joshua's time (24:29-31) and that Joseph's bones are finally laid to rest in the land of promise (24:32; cf. Gen 50:25; Ex 13:19).

Canonical Synthesis: Covenant Renewal

Many canonical connections have already been noted, but one more should be included. Just as Moses' call story serves as the model for future call accounts, so does Joshua's covenant renewal set the standard for later similar observances, rare as they are in Israel's history. Samuel leads covenant renewal in about 1050 B.C. when Saul becomes king (1 Sam 12:1-25). Josiah renews the covenant in about 622 B.C. (2 Kings 23:1-3), as do Ezra and Nehemiah (c. 440 B.C.; Neh 9:1-38). These instances are separated by years, generations at times, of covenant breaking such as that foreseen by Moses. Still, Joshua sets a standard that removed all excuses from the lips of the unfaithful. He places life and death before the people as only a man who experienced slavery, Sinai, desert and conquest could do.

Conclusion

Joshua seems like the closing act and a notice of future acts at the same time. God's promises have materialized due to divine election, divine power and one faithful human generation. But readers can hardly think the sin problem has been solved or all nations have been sufficiently blessed. Moses' dire predictions preclude such delusions. New details soon emerge that demonstrate how right Moses was in Deuteronomy 31:16, 29 yet also how right he was in Genesis 3:15, 12:1-9, 15:1-6, Leviticus 16:21-22 and Deuteronomy 18:15-22. An uneasy peace settles over the canon even as the Israelites bury Joshua, Joseph and Eleazar (24:32-33).

8

The God
Who Disciplines
& Delivers

Judges

. . . .

READ ON ONE LEVEL, JUDGES IS A FAIRLY STRAIGHTFORWARD BOOK. ITS theology mirrors the warnings in Deuteronomy 28:15-68, for the people commit idolatry, suffer the consequences of their sin, repent and cry out to Yahweh for help, receive aid and then turn to their idolatry again (cf. Judg. 2:6—3:6). The idolatry involved sounds similar to that in Exodus 32—34 and Numbers 25, as does the Lord's response to the transgression. Further, Israel has a steady stream of leaders who seemingly take Moses and Joshua's place yet who do not all match the standards set by those men or by Deuteronomy. Finally, Israel faces new and tough opponents who have no intention of handing Canaan over to their Hebrew foes.[1] The overall impression is one of self-inflicted chaos suffered by a people who forget who they are and how they got to Canaan.

Read on another level, however, the book is more complex, horribly twisted, dark and brutal. Murder, rape, idolatry, perversion and betrayal become the backdrop for theology. Irony pervades the whole.[2] Major character flaws appear in persons who are supposed to lead the people back to God or at least away from the enemy. Failure abounds. Defeats are normal.

This mixture of the expected and the unthinkable fits the theological purposes of the author of the Former Prophets. The book describes what occurs when a covenant people forsake that covenant and do whatever each individual or tribe sees fit rather than following the revealed word of the Creator of all lands and peoples (cf. 17:6; 21:25). It does so by describing what reads like a cycle of sin, repentance, deliverance and repeated sin but what in reality amounts to a descent into an ever-deepening moral abyss that threatens the existence of Israel in the land.

This descent unfolds in three parts in Judges. First, the author anticipates the descent in the book's introduction (1:1—3:6). Israel's early military success and later failures are recounted as a reminder that Israel has come to Canaan as a result of God's work on their behalf (1:1—2:5). Following this historical introduction, a theological introduction states that idolatry led Israel to forsake the covenant. Therefore the Lord decided to "test" the people by allowing their enemies to stay in the land (2:6—3:6). In this section Yahweh acts as the God who tests the people, a role not assumed with such force since Genesis 22.

Second, the descent is articulated in the book's longest segment (3:7—16:31). Here a series of twelve major and minor judges of varying character lead Israel to freedom from oppressors. These leaders decline in theological substance until the last one proves as much a man of sexual, intellectual and physical appetite as a man of God. In these chapters the Lord calls the judges as a response of Israel's cries for help yet also sends the oppressors to punish Israelite idolatry. Yahweh is the God who responds in these texts. The Lord responds both from his own sense of justice and to the life decisions of the chosen people. At all times Yahweh is faithful to the covenant, but sometimes Israel does not enjoy this faithfulness.

Third, the full depravity of a nation who does as each person sees fit emerges as the descent is completed (17:1—21:25). Terrible acts occur, as despicable as appear anywhere in ancient literature. At this point Yahweh is the God who releases the people to their own wickedness. Now the nation punishes itself. Now the sin problem in the holy nation appears to be as real as the one in the world at large. Further canonical writings will be necessary to relieve these theological burdens.

In Judges, no issue matters more than Israel's commitment to covenantal monotheism. Any deviation from this principle results in disaster for the nation. Every time the author states that Israel displeases God it is idolatry that causes the relational disjuncture. Other sorts of sins can be forgiven as individuals turn to the God who forgives, but those who worship idols cut themselves off from theological reality and a relationship with the living God. Only judgment can result.

The God Who Tests Israel's Faithfulness: Judges 1:1—3:6

The opening phrase in Judges ("After the death of Joshua") links the book to its canonical predecessor by citing a common character and using a familiar strategy.[3] When this phrase is coupled with the book's final phrase ("everyone did as he saw fit"), the message of Judges becomes clear. Joshua's death initiates a new era of covenant breaking that Joshua's covenant renewal efforts in Joshua 23—24 sought to postpone. The historical scene influences Israel's theological commitments at this point: left without strong leadership and confronted with powerful enemies who advocate their own systems of belief, Israel changes its faith commitments. The biblical ideal is for precisely the opposite result to occur. Faith ought to drive the people's entire existence.

Many scholars consider Judges 1:1-36 a composite collection of sources that varies from the portrayal of the conquest in Joshua 1—12.[4] K. L. Younger counters this opinion by noting that Assyrian records also depict military campaigns in a manner calculated to show that nation's success in a particular geographical region rather than its temporal progression toward those victories.[5] He then concludes that Judges 1 focuses on the tribes as separate but related entities and Israel's initial victory and subsequent failure to subjugate their enemies.[6] Thus the opening chapter resonates with the problem recounted in Joshua 13—21: God has been with Israel (cf. Judg 1:19, 22) and has given Israel the land (cf. Judg 1:4), but the people have not driven out the Canaanites. Such failure amounts to a lack of faith and obedience. Therefore, Brevard Childs concludes, "far from being a foreign element or useless fragment, the introduction strikes the keynote to the whole witness of the book."[7]

God's response to the lack of faith is to turn Israel over to the foreign nations and allow their gods to become a snare to them (2:1-5). In this way the Lord may test the people's resolve to serve the living God (2:21-23). Israel fails the test through intermarriage and resultant idolatry (3:1-6). This failure reminds readers of the disaster at Baal-Peor (Num 25:1-18). Canaan's gods prove a snare to Israel because they are antithetical to the principles stated in the Law. Canaanite religion was polytheistic, laden with sexuality derived from its emphasis on fertility and replete with images.[8] It embodied all that was wrong with Canaan in God's eyes (cf. Lev 18:24-30), connected the chosen people to the practices God condemned when praising Abraham's faith (Gen 15:16) and made them vulnerable to being on the wrong side of Yahweh's wrath in a situation of holy war (Deut 18:15-68).

Judges 2:16-19 presents the book's overall theological problems. When Israel follows the Canaanite gods, best represented by Baal, Yahweh gives them over to oppressing nations (2:11-15). This part of the test often drives the nation to ask for God's help, which comes in the form of judges who lead the people to freedom (2:16-18). Just what a judge is has caused a great deal of scholarly discussion. The word *judge* translated noncontextually has judicial implications, and at least one judge does fulfill this function (see 4:4). G. F. Moore states that in the context of the whole book the word means "defend," "deliver," "avenge" and "punish" as well as to "rule" or "govern."[9] J. Alberto Soggin says that the major judges, or those who are given more space in the accounts, have a military function.[10] In other words, these individuals are to approximate the work done by Joshua, who was a military and religious leader, though in a different context. Israel refuses to listen to the God-sent judges (2:17) or only follows Yahweh as long as a particularly strong judge lives (2:19).

All these introductory matters are necessary to explain how the chosen people have come to enjoy little rest in the land where they were to find complete rest. Israel's blessings have always been held in tension. They have God's promises, yet these promises are not unconditional. That is, they are unconditional in that they are given solely by electing grace. But they are not unconditional in the sense that the nation may act however it wishes and still have the good things the Lord alone is able to bestow on them. Faith and obedience seal the covenant in Israel's favor, and Yahweh wants it so. Israel has acted in such a way that the Lord decides to find out exactly what their true desires are.

Canonical Synthesis: Lack of Rest in the Land

This section causes a pause in the canonical theology of Israel's rest in the promised land. The people have the physical fulfillment of the promises to Abraham, but they do not yet enjoy the benefits of personal faithfulness that are the true core of what God was beginning to do by calling Abraham from Ur. They do not see that solving the sin problem by creating a system of forgiveness within a nation that could act as a kingdom of priests to the whole world was Yahweh's aim, not simply to give the chosen people a piece of ground, however significant that endowment was. The fact that the judges cannot motivate the people to obey the covenant also provides a leadership dilemma that will bedevil the rest of the Old Testament but that also becomes the Bible's main theological point in 2 Samuel 7:1-17, in the Latter Prophets and in the New Testament.

This passage also raises the issue of when, why and how God tests covenant persons. In Genesis 22 the text states directly that Yahweh determines to test Abraham to see if Yahweh or Isaac means more to him. This test shows that faith must take precedence over the physically observable blessings God gives the faithful. The same is true in Judges. Israel acts as if living in Canaan is all of the covenant they want to consider. God does not allow them this luxury. The Lord has committed unreservedly to Israel (2:1), and he expects the same from the covenant partner. E. R. Dalglish observes that Yahweh's unswerving faithfulness is good news for Israel, for they have only to return to single-minded monotheism to receive the full covenant blessings again.[11] Passing the test is in the people's best interests, and it will decide in part how the sin problem is resolved for all nations.

The God Who Responds: Joshua 3:7—16:31

Duly warned that what follows is not going to be a theological success story, interpreters now encounter the lives and careers of the judges themselves. It is fair to say that the judges usually exhibit higher covenant commitment than does the populace as a whole, but in some cases this generalization does not hold. They err in many of the same ways the people do and at times do even worse things than the people. The decline of the people in these chapters is matched by the moral slide of the judges.

There is no movement toward Yahweh until the people have been oppressed by Yahweh through the foreign nations. When all else fails, Israel turns to God. The cycle of the narratives presents opposition between worldly power and ethical Yahwism. In the first narratives of the judges (Othniel, Ehud, Deborah), the separation from Yahweh originates among the people— "they did evil." With Gideon, the turn from Yahweh issues from the judge himself, and the people continue their earlier pattern. Instead of teaching the people, the judge learns from them. Finally, with the last judge, Yahwism has become empty covenant and empty vow, meaningless to Israel.[12]

Still, the judges are the Lord's means of helping the chosen nation, and they are the human instruments by which God remains faithful to his own character and to the Israelites. Perhaps this fact magnifies the desperate times and the low quality of the nation's character.

Deborah is the most impressive of the first three judges, though Ehud's career provides the book's first mean-edged yet humorous account. Deborah has a dual function in the story, for she is both prophet and judge (4:4).[13] All Israel comes to her, a judge, for advice (4:5). As prophet, she declares that God wants Israel to fight their enemies and expect God to give them the victory (4:6-7). She convinces Barak to lead Israel's forces, and the people do indeed win a great victory, which she immortalizes in song (5:1-31).

Gideon's career mirrors the nation's relationship with Yahweh in this era. He receives a call from God to lead the nation (6:11-18). This call corresponds to Moses' at several points.[14] Thus he has divine support, and this support results in a miraculous victory over the oppressors, the Midianites (6:11— 7:25). Israel enjoyed similar divine help in Joshua 1—12, only to step away from the Lord. Like Israel, having won the victory, Gideon turns to questionable religious practices. He takes gold from the Israelites and makes a golden ephod, a situation too much like the golden calf incident for theological comfort. Israel uses the ephod to rebel against God (8:27). It took faith for Gideon to deliver Israel, but that faith does not remove idolatry from his or Israel's immediate future.

At the end of Gideon's career the issue of kingship emerges. Deuteronomy 17:14-20 sets forth specific rules for the kings that Moses predicts will rule Israel. This text says a king must be chosen by the Lord, must be an Israelite, must not serve for the wealth it may bring, must not multiply wives for himself and must rule based on the standards in God's written word. To his credit, Gideon knows that his calling does not include kingship, and he encourages Israel to let God rule them, yet paradoxically he does so while making the golden ephod. Such mixed messages become extremely common in the chapters that follow.

Gideon's son Abimelech has no theological scruples about becoming king. He seizes power and rules for three years before meeting his end at the hands of a woman who aims a millstone at his head (9:1-57). This episode illustrates Israel's unwillingness to follow God's standards for the nation. It also offers the first glimpse of the many ineffective rulers who displease Yahweh in the Former Prophets' description of the Israelite monarchy. Abimelech is not chosen by God, does not protect the people, does not follow the Law and does not lead the nation to serve the Lord. In other words, he is "the wrong person for doing what a king should do."[15] It is equally true that the people who make the murderous Abimelech king are self-serving opportunists.[16] They have no interest in serving Yahweh either, so people and king alike are theologically and ethically bankrupt. God's response is to repay the wickedness of both Abimelech and those who give him power (9:56-57).

After two more minor judges are mentioned (10:1-5), the text notes that Israel serves gods from Canaan, Aram, Sidon, Moab, Ammon and Philistia (10:6). This list is the text's most extensive comment on the comprehensive nature of Israel's idolatry in Judges, and it probably summarizes the entire era.[17] At this point Yahweh gives the Israelites over to the Philistines and Ammonites (10:7-9). When the people cry out, God responds in two ways. First, Yahweh reminds them of all the previous deliverences they have conveniently forgotten (10:10-12). Second, God tells them to gain relief from their idols (10:13-14). But the Lord's compassion overwhelms this appropriate wrath when the nation repents (10:15-16). True repentance is the proper response from Israel, and this reaction meets with God's approval. God neither permanently releases Israel to their enemies nor allows them to destroy themselves at this time.

Despite this respite, the nation's covenant commitment does not become long-lasting. Just as tragically, even Spirit-empowered judges like Jephthah (11:29) and Samson (13:25; 14:6, 19; 15:14, 19) are unable to be faithful to the covenant themselves. Jephthah speaks favorably of Edom's god in a diplomatic letter (cf. 11:24), a pragmatic move that depicts him as a man hardly inclined to remove the nongods that Moses denounces.[18] Worse still, he pollutes worship of Yahweh. He vows to sacrifice whatever emerges from his house when he returns if God will grant him victory in battle (11:30-31), no doubt expecting an animal to emerge from the one-room home in which he most likely lived.[19] Instead his daughter comes to meet him, and in violation of laws related to redeeming first-born children (cf. Num 18:16; Lev 27:1-2) and of laws opposing human sacrifice (e.g., Lev 18:21), he keeps his vow. This sacrifice also stands in sharp contrast to the principles implicit in the freeing of Isaac in Genesis 22. At best Jephthah is a man who mixes worship of Yahweh with polytheistic practices and who does not know God's real standards.[20] As such he represents the spiritual state of the people as a whole.

Samson is an even more uneven character than Jephthah. God's angel announces Samson's birth, which sets him apart in a dramatic fashion not in evidence since Gideon's call experience (13:1-23). Without question this judge is, like Israel itself, chosen by God for special purposes. Samson's uniqueness is highlighted by the fact that he is a Nazirite from birth, a calling that Numbers 6:1-21 indicates means he must abstain from strong drink, must avoid dead bodies and must not cut his hair. He is to be holy to the Lord.[21] God blesses him with a filling of the Spirit of the Lord (13:24-25). Thus he is able to do mighty acts of strength and bravery because Yahweh desires to use him to punish Israel's enemies (cf. Judg. 15:4). God's response to the chosen people's pain is to give them an incredibly gifted leader.

Samson has a strong desire for Philistine women, despite what the Law says about intermarriage with those who do not worship Yahweh (cf. Deut 7:3) and despite his parents' protests against this breach of tradition.[22] His inclinations lead him toward a Philistine wife (14:5-20), prostitute (16:1) and paramour (16:4-17). Long after he has broken his other Nazirite vows, his last Philistine lover cuts his hair, God's power leaves him, and he is blinded and taken captive by the enemies he has tormented (16:18-22). Like Jephthah, Samson is a fitful Yahwist, committed enough to be useful to God for a time but not able to serve his whole life due to mixed beliefs and misguided passions. In the end he gains revenge by killing worshipers of Dagon, a Canaanite crop god.[23] Like the people of his day, Samson ends his life in bondage, doing everything he can to strike a blow against his foes. Everything, that is, except committing unreservedly to the God who has responded mercifully to each of the nation's heartfelt pleas for deliverance.

Canonical Synthesis: Deborah and Prophecy

Deborah's contribution has important ramifications for understanding the role of prophets in the canon. Before this text, Abraham (Gen 20:7), Aaron (Ex 7:1), Miriam (Ex 15:20) and Moses (Deut 18:15-22) are called prophets, and a group of Israelite elders prophesy once (Num 11:24-25). Abraham is called a prophet because of his intercessory capabilities that derive from his special relationship with God.[24] Aaron gains this designation because he will speak God's words for Moses. Miriam sings the great wonders of God in the passage where she is called a prophet. Moses emphasizes the accuracy of prophetic prediction and the God-sent prophet's fidelity to the covenant in Deuteronomy 18:15-22. The elders are able to prophesy only because Yahweh's spirit comes upon them. The prophets speak for God because they speak God's words. They also praise the revealed acts of God. Each prophet has a distinct personality, as even a quick glance at the individuals listed indicates, but they are all united in accuracy based on their adherence to God's word.

Deborah embodies most of these characteristics, which marks her as a true prophet within the history told in the Former Prophets. She predicts the future accurately, since the Israelites do win the victory she says will occur. She composes a victory song like the one Miriam writes in Exodus 15:1-18. Her main concern is that Yahweh's enemies perish, so she stands strongly in favor of the covenant. The only element missing is a statement about the Spirit of God's leading her, but given her adherence to Moses' standards for a prophet this filling is a foregone conclusion.

By speaking God's word about the future accurately, Deborah initiates the Former and Latter Prophets' emphasis on how God's word spoken through the prophets determines history. Later in the canon prophetic predictions will give readers advance knowledge of what will happen far in the future. Further, her fidelity to the revealed word also begins the judges era positively, so she provides a balance for Samuel, who will end the era of the judges by exerting a godly ministry. Finally, her spiritual strength condemns judges who falter in their covenant commitments.

A second reference to a prophet initiates the accounts about Gideon, which span Judges 6:11—8:35. This prophet, whose name is not given, tells Israel that their suffering at the hands of the Midianites results from their disobedience (6:7-10). The prophetic word accurately interprets the nation's situation and provides a backdrop for the next divine response to the people's cries for help (cf. 6:6).

Canonical Synthesis: The Era of the Judges

The canonical portrayal of the judges reflects the two-sided nature of most of their careers. In the last speech of the last judge, Samuel claims that the judges were sent by Yahweh to help Israel in response to their cries (1 Sam 12:10-11). Only through the work of the judges did the people enjoy any rest in those days (1 Sam 12:11). Acts 13:20 also implies that the judges emerged as a direct result of God's will.[25] Hebrews 11:32 states that Gideon, Barak, Samson and Jephthah exercised faith in the execution of their duties. At the same time, 2 Kings 23:22 remembers this era as a time in which Passover was not celebrated, Psalm 78:56-58 speaks of these days as a period of idolatry and sinfulness, and Judges 3:7—16:31 clearly portrays the judges' era as uncertain times religiously as well as politically. The judges are no permanent solution either to the sin problem or to Israel's leadership crisis caused by Joshua's death.

God's response to Israel's problem extends beyond the judges, as has already been noted. Prophets and kings have a place in God's plans as well, and the prophets make a positive contribution to the Lord's people in these accounts. Deborah and the unnamed prophet demonstrate that God's prophets are sound interpreters of the Law, faithful carriers of divinely revealed future events and accurate mediators of God's will. Kings are now part of Israel's history, just as Moses predicted in Deuteronomy 17:14-20. How they will figure positively in God's response remains to be seen, since Abimelech symbolizes all that will be wrong with future monarchs. Still, the issue of the kingship as it relates to God's will has been introduced and will not go away in the rest of the Former and Latter Prophets.

The God Who Releases Israel: Judges 17—21

Perhaps the only punishment more frightening than foreign invasion and domination is civil war. The former at least leaves a country with an outside, common foe, but the latter leaves a nation tearing at itself, extracting a terrible price from family that must be paid by family. In civil war a nation has only itself to blame for the carnage that occurs, so the cohesiveness needed to overcome the devastation of war is often lacking when conflict ceases.

Nowhere in Judges 17—21 does the text state that the Lord brings a foreign nation to chastise Israel, but the chapters do present the chosen people as turned over to the effects of their own iniquities. The major effect is civil war brought about through the unrestrained wickedness of the people. God has responded in righteousness and in mercy so far in the book. Now the Lord responds by releasing the nation to their own violent, destructive tendencies, which are the natural result of their half-hearted faith in Yahweh and their outright love of other gods.

Judges 17—19 presents the sort of character vacuum that causes Yahweh to leave the people to their own devices. The first two chapters reveal a nation that has so corrupted its worship that it can hardly tell the difference between Moses' covenant and Canaanite religion. This misguided syncretism leads to unprecedented moral outrages in the third chapter. Veneration of idols and abuse of Yahweh's name lie at the heart of this theological and ethical collapse.

A man named Micah steals silver from his mother and then confesses his theft to her. Delighted to find the silver, she dedicates the metal for an idol, after which her son hires a Levite from Bethlehem to be the priest of his idol and his household (17:1-13). Totally misunderstanding the Mosaic covenant, Micah thinks God will bless him because he has a Levite to preside over the worship of the idol (17:13). In the next episode, some Danites wish to conquer a quiet city, and they ask the Levite to ask Yahweh if they should attack. The idol priest says the Lord is with them (18:1-6). When they conquer they are so pleased with the Levite that they take him as their priest, all the while promising him more pay and recognition. They threaten to kill Micah, who wants his priest back (18:7-30). Once settled, they worship the idol Micah's mother made (18:31).

Without question these accounts portray a shocking array of covenant violations, all under the guise of normative worship. There is no doubt that the people in these stories are totally immersed in Canaanite worldviews that make even the Ten Commandments irrelevant to them. As J. Barton Payne summarizes the situation:

> Even if we restrict our observations to the first table, the following violations at once appear: Micah dishonored his mother (Judg. 17:2); the Danites threatened murder (18:25); Micah stole and was stolen from (17:2; 18:24); Moses' great-grandson Jonathan was false to his contract and to his benefactor (17:10, 11; 18:20); and the Danites seem to have been so covetous of Micah's idols as to have needed no more specific incitement for their expropriation of them than the simple suggestion (18:14), "Now therefore consider what you have to do" (cf. v. 23).[26]

This list of offenses and the reason for their existence is explained in Judges 17:6: "In those days Israel had no king; everyone did as he saw fit." Faith and obedience mean little, as the next accounts prove.

Perhaps no more morally repugnant story appears in Scripture than the one in Judges 19. Once again a Levite is prominent in the narrative. This man has a concubine who flees from him to her father's house (19:1-2). What sort of relationship is this? Lillian Klein says that

> the Levite appears not to have acquired the slave-girl or concubine to counteract his wife's infertility; no mention is made of another woman as wife. Given these conditions, the Levite seems to have bought the girl for purposes of sexual gratification or housekeeping (or both), possibly because he could not afford the bride price of a wife.[27]

There is no allowance in the Law for concubines for Levites, but there are specific standards priests are to follow for marriage (cf. Lev 21:1-15), so Klein's depiction of the Levite as a man who wants sex without having to marry a woman seems fair. This Levite is not yet as covenantally corrupt as his brother Levite in the preceding section, but he is not exactly exemplary even at this point in the account.

Having reunited, the couple journey through the territory of Benjamin and are given hospitality by an old man (19:16-21). During the night, in a scene reminiscent of Genesis 19:1-11, a mob forms, demanding to have sex with the Levite (19:22). Instead the Levite sends out his own sex object, the concubine, and the rabble rape her all night long (19:25). The horror of this scene is multiplied in two ways: in the morning the Levite callously tells her to get up and go when she is dead at the doorstep, and when he discovers her death he cuts her in twelve pieces and mails her remains to Israel's elders (19:27-30). He is outraged that the mob has killed her when he exposed her to the killers in the first place. The difference between his abuse of the woman and the crowd's is one of degree, not of kind. Perhaps he sends the limbs and lungs to the leaders to find out if any conscience remains in Israel,[28] but one wonders if he has any left himself.

Neither God nor the author has assessed the situation yet. In the absence of covenantal faithfulness and a repentant cry from the nation, the Lord does exactly as promised in Judges 10:13-14. God leaves Israel to be delivered by the gods in whom they trust and lets the people be crushed under the weight of their own sin, which is the only substance their gods possess. Thus Israel's sin, their god, delivers them into ever greater and more depraved acts.

Faced with the evidence of the Benjaminites' atrocity, the people finally rouse themselves from their moral slumber. They demand that the killers be turned over, but their community protects them (20:8-16). This refusal results in civil war. But it also results in the opponents of Benjamin asking Yahweh for battle instructions. God's desire to punish all Israel is evident in the fact that twice God sends the inquirers to defeat at the hand of the Benjaminites (20:17-23). The third time Yahweh gives the inquirers the victory (20:24-48). The victory requires tens of thousands of lives, however, and ends with the tribes' swearing not to give their daughters in marriage to Benjaminites (21:1-7).

God has restored order, but the nation lies in shambles because of its own sin. Unity has been shattered. Morality hardly exists. Marriage in Benjamin is reduced to the stealing of women as they dance at a festival (21:13-24). The narrator can only repeat that such things happen when there is no king and the people do what is right in their own eyes (21:25).

If there is any good news at all at the end of the book, it is that Israel continues to cry out to or inquire of God periodically and Yahweh's character does not allow him not to answer. Yahweh has not yet seen fit to punish the chosen nation by driving them from the land. Hope remains that the promises to Abraham still carry weight, still offer Israel the chance to be the holy people in the holy land. Michael Wilcock asks:

> And why is it possible? Because even when, as in all five chapters [Judg 17—21], the Lord sits disapprovingly on the sidelines, speaking only when spoken to and for the rest leaving Israel to muddle through in her own way, since that is what she has decided she wants to do—even then, he is there. He has not abandoned his people. Indeed, unasked and unobtrusive, he is ensuring that they will never finally destroy themselves by their own wilful folly. What we have here is in the end a story of grace.[29]

Israel still has a chance to avail themselves of the riches of this grace.

Canonical Synthesis: The Cost of Sexual Depravity

Canonical uses of these chapters are rare. Hosea 9:9 and Hosea 10:9 refer to the battles of Judges 20 to warn eighth-century B.C. hearers to avoid the depravity and defeat that occurred in those days. The mob's attempt to rape the men in Judges 19 approximates the episode in Genesis 19:1-11. Charles Fox Burney notes the many linguistic parallels between the two texts,[30] while Klein notes both similarities and differences between the two accounts.[31] At the least one can argue that the sheer depravity of the mob's desires are at variance with the rules for sexual conduct set forth in Leviticus 20:13 and Deuteronomy 22:23-27. Paul cites such sexual practices as indicators that people of depraved mind have been "given over" to their sins by a God who has attempted unavailingly to get them to live according to revealed truth (Rom 1:26-27). This interpretation of Paul's social context matches the tone in Judges, since uncontrolled sexuality marks both settings.

Conclusion

Several theological matters are at risk at the end of Judges. First, Israel's involvement with other gods breaches the fundamental principle of the Law and multiplies the sin problem on earth. The book's themes sound very much like the situation in Genesis 3—6 before the Lord destroys the world and like Israel's condition in Numbers. Canaan remains as polytheistic and immoral as before, and Israel adds its own unique brand of iniquity to the scene. Second, Israel's status as holy nation (Ex 19:5-6) is desperately in peril. The people do not keep the covenant, which in turn precludes their opportunity to be priests to themselves or to their neighbors. Thus they are not a blessing to all nations (Gen 12:1-9). Third, based on Deuteronomy 27—28, Israel is dangerously close to abandoning the land for exile. All the hard work done by Moses, Joshua and the previous generation may be annulled by unfaith-fulness now.

Fourth, the issue of sound leadership for Israel remains unsettled. Moses set standards for kings that would keep the covenant in the forefront of Israelite life (Deut 17:14-20), but Judges 17:6 and Judges 21:25 state that no such king arises in this era, obviously asserting that Abimelech does not meet these criteria. Moses also promised that a prophet like himself would emerge (Deut 18:15-22), but despite the appearance of Deborah and the unknown prophet no ongoing prophetic presence exists. God sends the judges, yet these individuals prove rather unreliable guides for Israel's covenantal or governmental commitments. Israel's leadership seems as weak and ethically unstable as the nation itself. How judges, kings and prophets will impact Israel's future remains to be seen, but Deuteronomy leaves no doubt that the sort of disasters found in Judges cannot continue. Kings cannot be blamed for what happens in Judges (Judg 17:6; 21:25), but they may be culpable for what occurs later.

Fifth, faith and obedience, the twin pillars of the theology revealed to this point in the canon, are evident in only a few Israelites. The existence of a minority of believers means the promises to Abraham are not defunct even on the human side. It remains possible that the people will yet return in larger numbers to the God who has created, redeemed, sustained and gifted them. Each time a group cries out to the Lord for help faith and obedience are revived, if only for a time. Hope clings to the text, though barely.

All these concerns are summarized in Judges as Israel's love for other gods. The author states from the beginning that polytheism is the greatest threat to Israel (2:11-23). Judges 10:6 cites six different nations from which Israel chooses idols. At every turn the author states that this idolatry causes Yahweh to send oppressing armies or to give Israel over to their own sins. The principle of worshiping one God, and one God only, is a centering theme here as much or more now as in the Law. Monotheism will be the theological touchstone that interprets the rest of the Former Prophets.

9

The God
Who Protects,
Blesses & Assesses

Samuel

· ·

T HE BOOK OF SAMUEL[1] RESTS COMFORTABLY AT SEVERAL STRATEGIC HISTORI-
cal, theological, canonical and critical crossroads. These accounts link Israel's
era of uncertainty under the judges' leadership, the rise of the monarchy
under Saul and the monarchy's qualified flourishing under David. They also
chronicle Israel's struggle to subdue the enemies left unconquered since the
conquest itself (cf. Judg 2:1-5). Such historical details have tremendous
military, social, economic and political implications. Further, Samuel continues the Old Testament's emphasis on Yahweh's uniqueness, on Israel's elect
status, on human failure, on divine sovereignty and on divine blessing. While
doing so, the book depicts God's pledge to David of an eternal kingdom (2
Sam 7:1-29), a promise that dominates the theological scene in the rest of
the canon. Finally, Samuel's diverse range of ideas and characters has
produced a variety of critical opinions about the book's authorship, date, use
of sources, opinion of the monarchy and so forth.[2] Due to the multiplicity of
these critical positions and the difficulty of proving them, many commentators
prefer to deal with the received, canonical text rather than try to re-create
the text's compilation and interpret it accordingly.[3] Traditional historical-critical works continue to appear.[4]

As could be expected, Old Testament theologies have tended to discuss
Samuel in the context of the individual theologian's approach. This natural

tendency does not allow each writer to comment on Samuel in its canonical context, as this volume attempts to do. Still, the movement toward analysis of the received text among many commentators aids canonical analysis, as does the existence of several monographs dedicated to the monarchy's and messianic promise's respective places in Old Testament history and theology. Thus it is possible to examine Samuel's theological contribution in a way that reflects major scholarly currents.

Following Judges' bleak portrayal of Israel's hapless misadventures in the promised land, Samuel provides perspective on how the chosen people will remain inhabitants of Canaan for another five centuries. Israel survives because their covenant partner, the only God, is one who protects, blesses and assesses with pure grace and unquestioned integrity. In the midst of moral decline, Yahweh protects his glory by protecting the faithful, the divine reputation and worship in 1 Samuel 1—7. These accounts create a situation in which kingship has an opportunity to be more than it was under the self-consumed Abimelech's abortive reign (Judg 9:1-57).

Next, 1 Samuel 8—12 states that God institutes kingship.[5] By doing so Yahweh refashions the direction of Israel's identity and history and corrects certain theological misconceptions. Though God chooses Saul to rule, 1 Samuel 13—15 claims that Yahweh also assesses and later rejects him. Kings are thereby held responsible for their actions and shown to be as subject to God's laws as any Israelite is. With Saul set aside, the book's longest unit (1 Sam 16—2 Sam 5) claims that it is Yahweh who elects, protects, exalts and enthrones David. This king has a determination to serve, however imperfectly, only one God. David's desire to honor Yahweh culminates in plans to build a temple, which is followed by the Lord's making an eternal covenant with him (2 Sam 6—7). The covenant flows from the Abrahamic covenant yet provokes extensive canonical statements on its own merit.

Despite his favored status, David, like Israel, proves a fallible covenant partner. His sins cause God to punish him, while the eternal covenant causes God to protect the repentant king (2 Sam 8—20). Finally, 2 Samuel 21—24 presents Yahweh as the God whose protection of David earns David's praise. By now the Lord richly deserves the monarch's devotion.

To be sure, there are many perplexing theological details in Samuel that must not be minimized. God's character and God's followers' character often appear to be at risk, just as they have been in previous canonical books. The author's ability to present the human frailties of David and others gives the work historical credibility. The author's careful presentation of God's multifaceted personality marks the book as an honest, penetrating theological effort. It seems that the author expects readers to risk developing a theology that both challenges their thinking and scrutinizes their behavior.

The God Who Protects His Glory: 1 Samuel 1—7

Judges ends with a story of Benjamite men taking wives from among girls who dance at a festival held in Shiloh. Samuel begins with a Shiloh scene, a canonical connection that immediately fastens attention on past sins and present worship needs. At first the text seems to present for its own sake an account of a barren woman being given a son, a wonderful event in its own right. By the end of 1 Samuel 3, however, this birth emerges as God's way not only of protecting faithful persons but also of safeguarding the divine word. Likewise 1 Samuel 4—6 demonstrates how God protects his reputation against Israelite superstition and Philistine polytheism. Battles are won and lost and enemies are eventually humiliated, yet God's glory takes precedence over such events. Just as significant is the fact that all these things are done so that Israel's worship might lead to national well-being born of covenant obedience (1 Sam 7). In short, God's glory is integral to Israel's success.

The book's namesake and first great character has a birth similar to Samson's (see Judg 13:1-7) in that a barren woman is given a child. Here God's mercy follows the mother's (Hannah) prayer for a son and pledge to give him to the Lord (1:1-20). Hannah's prayer at the Shiloh sanctuary and her family's annual pilgrimage there demonstrate her piety and faithfulness. Her song of praise when Samuel is born solidifies her status and sets forth the book's major teachings about the Lord at the same time.

Hannah's praise includes several theological statements. She says God is holy (2:2), unique (2:2), all-knowing and thus able to judge (2:3), the one who empowers the weak (2:4-5), the source of physical life and death (2:6) and the one who strengthens the faithful (2:9-10). Each of these themes emerges later in the book, but four of them deserve specific emphasis. First, her confession that "there is no one besides you" (2:2) parallels Deuteronomy 32:39, where God's uniqueness and power over life and death are highlighted. Hannah's faith gives hope for a new dawning of righteousness among the people based on the first commandment. Second, her conviction that God exalts the poor from the dust (2:7-8) sets the stage for God's choice of Saul and David, men of humble origins who become kings of Israel. Third, Hannah's assertion that Yahweh "will guard the feet" of the godly but banishes the wicked to darkness (2:9) prefigures what occurs with the Lord's protection of David and rejection of Saul. Fourth, Hannah's mention of the king (2:10) sets the stage for the monarchy's rise and fall in Samuel and Kings. Yahweh retains the status of judge of all the earth and gives authority to the anointed, chosen leader at the same time (2:10). This reference to the king continues the canon's hints about the monarchy begun in Genesis 17:6, 16, where Sarah and Abraham are told their descendants will include some kings; in Genesis 49:8-12, where Jacob says Judah will hold the ruler's staff; and

Deuteronomy 17:14-20, where Moses sets forth rules the kings must obey.[6] Hints will become full-blown discussions in Samuel's next segment.

Hannah's song also resembles David's praises near the end of Samuel (2 Sam 22:1—23:7).[7] There the aging warrior king thanks God for choosing, exalting and protecting him. He also rejoices in Yahweh's uniqueness (2 Sam 22:31). Thus these two praises help frame the book by providing expansive praise in the era of the judges and in the reign of the most famous monarch.[8] These dual praises present a stark contrast to the failures depicted at the beginning and the end of Judges.

Hannah's faithfulness and blessedness are wonderful, but the child himself swiftly becomes the issue. Eli, the priest at Shiloh, is old, and his sons are men who do not know the Lord (2:12-17). They place worship at risk due to their despising of God's standards for priests and sacrifices (2:17; cf. Lev 1—10). A "man of God," a phrase that R. P. Gordon notes "in most of its occurrences, is virtually a synonym" for the word *prophet,*[9] denounces Eli. As in the accounts of Deborah and Gideon (Judg 4:4-10; 6:7-10), the prophet also predicts the future. He says Eli's house will be rejected for their lack of covenant obedience and a new priestly family will emerge (2:27-36). Until then Samuel receives God's call and God's word, both of which indicate he will replace Eli and his blasphemous sons (3:1-21).

God protects divine revelation and proper expressions of worship by choosing Samuel (1 Sam 1—3). Samuel achieves even more than Deborah, Gideon or Ehud did, for he leads worship, has prophetic power (3:19) and also delivers Israel from foreigners (see 7:10-11). God is with Samuel (3:19), which means he will be empowered to do great things.[10] At a crucial moment in Israelite religious history, Yahweh intervenes by preserving the backbone of covenant faith. With word and worship rescued, God's glory remains with faithful persons like Hannah and Samuel. But the spirit of the age of the judges has not yet died by any means, as the presence of Eli's sons indicates.

Having protected his word and worship, Yahweh next protects his reputation among the nations, a task Israel has hardly performed well. Israel treats the ark of the covenant as a magic charm to be used in battle rather than as a symbol of God's presence among the chosen people (4:1-4).[11] Their misconception about the nature of God's character proves "their insensitivity to spiritual things."[12] God allows the Philistines to defeat Israel and lets the enemy capture the ark. Eli's sons die in the conflict, Eli expires upon hearing the news, and Eli's daughter-in-law names her newborn son Ichabod, which means "no glory," since she believes God's glory has left Israel (4:5-22).[13] But has it? Has this historical defeat produced such a theological catastrophe? Has God become unable to protect his honor and his people?

The Philistines believe so. They place the ark in the temple of their primary deity, Dagon, "god of corn and of the fertility of the ground."[14] Gordon comments, "It was common practice in the near east for victorious armies to carry off enemy idols and install them in the temple of their chief god in symbol of the latter's sovereignty over the subject people and its gods."[15] The Philistines soon discover, however, that Yahweh is not subservient to Dagon even if Israel is subservient to Philistia. Dagon bows to Yahweh (5:1-5). Yahweh afflicts the Philistines with death, pestilence and illness until they send the ark home (5:6—6:18). Once back in Israel, the ark brings death to Israelites who do not respect Yahweh's holiness (6:19-21). Twenty years of mourning follow (7:1-2). God's reputation as sovereign cannot be compromised within or outside Israel. The severity of God's actions in protecting the ark as a holy symbol magnifies the importance of rejecting idolatry and embracing appropriate worship. Israel's fortunes languish, but Yahweh's power insures the Lord's prominence. Yahweh rules all lands, all people, all the time. Superstition and polytheism have no power against or over the Lord.

Like Moses in Exodus 32—34, Samuel mediates a renewed relationship between God and Israel. Samuel counsels the people to serve God alone (7:3). Israel removes the Canaanite gods, fasts, confesses their sin and cries out to God (7:4-8). Then Samuel offers sacrifices on their behalf (7:9). God's deliverance releases them from the Philistines' grip, so peace is restored (7:10-14). This obvious Judges-type scene is the last in the Former Prophets, for Samuel is the final judge (7:15-17). He has been successful, yet his ministry concludes the premonarchic era. Due to his mediation, though, God protects the covenant relationship with Israel, one of the chief sources and evidences of divine glory. God's word, worship, sovereignty and relational kindness remain intact, but they have not survived without God's determination to make them do so.

Canonical Synthesis: God's Incomparability

Two canonical features merit special attention. First, the end of the period of the judges marks a turning point in Yahweh's approach to Israel's life in the land. The judges give Israel relief from enemies, yet they do not lead the people into rest. God is powerful enough to give rest if Israel will but cooperate and has indeed stamped his name, or reputation, firmly on the land.[16] Still, idolatry and its attendant worldview easily rival Moses' teaching in Israel's affections, which means the Abrahamic covenant remains only partially fulfilled. Whatever new direction Yahweh chooses will surely deal with these matters. It will also surely focus on a way to eliminate the human race's seemingly indefatigable ability to mar the earth with idolatry and violence.

Second, 1 Samuel 4—6 prefigures later treatments of the folly of idolatry. No one satirizes idolatry more effectively than does Isaiah.[17] Echoing Deuteronomy 32:39, 1 Samuel 2:1-10 and 2 Samuel 22:32, Isaiah asks to whom one can compare God (Is 40:18; 46:5). He then argues that idols are made by people, not vice versa, and thus have no power of their own (Is 40:19-20; 41:7; 44:9-20; 46:1-7). God has made all things (Is 44:24; 45:18-19), which leaves no room for other so-called gods or the images that represent them. Therefore idolatry is evidence of a twisted, deceived, uncomprehending mind (Is 44:18-20; 45:1-7). Since only God exists (Is 45:18-21), only God can save (Is 45:22). Jeremiah 10:1-5 considers idols like "a scarecrow in a melon patch" because they cannot speak, walk, do good or cause harm. In contrast, there is no one like Yahweh (Jer 10:6), for Yahweh is living, active and everlasting (Jer 10:6-10). Psalm 86:8-10 confesses that there is no other God who exists, hears prayer or deserves worship, while Psalm 97:7 pours shame on those who venerate idols.

The canonical list could be extended, but the point is clear: God's status as Creator eliminates all competition. Ancient peoples believed that a god's power was evidenced by the power of that god's worshipers. Isaiah, Jeremiah and the psalmists disagree. They argue that Yahweh's power is separate from Israel and is bestowed on Israel only by grace through Israel's faith. The Philistines discover that Yahweh "was supreme even in the heart of Philistine territory and in the center of their pagan faith. Israel was a weak and rather divided nation; but her God was all-powerful, as she increasingly came to appreciate."[18] The writer of Samuel intends for readers to learn the same lesson. Israel may fail to protect its glory, which is its connection to the Lord, but God will not fail to protect his glory regardless of the circumstances.

The God Who Institutes Kingship: 1 Samuel 8—12

So far the author of the Former Prophets has taken readers through two major historical movements. The first centers on Joshua's life and leadership. Joshua provides a link between the Mosaic era and the conquest era, as well as a tie between the desert and the promised land. The second great movement begins with Othniel, the first judge, and ends with Samuel, the final judge. This era concludes with Israel in the same condition as when it began. A great historical and theological holding pattern seems to have occurred, a fact not lost on the people of Samuel's day. Whatever else unites the two movements, one fact is especially clear. God calls the leaders, and the leaders are bound to obey God. Yahweh's initiative and Yahweh's standards guide the process.

It is somewhat surprising, then, that Samuel attempts to appoint his sons, who are unrighteous men, to be judges over Israel (8:1-3). William Dumbrell comments that such an ordered succession was impossible, since "what appointments were needed were made by Yahweh as a crisis in Israel occurred. Moreover, the office of judge had ascribed the final governmental decisions to Yahweh alone. Not only could no successor be predicted from a human point of view, but even the center from which a consequent rule would be exercised was not known in advance."[19] Israel's elders are not satisfied with the arrangement, so they request a king to judge them, fight their battles and generally help them be like other nations (8:4-5). Their request inaugurates the Former Prophets' third and final great movement, in which Israel is led by kings. As with the first two movements, this last one has theological ramifications connected to, yet greater than, its historical implications. God grants their wish, calls a king, gives them victory and offers cautions about royal abuses of power in 1 Samuel 8—12. At no point does Yahweh lose control of the situation.

As has been noted, the arrival of kingship has already been announced in the canon. Genesis 17:6-16, Genesis 49:8-12, Numbers 24:7 and Deuteronomy 17:14-20 have prepared the way. Scholars have long noted the ambivalence that Yahweh and Samuel have concerning the monarchy and have posited various redactional theories to solve the problem.[20] Given the canonical preparation, however, a theological reading of 1 Samuel 8—12 must view the episodes as natural outgrowths of earlier texts and must strive to apply those texts to the current situation. Genesis 17:6-16 links the Abrahamic covenant to whatever role the monarchy plays. Genesis 49:8-12 focuses on Judah's prominence in kingship, a factor that does not have great significance until David's emergence. Deuteronomy 17:14-20 has tremendous importance. There Moses anticipates the elders' request and then states that kings must be chosen by God, be Israelites, be covenant keepers and be committed to a simple lifestyle, or at least one simpler than was typical of ancient rulers. These standards guide the author's assessment of the situation and indicate that Yahweh is already guiding history with kingship in mind.

Still, Israel's request for a king is an outright rejection of Yahweh's work through Samuel and the other judges. After all, in 1 Samuel 7 the people are secure due to covenant fidelity and Samuel's leadership, yet in 1 Samuel 8 they desire a king even if this change brings them higher taxes, oppression, forced labor and military conscription (8:10-18).[21] Further, though they are in no current danger, they want a king so they can be like other nations (8:5, 19-20), which is a direct repudiation of their calling as a nation of priests set apart as holy to Yahweh (cf. Ex 19:5-6).[22] Since God has placed them in the land and called their leaders, their request rebukes God (8:6-8). Ironically, only their rebellion has necessitated any danger or fear on their part (8:8). They fault Yahweh when they have only themselves to blame, a fact Joshua and Judges make abundantly clear.

God calls Saul to lead Israel, raising him from the smallest tribe (9:1-21). This summons comes in response to Israel's cries (9:16), just as Moses' calling did in Exodus 2:23-25. God's mercy drives his initiation of kingship. As Yahweh's representative, Samuel anoints Saul, a ceremony that symbolizes the Spirit anointing that Saul receives later (10:1-13). In turn God's Spirit enables Saul to defeat the Philistines and thereby rally all Israel to his side (11:1-15). There can be no doubt that Yahweh has chosen and blessed Saul, or that at this point in time Saul abides by Deuteronomy 17:14-20, or that a return to the judges system is unlikely if not impossible.[23]

Samuel's speech in 1 Samuel 12 instructs Israel in how they can flourish under a monarchy. He examines their history from the exodus onward in order to link their asking for a king to past rebellions (12:1-18). With this background in place, he calls them to fear and serve Yahweh based on God's great acts on their behalf, an exhortation that summarizes the Pentateuch (12:24-25). This challenge is undergirded by Samuel's conviction that Yahweh will not abandon Israel because of the importance of maintaining his character and reputation (12:22). Adherence to Yahweh will result in success, but forsaking Yahweh will lead to disaster, just as Deuteronomy 27—28 has already warned (12:19-25). The monarchy is no more doomed to failure than the system of the judges or the leadership of Moses and Joshua was. It will rise or fall based on its acceptance or rejection of Deuteronomy 17:14-20.

Canonical Synthesis: Divine Kingship

Few canonical passages deal with Saul's reign. Chronicles skips his early years in order to report his death, which the author attributes to his disobedience to God's word (1 Chron 10:1-14). Hosea 13:9-11 does mention Israel's request for a king, however, stating that God gave Israel a king in anger, only to remove him later. Hosea's point is that kings cannot save a disobedient people from impending disaster. Kings rise and fall according to divine authority, just as nations do. Like 1 Samuel 8:1-9, the text in Hosea denounces the people's motives in asking for a king. The nation wants a king to do what only Yahweh can perform. Israel's request amounts to an independent decision on their part that can only lead to disaster.[24]

God's installation of a king in no way indicates that Yahweh has relinquished ultimate authority to a human being. Deuteronomy 17:14-20 implies that Israel's kings answer to a higher ruler.[25] When he is asked to become king, Gideon replies that Yahweh rules over Israel (Judg 8:23). Isaiah 6:1-2 envisions the Lord on a throne, surrounded by heavenly beings, a vision shared by Ezekiel 1:26-28. Zechariah 14:16-21 depicts Yahweh as King in Jerusalem at the end of time. Psalms 47, 93 and 96—99 celebrate the notion that the Lord, the Creator, reigns supremely over creation. Seen this way,

Israel's kings are to be God's agents on earth who see that Yahweh's rule of law is kept intact. As Christoph Barth comments:

> God's deeds in history might suggest at times that he has only just been enthroned, and Israel hopes for his future enthronement when his kingdom seems to be hidden or invalidated by present disorders. Yet he never ceases to sit on the throne and to rule the world.[26]

The God Who Assesses and Rejects Saul: 1 Samuel 13—15

Since Yahweh remains sovereign, and since Yahweh has standards for kings, it is inevitable that Yahweh will assess Saul's effectiveness by his faithfulness to those standards. As this assessment unfolds in 1 Samuel 13—15, it becomes apparent that the Lord does not judge according to whether or not Saul performs as well as kings of other nations, though Israel does so (see 1 Sam 8:4-5). God determines Saul's future by the king's obedience to divine commands. When Saul fails in this manner, Yahweh removes him as divinely anointed ruler. The human agent who carries God's assessment is Samuel the prophet. This prophet-king scenario will be repeated several times in later texts.

Saul's failure unfolds in three acts, none of which affects Israel's success in battle. First, he offers sacrifices himself when Samuel fails to come as promised and his army dwindles before a major battle (13:1-9). Samuel informs him that he has done foolishly, so foolishly that he has forfeited the chance for God to give him an eternal kingdom (13:10-13). P. D. Miscall thinks Saul's error lies in not having enough initiative to attack without offering sacrifices.[27] Robert M. Polzin believes Samuel is as much a failure in this episode as Saul, since the prophet tries to keep the king under his control.[28] Kyle McCarter notes Samuel's lack of punctuality but then comments, "He [Saul] has disobeyed Yahweh, or rather Yahweh's prophet. Thus he has violated the terms of his appointment as king. Kingship requires obedience."[29] Gordon observes that Saul's sin may be that he usurped the priest's role as described in Leviticus, but the text does not say so. What the text does indicate is that Saul has willfully disobeyed.[30] McCarter and Gordon get to the heart of the problem, though Miscall and Polzin locate some of the factors in Saul's decision-making process. What matters most is that God seeks another king (13:14) and that Saul's decision, not dark fate, brings God to this conclusion.[31]

Second, Saul makes a rash vow that his own son says "troubles" the people (14:1-30). Though God fights for Israel against the Philistines (14:15-23), and despite Jonathan's victories that prove God is with Israel, Saul swears that the army will not eat until he has been avenged (14:24). This oath is akin to Jephthah's ill-conceived vow (Judg 11:31-40)[32] and reveals that Saul is "out of touch with God and indeed with nature and human needs as well."[33] It also implies that Saul sees war more as vindication for himself than as vindication for Yahweh and security for the people.[34] In other words, he acts like other kings. Only the people's intervention keeps Saul from executing Jonathan as Jephthah sacrificed his daughter (14:31-52).

Third, Samuel brings an explicit command from God that Saul must destroy the Amalekites in battle (15:1-3). The reason is Amalek's ancient opposition to Israel (cf. Ex 17:8-16; Deut 25:17-19), and the method of war is spelled out in Deuteronomy 20:16-18. To disobey means a refusal to honor God's written or revealed word. Though God gives the victory, Saul spares his royal counterpart and the best of the spoil, destroying only worthless booty (15:1-9). Again he has acted precisely as virtually any other king would, thus misunderstanding what constitutes success in his work.

Yahweh rejects Saul and sends Samuel to tell him so (15:10-12). Saul has set up a monument to himself, more evidence of his attitude about the war (15:12). When confronted, he owns his disobedience only under much pressure. Even then he believes he has done well and confesses only because he wants to retain power (15:30), a desire that later becomes an obsession. Samuel's condemnation is simple: Saul has rejected the word of Yahweh, who has always insisted that obedience precedes sacrifice (15:19-23). Thus his rejection is final (15:26-29). Again it must be stressed that Yahweh decides to reject Saul. The One who chose Saul can also replace him.

This initial instance of kingship foreshadows God's assessment of every future king in the book of Kings. There the author falls into a comfortable pattern of noting a ruler's ascension, length of rule and effectiveness. Always success is measured by adherence to Mosaic monotheism. Anything less results in mixed reviews, or worse. Saul himself never overtly worships other gods, yet he determines the nature of his religion himself, which in itself is a type of syncretism. As king, he forgets to yield his will to his own sovereign. For this he pays an awful price, turning himself into a tragic figure.[35]

The God Who Elects, Protects and Exalts David: 1 Samuel 16—2 Samuel 5

With Saul now unsuitable for leadership, the Lord selects David to be the new king. Saul lives on, hardly willing to give up the throne. Thus Yahweh must protect the chosen one until Saul's reign runs its course and David can take control. This process consumes a long segment in Samuel, which highlights the uniqueness of David and his relationship to Yahweh. In 1 Samuel 16—18 the Lord chooses David and raises him to prominence in Israel. With the exception of 1 Samuel 28, all of 1 Samuel 19—30 examines God's protection of David when Saul and others endanger the chosen one.

Finally, 2 Samuel 1—5 discusses how Yahweh engineers David's rise to power. Interspersed in these accounts are episodes that describe Saul's descent into jealousy, madness, the occult and death (see 1 Sam 28, 31). His demise underscores David's rise.

God's selection of David is as unexplained as that of Abraham, Jacob, Moses, Saul and others. That is, God informs Samuel one of Jesse's sons must be anointed king (16:1). Yahweh does say that human beings examine outward appearance while he "looks at the heart" (16:7), yet no details about the nature of David's heart are given. All that can be said is that God values character above all other personal details. The overall canonical discussion must help interpreters decide what God sees in David as well as how God will bring him to power.

Once Samuel anoints David (16:13), God begins to make him powerful by giving him "the Spirit of the LORD" (16:13). This gift confirms David's election not just as king but as Yahweh's king. Though Saul seems to forget this point, it was God's spirit upon him that led to his early victories (10:9—11:15). As Walther Eichrodt concludes:

> It is not military ability nor the gifts of a statesman, not the setting up of a definite law of the kingdom nor a position of authority in domestic affairs which make the king, but the proof in his person that he is a man filled with divine power, and therefore capable of greater things than other men.[36]

Now David receives God's spirit for the purpose of ruling, while Saul loses his special anointing for leadership (16:14). Saul's new nonelect status includes enduring a punishing spirit from Yahweh that replaces the blessing presence of the past. John Calvin says that through this troubling spirit Saul's sins are "punished by it as by a lash [I Sam. 16:14; 18:10]."[37] Saul receives relief from the terrorizing spirit when David, who has been recruited for the task, plays music for the distraught monarch (16:14-23). David's emergence in Saul's court is a second way God begins David's rise to the throne.

Samuel's anointing of the chosen ruler introduces the growing importance of prophets and prophecy in Israel. God has already guaranteed the veracity of Samuel's prophetic pronouncements (3:19-21). The Lord has also used him to deliver directions for battle and to condemn Saul's disobedience (13:13-14; 15:1-3, 22-23). Samuel accurately predicts events in Saul's life (10:1-13) and provides a deterrent to royal excess.[38] Samuel has been God's messenger. Now he serves as God's representative in the transfer of political power, a role later prophets will fulfill as well.

Yahweh magnifies and defends David in several ways in the rest of the section. The famous story about Goliath allows David to become Israel's most celebrated soldier (1 Sam 17), introduces him to Jonathan, who becomes his close friend and protector (18:1-5), and paves the way for David to marry Michal, Saul's daughter (18:20-30). God's presence (18:12), Jonathan's friendship (19:1-7; 20:1-42), Michal's devotion (19:11-17) and the Spirit of the Lord (19:19-24) save David from certain death. Saul drives David away, seeks his life and kills those who protect him (1 Sam 21—24). David survives, though, even when he flees to Philistia (1 Sam 25—27; 29). God has already proven sovereign over the Philistine gods (see 1 Sam 5), so David is safe there.

One episode in David's outlaw period highlights God's work in his life. David's followers are insulted by a man named Nabal, so he prepares to punish the offender (25:1-13). Nabal's wife, Abigail, saves David from bloodshed by convincing him God will give him a "lasting dynasty" (25:28) and deliver him from his enemies (25:29). His own confession is that God has kept him from doing evil of the sort Saul attempts to do to him (25:39). When Nabal dies, David learns how well God does protect (25:36-38). Abigail's intervention reminds David "to live by faith in the Lord God, and not by his own impulses"[39] and functions like a prophetic word in its delivering power and instructive nature.

By contrast, Yahweh does not protect Saul nor give him a prophetic word to guide him (28:3-7). That is, the only prophetic word comes from the deceased Samuel (25:1), who prophesies Saul's death when he is summoned by a medium (28:8-25). The only way Yahweh speaks to Saul is through a punishing, maddening spirit or through a dead prophet called up by a woman whose powers Moses considered detestable, or evil (Deut 18:9-13). God's final word to Saul is to let him die in battle (31:1-13) while David is protected from political and physical harm (1 Sam 29—30). Saul's latter years do not negate his earlier greatness, but they do magnify how far a disobedient person may decline spiritually, emotionally and politically. David F. Payne notes that Saul's death teaches Israel that having a king will not save them. Rather, "the essential thing was for the Israelites to have the right kings."[40]

With Saul gone from the scene, Yahweh exalts the chosen one to the throne. Again, though, there are barriers to this exaltation. David's tribe (Judah) makes him their king (2:4), but the rest of Israel follows Saul's son Ish-Bosheth (2:8-11). Finally assassins remove David's rival, though David does not reward the killers with anything but death (4:1-12). By now David's confession is to call Yahweh the One "who has delivered me out of all trouble" (4:9), and he seems to understand, at this point at least, that he has not been delivered to act like a typical petty tribal chieftain. Rather he has been redeemed to affirm his faith in his protector.[41]

Four final episodes complete David's exaltation. First, the rest of Israel accepts him as monarch (5:1-5). The process of ascension has taken many years, but Yahweh's chosen one has risen inexorably to power. Samuel's author emphasizes that this exaltation occurs without any rebellion or duplicity on David's part.[42] God has done it. Second, David's forces capture Jerusalem, and he makes it the seat of government (5:6-9). The text attributes this victory to Yahweh's presence with the king (5:10). David's greatness comes as a gift from "Yahweh of hosts," who as sovereign divine ruler has all the armies of heaven at his disposal.[43] The greater King has bestowed earthly glory on the chosen one. Third, Hiram of Tyre recognizes David's power by building him a house, or palace (5:11-12). Fourth, Yahweh directs David's wars against the Philistines, thus guaranteeing victory over his enemies (5:17-25). After one victory David's men collect Philistia's lifeless idols (5:21), which contrasts sharply with how Yahweh operates when Israel suffers defeat (1 Sam 5).

Canonical Synthesis: David and Psalms

This section of Samuel initiates the canon's emphasis on David as psalmist. David plays music for Saul (1 Sam 16:17-23) and sings a lament when Saul and Jonathan die in battle (2 Sam 1:17-27). At the end of his life David sings a song of praise that highlights God's deliverance from Saul and other enemies (2 Sam 22:1—23:7). In the psalter, Psalm 18:1-30 matches 2 Samuel 22:1-30 nearly word for word. This dual canonical attribution to David not only makes it plausible that David wrote this material[44] but also makes it likely that the psalm acts as a summary of God's great acts on his behalf in both books. Seen this way, Psalm 18 and 2 Samuel 22 interpret 1 Samuel 16—2 Samuel 5 as material that focuses on God's preservation of David in even extreme circumstances.

Twelve other psalms have titles that trace them to specific events in Samuel (Ps 3, 30, 34, 51, 52, 54, 56, 57, 59, 60, 63, 142). All but Psalms 3, 51 and 60 are set within 1 Samuel 16—2 Samuel 5. Scholars disagree over the historical value of the titles,[45] but enough evidence exists to conclude that they have reasonably solid historical analysis backing them. The following summary indicates that most of the psalms deal with David's narrow escapes during the time in which he flees from Saul as he waits for his election to be recognized.

1. Psalm 30 celebrates the dedication of David's house, which probably though by no means certainly refers to 2 Samuel 5:11-12. Here David's fame spreads to Tyre, whose king builds him a house.

2. Psalm 34 thanks God for delivering David from the king of Gath (cf. 1 Sam 21:10-15).

3. Psalm 52 chastises evil men after Doeg the Edomite kills the priests who aid David's flight from Saul (1 Sam 22:9).

4. Psalm 54 gives thanks for God's deliverance from the Ziphites' treachery (1 Sam 23:19; 26:1).

5. Psalm 56 expects deliverance from the Philistines, probably in the episode in 1 Samuel 21:10-15 but possibly in the accusation scene in 1 Samuel 29:1-11.

6. Psalm 57 parallels 1 Samuel 22:1 and 24:3, for it focuses on David's fleeing from Saul at the cave.

7. Psalm 59 marks David's escape from Saul with Michal's help (1 Sam 19:11-17).

8. Psalm 63 stresses David's search for God during David's time in the desert, a setting that matches 1 Samuel 22:5 and 23:14.

9. Psalm 142 returns to the cave episode (1 Sam 22:1; 24:3). Here David prays for deliverance.

Two canonical details stand out in the preceding summary. The first is that God's protection of David is a major theme. The second is that the persons who affixed the titles were aware of the major events depicted in Samuel that relate to David's early years. Thus the canon's collectors' attempt to provide a format that interprets Israel's past as it is presented in Scripture. History becomes the background for worship, just as surely as worship strengthened David during difficult historical circumstances. Where theology and history intersect in the canon, worship occurs.[46]

The God Who Makes an Eternal Covenant with David: 2 Samuel 6—7

Few texts (if any) generate the exegetical opinions[47] and canonical responses that 2 Samuel 6—7 does. Two events dominate the passage. First, David takes the ark to Jerusalem, thus making that city the center of Israelite worship (6:1-23). Second, the king desires to build a temple to house the ark but is denied the right to do so, only to be offered an eternal kingdom instead (7:1-17). David is rightly astonished at this turn of events and states his well-placed gratitude to the Lord (7:18-29). Most prophetic texts that fasten their hopes on a coming Messiah ("anointed one") have their starting point in 2 Samuel 7:1-17, and the psalms that stress Jerusalem's primacy have 2 Samuel 6 and other related texts in mind. Thus it is appropriate to separate these chapters from 1 Samuel 16—2 Samuel 5 despite the fact that both segments chronicle David's exaltation by Yahweh.

God's ark has resided in Abinadab's house since 1 Samuel 7. David attempts to move it to Jerusalem, only to discover that the holy God still protects the ark to the point of killing those who presume to touch it needlessly (6:1-11). When the ark comes at last to Jerusalem, the symbol of "the name of the LORD Almighty, who is enthroned between the cherubim" (6:2) rests in David's capital. This fact does not mean David controls Yahweh at all, which 2 Samuel 6:1-11 makes clear. God remains independent of whoever houses the ark, so David is privileged that the Lord decides the ark may stay in Jerusalem.

With the whole nation under his control, with the government centralized in his city and with his enemies quieted for the moment (7:1) David seeks to honor God by building a temple (7:2). Nathan the prophet provides the necessary communicative link between the king and the Lord, a function fulfilled by Samuel in the past. The word Yahweh gives Nathan for David provides a virtual summary of Old Testament theology.

First, Yahweh reminds Nathan that the Lord has never commanded a temple to be built (7:6-7). God is quite able to meet with the people under the conditions set forth in the Pentateuch.[48] David need not fear any anger or disappointment on Yahweh's part over the lack of a temple. References to Egypt and Israel's earlier shepherds encompass both the nation's history and the canon's contents. God has never needed a place to live. As Creator, Yahweh transcends such needs or wants.[49]

Second, Yahweh summarizes David's career in two parts. From humble origins God chose him to lead Israel (7:8) and then protected and exalted him against all his enemies (7:9). Apparently the Lord did not do so to gain a temple. Third, Yahweh claims that David has been chosen so that Israel might receive rest in the promised land, a goal highlighted in Joshua and Judges (7:10-11). David has been elected and protected so that Yahweh's promises to Abraham might be fulfilled (Gen 12:1-9). This reference, coupled with the comment in 7:9 that Yahweh will give David a great name, ties this special event firmly to the earlier pledge.[50] Great historical events, themes and personages seem to be converging here.

Fourth, having touched upon canonical and historical points ranging from Abraham to the era of the judges, Yahweh instructs Nathan to predict both the short- and the long-term future. David will have a son who will rule after him, a prediction Solomon fulfills (7:12; cf. 1 Kings 1—2). This son will build a temple, another promise Solomon fulfills (7:13; cf. 1 Kings 6:1—9:9). Yahweh promises to love and correct Solomon, pledges 1 Kings 3—11 amply proves are kept (7:14-15). These statements carry the canon far forward.

Fifth, the Lord makes promises that reach well beyond Solomon's time. Yahweh says David's throne will be established forever (7:13, 15). This pledge is based on a filial relationship, for God will be the king's father and the king will be God's son, an image applied to all Israel in Exodus 4:22.[51] As always, God's covenant is inextricably linked to a relationship with the covenant partner. The eternal nature of the covenant is stated in absolute, unconditional terms.[52] This blessing honors David, but it also offers the nation as a whole stability, hope, leadership and rest.[53] Having stated the promise, the text leaves it to history and to the canon to spell out specific details of its fulfillment.

David's response is as ideal as Yahweh's blessing. He praises Yahweh for choosing, exalting and making promises for the distant future (7:18-19). David knows God's acts are done to honor God's character and fame, not his own (7:20-21). Therefore David confesses, "There is no God but you" (7:22), a monotheistic faith he never forsakes even at his worst, and recognizes the unique Lord's unique relationship with the unique people (7:23-27). Believing all God's words true (7:28), David confidently expects Yahweh to do all that has been promised (7:29). His confession could hardly be improved.

Canonical Synthesis: The Messianic Promise

There are so many canonical connections to this section that it is necessary to be selective in noting them. As has been stated, Solomon's career, as depicted in 1 Kings 1—11, fulfills many of the nearest predictions. Perhaps the most significant aspects 2 Samuel 6—7 addresses are his temple building and his establishment of the Davidic dynasty. God places his name on the temple (1 Kings 9:3), which in turn establishes Jerusalem as a specially chosen city. Despite Solomon's idolatry (1 Kings 11:1-8), Yahweh does not end the dynasty because of the promises made to David (1 Kings 11:11-13). Solomon stands as the link to David's fidelity and the dynasty's later consistent covenant breaking.

Isaiah, Jeremiah, Ezekiel and the Twelve all look to the Davidic dynasty for an ideal king to solve the nation's sin problem. These references will be discussed in the chapters that deal with those books. But even a cursory glance at these prophecies reveals this tendency. Isaiah 9:2-7 and Isaiah 11:1-9 mention ideal Davidic rulers in texts that look forward to ideal times. Jeremiah 23:1-8 links Israel's deliverance in the last days to one of David's relatives who will provide righteous leadership for the chosen people. Jeremiah calls the Davidic ruler a shepherd, the very term Ezekiel uses to describe the coming king (Ezek 34:1-31). Micah 5:1-5 looks to Bethlehem to provide a shepherd who will bring peace to Israel, indeed to the end of the earth. The list of texts could be extended.

By the time these texts are written centuries after David's death the sense of "eternal kingdom" has come to mean "lasting peace throughout the world" (cf. Is 11:1-9; Mic 5:1-5). The prophets' interpretation of 2 Samuel 7:1-17 is particularly accurate if Walter Kaiser's thesis that God's promises amount to a "charter for mankind" (cf. 2 Sam 7:19) that impacts all nations is correct.[54] The prophets believe that this king will help Israel be the nation of priests God wants them to be (cf. Ex 19:5-6). In this way Israel will initiate peace and righteousness in all lands.

In Psalms, the royal psalms focus on the Davidic promises, especially the pledge that the king will be God's "son" (2 Sam 7:14). Again Israel itself is often called God's son (cf. Ex 4:22; Deut 14:1; Hos 11:1),[55] but in the psalms God's anointed, the king, also receives this designation (Ps 2:7).[56] Both Israel and David have a covenant with the Lord that amounts to a family relationship.[57] Just as important is the fact that Psalm 89:27-29 links the theme of the son with the eternal covenant in much the same way as 2 Samuel 7:1-17. Here the text even defines "eternal" as long "as the heavens endure" (Ps 89:29), not as long as the dynasty endures.[58] It also wonders how the promise of duration can be fulfilled if the dynasty has been displaced (Ps 89:38-52). Therefore it leaves open the matter of how the Davidic king anticipated in the prophetic writings will even have a chance to emerge.

The New Testament applies these texts to Jesus Christ. In him they find one who fulfills all requirements. Jesus comes from David's family (Mt 1:1-17). Jesus is confessed as God's son in texts that quote Psalm 2:7 (Acts 13:33; Heb 1:5; 5:5). Revelation 19:16 declares him "KING OF KINGS AND LORD OF LORDS," a phrase that encompasses all royal requirements set forth in the Old Testament. Other canonical connections will be mentioned later, but it is clear that New Testament authors believe Jesus must meet these earlier standards to be the savior who eradicates the sin problem, who embodies all that is entailed in the charter for the human race.

The God Who Judges Yet Protects David: 2 Samuel 8—20

In many ways 2 Samuel 7 constitutes the epitome of faithful kingship. David's relationship to God could hardly be more ideal, which means the monarch fulfills Moses' standards set forth in Deuteronomy 17:14-20. This glorious arrangement continues in 2 Samuel 8—10, where David governs justly, makes sound decisions and receives Yahweh's favor. In 2 Samuel 11—20, however, the book's tone shifts dramatically. David sins, and not even his prior relationship with God saves him from appropriate loss. When the king is judged the whole kingdom suffers; such is the responsibility of leadership. Unlike Saul, David thinks Yahweh's judgments are fair and accepts them. Thus he is able to praise God and accept further correction in 2 Samuel 21—24. Part of David's greatness lies in his unflagging devotion to Yahweh despite being under the Lord's discipline. He is like Moses in this regard.

David's ongoing faithfulness is blessed considerably in 2 Samuel 8—10. Here David's kingdom reaches great heights as he conquers enemies (8:1-18), shows kindness to his friend Jonathan's progeny (9:1-13) and avenges himself on insulting neighboring nations (10:1-19). Such achievements are possible because of God's favoring presence (8:6, 14) as well as David's commitment to Yahweh (8:11) and to ruling justly (8:15). Historical conditions were also favorable at this time. H. W. Hertzberg combines all these factors when he claims that

David's kingdom was not only the first but also the greatest state to arise on the soil of Palestine. And while that was only possible because at the time, in the tenth century, there were no great states of considerable power either in Asia Minor and Mesopotamia or in Egypt, nevertheless the chief cause lies in the person of King David, who was exceptionally skilful both at politics and in war.[59]

Even more important, he writes, is the fact that

behind what is catalogued here in such a matter-of-fact way lies the supreme achievement of a man of whom it is twice intentionally said "The Lord helped him." Evidently his contemporaries and their successors regarded these deeds as a miracle.[60]

Everything David does prospers because he serves the God who directs history.

Swiftly, sadly and unexpectedly everything changes. David stays home from war, commits adultery, gains a conspirator and then kills his lover's husband (11:1-27). David has broken all the laws Moses set forth for kings in Deuteronomy 17:14-20. A desire for power, sex, oppression and self-seeking has emerged. Despite David's favored status, God considers his activities evil (11:27). He will endure the results of his sin, for if God punished other covenant bearers such as Abraham, Jacob and Moses, and if God chastised Saul for his behavior, then surely Yahweh will assess and judge David as well. God's character demands a response.

Just as Samuel bore God's punishing word to Saul (1 Sam 15:17-23), so now Nathan performs this prophetic task with David (2 Sam 12:1). Combined with his role as bearer of good news in 2 Samuel 7:4-17 this episode completes the portrait of Nathan as a full-fledged, fully functioning messenger of God. He confronts David, secures his repentance, predicts punishment and leaves the king to his future (12:1-15). David's illegitimate child dies as Nathan predicted, but rebellion and public humiliation loom in the future. Solomon comes from David's marriage to Bathsheba, however, so some good will eventually result (12:24). God continues to bless David's future even while punishing his present.

Yahweh continues both to maintain a commitment to the covenant with David yet also to punish the sinful king in 2 Samuel 13—20. David's family is torn apart first by incest and then by Absalom's rebellion (13—15). Though the first incident is not part of God's chastisement, it does lead to the rebellion that was part of the punishment Nathan anticipated (12:11-12). David survives because Yahweh had decided to defeat the counsel Absalom receives (17:14) and because God delivers him in battle, thereby freeing him from Absalom's grasp (18:28-33). Only the Lord's intervention keeps David in power during the debacle with Absalom and the subsequent threats to his authority in 2 Samuel 19—20. At the same time, though, all the harsh moments come as a result of God's displeasure at David's actions. Again this tension mirrors that of previous clashes between God and earlier characters, as well as between the Lord and Israel itself.

Canonical Synthesis: David's Penitence

This era in David's life is not discussed at great length in the canon, yet it is not bypassed altogether. In 1 Kings 1—2 there is intrigue over whether Adonijah or Solomon will succeed the dying David. Nathan and Bathsheba encourage the aging monarch to decide the matter in Solomon's favor. So he does, telling Solomon to eliminate Joab, the man who executed Uriah. The ugly chapter is thereby closed. Later 1 Kings 15:4-5 observes that David never served other gods; his only major flaw was the sin with Bathsheba. The historian feels free to praise David's adherence to monotheism yet does not shirk a deeply felt obligation to write a truthful history about this very human being with whom the Lord made an everlasting covenant.

Psalms 3—5 mirror Samuel's twin theological themes of overlapping divine protection and assessment. The earlier psalm asks for protection and sustenance in the midst of an uprising. Traditionally attributed to the incident with Absalom the passage celebrates Yahweh's willingness to save. Psalm 51, by contrast, presents the Bible's most detailed and heartfelt confession of sin. Its title links this penitential psalm to the adultery with Bathsheba. Unlike Saul's, David's admission of guilt contains no excuses or hopes for retaining governmental power. Rather the psalmist owns the sin, recognizes its effect on the one praying and those around him, and realizes that all sins are ultimately against God. Great sin calls for thorough repentance. David does not falter in doing what is necessary to restore a right relationship with his God.

Oddly enough, Chronicles never mentions David's moral failure. Instead the narrative skips from 2 Samuel 11:1 to 2 Samuel 24:9. Without question the two historians differ in their approach. How and why they do so will be analyzed in the chapter on Chronicles. It is sufficient to say at this point that the Former Prophets recount Israel's glories in the context of its ultimate failure, while Chronicles admits Israel displayed some weaknesses during its great history. This distinction highlights differences of interest and intention, not of error versus truth.

The God Who Deserves David's Devotion: 2 Samuel 21—24

Sin has an adhesive quality that only steadfast devotion can combat. Even the greatest men and women sin, so devotion and repentance are necessary for the faithful in any era. David exhibits these characteristics in this final segment in Samuel. He attempts to make good Saul's sinful acts (21:1-14), yet he also has to confess his own transgressions (24:1-25). He sings of God's help in two poems (22:1-51; 23:1-7), yet he also depends on aid from unscrupulous human beings (21:15-22; 23:8-39). He sins but always returns to Yahweh, which demonstrates his core commitment to the Lord. David fails, yet he moves forward toward God afterwards. Thus his devotion is as real as his sin.

Some scholars consider 2 Samuel 21—24 a rather disjointed intrusion into the deuteronomistic history. This conviction grows out of the work of Leonhard Rost and others who believe 2 Samuel 9—20 and 1 Kings 1—2 derive from a source that stresses the struggles related to determining David's successor.[61] These commentators often argue that the succession narrative sets forth an apologetic for Solomon's rise to power[62] and that 2 Samuel 21—24 therefore breaks into this clear historical-theological-ideological account.

Other critics think this segment critiques overly enthusiastic devotion to the Davidic dynasty. R. A. Carlson concludes that the narratives in 2 Samuel 21 and 24 are careful to demonstrate David's flaws.[63] Walter Brueggemann says that 2 Samuel 21—24 acts as a "deconstruction" of David in direct contrast to the tremendous promises and praise heaped upon him in 2 Samuel 5—8.[64] Viewed this way, the passage cautions readers against magnifying David to inappropriate proportions. Rather they should see him as the chosen of God but also as a very human king totally dependent on Yahweh.[65]

As was stated earlier in this chapter, Brevard Childs and Polzin treat 1 Samuel 1—2 and 2 Samuel 21—24 as canonical and literary end pieces.[66] Childs particularly links Hannah's praise in 1 Samuel 2:1-10 to David's song in 2 Samuel 22:1-51. Polzin extends the canonical importance of 2 Samuel 21—24 to include several crucial canonical seams.

Two things are obvious about the placement of this poetry in the books of Samuel. First, David's song (22:1-51) and last word (23:1-7) recall Jacob's poem at the end of Genesis (Gen 49:1-27) and Moses' song and blessing near the end of Deuteronomy (Deut 32:1-43; 33:1-29). At the same time, David's final poems combine with Hannah's song and David's elegy in 2 Samuel 1 to form a magnificent triptych that graces the books of Samuel at the beginning, middle and end.[67]

Childs and Polzin demonstrate that 2 Samuel 21—24 aids canonical cohesion rather than creating historical-sequential disruption. Both 1 Samuel 1—2 and 2 Samuel 21—24 focus on praise of what God has done rather than on what David or Hannah has achieved. Human frailty, whether the inability to conceive or the ability to conceive in an adulterous relationship, is overcome by divine grace.

While a unitary approach to Samuel best serves Old Testament theology, all the opinions noted share a concern that David's humanity stands in tension with God's promises. The text has balanced these two realities since the incident with Bathsheba, so the concern is definitely valid though not new to these chapters. Thus it is appropriate to discern how human sin impacts what God does and how divine favor affects human behavior and determines the course of future events. At the intersection of these issues stand human praise and devotion. Worship links a faltering David to an unfaltering Yahweh. The result is a continuation of the Lord's commitment to the chosen people.

Both major narratives in 2 Samuel 21—24 describe events by which God judges Israel. In the first episode (21:1-14), the Lord has sent a famine because of Saul's unrecompensed mistreatment of the Gibeonites. Only after David hands over seven of Saul's relatives to be killed and David orders the bones of Saul, Jonathan and the seven unfortunate victims buried together does God turn aside a famine. This strange story reemphasizes Saul's failures, David's obedience, Israel's dependence on the God of creation and Yahweh's gracious response to the people's pleas for relief (21:14).[68] It also finally brings down the curtain on Saul's career. David and his line have prevailed over all who seek to defeat them. The description of great acts that follows underscores the role of David's followers in his ability to prevail (21:15-22), as does its companion text in 2 Samuel 23:8-39. They, too, contribute to God's exaltation of the king (cf. 21:17).

David understands that God's great acts on his behalf merit praise for Yahweh's character and work. Thus the confessional song of praise found in 2 Samuel 22:1-51 highlights the importance of worship in David's life. The psalm, also found in Psalm 18, covers the major epochs in the king's life. In doing so it stresses God's support during the deliverance from times of extreme external pressure such as that David endured in 1 Samuel 16—31 (cf. 2 Sam 21:1-20). David further claims that his own spiritual commitment brought reward (21:21-30). He also states that God's words and ways are flawless (21:31) and asks if there is another deity at all (21:32), a question that at the least reveals implicit monotheism.[69] Finally, David praises God for keeping him in power by defeating foes both at home and abroad (22:40-51). Again he knows and confesses that Yahweh deserves credit for the positive events in his life.

The king's last words contained in 2 Samuel 23:1-7 complete the summary of his life. He mentions the eternal covenant first promised in 2 Samuel 7:1-17 (cf. 23:5). It is this promise that separates David from even the righteous monarchs who serve later in Israel's history. Great kings integrate righteous character and righteous leadership,[70] but only he receives the blessing of an endless dynasty that is preserved by a gracious God.[71] Such a unique blessing merits heartfelt devotion to the one Lord.

In the book's last scene God once again demonstrates both a commitment to assessment and a desire to bless. Yahweh chooses to punish Israel by inciting David to take a census, for which the Lord then sends a plague (24:1-17). Two events demonstrate David's devotion. First, he confesses his sin and places himself and the people in God's hands, which parallels his reaction to Nathan's accusation after his adultery with Bathsheba (24:10-17; cf. 12:13). Second, he buys a threshing floor that becomes the site for Solomon's temple (24:18-25). There he offers sacrifices, further proof of his desire to worship Yahweh (24:25).

Canonical Synthesis: David and Worship

Canonical reflection beyond that mentioned in this section's introductory paragraphs must include two further details. The first is that the reappearance of 2 Samuel 22 in Psalm 18 reinforces the canon's perception of David as a great worshiper of Yahweh. Despite his other great achievements, the books of Psalms and Chronicles focus on his contributions to Israelite praise, lament, confession and temple organization. His devotion endures longer than anything save his dynasty. The second is that the purchase of the worship site will eventually actualize Moses' anticipation of a single worship center (cf. Deut 12:1-14). Solomon's temple fulfills this prediction, but it is David's decision to buy the threshing floor that begins the temple-building process. The purchase therefore celebrates God's grace in David's time[72] yet also creates a space where this benevolence can be enjoyed by all Israel.

Conclusion

Samuel balances Joshua by depicting success in the land centuries after Israel enters Canaan. Sandwiched between these books, Judges offers a somber picture of how seriously God takes sin and how seriously the holy, chosen people should take it as well. Though David's character is far from flawless, his faithful response to divine election and personal exaltation helps establish his people in the promised land. God's promise of an everlasting throne offers hope that Israel may have a great future that will prove them sound stewards of God's creation, a true means of Abraham's blessing other nations and an international testimony as a holy nation of their holy God. What remains to be seen is whether this promise will be realized or whether a new generation will sink to Judges-like depths.

10

The God
Whose Word
Shapes History

1-2 Kings

. . . .

P ERHAPS MORE THAN ANY OTHER CANONICAL WORK, THE BOOK OF KINGS
argues for a single-minded commitment to the one God who exists, creates,
makes covenant and gives the land. Here the day-to-day struggles of
Yahweh's faithful servants against the proponents of idolatry unfold. Here
kings and kingdoms rise and fall, each one dependent on God's will for its
existence. Here the full impact of Israel's covenant obedience or disobedience
becomes evident, and here the likelihood of losing the promised land
becomes a reality for the first time. All that has unfolded in Joshua, Judges
and Samuel culminates. Israel ascends to its greatest religious, economic and
political strength during Solomon's reign (c. 970-930 B.C.), only to divide at
his death, then disintegrate and suffer exile by 587 B.C. This demise has
profound historical and theological implications for the rest of Scripture.

Israel's destruction seems highly unlikely early in the book. God keeps
the Davidic covenant by placing Solomon on the throne in 1 Kings 1—2.
Yahweh's faithfulness has been unerring in the succession process. Then God
gives Solomon extraordinary wisdom and affirms his decision to build the
temple, promising to dwell at the central worship site (1 Kings 3—9).
Solomon receives honor and riches, yet he turns to syncretism and idolatry
by the end of his life, an apostasy that leads Yahweh to tear the kingdom
into two parts when Solomon dies. The nation's dying begins at this point,

but more than three hundred years pass before Yahweh's patience and Israel's life are exhausted.

Once the death throes start, the Lord opposes every sort of threat to strict Yahwistic monotheism. Yahweh rejects syncretism (1 Kings 12—16), fights Canaanite idolatry (1 Kings 17—2 Kings 1) and works miracles on behalf of faithful worshipers (2 Kings 2—13). Most prominent of all the committed monotheists are the prophets, who declare God's covenant truths to the people and who suffer persecution for their dedication. They are the human instruments for working miracles as well as for proclaiming the truth. Finally, God's opposition to covenant infidelity concludes with the destruction of both portions of the now-divided Israel (2 Kings 14—17 and 2 Kings 18—25). Assyria and Babylon conquer the covenant people, but God sends them to do so. Yahweh controls history in Kings as certainly as he does in Exodus or Joshua, but this time God's sovereignty does not work in Israel's favor. Rather all the consequences for rebellion outlined in Leviticus 26, Deuteronomy 27—28 and Joshua 24 come to pass.

At several key junctures in the account the author mentions three sources used in this centuries-long history (e.g., 1 Kings 11:41; 2 Kings 13:8). All these references are to information about kings. Other data may have been used as well, since many of the stories depict events related to the prophets. The writer seeks to tell Israel's history in an accurate fashion. As part of the great history based on Deuteronomy's principles the book recounts Israel's past from a specific theological viewpoint. Still, this fact in no way detracts from the account's reality. As Brevard Childs concludes:

> The manner in which the reader is constantly referred back to the writer's sources indicates that he did not envision his composition to be in contradiction with his sources. He was not attempting to rewrite history nor to supply hitherto unknown information. Neither was he writing a "theological history" which operated on its own principles apart from the history found in the official records. Event and interpretation belonged together and he needed only a selection from a larger historical sequence to demonstrate his thesis.[1]

Theology and history are inseparable in Kings, not because of any sort of special pleading on the author's part but because the writer was convinced that historical effects were caused by theological principles that were heeded or ignored.

In Kings, the prophets are the most consistently significant characters. Israel's prophetic movement united a concern for history and the belief that a failure to live up to the theological agreements found in the Pentateuch led to national disaster. In Kings the prophets preach the word, both by predicting the future and by explaining the past. Prophets anoint and denounce kings.

They are Yahweh's messengers and friends, as well as Israel's conscience and protectors.

Within the scope of the narrative the prophets' message has at least five distinguishing characteristics. First, they assess the past and present based on Israel's adherence to the covenant. Second, they predict the future based on the Sinai covenant and the Lord's covenants with Abraham and David. Third, they assess characters based entirely on a person's faithfulness to covenantal fidelity. Fourth, prophets stress repentance as the people's hope for escaping disaster. Fifth, the prophets consider those who stand against idolatry the truest supporters of Israel's government. All these ideas are included in the prophetic books that make up the next segment of the canon.

As the last book of the deuteronomic history and the conclusion of the Former Prophets, Kings plays a pivotal role in the canon. The book describes the tragic end of Israel's national story, which begins with Abraham. It also introduces readers to the prophets' tremendous influence on biblical litera-ture, provides a prophetic interpretation of Israel's past and prepares the way for Isaiah, Jeremiah, Ezekiel and the Twelve. Kings brings together such major theological issues as covenant keeping, divine promise, the responsibilities of leadership and the prophets' attempt to effect reconciliation between God and the chosen people. It also brings readers face to face with the reality of exile and its attendant need for theological reflection on that disaster. When the book ends the nation is defeated, the temple is destroyed, the people are scattered, the land is lost, and the future of the covenant relationship between God and Israel is very much in doubt. Thus it is not overstating the case to say that Kings portrays a series of historical-theological crises that culminate in the loss of much that Moses and Joshua and David worked to give Israel.

The God Who Keeps Covenant with David: 1 Kings 1—2
When the book begins Israel stands poised to enjoy its greatest days. During his reign (c. 1010-970 B.C.), David assembles a considerable regional king-dom. He has defeated neighboring lands such as Moab, Ammon, Edom, Philistia and Syria, thus expanding Israel's borders and enlarging its treasuries (see 2 Sam 8:1-14; 10:1-19). He has centralized Israel's government by capturing Jerusalem (see 2 Sam 5:6-10; 6:1-23). More significantly, he has centralized worship in Jerusalem by housing the ark there, a sure sign that Deuteronomy's statements about a central sanctuary may soon be fulfilled (cf. 2 Sam 6:1-19; Deut 12:5, 11, 14, 18, 21, 26; 14:23-25; 15:20; 16:2, 6-7, 11). As a result of the king's commitment to monotheism the people seem to display more fidelity to the covenant. Of all the personal flaws David exhibits and all the problems he encounters, none is a result of idolatry.

Most important of all, however, is the fact that the king has been promised an heir to rule when he dies and an eternal kingdom that transcends himself and his successor (cf. 2 Sam 7:1-17). Therefore the struggle to succeed David when he becomes old and decrepit takes on tremendous importance. This new king will build the temple David longed to construct and will enjoy a special relationship with Yahweh (2 Sam 7:13-16). At the same time, he should also meet the qualifications for monarchs Moses sets forth in Deuteronomy 17:14-20. This person has a significant historical opportunity that can be realized only through the fulfilling of significant theological stipulations.

Through much intrigue and the crucial intervention of David himself, Solomon bests his brother Adonijah's challenge and becomes king (1 Kings 1:1-53). David's advice to his son echoes that given by Moses to Joshua and by Yahweh to Joshua. David tells Solomon to have courage and to adhere carefully to Moses' law (1 Kings 2:1-4; cf. Deut 31:7-15; Josh 1:1-9) and then exhorts him to keep the Davidic covenant's standards (1 Kings 2:4). David also gives Solomon some astute, even cold-blooded, political advice, which he follows almost to the letter (2:5-46). Some scholars conclude that the account blames David for the bloodshed;[2] others think it seeks to exonerate him;[3] and still others think that the men are simply depicted as persons responsible for their own actions.[4] Regardless of who bears the blame for the resulting bloodshed, one thing is clear: Solomon may ignore the political advice and live to tell the tale, but the stories of Saul and David both indicate that he cannot neglect the covenant counsel and escape unscathed. His is a kingdom placed under a divine ruler who governs the chosen people. Faith in and obedience to divinely revealed truth will therefore determine the limits of his success. David's psalm in 2 Samuel 22 makes this point clear. Kings live in two worlds, David seems to say, yet their power and influence derive from the world in which they do not live.

Canonical Synthesis: God's Fidelity to David
Canonically speaking, these two chapters are interpreted in Kings as the reason that God delays Israel's punishment after the people fall into idolatrous practices, as evidence that God blesses David's lineage when his descendants obey the covenant and as God's faithfulness to the covenant king. Late in life Solomon turns to idols (1 Kings 11:1-10), so Yahweh shrinks the Davidic kingdom to two tribes. Only for David's sake (1 Kings 11:11-13) does the Lord spare any portion at all. More than two hundred years later (c. 701 B.C.), it is still for David's sake that God defends Jerusalem during Hezekiah's era (1 Kings 19:34; 2 Kings 20:6). At the same time, kings who rebel against Yahweh by allowing idolatry to flourish are compared unfavorably to David (1 Kings 14:8, 15:1-5; 2 Kings 14:1-6), while faithful monarchs

are considered like David (2 Kings 18:1-8; 22:1-2). The author of Kings knows of no better standard for kings than to measure them against their "father."

Two texts in the Writings agree with these statements. Psalm 72 appears as a late Davidic prayer (72:20) that Solomon, "the royal son" (72:1), will judge righteously so that God's people may prosper, whether they are rich or poor (72:2-4). The prayer asks that the new ruler may have a great name and a great kingdom (72:5-17), all the while confessing that only God can do such marvelous deeds (72:18-19). Similarly 2 Chronicles 28:1-10 depicts David as stressing obedience to the Mosaic law as the means for the dynasty's success and the building of the temple as the chief aim of Solomon's reign. Again kingship is defined as public service and the facilitating of monotheism. God alone must be worshiped, and God's people alone, not the king's whims, must be served. Deuteronomy 17:14-20 could hardly find clearer interpreters than the authors of these passages.

The God Who Gives Wisdom: 1 Kings 3—11

Solomon is undoubtedly one of the most fascinating individuals in Scripture. His rise to power occurs because of God's promise to David in 2 Samuel 7:1-17 yet also because of careful human maneuvering by Nathan, Bathsheba, David, and others (1 Kings 1:1-53). God fills him with great wisdom and then blesses him with wealth and renown. Solomon builds the temple to honor Yahweh. Yet by life's end he unwisely turns to foreign wives and their foreign gods, seemingly oblivious to the implications of his actions. Solomon has great organizational abilities yet creates animosity by the way he orders the government and the people. Above all these paradoxes, however, stands Solomon the man of wisdom, for it is primarily as a wise man that the canon chooses to remember him, in both the Former Prophets and the Writings.

God gives Solomon the wisdom he possesses. Because of the king's love for Yahweh and covenant commitment early in his reign,[5] God offers Solomon whatever he wishes (3:1-5). When the king asks for wisdom (3:6-9) the Lord grants his desire, plus honor and riches (3:10-15). Solomon demonstrates his God-given wisdom by deciding a difficult case (3:16-28), by organizing his government in a way that defuses many old sectional rivalries (4:1-19), by providing for a large court (4:20-28) and by becoming a great producer of wisdom materials (4:29-34). It is crucial to understand that all these achievements are a divine gift that flows from reverence for God and for God's law.

Though all the evidences of his wisdom are significant, the generating of proverbs and songs noted in 1 Kings 4:29-34 may bear the greatest canonical weight. This notion links Solomon and Israelite wisdom writing to the substantial ancient Near Eastern tradition of wisdom literature.[6] It also links him to the writing of many of the proverbs that appear in the book of Proverbs (Prov 1:1; 10:1; 25:1), and perhaps the mention of songs ties him to the Song of Songs.[7] His thorough knowledge of botany and biology demonstrates his mastery of data that were highly valued in ancient intellectual circles.[8] Put together, this report of his brilliance introduces Solomon as the father of Israelite wisdom literature, as the nation's greatest sage.[9] Thus it is not surprising that Proverbs, Ecclesiastes and Song of Songs are in some ways tied to Solomon. Without Solomon, Israelite wisdom has less discernible canonical origins. Without God, Solomon has no wisdom at all. With Solomon's wisdom comes the understanding that God makes the wise to be wise, as well as the sense that wisdom has its intellectual foundations in the Davidic covenant as much as in the ancient cultural milieu.

Wisdom and heeding his father's admonitions lead Solomon to build a temple in Jerusalem. He is aided in this endeavor by Hiram of Tyre, his father's ally and ruler of Tyre (5:1-12). Both kings were aggressive proponents of trade, and both built worship centers in their respective lands.[10] In his diplomatic letter requesting Hiram's aid, Solomon cites a desire to honor Yahweh for blessing David with the promises in 2 Samuel 7:1-17 as his reason for undertaking the project (5:3-5). Much as in the tabernacle accounts, God agrees to dwell in the temple, which is built in the country's capital, as long as Solomon obeys the covenant (6:11-13). God's presence in the temple is not guaranteed by the Davidic covenant. The temple is not mentioned specifically as part of the eternal kingship.

When Solomon dedicates the temple, he unites the people in worship at the central sanctuary that fulfills Moses' prediction of God's choosing one place where the people must worship. Israel's tendency to worship many gods (Judg 10:6) can now perhaps be avoided (cf. Deut 12:1-9). Further, the temple's dedication completes the promise of land made to Abraham, taught by Moses and secured by Joshua and David. The exodus remains the focal point by which Israelite history is dated (6:1), and the deliverance from slavery continues to define Yahweh's relationship with the people (8:50-53). Only because Israel is God's chosen nation does Solomon pray that the Lord will watch, guide, rebuke and forgive those who open the temple and those who use it through the years (8:22-53). In a real sense this episode concludes the Law's emphasis on Israel finding rest in their own land.

Yahweh's response to the dedication ceremony and Solomon's prayer highlight the temple's role as symbol of and dwelling place for God's name, or presence. It also reiterates that monotheism is mandatory for future blessings to occur. God makes the temple holy by dwelling there (9:1-3). This presence will be removed, however, if the king fails to exhibit "integrity of heart and uprightness" (9:4) going beyond mere external observance of religious ritual. God will reject the temple and the monarchy if other gods are venerated there, since such activity obviously would negate the temple's very reason for existing. Polytheism will cause Yahweh to invoke the punishments described in Leviticus 26, Deuteronomy 27—28 and Joshua 24:19-20. God will "cut off" Israel, "reject" the temple and make Israel an "object of ridicule" among the nations (9:7). All this will happen even though God has chosen this place. Israel's chosen status does not mean that any single generation may take Yahweh's favor for granted. Exodus 32—34 surely made this point clear, as did Numbers 13—14.

Solomon's and the people's actions in the dedication ceremony serve as positive models of what worship in Israel was always meant to be. Here, as in all the Old Testament, worship consists of praise (8:14-21), confession (8:23-51) and petition (8:46-53) offered in humility. True worship assumes Yahweh is near, personal, faithful and active on behalf of the committed. Solomon's petitions also depict an approachable God who punishes sinners yet who also restores the penitent (8:34). The covenant God is both powerful and loving.

Worship begins in worshipers' hearts, but it takes place in the physical setting of the temple. Proper worship procedures have already been outlined in Exodus and Leviticus. Prayer, sacrifice and the Levites' intercessory ministry characterize God-honoring worship. Temple observances by no means imply that God can be contained in one place or manipulated (8:27). The central sanctuary helps the people do God's will, not aid Yahweh in doing Israel's bidding.

After an extended era of glory, Solomon rejects wisdom and monotheistic worship later in his life. He marries many foreign wives in order to secure peace with surrounding nations, builds worship sites for their respective gods and even participates in polytheism. These activities violate Exodus 34:11-16 and Deuteronomy 7:1-5, which warn against intermarriage with polytheists from other lands; Deuteronomy 17:14-20 states that kings must adhere to the covenant and must not multiply wives as evidence of their greatness. Solomon's idolatry clearly breaches the agreement between the king and Yahweh reflected in 1 Kings 6:11-13 and 1 Kings 9:1-9. It also shows that this man of wisdom has become foolish and has set a foolish example for the people to follow. A shared idolatry between leaders and people can only result in a society that recalls the era of the judges.[11]

When kings sin it is the task of prophets to rebuke that sin. Samuel confronts Saul in 1 Samuel 13:8-14 and 1 Samuel 16:10-35, the second time telling him that someone else will take his place. This predictive prophetic word guides the text through 1 Kings 2:10, when David, Saul's successor dies. Likewise Nathan points out David's sin with Bathsheba in 2 Samuel

12:1-14. Nathan's earlier delivery of the promises in 2 Samuel 7:1-17 leads to Solomon's accession and points toward the distant future. God reveals to Solomon that his sins have led Yahweh to divide the kingdom into a ten-tribe northern nation and a two-tribe southern country (11:11-13). Ahijah the prophet anoints Jeroboam to lead the new land, and it is only because of the Davidic covenant that anything is left to Solomon's descendants (11:11-40). Solomon has proven to embody all the negative traits Samuel warned kings could possess (1 Sam 8:10-18), and Ahijah desires "to see on the throne a better protector of Yahweh's people in place of the despot."[12] He also desires to protect monotheistic faith from syncretism and polytheism.

Canonical Synthesis: Solomon and Wisdom

As has been stated, Solomon produces conflicting theological reflection in the canon due to his early commitment to Yahweh that recedes into polytheism by his later years. Proverbs, Song of Songs and Chronicles focus on his wisdom and his role in building the temple. By doing so these books highlight the fact that Yahweh gives him wisdom uniquely designed for monotheistic faith. First Kings 11 cites his unwillingness to place covenant fidelity above foreign policy and affairs of the heart, a fickleness perhaps duly noted in Ecclesiastes. Like the covenant, wisdom, even God-given wisdom, must be maintained by responsible human faithfulness. Neither unique giftedness nor the privilege of being David's heir guarantees divine favor and approval when foolishness, defined in 1 Kings 11:1-13 as polytheism, is chosen over wisdom, which is defined in 1 Kings 3-10 as the ability to make astonishingly consistent, correct decisions based on covenantally generated truth. The very existence of this inconsistency in Solomon paves the way for the canon's later discussion of wise versus foolish behavior.

The God Who Rejects Syncretism: 1 Kings 12—16

Two issues dominate this section of Kings. First, the author discloses God's attitude towards syncretism, the theological halfway house between Mosaic monotheism and outright polytheism. Second, the text highlights the strategic importance prophetic circles play in correcting Israel and Judah's theological vision. These themes unfold against the background of a people divided into Davidic and non-Davidic kingdoms born of Solomon's spiritual adultery. God's promises to Abraham and David have not altered, but the glory reached at the temple dedication ceremony recedes due to human failure.

God protects Ahijah's prophetic word in 1 Kings 12:1-24. Ten northern tribes proclaim Jeroboam king, thus leaving Rehoboam, Solomon's son, with two tribes over which the Davidic dynasty may rule. Once in power, Jeroboam considers the central sanctuary and its regulations detrimental to his political power base. He fears frequent trips to Judah will turn the people's hearts back to David's kingdom, despite all Yahweh has told him through Ahijah (12:26-27). Consequently he sets up shrines in Dan on his extreme northern border and a more important one at Bethel on his southern boundary. With Jerusalem's uniqueness thereby compromised, he erects golden calves to represent God's presence in the new worship centers. In the polytheistic environment of Canaan these images quickly come to be venerated as idols (12:28-30), which shatters the first two commandments (Ex 20:3-6). Further, non-Levites are appointed priests for the new denomination (12:31), and new festivals are initiated (12:33). The forms of Mosaic faith are retained, but its substance has been altered a great deal.

Scholars have offered a variety of opinions about Jeroboam's motives. Herbert Donner believes the calves were erected "certainly not as cult objects but—remotely comparable to the ark of Yahweh—as animal-shaped pedestals for Yahweh, who was thought to be standing on them invisibly."[13] Martin Noth agrees, arguing that "they were probably not intended to be thought of as divine images, especially as theriomorphic images were unknown in the Near East—as opposed to Egypt."[14] Like Donner and Noth, John Bright and Simon DeVries question the text's objectivity and factuality yet find the author's viewpoint basically valid. Bright understands the situation correctly when he notes that the "bull symbol . . . was too closely associated with the fertility cult to be safe."[15] Thus the use of images could easily lead to "a confusion of Yahweh and Ba'al, and to the importation of pagan features into the cult of the former."[16] Whether he knew it or not, Jeroboam could not draw the line where the religion began. DeVries concludes that

all around Israel, and in the numerous Canaanite enclaves within its territory, were half-Yahwists to whom the calf or bull was the symbol of male fecundity. Officially or unofficially, Baalism was in the land; it was destined in the days of Ahab to gain the mastery. Thus the golden calf could have done nothing but confuse and mislead.[17]

Jeroboam's new religion also made it possible for those influenced by the surrounding culture to identify Yahweh with one of the Canaanite gods.[18] In other words, Jeroboam's cult was a syncretistic masterpiece, for it allowed monotheists, polytheists and civil religionists some grounds for a common religion.

God has no illusions about the intent of Jeroboam's heart or the sure results of his religion's implementation. Two prophets, Ahijah and an unnamed individual, denounce him. Undeterred by the first (13:33-34), he remains unmoved even after Ahijah, who predicted his rise to power, condemns his idolatry (14:1-20). So great is the attraction of allowing syncretism and polytheism to flourish as a means of maintaining power that Rehoboam embraces Jeroboam's methods (14:21-24), as do all but one (Asa) of the kings that rule either country for the next several decades (15:1—16:20).[19] Asa and the prophets consider syncretistic practices a direct violation of the Sinai covenant (13:1-3; 14:6-9; 15:11-15).

Based on the threats embedded in Leviticus 26 and Deuteronomy 27—28, Yahweh begins to punish the people in a way calculated to motivate them to repent. The unnamed prophet prays for the king, obviously hoping the monarch will change (13:6). Ahijah, however, announces judgment without anticipating any change. Both men predict a future event. The first says a king named Josiah will someday destroy Jeroboam's altar (13:1-3), a prediction that does not come true until 640-609 B.C., or more than two centuries later. Ahijah says idolatry will eventually force God to send Israel into exile (14:14-16), which occurs in 722 B.C. Ahijah's prophecy particularly meets the Mosaic threats (cf. Deut 28:36-37). Disobedience will indeed lead to a loss of the land purchased at so dear a price. Here disobedience amounts to any divergence from the Ten Commandments, and here it is the prophets who announce what history holds according to the Lord's interpretation of the Mosaic covenant. God's prophets declare accurately God's opinions on the chosen people's first steps toward devastating defeat.

By the end of this section Israel digresses past syncretism to outright polytheism, a development hardly surprising in light of how easily the populace could use Jeroboam's religion to turn to Baalism. Omri (c. 880-874 B.C.) establishes Israel's capital city, Samaria, and continues Jeroboam's practices (16:21-28). His son Ahab (c. 874-853 B.C.) hastens the polytheistic process by marrying Jezebel of Tyre, where Baal was worshiped, and then venerates Baal himself (16:29-33). Such covenantal adultery provokes Yahweh's wrath, just as it did at Baal-Peor (Num 25:1-18), in the incident of the golden calf (Ex 32:1-10) and in the era of the judges (Judg 10:6-14). Yahweh remains as fiercely protective of the covenant relationship as in those episodes. The only issue is how this wrath will be expressed in the current situation.

Canonical Synthesis: National Renewal and the Prophetic Word
In later canonical texts, the division of the kingdom, which in itself begins to reverse the promise of land begun in Genesis 12:1-9 and completed as recently as 1 Kings 8:1—9:9, is depicted as a serious yet temporary setback. Isaiah (10:20-23), Jeremiah (3:18; 31:9), Ezekiel (37:15-17) and Amos (9:11-15) envision the time when a reunited Israel will again serve Yahweh after exile. While the division signifies disintegration and well-earned chastisement, the nation's restoration will prove that God has not given up on forging a holy nation from the ranks of the chosen people. This reunification is portrayed as both a near and a long-distant future event. Thus it invites hope

regardless of the audience's particular historical setting. Haggai, Zechariah, Malachi, Ezra and Nehemiah stake their life's work on this promise of a renewed, reestablished, whole Israel. Several psalms, including Psalm 107 and Psalm 126, agree. God made the covenant with all Israel, so the whole group must also somehow be involved in the healing and rejuvenation.

This section also revisits the canon's discussion of true and false prophecy. False prophets make a spectacular debut in the stories about Balaam (Num 22—24). Like Samuel and Nathan before him, Ahijah acts as an ideal, covenantally based prophet. His predictions about Jeroboam's emergence and loss of a son (1 Kings 11:29-34; 14:1-17) are both tied to breaches of faith, and both come true, all of which mark Ahijah as a legitimate prophet (see Deut 18:14-22). True prophecy carries the full impact of the power of God's word, so it will succeed no matter who opposes it. The issue is truth and how truth impacts history. Childs observes, "Timing and hermeneutics have nothing to do with the true and the false. The distinction is unrelated to the ethical sensitivity of an alert prophet, but is measured completely by the effect of the word of God."[20] Who speaks for God and who does not becomes an even more serious matter in the accounts of Elisha and Elijah, and it reaches a crucial juncture in Jeremiah. God's word is so integral to Israel's survival that any twisting of it leads to death. Israel must live by God's word (Deut 8:3; 32:47).

As 1-2 Kings itself unfolds, Jeroboam's syncretism is listed consistently, almost grindingly, as a canonical condemnation of later kings' departure from covenantal faith (see 1 Kings 15:34; 16:2, 3, 7, 19, 26, 31, 52; 2 Kings 3:3; 9:9). This aberrant national cult leads Israel toward ultimate destruction by Assyria, according to 2 Kings 17:19-23. The fact that this cult does not utilize idols to the extent Baalism does hardly matters.

The God Who Rules Nature and Nations: 1 Kings 17—2 Kings 10

With the spread of Baalism as a viable religion in Israel through the support of Ahab and Jezebel (1 Kings 16:29-33), those who attempt to serve Yahweh must combat a growing public perception that Mosaic faith is no longer viable. Its separatist tendencies set its adherents apart from those who embrace Jeroboam's state religion and from the followers of Baal. Yahwists eschew idols, multiple sanctuaries and compromise, while their counterparts welcome all three. These Yahwists are the minority, however, in an era when minorities are persecuted. The author takes the Yahwists' side, but the text never suggests that this group holds a majority of Israelites. Quite the opposite is the case.

Each faction in Israel has prophets to argue its case. Prophets committed to Yahweh, Baal, Jeroboamism and sheer financial gain appear in this segment. Two men, Elijah and Elisha, serve as the chief preachers and theologians who press the Yahwists' claims, and they are joined by other named (e.g., Micaiah) and unnamed prophets who suffer for covenantal fidelity. For the first time the canon links prophetic proclamation and suffering, a combination that will endure through the rest of the Old Testament. Commitment to the truth may be the right lifestyle to uphold, but it is not a safe lifestyle to choose.

Elijah's career strikes at the very tenets of syncretism and Baalism. His name means "Yahweh is my God," and he believes it his mission to help others make this confession instead of declaring allegiance to Baal. He promises there will be no rain until he says so (17:1) because Baalists believed their god made rain, unless, of course, it was the dry season and he needed to be raised from the dead. Elijah claims that Yahweh, not Baal, controls nature. When his stand for God forces Elijah into hiding the prophet takes refuge in Tyre, Jezebel's homeland (17:7-10). There, in Baal territory, he feeds a starving widow and her son, and he raises the son from the dead (17:11-24). These activities indicate that Yahweh is the living God who feeds the hungry, cares for the helpless and has the power to give or take life. Baal may experience a season of death and rebirth; Yahweh has no such flaw. F. C. Fensham explains that "Yahweh has power over things in which Baal has failed. . . . In the absence of Baal who lies impotent in the Netherworld, Yahweh steps in to assist the widow and the orphan, and this is done even in the heartland of Baal, Phoenicia."[21]

Upon returning to Israel, Elijah proceeds to push his message even further. No longer content to imply that Yahweh is not a local deity and to show that the Lord can do things Baal cannot, Elijah determines to eliminate Baal as a viable god. The challenge on Mt. Carmel (18:16-40) proves God hears prophets while Baal has no ability to do so. Elijah calls for a commitment to either Baal or Yahweh but not to both or to any form of polytheism. Both Elijah and the prophets of Baal believe their deity deserves allegiance. Elijah's experiences in Phoenicia have solidified his conviction that there is no god but Yahweh. He does not believe that Yahweh is merely the strongest deity, despite some scholars' arguments to the contrary. Leila Leah Bronner assesses Elijah's opinion correctly when she says,

> It is true that the faith of many of his contemporaries was of this rudimentary order; the clash between God and Baal was to them a real struggle between rival deities. But Elijah's lofty conception of God virtually excludes all other objects of worship and makes all the gods idols. Elijah apparently proved by his actions that he believed the God of Israel not to be limited by the territory of Israel, and he demonstrated that God can perform miracles in Phoenicia as well, thus showing his belief in a universal deity.[22]

No one answers when the Baalists pray to Baal (18:26-29) because Baal does not have a voice, an ear or a heart. He is not there, nor is he real. Fire descends from the only God who exists.

Clearly 1 Kings 17—18 demonstrates God's rule over nature in a way that eliminates the nature god Baal from consideration as a living deity. In 1 Kings 19—22 the Lord establishes sovereignty over nations as well. Elijah flees Jezebel's threats and then encounters Yahweh, who tells him a remnant of faithful Israelites still exists and that he must anoint new kings of Israel and Syria (19:1-18). God's word reaffirms Yahweh's sovereignty over all nations and Yahweh's commitment to the prophetic word. God's word cannot be silenced, for it constantly produces believers, protects believers and empowers believers. It also creates the future for Israel and for other countries.

God's word also condemns kings. When Ahab spares Ben-Hadad of Syria in a scene reminiscent of Saul and Agag (see 1 Sam 15:1-33), an unnamed prophet denounces Ahab for letting God's enemy live (1 Kings 20:31-43). God has determined to allow Ahab to defeat Syria because the Syrians believe Yahweh is a geographically limited, functionally bound deity (20:1-30). When they lose a battle in the hills they call Yahweh a hill god (20:23). When they lose in the plains they have no theology to explain their experience. They are merely exposed as Yahweh's enemies, and Ahab hopes to buy peace with them by letting their king live. In effect he opposes God by supporting the Lord's foes. Therefore God will punish Ahab, Israel, Ben-Hadad and Syria (20:41-43). God rules these persons and nations.

The prophetic word chastises Ahab in 1 Kings 21—22 as well. Once again the king rejects Moses' criteria for monarchs, this time by killing a subject (with Jezebel's help) and taking his land (21:1-16). Elijah promises Ahab he and Jezebel will die for these crimes and even specifies how they will die (21:17-26). Micaiah, a jailed prophet, claims that Ahab will meet his death in battle with Syria (22:1-18). This word from God not only comes true (22:29-40) but also comes in direct contradiction to the word offered by four hundred court prophets who all tell Ahab he will conquer (22:1-12). Micaiah says the lying prophets are God's means for destroying Ahab (22:19-23), a comment that has spawned a host of scholarly opinions.[23] Though it is impossible to sort out all these ideas here, it is possible to make a few observations.

First, Micaiah shapes his account of the lying spirit to rebuke, emphatically, the court prophets. These are not true prophets. They are court functionaries on the king's payroll who are a striking contrast to persecuted prophets like Elijah and Micaiah. Listening to them will get Ahab killed, which will in turn fulfill Elijah's prediction (21:17-29). Second, it is hard to fault Yahweh here, since the Lord states before Ahab goes to battle that he ought to ignore the royal liars for hire. Instead Ahab chooses to try to avoid the divine word and suffers fatal consequences. Third, this text focuses on God's sovereignty and the unerring accuracy of the Lord's revealed word. No one may operate outside of God's jurisdiction, and no one can avoid the force of God's word. The episode underscores the Lord's rule over nations, for it is Yahweh who decides what countries win which battles and which individuals govern those countries.

God's control of nature remains a guiding principle as Elijah exits the text and Elisha takes his place as God's lead messenger. Having gotten fire from heaven one last time during an encounter with representatives from Ahaziah, Ahab's son (2 Kings 1:1-18), Elijah prepares to go "to heaven in a whirlwind" (2:1). Elisha stays with him and sees his mentor go to his reward (2:1-12). As the one who has carried God's word, as the one who has protected Israelite religion from the ravages of idolatry, Elijah has truly been "the chariots and horsemen of Israel," the nation's true strength.[24]

Now fire takes Elijah away from Elisha. Just as fire from heaven once proved that Yahweh, not Baal, rules fertility, so now the same fire proves that the Lord rules death. Further, just as fire once protected Elijah from harm (1:9-12), so now heavenly fire removes him from all persecution and danger. Kings and queens can no longer threaten him. God rules Elijah's personal history, as certainly as God rules international history.

This unusual fire proves that Elijah is the prophet God approves, the prophet par excellence. Mordechai Cogan and Hayim Tadmor comment that this nondeath "invested him with the quality of eternal life, surpassing even Moses, the father of all prophets, who died and was buried (albeit by God himself: Deut 34:5-6)."[25] Because he does not endure death, Elijah later becomes the symbol for all prophets, including the forerunner of the Messiah (Mal 4:5-6). The New Testament patterns its portrayal of John the Baptist (Mt 3:1-12; Jn 1:19-23) and one of the two witnesses in Revelation 11:1-14 after Elijah's ministry. Elijah also appears with Moses on the Mount of Transfiguration, where he represents all the Old Testament prophets (Mt 17:3).

Though Elijah has left the scene, his protégé Elisha remains. If anything, his ministry exceeds Elijah's in its emphasis on Yahweh's sovereignty over nature and nations. Miracle after miracle demonstrates to every conceivable group inside and outside Israel that Elisha is truly God's prophet and Elijah's successor (2:13-18, 19-22, 23-25; 4:1-7, 8-37, 38-41, 42-44; 5:1-27; 6:1-7, 8-23; 6:24—7:20; 8:1-6). Elisha works miracles ranging from making an axhead float (6:1-7) to raising the dead (4:8-37). Whether as preacher or miracle worker, Elisha is at all times God's messenger. Without God's Spirit the prophet has no power and nothing worth saying.[26]

Beyond these miraculous powers, Elisha wields as much political influence as any biblical prophet, which demonstrates God's power in the realm of government. He prods Israel's kings to do what is right (3:10-27; 6:24—7:20; 13:10-19). He helps Israel's armies triumph over Syria (6:8—7:20). Emulating Samuel, he is also the person who anoints those Yahweh chooses to be king (9:1-13). Even more to the point, Elisha reveals who God chooses as king of Syria (8:7-15) and heals Naaman of Syria's leprosy (5:1-27). These actions underscore God's rule over covenant and noncovenant nations alike. Yahweh is capable of healing individuals or nations. Yahweh is equally capable of judging persons or countries. All of nature is at the creator's disposal, and all human events are under the lordship of the sovereign judge. Elisha is the human means by which these truths became evident.

As preachers of Yahweh's uniqueness and messengers of God's authority over human events, Elijah and Elisha are truly the "chariots and horsemen of Israel" (2:12; 13:14). They, and God's promises to David (8:19), are Israel's only defense against the defeat promised by Moses in Deuteronomy 27—28 and predicted by Ahijah in 1 Kings 14:15-16. It is to the fulfillment of these pledges that the author turns next.

Canonical Synthesis: The Power of the Prophetic Word

This portion of Kings reemphasizes aspects of Yahweh's personality that are introduced earlier in the canon. Elijah's ministry highlights God's control of nature, care for the helpless, power over death and supremacy over mere idols like Baal. Both Elijah and Elisha demonstrate that the Lord rules Israel, Judah, Syria and the rest of the earth. Thus Yahweh deserves sole allegiance instead of being considered merely one among many religious options. Baal cannot answer prayer, cannot bring fire from heaven, cannot save himself in his own mythology. By contrast, Yahweh has no limitations. The author of Kings applies the truths of the Law to the events that occur during the monarchy.

The prophets are inextricably linked to Yahweh in 1 Kings 17—2 Kings 13. They are God's messengers, or spokespersons, here.[27] They carry the Lord's message to kings (2 Kings 3:14-19; 6:8—7:20; 8:7-15; 9:1-10) just as Moses (Ex 5—12), Samuel (1 Sam 13—16), Nathan (2 Sam 12:1-15) and the previous prophets in Kings have done. Later in Scripture, Isaiah, Jeremiah, Amos and John the Baptist will carry on this tradition. Common folk hear the messengers too, but the text highlights the prophets' statements to the people's leaders. As God's messengers, the prophets are vehicles of divine revelation both to the great and to commoners.

These texts make it clear that because the prophets share God's word, their words cannot fail. Elisha waits for God's word (2 Kings 3:15). That word must be shared, regardless of how difficult it is for the prophets to preach it

(2 Kings 8:7-15). In return Yahweh vindicates their statements. Israel does win the battles Elisha says they will win (3:15-25; 6:24—7:20; 13:24-25). Hazael does rise to power in Syria as Elisha predicts (8:7-15). Ahab dies in the manner the prophets claim he will (1 Kings 22:37-40), as does Jezebel (2 Kings 9:27-37). God's own predictions that Elisha will succeed Elijah, that Hazael will succeed Ben-Hadad and that Jehu will rule Israel (1 Kings 19:15-18) come true. As long as it is truly God's word that is shared, not just what the kings want to hear (1 Kings 22:1-12), that word cannot fail. All subsequent canonical prophets enjoy a similar assurance.

God's encounter with a fearful Elijah in 1 Kings 19:10-18 presents Israel as a divided people. Yahweh does not deny that Israel has, as Elijah says, broken the covenant (19:10, 14). The Lord states, however, that he has "caused a remnant"[28] of seven thousand persons to remain faithful (19:18). Despite how it looks, Elijah is not alone. Two groups exist, a vast number of committed covenant breakers and a small "remnant" of covenant keepers. In this section the prophets are the most visible members of the remnant. They are joined, though, by others, including the Tyrian widow (1 Kings 17:7-24), the Shunammite and her husband (2 Kings 4:8-37) and the man who feeds the faithful prophets (2 Kings 4:42-44), to name a few. Isaiah, Jeremiah, Ezekiel and the Twelve are the most famous remnant members in the Latter Prophets, but they are joined by such characters as Isaiah's family, Baruch and Zerubbabel. Isaiah builds much of his theology around the remnant concept, as will be noted later.

Naaman's healing (2 Kings 5:1-27) demonstrates the canon's emphasis on God's willingness to include Gentiles in the remnant. From Abraham's call (Gen 12:1-9) onward, the Lord expects Israel to reach out to other nations. Moses marries a Cushite (Num 12:1). Rahab is a Canaanite. Jonah preaches to Assyrians, while Daniel bears witness to Babylonians. Ruth hails from Moab. Yahweh, the Creator of all persons, stands ready to accept anyone who believes. The question is whether Israel is in any condition to offer true faith to the Gentiles.

Finally, Elijah dominates canonical reflection on the texts. His unstinting opposition to syncretism and Baalism is notable, but it is as the greatest prophet that he is remembered. Malachi 4:5-6 expects Elijah to announce the day of the Lord's judgment. Jesus claims John the Baptist was this "Elijah" (Lk 7:24-35). Both John and the one announced by Malachi proclaim coming times of decision, and both offer nonremnant individuals the chance to change before punishment falls. Elijah's presence at the transfiguration (Mk 9:2-8) indicates his status as greatest prophetic messenger. It also highlights his nondeath and implies that no greater prophet will arise. Given the status assigned Elijah by the canon, it is disturbing to realize that the chosen people do not respond to his monotheistic message. If he, Elijah, Micaiah, Ahijah and the other prophets cannot turn Israel to Yahweh, then the future hardly looks hopeful.

The God Who Finishes Kingdoms: 2 Kings 14—25
Throughout the canon Yahweh appears primarily as Creator, sustainer, deliverer, revealer and comforter. When necessary, though, the Lord acts as judge, as terminator of sin, sinners and, when appropriate, nations. By the time of Elisha's death (c. 800 B.C.) Yahweh has patiently endured syncretism, Baalism and idolatry for 130 years. More time will be given, but time is expiring for both Israel and Judah, especially for Israel, who exists under the threat of Ahijah's prediction of doom (1 Kings 14:14-16). Until these destructions occur the author maintains a consistent historical theory: covenantal fidelity alone can spare Israel; prosperity is not necessarily evidence of righteousness; and God will use foreign nations to punish the elect people. When God exercises this latter option, Israel experiences divine wrath in much the same way the Canaanites endured it during the conquest. God is fair and holy, which means not even the chosen ones can sin forever and avoid judgment. God will finish their kingdoms, leaving the canon to divulge what must occur next.

Israel and Judah achieved military and economic success during the first half of the eighth century B.C. Due to Syria's defeat by Assyria in about 802 B.C., both Israel and Judah enjoyed a respite from constant war.[29] During this regional power vacuum, Jeroboam II of Israel (c. 793-753 B.C.) and Uzziah of Judah (c. 792-740 B.C.) were able to extend their collective borders to where Solomon's had been (see 1 Kings 8:65; 2 Kings 14:25). This time of prosperity was not accompanied by covenant faithfulness, a fact the author makes plain (2 Kings 14:24; 15:4) and canonical prophets from that era such as Amos and Hosea emphasize. Without spiritual renewal, prosperity is merely a blessing before terrible consequences, for, as Noth observes, "the great power of Assyria loomed sinisterly in the background."[30] An awesome instrument of destruction would soon be ready for use to punish the disobedient people.

After Jeroboam II's death in about 753 B.C., Israel endures a series of short-term monarchs. Intrigue and deception cause chaos in Samaria just as Tiglath-Pileser III (c. 745-727 B.C.) turns Assyria into an adventurous, conquering, occupying, exiling, murderous world power. Five kings in twenty years rule Israel, none of whom does anything to check the nation's moral slide (2 Kings 15:8-31). Meanwhile, in Judah the situation is slightly better because of Uzziah's and Amaziah's basically moral leadership (15:1-7). Still, with high places not removed from Judah, the seeds of destruction exist in both kingdoms.

When Samaria falls to Assyria during Hoshea's reign (c. 732-722 B.C.), more than two centuries have passed since Ahijah's prophecy of destruction. God's word comes true as Israel doggedly pursues self-destruction. No reform occurs. No real lasting repentance due to prophetic utterances and activities emerge. No prophet is truly taken seriously, so totally have the people given themselves to a polytheistic worldview. No leader calls a halt to non-Mosaic worship patterns, for David's example is forgotten. Thus the spare, unadorned description of Israel's fall in 2 Kings 17:1-6 is almost anticlimactic, and the text asserts that only God's grace has delayed the fall this long. The nation has been theologically dead for decades.

The author devotes the most words to the reasons behind the devastation. According to 2 Kings 17:7-23, the loss occurs because of theological amnesia (17:7-13), polytheism (17:14-20) and syncretism (17:21-23). Their theological amnesia includes forgetting the exodus (17:7), the reason for the conquest (17:8), the basic covenant commands (17:9-12) and the importance of heeding divinely inspired prophetic revelation (17:13). Having cast off the covenant, idolatry becomes easier, both before and after the kingdom's division in about 930 B.C. Astral deities, fertility deities and deities who require human sacrifices capture Israel's fancy (17:16-17). Jeroboam's syncretistic cult's status as state religion institutionalizes covenantal infidelity (17:21-23). Placed together over two centuries these flaws can only result in the devastation threatened in Leviticus 26 and Deuteronomy 27—28.

Judah learns nothing from Israel's exile (17:18-20). Ahaz (c. 735-715 B.C.) worships Assyria's gods (16:1-20). It is possible that Ahaz is coerced to do so to receive Assyria's help against his enemies,[31] but it is equally possible that he does so because he believes these gods will make him more powerful.[32] Regardless of the specific circumstances, neither Ahaz nor Judah is loyal to any particular system of worship. The king does nothing to steer his people from the fate that befalls his northern relatives. He probably thinks he is helping the people by making an alliance with a dangerous opponent.

Ahaz's approach to the Assyrian threat is in direct opposition to that of the author of 1-2 Kings. The writer is aware of Assyria's existence yet argues that Israel and Judah have nothing to fear if they serve Yahweh. Theology infuses and informs the author's view of history. Since God rules history, God will determine Israel and Assyria's future. Mere circumstances do not determine what will occur. God does, and Judah will be next to die.

The canonical prophets from this era agree with the author's viewpoint. Hosea portrays Israel as an adulterous spouse (Hos 1—3), as a nation dying of religious stupidity (Hos 4:1-6), as a violent and unjust society (7:1-7) and thus as a nation ripe for judgment (8:7-10). Still God has compassion on them (11:1-11) and will renew them in the future (14:1-9). Similarly, Amos indicts

Israel for immorality and covenant breaking (Amos 2:6-16). The people's sins will lead to exile (4:1—6:14). Only after punishment will restoration ever come. Exile is inevitable, though not irreversible (9:11-15). Near the same time Isaiah warns Judah to repent and avoid the punishing Assyrian forces. Fearing God and turning to God's word will stave off destruction (Is 8:1-22). It is rather odd how little the Scriptures reflect on Israel's actual defeat. Only 2 Kings 17 offers many details. That author's point is clear: Israel's defeat signals the beginning of the complete loss of the promised land (2 Kings 17:21-23).

Judah's disintegration is slowed by the ministries of Hezekiah and Josiah, the only two kings given unqualified praise by the author. Hezekiah (c. 715-687) repeals Ahaz's pro-Assyrian policy and initiates sweeping, though hardly long-lasting, spiritual reforms, including the destruction of idols and high places (18:4-8). Mosaic law and Davidic examples are followed. Despite his faithfulness, though, Hezekiah endures a terrible Assyrian invasion that leaves only Jerusalem, of all Judah's cities, intact (18:1-18). Like Abel, Hagar, Joseph, David and others, Hezekiah suffers without deserving to do so. His faithfulness leads to his predicament, a situation that at first apparently validates Ahaz's foreign policy and personal theology.

A theological war takes precedence over military war in 2 Kings 18:17—19:34, and this theological test of wills settles the military confrontation. Assyria does claim that Judah's armies cannot defeat them (19:19-24), but the theological comments are aimed at Yahweh's power and will, not just at Judah's beliefs. Assyria's representative tells Judah's warriors not to trust in Yahweh because Hezekiah has angered the Lord by removing the high places in his honor and by limiting official worship to one small temple. Therefore, he claims, the Lord has sent Assyria to punish the people for devaluing their deity. This sort of propaganda about gods abandoning their adherents was a standard ploy when Assyria invaded other lands. Cogan notes that the Assyrians routinely told their enemies that their gods were angry with them, that the gods had abandoned them and that these gods counseled them to surrender to the Assyrians.[33] What the speaker in this text has not grasped, however, is that he addresses committed Yahwists, not the typical polytheists he is used to manipulating. He concludes by arguing that no other god has saved a nation, so it is unlikely that Yahweh will deliver Judah (18:32-35). Like other ancient polytheists, he measures the worth and power of individual gods by the success and grandeur of those who worship them. By his standards, Yahweh must be no stronger than gods from other small kingdoms, so it is ludicrous to believe this deity can save the city. His argument makes sense given his presuppositions, but it is just such presuppositions that the canon attacks.

Unlike the majority of his predecessors, Hezekiah realizes that he must reach a theological solution in order to find a historical-political resolution to his dilemma. To this end he prays for help, confessing that all other gods are wood and stone, but Yahweh, and Yahweh alone, is God (10:17-19). He pits his faith against Assyria's propaganda, which constitutes a direct break with prevailing worldviews. Hezekiah desires freedom for himself and for his people, yet he recognizes Israel's first priority is to glorify and bring recognition to Yahweh.

God responds in two equally compelling ways. First the Lord has Isaiah reassure Hezekiah that Assyria's blasphemy will not go unpunished (19:20-28). Assyria has attacked God, and God will have the last word.[34] Hezekiah believes God, and this faith is rewarded.[35] God promises to defend Jerusalem for David's sake and for the sake of God's own glory (19:32-34). This defense will allow a remnant of Judahites to survive and begin the nation afresh through the power the Holy One of Israel (19:22, 29-31). The prophetic word is as concrete as the deed itself. Second, God puts to death 185,000 Assyrians, thus driving the invaders from the land (19:35-36). Scholars differ over the particulars of this event, yet many do affirm the miraculous nature of the deliverance depicted.[36] God proves Assyria's theology wrong and at the same time shows that monotheism yields practical results in history. Hezekiah and Isaiah demonstrate that faithfulness empowered by divine revelation overcomes the direst of predicaments and the finest polytheistic propaganda. Still, though Assyria will not destroy Judah, Isaiah predicts that Babylon will eventually do so (20:16-18).

One more bright spot illuminates Judah's history before Yahweh closes that history. After a renewal of idolatry and pacifying Assyria during Manasseh's reign (c. 697-642 B.C.), Josiah, a boy king of a mere eight years of age, ascends the throne (22:1). During his reign (c. 640-609) he mirrors Hezekiah's monotheistic commitments and becomes the second, and last, monarch to receive unqualified praise in the text (22:2).

Like Hezekiah, Josiah responds positively to the revealed word of God. Josiah leads a religious reform after the discovery of "the Book of the Law in the temple of the LORD" (22:8-10). God confronts the king through the written word, a word the king understands to be an indictment of Judah's covenantal disobedience (22:11-13). Josiah sends envoys to Huldah the prophet to interpret the written word for him.

Huldah offers a two-pronged interpretation that fits the message of the canonical prophets. First, she interprets the book for the people. She says their idolatry will lead to the consequences outlined in Deuteronomy 28:15-68 (22:14-17). Second, she extends a positive word to Josiah. He will die before Jerusalem falls (22:14-20). Whenever Isaiah's prediction of Babylon's victory over Judah comes true, Josiah will not have to endure it. Both infallible words will come true. Huldah continues the great prophetic tradition of faithfully and accurately proclaiming God's word, though this time the focus is on an interpretation of an already existing written word.

Josiah's subsequent purging of polytheism restores the importance of the Mosaic covenant in Judahite society.[37] Moses' writings have been neglected through the centuries, but Josiah restores them to prominence for a brief time. His personal faith grows when he hears at least a significant portion of the Law. This hearing motivates him to act. When he acts it is with the confidence that he is doing God's will, based on God's word, in the service of God's people. By doing so he embodies biblical traits for a member of the holy nation and the requirements for a holy king.

Other kings rise after Josiah, but none even slows Judah's death. Yahweh has no reason to spare the nation other than an extraordinary personal patience that has already extended over three hundred years since Solomon's idolatry. Now the Lord finishes Judah in righteous indignation. Two smaller deportations precede the final defeat (24:1-17); then the curtain falls during the hapless Zedekiah's era (c. 597-587 B.C.).The description of the devastation includes loss of city, temple, populace, land and monarchy (24:18—25:21). Only a few people remain for Babylon's appointed governor to rule. These few assassinate him and flee, thereby reducing the population further (25:22-26). The holy nation has been reduced to a mere handful in a holy land that is for all practical purposes destroyed.

Just the smallest sliver of hope remains for the conquered people and their discontinued monarchy. The book concludes with an unexpected account of Jehoiachin, the king who rules Judah for three months during 598-597 B.C. and is exiled in 597 B.C. The account states that he is treated well after his conqueror dies in about 562 B.C.38 Gerhard von Rad believes the prominence of the Davidic covenant in Samuel and Kings indicates that Jehoiachin's survival means God has not rejected David's lineage. This message "is just hinted at, and with great reserve,"[39] but must be considered carefully because "the Deuteronomist saw yet another word as active in history, namely, the promise of salvation in the Nathan prophecy, and it, as well as the threat of judgment, was effectual as it ran through the course of the history."[40] Noth disagrees. He thinks the passage ends Israel's tragedy with a note of benevolent finality.[41]

Given the overall flow of Kings, it is possible to conclude that this final episode does not exclude hope. The historian certainly believes the nation's history has taken a horrible, ominous turn. Still, better days are possible, because such days have always been possible. This fact is what makes the situation tragic. A new and better day may emerge after punishment, just as Deuteronomy 30:1-10 indicates. Whatever hope may emerge, the author has stated since 2 Samuel 7 that David's family will be a key element in that possibility. God stakes the future on David, regardless of David's descendants' failings. Israel may be out of the land, but some Israelites still exist, and David's lineage has not been eradicated.

Canonical Synthesis: Exile and the Remnant

Judah's defeat and subsequent exile provide significant canonical signposts. Their description at this canonical juncture highlights their pivotal importance. Moses threatens the people with the loss of the land promised to Abraham (Deut 27—28). Few warnings could carry more theological, relational and practical weight. Exile is what Israel narrowly avoids in Judges, what Samuel reminds the people of in 1 Samuel 12 and what Solomon fears in 1 Kings 8:22-61. In the Latter Prophets, Isaiah predicts the exile (39:1-8; cf. 2 Kings 20:12-21), as do Jeremiah (7:1-15), Ezekiel (20:1-49), Amos (2:4-5; 6:1-7), Micah (3:12), Habakkuk (1:5-11) and Zephaniah (1:4-13). Jeremiah and Ezekiel live during the exile, whereas Haggai, Zechariah and Malachi live in its wake. No other historical event impacts their life and ministries more significantly.

The exile's role does not lessen in the Writings. In Psalms 89—90 it is depicted as the culmination of Israel's covenant breaking, whereas Psalms 90—150 focus in part on overcoming the effects of this crucial event. Lamentations mourns Jerusalem's destruction. Daniel and Esther live in exile, while Ezra and Nehemiah attempt to rebuild Jerusalem in postexilic times. Chronicles closes with a call to rebuild the temple (2 Chron 36:13). All these texts wrestle with what the exile means in their particular setting.

Though a great number of options are possible, it is evident that the Old Testament interprets the exile in at least two basic ways. First, the Prophets and the Writings uniformly argue that the exile is God's understandable punishment for Israel's infidelity. Jeremiah 44:20-30 is a prophetic text that epitomizes this belief. There the prophet declares that the exiles have only themselves and their idols to blame for their plight. Yahweh punished only when the sin became unbearable. Similarly Psalm 106, Daniel 9:1-20 and Ezra 9:5-15 agree during extended confessions of sin that this punishment has been well-earned and has come from a righteous, patient God. No failure on God's part may be claimed. Only the people are to blame.

Second, the exile is not viewed as permanent. It is portrayed as an opportunity for scattered Israel to repent and for faithful Yahweh to create a new exodus to the holy land. Isaiah 35:1-10, Jeremiah 23:1-8 and Ezekiel 34:11-16 claim that God's people will return to the land to proclaim the greatness of Yahweh's redemption. Hosea 11:8-11 states that the Lord's compassion makes it impossible for divine wrath to be God's final work with the chosen ones. The presence of Haggai, Zechariah, Malachi, Ezra and Nehemiah in Jerusalem in postexilic times reemphasizes this point, as does the presence in the canon of the psalms of ascent (Ps 120—134), which rejoice in restored worship in Jerusalem. God has not forgotten how to be merciful or how to redeem. This new situation will magnify those characteristics.[42] If Jerusalem's fall underscores the covenant consequences, then the eventual return to the land highlights the covenant blessings.

This section also stresses three other vital canonical principles. First, it reinforces the idea of a faithful remnant. It is fitting that 2 Kings 19:29-34 has Isaiah mention the remnant and David's importance together, since this prophet will stress these ideas extensively in the book of Isaiah. Hezekiah, Isaiah, Josiah and Huldah prove that Israel may be sinful but that, as in Elijah's time (1 Kings 19:15-18), God will never be without obedient followers. Second, it solidifies the trustworthiness of the prophets' words. Knowing who speaks for God makes the prophetic books that follow especially meaningful and establishes God's ability to reveal the future in appropriate ways at crucial times. Third, it highlights monotheism as the covenant's core principle. When Yahweh alone is worshiped, there is small chance that the whole covenant will be broken. When the opposite is true, all sorts of evil become possible.

Conclusion

When Kings ends, Israel's history has been told from Abraham's era (c. 2000 B.C.) to Jehoiachim's old age (c. 560 B.C.). Canonical theology has introduced and traced the implications of Abraham's promises, the Mosaic covenant and the stunning pledges made to David. God's uniqueness, Israel's calling as holy nation, Canaan's status as holy land and David's lineage's role as permanent rulers have all been firmly established. Sin has derailed the ongoing fulfillment of these themes, however, so sin remains the enemy it has been since Genesis 3. Faith, obedience and sacrifice combat sin, but a permanent solution has not yet emerged. The Latter Prophets make great progress in this area, though, in the next canonical segment.

11

The God
Who Saves

Isaiah

. . . .

FEW OLD TESTAMENT BOOKS MATCH ISAIAH'S ABILITY TO USE RECEIVED BIBLICAL theology while introducing new theological concepts. Placed strategically at the beginning of the Latter Prophets, this book reflects the major ideas already divulged in the Law and the Former Prophets. Isaiah discusses covenant giving and covenant breaking, the role of the prophets in warning and encouraging the chosen people, God's sovereignty over all nations and the Davidic promises, to name just a handful of relevant topics. At the same time, the prophecy links the remnant and the future, the eternal nature of the Davidic kingdom and the contemporary sins of that institution and the interaction between God and the Gentiles in ways not yet seen in the canon. This meshing and shaping of the new and the old makes Isaiah a formidable theological document.

Joshua, Judges, Samuel and Kings introduce the work of the prophets, but their specific literary contribution to biblical theology obviously unfolds more clearly in Isaiah, Jeremiah, Ezekiel and the Twelve. This contribution has many facets and utilizes a variety of characters and settings. It is accurate to say, however, that all these variations flow from a few common themes. B. D. Napier observes that the prophets stress seven basic topics.[1] First, they claim that their words and their symbolic acts are inspired by God. Their messages come from God and are therefore God's word. Second, they reflect on Israel's election. God has chosen Israel and blessed them with special status as the recipients of the Abrahamic, Mosaic and Davidic covenants.

Third, they argue that the chosen people have rebelled against the Lord by breaking the covenant they have pledged to keep.

Fourth, because of this covenant breaking Yahweh will judge the people, just as Leviticus 26 and Deuteronomy 27—28 promise. The Lord's character demands that sin not be allowed to remain unchecked. Fifth, despite this punishment, the Lord still has compassion for the chosen ones. Judgment is never God's final word. Sixth, God's compassion means that redemption will emerge out of the pain of punishment. Punishment always occurs to effect renewal; it is never an end in itself. Seventh, this renewal will extend to all nations. God is the creator of all nations and races of people, not just of the Israelites. Therefore restoration must include all creation for the Creator to receive adequate glory from the proper and necessary results of judgment.

These foundational concepts leave open a host of issues. How, when, why and where these themes will transpire are examined in more than one way in the prophecies themselves. The historical settings that spawn the themes shift. The persons who create the context for the ideas do not stay the same. Despite the changes that naturally occur as the books relate to their specific historical settings, the prophetic literature's unique theological viewpoint remains constant. The various settings, authors and audiences give the theological interpretations of events added texture, relevant substance, more creative energy.

As a group, the Latter Prophets provide the canon with an interpretation of the history that has already been described in the Law and the Former Prophets. This interpretation agrees with the perspective found in Joshua—Kings: Israel's consistent rebellion against God produces judgment, but a remnant of faithful persons who never turn away from the Lord will always exist (see 2 Kings 17:3). At the same time, the Latter Prophets move beyond the past to envision how God will work in the future. In this way they predict what will happen by understanding what has happened. As individuals entrusted with the very words of God, they also occasionally envision future events that are not specifically anticipated in the Law, and they know the details of some events, such as the exile, that are mentioned only in anticipatory form in the Law.

After two centuries of debate over Isaiah's authorship and date, the situation has shifted in the twentieth century, and it has done so in a way that makes theological dialogue between the differing camps more possible. At this point critical and conservative scholars alike are dealing with texts as they have been received in the Hebrew canon. Some of these writers are interested in the literary unity of the text,[2] some in the book's theological coherence,[3] some in its editorial structuring[4] and some in its role as canonical document.[5] Disagreements over authorship issues remain a significant point of contention, but this difference no longer precludes discussion of matters that reflect Isaiah's theological unity.

For example, Brevard Childs and J. A. Motyer do not agree about who wrote all of Isaiah. But Childs writes that even if Isaiah did not write the whole book the canon treats the prophecy as if he did, and the community of faith has traditionally read the book in that context.[6] Motyer notes that the issues raised by critical scholars are not trivial, yet he correctly decides that this fact does not negate the value of treating the prophecy as a united theological work.[7] Both authors conclude that theological reflection on Isaiah must begin with how the entire book and its parts cohere. This volume shares Motyer's viewpoint and appreciates the spirit of all scholars who attempt to work with the unity of the canonical form of Isaiah. Pitting sections of Isaiah against each other does not do justice to the prophecy's theological achievement.

There is a significant amount of agreement across traditional and nontraditional lines about Isaiah's theology. Most theologians observe that Isaiah's primary focal point is God's holiness.[8] From this focal point several other key concepts naturally follow. For instance, John Oswalt observes, "Because God alone is great, and because he alone is holy, the worship of other gods is sheerest folly."[9] In other words, the Lord's holiness, or uniqueness, leads to the conclusion that there is no other God. As Christopher North says, the book of Isaiah is "explicitly monotheistic," especially in chapters 40—66.[10] John Skinner adds, "Isaiah is a monotheist in the strictest sense of the term."[11]

Because there is only one God, it follows that this God is the Creator of the heavens and the earth. John Watts notes that when Israel doubts God's ability to help them in exile, the Lord reminds them who created all things.[12] Surely the Creator can sustain the people in their struggle to maintain their faith and physical well-being. The Creator who redeemed Israel from Egyptian slavery will lead the people in a new exodus, one that will bring them from the ends of the earth back to their ancestral home.[13] This new exodus will result in the restoration of Jerusalem, which takes on added significance as Zion, God's dwelling place.[14]

Though God saves, it is also true that Yahweh will judge sinners on the day of the Lord. This separation of the remnant from their rebellious opposites will occur temporarily in space and time but permanently at an unstated time in the future. Thus it is clear that Yahweh rules all history, past, present or future, which leads Watts to conclude that the heart of Isaiah's theological vision "is that Yahweh is the Lord of history."[15]

Related to all these themes is the book's emphasis on the coming Davidic Savior. Whether depicted as king or servant, it is this individual who sparks the most interest in biblical theology as a whole, particularly in the New Testament.[16] It is this figure that the prophecy anticipates, and it is this character who will rule all creation when history flows into perfection. It is therefore impossible to neglect this person's role in all the book's other theological emphases, and this person helps provide a context for how the Abrahamic, Mosaic and Davidic covenants complement one another.

With this sort of scholarly coordination on the book's major ideas, it is possible to suggest how the prophecy's theological ideas cohere. No doubt there are other valid ways of conceiving the book's thought, but this scheme keeps faith with its contents. Isaiah 1—12 begins the prophecy by introducing the God who condemns and calls. Israel's unfaithfulness to their covenant obligations is duly described, and Isaiah's prophetic ministry is announced. The fact that Isaiah's call to ministry is not described until Isaiah 6 reflects the historical pattern of the Lord's sending prophets in response to Israel's sin. This section also begins the book-long tendency to alternate between the author's present and the near or distant future. The most compelling figure in this dialogue is the Davidic king promised in Isaiah 7—12. The most compelling event is the promised and much-to-be-feared day of the Lord, or day of judgment.

Next, Isaiah 13—27 describes Yahweh as the God who eliminates prideful nations. Israel's own pride and resultant lack of faith lead God to use nations like Assyria to punish the chosen people. A similar pride and lack of faith lead Yahweh to condemn the surrounding countries. This judgment segment places Israel's relationship to the Lord squarely in history and at the same time reveals that Israel's God rules all creation. Despite the present degeneracy of these peoples, the Lord will redeem some of the worst offenders in the future, therefore keeping the present-future conversation alive.

Isaiah 28—39 continues the punishment theme by announcing a series of woes on the wicked. This is followed by a description of future hope and concluded by a historical account of Jerusalem's deliverance from the crisis of 701 B.C. (cf. 2 Kings 18—19). Throughout this section it is clear that Yahweh is the God who secures and protects the faithful remnant. Hope exists in the midst of pain, yet only for the remnant and in an ultimate sense only in the future. At all times this hope flows from a relationship with the Lord, not from military alliance or political maneuvering. The section ends with the ominous notation that Babylon will invade and conquer Judah, a fact already established canonically in 2 Kings.

Pain and hope in the present and the future continue to intersect in Isaiah 40—55. Here the God who saves through suffering sends a servant to initiate a new exodus from literal and spiritual exile. As in Isaiah 28—39, only exclusive allegiance to Yahweh will result in freedom from bondage and security from punishment. Some of the strongest monotheistic statements that grace Scripture appear in this segment. The servant's identity sparks significant theological reflection in the New Testament.

Finally, Isaiah 56—66 depicts the God who renews creation. Once more faith in this God acts as the only catalyst for a bright future. The totality of this re-creation is reflected in the prophecy's final verses, which envision a new heaven and a new earth, concepts that also conclude the New Testament canon (cf. Rev 21—22). Only Yahweh can effect this transformation, for Yahweh is Creator, sustainer and sole deity. Only the Creator can be the re-creator.

Isaiah's vision is unrelentingly monotheistic. Idols and other variations of worship objects appear but are allowed no relevance as active participants in the running of human or divine affairs. As Christopher Seitz observes, "In the Book of Isaiah, Israel's God is not in a contest to prove his superiority over the gods of the other nations: Israel's God is the one God of all nations."[17] Embracing this concept offers all remnant persons a future, but ignoring this principle consigns all majority individuals to the darkness inherent in the day of the Lord.

The God Who Condemns and Calls: Isaiah 1—12

Though salvation is God's ultimate goal in Isaiah, the book hardly takes a mild approach to achieving that purpose. God does not treat Israel like a spoiled or ailing child. Rather the Lord empowers Isaiah to preach messages that cut into the hearers' souls and that protest their activities. God declares the nation's sin (1:2-31) and describes the future as bright beyond and because of the day of judgment (2:1—4:6). The Lord compares Israel to a bad vineyard (5:1-7) and a land deserving of woe (5:8-30). God calls Isaiah (6:1-13) to present the people and their king with the opportunity to believe and be saved but has to project that salvation into the future when the gracious offer is refused (7:1—11:16). Then Israel will know that the Lord is their salvation, a fact that Isaiah and the other remnant believers have accepted from the start (12:1-6). God's anger at sin and God's call of a prophet to warn and instruct the people go together a surely as punishment follows stubborn rebellion.

God's condemnation of Israel in Isaiah 1:2-31 proceeds along familiar canonical lines. Yahweh, the Creator, calls heaven and earth as witnesses of Israel's covenant breaking (1:2). Israel, God's child (cf. Ex 4:23), has rebelled and has refused to repent despite divine chastisement (1:2-9). Thus they will be overthrown like Sodom and Gomorrah (1:10; cf. Gen 19:1-29), even though they offer the sacrifices required in Leviticus (Lev 1:11-14). God is willing to forgive but has no reason to do so (Is 1:18-19). The present is bleak. The references to Jerusalem's solitary status probably imply that the setting is the invasion by Sennacherib depicted in 2 Kings 18:13-16.[18] Jerusalem may survive, but only as a lonely reminder of the nation that once was the glorious home of the covenant people. Only God's grace allows this small portion to stand.

Beyond this current devastation lies a wonderful future forged by Yahweh through terrible means. In "the last days" Jerusalem will draw all nations to itself, thus making Israel the kingdom of priests and universal blessing they have been called to be since Genesis 12:1-9 and Exodus 19:5-6. God will judge the people there (Is 2:1-5). This new reality can emerge, however, only as the aftermath of a cataclysmic day of Yahweh that purges divination, materialism, arrogance and idolatry from the land (2:6-22). In that day the Lord alone will be worshiped, as has always been proper yet never observed (2:17). Only the righteous will survive intact (3:10; 4:2-6). In that day the Lord will reign, Jerusalem will be God's dwelling place, and the faithful will be shielded from harm forever. Isaiah's realistic vision of his own circumstances forces him to envision these events in the future, for he sees no possibility of their coming true any time soon. Ultimate hope thereby gets forced into a nonimmediate context. What is truly frightening is the fact that an Assyrian invasion, a horrible experience, in no way approximates what Yahweh's final punishment will be like. God's judgment therefore takes on beyond-normal proportions for the first time in the canon.

The text returns to the present in Isaiah 5:1-30 but does not soften in tone. Israel has been like a wild vineyard that has not fulfilled its purpose. Israel has been filled with bloodshed, injustice and idolatry (5:1-7). Thus the land will be filled with woe, and the chosen people will be exiled at the hands of a fierce, unsparing foe (5:8-30). God condemns the holy nation as drunkards (5:10, 22), arrogant (5:13-17), lovers of evil (5:20) and objects of wrath (5:26-30). Covenant breaking hardly does justice to the level of their depravity. Throughout the book the Lord's attitude toward Isaiah's contemporaries rarely mellows. The prophecy indefatigably presents the group as guilty, ripe-for-judgment sinners. Their sins are anticipated in the Law, and their fate is spelled out clearly in the Former Prophets, so Isaiah 1—5 serves as a canonical bridge between what has been and what will be.

Isaiah's call has immense theological importance for the book as a whole. In the year Uzziah died, or near 742 B.C., Isaiah receives a vision of the living God (6:1). The Lord is "seated on a throne, high and exalted," a phrase that magnifies Yahweh's kingship and sparks other reflections on God's role as cosmic King (cf. Is 13—23; 37:23-24; 40:18-22). This King more than fills the temple (6:1) and is attended by seraphim praising his holiness (6:1-3). God's holiness confronts Isaiah's sinfulness, and the man confesses his unworthiness, whereupon the holy God forgives (6:4-7). Out of gratitude, Isaiah volunteers to speak for the Lord (6:8). This scene should be typical of Israel's relationship with God but is the exact opposite of the actions described in Isaiah 1—5.

Thus when the newly appointed prophet is commissioned, he hears that the people will not listen and is informed that he must preach without positive results (6:9-10). His mission is to uncover the remnant of the faithful who will become "holy seed" for the replanting of the holy people in the holy land (6:11-13). In other words, he must do as Ahijah, Elijah, Micaiah and Elisha have already done. His role is not a new one, and it remains a hard one. As God's prophet, he will have God's support, but that support has never resulted in ease for the committed.

The prophet's first recorded preaching mission is to Ahaz of Judah (c. 731-715), who must choose between being invaded by Syria and Israel, asking for Assyria's help or trusting a revealed word from God. Like Ahab, Ahaz refuses to express faith in Yahweh's truthful servant (7:1-9). Therefore Isaiah offers an oracle that encompasses the present and the future. He does so while implying that God will give an extraordinary sign that will highlight the futility of Ahaz's unbelief. He says a "virgin will be with child and will give birth to a son, and will call him Immanuel" (7:14). Further, the land will soon be rid of the Syrians and Israelites and Assyria will come against Judah (7:15-17).

There has been strenuous scholarly discussion of what these promises mean and how Isaiah conceived of their fulfillment,[19] but some agreement does exist. First, many writers believe the Immanuel promise relates to the hopes placed on the Davidic lineage since 2 Samuel 7:1-17. Some think Hezekiah is the promised child,[20] while others point to "the divine son of David"[21] as the prophecy's fulfillment. In some way the eternal kingdom pledged in 2 Samuel 7 must come into play here. Second, most commentators understand the promises to include relief from foreign invasion, which highlights Yahweh's power and love for the chosen people and the chosen city. Third, most experts conclude that Isaiah's words unequivocally denounce Ahaz's unbelief. As Otto Kaiser comments, "Because Ahaz did not accept the offer of the God of grace, he will not escape his punishment. And therefore this is also a true sign, a proof, permeating the whole of the subsequent history . . . that the sinner does not escape his punishment and that God's word prevails."[22]

These convictions demonstrate that the Lord is a God who keeps promises, rules history and judges sinners. Thus God's word cannot fail now anymore than it could in Ahijah's or Elijah's times. David remains the nation's best hope for the future, and God remains the country's surest defense. Immanuel will be from David's lineage, even through Ahaz's lineage. God's prophet feels compelled to speak the truth as much now as in Micaiah's era. The prophet feels comfortable moving between the present and the future because the Lord of all history knows the end of time as well as the beginning. Kings who read history through a solely secular lens will not have the insight to rule effectively even in the secular realm. They know neither the end nor the beginning of time.

Isaiah heightens the importance of faith, the remnant, God's word, divine punishment and the coming Davidic king in the remainder of the section. Having received Ahaz's refusal to believe, Isaiah is told by Yahweh not to fear but to believe, trusting the law and testimonies for guidance. God's word may be trusted when all else fails and will be the only source of light when the darkness associated with the day of the Lord shadows the earth (8:11-22). While the people and their king fear the Syrians and Israelites and will come to fear the Assyrians, the prophet and the rest of the remnant must fear only God, for God alone is holy (8:11-15).[23] Thus only God's word can be trusted.

Trusting in God's word will bring the remnant through the current crisis, but waiting for the Davidic king will sustain them in the future. It is possible, though not provable beyond a reasonable doubt, that Isaiah 4:2 refers to the Davidic king, for it mentions "the Branch of the LORD" as part of the renewed Israel that will take shape after judgment. This title has specific messianic and Davidic connotations in Jeremiah 23:5 and 33:15.[24] At the very least this phrase begins a specific interest in a God-ordained individual who will oversee Israel's future restoration. Immanuel heightens this expectation, for the child is the key to victory and renewal in some tangible way. Isaiah 9:1-7 relieves the tension. A future Davidic king will be wise, powerful, everlasting and able to achieve peace, establish justice and uphold righteousness forever (9:6-7).

What is astounding about this text is that it attributes to the coming king divine names. He will not merely be mighty but will be called "Mighty God." He will reign forever, seemingly without succumbing to death. Such characteristics are beyond what is possible for a normal ruler governing within the boundaries of common human history. This person takes on God's traits in a clear, nonadoptive sense.[25] This individual is called God yet stands alongside the Lord of hosts, whose zeal seals his reign. When this king rules, God's kingdom will spill out of heaven and consume the earth in as thorough a manner as the day of the Lord will bring punishment.

Between the crisis with Ahaz and the king's coming there will be woe on all those who reject God's covenant (9:8—10:4). Assyria will devastate Israel, only to be judged themselves for thinking they are more than an instrument in Yahweh's hand (10:5-19). Given this knowledge of what will be, the remnant may "rely on the LORD, the Holy One of Israel" (10:20). This remnant, who by this point in Isaiah are clearly identified as those who believe in and rely upon Yahweh, will be the only persons who will escape judgment, either in the short- or in the long-term sense. And it is this remnant, this burned stump (cf. 6:13), that Isaiah's preaching will create and encourage.

In this immediate context of international war, the Lord again announces eventual never-ending, worldwide peace. Again this peace will be mediated by the Davidic king (11:1-9). After the day of Yahweh the Davidic judge of the earth will draw all nations to himself to give them a "place of rest" (11:10). This rest, this new exodus,[26] will be for the remnant but not limited to them. God's purging of the earth will create a remnant from all nations, a fact that means the Lord rules all creation (11:12-16).

Isaiah's first section ends with a hymn of praise that confesses that God saves, protects and comforts (12:1-6). The Holy One deserves to be mentioned to all nations. This final segment underscores the ways the rest of Isaiah 1—12 presents the God who saves. In the disasters that plague Isaiah's era, the Lord will save the remnant who believes. In the disasters that will come long after Isaiah is dead, the Lord will still save the remnant. This salvation will come through judgment, faith and the coming King. It will come despite the sin so graphically depicted and condemned, and it will come as the word of God presented by the God-called prophets.

Canonical Synthesis: The King and the Remnant

Isaiah 1—12 gathers many canonical ideas that have already been introduced. In fact Isaiah 8:20 encourages readers to remember these biblical notions as an antidote to the covenant people's sin. Isaiah's initial verses bring Israel's covenant status to the forefront. God's people have rejected the holy God that Exodus 20—Leviticus 27 describes in such detail. The people substitute mere ritual observance for the heartfelt commitment Deuteronomy commands. Exile predicted in Deuteronomy 27—28 and described in 2 Kings 17 awaits the disobedient nation. God's word through the chosen messenger offers the nation knowledge of God's ways and then condemns them as they reject the Lord's grace. Later prophecies and portions of the Writings will confirm Isaiah's claims.

Isaiah 1—12 also clarifies certain canonical notions. For example, the Davidic promises, first given in 2 Samuel 7, are discussed in more detail. The eternal kingdom mentioned in Samuel now includes all nations, total peace, complete justice, full wisdom and God's presence with the remnant. Only this sort of comprehensive portrait can bring redemption to the sinful situation depicted in Genesis—Kings and in Isaiah 1—5. Thus only a person who transcends history may save the sinners who occupy history. Only a Davidic king whose dimensions become larger than history can transform history into holy territory fit for the Holy One of Israel.

These texts also clarify the identity of the chosen people. Here national Israel consists of the remnant and those whose hearts are hardened (cf. 6:10-13). These two parties stand on opposite sides of the day of the Lord, separated by their willingness or lack of willingness to believe God's word and to act upon that belief. Isaiah pushes forward the concept of Israel against remnant Israel begun in Exodus 32—34, the book of Numbers and the episodes involving Elijah by extending the notion into the end of time. This theological shift has not occurred previously. Before the emphasis was placed on how the remnant and the rebellious ones took their places within recorded human history. These texts also include non-Israelites in the remnant, thereby solidifying an idea introduced by Rahab's conversion, as well as by Naaman's healing and subsequent confession. Those who believe and forsake all other gods are accepted by Yahweh regardless of their ethnic background, while those who reject the Lord are themselves rejected even though they may be Abraham's direct descendants.

One other canonical development merits attention. For the first time the canon begins to move beyond the past, present and short-term future to envision the end of time, when God will redeem all things. As the Bible unfolds these beginnings will grow into extensive end-time (eschatological) writings and then into the specialized literary treatments of the future found in apocalyptic books and passages. Isaiah writes like one who believes himself at a midpoint of history, too far from the beginning to return there yet too far from final hope to get there either. What remains, then, is hope for better times based on Yahweh's historically proven character.

The God Who Eliminates Prideful Nations: Isaiah 13—27

Of all the present realities Isaiah understood, surely Judah's weakness was at the top of his list. The prophet lived in a decidedly politically insignificant country, one with no real means of adequate self-defense, one that needed outside help to survive (cf. 7:1-9). It is also true that Isaiah lived in an era in which the power of a god was measured by the power of nations that worshiped it. In Isaiah 13—27 the book addresses both these beliefs. First, the text locates Judah's growth, renewal and prominence well into the future. Second, the author shatters the latter theory by affirming Yahweh's sovereignty over all countries, Yahweh's right to judge all nations and Yahweh's special opposition to prideful, self-confident kingdoms.

Several nations addressed in Isaiah 13—27 have already been mentioned in Isaiah 1—12. Assyria, Philistia, Syria, Edom, Moab, Ammon and Egypt are listed in 11:11-16 as places from which the remnant shall return after exile.[27] Other lands, such as Tyre (see 23:1-18), are added here, but Babylon is the

most significant newcomer. When Isaiah declares the future destruction of
that power he projects his message down to 539 B.C., when Persia displaces
Babylon, Assyrian's conqueror in 612 B.C., as the major world power.

The text says that the first Babylonian oracle comes from Isaiah himself
(13:1). Many scholars have sought to date the Babylonian oracles later, but
these texts may be dated plausibly within Isaiah's lifetime because of
Babylon's activities while Assyria was weak (c. 720-708 B.C.).[28] Babylonian
envoys visit Hezekiah, perhaps to encourage a joint opposition to Assyria
(cf. 2 Kings 20:12-19; Is 39:1-8). If so, Egypt and Babylon share in common
the inability to deliver Judah from Assyria. The Babylonians are boasters who,
like Egypt, cannot deliver what they promise. Arrogance does not equal
ability. Two other texts also anchor these statements in Isaiah's era. Isaiah
14:28 says the next oracle came the year Ahaz died (c. 715 B.C.), while Isaiah
20:1 sets a message after a specific event in Sargon's reign.[29] These references
help highlight the section's futuristic orientation.

The oracle about Babylon sets the stage for the rest of the judgment
depicted in this segment of the prophecy. On the day of Yahweh the Lord
fights against Babylon so that pride and haughtiness might be eliminated
(13:11, 19). As Gerhard von Rad comments, the battle takes on supernatural
proportions.

> Yahweh comes in person to the battle, the stars are to withhold their light,
> the earth quakes, the carnage is terrible. The poem ends with an allusion
> to the complete desolation of the empire. . . . The war is made to take on
> gigantic dimensions; not single warriors but whole nations stream to the
> muster. At the same time, the events described have their parallels in real
> warfare.[30]

Babylon's pride is such that it seeks to displace God (14:12-14). Therefore
God will sweep the nation away from the earth (14:22-23). God will displace
them.

Other nations fare no better. Assyria, whose defeat by God's hand is a
major theme in Isaiah,[31] will be destroyed as well (14:24-27). That country's
arrogance has already been described in Isaiah 10:5-19. Likewise Moab
(16:6-7), Egypt (19:11-15) and Tyre (23:7-9) have all exalted themselves, only
to learn that Yahweh will punish their arrogance. Isaiah foresees a worldwide
destruction of catastrophic, divinely induced proportions (24:1-13). Such is
God's will, so it will occur (14:26-27).

Only the remnant will survive. Again the remnant will consist not only of
Israelites but also of strangers, Gentiles who will believe (14:1).[32] This
multinational group will dwell in Zion (14:32), feasting on God's mountain
(24:6-12). Idols will be removed (17:7-8; 19:1-4), and Israel, Egypt and Assyria
will all be God's chosen people (19:23-25). Tyre will undertake shipping and

trade for Yahweh's sake (23:17-18), which indicates that every realm of life will be dedicated to the Lord. Just as exile purifies Israel and leads Israel's remnant to acknowledge Yahweh alone as Lord (26:13; 27:9-11), so judgment will reveal the remnant that exists in the world's nations. Though the Davidic king's role in this brighter future is not as prominent in this section as it is in Isaiah 1—12, the concept is not absent. Moab's only hope is for a righteous, faithful, loving, Davidic king who is the same person as the one described in Isaiah 7:14, 9:1-7 and 11:1-10.[33] Also, Egypt's willingness to be part of the remnant will occur because of God's self-revelation and sending of a "savior" to deliver them (10:20-22). These images at least remind one of the coming King.[34] Though this section's description of God's elimination of arrogant wickedness has a wider scope than those in Isaiah 1—12, the basic principles remain the same.

Canonical Synthesis: God's Final Judgment

Earlier canonical texts have prepared readers for Isaiah's claim that Yahweh may judge all nations and create a multiracial remnant. In the Pentateuch, God judges Egypt, a nation he has created, on behalf of Israel, a created people chosen for a specific task. The same principle holds in the Former Prophets, for there Yahweh repeatedly fights for the small yet unique Israelite nation. Since the Lord has been chastising Egypt, Philistia, Moab and other nations for centuries, it is hardly shocking when Isaiah proclaims Yahweh will again punish these countries. At the same time, Moses' Ethiopian wife (Num 12), Rahab (Josh 2:1-24; 6:22-25) and Naaman (2 Kings 5:1-19) prove that God's people are not distinguished by race alone but by a commitment to the one God who creates and judges.

Subsequent prophetic books include lists of nations Yahweh will punish similar to the one in Isaiah 13—23. Jeremiah 46—41, Ezekiel 25—32, Amos 1:2—2:16 and Zephaniah 2:1—3:5 all stress Yahweh's sovereignty over every inch of the earth. They also emphasize the Lord's condemnation of sin in Israel and elsewhere, Yahweh's protection of the remnant and God's disgust with humankind's arrogance and viciousness to one another. Every passage demonstrates the Lord's specific involvement in judgment, whether that punishment occurs through human means in history or through direct, divinely produced events. This punishment purges the earth of evil so that the earth may return to its initial innocence.

Isaiah 24—27 is so committed to the future, final judgment, resurrection and the defeat of evil that many commentators consider this text apocalyptic literature.[35] Apocalyptic writing generally reviews long periods of time and divides these periods into ages, utilizes symbolic language, views human history as a battle between good and evil, sometimes uses pseudonymity of authorship and transfers God's judgment from the historical to cosmic realms.[36] Given these generic characteristics, it is best to conclude that these chapters "break new ground in the history of Old Testament prophecy, but do not yet qualify for the title apocalyptic."[37] They provide a bridge from traditional prophecy to apocalyptic.[38] Thus this section provides a context for Daniel's and Zechariah's visions and by extension those in the Apocrypha and the New Testament as well.

Perhaps this passage's greatest contribution to biblical theology is its emphasis on what happens when human history as it has been known since creation ceases. At this climactic moment Yahweh's uniqueness will be absolutely evident. Yahweh will purge the earth, judge the wicked, banish death forever and hear the remnant's praises (25:6-9). No other god is in this scene. Yahweh alone opens eternity to the remnant. Though many other biblical passages deal with the end of time and life after death, by the end of Revelation its author can conceive of no better way to express these ideas than to echo these images from Isaiah 25:6-9 (cf. Rev 21:1-8). Isaiah sets the standard by which subsequent writers must judge their eschatalogical ideas. The one God who created history will also re-create it.

The God Who Secures the Remnant: Isaiah 28—39

Isaiah 28—39 returns to the book's earlier habit of alternating between Isaiah's setting and the future. It revisits the people's choice between trusting Yahweh or looking to foreign nations for deliverance.[39] Now the decision is whether to trust Egypt to save them from Assyria, but the principle remains the same. Speaking for God and for the remnant, Isaiah counsels faith in Yahweh. By the end of Isaiah 39 his point is amply illustrated, for a faithful prophet and an obedient king will deliver Jerusalem from Assyria. God undertakes this miracle only to protect the remnant and to demonstrate the emptiness of polytheistic political propaganda.

God pronounces woe on the people for the same sins condemned in Isaiah 1—5. The chosen people have become drunkards (28:1, 7), and their prophets, priests and sages have ceased to have clear visions and offer sound advice (28:7; 29:14). Judah trusts Egypt to save them from the Assyrians (30:1-7; 31:1-5), who destroy Ephraim (Israel) as easily as one eats summer fruit (28:1-4). Therefore they will endure immediate woe, represented by the fall of Samaria and the crisis with Sennacherib. They will also endure the permanent woe created by the day of Yahweh. Their destroyers will also be destroyed (33:1), as earlier chapters have already indicated.

Despite all this misery, a believing remnant will find a home in Zion. Now the remnant is characterized as those whom God comforts with strength, beauty and justice (28:5-6). They are the meek and poor who exult only in

Yahweh (29:19). They are the true children of Abraham (29:22-24) who find their rest in Zion (30:19-33). The remnant will find refuge under the coming King's leadership (32:1-20). They will return to Zion from the ends of the earth (35:8-10). Within the narrative in Isaiah 36—39, the remnant consists of Hezekiah the believing king, Isaiah the faithful, now aging prophet, and officials who stand with their king. This section includes both a verbal image and a human actualization of the remnant concept.

Canonical Synthesis: The Remnant and Deliverance

These chapters also present immediate and long-term presentations of deliverance. God's promises to help the remnant unfold in 701 B.C. when Hezekiah and Isaiah are delivered from Assyria while living in Jerusalem/ Zion. As Isaiah 25:6-9 has shown, however, a permanent peace will occur when Yahweh gathers the remnant to Zion and suspends death. Thus the deliverance in Isaiah 36—37 is initiated by God, yet it is not all God will do. It is a marvelous first step toward similar yet greater events to come.

Kingship remains a major issue in the present-future exchange. Richard Schultz observes that in Isaiah 6—11 Ahaz refuses to believe and in Isaiah 28—33 an unnamed king is tempted to rely on Egypt, but in Isaiah 36—39 Hezekiah trusts God, which provides anticipation of an even-greater King's rule.[40] The images in 32:1-20 link it with earlier royal texts.

The King's reign will bring an end to the people's blindness and deafness (cf. Is 6:9-10) and usher in a time of righteousness and peace (cf. 9:6-7 [5-6]; 11:5-9) after the Assyrian threat is past (31:8-9; see also the reference to "quietness and confidence" in 30:15 and 32:17).[41]

Motyer concurs and adds that this vision of a new King and new society fits the tendency of "biblical eschatology to allow the ultimate vision to brighten the intermediate dark days."[42] Without this King there can be no bright future, and the text introduces no other king than the Davidic ruler mentioned in Isaiah 7—11. So far the text maintains its emphasis on the King as the key to the remnant's future with Yahweh.

Isaiah 36—39 is one of the few lengthy Old Testament texts repeated in Scripture. Its dual appearance allows its canonical function to become clearer. In 2 Kings 18—20 the account provides a bridge from Judah's survival to its downfall. Hezekiah shows the Babylonian envoys his entire kingdom, which 2 Chronicles 32:24-26 may consider raw human pride. He at least considers the always-rebellious Babylonians his allies against the vicious Assyrians. Regardless of his exact motivation, both 2 Kings 20:12-21 and Isaiah 39:1-8 record Isaiah's prediction of future Babylonian rule over Judah. This event, dated near the end of the eighth century B.C., prefigures what will occur in 587 B.C. In both Kings and Isaiah the accuracy of the prediction demonstrates that God knows what will occur before it happens. Thus God rules history, and God reveals the future through prophetic messengers.

The twin texts also highlight Yahweh's redemptive power over the arrogant forces of evil, in this case represented by Assyria. God saves Jerusalem, just as Isaiah promises (2 Kings 19:20-37; Is 37:21-35). The Lord may destroy or save, depending on the obedience of the people. This historical illustration of these two principles validates the messages on these subjects found in Isaiah 1—35. It also keeps alive the present-future theme.

The God Who Saves Through a Suffering Servant: Isaiah 40—55

Isaiah 40—55 assumes the previous thirty-nine chapters' themes, historical context and present-future time frame have all been absorbed. Therefore readers must recall that Israel has been defeated for more than two decades and that in Judah only Jerusalem has survived a thorough Assyrian invasion. Most of the chosen people are in exile, and all of them have suffered terribly. Sin, punishment and renewal have been themes since Isaiah 1—4, so it is likely that they will remain important in the rest of the book as well. Sin, punishment and renewal have also been portrayed as occurring in Isaiah's time and in the distant future. This orientation toward time can be expected to continue. Given these considerations, it is not necessary to read Isaiah 40—55 solely as an exilic work or as a totally predictive prophecy. Rather it is necessary to encounter these chapters in light of what the book as a canonical whole has already set forth and still seeks to accomplish.

In many ways biblical theology reaches one of its highest points in these chapters. First, few texts place a greater premium on monotheistic faith. Following the polytheistic propaganda and divine response in Isaiah 36—37, this section magnifies Yahweh's uniqueness. Second, these chapters present a picture of a suffering servant who embodies the best characteristics of Abraham, Moses, David and the prophets. All vital messianic images merge. Third, Isaiah 40—55 envisions the renewal of a remnant united behind the servant. Fourth, this segment predicts the rise and fall of the kingdoms that rule the promised land in the rest of the Old Testament era. Even more than in any other portion of the book, Isaiah's theological-historical vision staggers the imagination.

Isaiah 40:1 announces comfort for the besieged Jerusalem that has been left lonely and desolate (cf. Is 1:8-9; 36:1). This comfort will emerge because of Yahweh's character. God's glory must be seen (40:3-5), and it will be seen when Yahweh shepherds the people again (40:6-11). For those who believe Assyria's gods are more powerful than Yahweh,[43] the text states that the Lord is the Creator and ruler of history (40:12-17, 21-24, 26), so no idol is comparable (40:17-20, 25). Other gods are images, not persons. Isaiah speaks of them as "whom" (40:18), only to dismiss them as "it" (40:19). No real God "can be represented by the works of human hands."[44] As Creator, Yahweh is everlasting, which means his power to save can never diminish, which in turn means Israel will be renewed (40:27-31). The Creator is also therefore comforter, shepherd and sustainer.

Yahweh's uniqueness continues to be manifested in 41:1-29. First, God calls nations to rise against one another (41:1-4, 25), a truth proclaimed since Isaiah 1—5. Yahweh's everlasting nature makes this long-term sovereignty possible (40:28; 41:4). Second, Yahweh called Israel to be his servant from Abraham's time (41:8), redeemed them (41:9) and now promises to help them again (41:10-16). Once again Yahweh will lead the people through the desert (41:17-20). A new exodus will unfold. Third, God continues to predict the future, as has been the case in the past (41:21-19). Fourth, idols, which are less than nothing, cannot do such things (41:22-24). God alone rules. To link these ideas to earlier passages the text proclaims that the redeemer is the Holy One of Israel (41:14). This fact has not changed.

Part of Yahweh's revelation of the future includes a description of an ideal servant who will do all Israel has failed to do in its role as God's servant. Bernhard Duhm notes at least four texts in which this servant appears: 42:1-4, 49:1-6, 50:4-9 and 52:13—53:12. He also correctly concludes that these texts speak of an individual, whereas passages such as 41:8, 42:19, 43:10, 44:1-2, 21, 45:4 and 49:3 (within 49:1-6) refer to all Israel as God's servant.[45] Almost uniformly Israel is depicted as a frail, failing servant, while the individual servant performs God's will without fail. The former servant will be reformed and redeemed, but the latter requires no redemption. As Isaiah 40—55 unfolds, the individual servant becomes the model for the corporate servant, which is identified with the remnant in the rest of the book.

Many scholars disagree with this assessment. Besides this option, at least seven (if not more) other possibilities have been suggested. These ideas include that the servant is Israel,[46] a prophet,[47] a royal servant,[48] a specific historical figure,[49] a second Moses for the second exodus,[50] a corporate personality[51] or a symbolic individual who embodies a combination of the best servant traits found in Scripture.[52] Each viewpoint has strengths and weaknesses, but the text itself points to a servant who renews God's servant Israel through teaching, leading, dying and dividing rewards. Thus this person must achieve in the future even more than Abraham, Moses and David have accomplished in the past. In this person the covenants will be actualized, and the one God who reveals him will be glorified.

God's servant is called by God, filled with God's Spirit, willing to suffer and incapable of failure (42:1-4). The Creator calls the servant to be a light to the nations, a healer and the fulfillment of divine prediction (42:5-9). These images echo Genesis 1—2, Genesis 12:1-9 and Exodus 19:5-6. The individual servant is an agent of salvation for the blind corporate servant who has suffered Yahweh's wrath (42:10-25). The references to justice also remind readers of the work that will be done by the Davidic king in 9:6-7 and 11:1-11.

Isaiah 43—48 attacks the barriers that keep Israel from being an effective servant. The fault is not God's. The Lord has created and called Israel because Yahweh loves Israel (43:1-7). God is their Holy One (43:3). The problem is that they have sought strange gods (43:12), idols (44:9-20; 46:1-2) that have no life. To combat this error the Lord offers the following litany of truths.

1. God alone is the Creator (43:1, 7; 44:2, 21, 24; 45:7, 9-12, 18; 48:12-13).

2. God alone redeems (43:1, 11-21, 25-28; 44:6-8, 22-24; 45:17, 21; 47:1-4; 48:17-19).

3. God alone reveals the future (43:8-10, 14-21; 44:6-8; 44:24—45:1; 45:21; 48:3-5, 14-16).

4. God is incomparable (44:7, 24; 46:5-11) and holy (43:3, 15; 45:11; 47:4).

5. Yahweh is God, and there is no other (43:10-13; 44:6-8; 44:24—45:7; 45:14-25; 46:8-11).

These teachings stress explicit monotheism as the only basis for a theology of hope. They also provide rich, ironic descriptions of the utter folly of venerating idols (cf. 44:9-20; 46:1-2). Israel's future depends upon their commitment to these principles, just as their past has been determined by them. The people may pray to a god that cannot save because it is hand-made (45:20), or they can turn to the God who rules history and who will lead the remnant home from exile. No other god has validity in Isaiah's eyes.

Besides calling the servant, Yahweh will prove master of history by revealing that Cyrus will be God's instrument for making it possible to rebuild Jerusalem (44:24—45:7; esp. 44:28; 45:1). This passage parallels 1 Kings 13:2 in its promise by name of a future person who will be used by God. Some commentators believe that this text was added after Cyrus's career as Persia's leader (c. 559-529 B.C.), conqueror of Babylon (c. 539 B.C.), releaser of Israelite captives (c. 538 B.C.; cf. Ezra 1:1-4) and benefactor for the rebuilding of Israel's temple (cf. Ezra 1:5-11). Most commentators think that his career was unfolding as the third segment of the book (Is 56—66) was being written. Anyone who dates this passage prior to the temple's rebuilding in 520-516 B.C. treats the text as predictive, and all who date it before 538 B.C. find the whole predictive. The only issue to be decided is how many years in advance the promise is made.[53] The main point is that Yahweh proves superior to idols by revealing the future to the chosen people, and the astounding accuracy of the revelation ought to inspire Israel to faith in their God.

Isaish 49—55 deals with a second problem Israel must overcome. Some people worship idols, but others truly find it hard to believe that God still loves them. They feel as if Yahweh has forgotten Zion (49:14; cf. 40:27). So the last three servant songs are set within a section in which God reassures the people that the one deity who can save will indeed save them, even though recently they have been under divine wrath.

Both servant types appear in 49:1-6.[54] Yahweh called the nation from birth (49:1), a phrase that refers to Israel in 44:2 and 24, and then prepared this servant for service (49:2). Rather than glorifying God, however, this servant succumbed to weariness and discouragement not unlike that expressed in 40:27-31 (49:3-4). Therefore the second servant, who is also called from the womb (49:5), is commissioned to the twofold task of restoring Israel (49:5) and being a light to the Gentiles (49:6). God's desire is that salvation, which in view of Isaiah 40—48 must be defined as worship of the one God, will stretch to the "ends of the earth" (49:6).

Only through this second servant will the remnant become courageous enough to fulfill Exodus 19:5-6. Then kings will give honor to the Holy One of Israel (49:7), their Creator and Lord. When Yahweh redeems the people from exile (49:8-13) they will learn God has not forsaken them (49:14-23), and they will know the Lord can release them from the tyrant (49:24—50:3). Again God's goal is to teach Israel that they can have faith that Yahweh is the Lord (49:23) and the Lord is their redeemer (49:26). Salvation can be mediated only to those who express monotheistic convictions about Yahweh and who trust in his permanent love (50:1-3).

Now the individual servant joins the Lord in trying to strengthen the nation in the third song (50:4-9). Like the people, the servant has suffered greatly (50:4-6), yet he has not ceased serving Yahweh or become faithless as they have (50:7-9). Why? Because the servant stands with God and thereby receives God's empowering presence (50:7).[55] God is near, so the servant does not falter (50:8). Given the divine revelation and the servant's testimony, the people should fear the Lord, obey the servant and walk in the light (50:10-11). There is no distinction between Yahweh's work and that of the servant who does God's will.[56] Only the nation lags behind the divine activity.

The exhortative nature of the section continues in 51:1—52:12, where Yahweh again bases the promise of future salvation on redemptive acts in history. Three times the Lord tells Israel to listen (51:1, 4, 7), three times Yahweh orders them to awake (51:9, 17; 52:1), and as a single, concluding imperative God commands the people to depart (52:11). Together these commands and their succeeding messages constitute the promise and proclamation of salvation to come.[57] This salvation will endure forever (51:6, 8). It will restore Eden and Zion and will continue to fulfill the Abrahamic covenant (51:2-3). It will establish Yahweh's justice through God's law (51:4-7). It will be a new exodus in which Yahweh's ransomed remnant will return to Zion because their Lord still has power over nature and still overpowers polytheistic myths (51:9-11). Yahweh refers to Babylonian creation myths to demonstrate their inabililty to defeat the One whom 51:12-16 identifies as the real Creator.[58] God's people must hasten to depart on this new exodus in as much haste as their ancestors left Egypt the first time (42:1-12; cf. Ex 12:33-36).

In other words, all the great covenants will be kept and all the great events reenacted in a new way. God's creation of Eden and God's choice of Jerusalem as Zion will be renewed (51:3). The Abrahamic (51:2) and Mosaic (51:4, 7) covenants will be actualized, and the holy land will be inhabited again. Only the Davidic covenant seems missing, but Isaiah's earlier texts indicate that lasting justice, which is promised in 42:4, 51:4 and 51:7, will originate with the King from David's line. David's connection with Jerusalem/Zion also brings that covenant into view. Thus the servant may be connected with the Davidic promise, since he is the one most linked with restoring Israel, bringing light to the Gentiles and generally doing the spiritual work mentioned in Isaiah 9:6-7 and 11:1-11. Once the people heed the servant, they will become the fulfillment of Exodus 19:5-6. At last the holy nation will be in place. Most of Old Testament theology is compacted here.

The fourth servant song Duhm identifies is the most important for biblical theology, since the New Testament writers find it a compelling portrait of Jesus' ministry and death. This passage expands the servant's suffering role first mentioned in 50:4-9, for God declares the servant will prosper and be exalted but only after enduring terrible pain (52:13-15). The nations will be startled at the servant's experiences (52:13), as will the Israelites (53:1). Both groups must be included because both have been promised "light" (cf. 9:2-7; 49:6; 50:10-11).[59] What amazes the Gentiles and makes the Israelites doubt unfolds in four specific parts.

First, Isaiah 53:1-3 describes the servant's manner and his rejection by his peers. He has no physical beauty to draw people to him, so those judging by outward appearance, in this case apparently everyone involved, turn from him (53:2). He suffers sorrow and grief (53:3). Second, Isaiah 53:4-6 describes the servant's suffering as substitutionary. Though observers consider him afflicted by God (53:4), he actually suffers for others to heal others (53:5). Thus "the servant does not suffer fruitlessly. Because he suffers the pains of others, others are released from pain."[60]

Third, Isaiah 53:7-9 discusses the servant's death. He dies humbly (53:7), unfairly (53:8) and poverty-stricken (53:9). Again the passage stresses "the fact that the Servant took it upon himself to act vicariously, that submissively and unresistingly, and therefore deliberately, he took this mediating office upon himself even unto death, and that in so doing he complied with

Jahweh's purpose."[61] The speakers fully understand the seeming injustice of the situation yet realize they have benefited from it in a way Yahweh specifically intends.

Fourth, Isaiah 53:10-12 announces the servant's future reward for his ministry. All along the passage has confessed that the servant bears guilt, or is a "sin offering." Walther Zimmerli notes that Isaiah's phrase in 53:10 links the servant to the sacrificial system and to the suffering prophets.

> According to Leviticus 10:17, the animal sacrificed as a sin offering "bears" or "takes away" the guilt of the community. Above all, according to Leviticus 16:22, on the great Day of Atonement the scapegoat chased out into the desert to Azazel, upon which the guilt (and punishment) of the community is placed, bears away this guilt. Here, too, there is a striking point of contact with the prophet of the early exilic period, who lay sick for days bearing the guilt of Israel (Ezek. 4:4-8).[62]

A human sacrifice for sin occurs nowhere else in the Old Testament, and von Rad prefers to read the phrase "in the more general legal sense of 'substitute' or 'compensation'" because, he notes,

> if this alludes specifically to the sacrifices offered in the cult, a special importance would accrue to the expression from the theological point of view; for the suggestion that the servant's sacrifice surpassed the sacrificial system would certainly be unparalleled in the Old Testament, and it perhaps also contradicts Deutero-Isaiah himself (Is. XLIII. 22f.).[63]

What must be recalled is that Isaiah 40—55 exists in the realm of new things (e.g., 43:19) God will do in the future. Thus the reference may indeed intend to state that a time will come when the sacrificial system will be surpassed, but that time has not yet come.

Having been a sin offering, obviously dead, the servant will "prolong his days" and receive blessing from Yahweh (53:10-12). North observes that Canaanite and Babylonian myths depict gods who die and rise again.[64] Perhaps these verses, like 51:9, displace the gods the Israelites are tempted to worship. Regardless, there is no doubt that the victory lies beyond the grave.[65] The victory consists of the servant causing many to be made righteous (53:11), of interceding successfully for the sinners (53:12). In effect the observers/speakers here celebrate their own salvation through the servant's work. They are "his seed," "his fruit," "his spoil." Those who stray as sheep in 53:6 return as children in 53:10.[66] In this way the group has become the remnant through God's forgiveness mediated through the servant's death.[67]

Isaiah 54—55 asks the Israelites and the nations to respond to God's gracious salvation. In this way it parallels the challenge in 50:10-11 in the third song.[68] Israel has been barren (54:1), afflicted (54:11) and without comfort (54:11; cf. 40:1-2). They have experienced Yahweh's wrath (54:8).

Now, however, they may take solace in the fact that the Creator is their husband who can protect them from any harm (54:4-8, 11-17). God promises them this covenant is as permanent as Noah's (54:9; cf. Gen 9:8-17) and as universal in opportunity.

God cements the Gentiles' salvation by referring to the Davidic covenant. This agreement is everlasting and is founded in love (55:3). It is based on one who witnesses to the nations, commands the people and is glorified by God. This verse transforms the nations from cringing in David's presence in 2 Samuel 22:44-46 (cf. Ps 18:43-45) to enjoying a loving relationship with the Lord.[69] James Smart correctly states that the tasks assigned to the Davidic figure in Isaiah 55:3-5 are those of the servant in the rest of Isaiah 40—55.[70] Why bring David into the discussion now? To merge the Davidic king and the servant images. Motyer says, "The answer is that the book of the King (chapters 1—37) portrayed the Messiah as the fulfillment of the ideal in its royal aspects, but now Isaiah brings the values of the Servant-Messiah within the basic Davidic-Messianic model."[71] God has revealed this means of redeeming the remnant, and God's word cannot fail (55:10-11). Any possibility of such failure renders the claims to interpret the past and to reveal the past in Isaiah 40—55 null, void, unworthy of heeding. Those who seek (55:6-9) will rejoice (55:12-13).

Canonical Synthesis: The Servant and Jesus

This section of Isaiah is a minicanon unto itself. It mentions Eden, Abraham and Sarah, Jacob, the exodus, the law, Zion, David, the return from exile and the uniting of Israelites and Gentiles as a holy remnant to the holy God. All the Old Testament's major redemption themes converge here. Their fulfillment depends entirely on God's sovereignty and the servant's ministry. Salvation for all people rests on their believing the report about the servant (53:1). If they believe, then Yahweh will restore them by forgiving their sins, because the servant has borne those transgressions. Under these conditions the future is very bright. Through the servant God will bless all nations (cf. Gen 12:1-9), make Israel a holy nation (cf. Ex 19:5-6), legitimate the law (cf. Deut 8:3), give David an everlasting kingdom (cf. 2 Sam 7:7-17) and provide a future for the remnant.

The New Testament writers think Jesus is the servant Isaiah portrays. Matthew 8:17 and 12:18-21 cite Isaiah 53:4 and 42:1-4 respectively as reference points for Jesus' healing ministry. Matthew 26:67 and Luke 22:63 may reflect Isaiah 50:4-9, since they speak of Christ enduring mocking, hitting and being spat upon. John 12:38-40 cites Isaiah 53:1 and Isaiah 6:9-10 together as evidence that the coming Savior would face unbelief. Paul quotes this same Isaiah 53:1 to argue for the necessity of preaching to engender faith

(Rom 10:16). Isaiah 53:5 is used as evidence for Jesus' atoning death in 1 Peter 2:24 and Romans 4:25. Philip tells the Ethiopian eunuch that Isaiah 53:7-8 refers to Jesus (Acts 8:26-39). Matthew 27:57 says Isaiah 53:9 predicts the fact that a rich man will loan Jesus his grave. Paul may reflect on Isaiah 53:12 when discussing how Jesus' death makes sinners righteous, and Jesus himself cites that passage when attempting to explain his death to his disciples (Lk 22:37). The apostle Paul uses Isaiah 49:6 to legitimate his own ministry to the Gentiles (cf. Acts 13:44-52; 26:19-23).[72]

Perhaps the list could be extended, but the point is clear. The Gospel writers and the apostle Paul believed that the servant passages help them identify Jesus as the promised Davidic king. Paul viewed the church as the ideal remnant of Jews and Gentiles and cast his own ministry and that of the church in terms of servanthood (cf. Rom 1:1; 9—11; 15:1-2). They did not use extraordinary (allegorical or midrashic) interpretative methods to draw these conclusions. Rather they decided that the servant was the key to the various Old Testament covenantal promises being fulfilled and then determined that Jesus was that servant. One may conclude that they were wrong, but not because of exegetical gymnastics on their part.

Canonical Synthesis: Monotheism and Gentile Conversion

Though scholars disagree on a host of issues related to Isaiah 40—55, they generally agree that these chapters stress monotheism. J. J. M. Roberts and North believe this emphasis grows out of the text's conviction that Yahweh created all things, which means this God has no rival.[73] John McKenzie and Skinner think the main purpose of Isaiah 40—55 is to discuss salvation and that the text's insistence on Yahweh as Creator and only God intends to remove from the Israelites' minds any notion of looking for deliverance in another deity.[74] From the notions that God alone is God, that Yahweh is the Creator, that Yahweh is the Savior, it is plausible to conclude, as Isaiah 40—55 does, that Yahweh rules history.[75]

These themes link Isaiah 40—55 to the earlier portions of the canon. Yahweh's role as Creator begins the canon, serving as the foundational element for what follows. Exodus and Leviticus emphasize God's holiness and Israel's response to this trait. The Former Prophets teach that Yahweh rules world history if they teach nothing else. Isaiah orders his own theology along lines consistent with Israelite history and the rest of the canon. Later prophetic books will take a similar approach, both by reflecting on the Law and Israel's history and by displaying familiarity with Isaiah's use of that material.

Isaiah 40—55 also advances the canon's treatment of salvation for all persons to a new level. H. H. Rowley asserts that the author makes Israel responsible for taking God's standards to the world. Indeed belief in one God makes this a natural responsibility.

> With him it was not a distant hope that one day the peoples would spontaneously flock to Zion to learn the law of God. He believed that the people of God was called to proclaim that law. With him universalism was the corollary of monotheism and the world-wide mission of Israel the corollary of her election.[76]

Only through globally oriented ministry can Israel fulfill Genesis 12:1-9 and Exodus 19:5-6. Such figures as Rahab and Naaman have already embraced this salvation in the canon, and they will be joined later by Ruth and Jonah's Assyrians.

The God Who Creates New Heavens and Earth: Isaiah 56—66

Isaiah 55 concludes with exhortations and promises about what Yahweh will do to redeem the remnant. Isaiah 56:1 begins with commands about what the remnant must do until final salvation comes: keep justice and do righteousness. Motyer rightly says that in this way the recipients of these chapters are a community waiting for God's glory to come.[77] Personal righteousness derived from recognition of Yahweh's righteousness is a book-long theme[78] and is the means by which the remnant is separated from the unbelievers. This winnowing process continues in Isaiah 56—66.[79] Zion has been the ultimate place of final salvation for the remnant throughout the book and continues to be so here.[80] As in Isaiah 24—27, the ultimate rewarding of the remnant and renewal of the earth will occur at the end of time (cf. 66:17-24). It is this salvation that the book has consistently pointed toward, and it is with this salvation that Isaiah ends. As could be expected, the one God, the Holy One of Israel (60:14), will be the One who saves. Thus the great themes begun earlier help bring the prophecy to its conclusion.

Yahweh calls all the remnant, whether Israelite or Gentile, to obedience while waiting (56:1-8). They are to keep the sabbath, which is synonymous with proper worship, and to practice righteousness, which is synonymous with keeping the law in 51:4-7. This lifestyle will give discipline to their faith and substance to their confession. Leaders and followers alike attack and kill the remnant (56:9—57:13). Idolaters cannot stand the presence of the faithful here any more than they could in Elijah's era. God's wrath against the wicked, though, will free the remnant from their foes (57:14-21).

God tells the prophet to declare their sins to the people (58:1). As in 1:2-31, the Lord loathes pseudoreligion that consists of outward observance devoid of inward faith (58:2-5). Repentance remains the key to renewal (58:6-13; cf. 1:16-20), but judgment continues to be what the nation chooses (59:16-19; cf. 2:1—4:6). For the remnant, however, God will reign over them in Zion

(59:20; cf. 25:6-12) because the covenant with them is everlasting (59:21; cf. 51:6; 54:10). Little has changed since Isaiah 55, then, for the calls for faith in Isaiah 40—55 are not certain of a proper answer, but for those who do respond correctly salvation is certain and permanent, though not without cost.

What is certain is that God's light will destroy the shocking darkness of the sins depicted in Isaiah 56—59.[81] This reversal will occur because God himself will come to dispel the darkness (60:1-3), a promise that sounds very much like Isaiah 9:2-7.[82] When Yahweh arises, the remnant will gather together in Zion to bow down before the Holy One of Israel (60:4-14), and all unbelieving Israelites and oppressing Gentiles will be punished (60:12-14). Time will cease, for the sun is no longer needed where God is the light (60:19-21). Clearly these images push towards eschatalogical restoration. For now, though, the city must wait for this redemption.[83]

In Isaiah 1—35 the Davidic king enters the picture as the anointed one who will resolve Israel's sin problem. The servant assumes this role in Isaiah 40—55, with 55:3-5 providing a link between the king and the servant. Now a third anointed individual appears to do the same work in 61:1-3. This person has God's Spirit upon him (61:1; cf. 11:2; 42:1), he proclaims freedom, joy and righteousness to the remnant (61:1-3; cf. 42:1-4),[84] and he is "free from preoccupation with self."[85] It is his purpose to unite Yahweh with the remnant, not to gain notoriety for himself. Again the good news is that Yahweh will bless the people not merely with material wealth but also with the right to be the Lord's priests (61:6; cf. Ex 19:5-6) who are filled with joy and righteousness born of a love for Yahweh (61:10-12). Jesus reads this passage aloud in the synagogue at Nazareth and declares that he fulfills the promise (Lk 4:16-21). At the least Jesus uses Isaiah 61:1-3 as a pattern for his ministry. Luke's use of the text indicates he believed that Jesus meant the anointed one in Isaiah and Jesus were the same person.

Reassurance and joy continue in 62:1-12. God has chosen Jerusalem, and this elect status explains why Yahweh will save this city.[86] God has married Jerusalem (62:4-5; cf. 54:6-7), protected it (62:6-9; cf. Is 36—37) and saved it (62:10-12; cf. 11:10-12). The results will be that all nations shall see this vindication (62:2; cf. 52:13) and Israel will be a holy people (52:12; cf. 4:3; Ex 19:5-6). Thus Isaiah 60—62 presents a fabulous portrait of redemption, both for Israel and for the nations.[87] Zion is the focal point in these chapters because it is the final location of this salvation. Thus the imagery of Zion forecasts the final grace of God to the remnant in the end times.

Isaiah 63—66 provides a panoramic view of history from Israel's election through Abraham (63:16) to the end of time, when the remnant will dwell in a new heaven and earth (65:17-25) while the unbelieving live in a place of permanent torment (66:18-24). Along the way, the prophet summarizes Israel's spiritual heritage, Yahweh's nature and dealings with the chosen people and the difference between the remnant and the rebellious.

God's character provides reference points for Israel's history. Because of God's love, goodness, mercy and identification with human suffering, the Lord elected Israel (63:7-9). Because of God's holiness, Israel's sin was punished (63:10). Because Yahweh cannot forget Moses' era (63:10), the Lord hears the confession and cries of the people for the new exodus to take place (63:11—64:12). Because God is Israel's father (64:8), they have hope for the future. The remnant has been honest about the country's unsavory past, so it is likely God will respond.

The way the Lord responds to 63:11—64:12 is to judge for the direct purpose of identifying and blessing a remnant. God will judge (65:1-7) but not indiscriminately, for Yahweh considers the remnant wine within a cluster of grapes (65:8). Only the wicked will die by the sword (65:8-12). Now God explicitly defines the remnant as "servants" (65:9, 13-16). They are the ones the work of the suffering servant and the anointed one in 61:1-3 bring to the Lord. They are the ones who refuse to remain blind (cf. 43:18-19), who keep justice, do righteousness and suffer for their faith (cf. Is 56—57). To create this company of the committed, the Lord works through Israel's history.

This separation of remnant from unbelievers will occur at the end of time. God, who was firmly established as Creator in Isaiah 40—55, will create a new heaven and earth with a re-created (presumably) Jerusalem as its focal point (65:17-25). This place will be devoid of sorrow, pain over childbirth and wasted labor. In other words, it will be a return to Eden. The serpent will eat dust (65:25), another reference to Genesis that reaffirms the reversal of the curses that have plagued the human race since the fall into sin. These images also sound very much like Isaiah 11:1-10, which reminds readers of the Davidic king's role in this scene. Faith and humility, not ritual for ritual's sake, provide the way into the new creation (66:1-4).

Before the end comes the Lord will comb the nations one final time for Gentile members of the remnant (66:18-20). This great missionary activity[88] will produce converts (66:21-23). At the same time, not all will believe, for some persons shall be exposed to worms and fire forever (66:24). The damnation of the nonremnant provides a sobering apocalyptic conclusion to Isaiah.[89] While the day of the Lord envisioned since 2:1—4:6 will be joyful for the Lord's servants, it will be horrifying for the wicked. There can be no salvation unless there are people and situations from which one may be delivered.

Canonical Synthesis: The Righteous, Suffering Remnant

This section, like its predecessor, contains themes that appear earlier in

Scripture. The first of these themes concerns the remnant. Israelites must be separated from Israelites and Gentiles from Gentiles. Sometimes the remnant shrinks to a single person. Sometimes it is seven thousand strong, as in Elijah's day. Regardless, the remnant and only the remnant will receive Yahweh's blessings. Paul cites Isaiah's views on the remnant in Romans 9—11, where he argues for a multinational group who will serve Jesus. Neither Jew nor Gentile may be eliminated from the remnant, Paul says, on the basis of race alone.

The second theme is the need for personal righteousness that includes the willingness to suffer for faith. Joseph, Moses, Joshua, Caleb, Elijah, Micaiah and others model this lifestyle for the faithful in Isaiah 56—57 and 63:11—64:12. Jeremiah, Ezekiel, Hosea and others will have the chance to apply this principle later in the canon. The third theme is the greatness of Yahweh's person. No other god works on behalf of the people (64:4), a claim that disagrees with all the teachings of the prophets and priests from other ancient religions. Only God exists, and only God is good, merciful, kind, wrathful and rewarding. On this point there could not be greater agreement between Isaiah 56—66 and the Former Prophets.

Canonical Synthesis: Isaiah and the Canon

Isaiah's place at the front of the Latter Prophets just after the tragic history in Joshua—Kings offers the reader an interpretation of the latter part of the history just told, a unique contribution to prophetic theology and an introduction to prophetic literature. Isaiah's work in 2 Kings 18—20 prepares readers for this prophecy's appearance, though not necessarily for its scope and brilliance. Isaiah mentions Eden, Abraham, Jacob, Moses and David in his reconstructions of Israelite history and his interpretation of those events. Building on the Davidic promises in 2 Samuel 7:1-17, Isaiah concludes that all covenants will come to fruition when this one is fulfilled. Eden will be restored, nations will be blessed, sins will be forgiven, the law will be fulfilled and David will have an eternal throne when the anointed King, servant and healer (61:1-3) ministers to the remnant who will inhabit the new heavens and the new earth. Isaiah clears the ground for this view by describing Israel's sin and Yahweh's uniqueness. Only if there is no other god does breaking the Mosaic covenant make any difference. Only if there is no other god may one trust this revelation of the future.

Isaiah's contribution to canonical theology is to take principles embedded in history and text and expand them to include all of time. In this way this book introduces apocalyptic principles in an impressive manner. He approximates the Former Prophets' view of sin as covenant breaking yet takes sin's consequences well past exile. Isaiah accepts the Davidic promise and then describes the implications and actions of the person fulfilling those promises in detail. He believes God is holy and the Lord of history, so he applies these principles to history in explicitly monotheistic terms. Isaiah's vision of Jerusalem (1:1) stretches from about 740 B.C. to the final judgment.

Isaiah did not invent all or perhaps even most of the elements of the prophetic message the book presents. Still, within the canon this prophecy provides a comprehensive preview of the works that follow. Jeremiah, Ezekiel and the Twelve also consider Israel's history, the meaning of sin, the fulfillment of the Davidic promise, the end of time, the new exodus from exile, God's role as father, husband and Savior of Israel, the fate of the nations, and the nature of God and the remnant. Many of the prophets either reflect on Isaiah's work or have a similar view of what prophecy should include. Either way, this lengthy chapter about a lengthy prophecy hopefully will offer some indication of what is to come. Isaiah was hardly alone in his beliefs.

12

The God
Who Enforces
the Covenant

Jeremiah

. . . .

J EREMIAH IS A CHALLENGING BOOK BY ANY STANDARD OF MEASURE. IT IS A LONG prophecy that does not proceed in exact chronological order. This work contains several different kinds of poetic and prose materials. It covers a career that spans at least four decades and does so by including biographical material that is said to come from his only disciple. To complicate matters further, the Hebrew and Septuagint versions of Jeremiah differ, the most striking change being the fact that Jeremiah 46—51 is placed after 25:13 in the Greek text.[1] Such details make it difficult to determine an exact historical basis upon which to interpret the prophecy.

Despite these challenges, experts agree on many of Jeremiah's theological emphases. Almost without exception they conclude that Jeremiah preaches adherence to the Mosaic covenant in a manner quite similar to that found in Deuteronomy and the Former Prophets. Some believe this theme occurs because the book was written by "deuteronomists" who preached to exiles,[2] while others attribute the idea to earlier influences,[3] but the conclusion remains the same. In particular most scholars focus on the fact that Jeremiah calls the people to repent or face punishment and therefore blames Jerusalem's fall on the nation's unwillingness to obey Yahweh. More specifically, according to Moshe Weinfeld, Deuteronomy and the Former Prophets include the following theological concerns:

1. the struggle against idolatry
2. the centralization of the cult
3. exodus, covenant and election
4. the monotheistic creed
5. observance of the law and loyalty to the covenant
6. inheritance of the land
7. retribution and material motivation
8. fulfillment of prophecy
9. the election of the Davidic dynasty[4]

All these considerations appear in Jeremiah under the larger heading of covenant preaching. These themes force Jeremiah's readers to apply covenant principles to their own lives. Jeremiah's most famous text refers to a "new covenant" (31:31-34), a phrase with enormous implications of its own.

William Holladay notes that the prophecy also includes other theological principles drawn from a number of biblical texts. Besides the covenant, which he considers Jeremiah's chief concern, Holladay concludes that Yahweh's roles as Creator and Lord of history deserve mention.[5] He believes the prophecy uses an extensive number of earlier texts stretching from Genesis to Psalms, with Deuteronomy and Hosea providing the greatest influence.[6] In other words, Holladay conceives of Jeremiah as a biblical theologian who uses the best of the received traditions to formulate his messages. Though most of those messages were not necessarily written for later readers, they certainly would have spoken to perceptive subsequent audiences.

A canonical approach to theology accepts Jeremiah as a document written for God's people by God's servants. It does not seek to read the book according to a specific historical reconstruction or to act as if Jeremiah were no more difficult to analyze than, say, Haggai, a short and well-dated prophecy. Rather it interprets Jeremiah as it appears in the Hebrew version and observes its connections to previous biblical books and its influence on later Scriptures. Part of Jeremiah's canonical significance is due to its diversity, creativity and difficulty.

Certain important details emerge from a canonical approach to Jeremiah. Brevard Childs states that "a most significant feature of the canonical shaping lies in the close relation established between the law and the prophets."[7] The book itself presents Jeremiah as one who knew, appreciated and proclaimed the law, not as one who discovered a new legal tradition through Josiah's reform. Therefore, Childs says, "to take this interpretation seriously rules out both an alleged conflict between the law and the prophets, and also a legalistic subordination of the latter into a minor role."[8] Childs also argues that a canonical approach helps elucidate the conflict between true and false prophecy, an issue that is settled more by interpretation of the text than by psychological analysis of Jeremiah.[9] Besides these matters, a canonical approach allows readers to examine the value of prophetic biography. Rather than considering the narratives only in light of their value for illuminating the sermons, a canonical approach encourages comparing the stories about Jeremiah to those about Ahijah, Elijah, Elisha, Micaiah and Isaiah in Kings to determine their theological message.[10] Seen this way, biography is as important as poetic or prose sermons for developing theology.

Dealing with Jeremiah in canonical order reveals at least nine separate segments, each of which reflects canonical continuity and some of which influence later biblical thought. Jeremiah 1:1-19 reports Jeremiah's call in a way that reminds readers that the God who called Moses also summons Jeremiah. Next, Jeremiah 2—6 depicts a God who instructs the prophet. Yahweh explains to Jeremiah the work he will do and the obstacles he will face in language reminiscent of Isaiah 1—5. In Jeremiah 7—10 the now-informed prophet proclaims that God rejects hollow worship. It is not enough to mouth platitudes; rather one must apply the covenant to daily life to please Yahweh. Jeremiah 11—20 presents the prophet's struggle to maintain faith in a God who allows the faithful to suffer, while Jeremiah 21—29 presents God as the One who vindicates true prophets and comforts sufferers.

At the heart of this book devoted to covenant preaching, Jeremiah 30—33 announces a brighter future and a new covenant. God will create the remnant through a means hinted at in Isaiah yet not fully developed there. Then, with salvation projected into the future, Jeremiah 34—45 describes Jerusalem's fall and Jeremiah's exile to Egypt, which emphasizes how God punishes covenant breaking and how the righteous suffer because of the wicked ones' deeds. To show that Yahweh rules the nations, Jeremiah 46—51 presents the Lord's condemnation of the nations, a theme declared earlier in Isaiah 13—23. Finally, Jeremiah 52, which is a near duplicate of 2 Kings 24:18—25:30, states that even in exile God protects the Israelites. Defeat is not the only or the final word. As Deuteronomy 30:1-3 indicates, even after exile the Lord will restore the penitent.

The God Who Calls: Jeremiah 1:1-19

By now the canon has presented several strategic call stories, including those about Moses, Joshua, Gideon, Samuel, David, Elisha and Isaiah. Norman Habel has argued that Moses' call account is a pattern other stories follow,[11] and this seems to be the case in Jeremiah 1:1-19. Like Moses, Jeremiah feels overwhelmed, incapable of fulfilling the job's demands. Like Moses but more particularly like Isaiah, Jeremiah is called to a difficult task. He must face terrible opposition during terrible times. Despite the seriousness of these issues, what truly matters is that God calls, God will protect and God will be present. What Moses, Isaiah, and the others learned Jeremiah will now also discover.

Jeremiah 1:1-3 states the length, major political figures, major events and key places in his career. He serves about 627-587 B.C.,[12] or from five years before the discovery of the law book and Josiah's subsequent reform (2 Kings 22:3) to the fall of Jerusalem. His ministry occurs during a terrible national downward spiral from hope to despair. The passage also reveals that Jeremiah was a priest, which may help explain his knowledge of Scripture and interest in cultic purity, and that he was from a small town, which may in part explain his rejection by Jerusalem's authorities. These verses anchor what follows in history. Whatever he attempts or achieves will unfold during a time 2 Kings 22—25 describes as Judah's death throes (1:3). There will be no reprieve such as the one that emerges in 701 B.C. at Isaiah's word.

The call itself is told in autobiographical form, as is Isaiah's. Yahweh says he has known Jeremiah since before his birth, that Jeremiah has been set apart for God's work and that Jeremiah will be a prophet to the nations, a task that resonates with Isaiah's interest in a remnant from many lands (1:5). Like Moses and Gideon, Jeremiah finds a reason to decline: he is too young (1:6). God reassures him by promising protection and, more important, divine presence, the same pledges given Moses (Ex 3:12) and Gideon (Judg 6:16).[13] Yahweh also promises to give him the words to say (1:7-9), a phrase approximating Deuteronomy 18:18, Moses' major statement on true prophecy.[14] With God's word he can "uproot up and tear down," "destroy and overthrow," "build and plant" the nations (1:10). Samuel and Kings have already shown that God's word determines history. Now that word will come from a new messenger, and that word cannot fail (1:11-12). Jeremiah's message, according to 1:10, will include the normal prophetic themes of sin, punishment and renewal. Always the prophets seek to renew through punishment, so the preaching of punishment without proclaiming its final goal is not full-orbed prophecy.[15]

Yahweh's next words are directed toward the future. Disaster will come "from the north" to destroy Judah (1:13-16). Proclaiming this message will bring opposition from every quarter (1:17-19), as it did for Elijah. Jeremiah's only help is in the Lord who calls, empowers, warns and instructs the called. His only hope and Judah's only hope is in God, and it is this truth he must take to the people. Canonical readers know he will not help Judah avoid defeat, so what matters most is how he obeys and how what he says continues to be significant to the canon and the community of faith.

The God Who Instructs the Prophet: Jeremiah 2—6

Isaiah 1—5 and Jeremiah 2—6 have similar functions. Peter Ackroyd believes

Isaiah 1—12 presents the prophet's message and person, with Isaiah 1—5 discussing the problems he will face and the possibilities that exist for Israel's future.[16] In much the same way, in Jeremiah 2—6 the Lord teaches Jeremiah why he must preach and what he will say. This instructional process has been introduced in 1:11-19 and continues along the lines charted there. Within these chapters Jeremiah listens to Yahweh, makes observations (4:10) and asks questions (5:3). God responds, thus establishing a dialogic framework that marks the book's poetic sections in particular. All phases of the prophetic message are covered, but the emphasis is on covenant rebellion. When this initial stage of Jeremiah's education is complete, God tells Jeremiah that prophets test and refine Israel (6:27-30) and then sends him to preach at the temple (7:1—8:3). The prophet learns that judgment will affect him as well as the people, so he begins to ask questions that will lead to serious conflict with Yahweh later.

God's instruction unfolds in at least six distinct sections. First, the Lord complains that the entire nation[17] has broken the covenant established at Sinai (2:1—3:5). In 2:1-3 the exodus is portrayed as a glorious spiritual experience akin to a wedding. Israel was God's bride who followed her husband "through the desert" when she was a youth in love (2:2). Because "Israel was holy to the LORD" (2:3; cf. Ex 19:5-6), God protected them and served them like a responsible husband. Thus the Lord bases all subsequent complaints against the people on the fact that they have rejected the pure love they once had for their deliverer.

The fundamental problems in the land are idolatry and immorality. Israel has worshiped "worthless idols and became worthless themselves" (2:5). As in the past, they turn to Baalism (2:8, 23), though Yahweh has given them the promised land (2:7). The priests, leaders and prophets, those charged with teaching the law, enforcing the covenant and pricking the nation's conscience, have instead led the people to pursue vanity (2:8). Therefore the nation's sin is unnatural in its rejection of Yahweh's love and serious in its consequences.[18] Because Israel has refused to respond to correction (2:30-37) and confesses without repenting (3:1-5), judgment must come (2:36-37; cf. Deut 27—28). Canonical readers know that it will come.

Second, Yahweh tells Jeremiah that Israel has time to repent but will not do so (3:6—4:4). Israel's husband is willing to receive the idolatrous wife back. Set in Josiah's era (c. 640-609 B.C.), this lesson demonstrates how long the people have been sinning and at the same time shows how long they have had to repent. The nation's best lesson was Samaria's fall in 722 B.C., yet Judah discerns nothing from this disaster (3:6-10; cf. 2 Kings 17:7-20), so this sin is even worse than Israel's. As Robert P. Carroll says, "Judah's response to Israel's divorce (i.e., destruction and deportation by the Assyrians) was to behave in the same way (i.e., to play the whore with false gods) and to view such behavior in a frivolous manner."[19]

Such behavior should cease and Israel should "repent" or "return" to Yahweh (3:7, 10). Repentance now becomes a constant theme, for some form of the word *repent* occurs more than one hundred times in the rest of the book.[20] For now the term means that the people should return to their first love (3:21-25), a process that involves circumcising their hearts (4:4), which Moses mentions in the context of election in Deuteronomy 10:16 and in the context of repentance and restoration after punishment in Deuteronomy 30:6. God instructs Jeremiah to be a Mosaic preacher who will present the fact that sin is not inevitable nor forgiveness impossible.

Third, Yahweh informs Jeremiah that disaster is coming "from the north" (4:6), an idea introduced in 1:13-16. This foe is like a powerful lion bent on destroying Judah (4:7). Many suggestions have been given as to the identity of this northern invader,[21] but it is appropriate to consider this phrase as a metaphor for all God-given military disaster.[22] By 587 B.C. it becomes clear that Babylon is the northern army that will fit Jeremiah's description. Like Isaiah, Jeremiah calls judgment day the day of Yahweh. On that day the kings, princes, priests and prophets responsible for not turning Israel's heart to the covenant God (2:8) will be punished (4:9-10). Whereas Isaiah told Ahaz not to fear, Jeremiah extends no such hope.[23] Jeremiah envisions only destruction.

Out of love for the people, the prophet interrupts the lesson to charge God with deceiving the people. Perhaps he thinks of the hopeful comments in 3:14-18 or 4:1-4. Perhaps he reflects on Isaiah's sermons on Yahweh's love for Zion. Regardless, the passage begins the book's revelation of Jeremiah's heart for the people as he intercedes for them.[24] He furthers this concern in 4:13-15 and 4:19-21, lamenting sin and begging Jerusalem to repent. Without question he has learned that prophets stand between God and the people, preaching the Lord's word on the one hand, pleading the people's case on the other (cf. Amos 7:1-6).

Fourth, to demonstrate that judgment is not without cause, Yahweh tells Jeremiah there are no righteous persons in the land (5:1-9). If Jeremiah wonders, like Abraham, whether there is a large enough remnant to spare Jerusalem, the Lord answers there is no one "who deals honestly and speaks the truth" (5:1; cf. Is 56:1). A careful examination of Jerusalem yields only idolaters and adulterers (5:8) from every class of people (5:4-6). The remnant has shrunk to so small a number that they have no influence in Judah.

Fifth, Yahweh will be avenged (5:10-31). For all their covenant breaking, for believing Yahweh has no power (5:12-13), judgment will come. But God will preserve a few to give witness to the nation's infidelity (5:18-19). This remnant, however small and weak, will become the nucleus of a future (cf.

Deut 30:1-3). As in 3:14-18, some hope, some building and planting (cf. Jer 1:10), will take place, but already Jeremiah learns to anticipate these positive results only in the distant future. Even this miniature hope emerges solely because of God's grace.

Sixth, Yahweh informs Jeremiah he must test and refine the people (6:1-30). War is coming (6:1-5), siege awaits (6:6-8), so Jeremiah must attempt to glean the remnant (6:9). The prophetic message in its time always preaches to this end: to call out, define and identify the remnant. Judah as a whole rebels (6:10-12) and treats sin lightly (6:13-15), so Jeremiah wonders to whom he should, or if he should, preach (6:11). Yet he must preach or explode.[25] He learns prophets have a compelling calling. They are not happy holding in a divine message that is "bubbling forth," a phrase that is one definition for prophet. As tester of metals (6:27-30) he must burn the slag from the ore, leaving only the faithful. What he discovers over forty years about the tiny size of the remnant will shock him. For now, however, that work is in the future.

Canonical Synthesis: Prophecy, Law and Judgment

Within the canon, Jeremiah 2—6 demonstrates that the prophets stand ready to apply the law to their own setting. God instructs Jeremiah to adopt a view of Israelite worship that excludes having other gods, making idols, committing adultery[26] and lying. This view allows for the possibility of forgiveness for repentance. It blames the priests for mishandling the law they were supposed to teach (2:8) and longs for faithful shepherds to guide the people (3:15). All these concerns are clearly reflected in Exodus—Deuteronomy. Without question these chapters reflect the belief that covenant disobedience will bring exile, which is the chief threat posed for disobedience in both Leviticus 26 and Deuteronomy 27—28.

Further, Jeremiah 2—6 agrees with the view of history found in the Former Prophets. God elected Israel, delivered Israel and gave Israel Canaan, all out of love, yet the people seem determined to return to slavery (2:3-37). Josiah's era provided an opportunity for true repentance (3:6-18; cf. 2 Kings 22:1—23:25), but the moment passed, and God's wrath rages. There have been more false prophets than true (2:8; 5:13), and the nation has ignored the faithful messengers of God (2 Kings 17:13-14). Other prophets have shared Elijah's experience. Therefore Jeremiah 2—6 promises the judgment described in Kings. Again both the Former Prophets' and Jeremiah's perspective on history can be traced to Deuteronomy.

Finally, this section resonates with Isaiah and the rest of the canonical prophets. Isaiah's treatment of ethical and worship sins in Isaiah 1—5 parallels Jeremiah 2—6, and both men stress the day of the Lord as a great military disaster. Jeremiah 3:14-18 looks forward to a bright future for Israel and the nations, a theme Isaiah employs steadily throughout his prophecy and one to which Jeremiah will return. Jeremiah 5:22 asks Israel to consider their Creator and repent, while Isaiah 40-48 counsels the people to consider their Creator and believe. Jeremiah and Isaiah both know that their task is to prepare the remnant to serve. There is no other god to which anyone may turn in either prophecy. There are several clear links, then, between the messages both books espouse.

Jeremiah's ideas also connect with Amos and his near contemporaries Habakkuk and Zephaniah. Like Amos, he intercedes for the people (4:10; Amos 7:1-6). Like Habakkuk he dialogues with God, seeking answers to hard questions. Similar to Zephaniah, he learns that judgment will reverse creation, thus returning the world to chaos (4:22-26; cf. Zeph 1:2-3). In the canon Jeremiah paves the way for ideas in the Twelve. In history these individuals influenced Jeremiah.

Hosea seems to exercise the most influence on Jeremiah 2—6. From Hosea Jeremiah derives the metaphor of Israel as Yahweh's bride and the connection between Baal worship and spiritual adultery, as well as Israel's need to return to their first love.[27] In this way he takes messages preached to Israel one hundred years earlier and applies them to the current situation. Jeremiah sticks with the teachings of his prophetic predecessors just as he adheres to the revealed word in the Law. He is no innovator in his biblical theology.

The God Who Rejects Hollow Worship: Jeremiah 7—10

Now Jeremiah's work begins in earnest. Six messages make up this part of the book, each of which is prefigured in Jeremiah's lessons and each of which expands the prophet's influence, responsibility, ministry and level of danger. By the end of the segment he will have struck at the heart of Judah's sin and will have begun to sense that suffering looms on the horizon simply because he preaches the word. The people for whom he intercedes so earnestly in Jeremiah 2—6 want no part of his message.

God first sends Jeremiah to preach at the temple, where the priests' (cf. 2:81) influence is highest. In his opening call to repentance, he warns the people not to trust in deceptive words like "the temple of the LORD, the temple of the LORD, the temple of the LORD" (7:1-4). The mere existence of a worship site does not guarantee God's blessing presence, as the incident at Baal-Peor and Solomon's dedicatory prayer at the temple prove (Num 25:1-5; 1 Kings 8:27-30). Yahweh chooses to be in the temple and therefore is not trapped there. Since all the Ten Commandments have been broken, God sees that the people come to services only to feel secure in their sins (7:8-10). Their liturgy reinforces false doctrine.[28] Repentance is necessary, and it must result in justice and mercy (7:5-7). If not, God will remove this temple as easily as he removed Shiloh in Eli's era (1 Sam 4:10-11).

Jeremiah's sermon asks the hearers to declare in what they trust. Currently they trust their own deceit (7:9), idols (7:17-20) and the physical presence of a worship center. Yahweh's frustration is that faith and obedience have always preceded sacrifice, thus making liturgy and ritual positive in their effects. Some scholars read 7:22 as evidence that sacrifices did not enter Israelite life until very late,[29] but the text focuses on the substance of Israel's faith, not on origins. God wants a pure sacrifice or no sacrifice at all. Judah cannot trust even in a God-given system more than they trust the God who gave the system. Still, the temple is a significant theological symbol of trust, for it demonstrates the people's desire to have Yahweh dwell among them. Thus if the nation rejects the Lord the temple will be destroyed along with the rest of Jerusalem, and when the temple is gone the people will know that God has withdrawn as well.[30]

This sermon separates Jeremiah from his neighbors. He is remnant; they are not. After this sermon the threat of judgment hangs over the city until it is indeed destroyed.[31] Jeremiah threatens priests, prophets, kings and people (7:2; 8:1-3), so he has set himself against the whole land, just as 1:17-19 promises.[32] Therefore Yahweh tells him not to pray for them (7:16), for they will not listen to him any more than they have heeded earlier prophets (7:25-27). He is the remnant, and his ranks will not swell through hollow, self-deceiving worship. Israel's history continues along lines already stated in the Former Prophets (7:21-34; cf. 2 Kings 17).

The second message is that Yahweh will not tolerate improper use of Scripture. Judah has refused to return to the Lord despite the fact that repentance would be a normal response to their covenant obligations (8:4-7). Why? Because scribes, who were entrusted with transcribing the law, alter it to fit their beliefs (8:8). Because the wise, who were charged with teaching the application of the law, reject the law, which is the source of wisdom (8:9). Prophets and priests, the consciences and teachers, tell the people only what they want to hear (8:10).[33] Thus religious degeneration exists everywhere (8:11), and judgment approaches (8:12-17). Here the law and prophets come very close indeed, for the prophet must preach the law that has been neglected, altered and rejected. Misuse of God's revelation cannot benefit the nation in any way. Rather it separates them from the theological underpinnings that sustain them in the holy land.

The third message separates Jeremiah from the people as certainly as the temple sermon does. Still, he tries to retain contact by praying for them (8:18—9:2), apparently in disregard of Yahweh's command in 7:16. Jeremiah suffers with the people (8:21), senses the loss of God's presence in Judah and asks if there is no hope for healing (8:22). God's silence in this dialogic book indicates that "no healing is possible. The sickness is too deep. The idolatry is too pervasive. Judah refuses the medicine that is available."[34] In response Yahweh tells Jeremiah to beware of his neighbor (9:4). Those who preach such things are in danger. As a remnant preacher, Jeremiah stands outside of accepted society, outside of its felt obligation to protect him, outside the bounds of courtesy and decency. The remnant is not welcome here any more than it was in Isaiah 56—57.

Therefore the fourth message (9:7-24) highlights judgment again. It returns to the idea of wisdom (cf. 8:8-10), this time to define the term. Wisdom excludes self-glory in favor of knowing God and imitating Yahweh's love, justice and righteousness. These ideas have been developing as the touchstones of the remnant's behavior since Isaiah 56:1.

In the fifth message (9:25—10:16) the prophet begins to take seriously his role as prophet to the nations. He denounces Judah but adds Egypt, Edom, Ammon and Moab to this condemnation (9:25-26). Their sin is idolatry, so the prophet expresses what may be his clearest monotheistic statement in 10:1-16. Note the contrast between Yahweh and idols in the following lists.

1. There is none like Yahweh (10:6, 7).
2. Yahweh is King over the nations (10:7).
3. Yahweh is the true God (10:10).
4. Yahweh is the living God (10:10).
5. Yahweh is the everlasting King (10:10).
6. Yahweh is the Creator (10:11-13, 16).

Conversely,

1. Idols are made by human beings (10:3-4, 8-9, 14-15). They do not create (10:11).
2. Idols must be carried. They weary their adherents (10:5).
3. Idols cannot instruct through revelation (10:8).
4. Idols have no life. They do not exist (10:14).

Jeremiah's monotheistic confession parallels Isaiah 40—48 in virtually every detail, fits the spirit of the Former Prophets and derives its substance from the Law. Only those who adopt these fundamental beliefs may know God. This principle holds true for Gentiles as well as Israelites, for monotheism means Yahweh is not just Israel's God but "a light for the Gentiles" (Is 42:6; 49:6). Thus Jeremiah's preaching not only must show concern for his own people but also must expand to include all those whose sin he condemns.

Finally, Jeremiah's sixth message includes the nations in the day of the Lord (10:17-25). This punishment will come because of idolatry, but it also is due to their harsh treatment of Judah (10:25). Amos has much to say about cruelty in wartime among the nations (cf. Amos 1:2-15), so Jeremiah participates in an already established prophetic tradition of holding all countries accountable for their atrocities.

Canonical Synthesis: Faith-Based Worship

Probably the most important canonical connection in Jeremiah 7—10 is its emphasis on worship resulting from faith instead of ritual taking the place of both faith and worship. Deuteronomy repeatedly identifies true covenant obedience as originating in the heart (Deut 6:4; 10:12). Isaiah considers ritual a "trampling of [God's] courts" (Is 1:12) when no faith and action accompany those liturgical acts. Amos 4:4-5 satirizes sacrifices offered by a disobedient people, while Hosea 4:1-3 and 9:4 warn that sacrifice without true knowledge of Yahweh avails nothing. Malachi focuses specifically on how worship that is self-serving demeans the whole process (Mal 1:6—2:17). The canon never approves of sacrifices that flow from wrong motives. Put another way, worship is not directionally correct unless faith precedes the revealed obligation and is not functionally correct unless sacrifices are brought in obedience generated by faith.

The God Who Allows Prophets to Suffer: Jeremiah 11—20

Throughout the canon God allows the righteous to endure events that go beyond discomfort to include outright pain and suffering. Jeremiah's call includes a call to separation and pain (1:17-19). There is no more guarantee of ease for him than there was for Abraham, Jacob, Joseph, Moses, Elijah or at times the nation itself. Something about God allows him to let the remnant endure, indeed call the remnant to, harsh circumstances. This issue appears repeatedly in Jeremiah 11—20, a fact that has led to a host of writings on five passages known as Jeremiah's confessions but which may more properly be termed his "personal laments." As John Goldingay writes:

> They are not passages in which Jeremiah is confessing his sin, or even, generally, confessing the greatness of God. They are the lamentations of Jeremiah. As far as their form goes, they are like the laments in the psalter, in which believers pour out their suffering, their anger, and their longings to God.[35]

These texts form the backbone of Jeremiah 11—20, for they provide a framework around which Jeremiah preaches messages that are similar to those in Jeremiah 1—10. They also aid examination of the Lord's character.

Jeremiah's first lament unfolds after God instructs him to preach a sermon on covenant breaking that includes most of the deuteronomic themes Weinfeld mentions.[36] The passage serves as an excellent summary of the Law and the Former Prophets. Afterward Jeremiah learns of a plot against his life

(11:18-20), an incident not wholly unexpected given Yahweh's earlier warnings in 1:17-19 and 9:4-6 but still bone-chilling in its prospects. Due to this threat and the people's general wickedness, Jeremiah wants his enemies defeated, wants to know why the wicked prosper and wants to know why a righteous God does not do more to stop sin (11:23—12:4). God delivers him from this danger (11:18-20), but he wonders why danger is necessary at all. He may wonder if he can trust God fully.[37]

Yahweh responds in three parts. First, he asks Jeremiah how he will survive worse things if this episode causes him so much distress (12:5-6). Rather than being a callous statement, this question seeks to prepare the prophet for a painful future.[38] The Lord sets this occurrence in the fabric of the whole of Jeremiah's ministry. Second, Yahweh shares Jeremiah's pain, for everything the Lord loves is about to be overthrown (12:7-11). The God who grieved over the world's sin in Genesis 6:6 grieves here. This grief is pure, holy and justified, so it is part of Yahweh's character, not a new innovation or self-limiting process. The Lord's promise to be with Jeremiah in 1:17-19 was set in the context of pain, not ease. God is present to share suffering and sustain Jeremiah. Third, Yahweh places the coming devastation in the context of future renewal that will come as a result of Jeremiah's ministry of "plucking up" (12:14-17). Once again punishment is a horrible and necessary step toward restoration. It is also the way that Yahweh will address the prophet's concern about the wicked's prospering. Seen this way, Jeremiah's suffering has purpose because it is part of an overall plan to eradicate sin.

The second lament poses a crisis in Jeremiah's relationship to the Lord. As in Jeremiah 11—12, Jeremiah's pain is expressed after a normal series of prophetic duties. He does a symbolic act designed to show the people they are spoiled and will become spoil (13:1-14). He uses proverbs (13:12-14) and typical sermons (13:15—14:6). But he also intercedes for Judah (14:7-9, 19-22), only to be told to cease (14:11), for not even Moses and Samuel could change things now (15:11). Therefore Jeremiah laments his lack of effectiveness (15:10-14) and God's seeming unwillingness to heal his pain, and then accuses the Lord of being a deceitful, dried-up brook to him (15:15-18). Few biblical laments are more cutting or more willing to challenge God than this one.[39] Gerhard von Rad calls it a "terrible accusation."[40]

Yahweh reassures Jeremiah with language from his call experience,[41] but only after delivering a serious rebuke that charges him of leaving his prophetic calling.[42] Jeremiah must repent (15:19). His job is to preach God's word and to stand with the Lord, not the people (15:19). He is remnant, and Judah is not. Only as a remnant preacher does he receive Yahweh's protection (15:20-21). Jeremiah's choices are to either stand with God and suffer or stand with Judah and suffer even more. Such is the cost the remnant pays, yet it is light in comparison to what unbelievers pay. God is relieving his pain, not adding to it.

This separation emerges again in the third confession. Yahweh makes Jeremiah a symbol of remnant isolation by forbidding him to marry or attend funerals (16:1-9) and then offers another summary of the reasons for and nature of the coming destruction (16:1-21). This devastation is certain because the nation's sin is engraved on their hearts, where their love for Yahweh should be (17:1). Their hearts are so thoroughly deceitful that only Yahweh can know their depths and judge them (17:9-13). Surely the remnant must trade their sins for God, and the prophet does so by asking his own heart to be healed (17:14). Even the remnant must lament sin and not presume on the Lord's favor (17:14-18). Human responsibility and divine election are wed here, and the former begins in the heart (cf. 7:1—8:3). As Walther Eichrodt asserts, this text "cannot envisage any liberation from sin, or its evil consequences, without an inner transformation of the natural condition of Man."[43] Jeremiah repents and is accepted, while Judah does not and is rejected.

A. R. Diamond notes that a shift in emphasis occurs during the third and fourth laments. This change is from Jeremiah's complaining about God to his lamenting the people's actions.[44] Diamond's observation is basically true, though Jeremiah still wonders in the last lament what God's protection is really worth. Here Jeremiah preaches about the sabbath (17:19-27), reminds the people they are as much God's creation at God's disposal as any pot made by a potter (18:1-12) and condemns their theological amnesia (18:13-17). For his pains, his life is threatened again. The people decide to continue to heed their prophets, priests and counselors (18:18), the very leaders who are guiding them to defeat (cf. 8:14-17). Now he agrees that the nation deserves punishment (18:18-23), so the effect this lament has is to help Jeremiah side with Yahweh, as Diamond argues. Part of suffering's purpose is to force the prophet, the remnant, to depend on God alone, who is in fact the faithful's only defense (1:17-19).

So far Jeremiah has mourned the prosperity of the wicked, God's apparent unwillingness to ease his pain, his own sin and the direct plots against his life. All these concerns coalesce in the final lament. As in the previous three laments, Jeremiah does a symbolic act and preaches to the people. Each act has sought to turn them from disaster, yet the self-deception they treasure keeps them from obeying. Each act also worsens their situation, for they progress from spoiled thing, to folk from which the remnant must separate, to a pot in God's hand and now to a pot that is smashed (19:1-15). Again the prophet explains that idolatry will be their downfall (19:4-6). God's patience is evident, though here it is patience that reveals hardened sinners rather than penitent believers.

Pashhur, a priest, imprisons and beats Jeremiah for these messages (20:1). First Jeremiah promises punishment on Judah and Pashhur (the sort of man 8:8-10 denounces), then he laments again. Jeremiah seems to affirm his faith in 20:7-13, only to turn on God again in 20:14-18. He feels "deceived" and "overpowered" (20:7). Simply put, the second term means "rape." Having endured rape, he is held up for contempt and then cast off.[45] He tries to cease preaching but cannot (20:9). God remains his only protection (20:10-13), yet even so he feels as if he were better off never having been born (20:14-18). Jeremiah expresses the remnant's agony, and he does so out of a mature faith refined by experience. The remnant must be fully satisfied with life in God's presence. Nothing else is promised in such desperate times.

Canonical Synthesis: Redemptive Suffering

The canon affirms this section's testimony to the Lord's work in suffering. There is no need to attempt to diminish pain through cheerful talk, and the canon never does so.[46] Rather Joseph, Moses, Elijah and others prove their faith within the suffering context, not outside of it. The ones lamenting in psalms and David, Daniel and Job do as well. They learn that God has a larger redemptive role for suffering (cf. Gen 50:20; Jer 12:14-17), that God grieves at sin (Gen 6:6) and that the wicked will be eliminated. What cannot change, however, is the agony of the moment, for it is this agony that makes suffering redemptive. And in the agony of the moment Yahweh is present to deliver, whether in this life or the one Isaiah 66:18-24 envisions.

The God Who Vindicates True Prophets: Jeremiah 21—29

So far the prophet has proclaimed the words entrusted to him. In doing so he has apparently won few if any converts, has wrestled with his own relationship to Yahweh and has encountered strong opposition from other priests. No one stands with him, just as 1:17-19 promised. This section recounts Jeremiah's struggles with kings, prophets, priests, nations and common people, in other words, those he seeks to convince to serve the Lord. These episodes are much like the narratives in Kings that depict prophets trying to move an unmovable public. As in Kings, these stories demonstrate how true prophets preach messages that provide a theology of prophecy, kingship, nationhood and individual piety. At the core of this section is the text's determination to show that Yahweh does indeed vindicate the word of the inspired prophet, which is another way of saying God vindicates his own word.

Jeremiah 21:1—23:8 focuses on Yahweh's expectations for kings, which are stated in outline form in Deuteronomy 17:14-20. When Babylon begins its assault against Jerusalem in 588 B.C.,[47] Zedekiah sends representatives to

Jeremiah to see if Yahweh will deliver the city (21:1-2). They probably have in mind the deliverance executed in Hezekiah's time,[48] and they perhaps approach Jeremiah because he has threatened judgment for nearly four decades.

Zedekiah has obviously misread the situation in his time and Hezekiah's. He is no Hezekiah, a fact Jeremiah makes clear. He is just another monarch who oppresses rather than serves (21:11-14). There will be no deliverance (21:3-7), so those who want to survive should surrender to Babylon (21:8-10), which has become God's instrument of wrath. This strategy had spared the city in a similar situation in 605 B.C. (cf. 2 Kings 24:10-17). The king must put the people before his political or personal future.

Jeremiah 22:1-30 offers an analysis of Zedekiah's predecessors from Josiah (c. 640-609 B.C.) to Jehoiachin, called Coniah here (c. 598-597 B.C.). Sitting on David's throne makes kings responsible for administering justice and protecting the weak, the very things God's law, which they are to apply to daily life (Deut 17:14-20), is concerned to do. In contrast to this ideal, these kings build palaces by oppression and injustice (22:13-14). They have constructed monuments to greed and raw power rather than being satisfied with daily provision (22:15-16). Thus innocent blood has been shed (22:17; cf. 2:34; 7:6; 19:4) instead of the innocents' being sheltered. These scathing verses probably refer to Jehoiakim (c. 609-598 B.C.), who serves as the prophet's nemesis later in the book, and who will receive, Jeremiah says, an ass's burial (22:18-19). Jerusalem's lovers, its foreign allies and their gods, cannot save the city now (22:20-23). Exile is certain for the people as well as for their exiled former king Jehoiachin (22:28-30). King and people alike have made redemption impossible.

Despite his objections to the monarchy's covenant breaking, Jeremiah does not give up on David's lineage or the positive effect it will one day have on the people. The institutional monarchy may end, but Yahweh's promises to David in 2 Samuel 7:7-17 have not,[49] though the current royal failures push their fulfillment into the future.[50] Like Isaiah, Jeremiah conceives of a quite different "shepherd" for Israel, one whose wisdom and righteousness will make the people secure (22:5). Also like Isaiah, Jeremiah gives this king a name consistent with divine attributes,[51] "the LORD Our Righteousness" (23:6). The promise of the King coincides with the new exodus theme (23:7-8), which provides yet another link with Isaiah and the Former Prophets.

Jeremiah's theory of kingship mirrors that of his canonical predecessors. Deuteronomy 17:14-20 is the standard for rulers, and Jeremiah applies that standard as firmly to his situation as the Former Prophets' author does to Israel's postdesert history. Like Isaiah, he ties the nation's future to the emergence of a special shepherd from David's line. No other hope exists.

No other interpretation of history appears.

Having addressed civic leadership, the text moves on to religious leadership. Jeremiah's opinion of the false prophets has already been introduced in 4:10 and 14:13 yet will have greater priority in 23:9-40 and 27—29. Jeremiah mentions two types of prophets in 23:9-15: the old Baal prophets of the northern kingdom (23:13) and the immoral prophets of his era who cannot apply the covenant to the people's lives because they themselves are ethically and theologically corrupt.[52] Both types poison the nation (23:15). They confuse some hearers and confirm others in their sins. Jeremiah claims they have three basic flaws. First, they have not stood in God's presence and therefore do not possess God's word (23:16-24). Second, when they preach they have only their own impulses and beliefs to share (23:25-32). Third, because of their presumption the Lord bars them from revelation, which in turn means they will never preach an effective (true) message (23:33-40). They are not called, instructed or tested, as Jeremiah has been, and their lifestyle reflects their utter rejection of the covenant. They are nothing like the prophets Deuteronomy 13:1-11 and 18:14-22 envision.

Israel's people are as corrupt as their leaders. They must learn in exile what they refused to discern in the promised land. After Jehoiachin and some Israelites are exiled in 597 B.C. the prophet envisions two Israels, one a basket of good figs, the other a basket of rotten figs. The rotten figs are the unrepentant inhabitants of the land who are destined for punishment (24:8-10). The good figs are the Babylonian exiles (24:4-5). This group will come to embody God's ideal for a holy, covenantally obedient people, because they will possess the "whole heart" commitment to Yahweh Deuteronomy describes (Jer 24:6-7; cf. Deut 6:4-9). Their return to God will ignite a return to the land, as promised in Deuteronomy 30:1-3 and Leviticus 26:40-45. It will also put the idolatry and unbelief practiced by their counterparts to shame (25:1-13). The bad figs will not learn even in exile.

Jeremiah views Babylon as Yahweh's instrument for punishing the elect nation's sin (25:8-13). This belief coincides with Isaiah's attitude toward Assyria (cf. Is 10:5-11), as does Jeremiah's prediction that Babylon will eventually be punished for its own iniquity (25:12). Israel's exile will last seventy years (25:12) but will indeed end. Jeremiah also predicts disaster for Egypt, Philistia, Edom, Moab and Ammon. This judgment has already been traced to idolatry (cf. 10:1-16) and is charted in more detail in Jeremiah 46—51.[53] God's sovereignty over all nations is thereby underscored here. The Gentiles, no less than Israel, are not created to worship false gods and exercise naked power. Jeremiah fulfills his role as prophet to the Gentiles by making these facts known.

Jeremiah 26—29 returns to the reaction of the king, religious leaders and people to God-inspired prophecy. Most scholars believe Jeremiah 26 offers a brief summary of the longer sermon found in Jeremiah 7 (26:2-6) and then describes the persecution it caused Jeremiah and prophets who preached similar messages.[54] For calling the people covenant breakers and comparing the temple to Shiloh (26:2-6), he faces death at the hands of those who find more security in the temple than in covenant obedience (26:7-15). What saves Jeremiah is a favorable comparison of his message to Micah 3:12, a prophecy viewed as helping Judah repent in Hezekiah's era (26:16-18). Quite correctly they conclude that messages of doom may be transformed into messages of hope through repentance (26:19). They spare Jeremiah, but the prophet Uriah has already paid for such preaching with his life (26:20-23). True prophets face danger and death for the sake of the truth. Oddly, though the leaders speak of Hezekiah, there is no apparent move on their part to imitate the eighth-century B.C. king. God vindicated Micah's word. The question is why this generation does not apply Jeremiah's word in the same way.

Jeremiah's confrontations with false prophecy dictate the thematic movement in Jeremiah 27—29. Ten years before Jerusalem falls, the prophet warns the nations (27:1-11), Zedekiah (27:12-15) and the people (27:16-22) to serve Yahweh's chosen instrument, Babylon. Blocking their belief, however, are prophets, diviners, soothsayers and sorcerers who predict Babylon's demise (27:9-10, 14-16). The same opposition arises when Jeremiah wears a yoke to symbolize his message. A prophet named Hananiah breaks the yoke and predicts Babylon will be gone and all will be well within two years (28:1-11). Likewise Jeremiah writes a letter to those already in exile to counter claims of lying prophets who say the sojourn will be short, not seventy years long (29:8-10).

Canonical Synthesis: True and False Prophecy

God's ability to reveal a clear word to the people is at stake here, as is the vindication of those who dare to preach Yahweh's unpopular messages. Scholars have debated the criteria for true and false prophecy for some time. Carroll claims that true prophets can only be known after the fact. That is, historically speaking, Israel could not know until a prediction came true if an individual prophet told the truth, for there were no criteria available to inform them.[55] Thus Israel had to wait and see whether Jeremiah or his opponents were true prophets. J. A. Sanders agrees that no objective criteria existed to separate true and false oracles. What distinguished true from false prophecy was timing. Prophets who applied traditional themes to appropriate settings in a timely fashion were true prophets. So Hananiah's fault was one of interpretation, not presumption.[56] Von Rad also believes no set of standards were set but locates the true prophet's status in that prophet's experience with Yahweh.[57]

Other writers have attempted to locate principles beyond experience, timing and long-term historical substantiation. T. W. Overholt argues that the people trusted in three falsehoods that Jeremiah attacked: false security from the temple's existence (cf. Jer 7, 26), false prophets and false gods.[58] Because of their acceptance of these falsehoods the people became lax in their covenant commitments and developed an unfounded confidence in God's protection.[59] Believing lies "led to actions which were not based on a perception of religious and historical reality, and could therefore do nothing to heal the sickness at the core of the community."[60] Overholt's reconstruction of Israel's mindset is accurate, yet he also fails to say why Hananiah is necessarily false from the start.

Though they disagree over the particular details of the matter, E. W. Nicholson and Childs offer some sound general guiding principles for recognizing true and false prophecy. Nicholson correctly observes that Jeremiah 28:8-9 draws upon Deuteronomy 18:21-22 and 29:32 in its condemnation of Hananiah.[61] According to Deuteronomy, Hananiah preaches rebellion and makes people trust the three lies Overholt isolates. Childs states that "the content of Hananiah's message is wrong. . . . The test of the truth lies in God who makes known his will through revelation."[62] Like Nicholson, Childs considers the substance of what prophets say to determine who speaks for God. If the substance is correct, the interpretational or historically proven validity of prophecy will not be in doubt.

Jeremiah demonstrates in 27—29 the twin canonical standards for true prophecy. First, he is a covenant preacher who tries to change the people instead of allowing them to follow other gods commended by other prophets (cf. Deut 13:1-5). His whole ministry proclaims a turning back to the covenant. Second, because he is a covenant preacher he is able to make accurate, God-given predictions such as the ones about Babylon (cf. Deut 18:14-22). Only covenant preachers who define sin and repentance by Mosaic standards are in any position to have a predictive word from Yahweh. Hananiah is no such preacher. He preaches peace to a disobedient people in direct contrast to earlier prophets (28:5-9). Isaiah preached peace to Zion but only after declaring God's wrath at Jerusalem's sin and only during the reign of a righteous, monotheistic, praying, decisive king. Hananiah is no Isaiah, Zedekiah is no Hezekiah, and the remnant of believers has shrunk to a bare minimum. Therefore Hananiah's prediction cannot come from God, for he has no relationship with God and no sense of God's covenantal workings in Israel's history.

Who is a false prophet? Those who do not preach God's covenant; those who do not warn the people to flee immorality and idolatry; those who make predictions in spite of their theological ignorance. Such persons can only produce lies that the untaught masses believe (28:15). Based on Deuteronomy 13:1-11, Jeremiah knows Hananiah deserves death, and when he predicts that death it occurs (28:16-17). He knows the land will rest when Israel leaves (Lev 26:34-39). When he predicts a seventy-year exile it happens.

This section joins Numbers 22—24, 1 Kings 13 and 1 Kings 22 in the canon's discussion of true and false prophecy. What is clear from these very different texts is that God never comforts sinners in their sin. These passages also indicate that a direct word from God may be disobeyed only at the sinner's peril. They also promise long-term benefits to those faithful to the Lord. Only on these bases can true prophecy rest. The canon's witness is that Jeremiah was a true prophet, both by its inclusion of his prophecy and by direct statement in Daniel 9:2. A true prophet is not just someone whose predictions may be proven true but also one whose theological view of history makes such accuracy possible. It is such prophets that Yahweh vindicates, and Jeremiah received that authentication.

The God Who Promises a New Covenant: Jeremiah 30—33
So far Jeremiah's ministry has focused on tearing down and plucking up much more than on building and planting (cf. 1:10). Now he preaches hope beyond the destruction, though like Isaiah he projects this renewal into the future. The picture of God painted here is one of a Lord who begins anew with a restored people after the dust of destruction has settled. Yahweh even promises a new covenant that will insure this transformation, and it is this pledge that the New Testament considers the touchstone for the ministry of Jesus and the church. Mark Biddle notes that Jeremiah 30—33 revolves around promises to the people and promises to the city, with 30—31 featuring the former concept and 32—33 the latter.[63] This observation has thematic and linguistic plausibility and shows how the text redeems most of Jeremiah's audience. These chapters also renew the monarchy as well, so the whole nation has future hope.

God tells Jeremiah to make a permanent record of the promises that follow, a command that highlights their certainty of fulfillment (30:1-4). Though a terrible day of punishment approaches, the Lord will use that day to restore the people and reestablish the Davidic line (30:4-11). Thus Jeremiah joins Isaiah in viewing judgment as both purging and restorative (cf. Is 2:1—4:6; 28—35). In 23:1-8 the prophet sees the coming King as the embodiment of righteousness, and here as the restorer of Israel's fortunes. God will save the remnant from their oppressors (30:10-11). This act will heal their horrible sin-caused wounds (30:12-17), cause rejoicing (30:18-21), restore the people's covenantal relationship with Yahweh (30:22) and signal the end of the Lord's wrath (30:23-24).

This salvation will occur because of the love Yahweh has had for Israel from their first days (31:1-6; cf. Deut 7:8). It will happen only for the remnant (31:7-8) and will amount to a new exodus (31:9-22). Again Jeremiah's agreement with Isaiah and Deuteronomy is clear. God will heal the weary and force no one to suffer for the sins of others (31:23-30). Once more the prophet stands in full agreement with what his predecessors have said, though his statements are even more poignant for his audience, since they indeed experience God's wrath.

In his next comments, though, the prophet adds his own unique contribution to the prophetic teachings about how renewal emerges from punishment. Isaiah 55:3 echoes 2 Samuel 7 in its emphasis on God's everlasting covenant with David, just as Deuteronomy 7:6-11 speaks of the covenant with Abraham and his descendants as lasting for thousands of generations. Both these covenants are already in view in Jeremiah 30—31 when the people are informed of a new covenant. Thus the older promises lead into the most recent one, thereby giving it a historical and theological foundation.

Several concepts characterize the covenant. First, like the remnant with whom it will be made, it will arise in the future (31:31). Second, the covenant will help unite every tribe of Israel (31:31; cf. 30:3-4). Third, this covenant will reside in the people's heart, just as Deuteronomy had always hoped (31:33; cf. Deut 30:6).[64] Fourth, there will be no need to teach this covenant group to know Yahweh, for they will all know the Lord (31:34). Fifth, this covenant will never cease (31:35-37). Sixth, God observes that this covenant will not be broken (31:32). Seventh, God will forgive their sins (31:34). As important as they are, the first three ideas and the last one are not as groundbreaking as are the third, fourth and fifth. Prophetic literature has already begun to place true hope only in a future context, the other covenants helped create and unite the people, and the covenants were always heart-oriented commitments. These notions provide essential continuity for the other three concepts' implementation.

Yahweh's assertion that all the covenant people will know the Lord provides a profound shift in the definition of the elect. From Abraham onward the chosen nation has consisted of those who believe and nonfaithful persons, a situation that creates the notion of a remnant. Now, in effect, the whole covenant group will be believers, or what has been called the remnant up to now. All will receive the future blessings because none will fail to have had God place the covenant on their hearts. The unbelieving majority will no longer exist. This new group will receive the new city that Yahweh speaks of in Jeremiah 30—33.

How this remnant or new covenant people comes to know Yahweh is also new in the Old Testament canon. God will instill this knowledge directly in their hearts, leaving nothing to chance. God will regenerate the heart so that the written law will be kept and the relationship to himself maintained.[65] This action is foreshadowed in Deuteronomy 30:6, where it is said that Yahweh will circumcise the people's heart to know the Lord.[66] Even the power to keep what has been instilled will come from the Lord. Therefore according to Ronald Clements:

> In this way a covenant, which is recognized by the tradition to be a bilateral obligation, becomes effectively a unilateral one, since God himself ensures the fulfillment of the obligations that he makes. It becomes synonymous in effect, though not in name, with a covenant of promise.[67]

If disobedience is removed, if God's will has been directly implanted in the heart, if sins are forgiven because of this process, then, von Rad correctly concludes, "what is here outlined is the picture of a new man, a man who is able to obey perfectly because of a miraculous change of his nature."[68] All the covenant people will fit this description.

Since this covenant will transform the definition of the covenant people, it cannot be broken, and it will therefore never cease. The greatest problem with the Mosaic covenant is always human disobedience, according to the canon. God's instruction is merciful and gracious, yet it is forgotten, spurned and rejected by all but the few. This new covenant cannot be rejected by a portion or a majority of the elect nation, since rejection betrays one's status as noncovenant person. Once all covenant people are faithful there will be no reason for the making of other covenants. This agreement will incorporate the everlasting covenants with Abraham and David and will stand forever. With these elements assured, details such as unity, internalization and forgiveness will be secured as well. God alone has the power to effect such change in the diseased hearts (cf. 17:9) Jeremiah observes in his day.[69]

God completes the promise of restoration by focusing on the city. Every tower, gate and hill will be renewed (31:38-39). Like the new covenant, the new Jerusalem will endure forever (31:40). Jerusalem's destruction, a constant threat and assured result in Jeremiah 2—29, will be reversed. Added to the restoration of the Davidic leadership (30:8-11), priesthood (31:14) and people (31:31-34), the land's renewal finalizes the absolute reversal of the devastating punishment Jeremiah announces in 21—29.

As is so often true in Jeremiah 11—29, Yahweh supplements spoken revelation by ordering Jeremiah to undertake a symbolic act. This time he is told to buy a field just before Jerusalem collapses (32:1-15). Though he confesses that God is Creator (32:17), all-powerful lover of sinners (32:18), wise (32:19), all-knowing (32:19), miracle-working (32:20), delivering (32:21), conquering (32:22-23) and judging (32:24), he does not grasp why such a wise Lord would ask such a seemingly singularly stupid act. He thinks he has been told to pay for what soon will be confiscated.

Yahweh's reply is crucial for understanding the role of judgment in the Old Testament. God says that all the punishment will occur so that the blessings of new covenant, new people and new city may become realities (32:42). Because of their idolatry, wrath must unfold (32:26-35) to cleanse the land of polytheism, so that a holy remnant may embark on a new exodus and inherit the promised land (32:36-41). Thus, somewhat like Abraham's purchase of a burial cave in a land not yet his own (Gen 23:1-20), Jeremiah's acquisition is an affirmation of a certain future. Israelites will own this land again (32:43-46).

A second message solidifies the promises to the people and the city. In language reminiscent of Isaiah 46:8-11 and 48:1-6, Yahweh, the Creator, promises to reveal the future (33:1-3). Babylon will defeat the city, but it will be healed, a promise also made in Isaiah 62. This healing will coincide with Israel's being forgiven (33:7-8). It will also result in Gentiles' coming to the Lord because of the city's purity (33:9), a situation that parallels Isaiah's emphasis on Israel's being a light to the nations through the servant's ministry (Is 49:6). The city's greatness will emerge only under the leadership of a "righteous branch" from David's lineage, another image that links Jeremiah to Isaiah's vision of the future (33:14-16; cf. Is 9:6-7; 11:1-10; 53:1-3). Renewal will also include the affirmation of worship as defined in the Pentateuch (33:23-26).

Canonical Synthesis: Renewal and the New Covenant

Jeremiah's vision for renewal corresponds with the more comprehensive statements in Isaiah. The earlier prophet merges the Davidic, Mosaic and Abrahamic covenants in the work of the servant. Jeremiah locates the fulfillment of these agreements at the initiation of the new covenant. When the new covenant comes into effect, the others will be gathered into it, fulfilled and explained by it. Both prophets believe that a new age will come when a cleansed, faithful people of God inherit a glorious city in which they worship the Lord under the leadership of a Davidic descendant. God's law will be obeyed, and God will rule over subjects from Israel and the nations.

Ezekiel shares a similar view of the future. He also views the destruction of Jerusalem as payment for idolatry and rebellion (cf. Ezek 1—33) and thinks punishment will renew both people (Ezek 37) and city (Ezek 40—48) in the future. Ezekiel pins these hopes on a Davidic ruler who serves under a new covenant (Ezek 37:24-28). Ezekiel's situation and choice of imagery vary greatly from his those of predecessors, yet this change in technique does not alter the basic agreement with the prophetic heritage he inherits. The canon is definitely now heading in some specific directions that have their roots in what has unfolded so far.

The new covenant passage is vitally important to New Testament writers. Jesus, who says Isaiah 61:1-3 is fulfilled by him (Lk 4:18), informs his disciples at the Last Supper that the cup they take is the blood of the new covenant (Lk 22:20; cf. Mt 26:28; Mk 14:24). Paul cites Jesus' statements as evidence that Christians mark the new covenant as they take communion (1 Cor 11:23-26). The author of Hebrews 8:8—9:22 interprets Christ's death in light of Jeremiah 31:31-34 as meaning that Jesus' blood cleanses sin and initiates a new covenant with all who will believe. For the author of Hebrews, Christ's death gathers together and infuses with new meaning the covenants with David, Abraham and Moses. Jeremiah 31:31-34 provides the theological key that opens all these doors.

The God Who Enforces Covenant Consequences: Jeremiah 34—45

As the preceding section indicates, Jeremiah agrees substantially with Isaiah's conception of future renewal. This segment of the book highlights the prophecy's close agreement with the view of history found in the Former Prophets. As was stated repeatedly in the comments on Joshua—Kings, Deuteronomy 27—28 serves as an overview of Israel's national life. When they obey the Lord they are blessed; when they rebel they can expect ever-escalating consequences that will culminate in exile. At the defeat of Samaria, 2 Kings 17 offers an analysis of how the chosen people sinned through idolatry, rejected God's warnings given by the prophets and thereby went into exile. In other words, the latter passage argues that Yahweh enforced the covenant threats and consequences that Moses revealed. Jeremiah 34—45 illustrates the points 2 Kings 17 and Deuteronomy 27—28 raise. While doing so it demonstrates its connection with 2 Kings by describing some events in nearly identical language.

One of the major theological points made in the Former Prophets is that Yahweh patiently, mercifully delayed Judah's punishment by sending the prophets. Jeremiah 34:1-7 depicts the prophet warning Zedekiah to surrender to the Babylonians. He repeats his advice in 37:1-10, 37:16-21 and 38:17-28. During Jehoiakim's earlier reign he has his follower Baruch read God's word to the people and provide the king and priests with a copy (36:1-20). God's patience spans 605-587 B.C. in these accounts.

In response Zedekiah ignores Jeremiah and enslaves Israelites in direct opposition to Exodus 21:2-6 (34:8-16). Jehoiakim burns the scroll of Yahweh's word and has no fear in doing so (36:21-24). Zedekiah allows the prophet to be imprisoned for counseling the people to surrender (37:11-15; 38:1-6), despite the fact that he consistently asks Jeremiah for a word from God, no doubt hoping for a positive promise (37:16-21; 38:17-28). Though he has told the truth, in stark contrast to the false prophets, Jeremiah suffers greatly

(37:16-19). The observations in 2 Kings 17 are true, which means the consequences listed in Deuteronomy 27—28 must unfold. A disobedient nation spurns the merciful God.

Therefore, in language strikingly similar to 2 Kings 25:1-12, Jeremiah 39 depicts Jerusalem's fall, Zedekiah's capture and the temple's burning. Babylon allows Jeremiah to stay in the city, presumably because of his advice to Zedekiah and the people (39:11-14). Despite this freedom, the prophet loses even this privilege when some Jewish refugees return to the land, kill the appointed governor and then take him hostage when they flee to Egypt (Jer 40—43). Not only does Jeremiah not sanction the murder, he says it is unnecessary to flee, all to no avail (42:7—43:7). Now he will truly be a prophet to the nations in the wake of Yahweh's purging of the land.

Once in exile, Jeremiah continues to proclaim his view of Israelite history in two messages presented in Egypt.[70] The first condemns Egypt for its idolatry and states that Babylon will conquer that land (43:8-13). The second also deals with idolatry and its consequences, but it is addressed to the exiles (44:1-30). Here the prophet repeats the charge that Jerusalem fell because of idolatry and ignoring the prophets (44:1-6). Despite losing the land, the Israelites continue their idolatrous practices, which makes them liable to further covenant consequences (44:7-14; cf. Deut 28:64-68). Not only do the people refuse to change; they interpret events as meaning they did not serve Egypt's gods enough when Egypt was their hope against Babylon (44:15-19). Their view of history repudiates deuteronomic theology[71] in favor of the long-standing polytheistic doctrine that a god's power is seen in the power held by its worshipers. At the least, Thompson is right to call their theology "a strange syncretistic mixture."[72] Jeremiah promises that punishment awaits them (44:20-30), and he has history on his side now.

This section ends with a short message to Baruch, Jeremiah's convert and scribe (45:1-5). Baruch is warned not to be self-seeking during a time when one should be glad to be alive.[73] He has shared Jeremiah's and Yahweh's suffering, and will continue to do so. This postscript provides a direct message to all the faithful exiles of Jeremiah's era: serve Yahweh wherever your suffering places you. This text addresses its readers' situation, a pastoral function that surely speaks of the need to hear and heed the canon.

Canonical Synthesis: Deuteronomistic History

Without question the most vital event for the canon that happens in Jeremiah 34—45 is the destruction of Jerusalem. Since the impact of that event was discussed in the chapter on Kings, only a few brief observations will be given now. First, it is important to note the continuity between the prophetic view of Jerusalem's demise and that of the Former Prophets and the Law.

Deuteronomy 27—28 and Leviticus 26 present the possibility of what 2 Kings 17 and Jeremiah 34—45 say were the normal results of covenant disobedience. There is precise agreement that the rejection of monotheism can only lead to destruction. There is no new or novel reason for national defeat present in Isaiah, Jeremiah, Ezekiel or the Twelve. Second, it should be stated that Psalms, Daniel, Ezra and Nehemiah concur with this assessment of events. Third, this agreement solidifies a growing mass of evidence for the canon's view of history. Jeremiah presents events that confirm the Law's theoretical basis for a theological understanding of the past. Fourth, it is evident that the exiles Jeremiah knew were not the remnant that he and Isaiah believe will receive God's favor.[74] The new covenant and all its benefits lie in the future, perhaps with the "good figs" in Babylon (cf. 24:1-10) at some point but definitely not with idolaters such as these Egyptian refugees.

The God Who Judges the Nations: Jeremiah 46—51

Jeremiah's preaching about the nations has been fairly limited to this point. Other than the messages about idolatry in 10:1-16 and 43:8-13, the promise of Babylon's victory over Egypt's coalition in 25:7-26 and the statement on future Gentile belief in 33:9, the book remains focused primarily on Judah. The one overriding principle about the nations that has emerged is the role of Babylon as God's instrument of destruction. Still, Yahweh is portrayed as the one, living, true God in 10:10. God is depicted throughout the prophecy as the One who controls history. So it is not surprising that Jeremiah follows the example of Isaiah 24—27 and Amos 1:2—2:16 and denounces the idolatrous nations. The judgments against Babylon are particularly important because of Babylon's role in the book. These chapters demonstrate God's sovereignty over all that he has created, a principle that pervades prophecy. Clements says, "The genuine universality of Yahweh's concern with the affairs of men is accepted as a presupposition of the prophets and their preaching."[75]

Ten nations are listed in Jeremiah 46—51, with Babylon appearing last. Several of these countries, such as Egypt, Edom, Moab, Philistia, Syria and Ammon, are perpetual targets of such prophetic messages.[76] Though there is great variety in the tone, form and approach of these condemnations,[77] certain common theological concerns mark most of them. First, as in Isaiah 13—23, the nations' arrogance is attacked. This arrogance manifests itself as trusting in riches (48:7), personal prowess (48:28-30), national wisdom (49:7) and military might (50:29; 51:53). Second, and closely related to the first problem, the nations trust in false gods (46:25; 47:13; 48:35; 49:3; 50:2; 51:17, 44, 47, 52). Isaiah's descriptions of idolatry indicate that anyone who prays to idols should see the folly of such exercises (Is 44:9-20), and Jeremiah 10:1-16 has already expressed Jeremiah's agreement. God judges idolaters for worshiping themselves, for their gods are the works of their own hands.

Third, these nations tend to ravage Israel without compassion or awareness of their frailty before Yahweh. This failure is particularly noticeable in Egypt, that poor ally who raises Israel's hopes through the centuries (46:1-16), and in Babylon, which fails to grasp their role in God's plans (51:20-24). Both countries view history from the raw-power perspective inherent in idolatry. They have no notion of higher causes or a higher power to which they are accountable. Again the effect of such sin is that these countries worship themselves. Power supersedes service in their worldview.

Because of Babylon's significance for biblical history in general and Jeremiah's era to the return of the exiles in particular, it is not surprising that the condemnation of Babylon is the longest segment of this section. Since the great renewal of Jerusalem's fortunes could not begin until Babylon's demise (cf. 29:28), Babylon's future was a paramount issue for the people of Jeremiah's day.[78] Further, if Yahweh cannot handle Babylon, then the canon's emphasis on the Lord as Creator and Sovereign can hardly be maintained. As always, then, historical and theological concerns are inseparable.

The central theme in Jeremiah 50—51 is the defeat of Babylon and the renewal of Israel.[79] Closely related to this theme is Yahweh's determination to show Babylon's gods to be nothing more than images. All these matters are addressed in the section's opening verses (50:1-10). Yahweh promises Babylon will fall (50:2). Their gods, Bel, Merodach and the little gods, which John Bright says are referred to in 50:2 as "balls of excrement,"[80] will be shown to be powerless against the coming foe (50:2-3). Though plundered now (50:6-7, 17), Israel will leave Babylon (50:8-10) to seek the "everlasting covenant" Jeremiah 31:31-34 depicts (50:4-5). The agent of destruction against Babylon will be the Persians (51:11), a prediction that is fulfilled in 539 B.C. Yahweh the Creator will put idols to shame (51:15-19, 47), which will show again that the One who creates is the One who decides and reveals the world's future (cf. Is 40—48). Idols are blocks of wood and chunks of dung, but the Lord is the one living deity.

Jeremiah 50—51 indicates how foolish the exiles in 40—44 truly are. Israel's hope for survival does not lie in syncretism or polytheism but in the God who declares an accurate picture of the past and future. Only this God can claim to have sufficient power to effect Israel's release or even Israel's comfort in exile. The same Lord who promised Babylon's rise pledges its demise. The question is whether the elect nation will believe in Jeremiah's explanation of Yahweh's sovereignty over the nations or whether they will cling to non-Yahwistic worldviews spun by their conquerors.

Canonical Synthesis: Babylon's Knowledge of God

Beyond the fact that several prophecies have similar lists of condemned nations lie some other canonical principles. Initially readers may wonder how God can hold Babylon accountable for its idolatry, since this country has not received the covenant as Israel has. Besides the commonsense elements of rejecting idolatry stated here and in Isaiah, the canon portrays Daniel as instructing Nebuchadnezzar about the Lord (Dan 2:1-47). It also shows God dealing directly with Babylon's king (4:1-37) and his successors (5:1-9). Thus the canon explains that knowledge of Yahweh was not what Babylon lacked. Rather, like Israel, Babylon lacked faith in the canonical explanation of history and theology. For Babylon as much as for Israel, God's judgment is based on the general revelation of the folly of idolatry as well as on the special revelation of God's messages to them. Like the Israel of Jeremiah's day, the Babylonians reject both types of Yahweh's communication with them. They prefer their traditional polytheistic worldview to the one Daniel models for them.

The God Who Protects in Exile: Jeremiah 52

Jeremiah ends with a near repetition of 2 Kings 24:18—25:30. The one alteration is that Jeremiah does not include the account of Gedaliah's murder that is found in 2 Kings 25:22-26. Instead a statement of the number of exiles appears (Jer 52:28-30). Otherwise both depict the fall of Jerusalem, the fate of Zedekiah and the kind treatment given Jehoiachin in about 560 B.C., the thirty-seventh year of his exile. As was stated in the comments on 2 Kings 25, it is possible to read this text as at least a glimmer of hope for Israel's future. This reading seems more likely here than in Kings, for Jeremiah has attempted to show in 30—33 and 46—51 that the chosen people have a future return to the land in store. The prophecy has also stressed David's role in the long-term renewal of the land and people. Kings does not deny these claims but does not focus on them, preferring to stress the causes of the people's exile.

For Yahweh to bring a remnant home he must protect the faithful and the Davidic lineage in exile. The promises made in Jeremiah 27—29 demonstrate that the Lord will indeed bless and guide a remnant in Babylon. This passage shows that the royal line will also survive, thereby preserving the possibility of the emergence of a "righteous branch" (cf. 23:5-6; 33:14-16). Now all that has to occur for renewal to be possible is a seventy-year exile that shakes Israel in its very theological being. Hope exists, even if that hope is embodied by an ailing, aging king eating from the table of a dominant polytheist. From such misery and humiliation can emerge great character. Jeremiah's own life proves this point.

Conclusion

For good reason Jeremiah's new covenant passage is his most remembered contribution to canonical theology. This covenant preacher is able to create an image that incorporates his own theology into a model for future theology. He envisions a new covenant as also redeeming the wretched historical scene in which he lives into the means by which Yahweh effects great redemption later. This idea therefore gives him a way by which he can claim that Yahweh rules the past, present and future. It also provides a pattern for the rest of the canon to reflect upon and apply to other situations.

By now some canonical details are so fixed that subsequent books must affirm them, incorporate them or explain them in their writings. God's work with Abraham, Moses and David has a clearly everlasting nature. David is especially important, because it is his descendant who, whether depicted as king, servant or righteous branch, must lead Israel in the restored and glorified land. Abraham's family must continue for there to be a remnant for David's heir to lead. Moses' law must be obeyed in the new kingdom, or there will be no righteousness. Again the extraordinary promise in Jeremiah 31:31-34 means that God will take direct action to see that these everlasting covenants are fulfilled. What remains to be seen is how they will be completed and how the canon will continue to fill out the theological details that remain unexplained at this point.

13

The God
Who Is Present

Ezekiel

· ·

I SAIAH'S AND JEREMIAH'S STATEMENTS ABOUT GOD AND ISRAEL'S FUTURE ALREADY
hint at the issue that lies at the heart of Ezekiel. This matter has in fact been
relevant since the texts about the tabernacle and the golden calf in Exodus
25—40. It reasserts itself in Joshua and Judges as the text reflects on how
Israel comes to possess the land and yet afterward lives as virtual prisoners
within it. The topic that consumes both Ezekiel's body and mind is the
presence of God. Already the canon has stressed the importance of sacred
space where God chooses to dwell in the passages about the tabernacle and
the temple. It has argued that God's presence alone determines Israel's
success or failure in the promised land (cf. Ex 32—34; Num 13—14; Judg
10:10-16) and has concluded that only God can bring the people back from
exile. When one adds the issue of how sacred objects must be handled (e.g.,
Lev 10:1-3; 1 Sam 5—6; 2 Sam 6:6-7), the importance of this theme becomes
even more recognizable.

Ezekiel's ministry occurs at a time when the issue of God's presence was
particularly relevant to Israel. One of Jehoiachin's fellow exiles in 597 B.C.,
Ezekiel was called in 593 B.C. and served among the Jewish deportees until
at least 571 B.C. God's presence posed a particular problem for exiles, since
the common worldview of that time held that gods were territorially bound.
That is, they may have conceived of Yahweh as Lord of Judah but not of
Babylon, where Bel and Mardule were honored. Therefore they might have
wondered if their deity could indeed be relevant to them in their new setting.

At the same time, since their sins caused their removal from Jerusalem, they needed to be concerned about what was offensive in God's presence. Finally, they needed to know in what way Yahweh could be present. Their history proved that God could be present to bless or to judge. Again they required a better knowledge of why God chose to be present in either way. The time was ripe for a reconsideration and reshaping of the canon's prior concern with Yahweh's presence.

This volume seeks to analyze Ezekiel as it has been received. There is sufficient scholarly consensus to conclude that the book is by the prophet and people who accepted his beliefs or even to conclude that the whole text was written by the prophet himself. It is also true that the prophecy has a clear structure, is written in autobiographical form throughout, exhibits significant linguistic continuity, utilizes several typical phrases in every section and demonstrates a consistent theology. There is every reason to examine the canonical text rather than to reflect on a hypothetically reconstructed text.[1] Canonical analysis best reveals both Ezekiel's unique contribution to Old Testament theology and its place in the whole of Scripture.[2]

Though less is known about Ezekiel than Jeremiah, several facts about him are revealed in the text and help illuminate his theology. Besides being an exile, Ezekiel was a priest (1:2-3), which may explain his preoccupation with the temple, ritual and holiness. He was married (24:16) and enjoyed more prestige in the community than did Jeremiah (3:1; 20:1). Above all Ezekiel was a visionary who sometimes lost consciousness while receiving his visions. He did symbolic acts to explain his visions, and he had a strong grasp of the written word of God. Therefore, in mediating God's word he preached the canon, related his visions and acted out messages. His concern for his audience, for God's word, for holiness and for accuracy are evident.

Ezekiel's theology combines his own background and his audience's needs. Their need to know that Yahweh is present with them coincides with his priestly interest in cultivating the holy presence of God as prescribed in the Law, and his prophetic calling aids his proclamation against contaminating sins. His prophetic convictions also help him conceive of a holy God and holy people living together in a magnificent sacred space. His visionary impulses help his messages transcend their immediate physical and temporal contexts in a way that benefits audiences living long after his own. He seeks to describe sacred presence and discovers that an extensive use of symbolism is the best way he can convey such lofty thoughts.

Ezekiel's theological convictions unfold in the book's four parts. First, he encounters a God who is present to call in Ezekiel 1—3. This God is able to see all things and be in all places at once and is always present to bless the faithful. Ezekiel finds himself filled with this Lord's Spirit, or presence. Second, the prophet describes a God who is present to judge in Ezekiel 4—24. This segment depicts Yahweh withdrawing from the temple to the Mount of Olives and there ominously watching over the people, perhaps looking for repentance yet certainly preparing to judge. Third, Ezekiel 25—32 focuses on Yahweh's judging presence among the nations, an emphasis that links him with earlier prophets. Fourth, the text proclaims Yahweh is equally present to renew in Ezekiel 33—48. The same spirit that fills Ezekiel fills the dead nation as well, so God's presence heals here. The book closes the emphasis on presence by envisioning a future Jerusalem where worship is pure and the people's relationship with their Lord immediate and unmediated. At last the nation is ready to stand before the holy God.

Ezekiel is not easy to read. The book contains many strange images and can be repetitive. Because of its close thematic connections with Isaiah and Jeremiah it does not receive the same length of treatment as its predecessors here or in many other works. Still, the book makes an important contribution to theology through its depiction of Yahweh as the God who is different than humans, above and beyond the human sphere, yet who without altering character stands alongside and dwells within people. This sort of presence comforts, yet it also creates healthy respect for the covenant God.

The God Who Is Present to Call: Ezekiel 1—3

Ezekiel's call experience is different from that of Moses, Isaiah or Jeremiah in many respects, yet there are also striking similarities. Each individual either sees an unusual sign or has visions that are intended to highlight the odd nature of what occurs and to impress upon the one called the awesome power and presence of God. Ezekiel's vision of four creatures (1:4-14), wheels (1:15-21), a firmament (1:22-25) and a glorious Yahweh on a throne (1:26-28) are not ordinary. But neither is seeing a burning bush in the desert, viewing an enormous God enthroned in the temple or receiving visions of boiling pots while still a youth. Ezekiel's call brings before him "the appearance of the likeness of the glory of the LORD" (1:28). In God's presence this prophet falls on his face, a reaction paralleled in Moses' reluctance to serve, Isaiah's feelings of sinfulness and Jeremiah's self-deprecation and fear. God appears to Ezekiel, and this presence overwhelms him. He learns that God's glory does not just manifest itself in the promised land, which means that Yahweh is "the Lord, free from all earthly limitations, and able to command the whole universe."[3]

The God who is present to call is also present to commission. Ezekiel's task will be no easier than Isaiah's or Jeremiah's. Yahweh addresses Ezekiel as "son of man" (2:1), a name the Lord uses ninety-two times in the book.[4] It sets Ezekiel apart from the divine beings in the vision[5] and also highlights the prophet's dependence on God and God's Spirit to empower him.[6] God's Spirit enters him, helps him stand and makes it possible for him to hear and later share the word (2:2).[7] He is a true prophet, for he stands in God's presence and receives Yahweh's word. His messenger status authenticates his ministry.[8] God's direct work in his life will guarantee success in the things he is asked to do.

His audience will not be receptive, so Ezekiel must follow God's instructions fully. Israel is rebellious and stubborn, but he must not fear (2:3-7). These verses parallel Isaiah 6:9-10, where Isaiah is told of the people's unwillingness to hear, and Jeremiah 1:17-19, where Jeremiah is cautioned not to fear his enemies.[9] God's plan is that even if Israel disobeys they will have had a prophet in their midst to warn them (2:5; cf. 2 Kings 17:13-14). Ezekiel is told to eat a scroll of God's word, a document that symbolizes earlier writings[10] and the new revelation he will receive (2:8—3:3). His word will be Spirit-inspired and directly given by the Lord. His role as true prophet is thereby assured. Israel will reject this word, so the prophet must become as tough as flint lest he feel compelled to quit (3:4-11). God's Spirit conveys him back to his fellow exiles exhausted from the experience (3:12-15).

But his commission is not complete. Yahweh now informs him he is a "watchman" (3:16), an image often used in the Old Testament for prophets (Is 56:10; Jer 6:17; Hos 9:8; Hab 2:1). It is a particularly appropriate image for prophets since like the literal ancient watchmen they warn of threats on the horizon.[11] Israel's spiritual life is in Ezekiel's hands. God will hold him responsible for those whom he fails to warn who do not repent (3:16-21). For his pains, he will be persecuted by the rebellious people, and God will respond by shutting Ezekiel's mouth, which will effectively judge Israel by taking away their means of repentance (3:22-27). Israel truly does exist by God's word alone (Deut 8:3), and Amos 8:11-12 claims that a famine of Yahweh's word is the most terrible of all disasters. This final portion of Ezekiel's call and commission underscores the complete alienation of the God who gives the word from the people who refuse to live by it.[12]

Canonical Synthesis: God's Presence and God's Word

Three canonical observations are appropriate here. First, as has been noted, this call story shares in the canon's tradition of initial encounters between a holy God and God's servants. Yahweh's self-revelation leads to a stated task here as it does elsewhere. Second, these chapters demonstrate the universal quality of God's presence. In Isaiah 6 the Lord fills the temple. In Jeremiah 1 the Lord calls a nation from the north. Here Yahweh encounters an exile outside the land of promise. Of course, God creates the world in Genesis 1—2, calls Abram out of Ur in Genesis 12:1-9 and watches over Abram in Egypt in Genesis 12:10-20. Exodus—Joshua expresses the fact that Yahweh can lead Israel from Egypt to Canaan. Thus a canonical approach to God's presence reveals that the topic has come full circle. The same God who summoned Abram from Chaldea now calls a prophet from the exiles in the Chaldean region. Since God's character is holy in its essence (Lev 11:44), wherever the Lord goes and chooses to act becomes "holy ground" (cf. Ex 3:1-6).

Third, this passage highlights the inspiration of God's word. Probably as much as any text in the Old Testament, these verses illustrate what 2 Peter 1:21 means when it says prophecies were not human impulses, for the prophets spoke as they were borne along by the Holy Spirit. The prophets claim to speak the very words of God, whether received through vision, symbolic acts commanded by the Lord or in conversation with God. Their words thereby carry the accuracy, authority, urgency and applicability of the Lord speaking directly. They share this inspiration with Moses, whom the Pentateuch claims wrote (e.g., Ex 17:14) and received (e.g., Lev 1:1) direct revelation from Yahweh. Such assurances of divine inspiration may be particularly important in a visionary and symbolic prophecy like Ezekiel, since visions are experienced by a single individual whose honesty must be trusted by hearers.

The God Who Is Present to Judge: Ezekiel 4—24

Like Jeremiah, Ezekiel moves out from call and instruction to work among the people by doing symbolic acts and proclaiming God's word. Often his symbolic deeds lead to preaching opportunities, as in Jeremiah's experience (cf. Jer 11—20). This section presents God's moving out of the temple area in stages to a place where the people's actions may be observed, denounced and punished. It is also punctuated by three summaries of Israelite history that tie Yahweh's current work to the past. When the segment ends Israel will be nearly ready to receive the Lord's instrument of wrath.

Ezekiel's first task is to warn the people of the doom that will befall their beloved Jerusalem. He acts out a siege (4:1-8), the resulting famine (4:9-17) and the effects of warfare on the city (5:1-17). Finally he informs the mountains around Jerusalem that they will be filled with dead bodies (6:1-7). Israel's abominations mean the end has come (6:11—7:9) in the form of the day of the Lord (7:10-13), a time that will leave all wicked persons devastated (7:14-21). This day is portrayed as a time when God turns away from them because of their iniquity (7:22-26). Yahweh will be present but will look favorably only toward those who are bringing the disaster. Presence means punishment under these conditions, not protection.[13] It means graciousness has ended,[14] or at least now wrath must occur so that exile may create a remnant that believes (cf. 6:8-10).

Judgment may not be Yahweh's final word, but it is a necessary one at this point. The devastation will help the people know "I am the LORD" (7:27). This phrase punctuates the prophecy, occurring seventy-four times,[15] and its presence fastens attention on the nation's need to know the God of their history whose acts "reveal the true knowledge of his being."[16] The phrase revisits the attempt in Isaiah 40—48 to return the people to the God who met with Moses (Ex 3—4), who made a covenant with Abraham (Ex 3:1-6). Truly knowing God will restore them to their roots, purify their worship and secure their future. There is no benefit in their current ignorance.

Ezekiel 8—11 reveals how profound Israel's lack of theological knowledge has become. In 592 B.C.17 Ezekiel is taken in a vision to Jerusalem, where he reencounters God's glory in the worship place (8:1-4). Yahweh shows the prophet idols at entrances (8:5-6) and in the temple itself (8:7-13). Elders worship idols in God's house, for they think Yahweh has left the land because of the troubled times and therefore cannot see them (8:12). They doubt the possibility of the Lord's current presence. Outside, women are practicing a cult that involves a myth of a god's death and resurrection (8:14-15), while some men worship solar deities (9:16-18). In other words, the people venerate Babylonian, Canaanite and Egyptian gods in the Lord's sacred space where Yahweh has chosen to place his name (cf. 1 Kings 6:11-13; 9:1-3).[18] Israel does not know Yahweh their God or what constitutes proper worship.

The issue of presence emerges again in Ezekiel 9—11. God summons executioners to punish the people for violence and oppression (9:1-2, 9-11). All the while the Lord begins to move outside the temple itself (9:3). Again God's protecting presence gives way to a divinely appointed danger that only the faithful remnant will survive (9:4-8). The reason for this withdrawal of favor is that the people sin because they do not believe God sees what they do (9:9-11). They have adopted a polytheistic worldview that claims that a nation's gods are bound when their nation is bound. But Yahweh is not bound, and he does see. They must learn that in this case God seems absent because they have sinned.

Next, God commissions fire against Jerusalem (10:1-17) and then recedes out of the temple to the east gate (10:18-19). There is no longing for God here, so Yahweh departs,[19] all without ever losing sight of what happens. God continues to have intimate knowledge of their sins (11:1-12). Their chief failure is the same as that of Israel in the era of the judges: they reject the Mosaic covenant in favor of their neighbors' religious practices (11:11-12). Israel has spurned their only glory.

Two important details close the scene. First, the Lord reassures Ezekiel that there is a future for the remnant. As in Jeremiah 24, the Lord says that the exiles are the stock from which the holy remnant will grow. Those in Jerusalem believe they must be Yahweh's favorites (11:14-15), but their idolatry proves them wrong. They do not even yet have the opportunity to have the exile cleanse them and turn them to the Lord. God protects a remnant so they can inherit the land (11:16-17). The remnant will remove the idols (11:18). In language clearly related to Jeremiah 31:31-34,[20] the Lord states in 11:19-20 how the "true Israel"[21] will achieve such results. Yahweh will directly change their hearts, "replacing unresponsiveness with a new compliance to the will of God."[22] At the same time God will give the remnant a new spirit, a point not made by Jeremiah yet clearly central to Ezekiel's theology. The new spirit is a totally unmerited and free gift of God.[23] Together with the new heart it will produce covenant obedience and a renewed relationship with the Lord. Only by direct divine intervention can this transformation take place. Only the remnant will possess this power. Thus Ezekiel agrees in several key ways with Jeremiah's vision of a redeemed people of God. The new element he adds is the Spirit's role in this renewal.

Second, Yahweh's glory departs from the midst of the city to a mountain overlooking Jerusalem (11:23). The chosen place is now wholly unprotected. God's presence, though still evident, has taken a position that insinuates that of spectator or more probably a general who leads destructive forces. By not acknowledging the Lord's presence in proper ways the people have exchanged protective presence for a terrible, punishing force.

After again acting out the implications of exile (12:7-20), Ezekiel addresses the prophets and elders, or those responsible for the nation's demise. Jeremiah adopts a similar strategy in Jeremiah 21—24. The people believe that on the one hand the words of most prophets come to nothing (12:21-25) yet on the other hand conclude that Ezekiel's prophecies are about some distant time (13:26-28). God says Ezekiel has an immediate word, a word for the present (12:25, 28). The same nation that believes God does not see thinks the Lord has nothing current to say. For them, God is not present and is quite silent.

God's response is they have no word because they seek guidance from false prophets and idols (13:1—14:15). Ezekiel's list for identifying false prophets is like Jeremiah's: they tear down the nation (13:5), they speak their own words, not God's, because the Lord has not sent them (13:6), and they affirm the people in their sins because they say peace will come to a covenant-breaking people (13:8-16). This last point truly reveals their falseness, for it conclusively proves that they do not understand or correctly interpret the covenant. They want covenant blessing without covenant responsibilities. Some prophets turn to magic in their search for knowledge about the future (13:17-23).[24] These individuals do not just misread the covenant. They violate it in a way that makes Israel indistinguishable from polytheistic cultures (cf. Deut 18:14, 15-22). The elders are equally offensive to God because they practice a syncretism that includes seeking idols and asking direction from the prophet (14:1-5).

Such variations on pure worship will result in natural and military disaster (14:12—15:8). Only repentance can stem the tide of judgment (14:6). Otherwise the same Lord who in 11:19-20 moved directly to create a new remnant with new heart and spirit will act specifically by using lying prophets to punish those who seek them in the first place (14:7-9). This strategy appears in 1 Kings 22, where Ahaz is determined to do what the false prophets say, so God uses their lies to punish him.[25] In this way God "punishes sin by sin, and thus makes plain how those who thoughtlessly fall into guilt will have to face the inevitable consequences to which it leads."[26] Both sinners are responsible for their actions, since they are in effect partners in covenantal disobedience. Therefore it is clear that "the latter's mistake did not mitigate the former's error."[27] Only through the removal of such activities can it be known that the Lord is God (14:8) and that God's word is present in the land.

Ezekiel 16 views the idolatry depicted in Ezekiel 8—15 as just the most recent in a long line of covenantal infidelities in Israel's history. This chapter and its partner texts (Ezek 20, 23) invite comparison with the history of Israel portrayed in Genesis—Kings, Jeremiah 2—6, Isaiah 5:1-7, Hosea 1—2 and elsewhere in the canon. Joseph Blenkinsopp considers Ezekiel's messages "a radical rewriting of Israel's history" because Ezekiel 16 and 20 trace the nation's idolatry back to Egypt, assume rather than mention the patriarchs and do not include the cycle of sin, punishment, prayer and renewal found in the Former Prophets. He goes on to offer cogent reasons for Ezekiel's viewpoint, such as the mention of an idolatrous past in Joshua 24:2-14 and the fact that Ezekiel focuses on the first generation of Israelites instead of their faithful children.[28] He properly notes Ezekiel's preference for citing the sinful side of Israel's past. All these differences are more interpretational strategy than the writing of an alternative history. The goal of this history is the same as the others, which is to fasten attention on the fact that idolatry is the fundamental sin that turns the covenant from a blessing to a document of disaster.

God says Israel was like a baby exposed to die by uncaring parents,[29] but God gave her life (16:1-7). When she reached maturity Yahweh married her and decked her with jewels. So far the events in Genesis 12—Joshua 24 have been covered. Then the girl turned to Canaanite, Assyrian and Babylonian gods (16:15-29). Indeed she was shameless and tireless in her adultery

(16:30-34). Already her older sister, Samaria, has been punished (16:35-46), yet the younger sibling continues to sin (16:47-52) and must face judgment as well. Now the prophet has covered events found in Judges—2 Kings 24:20. The heavy sexual imagery in these passages serves a twofold purpose. Adultery is an excellent metaphor for covenant breaking, and the fertility rites associated with some of the cults required actual sexual experiences that broke marriage vows.[30]

Ezekiel 16:53-63 concludes the first historical review by envisioning the future. As in 6:8-10 and 11:14-21, the remnant becomes the bridge between the day of punishment and the time of renewal.[31] God will restore the remnant by remembering the old covenant and establishing a second, everlasting covenant (16:60). Then they will know that the Lord is God. Now Ezekiel presents material that links his message to that of Isaiah and Jeremiah. Isaiah 45:17 and 51:6-8 state that God's salvation is everlasting, while 54:10 speaks of a covenant of peace that cannot be removed and 55:3 proclaims an everlasting covenant mediated through David's lineage. Jeremiah 31:31-37 and 32:40 deem the new covenant unbreakable and everlasting. The close linkages between Ezekiel 6:8-10, 11:14-21 and 16:59-63 indicate that they are all based on this notion of a new, everlasting covenant. The parallels between Ezekiel 11:19-20 and Jeremiah 31:31-34 indicate that Jeremiah and Ezekiel agree that there will be a new covenant. Isaiah, Jeremiah and Ezekiel all believe that God must act directly upon the remnant through a new and everlasting covenant for Israel to be redeemed.

In Ezekiel 16, Ezekiel's review is both historical and canonical. It agrees with earlier books that God elects Israel solely out of love and compassion.[32] It focuses on the covenantal and physical adultery caused by idol worship and emphasizes loss of land as the most devastating means of punishing that infidelity. It also conceives of a long-term renewed relationship between God and Israel based on a new remnant, in a new covenant, because of divine intervention in the remnant's hearts. While emphasizing these points the passage follows the contours of Israelite history. The text has Ezekiel's personal stamp upon it, but it is in no way irreconcilable with the rest of the canon.

Having compared Israel to a vine for burning (15:1-8) and an adulterous spouse (16:1-52), the prophet now explains the nation's history during 597-587 B.C. in a third way. Israel is like a twig plucked off a tree by two great eagles, the first representing Babylon and the second symbolizing Egypt.[33] Under Zedekiah, Judah fears Babylon and asks Egypt to save them. They fear the wrong enemy, for it is Yahweh alone who judges covenant breaking (17:15). God is Zedekiah's enemy.[34] Covenant breaking will finish his kingdom (17:17-20), and the people will learn Yahweh's identity.

The Lord may close the kingdom for a time, but Ezekiel 17:22-24 continues the book's claim that the God who rules history will plant the people back in the land (17:22). God's word will do this planting, for God's word creates and directs history (17:24).[35] This time "all the trees," all the nations, will know that Yahweh has acted (17:24). As in Isaiah 40—66, what God does with the remnant witnesses to God's greatness. Therefore God's direct acts include making certain that light does flow from the chosen people to the whole creation.

Ezekiel 18—20 reflects on Israel's guilt by declaring each person's responsibility for his or her sin, by lamenting the end of the kingdom and by offering a second historical summary that highlights Israel's failure to serve Yahweh in spite of the exodus.[36] The prophet first reflects on a proverb found in Jeremiah 31:29-30 that means the children are suffering for the sins of their parents (18:1-2). Ezekiel's people believed they had done nothing to deserve their fate. All sin has corporate consequences, and it is possible to suffer for the sins of others, but these are not the only possibilities. The people refuse to consider that the sins enumerated in Ezekiel 8—17 might cause divine punishment. After all, they think God is absent, not present (cf. 9:9-11). They also consider the Lord unfair and incapable of ruling the universe, so Walther Eichrodt properly calls this "a blasphemous proverb."[37] They also imply Yahweh does not honor the law, since Deuteronomy 24:16 stresses that individuals are to be punished only for their own transgressions.

To contradict their claim that God's ways are not just (cf. 8:25), the text cites the spiritual status of three successive generations to prove that specific punishment handed down by the Lord depends on each individual's action (19:5-24). Then the Lord states that each person may repent and receive the new heart and new spirit mentioned in 11:19-20 (18:30-31). Sin and punishment are not inevitable. There is no fatalism with God, nor are there grounds for self-pity or self-satisfied piety.[38] The exiles he addresses may, one by one, become the whole remnant of Israel.[39] At the same time this emphasis on individual responsibility in no way eliminates the corporate nature of sin or punishment. After counseling individual responsibility in 18:30, the prophet declares in 18:30-32 that the death of any person contributes to the death of the house of Israel. Ezekiel seeks to instruct, challenge and encourage the exiles, not create a new doctrine of sin.[40]

God's pain over the death of sinners is also evident in Ezekiel 19—20. Israel's demise is so tragic it deserves to be remembered in a lament for the ages (19:1-14). After all, every age or era of their history is marked by covenant infidelity (20:1-4). No part of their past remains unstained.

Ezekiel's second summary of this unsavory past unfolds in 20:5-32. Though it is stated in nonallegorical form, it parallels the concerns in 16:1-52. Two controversial texts, however, that are not reflected in Ezekiel 16 require explanation. First, the prophet accuses Israel of idolatry in Egypt during their sojourn there. Joshua 24:14 admits such practices did exist, and Exodus 32 more than implies that the people already knew how to venerate idols. Still, the Old Testament nowhere else says God considered destroying them in Egypt, though it would be in keeping with the rest of the canonical witness had the Lord done so. In this and every other case Yahweh does not punish in order to protect the divine name or reputation, the very ground on which Moses intercedes for Israel after the incident of the golden calf (Ex 32:11-14). Not knowing God's true nature, God's name, has been repeated numerous times in Ezekiel as the key to all sin, so the Lord's concern is hardly rank egoism here.

Second, 20:25-26 speaks of God giving laws Israel could not follow as a means of punishing their wilderness-era disobedience. Which law is meant here is quite important, for if it is the *torah* itself then God's entire work with Israel may be called into question. Once again canonical analysis is helpful as a means of dealing with a difficult text. To begin with, it is vital to interpret this passage in light of 14:7-9. Ezekiel has already stated that when sinners reject the law and the prophets that Yahweh turns sinners over to sinners so that they might punish one another. That text, like 1 Kings 22, focuses on how false prophets are used for this purpose. Here the same principle may be applied to the cultic laws that polytheistic cults taught. When Israel rejected the law in favor of religions that required child sacrifice, Yahweh gave them over to that law as a punishment. Deuteronomy 28:64 states that part of the consequences for covenant breaking will be serving other gods. Therefore, as Moshe Greenberg observes, this situation parallels the hardening of Pharaoh's heart and Isaiah's preaching so ears will not hear.[41]

Several scholars disagree with this interpretation. Brevard Childs concludes that this passage means the law itself became a terror to the people when they sinned.[42] This interpretation does not take 14:7-9 and its comments about false prophecy fully into account. If there can be false prophets, then there can also be false law. If Yahweh uses one to punish it is possible to use the other in the same way. Eichrodt implies that over time Israel's syncretistic mindset came to link laws concerning the redemption of the firstborn to child sacrifice like that in Canaanite cults.[43] This situation no doubt may have occurred, yet Eichrodt still mistakenly identifies the law in 20:26 with God's law. Michael Fishbane states that God gave bad laws in order to insure the punishment of the nation's sin. He concludes that this fact means subsequent generations were punished for their ancestors' sins, which in turn means that Ezekiel 18 and 20 contradict one another.[44] If God in fact gives contradictory laws in this scenario, then Fishbane has a point, for then the nation would posses confusing divine revelation. But if a false law opposed to the true law is meant here, each successive generation chose the false law of pain and death over the revealed law of the loving God. Thus each generation is responsible for its own rejection of Yahweh's will and chooses to allow other sinners punish their sins. David expresses the danger of doing so in 2 Samuel 24:14.

The same God who spared Israel until now for his name's sake will produce a remnant for the same reason. The remnant's very existence will demonstrate God's holiness to the nations (20:41). It will restore the land and proper worship (20:40-42). Yahweh's mercy is evident in that Israel has not been judged based on their sins but on God's character (20:44). Yahweh's character refuses to judge without patient warning, and it declines to leave the nations with no witness to their creator.

Ezekiel 21—24 concludes the section on God's assessment of Judah along what are by now quite familiar lines. The prophet says the sword of Babylon will destroy Jerusalem (21:1-32; cf. 5:1-12). He states that punishment will fall because of idolatry, oppression and the shedding of blood (22:1-31; cf. 6:1-7, 14-27). A third historical summary appears, which is, like Ezekiel 16, a story of two adulterous women who are eventually destroyed by their lovers (23:1-49). Just as Israel gave themselves to false prophets and false cultic laws, so they have also given themselves to false allies. In every case God gives them over to the consequences of their actions. Thus, despite the similarities of style and substance, Ezekiel 16 and 20 focus on the nation's religious sins, while Ezekiel 23 pays more attention to condemning their political alliances.[45]

Until this point in the prophecy Ezekiel's visions have led up to the actual invasion of Jerusalem. Three texts provide dates from 593 B.C. (1:2; 3:16), to 592 B.C. (8:1) and 591 B.C. (20:1).[46] Ezekiel 24, however, dates to the beginning of the Babylonian siege in 588 B.C. (24:1-2). To illustrate the siege's horrible effects the Lord asks Ezekiel to undertake his most difficult symbolic act. His wife, his delight (24:16), will die, yet he must not mourn (24:16-18). This act is done to show the people they will lose their delight, Jerusalem, and there will be no mourning except over sin (24:19-24). At last what Ezekiel has warned will happen is about to unfold. God has come near to judge, for God's instrument, God's sword (cf. Ezek 5, 22) is at the city gates.

Canonical Synthesis: God's Empowering and Redemptive Presence

Some canonical reflection has been offered already, yet a few other points deserve consideration. One is the role of God's Spirit to this point in the canon. Here it is God's Spirit that fills the prophet with the divine word, that empowers Ezekiel to preach and that helps turn the remnant's heart into flesh instead of stone. Similarly the Spirit empowers Gideon in Judges 6:34, fills prophets in 1 Samuel 10:6-13 and is the agent of heart change in Psalm 51:10-12. Moses was endowed with the Spirit (Num 11:17, 25, 29), and the servant will be as well (Is 42:1-4; 61:1-3). Without the Spirit there can be no real relationship between the Lord and human beings.[47] This idea of Spirit and communion becomes even more important in the New Testament, since the Holy Spirit's presence is discussed as having a part in every facet of Christian faith and practice.

Another point that bears mentioning is the means by which God's presence changes from positive to negative. The Scriptures never speak of God being absent in the sense of not knowing, seeing or sensing all that happens. It does, however, as in Ezekiel 4—24, speak of God's withdrawing positive presence. In Exodus 32—34 it is the threat of the loss of this presence that drives Moses to restore the relationship between Yahweh and Israel. Moses knows that if God is not "with them" for good they have no hope. Virtually every biblical lament, whether in Psalms, Job or Lamentations, makes the same case. The writers do not doubt the Lord can hear, but they do question why Yahweh does not reestablish positive (in their view) presence.

Finally, it is important to draw a distinction between suffering and punishment. Abel and Job suffer, but their pain is not a result of their sin, and the same is true of Joseph and Jeremiah. For the faithful, their suffering is on behalf of others and is thereby redemptive. Punishment may have either a punitive or a purging impact, depending on the recipient's reaction. The people of Ezekiel's and Jeremiah's day made none of these distinctions. Rather they complained of any sort of disaster as if they were righteous. They rejected careful self-examination.

The God Who Is Present to Judge the Nations: Ezekiel 25—32

So far the text has barely mentioned the Gentiles. Babylon has been described as God's sword (Ezek 22), and two texts have said that the remnant will provide a witness to the nations about God (17:24; 20:41), yet little else has been offered. In this section, though, on the eve of Jerusalem's demise, the prophet addresses the sins the nations commit. God has seen their activities and knows their hearts. Therefore the day of the Lord will be Yahweh's personal response to what they have done. Through this judging presence God will manifest lordship over the whole creation. This section displays virtually the same concerns as Isaiah 13—23 and Jeremiah 46—51, though within the book's own particular theological context.

For example, as in Jeremiah 46, the Lord judges those who mistreat Israel during the Babylonian danger. Ammon (25:1-7), Moab (25:8-11), Edom (28:12-14) and Philistia (25:15-27) fall into this category. Punishment will teach them Yahweh's identity (25:17). Tyre also meets this description

(26:1-21), yet this city's chief sin is pride, a transgression that receives extensive treatment in Isaiah 13—23. Tyre has taken pride in its beauty (27:1-11) and wealth (27:12-36). This arrogance takes on Satan-like proportions in 28:1-11, where Tyre's king proclaims himself a god. His wealth and unquestioned leadership ability have led him to believe in his own infallibility.[48] His idolatry is the most fundamental kind, for he worships himself. Yahweh will take away Tyre's and Sidon's power (28:20-23) but will reinstate Israel. These events will teach all concerned a personal knowledge of Yahweh (28:24-26). Tyre's sin is particularly heinous because the Tyrians have enjoyed Eden-like advantages yet have used political oppression to defile the sacred place God has given them.[49]

Egypt and its associates will meet a similar fate for the same reasons (29:1—30:26). Pharaoh considers himself a god (29:9) and the greatest of kings (29:13-16). Egypt also venerates a variety of idols (30:13), some of which Israel worships in the temple (cf. 8:16-18). Babylon will conquer the proud, idolatrous land (30:20-26). Further, Yahweh made Egypt great (31:1-9) but now will devastate the nation (31:10-18). Thus Egypt will take its spot in the place of the dead (31:15-18; 32:20).

Who is in this place, and who is absent? Present are the past nations who have defied God, such as the Assyrians and the Edomites (32:20-32). Absent are any of God's faithful.[50] A great separation has taken place between the just and the unjust. Those who spread terror now dwell together (32:32). Where the faithful will go will be discussed later in the prophecy.

Ezekiel's treatment of the sinful nations does share its predecessors' denunciation of cruelty, arrogance and idolatry. It shows Yahweh directly, personally involved in punishment, which magnifies Yahweh's status as only God, not just Israel's God. Ezekiel clearly sets forth the monotheistic conviction that the God who created nations may judge them. The chief difference is that Babylon is not condemned here, a fact that underscores that country's role as divine sword.[51] Babylon will not be put away until all God's will has been achieved through them. Those who oppose Babylon stand against the One who sent them to punish.

The God Who Is Present to Renew: Ezekiel 33—48

Ezekiel's career and prophecy enter a new stage in Ezekiel 33. Many of the same themes and strategies from Ezekiel 1—32 continue, yet the fact that Jerusalem has now fallen (33:21-22) initiates a predominantly positive and comfort-oriented ministry on Ezekiel's part. By the time the book closes the prophet envisions a restored Israel, Davidic lineage, land and temple all existing in a ideal and holy space at the end of time. God's presence turns once again toward Israel's favor, especially when the Lord returns to the temple from the nearby hills (43:1-5) and promises this presence will be permanent (43:6-9).

Before the final renewal takes place, Israel's expulsion from the promised land must occur. Immediately prior to learning of Jerusalem's demise, the prophet experiences a renewal of his call to be a watchman over a rebellious and self-justifying people (33:1-20; cf. 3:16-21). The nation still lacks a sense of individual and corporate responsibility and a commitment to justice.[52] The loss of the holy city (33:21-23) leads to the people's flocking to hear Ezekiel preach yet does not drive them to repentance (33:24-33). Instead they seem to treat prophecy as a sort of entertainment.[53] Yahweh must do a direct work to change their hearts, a fact Jeremiah has already stressed and Ezekiel mentioned in 11:19-20.

God's specific action to restore begins with an exchange of leaders. The nation's leaders ("shepherds") are corrupt, so Yahweh will take charge of gathering the sheep from abroad (34:11-16) and of separating them from the goats (34:17-19). Creating the remnant, then, is a task the Lord must perform. Once collected, the flock or remnant will be placed under Davidic leadership and given a covenant of peace that provides permanent protection (34:20-31). This text corresponds to similar statements made in Jeremiah 33:14-26, where God's "servant David" is presented as the catalyst for the new, permanent covenant detailed in Jeremiah 31:31-34. It also echoes Exodus 5:22—6:8 in its renewal of "God's design: deliverance, community, knowing God, and a rich quality of life."[54] Images of the new exodus mentioned in Isaiah 40—55 also come to mind. The mention of Abraham in 34:24 reflects the concern shown in Isaiah 56—66 to bring earlier Israelite history to an appropriate climax. Thus the new covenant of peace becomes the fulfillment of the older covenants of promise. What human beings could not do the Lord has accomplished.

With these elements in place the text returns to the new heart image first expressed in 11:19-20. Israel will stand blessed in comparison to other countries (cf. 35:1—36:21) only when God acts solely for his holy name's sake to make a fully holy people (36:21-23). Given Israel's past, the only way a holy nation can be created is through the transplanting of a new heart through the agency of God's Spirit (36:24-27). This infusion of Spirit corresponds to Jeremiah's infusion of God's law in 31:31-34 and also indicates that "in 36:25-29 Ezekiel anticipates the day when the boundaries of the physical Israel will be cotermi-nous with the spiritual people of God. In his day a vast gulf separated the two."[55] Only through Yahweh's Spirit can all that constitute Israel have the same faith the remnant possesses (36:27). Only then will the Lord have complete covenant union with the chosen people (36:28).

God's Spirit takes on added significance in Ezekiel 37:1-14. Here the Lord's Spirit raises Israel from the dead, which means that Yahweh must create a holy people from nothing. Not even a heart of stone exists. This text reinforces the notion that one day there will be no remnant as such, for all those in Israel will be enlivened by God's Spirit and thus able to fulfill 36:26-27.[56] The same Spirit that empowers Ezekiel to preach (37:1) will empower Israel to live and return to the land (37:11-14). This Spirit will create a people cleansed of idolatry (37:15-23). Again this situation emerges not because of the repentance Ezekiel hopes for in Ezekiel 4—24 but as God's direct impact on Israel's individual and corporate hearts.

As in 34:20-24, the renewed people are led by God's "servant David" and presented with an everlasting covenant of peace in 37:24-28. The reason the covenant will not be broken is that the Lord will dwell in their midst forever (37:27). This presence will guarantee sanctity, obedience and witness (37:28), thus removing both the possibility of sin and the necessity of the Lord's withdrawing ever again to a position of judgment. Reconciliation will culminate in never-ending fellowship.[57] The designation of the Davidic heir as "servant" links Ezekiel's vision to the future expected in Isaiah 42:1-4, 49:1-6, 50:4-9 and 52:13—53:12,[58] and the affirmation of the covenant of peace reminds readers of Isaiah 54:10, 55:3 and 61:8.[59] Therefore Ezekiel uses his own distinct emphasis on the Spirit to tie together the king and servant images in Isaiah and Jeremiah, as well as those prophets' teachings about the everlasting and new covenants.

Once restored to the land, Israel will never be displaced. Defeats such as those inflicted by Assyria and Babylon will no longer be possible. Great nations may invade the land but will be repulsed by the Lord (38:1—39:16). These victories are not for Israel's sake alone. Rather they are to show God's holiness to the nations and to help them confess the Lord's greatness (38:23; 39:21-29).[60] Then the nations will realize that history, including Israel's previous defeats, unfolds to demonstrate the Lord's nature (39:21-29). Things do not just happen, nor do countries determine the flow of events. History depends on the holy God whose holy name must be honored for human life to have meaning. In the future it will be Yahweh's Spirit that creates history (39:29).

Ezekiel's conception of a restored Israel does not stop with a renewed people. He continues with his program by envisioning a rebuilt temple with revitalized worship in Ezekiel 40—48. This part of the prophecy counteracts Ezekiel 8—11, where the sacred space becomes so defiled that Yahweh refuses to choose to dwell there.[61] Now the Lord constructs a place in which to interact with worshipers who respect and honor the true God. Here Yahweh will dwell forever with the faithful.

Given Ezekiel's background as a priest, it is hardly surprising that the account of the restored Jerusalem begins with a description of a glorified temple. Since

Exodus 25—31 the canon has emphasized the importance of a central sanctuary where God's people may focus on their relationship with Yahweh. God chooses to meet Israel in this space, just as the people determine to focus on the Lord there. What makes the tabernacle or temple holy is the Lord's presence and the keeping of God's commands.[62] A lack of either reality renders the space common or other than uniquely holy. Ezekiel 8—11 declares that Israel has broken God's law and the Lord has forsaken the worship center. To complicate matters further, the destruction of the Solomonic temple by the Babylonians in 587 B.C. leaves the nation without even a potentially holy site. Thus it is reasonable to find Ezekiel foreseeing a future temple in Ezekiel 40—42.

Yahweh returns to the new temple in 43:1-5. Since the people will no longer sin against the Lord, Yahweh promises to dwell in their midst forever (43:6-9). Such permanence is precluded in earlier texts like Exodus 32—34 and 2 Kings 17 because of idolatry and deep-seated, ongoing rebellion against God and God's prophets. Those situations, however, occur in the old Israel in which remnant and nonremnant factions exist together. Given Ezekiel 33—39, it is clear that nonbelievers will no longer exist in Israel and have the potential to defile the temple. Thus Yahweh will have no need to vacate the sacred space or any reason to destroy it. God's presence for blessing is thereby assured forever because of the Spirit's creation of a holy community.

All the necessary components for appropriate worship in the new temple are also secured. A new altar will be dedicated and used appropriately by priests fully committed to serving Yahweh (43:13—44:31). Levites will no longer use their influence to lead the people toward idols (44:9-14). Land will be set aside for the holy site (45:1-6), princes will rule justly (45:7-9), businesses will operate honestly (45:10-12) and holy days will transpire according to God's wishes (45:13-25). Sabbaths and daily sacrifices will take place without fail (46:1-24). Israel will gain life from the temple as it constitutes the true focal point in the land (47:1—48:35). Ezekiel desires for the fixed temple to be as central to the new community life in the rejuvenated land as the tabernacle once was when Israel camped around it.

All these details point to the importance of God's presence for the chosen people's renewal.[63] Ezekiel's concluding statement about the glorified city is that God is there (48:35). All future glory and blessing depend upon the present and living God's offering life to the people.[64] This divine presence has become possible through the holy God's direct action in creating a fully obedient people. No other scenario in Israel's history can produce such glory, for Ezekiel 16, 20 and 23 have shown Israel unwilling and therefore incapable of turning to Yahweh permanently on their own. The new Israel, temple and land are totally the creation of the God who rules and completes history.

Canonical Synthesis: God's Renewing Presence

Several canonical texts support Ezekiel's claims concerning the Lord's renewing presence in people, city, worship and land. Haggai shares Ezekiel's desire for a new temple by encouraging Israel to rebuild the worship center in about 520-516 B.C. Despite its humble beginnings, Haggai expects this temple's glory to exceed that of its predecessors (2:1-9). Zechariah also wants the temple restored and shares Ezekiel's vision of a renewed Jerusalem that is holy to the Lord (14:20) and that provides life-giving water to the whole land (14:8).[65] Malachi parallels Ezekiel's concern for purity of worship within the community of faith. Like Ezekiel, Malachi desires a renewed people to inhabit the rebuilt Jerusalem. These three postexilic prophets who live in the land derive their theologically based restoration programs from ideas found in Ezekiel or at least from ideas akin to those in Ezekiel.

Other passages share Ezekiel's emphasis on Yahweh's presence in the holy city. For instance, Isaiah 60—62 stresses Zion's glory, concluding by stating that Jerusalem will not be forsaken (62:12). Similarly Psalms 46, 48 and 76 consider Jerusalem God's dwelling place.[66] All these references indicate that their authors think Yahweh's presence alone will guarantee a bright future for the chosen people. As Eichrodt observes:

> However differently they may express it in detail, they all agree that full fellowship with the God of election is the deciding factor in the fulfillment of Israel. For in that alone lies the guarantee that this people will reach the goal for which they are destined: to be freed of all sin and imperfection so as to be a credible witness to the Holy One, their God.[67]

Beyond these matters, Ezekiel as a whole agrees with or supplements five key elements found in Isaiah and Jeremiah. These details are also reflected in the Twelve. First, Ezekiel 21:25-27, 34:23-31 and 37:15-28 echo comments in Isaiah and Jeremiah on the coming Davidic king who will provide the holy leadership Israel's evil kings refused to give (cf. Is 9:2-7; 11:1-10; Jer 23:1-8).[68] Ezekiel calls the king God's servant, which may be a direct link with Isaiah's servant songs.[69] All these prophets look to 2 Samuel 7 as the focal point for Israel's future glory.

Second, all three prophets emphasize that the Davidic ruler will preside over an Israel that enjoys a new, or everlasting, covenant with Yahweh. Ezekiel 34:25-31 and 37:24-28 call this agreement a covenant of peace; Isaiah 42:6, 54:10-17, 55:3, 59:21 and other passages depict it as everlasting; and Jeremiah 31:31-37 and 53:14-26 call it both new and eternal. Jeremiah 33:17-18 and Ezekiel 44:9-31 agree that priests will administer the covenant, while Isaiah 59:21 parallels Ezekiel's overall convictions about God's Spirit producing this covenant. All three prophets believe a new situation is needed, and all three think once instituted the new covenant will never need to be superseded. None has any faith in the nation's willingness to repent, so all claim that God will have to act unilaterally to achieve this ideal situation.

Third, each of the prophecies states that only the faithful will constitute the people of God when the new covenant under the Davidic ruler becomes a reality. It is only the faithful who dwell in Zion with God in Isaiah 60—62 and 66:18-24. The new covenant people will all know the Lord, according to Jeremiah 31:31-34. Only the Spirit-changed righteous ones dwell with the Lord in the new Jerusalem in Ezekiel 40—48 (cf. 11:19-20; 36:26-27). There will be no unregenerate members of the chosen community, for God's direct work in the heart of the believers separates them from those who continue to reject the Lord.

Fourth, Isaiah 66:18-24 and Ezekiel 25—48 separate the wicked from the faithful at the end of time. Punishment will overtake the former group, while a new Jerusalem and constant communion with God await the other. These issues are not spelled out in careful detail, yet they are explained sufficiently enough to suggest specific avenues for future biblical authors (especially in the New Testament) to follow.

Fifth, all three prophets believe that Israel's sinful past make such future activities necessary. Isaiah 1—5, Jeremiah 2—6 and Ezekiel 8—11, 16, 20 and 23 concur that the chosen people have themselves chosen to break the Sinai covenant. Specific details may differ in these texts, yet the basic concerns raised are more alike than they are dissimilar. At the heart of all the covenant breaking lies idolatry, the sin that starts a chain reaction of spiritual infidelity. Thus, as much as Ezekiel and his predecessors embrace renewal, they do not fail to stress sin and punishment at the same time.

Conclusion

As the preceding comments indicate, Ezekiel certainly affirms the main emphases of canonical prophecy. At the same time, however, the book also contributes some unique perspectives to Old Testament theology. It offers an emphasis on the empowering nature of God's Spirit that is unparalleled in the Hebrew Scriptures. To Ezekiel, the Spirit inspires prophecy, empowers the remnant, creates the future community of faith, changes human hearts and raises Israel from the dead. These convictions about Yahweh's Spirit lead to Ezekiel's teachings about God's constant presence. God's Spirit may be anywhere, even in Babylon, and where the Spirit is the Lord is present, whether to bless or to judge. As long as the Lord is present there is hope for the future. For Ezekiel, such hope was more real than exile, more overwhelming than personal loss, more compelling than the people's self-serving despair. The one God who is present was, to him, the one God who could sustain the faithful in exile.

14

The God
Who Keeps
Promises

The Book of the Twelve

....

ONE OF THE MAJOR DIFFERENCES BETWEEN THE CONFIGURATION OF BOOKS in the English Bible and that of the Hebrew Bible occurs at the end of the prophetic literature. The English Bible considers the final twelve prophetic books separate prophecies and designates them as the minor prophets, a term that refers to their length, not their importance. The Hebrew Bible counts these books a single prophetic work that unfolds in twelve parts. To complicate the matter further, two major orderings of the prophecies have been handed down over the centuries, which makes it harder to determine what order is original.

The Hebrew manuscripts place the books in the same sequence as the does English Bible. The Greek tradition leaves the final six the same but offers the following order for the first six: Hosea, Amos, Micah, Joel, Obadiah and Jonah. Since this volume attempts to discuss the theology of the Old Testament as it unfolds in the Hebrew canon, that order will be followed and the books will be explained as one book. The other configurations are not unimportant, but each study must carry out its own approach as consistently as possible. To analyze these books as a whole treats the Hebrew tradition as important in its own right and at least has the value of attempting to explicate one important version of the canon.

Scholars are currently engaged in debating whether the Twelve was edited to be one book or was collected as a logical way to read several short prophecies. James Nogalski argues that more than one redaction (edition) of the Twelve was required for it to reach its final Hebrew form.[1] He points to strategic catch phrases and repeated words as indicators for how and why these redactions were made. Nogalski also thinks some of the Twelve, most notably Joel, were written in order to fill out the book and that editors contributed some linking passages to the text. Barry Jones, by contrast, concludes that the Greek version is more original than its Hebrew counterpart, which leads him to quite different decisions about how and why the Twelve came together as one.[2] Jones cannot accept both Nogalski's reconstruction of the Twelve's composition and the Greek sequence as original.

Though both these authors' works have definite strengths and weaknesses, it is not within the scope of this volume to address them at length.[3] Rather this chapter adopts a third position, which is to treat the books as if they were placed together because as a group they display many of the same literary and theological features as do their larger predecessors, Isaiah, Jeremiah and Ezekiel.[4] Such would not be the case if some of the smaller writings stood on their own. Together, though, they provide as comprehensive a prophetic theology as any of the three previous prophetic books. Thus it is best in this context to examine the books in canonical order and to observe how together the prophecies provide canonical support and expansion of the theological views already expressed in earlier passages.[5]

When this approach is implemented, it becomes apparent that by extending over three hundred years of history the Twelve provides a full portrait of the God who keeps promises. The time span allows the text to include the fulfillment of pledges made decades earlier, whether those pledges were of divine judgment or blessing. As great as the previous books are they do not have the scope both to offer and describe the completion of Yahweh's long-term threats and positive promises.

When considering the Twelve as a canonical whole it is appropriate to note the individual prophecies' historical setting, structural details and thematic emphases. Each of these elements will aid an understanding of how the individual books supplement the earlier prophecies and one another. There is no doubt that the original canonical readers could tell that the books placed together did not all unfold in chronological order. Thus familiar themes and characterizations of God, Israel and the nations probably took precedence in their minds as they read. It makes sense to examine how the Twelve uses both historical context and literary concepts to create the one book, for in the consideration of both lies the book's theological and canonical significance.

When one reads the Twelve as a partner with Isaiah, Jeremiah and Ezekiel, several specific prophetic ideas become readily apparent. These notions help order an effective analysis of the book's theology. For instance, the fundamental sin of covenant breaking receives treatment in all the prophecies but takes precedence especially in Hosea—Micah. Each of these texts discusses the general and specific contexts in which sin marred the Israel they knew in their particular historical contexts. They define and describe these transgressions and threaten punishment for them, but they anticipate chastisement coming later. In this way they read very much like early sections of Isaiah. As a group these six prophecies focus on the God who defines and condemns sin. At the same time they also proclaim that the Lord will eventually renew the land. Again the prophets anticipate this restoration in the distant future.

Nahum, Habakkuk and Zephaniah move beyond the description of sin and threats about punishment to specific promises about the approaching day of the Lord. Here Yahweh is portrayed as judge as surely as in Jeremiah. All nations will be devastated for their sins, regardless of size or present influence. Covenant and noncovenant people alike are included in the destruction. All creation is swept away by the end of Zephaniah—all, that is, except the remnant. Yahweh remains the God who spares a remnant to serve the Lord and inherit the Lord's blessings.

Just as Ezekiel looks beyond punishment to a brighter future based on God's presence in the remnant's midst, so Haggai, Zechariah and Malachi point toward God's eventual transformation of judgment to glory. Temple, city and people are all devastated by the Babylonians in 587 B.C. Thus the God who restores must reestablish these aspects of Israelite life for the renewal to be as complete as the devastation. The fact that Yahweh does just that reinforces the canon's insistence that punishment is always undertaken to effect cleansing and restoration. When Malachi ends, these prophetic principles and their counterparts in other texts span three centuries. Therefore the prophetic literature provides a theological body of work carefully grounded in history. Prophecy and reality never become separated.

The God Who Expresses Covenant Love: Hosea

Perhaps no prophet pays a higher price for his or her calling than does Hosea. Like other prophets he preaches the covenant truths already stated in the canon. Like other prophets he acts out his message. Unlike other prophets, he suffers profound personal agony through marital betrayal by his wife. By loving this woman despite her failure to remain faithful to him Hosea demonstrates for Israel the persevering love of God for a constantly straying Israel. This love is portrayed in two basic sections of the text. Chapters 1—3 express the love God has for an idolatrous and adulterous nation, while Hosea 4—14 describes the tough love the Lord has for a corrupt people. All of the chosen nation's sins are treated as breach of faith akin to adultery, however, so it is difficult to separate this image from any discussion of Hosea's theology.

The text states that Hosea's ministry transpires during the reigns of Uzziah, Jotham, Ahaz and Hezekiah in Judah, or a span of time stretching anywhere from about 767 to 687 B.C. The picture is clarified a bit by the further statement that he works during the reign of Jeroboam II of Israel, who rules about 782-753 B.C. It is probable that this mention of Jeroboam indicates that his ministry to Israel occurred during the prosperous days before the political upheaval that led to the nation's destruction by Assyria took place in 722 B.C.6 As the only known northern prophet in the canon, he tries to stave off the coming foreign invasion of his homeland by preaching the word while Israel still has time to repent. It is difficult to set the historical scene much more precisely than this. Canonically speaking, the historical setting tells readers that the prophetic word is sent to prevent punishment as much as it is to proclaim it. Texts such as 2 Kings 17 have already made this point clear.

Hosea's calling has sparked serious debate because of its unconventional nature.[7] Yahweh tells him to marry a prostitute and to have "children of unfaithfulness" to show Israel's spiritual adultery (1:2). Many scholars find it impossible to believe that the Lord would command a prophet to marry a woman with a questionable past and then purchase her freedom from slavery after further sin. So they suggest that she was chaste when the marriage occurred,[8] that the phrase may be a metaphorical representation of the fact that all women in Israel were adulterous through their idolatry,[9] that she was a fertility-cult prostitute ("sacred prostitute")[10] or that two women appear in the stories in Hosea 1—3.[11] The clearest meaning of the text is that the Lord did indeed ask Hosea to marry someone who was sexually promiscuous before marriage.[12] Whether or not she promised to be faithful in marriage is another matter. In this way his life parallels Isaiah's call to go naked and barefoot for three years (Is 20:1-6), or Jeremiah's commission to avoid funerals and forsake marriage (Jer 16:1-9) or Ezekiel's responsibility to avoid tears when his beloved wife dies (Ezek 24:15-27). All these acts break important social conventions too, so it is not out of the question for the Lord to require a similar sacrifice on Hosea's part, though his seems to be the greatest burden.

It is also possible that his marrying a compromised woman fits the history of Israel. After all, Ezekiel 20 considers Israel idolatrous even before the exodus, a view reflected in Joshua 24:2 and in Amos 2:4, which says Judah follows lies their fathers pursued, which is most likely a reference to idol worship in the nation's earliest history. The incident of the golden calf at least implies the people had some prior knowledge of idolatry before leaving

Egypt. Given these passages, it is certainly plausible that Gomer's having some prior sexual deviancy might fit the prophecy's view of Israel's pre-Sinai covenant worship habits.

From the start Hosea's marriage to Gomer demonstrates the grace and immeasurable, forgiving love Yahweh has for the chosen people. Gomer bears Hosea at least one child (1:3), yet she also bears at least one child outside the marriage relationship (1:8-9). Like Isaiah's sons, these children have symbolic names calculated to proclaim the prophetic message of coming disaster. These babies are "Jezreel," "Not Pitied" and "Bastard" (1:4-11), names that reveal God's wrath against Israel's monarchy and people and names that speak both of terrible pain in Hosea's household and in God's heart. Israel has cheated on God as surely as Gomer has betrayed Hosea (1:11—2:23).

The nature of Gomer's sin and that of Israel is the same. She is most likely a sacred prostitute for Baal, and the nation has involved itself in Baal worship (2:8-20). What Elijah battled a century earlier remains a threat at this stage of Israel's history. Gomer thinks that her lovers have fed and clothed her, though her husband has actually done so, and Israel mistakenly believes Baal makes the land fertile when Yahweh has truly sustained them (2:8). Through judgment and subsequent renewal the Lord will remove Baalism from the land (2:16-20). Hosea must follow a similar path of tough love to gain his wife's allegiance (2:8-15). When chastisement has done its work the people will once again know the Lord (2:20), a refrain reminiscent of Ezekiel's prophecy.

Hosea completes his symbolic activity by buying his wife back from the slavery she has embraced in 3:1-5. This personal grace reflects Yahweh's kindness to the idolatrous Israel (3:1). The means of permanent grace are the same as in the longer canonical prophecies, for the Lord promises that renewal will be sealed by the emergence of the Davidic monarch so prominent in the eschatalogical passages in Isaiah, Jeremiah and Ezekiel (3:5). In this text seeking the Lord and seeking the Davidic heir are synonymous activities, and this seeking constitutes appropriate fear, or reverence, for the Lord.

Canonical Synthesis: God's Love and Israel's Sin

The book of Hosea dates from times earlier than that of any of the previous canonical prophecies. By placing this material here the canon allows the book to be heard in light of more elaborate treatments of similar themes such as the Lord's anger at idolatry, the renewing nature of judgment and the importance of the Davidic heir for the renewal of the chosen people in Isaiah, Jeremiah and Ezekiel. Hosea influences Jeremiah's emphasis on the nation's adulterous religious practices (Jer 2—6), not the other way around, yet the pupil has the longer and more involved analysis in this case. Thus the canon allows the younger prophecy to appear first as the more thorough statement of this approach to Israelite history.

It is also true that the theological statements made about God's love for Israel in such texts as Jeremiah 2:1—3:5 and Ezekiel 16 and 23 are embodied by Hosea. Here spiritually oriented comments are displayed in the flesh through the prophet's love for his wife. His kindness and forgiveness make God's identical qualities real in history. If anything, the canon saves the most heartrending evidence for Yahweh's covenant love and remnant faithfulness until now. Though Hosea's life and ministry influence prophecies already presented in the canon, the Hebrew text chooses to place the master's life later as the prophets' most powerful statement of betrayal in the face of grace.

Despite the overwhelming sense of love and acceptance Hosea 1—3 exudes, it is also necessary to mark how strikingly this passage uses Gomer's actions to define Israel's sin. She is unfaithful, ungrateful and lacking in compassion and sound judgment. She is as thoughtless as she is adulterous. Her sin envelopes herself, her family, her society and her relationship to the Lord. Yahweh's mercy does not alter the reality of these failures, though it does deal with their consequences. The prophecy does not say what Gomer does with her second chance, but the rest of Hosea and the Twelve has plenty to say about what Israel does with each one of the fresh opportunities to serve Yahweh they receive over the next three centuries.

The God Who Contends with Israel: Hosea 4—14

Spiritual adultery, physical immorality and other acts that constitute covenant breaking continue to permeate the book. These issues provide intricate connections between passages that are otherwise very difficult to unify.[13] At the same time the Lord's determined love for Israel remains a constant factor. The dogged refusal on the people's part to respond positively to this love means that judgment is threatened, and this judgment will cleanse the remnant for service. Despite the ultimate promise of salvation, however, the themes related to the defining of the sins that make Israel fit for punishment take precedence over all hopeful statements.

Hosea 4:1-3 is brief, yet it contains a "comprehensive statement of Israel's guilt and of the punishment to come upon the entire land with all of its creatures."[14] God "contends" with Israel for all the sin in the land. In courtroom language the prophet proclaims a divine lawsuit against law breakers, a procedure that also occurs in 2:4-17, 4:4-6 and 5:3-15 as well as in Isaiah 1:18-20, Jeremiah 2:5-29, Micah 6:1-5 and Malachi 3:5.[15] Israel lacks fidelity, love and knowledge of God, which leads to lying, killing, stealing and adultery (4:1-2). The land mourns as its stewards commit sin after sin (4:3). The rejection of God for other gods leads to corrupt behavior. The breaking of the first commandment leads to the breaking of the others.[16] Israel's disobedience is as complete as Yahweh's love and holiness.

God places the whole nation under condemnation. The people exchange God's glory for idolatry, and the nation follows their example (4:4-9). Idolatry leads to immorality, including the use of Baal prostitutes, so punishment will come like a whirlwind (4:10-19). Israel worships sensuality, while "Yahweh, who would like to be present with his people in genuine faithfulness, remains unknown, even when his name is spoken."[17] Men and women (4:14), priests and kings (5:1-3) all turn aside, and these deeds preclude any healing (5:4-15).

Only true turning from sin to an intimate knowledge of God can save the land from devastation (6:1-3). When God is willing to heal the people they turn from, not to, the Lord (6:4—7:2). There can be no compromise with Baalism, as Exodus 20:3, Deuteronomy 6:4 and Joshua 24:15 have already stated.[18] Only a return to strict Yahwistic monotheism will suffice. Hosea agrees with Elijah on this point, yet the people side with Ahab in this era too. Knowing God is fundamental to their religion (6:6),[19] yet Israel casts off intimate knowledge of God as surely as Adam did in Genesis 3 (6:7). Judgment awaits those who forget their maker (7:3—9:9).

Hosea concludes that the people of his day are simply the latest example of how Israel has historically sinned with idols. In overtones also evident in Jeremiah 2:1—3:5 and Ezekiel 16 and 23, the text says Israel was graciously chosen by God (9:10a). But they commit idolatry at Baal-Peor (Num 25:1-18) and again during the time of the judges (9:10b—10:1). Since the current population does the same, Assyria will remove them and their high places (10:2-15). Like Isaiah 8:1-10, the prophecy considers Assyria Yahweh's means of judging the chosen nation.

God's history with Israel demonstrates true covenant faithfulness. The Lord has done more for Israel than the covenant demands. First, God chose Israel and redeemed them from Egypt (11:1). Nowhere does any Old Testament text so much as imply that this election was anything other than Yahweh's sheer unmerited mercy toward Israel. Second, the Lord called Israel despite the people's constant descent into Baalism and other forms of idolatry (11:2). Third, Yahweh established the northern kingdom because of Solomon's idolatry (1 Kings 11:1-40), yet the people turned from their healer, Yahweh (11:3). Fourth, God has sustained the nation. Fifth, Yahweh plans an Assyrian invasion for Israel's future, which means God's child will be punished (11:5-7). Sixth, after punishing the "son," Yahweh's future includes having compassion upon, then forgiving, the people (11:9-11). Israel's future depends on the Lord's unmerited mercy as much as their origins did. This history exposes the chosen people's history as outright shameful ingratitude.

Yet another historical survey further denounces Israel's actions. God's charge against the nation is stated in terms that parallel their actions and those done by Jacob in early life. Just as Jacob struggled with his brother and the Lord, so Israel has fought against God. Jacob overcame by wrestling with Yahweh, and the people must also find repentance by seeking the Lord (12:2-6). Yahweh will again prove victorious over the rebellious ones, but it remains to be seen whether the nation will turn.[20] Jacob found rest in a relationship with Yahweh, and his descendants may as well, yet they refuse to be at rest, which means they will face judgment (12:14).

A final historical summary concludes the prophecy's denunciation of the sinful chosen people. Through the events described in 1 Kings 11:1-40, the northern tribes grew to prominence as a nation (13:1). Having become noteworthy, however, they turned to all manner of idolatry (13:2-3). At this point in the summary the text reverts to the exodus. Based on this deliverance in history the nation should acknowledge no other god (13:4; cf. Ex 20:1-4). Further, the Lord cared for Israel in the desert (13:5) and then gave them a king (13:10-11), only to be rejected again and again. In the long term God will destroy death and redeem the people (13:14), but in the interim the land will fall (13:15-16). History will unfold at that time as Deuteronomy 27—28 has said it will.

Hosea concludes with the standard prophetic conviction that God's ultimate goal is to heal and save. Idols will be removed, wisdom will be restored and Israel will be renewed (14:1-9). It must be remembered, however, that this cleansing cannot occur without judgment. As N. H. Snaith observes, "Exile awaits Israel, and all chance of avoiding this has gone. Whatever message of hope there is in the genuine writings of Hosea, there is no hope of avoiding this national disaster."[21] God's ways are correct, but the wicked must stumble for this fact to be proven (14:9). Only destruction will ultimately eliminate Israel's idols, just as 2 Kings 17, Isaiah, Jeremiah and Ezekiel have already revealed.

Canonical Synthesis: Hosea, History and Prophecy

Hosea's use of common prophetic images and themes and masterful inclusion of historical summaries help anchor the text firmly in the canon. Such ideas as Israel's covenant breaking amounting to spiritual adultery, God's decision to judge this sin, the Lord's unyielding compassion and future renewal through terrible punishment have many counterparts in Isaiah, Jeremiah and Ezekiel. As will be noted shortly, they also have several parallels in the rest of the Twelve. B. D. Napier properly considers Hosea 11:1-11 a paradigm for all prophetic texts.[22] Besides adapting common themes, the book's consistent appeal to Israelite history gives it historical roots for its arguments. It is evident that Hosea knows the nation's history from Jacob to the exodus, the wilderness era, the settlement in Canaan, the choice of David, the rise of Jeroboam and the rebellion perpetuated by Jehu. At least a thousand years of history and texts ranging from Genesis through Kings are echoed. Though the northern kingdom receives priority, the whole history is reflected, and this whole history reveals a consistent pattern of idolatry. On this point Hosea could not agree more with earlier canonical books.

Taken together, the themes and historical details remind readers of certain matters. First, idolatry is the fundamental sin that poisons the covenant relationship. Idolatry even cuts off the people from their hope of repentance, for idolaters cannot recognize Yahweh's sovereignty in all life's issues. Second, God's covenant with David remains the nation's only chance for permanent renewal (3:1-5). This promise is less prominent than it is in Isaiah, yet is stated clearly nonetheless. Third, God desires to heal sinful Israel and will in fact create a faithful people. The God who rules history refuses to surrender control of the future.

When Hosea closes the chosen nation has begun a terrible spiral downward into sin that must lead to Yahweh's sending punishment. Idolatry, spiritual ignorance and moral impurity will not go unpunished. The situation will worsen until Israel's sin is even more carefully delineated and the Gentile countries are presented as at least as corrupt as the elect nation. The Twelve describes this descent with as much detail and as much alarm as do its canonical prophetic predecessors.

The God Who Rejects Apathy: Joel

Hosea presents a portrait of Israel as a nation bent on sinning and impervious to repentance. The people hear the word of the Lord yet prefer to ignore the message. Thus they are willfully and gladly ignorant of the truth. Hosea's prophecy indicates, however, that this attitude cannot be maintained forever. As in the days of Elijah, a choice must be made between the idols of their age and the one God. Joel heightens the sense that Israel must indeed decide whom they will serve. Here Yahweh rejects apathy and calls for decision.[23]

Two structural options have been forwarded for Joel. Both are based on the importance of the book's main image, which is a lengthy description and adaptation of a locust plague. Either critics divide the text into the description of the locust plague (1:1—2:27) and the coming eschatological age (2:28—3:21), or they separate the book's lament over the locust plague (1:2—2:17) and Yahweh's response to that lament (2:18—3:21). Though the first strategy does reveal the importance of the future in Joel, the second possibility allows both the book's literary and theological emphases to be seen. Viewed this way, the text stresses the God who causes mourning and the God who brings renewal. Throughout the book the text urges repentance as the key to renewal and argues that only the penitent will receive restoration. No room for indecision is allowed. These themes link Joel to each of the prophetic works that precede it.

The God Who Causes Mourning: Joel 1:1—2:17

After a summons to hear God's message and to proclaim what follows to future generations (1:2-3), tasks the canon's existence guarantees, the prophecy reveals its first governing metaphor. The land has been invaded by locusts yet will suffer even more when a swarming, devouring nation attacks (1:4-12). Scholars debate whether the invasion is past or present, literal or figurative, nature-induced or military-oriented. Probably the text uses a literal event to declare that a more terrible catastrophe will occur if the people do not repent. Seen this way, the locust plague initiates God's purging of sin from the land.[24]

This cleansing is nothing less than the day of the Lord, an event that calls for lamenting, wailing, fasting and solemn assembly (1:13-15). The announcement of the day in 1:15 closely parallels Isaiah 13:6 and Ezekiel 30:2-3[25] and brings to mind the fearful scenes portrayed in Deuteronomy 27—28 and 32.[26] Yahweh sends both plague and military defeat as punishment for covenant breaking. It is the Lord who causes this mourning over the loss of cattle and crops (1:16-20). The fierce foe does not come by accident but at the direct command of Israel's God (2:1-11). If Joel is read in isolation, no specific reason for this punishment is given. Read canonically, however, the Former and Latter Prophets have already given ample justification for divine wrath. What unfolds here relates to the whole of Israelite history, not just to Joel's era.

As in Jeremiah and Hosea, the solution to the problem is for Israel to repent. This call to mourning is for lamenting their transgressions. Fasting and weeping should produce clean hearts and changed lives (2:12-13). No other hope for avoiding the devastation exists (2:14). Still, Raymond Dillard observes, "Yet even in the face of repentance, God remains sovereign. Repentance no more controls him than do the magic incantations of pagan priests."[27] Mere ritual alone will not move God, though serious prayer may well do so (2:15-17). Perhaps humble repentance may yet stave off justified severity.

Canonical Synthesis: Repentance and the Day of Yahweh

This section of Joel is one of sixteen canonical passages that discuss judgment as the day of the Lord.[28] These texts declare punishment for Israel and the

Gentiles. They depict natural disaster, supernatural catastrophes and military invasions. They argue that God works through such occurrences to eliminate sin and create a cleansed earth for the faithful to inhabit. Here in Joel, the day is not a final event, but Zephaniah 1:7-8 and Zechariah 14:1 envision a final day of Yahweh that will bring history to a climactic point. Since human beings have no idea which they are facing, a quick, decided return to Yahweh is the only prudent response to an announcement that God's day has arrived.

The God Who Restores the Penitent: Joel 2:18—3:21

Nowhere in the Old Testament does Yahweh forgive and restore a stubbornly rebellious people. Repentance must precede pardon and cleansing, regardless of how much sorrowful confession and communal fasting take place. Isaiah 56—60 has already made this point clear. Nowhere does the canon expect that sinful human beings can maintain their commitments to the Lord without divine help. Ezekiel 39:25-29 and Jeremiah 31:31-34 state that God's Spirit must change hearts for repentance to become permanent. Thus it is not surprising to find Yahweh restoring Israel's fortunes through human repentance and the direct intervention of the Spirit in 2:18—3:21.

After the locust plague's full effect has been experienced, Yahweh pities the people (2:18). This reaction mirrors the Lord's love for Israel expressed in Ezekiel 16 and Hosea 11:1-9. God cannot, will not, give up the chosen, beloved nation. Therefore the Lord determines to restore the people's fortunes (2:19-26). The goal of this activity is the same as Yahweh's work in Isaiah 45:5, 21 and 49:23, which is to demonstrate that Yahweh is God and there is no other deity (2:27). Devotion to this monotheistic principle will eliminate the sort of transgressions that lead Yahweh to send judgment.

God's Spirit will complete and secure the restoration. All the Lord's people will receive the Spirit of God, just as the elders received Yahweh's Spirit in Numbers 11:29.[29] This time, however, the outpouring of the Spirit will signal the end times. Every believer will know the Lord's word and will, a situation approximating the assertion in Jeremiah 31:31-34 that all that constitute Israel will know the Lord due to changed hearts.[30] It is this Spirit that Ezekiel 36:24-32 says will turn the people's hearts from stone to flesh and thus create a restored community for the restored land. Scott Hafemann concludes correctly that "it is the future bestowal of this life-giving (divine) Spirit which forms the core of the prophetic expectation for restoration."[31] One cannot separate restoration from the pouring out of God's Spirit in the prophetic literature. It is also impossible to exclude persons from the faithful remnant based on age or gender.

Joel 2:30-32 further describes the day of the Lord as a time of odd events, of punishment for sin and of salvation for the remnant in Zion. Isaiah 13:9-16 has a similar vision of cosmic disorder and severe judgment, while Isaiah 60—62 focuses on Zion as the place of refuge for the remnant. Ronald Clements observes that Zion's protective role here marks this text as a classic restoration passage.[32] Joel 3:1-8 includes sinners from all nations in the devastation, and 3:9-15 portrays all those who have not decided to serve the Lord as waiting for Yahweh's decision for how they should be punished. The universal nature of this judgment may inspire books like Daniel to move toward apocalyptic, transhistorical descriptions of the end times.[33]

Joel concludes with an image of God roaring from Zion so that sin will be eradicated and God will be recognized as sovereign Lord (3:16-21). This same picture appears in Amos 1:2, so Yahweh's anger links both prophecies. Again judgment occurs to demonstrate the Lord's protection of the faithful and fierce opposition to the sinful (3:16). It happens to renew the holy land and the holy city (3:17-18). God's will is to redeem those who repent, not to destroy indiscriminately.

Canonical Synthesis: God's Spirit and the Day of the Lord

Besides the passages already noted, Joel 2:18—3:21 has strong ties to the Law's description of punishment for covenant breaking and to Acts 2:17-21. Walter Kaiser notes that several texts in the Pentateuch speak of judgment as a visitation from God (cf. Ex 32:34; Num 24:14; Deut 4:30; 31:17-18, 20). Such "visits" depict God acting directly to remove sin from the covenant people, and the concept parallels the notion of a day in which God attacks transgression.[34] The point is that judgment is more than a natural consequence. It is a specific action Yahweh does in history as the one God who rules history.

The text in Acts reflects Peter's belief that the Spirit's outpouring is part of eschatological restoration. All God's people know the Lord and share the Lord, a fact their Spirit intoxication underscores. A canonical reading of the prophets makes his interpretation plausible and accurate. Without the Spirit, there can be no complete renewal of the remnant, of the earth or of Zion.

Joel not only continues to build the prophetic literature's concern for the present and vision for the future but also furthers the Twelve's case against Israel's sin. Hosea offers repentance, but the people reject knowledge and mercy. Joel offers a bright future, yet no permanent repentance occurs. The book ends with Yahweh roaring; then Amos begins with the same image. Sin still angers God, for sin continues to plague the people. Joel has not dealt extensively with what specific errors anger Yahweh, but Amos will not hesitate to do so.

The God Who Roars Against Sin: Amos

Amos is much more specific about Israel's and the nations' sins than is either Hosea or Joel. This prophecy expresses exactly what constitutes covenant breaking for the chosen people and what amounts to sin on the Gentiles' part. Amos takes an almost encyclopedic approach while discussing Israel's breach of the Sinai covenant and the nations' breach of the universal covenant of the human race. Over and over the prophet denounces sinful behavior, and with each succeeding section the text includes another group of people until all are under God's condemnation. All, that is, except the remnant. Like Amos, they are victims caught in the web of the seemingly hopelessly ingrained sin that pervades that era. According to Amos, God roars against this sin and is determined to obliterate it. Yahweh's patience with sinners has not resulted in change, so judgment is about to unfold.

Amos works about the same time as Hosea. The book's superscription states that Amos preaches during the reigns of Jeroboam II of Israel and Uzziah of Judah. He preaches in the northern kingdom at Bethel and Samaria, probably about 760 B.C. If so, he may be the first "writing prophet."[35] Regardless of the exact date, he preaches to the northern kingdom three to four decades before the Assyrian conquest. Like Hosea, Amos attempts to move the nation toward repentance so that defeat will not become necessary. Instead of heeding Amos, the people continue the slide into sin described so graphically in the first six books of the Twelve.

Amos may be divided into five distinct parts, each of which furthers the Twelve's denunciation of sin and demonstrates Amos's ability to make specific claims about those sins. Amos 1—2 introduces the prophet, his major theme and the power and importance of his message. Yahweh is portrayed as roaring against sin (1:2) and ready to judge Israel, Judah and the surrounding countries for their iniquities (1:3—2:16). Amos 3—6 focuses on the sins perpetuated by the covenant people, with the main emphasis falling on the northern kingdom's activities. As in Joel, the day of the Lord is announced as the natural result of the people's refusal to change their lives. Here the Creator of the whole earth threatens the whole earth. Here the Lord demands to be heard. Amos 7:1—9:10 consists of five visions and an episode from the prophet's life. Now the Lord is the one God who executes punishment. Here God acts as the One who scorches the earth, measures the land for devastation and kills the wicked with a sword. Amos 9:11-15 closes the prophecy with a hopeful statement about how Israel will one day be rebuilt and be led by David's descendant. As with his canonical predecessors, Amos sees no other way for the nation to experience restoration. Yahweh must act directly to restore their fortunes, and the Davidic ruler must take charge of the land, or there can be no renewal.

The God Who Roars Against Sin: Amos 1—2

Placed after Joel, Amos picks up the theme of an lion-like Yahweh roaring against the people (cf. Joel 3:16; Amos 1:2). God's anger is directed not just at Israel and Judah but at six other countries as well. Each of these nations commits atrocities that require the righteous God to judge them. The following list shows the problems the text discusses.

1. Syria has shown excessive cruelty and violence in war (1:3-6).[36] They have treated people as if they were objects.[37]

2. Gaza has captured cities and sold its citizens into slavery (1:6-8). Most likely these cities were unprotected.[38] If so, this act was as vicious as it was cowardly.

3. Tyre has sold allies into slavery (1:9-10). Lies and personal gain dictate their foreign policy.

4. Edom has displayed anger against others that never wanes. This anger shows no compassion (1:11-12). It tears its victims like some sort of wild animal.[39]

5. Ammon has committed war atrocities such as ripping open pregnant women (1:13-15). The women and their unborn children hardly represent a threat to the Ammonite army. Injustice and terror are the only goals such behavior addresses.

6. Moab has desecrated graves (2:1-3). Their desire for revenge does not stop even when their enemy dies.

God's ability to judge these lands demonstrates his sovereignty over the whole earth. God knows and sees what they do, which reveals the Lord's omnipresence and omniscience. Yahweh holds these countries responsible for their actions despite the fact that they are not the covenant nation. They are guilty of perpetuating behavior that they do not want done to themselves, so the Lord has just cause to denounce them.

Yahweh also roars against Judah and Israel. Judah rejects the law and subsequently serves other gods (2:4-5). Such fundamental breaches of the Sinai covenant cannot go unpunished and have never gone unpunished in the history of Israel, whether in the desert (Ex 32—34; Num 25:1-18), or in the land itself (Judg 2:6-23). Israel has departed even further from covenant faith. They practice immorality associated with Baalism (2:6-8). Thus they have learned to buy and sell human beings to make the slightest profit. All these sins have occurred despite the Lord's revelation of divine standards mediated through the prophets and Nazirites (2:9-12). They have rejected both revelation and its attendant salvation, so the Lord will send judgment in the form of foreign invasion, just as Deuteronomy 27—28 warns (2:13-16).

Canonical Synthesis: Worldwide Sin

By now canonical interpreters are familiar with texts that list and condemn Gentile nations alongside the covenant people. Isaiah 13—23, Jeremiah

46—51 and Ezekiel 25—32 have all used this strategy as a part of their condemnations of sin and announcements of punishment. In this text the same sorts of concerns are evident; plus the passage makes the Twelve's statements about sin more specific. All these texts indicate that sin is worldwide in scope, dangerous to its adherents and utterly unacceptable to the Lord who made people and the earth for better purposes.

Amos's summary of how the Lord has dealt with Israel matches the historical viewpoint found in the Former Prophets, the Latter Prophets and the Writings. Israel moves toward destruction because it breaks the covenant, refuses to heed the prophets and ignores all opportunities to repent. Thus Amos 2:9-16 substantially agrees with the summary found in 2 Kings 17, Jeremiah 2:1—3:5 and Ezekiel 16 and 23. Summaries of Israelite sin such as those found in Psalm 78, Daniel 9:1-19 and Nehemiah 1:4-11 also fit this general mold. There can be no doubt that across the canon there is great agreement about what caused Israel to be destroyed. Polytheism fueled by covenant infidelity destroys the chosen people.

The God Who Demands to Be Heard: Amos 3—6

God commands attention[40] in this section by demanding that the people "listen" (3:1; 4:1; 5:1). What they hear is that they have neglected the privileges inherent in being God's chosen people.[41] By rejecting revelation they forget how to do right and are thereby turned over to the same sort of devastation all sinful groups receive (3:1-15). Israel has become a nation of luxury-addicted oppressors and religious syncretists (4:1-5; 6:1-7). Despite God's specific attempts to bring them to repentance, they remain unmoved, even unaware, about how and why Yahweh acts (4:6-13). God's "day" will sweep all such pretense away (5:8-27; 6:8-14). On that day the Lord will be heard.

Amos 4:13 and 5:8 state exactly why God has the right to punish all nations: the Lord is the Creator. Therefore it is Yahweh's prerogative to turn the light to darkness or to send the waters from their boundaries onto the land. B. K. Smith observes, "The one whose power could form the majestic greatness of the mountains and control the fierceness of the storm is one before whom the wise should tremble."[42] This fact has been true since Yahweh decided to punish the earth by flood. This God deserves and demands sole worship and righteous behavior yet has received neither, so the Creator will become the destroyer (5:18-27).

Canonical Synthesis: The Day of the Lord and Universal Sin

Amos 3—6 mirrors other texts that insist on justice motivated by faithfulness to the Lord and the Lord's word. Deuteronomy 17:14-20 considers the law the basis for and guarantor of all safety and fairness in society. Isaiah 1:13-17 also links worship irregularities with injustice.[43] When one forgets how to treat Yahweh mistreatment of other people soon follows. Sacred and secular concerns cannot be separated in any effective way. Jeremiah 22:1-5 highlights the king's responsibility to protect the weak and helpless against oppressors. The laments in Psalms argue that the Lord will not allow the weak to be overcome by the wicked (e.g., Ps 3—7), and Proverbs 14:31 counsels mercy, not oppression, toward the poor. Amos's convictions about justice are as canonically attested as are his beliefs about Israel's history.

Amos likewise describes the day of the Lord in language similar to that in previous canonical prophecies.[44] Isaiah says that on that day the proud will be humbled, idols will be demolished, armies will be routed, oppression will cease, luxury will be eliminated and leaders will be scarce (Is 2:9—4:6). Isaiah also envisions all nations assessed and natural disasters occurring at that time (Is 13:9-22). He considers judgment vengeance on God's enemies, as does Jeremiah (cf. Is 34:8-14; Jer 46:10). Ezekiel 7:10-13 states that the proud will be humbled, while 30:3 claims the Gentiles will be devastated. Joel states that the day will come with thorough defeat of the wicked and destruction of the land (Joel 1:15-18). Amos's messages on judgment are similar in their emphasis on punishment overtaking the wicked of every nation (1:3—2:3), in their comments against the proud (4:1-3; 6:1-7), in their winnowing of human life (5:1-3) and their emphasis on the removal of unacceptable worship practices (5:21-24). In Amos, as in the other prophecies, this day both punishes and removes sin, and it is Yahweh who alone plans and executes this terrible time.[45] God promises to judge and will do so.

The God Who Rises Against Israel: Amos 7:1—9:10

Five visions and a single narrative form the heart of this section. Each of these segments demonstrates the prophet's role and the Lord's character. They also solidify the book's depiction of Israel as a nation determined to sin and thus determined to receive the penalty for their actions. What is most striking is the fact that punishment could have been avoided had the people paid the slightest attention to the prophetic word.

Twice Amos has visions of destruction, prays for Yahweh to spare Israel and finds the Lord willing to wait patiently for repentance (7:1-6). By Amos's time God has endured Israelite idolatry for nearly two centuries (c. 930-760 B.C.). Repentance has not materialized (4:6-13), yet still the Lord relents. The third vision, however, is of God using a plumbline to measure Israel for destruction (7:7-9). Now God will not wait. Why? Because the people persist in improper worship (7:9) and because their religious leaders refuse to accept Amos's words as coming from the Lord (7:10-17). Instead they choose political approval.[46] Thus cut off from Yahweh, further visions describe the

devastation the nation has chosen over God's mercy (8:1—9:10). The day of
the Lord will come with all the features that have already been described.

Twice in 7:1—9:10 the text highlights the life-giving importance of God's
word. The first time is the incident at Bethel when the priest Amaziah accuses
Amos of being a typical prophet for hire along the lines of the court prophets
in 1 Kings 22. The twist here is that Amaziah assumes Amos attempts to stir
up political trouble in the northern kingdom. By refusing to hear Amos,
Amaziah really rejects the Lord's word, which exposes him, his family and
his hearers to danger (7:14-17). The second instance appears in 8:11-12,
where Yahweh promises a famine of divine revelation that will endanger
Israel more than a famine of food. This famine will take place because the
revealed covenant and prophetic word have both been ignored (2:4-16;
3:3-8).

Without God's word the nation cannot survive, for they live not on bread
but by God's word, according to Deuteronomy 8:3 and 32:47. Similarly
Deuteronomy 18:14-22 and 2 Kings 17 place great emphasis on prophecy as
God's direct communication with the people. Given the importance of the
prophetic word, it is likely, as H. G. M. Williamson argues, that Amos and
his preaching embody God's plumbline. When Israel rejects God's word,
judgment falls.[47] God's word provides both Israel's greatest chance for
knowledge of God's ways and reception of Yahweh's mercy yet is also the
evidence that they reject the Lord and choose punishment. The canon cannot
heal when it is not heeded.

Amos's visions resonate with experiences shared by Isaiah, Jeremiah,
Ezekiel and Zechariah.[48] These visions typically reveal God's greatness,
coming devastation or the Lord's creation of a better future.[49] Though they
differ in details, all prophetic visions demonstrate the prophets' close
relationship with God (cf. 1 Kings 22:19-23; Amos 3:7). Visions distinguish
prophets as those who know and experience Yahweh's revealed message.
Therefore Amos's historical frame of reference, views on the day of the Lord
and attitudes about the divine word find support throughout the canon.

The God Who Restores David's Fallen Tent: Amos 9:11-15

Though Amos focuses on Yahweh's anger at sin, the book closes on a
positive, hopeful note. "In that day," which surely refers to the aftermath of
the day of the Lord,[50] God will restore David's dynasty and the nation
(9:11-12). Israel will possess the promised land, and the land's fertility will
far transcend its current reality (9:13-15). God's people will then inhabit the
land forever (9:15). Given the lack of response to his message, Amos
discusses no other possibility for renewal. God must act directly to redeem
the people through the Davidic king, or the chosen people have no future.

Canonical Synthesis: Israel's Renewal

Amos 9:11-15, though shorter than many of its companion texts, agrees with previous canonical comments on Israel's future. Every preceding prophecy except Joel defines a bright future for Israel by first highlighting the centrality of David's lineage. They all emphasize the following order of events: the judgment of Israel and the nations' sins, the coming of the Davidic ruler and the restoration and permanent occupation of an ideal land. Always the Davidic descendant is the catalyst for renewal. Zechariah will echo this conviction later in the Twelve (cf. Zech 9:9; 12:7—13:6). Acts 15:15-17 cites Amos 9:11-12 as evidence that Gentiles will come to the Lord and thereby become part of God's people, the church. Luke probably cites the Septuagint, for he includes the phrase "that the rest of men may seek the Lord," which is missing from the Hebrew text.[51] Though the added phrase strengthens the sense of Gentile nations coming to the Lord, this idea is not absent in the Hebrew text and is prevalent in earlier canonical passages (cf. Is 19:19-25; 56:7). Acts and Amos agree that the Davidic king's rule will include nations beyond Israel that are called by Yahweh's name (15:17; 9:12). Acts obviously believes Jesus is the Davidic ruler and the church is the multinational body he rules.[52] Amos looks to a restored community all united under Davidic rule.[53] Acts finds Gentiles in many countries believing in Jesus, the son of David, and considers this phenomenon a reasonable interpretation of Amos 9:11-12.[54] Given the worldwide scope of the Davidic king's rule envisioned in Isaiah 11:1-10, the passage in Acts hardly overstates the king's potential kingdom.[55]

Amos provides a clear definition of covenant breaking. It is committing adultery, doing acts of violence, lying, oppressing others and perverting justice. At the heart of covenant breaking is idolatry. When Israel turns away from Yahweh, they of necessity break Yahweh's standards. Thus Amos also provides a clear picture of the punishment Leviticus 26 and Deuteronomy 27—28 threaten. God continues to promise judgment for covenant breaking, and there can be no doubt God will keep this promise. The good news is that renewal lies beyond this devastation. The God who roars will eventually also be the God who heals.

The God Who Judges Pride: Obadiah

Obadiah unfolds in three basic parts. First, verses 1-9 announce Edom's destruction for its pride and its hatred of Israel. Second, verses 10-14 denounce Edom for its part in the defeat of Jerusalem in 587 B.C. Third, verses 15-21 contrast Edom's fate on the day of the Lord with Judah's returning remnant. God's wrath at Edom's pride and viciousness permeate the prophecy.

Several earlier books have already prepared interpreters for the denunciation of Edom in Obadiah 1-9. Israel and Edom have battled since their patriarchs Jacob and Esau wrestled in the womb (Gen 25:19-34). Edom barred Israel from passing through during the wilderness period (Num 20:14-21), and David conquered this neighboring state (2 Sam 8:13-14). Edom revolted against Judah in about 850 B.C. (2 Kings 8:20-22) and could hardly have mourned Jerusalem's demise.[56] Isaiah 21:11-12, Jeremiah 49:7-22, Ezekiel 25:12-14, Amos 1:11-12 and Malachi 1:2-5 all inveigh against Edom's treatment of Israel.[57] Joel 3:19-21 says Judah will inhabit cruel Edom's land, Amos 1:6 and 1:9 condemn Edom's buying and selling of slaves, Amos 1:11-12 claims Edom's wrath never ceases, and Amos 9:11-12 indicates that Edom will again be ruled by a Davidic king. Only this last passage offers any hope that the Edomites will ever serve the Lord. The dismal prospects for Edom stated in Obadiah are hardly unprecedented in the canon.

Edom's pride (3-4) has betrayed them. They believe their mountain fortresses make their land impregnable,[58] but they have not counted on God's power. God will bring them down (4). This imagery sounds very much like Yahweh's statements against Babylon in Isaiah 14:12-16 and against Tyre in Ezekiel 28:17. Pride separates people from Yahweh, so the Lord must remove it.

Obadiah 10-14 says that Edom's pride led them to stand "aloof" when Jerusalem was defeated (11). At that time Edom gloated over Judah's ruin (12-13). Once again Edom acted as flesh traders when Judahites were captured and sold (14). These sorts of sins have already been condemned in Amos 1:6-12. Edom is loyal only to itself, which indicates arrogant self-consumption.

The day of the Lord will remove Edom's proud populace and exalt Judah's humble survivors. Edom will experience God's justice by having their deeds turned against them (15). They will learn the fundamental fact made so clear in Amos 1:3—2:3 that God's judgment will fall on every nation (15). Further, they will discover how special Zion is to God (17), a point underscored in Isaiah 62, Jeremiah 30—33 and Ezekiel 40—48. Finally, they will see Judah's exiles return to the land (19-20). God's rule in Zion on behalf of the remnant constitutes the kingdom of God on earth (21; cf. Is 25:6-8). God is sovereign, and God fights for Israel, thus fulfilling the promise made to Abraham to defeat his seed's enemies (Gen 12:1-3).[59]

Without question, Obadiah furthers the Twelve's emphasis on the Gentiles' sins and on Yahweh's right to judge the earth. Edom's activities demonstrate that only the Lord's direct intervention can save the Gentiles. No repentance is forthcoming. Therefore the day of Yahweh must come as a cleansing agent for all people, not just Israel. It is this very direct intervention that provides the backdrop for Jonah.

The God Who Sends Prophets to the Gentiles: Jonah

Jonah helps ease any fears that the Lord does not care for non-Jewish nations that may have arisen due to certain statements in Joel, Amos and Obadiah. Jonah proves that indeed God does love and care for even the Assyrians, the most vicious and powerful of all Israel's ancient enemies. Isaiah 19:19-25 has already made this point, but the flow of the Twelve requires a similar affirmation here. God sends a prophet to preach to the Assyrians so that they, too, may come to know the God who has created the heavens and the earth. Jonah's reluctance to undertake this task continues the Twelve's emphasis on the hatred Israel and the nations share for one another, a situation that makes it highly unlikely that they will be reconciled to one another before the day of the Lord.

As could be expected, the account of Jonah being swallowed by a fish has absorbed an inordinate amount of scholarly effort. Experts who doubt the possibility of this experience interpret the book as a parable, a parable-like story, an allegory or some other form of literature that tells an important lesson without being literally true.[60] Authors who insist on the probability of a miracle in this instance tend to argue for the historical accuracy of the account.[61] These writers also point out the similarities between Jonah and the acounts about Elijah and Elisha and thereby conclude that the mode of narration in Jonah approximates that of similar stories.[62] It is also true that the prophetic miracle accounts differ in manner of presentation from other events recounted in the same books only in their inclusion of miracles. Thus, as with so many other issues in Old Testament studies, Jonah's interpretation hinges on theological convictions held by its commentators.

Though the issue of the historicity of Jonah's experiences is an important detail and this volume accepts its factuality, focusing on this issue does not do justice to the book's theological substance. The same is true of emphasizing a second major concern of interpreters, which is the fact that Jonah predicts the destruction of Nineveh, but the populace's repentance renders that prediction void. Does prophecy fail? Is Jonah a false prophet by Deuteronomy's standards?[63] To frame Jonah in this manner is to neglect the major thrust of canonical prophecy. To interpret Jonah accurately, it is necessary to shift the focus from the prophet to the God who sends the prophet in the first place.

Jonah unfolds quite cleanly within a narrative framework. First, 1:1-16 recounts God's call to Jonah and the prophet's running from that calling. The God who calls here is a God who cares enough about Nineveh to explain their sins to them. Second, 1:17—2:10 covers Jonah's time in the whale and his decision to undertake the preaching mission to Nineveh. Now the Lord is portrayed not only as the One who coerces the prophet but also as the

God who preserves his life through the agency of the great fish. Third, 3:1-10 discloses Jonah's ministry to the Assyrians. The prophet's success with so small an effort highlights God's direct act in healing the people. Fourth, 4:1-11 reveals Jonah's anger at Yahweh's mercy. Again the point is the Lord's love for all people. In contrast, the prophet complains about God's kindness, despite the fact that he himself has benefited from God's deliverance. The irony throughout the account is palpable.[64]

The God Who Calls the Prophet: Jonah 1:1-16

To this point in Scripture readers have grown used to encountering call stories in which the recipients of the call express doubt or make excuses but always respond eventually to the Lord's summons. Jonah breaks this mold. He has been identified as an accurate prophet in 2 Kings 14:25, where he predicts military victory for Israel. Now, however, he runs from the Lord's call; he attempts to run from the Lord's presence (1:2-3). God's call does not stop with this refusal, for Yahweh causes a great storm to toss the ship in which Jonah travels (1:4-5). The pagan sailors attempt to save Jonah and then offer sacrifices to the Lord when the sea turns calm after Jonah is tossed overboard (1:6-16). Jonah confesses that he is rebelling against the God who created the heavens and earth (1:9). His offhand statement leads to the sailors' conversion (1:16). God's sending of Jonah has already begun to pay dividends among the Gentiles.

Canonical Synthesis: God's Love for All People

This scene underscores the Lord's concern for Nineveh. At the same time, it emphasizes God's direct action in the saving of human beings. God intervened in the lives of Abraham, Isaac, Jacob, Moses, David and the prophets in order to change the direction of Israel's future. The same impulse appears here on behalf of the Gentiles. Thus the book's major theme, Yahweh's mercy toward the whole human race,[65] emerges in the very first segment. The prophet does not accept the Lord's vision at this point. He does not resonate with texts such as Isaiah 19:19-25, nor does he grasp the full implications of his confession that Yahweh created the world. His view of God remains landlocked and culture-bound.

The God Who Delivers the Prophet: Jonah 1:17—2:10

Despite the obvious discomfort involved, the fish that swallows Jonah must be seen as an instrument of deliverance for the prophet. Leslie Allen observes, "The Lord of the sea is Lord also of its creatures, and his providential control extends over both. . . . The deliverance of Jonah is a prime factor in the story as a whole, not only for its own sake, but for its implications in the latter part of the narrative."[66] Jonah's psalm (2:2-9) stresses the Lord's alleviating his distress and also highlights the difference between the Lord who does save and idols who cannot do so (2:8-9). Once he clarifies his attitude, he is deposited on dry land (2:10).

Once again the prophet confesses a central Old Testament truth. Having noted the Lord's position as Creator, Jonah makes the logical comment that only Yahweh is a living, hearing, acting, saving God. The issue that remains to be resolved is whether the prophet will take this belief and translate it into ministry to the whole creation or not. Stated theology will not suffice. Jonah's theology must become as active as the Lord's concern.

The God Who Forgives the Penitent: Jonah 3:1-10

Jonah's message to Nineveh's people is that they will be destroyed in forty days (3:1-4). In response they follow the perfect sequence for repentance. They believe God's word (3:5), humble themselves (3:5-8), change their wicked ways (3:8) and place themselves under God's mercy (3:9). It is difficult to imagine a more thorough or unexpected response to a prophetic message. The prophets have not experienced a similar positive response to their preaching to this point in the canon.

The people of Nineveh hope that the Lord is merciful, and their hopes are fulfilled. God "relents," just as after the incident with the golden calf the Lord relents from destroying the people and starts over with Moses (Ex 32:12). God's forgiveness in this instance is hardly a failure of prophecy. Rather it fulfills the intent of prophecy in the whole canon. For instance, Hosea 6:1-3 counsels the people to repent and receive the Lord's forgiveness, yet no change occurs. Joel 2:12-14 encourages repentance and hopes for renewal in language very close to that in Jonah 3:9. Amos 4:6-13 mourns continuously the nation's refusal to repent and thereby avoid judgment. Prophecy is not offered to relieve God of the responsibility to warn before punishing. It intends to effect change in its hearers. The existence of the remnant makes this point clear. Jonah may believe he has failed if the city is not devastated; if so, he does not grasp the purpose of prophecy any more than he understands the practical implications of creation theology or monotheism.

The God Who Is Gracious and Compassionate: Jonah 4:1-11

One last time the prophet confesses theology that he does not translate into appropriate action. He confesses that Yahweh is gracious, compassionate and patient, yet he does not appreciate those qualities if they are directed toward Assyrians. As Creator, only God, compassionate one, in short everything that Exodus 34:6 and the rest of Scripture teach, Yahweh knows that the sinful in all lands need divine grace. God also knows that only direct divine action will turn the sinful of all lands toward renewal and forgiveness. Jonah sees Yahweh's kindness as an overly generous treatment of the Assyrians.[67] He cares about a plant that he did not make yet wonders why the Lord is so concerned for people the Lord made (4:10-11).

Canonical Synthesis: God's Character

This final scene captures again the essence of the Lord's nature. Here God creates, calls, sustains, reveals, judges and forgives. There is no other God to do these things or any other things for that matter. Even when God's chosen servants fail to see the implications of canonical faith, the Lord continues to act according to the principles stated there. God does not act oddly in Jonah. Yahweh acts as the text has taught the reader to expect.

It is good to note that the Lord's character remains intact in Jonah, but it is somewhat depressing to see that Israel continues to sin even in the face of a great miracle of repentance. If a prophet can despise the Assyrians in spite of the theology they (the prophets) possess, then it is likely that people whose theology is less developed will as well. Again it appears that little if any reconciliation between Israel and its neighbors will happen. Sin continues to distort and impair relationships on the international scene.

The God Who Testifies Against Sin: Micah

Micah completes the Twelve's emphasis on the description of sin by summarizing and expanding concepts already discussed. Set in the last half of the eighth-century B.C. (1:1), this prophecy rehearses the tragic fact that the punishment depicted in the next three books need never have occurred. Repentance could have staved off judgment, as Jonah proves, but the covenant people fail to change. Therefore, as Obadiah has already shown, punishment will overtake the people. Micah portrays the Lord as testifying against the earth for its inhabitants' refusal to heed divine warnings.

Isaiah and Micah are not just near-historical contemporaries. They both also employ a technique of shifting between present and future realities that helps shape their books. Like Isaiah, Micah moves back and forth between how the present needs reformation and how God will guarantee a bright future for the remnant. By doing so Micah continues to testify against sin yet also manages to declare how that sin will eventually be negated. As in the previous canonical prophecies, Micah believes the emergence of a Davidic ruler and the cleansing nature of the day of the Lord will provide the means of renewal for Israel and the nations. Thus, like those texts, Micah believes restoration lies well in the future.

This emphasis on now and then helps give order to a book scholars find difficult to outline.[68] Several structural options have been suggested, and these fall into three categories. Some writers break the prophecy at every new call to "hear" (1:2; 3:1; 6:1), a strategy that stresses the fact that each of these segments contains threats of doom and promises of hope.[69] Other commentators divide the prophecy into Micah 1—3, 4—5 and 6—7 based on thematic concerns.[70] In this approach each section deals with doom and hope, but the long-term benefits are centered in Micah 4—5. Finally, some experts believe the book has two basic parts, Micah 1—5 and 6—7.[71] These individuals conclude that the first five chapters focus on the sins of the whole earth, while the last two chapters stress Israel's sins. Though each possibility has strengths and weaknesses, this study adopts the second approach because it reflects the book's main thematic and temporal emphases.

Seen this way, Micah 1—3 highlights the God who testifies against the present sins of Israel and the Gentiles. God pronounces woe on all who sin yet reserves blessings for the remnant. Micah 4—5 presents a God who in the future exalts the remnant above all the people of the earth. Here Yahweh guarantees the future by sending a Davidic ruler. Micah 6—7 presents the God who removes sin for Abraham's sake. Yahweh keeps the covenant by removing barriers to its keeping. Therefore the Lord speaks against sin in the present and the future based on past promises. God testifies against sinners but also to the remnant's faithfulness.

The God Who Denounces Present Sins: Micah 1—3

Micah's catalog of contemporary sins mirrors that of previous texts. God's vehement anger over worldwide iniquity in 1:2-4 sounds very much like the powerful statements in Isaiah 1—6 and Amos 1—2, to name just two passages. Likewise the cause of the Lord's anger, idolatry (1:5-7), revisits the complaints of Isaiah, Jeremiah, Ezekiel, Hosea and Amos, and calling idolatry "harlotry" (1:7) is reminiscent of Hosea. Though it is quite creative in its own right,[72] the list of towns that will be destroyed (1:10-16) is not unlike Amos 1:2—2:3 or even Isaiah 13—23 or Jeremiah 46—51 in strategy and intent. Defeat and exile await the rebellious people, just as Deuteronomy 27—28 promises.

"Woe" awaits sinners (2:1). Sin is defined here as willful, calculated and deceitful defrauding of God and neighbor (2:1-2). It is birthed in pride (2:3), fed by liars who conceal revelation (2:6-11) and doomed from the start (2:3, 12-13). It is perpetuated at the highest levels by leaders who rule for personal gain, who rip their constituents to pieces (3:1-3). Leaders, priests and prophets alike fill the land with bloodshed yet somehow think God is with them (3:9-12). True prophets preach, yet their message, Yahweh's message, is rejected (3:4-8). Therefore they will soon look for a word from God but receive no answer (3:6-7).

Canonical Synthesis: Woe for the Wicked

Unmistakable canonical images are brought to mind from reading Micah 2—3. Several texts in Isaiah (Is 5:8-24; 10:1-4), Jeremiah (Jer 22:13-17) and Amos (Amos 5:7, 10; 5:18-20; 6:1-3) pronounce "woe" on the wicked. God condemns those who plan evil in Amos 8:4-6, Jeremiah 4:14, Ezekiel 11:12 and Proverbs 6:10.[73] Exodus 20:17 commands Israel not to covet, and Amos 8:11-12 warns of the consequences of a famine of God's word. Jeremiah 8:4-17 denounces wicked leaders who take the people to destruction. The list could be extended, but the point is clear: when God testifies against sin in Micah 1—3 that testimony is backed by the whole of Scripture. The sins of the present preclude blessing and beckon punishment for all but the remnant and their king (2:12-13).

The God Who Will Exalt the Remnant: Micah 4—5

Micah and Isaiah agree on the fundamental elements of the renewal that will emerge out of judgment. Micah 4:1-3 and Isaiah 2:2-4 are virtually identical. Both conclude that in latter days Jerusalem will be exalted as Zion, the dwelling place of God. As God's special home, Zion will be a haven of justice and peace for people from all lands. This sacred space will draw a holy, saved, international group of believers, which Isaiah 19:19-25 and 25:6-12 have already identified. Temporal reality will give way to an ideal permanent reality.[74] Thus the concepts of sacred place, sacred people and sacred time will reach their ultimate fulfillment.

The remnant will suffer before being redeemed. They eschew idols and walk with the Lord (4:5), yet they must be brought back from affliction and injury (4:5-7). They must endure exile as well as political and emotional travail (4:8-10). Their hope lies solely on the God whose plans cannot be thwarted by human schemes (4:11-13).

As does Isaiah 7—12, Micah 5:1-15 concludes that such benefits can come only through the emergence and ministry of a Davidic ruler. In Micah's time Israel must accept rebuff from invaders. From Bethlehem, David's hometown, will come a ruler "whose origins are from of old, from ancient times" (5:2). Now the monarchy is an embarrassment, but from Bethlehem will arise a new beginning that will result in the extension of God's kingdom throughout the earth.[75] The reference to the king's origins marks him as a supernatural figure, much as the description of the king in Isaiah 9:6 as "Everlasting Father" does there.[76] This king will provide rest, sustenance and peace for the harried people of God (5:3-6), which again parallels the work of the king mentioned in Isaiah 9:1-7. He will eliminate fear, hunger and all other obstacles to renewal.[77]

The remnant will then be special among the nations (5:7-9). Perhaps the most striking element of their restoration is the removal of all idols from their midst (5:10-15). Restoration must by necessity negate the cause of judgment. War, the natural result of serving idols instead of Yahweh, will also be eliminated (5:10-11). Peace like that described in Isaiah 11:1-10 will result. The full implications of sinful behavior will no longer be in effect.

Canonical Synthesis: Renewal and the Davidic Ruler

Delbert Hillers says that Micah 4—5 displays five concepts basic to many futuristic texts. First, Micah 5:10-15 indicates that renewal will come when foreign elements, especially idols, are removed. Second, the glorious future will emerge after a time of trouble (5:3). Third, oppression and injustice must cease for restoration to be complete (4:2-3). Fourth, a ruler capable of initiating peace must arise (5:2). Fifth, the whole world must be impacted by the new situation (5:7-9).[78] Renewal texts like Isaiah 9:1-7, 11:1-10 and 60—62 reflect many of these ideas, as do their counterparts in Jeremiah 30—33, Ezekiel 33—48 and Amos 9:11-15. God's plan is to use judgment to eliminate idolatry, injustice and oppression and then to use the Davidic ruler to establish peace in the whole earth. God's kingdom will thereby extend to all lands and all people through the agency of the chosen leader.

No doubt the best-known usage of Micah 4—5 in the Bible is the quotation of this text in Matthew 2:6 by scribes in response to Herod's asking where the promised king would be born. This answer is in keeping with the expectation of a specifically Davidic king and represents their interpretation of Micah 5:2 as a specific prediction. In their view, whoever the king is, that individual must begin life in Bethlehem. Matthew concurs with this interpretation and uses Jesus' birth in David's hometown as one of his starting points for proclaiming Jesus as the promised one. Such specifity keeps the promise from being a vague or metaphorical pledge. An actual person will come at a specific time in history to restore the people to God and vindicate the remnant's faith.

The God Who Removes Sin for Abraham's Sake: Micah 6—7

Having staked out the future, Micah 6—7 returns to the present and even looks back into the distant past. The effect is to show the common elements of covenant breaking that have marred Israel's past yet also to offer hope to those who will do God's will now. It is significant that the book closes with a statement on the removal of sin as part of Yahweh's promises to Abraham. Defeating sin both fulfills the purpose for which the Lord called Abraham in the first place and demonstrates God's specific love for Abraham's descendants.

Yahweh links the people's current transgressions to the past. Despite the exodus and conquest (6:1-5), the chosen nation has committed one act of treachery after another (6:9-12), which causes the remnant to despair (7:1-6). They have done as Omri and Ahab did in their time (6:16). To compound their covenant infidelity they have acted as if Yahweh is unreasonable, impossible to please (6:6-7). In reality the Lord has asked for faithfulness to himself and fidelity to the covenant. In other words, they have been asked to love God and neighbor (6:8; cf. Deut 6:4-9; Lev 19:18). They could walk with (6:8) and wait on (7:7) the Lord as the remnant has done but instead have chosen the consequences of covenant disobedience (6:13-15; Lev 26:23-26; Deut 28:36-46). Thus God has had no choice but to send punishing circumstances and terrible destroying armies against them.

Yahweh will redeem the situation for Abraham's sake. Israel's enemies will only gloat for a time, for Yahweh will restore the chosen people from all the lands from which they have been driven (7:8-13). At that time Israel's boundaries will have no end (7:11-13). The return from Egypt and Assyria has been promised in Isaiah 11:16 and 19:23-25,[79] and the expanding kingdom concept appears in Amos 9:11-12, as well as later in Zechariah 9:10 and Psalm 72:8.[80] God will shepherd Israel as in the days of the exodus, and this repetition of divine activity[81] will make the nations tremble (7:14-17). The reason for this new exodus and new conquest is to demonstrate Yahweh's kindness in keeping faith with Jacob and Abraham (7:18-20).

Canonical Synthesis: The Biblical View of History

Thus Micah conceives of a complete history from Abrahamic times to the end of time. God's promises to the patriarchs resulted first in exodus, conquest and David's dynasty; then came disintegration. After the disintegration will come a new exodus, new conquest, new David and new city of God. These promises mean that every successive generation has historically relevant pledges given them to sustain their present and give hope to their future. Like the previous prophecies, Micah interprets history with both a short- and a long-term perspective. By doing so the book neglects neither the realities of the present nor the possibilities of the future.

When Micah closes God's promises of woe and renewal have been foreshadowed yet not fulfilled. God testifies against Israel and the nations, demanding to be heard and obeyed. That no positive audience reaction has been secured indicates that judgment must fall. It is to this issue that the Book of the Twelve now turns.

The God Who Destroys Assyria: Nahum

After all that has been said about Assyria in 2 Kings, Isaiah, Hosea, Jonah and Micah, the time has finally come for this great and dreaded nation to be judged. Writing between the fall of Thebes (663 B.C.; cf. 3:8) and that of Nineveh (612 B.C.), Nahum signals the end of Yahweh's patience with international iniquity. The end has arrived for Nineveh, the mightiest power of its day, so Yahweh may chastise any country or person at any time. The fact that judgment is beginning also means that renewal will naturally emerge afterward. Therefore the God who destroys is also the God who renews.

Nahum's theology carefully balances the various components of Yahweh's character in the book's seven sections. Marked by alternating speeches made by the prophet and the Lord, the text may be divided into three main topics. First, 1:1-15 describes a patient yet appropriately jealous God who takes vengeance on adversaries but delivers the remnant. Second, 2:1-13 presents the God who opposes Nineveh by sending an effective army against the city. Third, 3:1-19 declares that Yahweh humiliates the arrogant. Each segment demonstrates the Lord's power, justice, righteousness, goodness and control of history. Though these qualities spell doom for the wicked, they proclaim good news of deliverance and hope for the faithful.[82] They proclaim the ultimate victory of Yahweh over evil at the end of time.[83]

Reading and interpreting Nahum as part of the canon help rescue it from uncharitable assessments made by commentators who contrast its message with other prophecies. For example, J. M. P. Smith declares Nahum a false prophet like Hananiah (cf. Jer 28) for stressing Assyria's sin and not dealing extensively with Israel's and for rejoicing over Nineveh's demise.[84] Similarly G. A. Smith considers Nahum a great prophet yet also a bitter man with less conscience and insight than other prophets.[85] These statements do not do justice to Nahum's role in the Twelve or place in Old Testament prophecy. Within the Twelve the book begins to keep Yahweh's pledges of punishment that are so prevalent in Hosea—Micah. Sin will not be allowed to flourish unchecked. As part of the Prophets, Nahum demonstrates Yahweh's control of both near and distant history. What Isaiah envisioned about Assyria has come true. Surely what all the prophets envision about the Davidic promise and God's eventual, eternal reign over re-created creation will transpire as well.

The God Who Is Patient and Jealous: Nahum 1:1-15

From the outset the prophecy establishes the Lord's character as the basis for the announced judgment on Assyria. In fact, 1:2-11 acts as a virtual catalog of divine qualities found in earlier texts, particularly from Genesis and Exodus. God is jealous (1:2), as the prohibitions against idolatry in Exodus 20:4-5 have demonstrated. This jealousy is zeal for righteousness, so it is appropriate in this context. At the same time, Yahweh is patient and just (1:3), points also made in Exodus 20:1-2, 6. God is in control of all nature (1:3-5), for the Lord is the Creator (Gen 1—2). Thus God is good (1:7), which means the wicked cannot endure divine presence (1:6-8). Plotting against the Lord, which here means sinning against other nations,[86] will only net Assyria death (1:9-11). Assyria's arrogance has been growing since Isaiah's era (cf. Is 10:13-15), but now the nation's power is gone and the world will finally be released from bondage (1:12-13). Pride will get what it merits.

God's jealousy has as its aim the destruction of idols (1:14). Monotheism remains the earth's only viable belief system. Nineveh worships the Lord in Jonah, only to return to polytheism. God's patience and protection aim to produce good news for the weak (1:15). God's nature has always been to keep promises of healing and ultimate victory for the faithful. From Yahweh's nature flows the necessity for goodness, which here means the appropriate rewarding of righteousness and evil.

Canonical Synthesis: God's Sovereignty over Assyria

Carl Armerding notes that Nahum has several parallels with Isaiah 51—52. Though some of the items he cites may be explained as common terminology in judgment-oriented texts, there are close ties between the images of redemption in Nahum 1:12-15 and Isaiah 51:21—52:7. First, 1:15 and 52:7 are similar, for both hail the arrival of one bringing good news of peace. Second, 1:15 and 52:1 both promise liberation from oppression. Third, both announce "a transitional moment in history."[87] The likenesses in these texts reflect Nahum's use of an earlier prophecy to explain the near victory of Yahweh over the same enemy the Lord turned away from Jerusalem in Isaiah's day (Is 36—37). In effect the reappearance of this wording means that Yahweh is able to defeat Assyria as in earlier times, but this time the victory will be final.

It is also necessary to observe that Nahum 1:1-15 indicates that the repentance described in Jonah either did not spread beyond Nineveh or did not last. God mercifully sent Jonah to warn the Assyrians of punishment, so Nineveh cannot argue that Yahweh is patient and good to the Jews but not to them. God's mercy was not received with long-term commitment. Therefore destruction will occur, but the Lord is not guilty of not reaching out to a city set for judgment.

The God Who Opposes Nineveh: Nahum 2:1-13

After noting the rationale for God's actions, the prophet declares the shattering of Nineveh (2:1). Nineveh will be plundered, pillaged and stripped (2:10) by powerful forces (2:3-4) that cause Assyria's best soldiers to fail to defend their capital (2:6). Women will be captured (2:7), riches will be taken (2:9) and the city will be torn, though it has been as mighty as a lion (2:11-12).

The reference to the lion is ironic, since lions were often used in Assyrian art as being hunted by Assyrian kings and since these kings loved to compare themselves to mighty lions.[88]

These terrors occur because Yahweh opposes Nineveh (2:13). Assyria's military prowess is no more able to save them from the one God any more than Egypt's might could save it in the days of the exodus. Further, God is using this occasion to restore Israel to former glory by defeating their oppressor (2:2). Yahweh works in this case to reinstate the remnant in the land. Israel's renewal begins here as it did in Exodus 2:23-25, with God acting to relieve the chosen people from a vicious tyrant. The fact that God opposes Assyria here "is a sign of the victory of God and the basis for hope that his power and justice will ultimately conquer all evil."[89]

The God Who Humiliates the Arrogant: Nahum 3:1-19

Isaiah 10:5-27 has already stated God's decision to judge Assyria for their arrogance in assuming that they, and not the Lord, have ruled history. Now Nahum continues the description of Nineveh's defeat by highlighting the city's humiliation. God's judgment comes because Nineveh is filled with lies, violence and oppression (3:1). Nineveh enslaves others (3:4) and is cruel (3:19). Therefore God is against them and will expose their nakedness (3:5), cover them in filth (3:6), make them an object of contempt (3:6) and show the city to be weak (3:8-9). Commerce and government activity will cease (3:16-19). Their pride will be eradicated.

Canonical Synthesis: God's Universal Power

Those who have suffered under their hands will rejoice in Assyria's decline (3:19). This joy reveals the wickedness of Nineveh more than the faulty attitudes of the released peoples. One could no more mourn Assyria's fall than one could regret the fall from power of Hitler or Stalin or Napoleon. God's judgment means that Yahweh is the universal Lord who is sovereign in both salvation and judgment.[90] It means that God's power and justice still dictate history.[91] Therefore to take excessive exception to the book's tone may be a worse attitude than being glad Assyria falls.

With the rebuke of Assyrian pride the Twelve's long-promised judgment arrives. No sinful nation, however powerful, can avoid divine wrath. Because judgment begins with a mighty people, the fullness of Yahweh's judgment becomes evident. Only Judah may have some hope for now (cf. 1:15; 2:2). Assyria lies fallen before the Lord. Can other nations be far behind? Universal sin, so carefully stated in Joel, Amos, Jonah, Obadiah and Micah, has been attacked. God has been patient yet has begun to move against evil in an evident fashion.

The God Who Inspires Faith in Crises: Habakkuk

By any standard of measure Habakkuk is a unique prophecy. Its format is more clearly dramalike in structure than that of any other prophetic book. The prophet takes the initiative to seek revelation from God. God answers questions posed by the seeking prophet. The historical situation is reflected yet hardly specific. A crisis of faith unfolds, yet it is the prophet, not one of the people, who endures this crisis. A clearly defined psalm closes the work. Put together these details mark this text as a creative, even unusual, prophetic effort.

At the same time Habakkuk uses and reworks a number of theological ideas already prominent among his predecessors. For example, the book announces national and international iniquity. It depicts Yahweh using a powerful and wicked nation (Babylon) to punish sinners in Israel and highlights the prophet's relationship to the Lord. Here God acts as revealer, judge, comforter, instructor, deliverer and absolute Lord of history. Yahweh is the Creator and sustainer of the whole earth. Such common notions mixed with unusual characteristics help this book make a strong theological statement about how the Lord punishes sin and delivers the faithful.

Habakkuk unfolds in four distinct sections. First, 1:2-11 demonstrates that God will punish Israel by sending Babylon to chastise them. This God reveals the future. Second, 1:12—2:11 states that Yahweh expects faith from the faithful as Babylon is punished for their sins. Third, 2:12-20 makes it clear that Yahweh crushes idolaters. Neither Israel nor Babylon can stand against the one God by serving images. Fourth, 3:1-19 claims that Yahweh always acts on behalf of the faithful. The prophet may take refuge in God's power. Set sometime before Babylon assumed control of Israel in 605 B.C.,[92] the book anticipates the fall of Jerusalem in 587 B.C. and the demise of Babylon in 539 B.C. Thus the reader is offered God's view of the future,[93] which includes the same fate for Israel and Babylon that Nineveh endured in Nahum.

The God Who Reveals the Future: Habakkuk 1:2-11

Prophetic visions of the future are both general and quite specific. The more specific comments usually address the events nearest the prophet, while the more general statements tend to promise, for instance, Yahweh's eventual defeat of evil. In this passage Habakkuk asks the Lord a specific question, "Why do you tolerate wrong?" (1:2-4). Like Isaiah (Is 6:9-10), he wonders "how long" sinners will prosper. God's reply is "I am raising up the Babylonians" to destroy Israel's wicked (1:5-11). As in the earlier case of Assyria, a strong and vicious Babylon will act as God's instrument of wrath against the rebellious chosen people. Now Habakkuk knows the future!

Canonical Synthesis: Babylon as God's Instrument of Wrath

This role has been staked out for Babylon for some time in the canon. Isaiah 39, Jeremiah 27—29 and Ezekiel 24—32 particularly stress Babylon's future prominence in and dominance over Israel. God wills to use them this way. At the same time, Isaiah 13:1—14:27 and Jeremiah 50—51 indicate Babylon will suffer God's wrath in due time. Like Assyria (Is 10:5-27), Babylon's cruelty and arrogance will create their downfall. Their love for other gods will be their undoing. These facts make the judgment statements in the next section of Habakkuk fairly predictable, but the prophecy's artistry saves the prophecy from being tedious.

The God Who Inspires Faith in Crises: Habakkuk 1:12—2:11

God's answer satisfies only the most basic aspect of Habakkuk's question. Babylon's activities against Judah explain how one segment of sinners will be removed. But if wicked Babylon destroys wicked Judah, then the wicked still prosper, and Babylon may be worse than Judah, since that whole nation worships idols (1:13-17).[94] Surely the everlasting Lord (1:12) can do better, so the prophet waits for a more sufficient response (2:1). At stake here is the very nature and character of God as shown by how Yahweh rules history. Also at stake is whether the Lord allows idols any glory for their adherents' triumphs.

This time Yahweh's reply eliminates any sense of the wicked's prospering permanently. Before divulging the fate of the wicked, though, the Lord first secures the righteous. God instructs Habakkuk to write the revealed vision/ response as a lasting testimony (2:2). Yahweh's judgment of the wicked may seem slow, but it will come (2:3), and it will devastate the wicked (2:5). The posture Habakkuk and all others who call upon the Lord must assume is one of faith (2:4). The just person lives on faith, just as the covenant people are to live on the word of God (Deut 8:3). This faith in the God who reveals and promises will sustain Habakkuk and demonstrate that he is righteous in the Lord's sight.

Canonical Synthesis: Faith and Righteousness

So far Yahweh has asserted himself as a God who reveals and calls for faith. These details help Habakkuk know Yahweh's character. Now the Lord explains his work that is based on that character. God will bring "woe" upon Babylon for all its greed, arrogance and cruelty (2:5-11), which declares that wickedness will not long endure upon the earth. God not only secures the righteous but also eliminates evil, though this process may unfold over time (2:2-3).

It is important to note the inextricable connection between righteousness and faith here. M. E. Széles observes that the Old Testament consistently defines "righteous person" as one "who goes back to the prescriptions of the Law that conform to the expressed will of God and who accepts its binding validity and submits to it wholly."[95] At the same time, Peter C. Craigie concludes, one who is faithful must persevere in the belief that God's will is normative and must order life accordingly.[96] Seen this way, one may not be righteous without faith in God and God's word and may not be faithful unless righteousness is sustained over time. Here Yahweh tells Habakkuk to believe and to act on that belief. Living by faith will show that the prophet has the characteristic of uprightness, and firm reliance on God will secure his future.[97]

No doubt 2:4 is the most important verse for canonical theology in this section. It agrees fully with Genesis 15:6, where Abram believes God and that faith is counted as righteousness. Both texts find it impossible to separate the two concepts, and both make righteousness dependent on faith, or faithfulness. Further, each time an Old Testament character acts based solely on the Lord's promises these same principles apply. Before they act God calls them, during their lives they honor God, and at all times Yahweh sustains them.

In the New Testament Paul cites 2:4 in Romans 1:17 and Galatians 3:11 as the basis for his conviction that faith makes sinners righteous in God's eyes and that therefore faith precedes works as the fundamental premise of Christian faith. Hebrews 10:32-34 uses 2:4 as an exhortation for believers under pressure to remain faithful to Christ. Thus Paul uses Habakkuk's underlying theology to construct theology, while the writer of Hebrews uses Habakkuk's situation to enhance perseverance in a similar situation. Both agree with the Old Testament's conviction that faith is the foundation for godly behavior.

The God Who Crushes Idolaters: Habakkuk 2:12-20

With reassurances about Yahweh's character and deeds in mind, the prophet joins in pronouncing Babylon's woe. First, woe will come as Babylon wearies itself trying to become prominent, for God alone will be known by all people everywhere (2:12-14). As Habakkuk has learned, God offers self-revelation in abundance. Second, woe will come as Yahweh judges Babylon for its bloodthirsty ways (2:15-17). Third, woe will engulf Babylon because God, not idols, rules human history (2:18-20). Idols are the work of human hands, but the Lord is other than such blocks of wood and pieces of metal (2:20).

Canonical Synthesis: The Folly of Idolatry

Habakkuk's conclusions are shared by the bulk of the canon. Isaiah 42:7 and 44:9-20 portray the folly of thinking there is spiritual profit in idolatry.

Jeremiah 2:26-28 agrees, noting how foolish Judah's idolatry is, and Jeremiah 10:1-16 argues that the nations are equally foolish for venerating images. Psalm 115:4-8 applies these ideas in a text that focuses on how Israel and nature glorify God. Anti-idolatry texts of other types are plentiful in the rest of the canon as well, but these passages are nearly identical in tone, wording and purpose to Habakkuk 2:12-20. God must be known and glorified for the world to have hope, so competing gods must be shown to be the vanities they are.

The God Who in Wrath Remembers Mercy: Habakkuk 3:1-19

Habakkuk concludes with a prayer/psalm of trust. His first two questions are essentially laments offered by one of the faithful, while 2:12-20 is a song of woe for Babylon. The fact that it ends with praise and trust marks the prophecy as a kind of minipsalter shaped by a prophetic tone and emphasis. Judgment of evil and trusting God during difficult times remain the main themes, though they are joined by Habakkuk's concern that the Lord be merciful through the punishment.

The psalm longs for God to redeem the faithful by removing the wicked. This act would mean mercy for the oppressed. It is this mercy that the prophet longs to see, and Habakkuk knows that only God can manage this work. The prophet focuses solely on what God can do.[98] Habakkuk asks God to reveal himself as during the exodus era, when Yahweh freed Israel by crushing their oppressor (3:3-15). Such would be a renewal of divine, revelatory work; such would be mercy for the righteous who live by faith. For this sort of work the prophet is content to wait (3:16). By faith he will wait, though all seems bleak around him (3:17-19). He will do so despite the fact that Israel and Israel's conqueror must fall before his faith will be vindicated. God's word alone is enough to fuel this faith.

Canonical Synthesis: God's Intervention in History

Besides showing the overlap between prophecy and the psalms, this text stands alongside other poetic canonical reflections on God's extraordinary appearances in history. Many of these poems are offered in the midst of narratives, such as Exodus 15:1-18, where Moses praises God for deliverance at the Red Sea. It is clear that Habakkuk 3:1-19 asks for a similar event. Judges 5:4-5 celebrates Yahweh's going forth to battle against Sisera in Deborah's day. Once again the Lord needs to work against a foreign invader. Psalm 68 views the Lord as the great warrior who releases captives. Finally, Deuteronomy 33:2-5 depicts Yahweh assuming kingship over Israel at Sinai by giving Israel Moses' law. These texts memorialize God's word, God's mercy and God's power as sovereign over history's arrogant oppressors. In his own day the prophet asks for new revelation, renewed punishment for the wicked and a new Israel who, like Deborah, will serve Yahweh. God's positive answer to his prayer will mean that Assyria, Babylon and Israel will all be judged for the sorts of sins described in earlier parts of the Twelve.

The God Who Punishes to Create a Remnant: Zephaniah

Zephaniah leaves no doubt that God is about to punish the sins of Israel and the nations. All creation will suffer for transgressions committed by the human race (1:2-3). Assyria, Babylon and Israel will be joined in judgment by other countries who have offended the Lord (2:4-12). Though God's just anger continues to be a main theme, the fact that this wrath falls in order to forge a multinational remnant also receives major attention (3:6-20). The goal of God's judgment is redemptive, not simply punitive. Once again it is the familiar concept of the day of the Lord that provides the context for these activities.

Zephaniah's superscription (1:1) places the prophecy during Josiah's reign (c. 640-609 B.C.), though no specific statement about whether it precedes or comes after the great reform of 622 B.C. (cf. 2 Kings 22:1—23:30) is offered. Scholars have debated how much of the book stems from that era,[99] but J. J. M. Roberts rightly concludes that "there is no good reason to doubt the correctness of the superscription's historical information."[100] Like his contemporaries Jeremiah, Nahum and Habakkuk, Zephaniah preaches before the destruction of Jerusalem in 587 B.C. The book reflects a crisis theology intended to move Judah toward repentance. Lacking the ability to save the people from themselves, the prophet states how Yahweh will use the day of the Lord as a tool to destroy the wicked and the means by which the righteous will be saved. In other words, Zephaniah explains in explicit detail ideas that Nahum, Habakkuk and the previous prophecies began to express.

Though a variety of structures have been suggested,[101] the prophecy sets forth its message of the God who punishes to create a remnant in three parts. First, 1:2-17a depicts the God who sweeps away sin. Second, 1:17b-3:5 describes the God who consumes the nations. Third, 3:6-20 examines the God who creates the remnant. Thus the prophecy demonstrates Yahweh's righteous character, sovereign power over the nations and redemption of the faithful. These themes are staples of other prophetic texts that feature the day of the Lord.

The God Who Sweeps Away Sin: Zephaniah 1:2-17a

Rather than leading up to a pronouncement of judgment by listing sins first, Zephaniah begins with a striking statement of total, devastating punishment: God will sweep away everything created in Genesis 1:1-26 (1:2-3). While creation is the context of wrath, the objects of God's anger are the wicked of the earth (1:3). Yahweh will reverse creation as in the days of the flood.[102] This blanket promise renders most of Habakkuk's concerns void, since presumably all wicked persons on the face of the earth will suffer at this time. Zephaniah's vision of judgment is comprehensive if nothing else.

Old sins are the cause of Yahweh's wrath. Baalism, idolatry, astral deity worship, syncretism and apostasy are but the beginning of the specific offenses the book mentions (1:4-6). Further, royalty have turned to foreign ways and have perpetuated violence and fraud (1:8-9). Jerusalemites have become so apathetic about Yahweh that they think the Lord will never act against them (1:12-13). Polytheism has made them believe Yahweh is like them. They worship themselves,[103] so what else would they think?

Yahweh specifies the nature of the sweeping. The day of the Lord will come. It is near (1:14), bitter in its results (1:14), able to cause distress, despair and gloom (1:15), murderous in its intent (1:15) and comprehensive in nature (1:16). A great enemy will come, thereby causing alarms to be sounded at corner towers.[104] Blindness and shame will overtake the people (1:17a). Judgment will be as pervasive as the idolatry in Judah.

In just a few verses Zephaniah shows amazing solidarity with the whole canon. As has been stated, 1:2-3 evokes memories of Noah's flood, which indicates that Zephaniah views the day of the Lord as a revisiting of that event. The text also resonates with the reasons for divine displeasure and consequent judgment found in Deuteronomy 27—28,[105] a fact that further links the prophecy's view of history with the Former Prophets. Zephaniah's emphasis on the day of the Lord links the book to the Latter Prophets, and specific phrases from other prophecies appear here.[106] This section ties the book to the canonical beliefs that the Creator may judge creation, that the covenant people forfeit the promised land through idolatry and that the day of the Lord is the means by which these truths are actualized in history.

The God Who Consumes the Nations: Zephaniah 1:17b—3:5

As Isaiah 13—23, Jeremiah 46—51, Ezekiel 25—32, Joel 3:9-20 and Amos 1:3—2:3 have already indicated, Judah will not be the only country punished by the day of the Lord. Nations as great as Assyria (2:13-15) and as relatively small as Philistia (2:4-7), Moab, Ammon (2:8-11) and Ethiopia (2:12) will be punished as well. Every point of the compass is thereby covered, which speaks to the day's thoroughness.[107] The reasons for the devastation remain the same as in the previous books: arrogance (2:10) and idolatry (2:11). There can be no knowledge of God when these issues are left unresolved. All that can result is a type of self-worship (2:15) not unlike that seen in Judah in 1:12-13. Judah's inclusion in the listing of sinful nations (2:1-2; 3:1-5) indicates that their actions negate their favored status. As John Watts observes, "It [Judah] has become so foreign in its ways that it seemed to belong more to them [the nations] than to God."[108]

But one group will emerge from the devastation. The "humble of the land" who seek the Lord, the law, righteousness and humility (2:3) will become the remnant that will possess the land (2:7, 9). Those mentioned in 2:3, 7 and 9 are clearly Israelites, but 2:11 offers the possibility of extending the identity of the remnant to people from other lands. When idols are destroyed those who recognize God's worth will turn to Yahweh. Just as the wicked in Israel are treated like the wicked Gentiles, so the righteous among the Gentiles, those who worship the Lord, are equated with the Israelite remnant. Thus the vision of the remnant in Isaiah 19:19-25, Amos 9:11-12 and elsewhere is reinforced here.

Canonical Synthesis: God's Righteousness and the Remnant

Yahweh's sovereignty and flawless righteousness are evident. God consumes the nations for their sinfulness yet includes all nations in the remnant. Therefore if the imagery in 1:2-17a reflects ideas from the Law, the Former Prophets and the Latter Prophets, then 1:17b—3:5 contains notions found in the Latter Prophets and the Writings. While the Latter Prophets teach a remnant will survive, the Writings, especially wisdom psalms like Psalms 1 and 37 and the book of Proverbs, explain how one may claim to be among "the humble of the land."[109] The full range of concepts associated with Yahweh's righteousness and how human beings may reflect that righteousness are therefore contained in capsule form in Zephaniah.

The God Who Creates the Remnant: Zephaniah 3:6-20

Judgment is intended to deal with all who consider God's patience an excuse to sin (3:6-7), but it is also meant to create and bless a people committed to Yahweh. To this end Yahweh states that divine indignation (3:8) will "purify the lips of the peoples" (3:9) and cause worshipers to come from "beyond the rivers of Cush" (3:10). While 3:10 may refer specifically to exiled Israelites, the plural word *peoples* indicates that the remnant has a multinational identity.[110] Some scholars speculate that a textual corruption may change "my people" to "peoples" here, but there is no manuscript evidence to support this reading.[111] Given the presence of 2:11, the prophecy's overall context argues for this definition of the remnant. As has already been stated, Zephaniah's conception of the remnant is hardly a novel one in prophetic literature. The Creator of all people reserves a remnant from all peoples.

To this humble remnant (3:11-13) belong all Yahweh's blessings. God pledges presence (3:15), courage (3:15), delight (3:17), quietness (3:17), joy

(3:17), deliverance (3:19) and honor (3:20)—in a word, restoration (3:20). These promises reverse judgment as surely as judgment reverses creation. God's will is to bless, not curse; to heal, not kill. Renewal results from punishment. It is the ultimate purpose of judgment, and the remnant's rejoicing gives human voice to this theological principle (3:14-20). This view of punishment fits the pattern set in Genesis 1—11, Deuteronomy 27—28, Isaiah 40—66, Jeremiah 31—34 and other texts. God always retains a remnant beyond the devastation to promote renewal.

Zephaniah concludes the emphasis on judgment begun in Nahum. At this point in the Twelve all polytheists on earth stand under divine condemnation. The sins chronicled in Hosea—Micah will be punished. Still, renewal is the goal beyond devastation, so hope for the future exists. This hope rests unexplained, but the next three books address this matter.

The God Who Renews the Temple: Haggai

Zephaniah concludes without stating how renewal will occur in history. Haggai, Zechariah and Malachi address this matter and offer a consistent pattern for how final restoration will unfold. These prophecies are perfectly honest about how preliminary and preparatory to complete renewal their era is, but they are hopeful that the foundations that have been laid will be vital for the future. Peter Ackroyd observes that Haggai and Zechariah 1—8 are especially aware that they are living in a new age marked by God's blessing. The mark of God's blessing is God's presence, and the focal points of this blessing are the temple and the community of faith.[112] In other words, Haggai and Zechariah 1—8 stress the temple, the city and the people. It is also fair to include Zechariah 9—14 and Malachi in this summary.

Haggai and Zechariah are near contemporaries. Haggai's messages may be dated during 520 B.C., while Zechariah's unfold during 520-518 B.C.113 Both prophets work after the defeat of Babylon by Persia in 539 B.C., in itself a fulfillment of promises made in Isaiah 13:1—14:23, Jeremiah 50—51 and Habakkuk 2:2-20, the 538 B.C. decree of Cyrus that allows Jews to return to their homeland, another event promised in multiple texts (e.g., Is 35; 44:28—45:1; Jer 29:1-14) and the initial return of the Jews in about 538-535 B.C. (cf. Ezra 1—2).[114] These are all unquestionably momentous events. They could rightly be considered evidence that Israel's seventy years of exile (Jer 29:1-14) had given way to a new era in which Israel once again might inhabit the promised land, renew the covenant and enjoy Yahweh's blessings. Prophecy was coming true in their lifetime, and the question was how much and what sorts of prophecy were being fulfilled.

Haggai contends that full national renewal cannot take place until the temple is rebuilt. Ezra 3:8—4:24 indicates that the exiles tried to build earlier but were stopped by political enemies. Haggai thinks the time has come to begin again. He offers four messages that motivate the people to build. First, in 1:1-15 he proclaims that God deserves honor, so the people should construct a temple that demonstrates their commitment to Yahweh. Second, 2:1-9 presents the God who promises greater glory for the new temple. This pledge is possible because of the Lord's assured presence in the new worship center. Third, 2:10-19 states that God purifies the people so that they may be a proper remnant. Fourth, 2:20-23 claims that Yahweh renews the covenant with David. With the people back in the land, the temple in place and the Davidic covenant reaffirmed, Haggai declares that full renewal is not only feasible but already under way.

The God Who Deserves Honor: Haggai 1:1-15

Haggai preached to a puzzled people. They expected great blessings because of the preexilic prophets' declarations (1:9)[115] yet experienced God's judgment (1:6).[116] Haggai seeks to clarify matters by declaring that they are struggling because they have not seen fit to honor the Lord of hosts by rebuilding the temple (1:2-11). Their delay in building shows that they are hardly purified and obedient servants of God[117] and even leads Yahweh to call them "these people" rather than "my people" in 1:2.[118] Since God receives no honor they do not receive the benefits of God's pleasure (1:8). Haggai's solution is clear: they must rise and build.

To their credit, Israel's leaders and people respond positively to Haggai's challenge. They prove a worthy remnant by obeying Yahweh and the prophet (1:12). God's presence results in the stirring, motivating and empowering of the people's spirits and bodies (1:13-14).[119] They work within twenty-three days of hearing Haggai's message (1:1, 14-15). This response separates this generation from the countless unheeding audiences endured by earlier prophets. They recognize that the God who brought them back to the land and who controls nature (1:2-11) merits the honor a temple signifies.

Canonical Synthesis: The Temple and God's Renewing Presence

It is important to note Haggai's connection to the whole of Scripture. Haggai accepts Yahweh as the all-powerful Lord of hosts who created and rules the universe, so he affirms the teachings on those subjects found in Genesis, Isaiah, Psalms and elsewhere.[120] At the same time Haggai concurs with the emphasis on a central sanctuary found in Exodus, Leviticus, Deuteronomy and the Former Prophets. A temple signifies God's presence (1:12-14; cf. Ex 32—34; 1 Kings 8) and demonstrates commitment to the Lord (1:2-6; cf. Ex 35—40; 1 Kings 5—7). Just as important, Haggai agrees with the view of the future displayed in Deuteronomy 28:64-68 and 30:1-10, Isaiah 60—62,

Jeremiah 30—33 and Ezekiel 40—48. Haggai sees a better future because of God's intervention in history.[121] He contends that this greater future is linked to Israel's seeking God's kingdom by constructing a sacred center.[122] Thus Haggai indeed anchors God's work in the now of 520 B.C. (1:1, 15) yet anticipates God's greater work in an unspecified later. His view of time is obviously like that of his predecessors.

The God Who Promises Greater Glory: Haggai 2:1-23

It is possible to link Haggai's last three messages as part of God's overall plan for greater future glory. The first pledge is that the new temple will have greater glory than Solomon's (2:9). Anticipating discouragement over the disparity between the physical beauty, or "glory," of the former building and the new one (2:1-3), God has Haggai encourage the people and their leaders (2:4). Three promises are offered to help the people believe that their little temple will be more glorious than its predecessor. First, Yahweh promises to be with Israel in a manner like that of the exodus (2:4-5). God has not forgotten the Sinai covenant. Second, Yahweh's Spirit will abide among them, thereby eliminating any reason for fear (2:5). Third, the God who rules the earth will fill the temple with the treasures of the nations (2:6-8). Abiding divine presence and universal acknowledgment of Yahweh will grace this temple.

Earlier passages inform the promises in 2:1-9. Exodus 29:45-46 says that Yahweh brings Israel out of Egypt in order to dwell among them.[123] Similarly, Exodus 33:12-17 reports God's promise to be present in Israel as the nation goes to conquer Canaan. Finally, Isaiah 63:7-14 states that God's Holy Spirit was grieved when Israel sinned in the desert yet also later led the people to the land. The Spirit's function in each of these texts is to guide, sustain and give victory to Israel, and the Spirit serves the same purposes in Haggai 2:1-9.[124] The context of Isaiah 63:7-14 makes it very applicable to Haggai 2:1-9, since both texts deal with God's glory and the renewal of the nation in the holy land.

Haggai's third message (2:10-19) emphasizes the decisive renewal of the people. Before the temple building began everything they did was unclean (2:10-14). Now, however, the Lord will bless them as the holy remnant. All their needs will be met (2:15-19), which reflects a return to the blessing mentioned in Leviticus 26:3-13 and Deuteronomy 28:1-14. God will honor their repentance. Israel has not heeded a prophet and enjoyed God's blessings in this manner since the days of Josiah (c. 640-609 B.C.) and Hezekiah (c. 715-687 B.C.). They receive glory not seen for decades.

Finally, Haggai's fourth message deals with the glory of the Davidic lineage. Here the prophet says Zerubbabel, a Davidic descendant and current leader of Israel, is special to the Lord. He will be "like [a] signet ring" of the Lord (2:20-23). This promise is set for "that day" in the future (2:23). C. F. Keil says that this message informs the remnant that David's lineage is being preserved for future glory.[125] Kaiser observes that whenever God overthrows the kingdoms of the earth a Davidic descendant will be strategic to this victory.[126] Zerubbabel himself is not the coming king, but his existence means a future son of David has the chance to emerge. David's line has not been extinguished, so neither has Israel's future hope.

Canonical Synthesis: The Temple, the Remnant and the Davidic King
This final sermon completes Haggai's identification with the future depicted in earlier texts. Like Isaiah 7:14, 9:2-7 and 11:1-10, Jeremiah 23:1-8, Ezekiel 34:20-24, Hosea 3:1-5, Amos 9:11-12 and Micah 5:2-5, Haggai 2:20-23 links future renewal of people, worship and land to the ministry of the coming king. Zerubbabel is no more that king than was Solomon, Hezekiah or Josiah, yet he symbolizes the promise initiated in 2 Samuel 7:7-17 as much as they do. This king will finalize the renewal begun by the construction of a temple by a faithful remnant.

Without question the renewal begun in Haggai is a humble one. Much remains to be done before God's final victory occurs. Still, the people repent when their ancestors did not. They respond like a true remnant. Also, the Davidic and Mosaic blessings remain in effect. Most of all, the temple has been restored as the chief representation of Israel's honoring of their God. Significantly, no mention of idolatry appears. The worship that is reinstated here has no hint of idolatry to mar it, so this renewal may be incomplete, but it is hardly insignificant.

The God Who Renews Jerusalem as Zion: Zechariah
Though he works at the same time as Haggai among the same people for many of the same reasons, Zechariah's personality and presentation are quite different from his contemporary's.[127] Zechariah is a visionary who uses symbolic language to make his points. In this way Zechariah is very much like Ezekiel. Both prophets envision a renewed Jerusalem with a restored temple at its center. Both believe the Davidic king will be integral to this restoration, both emphasize God's Spirit, and both focus on the future. Zechariah agrees with Haggai's concern for temple construction, yet he offers hope for a comprehensive cleansing of the entire holy city of Jerusalem as the capital of God's kingdom on earth. Jerusalem is ultimately his primary interest. As Watts writes:

> The theme of the book is the kingdom of God. This theme is presented in many variations interwoven with other themes. Jerusalem's relation to

the kingdom is a thread which runs through the whole book. The Lord's intention to reestablish his dwelling there is the reason for building the Temple. God's coming and dwelling in Jerusalem are signs of her election. She is the centerpiece of the drama of "that day." When all else falls under the Lord's final judgment, Jerusalem will stand exalted and confirmed.[128] Scholars typically divide Zechariah into two major sections, chapters 1—8 and 9—14, and then subdivide these segments. Most critical scholars believe these two parts were written by different authors working decades apart, while conservative commentators think the whole book was penned by Zechariah.[129] Experts from both sides of this issue conclude that thematic unity exists across the entire book despite clear differences in subject matter in Zechariah 1—8 and Zechariah 9—14.[130] It is not entirely inappropriate to examine the book's theology as it unfolds in all fourteen chapters of the canonical prophecy. Zechariah's main theological emphases thereby become evident.

Zechariah may be separated into five parts. First, the prophet introduces the book by affirming the justice of the Lord's past dealings with Israel (1:1-6). Second, a series of eight visions describe God as "jealous for Jerusalem and Zion" (1:7—6:15; cf. 1:14). Each vision extends Yahweh's rule over creation. At all times Jerusalem and the temple are the focal points for God's activity. Third, in 7—8 the text declares the God who forgives and blesses. Fourth, as a prelude to final restoration in 9—11, the text portrays God as Israel's shepherd and protector. Now the prophecy highlights the coming of the promised Savior to lead the chosen people. Fifth, in 12—14 the prophecy focuses on the God who dwells in Zion. When the Lord's presence fills the city full renewal will result, and Jerusalem will be holy to the Lord (14:20-21). Temple and city will both declare Yahweh's glory at that time.

The God Who Deals Justly with Israel: Zechariah 1:1-6

Zechariah's opening verses, which are dated in 520 B.C. (1:1), state the prophet's agreement with the understanding of Israelite history found in the Former and previous Latter Prophets. The text argues that Yahweh's anger at the people (1:2) has been due to an unwillingness to repent (1:3) at the word of the "earlier prophets" (1:4). Thus God's word overtook them, or sent them into exile (1:5), which in turn effected a long-delayed repentance (1:6). A clearer, more succinct digest of the whole canon from Deuteronomy 27 through Zephaniah 3 could hardly be written. The thrust of this view of history is that the Lord has always been just in all dealings with the chosen people. Jerusalem's devastated condition stands as a testimony to the sins of the past.

The reference to earlier prophets in 1:4 indicates Zechariah's conscious personal identification with those who called Israel to repentance in the past.

At the least Zechariah stands in a long line of divinely called messengers.[131] It is also possible that he had a collection of prophetic writings at his disposal,[132] or even that he considered certain prophecies canonical.[133] Regardless of the exact situation, this notation demonstrates Zechariah's dependence on the example set by Jeremiah and others. For Zechariah, to be a prophet meant to teach the truths of covenant blessings and consequences. His whole book must be read in this context.

The God Who Is Jealous for Jerusalem and Zion: Zechariah 1:7—6:15
When Zechariah says in 1:6 that Israel has repented the text signals a new era in Israelite history.[134] God is once again jealous for Jerusalem and Zion (1:14), which means the city's enemies must be scattered and all impediments to its rebuilding removed. To symbolize this renewal of blessing, eight visions are given to the prophet, with the first setting the stage for the others. In the initial vision the prophet sees riders and horses that patrol the earth (1:7-10). When he is asked why no mercy has been shown to Jerusalem, the Lord expresses jealousy for Jerusalem but anger for the nations (1:14-15). God promises mercy and comfort in the form of the rebuilt temple (1:16-17). Though no prospects of renewal are apparent now, the Lord has already decided to judge the nations at ease and to restore Zion.[135] History has already been decided by the Lord of history, and Jerusalem's renewal is the key to the future.

Each of the next seven visions supports the notion of a reinvigorated Israel. The first vision indicates that Yahweh is sovereign over Israel's enemies (1:18-21), while the third depicts the measuring of the refurbished city that is God's chosen inheritance (2:1-12). Next, a fourth vision finds the Lord defending the high priest against the evil Satan, or accuser (3:1-10). This episode indicates the full restoration of the priesthood, which means authentic worship will occur soon. The fifth vision encourages Zerubbabel by guaranteeing that the power of God's Spirit will enable the temple to be completed (4:1-14). In the sixth vision, a scroll representing God's authority sweeps over the land, denouncing all covenant breakers (5:1-4). Only the righteous will inhabit the new Jerusalem.[136] The seventh vision likewise banishes the wicked from the land (5:5-11), and the eighth returns to the horses and riders, who this time declare Yahweh's ownership of the whole earth (6:1-8). The same God who controls the nations and their destinies is able to rebuild the city, restore the temple, renew worship and remove the wicked, thus clearing the way for the remnant.

Canonical Synthesis: The Davidic Branch
Besides the high priest Joshua and the Davidic descendant Zerubbabel, one

other individual is crucial to the renewal. This person will finish in the future what these men have begun. In 3:8 and 10, the Lord says "my servant, the Branch" will come to remove Israel's sin and allow them to dwell in peace. This imagery appears to unite the imagery of branch and root in Isaiah 4:2, Isaiah 11:1 and Jeremiah 23:1-8 with the servant passages in Isaiah 42:1-4, 49:1-6, 50:4-9 and 52:13—53:12.[137] It also uses the same symbolism of the vine as that found in Micah 4:4.[138] The connection to Joshua further ties the figure to priestly lineage, much as Psalm 110 claims the Davidic ruler will be a priest after the order of Melchizedek (Ps 110:4). Thus 3:8-10 combines royal, priestly and servant metaphors as a description of the one who can rebuild the temple, destroy sin and serve the Lord and the people.

Similarly in 6:12-13 the branch is connected to the building of the temple. Here Yahweh tells Joshua the person from 3:8 will restore the temple and have an ongoing kingdom. Carol Meyers and Eric Meyers state that the phrase "from his place he will shoot up" is literally "from under him someone will sprout up," and it is therefore a reference to a future Davidic descendant and to the permanent nature of the Davidic promise (cf. 2 Sam 7:1-17; Jer 33:17). This individual will build the temple at some distant time.[139] Thus Joshua and Zerubbabel are God's servants and are building the temple. To encourage and praise them, the Lord says that at some future time the Davidic heir will construct a temple that will be even more glorious. Their work is a forerunner and pointer to that person and that work. This view of now and later concerning the temple will be matched in Zechariah 9—14 in passages about Jerusalem.

Further, 6:13 promises glory and power to the Davidic branch. The text then proceeds to speak of unity between the throne and the priesthood. What has divided scholars is the means by which this peace will come, for some experts think 6:13 unites the priestly and royal offices in one person on one throne,[140] while others conclude that two persons are mentioned, the king and a priest beside him.[141] Again, as in the temple building itself, the text appears to encourage and praise Joshua and Zerubbabel by stating that the unity of purpose they so clearly share is a living portrait of the even greater glory that will come later. Since it is possible to unite the two offices contextually[142] and since the branch alone leads Israel from David's throne in all the branch passages in the canon, it is plausible to conclude that the Davidic branch will do both men's work in the future. The difficulty with this interpretation remains the meaning of "and there will be harmony between the two of them." The one-person interpretation must take "the two of them" to be two offices rather than two individuals.

The previous canonical comments about the branch help interpret the term here. There can be no doubt that "branch" refers to the Davidic ruler in Isaiah 11:1 and Jeremiah 23:1-8, and there is no reason to doubt that identification of the term here. The prophetic hope remains fixed on the promised one who will lead Israel to ultimate glory. What is interesting is that 3:8-9 and 6:12-13 also link the branch to servant and priest imagery, thus tying it to the servant songs and Psalm 110. In Zechariah, then, a converging of ideas takes place that highlights a multifaceted Davidic heir.

The God Who Forgives and Blesses: Zechariah 7—8

Zechariah 7—8 fuses past, present, future and distant future to declare that God's jealousy for Jerusalem will result in forgiveness and blessing for the people. A question about fasting (7:1-7) leads Zechariah to repeat the view of Israelite history reflected in 2 Kings 17, Jeremiah 2—6, Ezekiel 16, Hosea 1—3 and elsewhere. The people broke the covenant by oppressing one another, so the Lord sent them into exile (7:8-14). Significantly, there is no mention of idolatry. Rather the emphasis is on how fasting should lead to love of neighbor and love for the Lord, themes already developed in Isaiah 58.

Yahweh determines to intervene in this depressing scenario. Direct divine intervention in history will better the people's situation. Because of divine love for Jerusalem, God will choose to be present there again, this time as the One who blesses (9:1-9). Because of the remnant's responsiveness to Haggai and Zechariah the Lord will do good to Jerusalem, causing joy and gladness (8:10-19). Because of the city's restored favor, citizens of many nations will come there to seek the Lord (8:20-23).

In effect, all God's purposes for Israel will be fulfilled. The people will serve the Lord as a holy nation that draws all nations to its capital, where God's presence is evident. Negative history will thereby be reversed. Canonical promises such as the one to Abraham that all nations will be blessed through him will come to pass (cf. Gen 12:1-9). Since Zechariah 7—8 must be read in context with 1:7—6:15, the Davidic promises will also come true (cf. 2 Sam 7:1-17). God's stated purpose for Israel in Exodus 19:5-6 will reach fruition. Zephaniah and Isaiah's vision of a multinational people of God will materialize (cf. Zeph 3:8-9; Is 19:19-25). History will embody God's will.

The God Who Is Israel's Shepherd and Protector: Zechariah 9—11

Zechariah 9 continues the picture of future glory begun in the previous chapter. Verse 1 begins a burden, or oracle, that continues through 11:17. Another burden stretches from 12:1—14:21, and Malachi 1:1 also begins with a burden. This recurring term helps bond Zechariah 9—14 and the book of Malachi[143] and has led some scholars to doubt Zechariah's unity.[144] In its present context the first burden explains that all Israel's oppressors and ancient foes will be defeated by the Lord (9:1-8; cf. 9:4). Coupled with 8:20-23, 9:1-8 demonstrates God's sovereignty beyond Judah.[145] All the earth belongs to Yahweh (9:1), God watches the whole earth to make sure Israel is safe (9:8), and the Lord has determined to give the nations to the chosen people (9:7-8). Anyone remaining in these lands will serve the Lord. Joyce Baldwin comments that

> the first section of this second part of the book establishes from the start two important facts: the Lord's victory is certain, and He intends to bring back to Himself peoples long alienated from Him. These truths underlie all that follows and culminate in the universal worship of the King, the Lord of hosts, in 14:16-19.[146]

By now readers of prophetic literature know that the Davidic ruler must be part of this victory. In 9:9 he appears, both triumphant and meek, riding on a donkey. Thus this king unites the humility and power inherent in Deuteronomy 17:14-20's description of a king who serves the people, follows the covenant and receives Yahweh's blessings. Peace will result from this king's rule (9:10), for he will seek "the establishment of moral order and social righteousness" in the power of God's Spirit.[147] These images approximate the rule of the king mentioned in Isaiah 9:2-7 and 11:1-9 as well as the self-effacing ministry of the servant in Isaiah 42:1-4 and 52:13—53:12.[148] Because of this reign of peace, God will set all "prisoners of hope" (9:12) free (9:11-15).

All these wonders will occur because Yahweh shepherds Israel like a flock (9:16-17). When this portion of Zechariah is written the people suffer under poor shepherds (10:1-2), a common prophetic image for wicked rulers (cf. Jer 25:34-38; Ezek 34:7-10). But Yahweh will be their shepherd, which means Israel will prevail over the leaders of other lands (10:3—11:3). No one is capable of frustrating the sovereign shepherd's purposes, a fact Ezekiel 34:11-31 declares in an earlier passage that connects the Lord's shepherding of Israel, the Davidic ruler and Israel's ultimate restoration. All worthless human shepherds will be driven from the land as a prelude to that day (11:4-17).

There is no doubt that these chapters agree with the portrait of the coming Davidic descendant already drawn in Samuel, Isaiah, Jeremiah, Ezekiel and Micah. The king's character will incorporate righteousness, humility and power. His appearance will manifest God's grace and righteousness on earth.[149] Waiting for this person who will embody so many desirable characteristics offers hope to the people.[150] His coming extends hope to many nations, since the extent of his kingdom will include all of creation. This person will truly be a universal master.

The God Who Dwells in Zion: Zechariah 12—14

Zechariah's final section completes the restoration of the holy city by describing the eventual decision by God to dwell in Zion. This action will finally drive wickedness from the chosen people, city, priesthood and royal throne. Then the nations will consider Jerusalem to be Zion, the dwelling place of God, their capital city. Then the city will be holy to the Lord (14:16-21). Before that time the God who created the heavens, the earth and the human race (12:1) will strengthen Judah and Jerusalem (12:2-8). Any nation who comes against the city will be destroyed "on that day" (12:9). The Creator's blessing secures the chosen people.

Besides the Lord's favor, a particular tragedy will change the people's heart so they will be prepared for God's coming to Zion. Israel will mourn over one they have pierced (12:10). Scholars have suggested several possibilities for this person's identity, including the coming king, a prophet or some later historical figure.[151] Others have stated the impossibility of determining his identity.[152] The context of 12:10—13:9 helps produce a composite portrait of the pierced one. First, the three references to the house of David at least hint that he is a royal figure.[153] Second, the Spirit of God must be poured out for the people to repent of this sin (12:10).[154] Third, as a result of this repentance there will be a fountain of cleansing that covers all human misconduct, as well as ritual and sexual impurity (13:1).[155]

Fourth, the cleansing will lead to the removal of idols and lying prophets, two vital ingredients in Israel's past failures (13:2-6). Polytheism remains alive and well in Zechariah's time and later.[156] Fifth, God strikes a shepherd whose death causes God's people to be scattered (13:7). This shepherd has high standing, since he stands next to God.[157] Sixth, the scattering will test Israel and create a remnant who will serve the Lord (13:8-9). Thus "Israel and Yahweh will come to perfect harmony, as the covenant stipulated (13:9/Ex. 19:5)."[158] Without question, the person's death is necessary for Israel's repentance that leads to the remnant's emergence.

The final renewal of Jerusalem will occur when God descends to the city to defeat foreign armies laying siege to Israel's capital (14:1-5). Perfect weather, continuous light and living water will result, for Yahweh will rule the earth (14:6-9). Now beaten (14:10-15), the peoples of the world will worship God in a city completely holy to the Lord (14:16-21). Every major institution will become what God had intended at its inception. God's grace defeats sin and thereby overcomes all human rebellion against God's will.[159]

Canonical Synthesis: The One Who Is Pierced

Like Zechariah 9—11, Zechariah 12—14 has multiple connections with earlier texts related to the Davidic promise. Its most interesting parallels, however, are to Isaiah 52:13—53:12. Both the shepherd in Zechariah and the servant in Isaiah are righteous yet smitten by God, effect sorrowful repentance and divine forgiveness through their deaths and help produce a believing remnant. Thus there is an evident "association of ideas" between the texts.[160] Zechariah 12:10—13:9 seems to link the two figures to identify serving, shepherding and suffering with the coming Davidic ruler.

Several New Testament passages refer to Zechariah 9—14. Most of these texts are clustered in the description of Jesus' last days. For example, Matthew 21:5 and John 12:15 cite Zechariah 9:9 in the context of Jesus' triumphal entry into Jerusalem. Both Gospels thereby present Jesus as the coming Davidic shepherd whose humility is compatible with the prophet's portrayal. Similarly Matthew 26:31, Mark 14:27 and perhaps John 16:32 refer to Zechariah 13:7 to describe the scattering of the disciples on the night before the crucifixion. Their dispersal comes as a result of their shepherd's death yet also leads to the creation of a new believing remnant after the resurrection (Mt 26:32; Mk 14:28). In Zechariah and in the Gospels the smiting of the leader and the creation of the remnant are the direct work of the Lord, and this smiting constitutes both a time of judgment and the basis for hope. It is clear that Zechariah's connecting of Davidic lineage, shepherding, suffering and renewal was particularly compelling to the Gospel writers, who believed that Jesus fit the comprehensive description of the Davidic ruler found there.

The God Who Restores the People: Malachi

About seven decades after Haggai and Zechariah exhorted the Israelites to rebuild the temple, Malachi, the last of the canon's prophets, ministered in Jerusalem. By now the temple was functional, but worship was superficial. Jerusalem was again home to many Jews, yet Nehemiah found it necessary to rebuild its wall, repopulate it and help the people renew the covenant. The people were faced with social, economic and spiritual depression.[161] Malachi's message confronts these problems by fastening the people's minds on theology. This prophecy contends that postexilic Israel will flourish only when the people are renewed by a fresh vision of Yahweh's love for them and a recommitment of their willingness to love, honor and serve their Lord.

Malachi expresses the cost of renewal and explains how barriers to restoration may be removed. It does so in a measured[162] yet passionate[163] style that utilizes questions, answers, exhortations, oracles and narrativelike descriptions of activity while presenting its message. In particular, questions form six distinct segments that isolate the sins that delay the people's renewal. To effect restoration, Yahweh is presented as the God who loves Israel (1:1-5), the God who corrects priests (1:6—2:9), the God who denounces infidelity

(2:10-16), the God who establishes justice (2:17—3:5), the God who never changes (3:6-12) and the God who exposes arrogance (3:13-15). Following these foundational sections, 3:16—4:6 present Yahweh as the Lord who creates the remnant. The emergence of the remnant at the end of the book highlights the people's ultimate renewal. As in the earlier prophecies, however, only Yahweh's direct intervention in history through the day of the Lord makes this renewal possible.

The God Who Loves Israel: Malachi 1:1-5

For the Israelites of about 450 B.C., life under Persian rule in a Jerusalem devastated by time and neglect is so desperate they question God's love (1:2). Yahweh's response is based on Genesis 25:19-26, where God's choice of Isaac over Esau is first expressed by divine utterance. God's election of Israel spans sixteen centuries by Malachi's time. God explains that Jacob's descendants (Israel) will continue to be favored over Esau's (Edom).

Canonical Synthesis: God's Electing Love

God's relationship with the chosen people in Malachi's present is based on the promises made to the patriarchs in the past. All future hope is possible because the God who remains loving and faithful for more than a thousand years will maintain that loyalty indefinitely. Yahweh's love cannot be in question. Any pain the nation encounters must of necessity originate elsewhere.

Israel's election and Edom's punishment are ultimately for Yahweh's glory. God's work in judging Edom is meant to demonstrate the Lord's authority over the whole earth and to express God's character traits to all people. In this way 1:5 reflects concepts found in Joel 3:14-17, Jonah, Micah 5:4-5 and Zechariah 14:16-21, all of which emphasize the Lord's rule beyond Israel's borders. Unless Yahweh is exalted, neither Israel nor Edom will ever serve the living God. Idolatry will devastate both.

The God Who Corrects Priests: Malachi 1:6—2:9

Having removed a fundamental misconception about the ongoing nature of the covenant with Israel, the Lord moves to deal with the real issues at hand. God's people show that they despise the Lord by corrupting their worship practices. Though unacceptable sacrifices are mentioned (1:6-14), the major problems are that Israel despises God's name (1:6) and does not set their hearts to give Yahweh glory (2:2). They are arrogant and dismissive of God's revealed standards for worship (1:13). Instead of recognizing the worldwide authority of the king of the world (1:11, 14), they treat Yahweh as less important than earthly rulers (1:8).

God places the blame for this situation on the priests (2:1). Priests are charged with teaching the law and supervising appropriate worship, but they have abdicated their responsibility (2:5-9). By doing so they place the nation in risk of the covenant curses expressed in Deuteronomy 27—28 (2:1-4).[164] Thus this text affirms the priests' importance and rebukes their current activities at the same time.[165] It is crucial for the people's restoration that the priests recapture their theological vitality and reinstitute the principles that lead to blessing. Only then can the people participate in the spreading of God's glory to other peoples (1:11, 14).

The God Who Denounces Infidelity: Malachi 2:10-16

The result of the breakdown in worship is infidelity in spiritual and family matters. The two have been linked previously in Jeremiah 2:1—3:5, Ezekiel 16 and 23 and Hosea 1—3. Here the text asserts that Israel has forsaken the God who creates and makes covenant in favor of foreign gods (2:10-12). Once again idolatry emerges as the natural result of rejecting a relationship with Yahweh and neglecting covenant faithfulness. Even the sanctuary has been tainted with idolatrous practices (2:11).

Since the nation feels free to break faith with the Lord, it is hardly surprising that they will break faith with their spouses. God gives them life so that they can produce righteous offspring (2:15). Therefore God hates unwarranted divorce (2:16) and refuses to bless those who practice it (2:13-14). One type of faithlessness has led to another, when the ideal is for the covenant people to model Yahweh's loyalty and steadfastness in their homes.[166] Breaking the commands about the Lord (Ex 20:1-11) make it impossible to keep those related to community life (Ex 20:12-17). Those who do not love Yahweh find it impossible to love their neighbor (cf. Deut 6:4-9; Lev 19:18).

The God Who Establishes Justice: Malachi 2:17—3:5

Malachi's next question returns to the matter of Yahweh's character. This time it is not the Lord's love that is in question, as it was in 1:1-5, but God's justice. Israel argues that Yahweh does not merely ignore right and wrong behavior. They claim the Lord favors the wicked (2:17), which is an obvious attack on God's nature. Therefore, the prophet says, they weary Yahweh, or "put his patience to the test,"[167] a practice attributed to the wicked in Isaiah 43:24.[168] Their opinion of God places them in danger of punishment by the Lord whose justice they assail.

Yahweh's response is reminiscent of Habakkuk. Just as the earlier prophet's concerns were addressed by the revelation of coming judgment (cf. Hab 1:5-11; 2:2-11), so here God promises a dramatic evidence of divine justice. God will send a "messenger" to "prepare the way" for the Lord (3:1).

This language is also similar to Isaiah 40:3-5, where Isaiah has a herald prepare the way for the Lord's glory being poured out on suffering Israel. Once the messenger's work is done, Yahweh will come to "his temple" to cleanse it from impure practices like those mentioned in 1:6—2:9 (3:2-4). The Lord's appearance will also purify the land of unjust practices (3:5-6). Israel's concerns about justice will be addressed in a manner as awe-inspiring and thorough as the Babylonian invasion of Habakkuk's era (c. 605 B.C.). God's justice necessarily emerges in judgment.

Canonical Synthesis: The Coming Preparatory Messenger

Several suggestions have been offered about the messenger's identity. Options include Malachi himself, since his name literally means "my messenger," the angel of death, the prophets in general or a prophet who is identical to the "Elijah" in 4:5-6 who will prepare the way for God's coming.[169] Though caution must be exerted on this point, it is probably best to choose the last possibility, thereby linking the task of preparation undertaken in Isaiah 40:3-5, the figure in 3:1 and the forerunner of the Lord in 4:5-6. This decision allows vital connections between the canon in general and Malachi in particular to be made. Thus Israel will gain a clear vision of God's justice when a prophetic forerunner prepares the way for the Lord's judgment of Israel from the temple. At that time false priests, sorcerers, oppressors, adulterers, liars and blasphemers will experience divine wrath (3:2-5).

Malachi's vision of the day of the Lord resonates with several earlier passages. Like Joel 2:11, Malachi 3:2 wonders who can endure the day, all the while marveling at the wicked's call for justice in a manner similar to Isaiah 5:19 and Amos 5:18-20. The wicked will find themselves refined like metal (3:3), an image introduced in Isaiah 1:25, Jeremiah 6:27-30 and Zechariah 13:9. The list of sins in 3:5 is a veritable summary of a host of laws found in Exodus and Deuteronomy.[170] As in all the prophecies dealing with judgment, the Lord's direct activity creates the removal of the sinful. Still, Malachi's introduction of a forerunner provides a new element of this intervention, one that Mark 1:2-3 identifies with the ministry of John the Baptist.

The God Who Never Changes: Malachi 3:6-12

Though Israel accuses Yahweh of having shifting standards of love, blessing and justice, the Lord has not changed (3:6). Neither has Israel. God continues to spare people who break the covenant repeatedly, with faulty tithes and offerings in this case (3:8-12). Only repentance can replace the covenant curse they now endure with the covenant blessing they desire (3:7). In other words, the principles found in Leviticus 26 and Deuteronomy 27—28 still apply. If Israel continues to live as their ancestors did in the era of the judges and the divided kingdom, then they will pay the penalty they have chosen for themselves. Regardless of their decision, Yahweh remains sovereign, just and kind.

The God Who Exposes Arrogance: Malachi 3:13-15

All of Israel's claims against Yahweh amount to an arrogant refusal to recognize their sinfulness and God's holiness. The people oppose the Lord verbally and argue that God blesses the arrogant (3:13-15). If so, they would all be blessed! Instead they meet the fate of the arrogant announced in Isaiah 2:6-22, 10:5-19, 13:1-22 and 58:1-14 and Jeremiah 7:1-83. They must be taught that God rules the world justly and that human defiance must be removed so that divine power may be viewed for what it is: the human race's only hope for forgiveness, renewal and blessing.

The God Who Creates the Remnant: Malachi 3:16—4:6

As in Haggai, the Lord's work through Malachi receives a positive response. It is the remnant, those who fear the Lord (3:16), who turn from arrogance and corrupt worship. These persons have their name written in God's book (3:16). They will be spared on the day of the Lord, for God separates the wicked and the righteous then (3:17-18). Though there will be terrible suffering for the sinner, the remnant will rejoice in their final healing (4:1-3). These things will occur because God will act directly and definitively on their behalf (4:3).

How will Yahweh create this remnant? Through the law revealed to Moses, creating expectancy and humility in their hearts (4:4), and by the sending of Elijah the prophet (4:5), who will prepare God's people for God's action (4:6; cf. 3:1). Once again it will be a combination of canonical writings and prophetic preaching that will bring the people to a realization of their need for repentance and turning to the Lord. This pattern has been true at least since Isaiah 8:11-22, where Isaiah is told to emphasize the law and testimonies as he strives to help the remnant adhere to Yahweh during difficult days.

Conclusion

Malachi brings both the Twelve and the Prophets to a close. As the concluding segment of the Twelve, the prophecy completes the book's charting of Israel and the nations' sin, the inevitable punishment of that sin and the renewal that follows judgment. Set in about 450 B.C., Malachi finishes the Twelve's historical odyssey from before Assyria's defeat of Samaria, through Babylon's destruction of Jerusalem, to Persia's dominance over the chosen people and the promised land. Thus the Twelve covers three centuries of decline, defeat and initial recovery. Malachi also emphasizes the future envisioned by the rest of the Twelve, which focuses on God's intervention in history on behalf of the remnant.

In other words, Malachi caps the Twelve's determined depiction of the God who keeps promises. These promises include blessings for the remnant that turns from sin as well as woe for the wicked who refuse to obey Yahweh. As the Former Prophets have already indicated, God's word determines the course of history as Israel and the nations either believe it and obey or reject it and worship other gods. All the grief promised by the preexilic prophets comes true, so the victory pledged to the remnant will surely materialize as well.

Synthesis of Prophetic Theology

There can be no question that the prophetic literature builds upon the theological ideas found in the Pentateuch. God remains the Creator, sustainer, deliverer, Holy One and renewer of the covenant. Yahweh continues to be presented as the only deity, the sole Lord of all that exists. In particular the Lord remains the God who has created, blessed, sustained and judged Israel depending on whether the people have kept or broken the Sinai covenant.

The covenant principles found in the Law lead the prophets to approve or denounce the chosen nation's activities during their own lifetimes. The covenant blessings and consequences announced in Leviticus 26 and Deuteronomy 27—28 help the prophets assess Israel's past, and these same concepts give them hope that the Lord has not finished with sinful Israel. The God who forgave once can surely do so again, as Deuteronomy 30:1-10 indicates.

Still, the prophets shape these notions into memorable literature that charts its own course as it analyzes the past, present and future. As for the past, the Former Prophets set the tone for what follows. These books integrate hard facts and prophetic interpretation. For example, the author of Kings presents events he believes happen. Parables and proverbs appear, of course, yet are identified as such (cf. 1 Kings 22:18-28; 2 Kings 14:9-10). The author could have chosen a mythic format similar to those adopted by other nations but does not do so. There is no pantheon of gods, no hierarchy of gods, no other gods at all. There is no cyclical view of human events, no gods who act only slightly better than humans, no failure of Yahweh's character. The humans depicted here are hardly mythic either. The best of them are frail, fallible and weak. They fear death, give bad advice, sin in their old age and fight the wrong battles. They are real people in real situations. God meets them where they are, only occasionally working a miracle, and only then to protect the faithful.

Above all else, the text focuses on Yahweh. God allows no rivals, because to do so would allow people to believe and live a lie. The historian of Joshua—Kings claims that ignoring this view of history can be deadly, for it leads to national defeat (2 Kings 17:7-41). Thus it is crucial that every reader adopt this view of history. Only those who embrace this theology will find hope for the future, for if Yahweh is but one of many gods or is not like the text says, then there is no reason to think Israel will emerge from oblivion. Why believe in a real future history if a mythic history, however well-crafted, artistic, beautiful and well-meaning, lies in the past? Exile was real, and only a real God relating to actual human beings in space and time events can make renewal real.

The historian argues exhaustively that idolatry, refusing to heed the prophets and general covenant infidelity caused the nation to disintegrate and eventually sink into exile. Capped by 2 Kings 17, these books chronicle a fall from victory to defeat. At the same time, the Davidic promise set forth in 2 Samuel 7 leaves room for future hope that the nation will rise toward the Lord and renewal at some distant time. After all, an eternal covenant is promised to David.

Nothing in the Latter Prophets sets aside this view of the past introduced in Joshua, Judges, Samuel and Kings. Isaiah establishes the tone for following books by focusing on the idolatry and covenant breaking rampant in eighth-century B.C. Judah and Israel in Isaiah 1—6 and then stressing the coming Davidic heir in Isaiah 7—12. Isaiah 13—23 emphasizes Yahweh's sovereignty over the nations, and the rest of the prophecy expands the discussion of these issues. Jeremiah 2—6, Ezekiel 16, 20 and 23 and various passages in the Twelve reaffirm Isaiah's view of the parallels between Israel's past and the current situation. As long as the current generation lives like their predecessors there will be no spiritual, military or economic glory for the people of God. Likewise Jeremiah 46—51, Ezekiel 25—32, Amos 1:3—2:3 and other passages agree with Isaiah that the nations of the world all belong to and are thereby assessed by the Lord.

Given the sinfulness of the covenant nation and the nations, the near future holds some events already described in the Former Prophets. Isaiah, Hosea and Amos expect Israel to fall, and the Assyrian invasion depicted in 2 Kings 17 does indeed overwhelm the northern kingdom. Nahum celebrates the fact that Assyria itself falls to the Babylonians, an event prefigured in 2 Kings 20:12-21 and one that proves that the wicked do not prosper forever no matter how powerful they are. Jeremiah, Ezekiel and Habakkuk expect Babylon to destroy Judah, a reality described in 2 Kings 25 as well as in Jeremiah 39 and 52. The exile anticipated for covenant disobedience in Deuteronomy 27—28 becomes a fact as the prophets divulge the proof of their historical ideology.

As for the distant future, the promise to David acts as the major catalyst for positive change and punitive judgment. Isaiah 7—11 and 40—66 highlight a king and suffering servant who redeems the people from their sins and ushers in a kingdom of peace and glory. Jeremiah 23:1-8 and 33:14-22 link the Davidic ruler to the coming new-covenant era mentioned in 31:31-34 when all the covenant people will know the Lord. Ezekiel 34:20-24 places the Davidic heir squarely in the center of a coming spiritual renewal of the people of God, as do Micah 5:2-5, Zechariah 9:9-13 and Zechariah 12:10—13:9. For renewal and perfect peace to emerge, however, the wicked must be removed from the earth, which entails judgment for all who reject God's word.

Only the remnant will enjoy the benefits of God's blessings when the Davidic king comes, or on the day of the Lord. Jeremiah 31:31-34 claims that at that time the people of God will consist only of believers. In effect there will be no remnant among the people of God, for there will be no unbelievers associated with "Israel." Zephaniah 3:8-9 indicates that this remnant will include persons from nations other than Israel, an eventuality set forth as early as Isaiah 19:19-25, or even as early as the episode with Rahab in Joshua.

Ezekiel 11:19 states that the remnant will be created by direct action of God's Spirit upon the hearts of those who constitute the new people of God. Again Isaiah, Jeremiah and Ezekiel tie the Davidic king to the Spirit's work in creating the believing community. At this juncture in time the people of God, regardless of race, will all know the Lord because they will all be recipients of a direct work of the Spirit of God on their hearts that makes them participants in a new covenant. The Davidic king will be the key person in the supervising of this covenant. Judgment day is called the day of the Lord everywhere in the prophetic literature. The defeats suffered at the hand of Assyria, Babylon and Persia are viewed as days of the Lord, of course, yet the final judgment is the conclusive day of the Lord. God the holy Creator, sustainer, deliverer and healer will become the God of final, lasting, permanent punishment. All wicked ones will cease to harass the faithful.

The faithful remnant will enjoy the fruits of the kingdom of peace initiated by the Davidic heir. God will rule on earth at this time, according to Isaiah 25:6-8 and Zechariah 14:1-21, a reign that coincides with the work of the Davidic ruler mentioned repeatedly in those books. It is on behalf of this remnant that the Lord will initiate judgment, and only this remnant will endure its fierce coming.

Ultimately the prophets lived in three distinct yet inseparable time frames. They felt inextricably linked to the covenant people of the past. Their covenants were the same ones mediated through Abraham, Moses and David. Their histories were intertwined with their forebears. All the same, their present was defined by their current adherence to the Lord's standards. Their faith that led to obedience was possible only because of what had already transpired. Finally, their future was as tangible as their present because they did not know when God would break into history with the appearance of judgment, the Davidic heir or the final rule of God on earth. They awaited fulfillment of the final results of the historical scheme they believed was revealed by the Lord even as they lived out their faith and obedience in light of the past. They lived responsibly because they lived obediently and hopefully. Their words interpreted the past, gave meaning to the present and instilled hope for the future because they were the very words of Yahweh.

Permeating all these prophetic themes is the conviction that there is no other God. No other deity exists, so only the Lord may judge, renew or save. Idols are merely the work of human hands, but Yahweh is the maker of human hands. Therefore Isaiah 44:9-20, Jeremiah 50:1-3, and other passages feel free to proclaim the utter inability of idols to save. By the end of the Twelve, postexilic Israel hardly dares to consider the existence of other gods, since they have come to at least marginally accept the prophetic view of history. Only the Creator can reveal standards by which they must live, and it is this revealer who must be obeyed.

15

The God Who Rules

Psalms

. . . .

NO OTHER OLD TESTAMENT BOOK HAS THE THEOLOGICAL AND HISTORICAL scope that Psalms displays. As a theological document, the book embraces the full range of biblical confessions about the Lord's character, activity and concerns. Here God is called Creator, sustainer, protector, Savior, judge, covenant maker and restorer. Here the whole range of divine actions that give content to those names unfold, and here the historical settings that provide the context for theological reality and reflection are stated as well. All the major events of Israelite history—creation, the life of Abraham, the exodus, the conquest, the monarchy, the exile, the return to the land—are mentioned to anchor the book's confessions to daily human life. Given the comprehensive nature of the psalms' comments about God's supreme power within history, it is proper to analyze their theological contribution under the overall theme of the God who rules. It is this God that Israel celebrates, confesses and worships.

Because of its great theological and historical scope, Psalms is a perfect book to begin the Writings, the last of the three major canonical divisions.[1] Psalms probes the depths of suffering and discusses the origins and applications of wisdom, topics that occupy Job and Proverbs, the next two books in the canon. It also emphasizes the importance of the Davidic covenant, the career of Solomon, the struggle for meaning in life, the pain of exile and the challenge of renewing true worship in the land after the exile. Thus a theological orientation for Ruth, Song of Solomon, Ecclesiastes, Lamentations,

Esther, Daniel, Ezra, Nehemiah and Chronicles is apparent in Psalms. These books have specific theological contributions of their own, but their canonical role is also to supplement ideas already introduced in Psalms and earlier texts. In this way the Writings have both a unity of their own and a shared unity with the whole of the Old Testament.

Scholarly approaches to the psalms have proceeded along fairly distinct lines in the past, though some new ground is being broken. Those familiar with the interpretational traditions outlined in earlier chapters of this volume will note how Psalms studies parallel schools of thought in Pentateuch and Prophets research. Much of the work done by Christian authors between the writing of the New Testament and the commentaries of Martin Luther (1513-1516) and John Calvin (1557)[2] was allegorical in nature and tended to take nearly every conceivable opportunity to apply passages to the life and work of Jesus Christ.[3] Luther and in particular Calvin stressed interpreting the psalms in their historical context and in their original language. Both took the superscriptions to the psalms to be accurate traditions about when the texts were written. Both stressed the Christ-oriented nature of the psalms, though they did not always agree that the New Testament cited psalms according to their original context.[4]

Several major scholars produced studies of Psalms between 1557 and 1906, but only a few can be mentioned here. In 1753, Robert Lowth explained the nature of Hebrew poetry as consisting of parallelisms. This term refers to the tendency of Hebrew poems to be either synonymous, antithetical or synthetic in successive lines.[5] Wilhelm M. L. de Wette produced a volume in 1811 that questioned the accuracy of the psalms' superscriptions, considered some psalms nationalistic pieces and doubted the appropriateness of interpreting many of the psalms as predicting Christ's coming. As he did in his works on Old Testament theology, he stressed the enduring religious truths that could be gained from the psalms.[6] At the other end of the theological spectrum, Franz Delitzsch's 1867 commentary on Psalms emphasized the reliability of the superscriptions' historical reconstructions, affirmed the interpretation of specific psalms related to the coming Savior and critiqued the views of critical scholars.[7] The renowned Baptist preacher C. H. Spurgeon published his seven-volume commentary and compilation of relevant quotations about Psalms from 1882 to 1886.[8] This series marked a high point in devotional and expositional treatments of the psalms. Finally, Charles A. Briggs and Emily G. Briggs's two-volume 1906 commentary on Psalms capped early critical work on the book. Briggs and Briggs undertake careful textual and linguistic analysis and generally date most of the psalms much later than does Delitzsch.[9] Their comments are clearly akin to Julius Wellhausen's opinions on the Pentateuch in their interpretative principles. At the end of this era the chief theological battles were over biblical accuracy and the nature of the psalms related to the Davidic covenant.

It is impossible to overestimate the impact of Hermann Gunkel's work on Psalms from 1906 to the present. By 1906 Gunkel had written his famous commentary on Genesis (1901) and had begun to sketch the basics of what would become his standard means of examining psalms.[10] This method, which is known as *form criticism,* seeks to group psalms according to their literary or liturgical type and then to suggest the life setting that initiated their writing. Between 1913 and 1933 Gunkel published works on the psalms that applied form criticism to the texts, a practice that revolutionized Psalms studies.[11] He categorizes the psalms into various types, such as the hymn, individual lament, thanksgiving song, community lament and royal psalms, and states the special literary characteristics of each.[12] Because he does not accept the superscriptions as historically accurate, Gunkel locates the psalms' origins almost exclusively in Israel's postexilic worship. Because of his historical and literary interests Gunkel's theological comments are limited, but his observations about the psalms within Israel's religious life lead to theological reflection, as will be noted.

H. J. Kraus also analyzes psalms according to their forms, settings and purpose in worship.[13] In this manner he mirrors Gunkel's procedures.[14] Kraus's major contribution, however, is his determination to move beyond historical and linguistic analysis to theological reflection. In his *Theology of the Psalms,* Kraus stresses the need to focus first on God's acts and character and then to state what it meant for Israel to exist as a worshiping community under Yahweh's lordship. To this end he subsumes all Psalms' convictions under the main issue of God's identity.[15] Kraus thereby assesses the contents of the psalms with a theological program in mind, a methodology quite conducive to an effective linking of exegesis and theology.

Several factors have emerged from Gunkel's domination of Psalms studies. First, form-critical analysis has properly and effectively analyzed the literary types of psalms and how they generally unfold. A clearer understanding of individual psalms has resulted, as has the recognition that these individual texts had many kindred compositions. Second, a better sense of the psalms as parts of worship has been gained, which helps retain their importance for today's community of faith. Third, despite these positive features, the psalms have been isolated from one another. No sense of book continuity really exists in the form-critical approach. Canonical context is lost, thus making Psalms unique in the way it "must" be interpreted. Fourth, by usually rejecting the validity of psalm titles and historical statements in the psalms themselves in favor of hypothetical and unsubstantiated religious festivals, many form critics cut off the psalms from Israelite history. This result is the opposite of what they intend, but the fact remains nonetheless. Fifth, these results point out the need for canonical analysis that weds form, history, content and theology. This need is particularly acute for theological reflection such as this volume attempts.

Some progress along these lines has been made recently. Though he does not make great strides in his own work, Brevard Childs's insistence on canonical theology emphasizes the possibilities associated with charting a new course. Childs notes that however a canonical approach proceeds, it should include an awareness of the superscriptions' role in forming Psalms, the growing awareness of God's future rule and the stressing of Davidic psalms in the New Testament.[16] Though not adopting Childs's program explicitly, J. L. Mays's *Psalms* (1994) does attempt to analyze the book's ongoing content connections while stressing psalms that expose canonical seams. He also emphasizes psalms that have influenced biblical theology and the church's worship traditions.[17] Childs and Mays, then, demonstrate that it is possible to begin to move toward a canonical, contextual, theological reading of Psalms.

In a seminal 1991 essay, John Walton suggests a way to link Psalms' canonical division into five books,[18] its superscriptions, its contents, its theology and Israelite history. Building on Gerald Wilson's analysis of the canonical structure of Psalms,[19] Walton states that Psalms 41, 72, 89 and 106 conclude with a doxology, or blessing, of Yahweh, that Psalms 1—2 introduce the book and that superscriptions group specific psalms together for specific purposes. Further, he states that Psalms displays a "content agenda" that includes an introduction (Ps 1—2), David's conflict with Saul (Ps 3—41), David's reign (Ps 42—72), the Assyrian crisis (Ps 73—89), reflection on Jerusalem's destruction (Ps 90—106), reflection on the return to the land (Ps 107—145) and concluding praises (Ps 146—150).[20] These divisions and content statements keep faith with the shape of Psalms and offer ways by which major theological themes may be discussed. They also allow for both essential diversity and necessary unity in Psalms interpretation.

The great length and breadth of Psalms necessitates a clear statement about how the book will be treated in this chapter. First, the canonical suggestions made by Childs, Mays, Walton and earlier writers such as Delitzsch will be followed: The book will be analyzed according to its five traditional parts, with the main theological emphases of each noted. Linkages to earlier canonical texts will be highlighted. Superscriptions will be taken seriously as historical and thematic markers.[21] Second, the psalms will be interpreted according to their literary types. Gunkel, Sigmund Mowinckel and Claus Westermann are correct in many of their designations of single psalms. Examining a text by its specific type often aids specific theological reflection. Form-critical suggestions about life settings will only rarely be adopted. Third, not every psalm will be treated. No selection could please everyone, yet several psalms have been isolated as crucial by a number of commentators. Particular attention will be paid to psalms with connections to the whole of Scripture. Fourth, the book's confessions about God will be given priority and the people of God and enemies of God given secondary importance. Kraus's conviction along these lines is correct at this point.

As has been stated, Psalms' Hebrew text structures the book in five parts. Part one spans Psalms 1—41 and focuses on the God who instructs, elects and delivers. The initial three psalms introduce these themes. All but four of these psalms are given superscriptions related to David, so the canon makes his life the focal point in these texts. Priority in this section is given to how the Lord delivers from trouble. Part two includes Psalms 42—72 and highlights the God who establishes and delivers. Psalm 72 is ascribed to Solomon and ends with the phrase "This concludes the prayers of David son of Jesse," which probably indicates that parts one and two were originally joined as the first Psalter. Psalms 66 and 68 summarize Israelite history, stopping with temple worship. God continues to deliver David and has placed Solomon on the throne. The promises declared in 2 Samuel 7 have begun to materialize.

Part three (Ps 73—89) stresses the God who rebukes and rejects. Only Psalm 86 is ascribed to David, though the superscriptions may place some of the texts near his era. Worship in Jerusalem, or Zion, is mentioned (cf. Ps 84 and 87), but the Davidic promise is conspicuously absent. Only the historical summary in Psalm 89 mentions David's election, and then only in the context of Jerusalem's destruction. The whole segment emphasizes the growth of wickedness in Israel, with the historical summary in Psalm 78 providing an apt description of Israel's covenant failures since the exodus.

Part four (Ps 90—106) portrays God as the One who remembers and sustains. Only three of these psalms are traced to individuals: Psalm 90 to Moses and Psalms 101 and 103 to David. Psalms 90—100 highlight God's power, especially as Creator, while Psalms 101—104 stress loyalty to the Lord. Apparently psalms connected to Moses and David are chosen to highlight how the Creator sustains the faithful. Psalms 105—106 offer a historical summary that ends with prayers for return from the ends of the earth, or from exile. No Zion poems appear.

Part five (Ps 107—150) presents the God who restores and renews. Several psalms celebrate God's steadfast love (107:1; 108:1; 117:2; 118:1), and the famous psalms of ascent (Ps 120—134) find pilgrims returning to Jerusalem for worship. The book concludes with five psalms of unrestrained praise for the God who rules the earth and blesses Israel. The postexilic era is reflected in this section. Psalm 119 anchors the nation and its covenant in the written word here, just as Psalm 19 does in part one. Israel's praise indicates that its history has moved from exodus to new exodus.

Regardless of the specific circumstances in the sections or individual psalms, the writers emphasize God's sovereignty over Israel and the rest of creation. As Creator, redeemer, judge and covenant maker the Lord rules as divine King, and as such he merits worship, whether in the form of praise or lament. As sovereign, Yahweh makes plain by his activity that there is no other god, though this fact is constantly in dispute. As Mays observes:

> Because it is the reign of God whose way in the world is being worked out through one people and one presence and one king and a particular kind of human conduct, the rule encounters the opposition of nations and rulers and people whose gods and power and autonomy are denied by the reign of the Lord. There is not a psalm that does not in some way or other reflect some dimension of this fundamental conflict.[22]

Because God's uniqueness is expressed through historical conflict, Kraus argues, Psalms' repeated claims that Yahweh alone is God is no mere theoretical statement.[23] Rather monotheism in the psalms is grounded in daily life by constant confessions that God lives, speaks, acts, helps, sees, hears, answers and saves.[24] No other god does any of these things in Psalms. Thus whatever name is given God (e.g., Elohim or Yahweh) in Psalms, there is only one God, and this God rules creation. In Psalms, as elsewhere in the Old Testament, the God who creates is the only God who exists. As Ludwig Köhler writes, "God is the ruling Lord: that is the one fundamental statement in the theology of the Old Testament."[25] This principle undergirds all the diverse material found in the Psalms.

The God Who Instructs, Elects and Delivers: Psalms 1—41

Seventy-three psalms are linked to David, and thirty-seven of those appear in this part of the book. The description of David's life in Samuel and Kings highlights how God delivers the chosen one from all manner of self-inflicted and external harm and also stresses the promise to David of an eternal kingdom. At the same time, David is portrayed as a grateful worshiper of Yahweh (cf. 2 Sam 22:1—23:7) and as the one king who, despite his obvious sins, most embodies the principles for kingship found in Deuteronomy 17:14-20 (cf. 1 Kings 15:1-5). Thus it is hardly surprising to find instruction, covenant, deliverance and praise stressed in a section so shaped by psalms considered Davidic. Psalms 1—3 and Psalms 8, 18, 19 and 22 characterize the linkage between the narrative material in Samuel and Kings and the poetic passages in Psalms. These texts introduce many kindred psalms that follow.

Psalm 1 has long been considered an introduction to the whole book because of its emphasis on the importance of following God's word. For example, Calvin writes, "He who collected the Psalms into one volume, whether Ezra or some other person, appears to have placed this Psalm at the beginning, by way of preface, in which he inculcates upon all the godly the duty of meditating upon the law of God."[26] Those who obey the Lord's word will live wisely, reject the lifestyle of unbelievers and prosper (1:1-3), while the wicked will be swept away (1:4-6). Therefore, Artur Weiser observes, this psalm, "standing at the entrance to the Psalter as a signpost," offers God-fearing people "clear guidance regarding the way in which they shall conduct their lives."[27] It also warns unbelievers of the fate awaiting them.

This introduction to Psalms has certain specific canonical linkages. First, its emphasis on meditating on God's word as the key to success sounds very much like Joshua 1:7-8, the opening episode in the Prophets. There the Lord tells Joshua that the written, revealed word will guide him; here the whole believing community is told the same thing. God's written word remains vital to the people of God. Second, the text's usage of wisdom themes such as righteousness as a lifestyle or journey (1:1), success growing from adherence to previously revealed principles (1:2-3) and the distinction between the faithful and the wicked (1:4-6) remind readers of past texts such as Deuteronomy 27—28, Joshua 1:1-9 and 1 Kings 2:1-10. They also set the stage for other "wisdom psalms"[28] such as Psalm 37 and for Wisdom writings such as Job, Proverbs and Ecclesiastes. Thus this one chapter introduces the Writings and at the same time links the Law, the Prophets and the Writings.

Psalm 2 helps its predecessor introduce the Psalter, for Psalms 1—2 both lack superscriptions, and 1:1 begins with a statement of who is "blessed," a concept that finishes Psalm 2 (cf. 2:12).[29] Virtually all scholars consider the second psalm a royal psalm, or one "in which the King is unmistakably in the foreground."[30] Later royal psalms include Psalms 18, 20, 21, 45, 72, 101, 110, 132 and 144,[31] so this text introduces a literary type that spans the Psalter. Mowinckel and Weiser deem this passage an enthronement psalm written after David's era, but William Holladay and Derek Kidner think it likely originated in David's reign.[32] No one can dispute the fact that this text marks the Davidic lineage as God's chosen family to lead Israel.

Four segments structure the passage. First, 2:1-3 depicts "kings of the earth" plotting against the Lord and the Lord's anointed. Second, 2:4-6 pictures God as laughing at such insolence and then as identifying the anointed of 2:2 as the king the Lord has installed on Zion (2:6). David and David's descendants are Yahweh's chosen, anointed ones. Third, 2:7-9 finds God calling David his "son" to whom the ends of the earth will be given as an inheritance. All who oppose the Davidic lineage oppose God's infallible decree concerning the present and future. Fourth, 2:10-12 counsels the kings to bow to God's will if they want to be "blessed" (2:12). Nations' fortunes are bound up in their kings' obedience to this divine election and blessing of David.

David's exaltation here resonates with many promises in the Former and Latter Prophets. Of course, 2 Samuel 7 begins the specific Davidic tradition, but texts such as Isaiah 9:6-7 and 11:1-10, Amos 9:11-15 and Micah 5:1-5 state specifically that the Davidic Savior will rule all nations. Every other prediction of the greatest anointed one includes direct ties to David's family. No other source is ever named. All power will eventually rest there.

Psalm 3 demonstrates the fact that David is chosen and blessed does not mean he and his descendants will live trouble-free lives. Quite the contrary, for David's own life is marked more by struggles and opposition than peace. This simple lament notes the writer's many foes (3:1-2), considers God his security (3:3-6) and asks the Lord to deliver from the wicked (3:7-8). Faith is palpable, but the fact remains that the God who instructs, elects and blesses allows the faithful to endure trouble of all sorts. Remnant living is not easy, not even for the one given the promise of an eternal kingdom.

The lament form is crucial for the rest of Psalms and the remainder of the canon. Westermann asserts that

> the individual psalm of lament is the most common psalm type in the Psalter. More than fifty of the 150 Psalms are of this type, Psalms 3—17 (with the exception of 8, 9, 15); 22—28 (except for 24); 35—43 (except for 37); part of 40; 51—64 (with the exception of 60), and many individual passages as well. Outside the Psalter we have Lamentations 3; Jeremiah 11; 15; 17; 18; 20 and many sections in the book of Job.[33]

To this list could be added laments of confession found in Daniel 9:1-19 and Ezra 9:1-15. Those who decide to serve the one God will be challenged and attacked by those who do not. Circumstances such as foreign armies' attacks and exile itself place faithful remnant believers in harsh situations. Their confession is that God has delivered them in the past and will do so again in the new distress. It is this faith that marks their prayers with hope instead of despair.[34]

Two other psalms with Davidic connections and lament overtones deserve mention at this point. Psalms 18 and 22 describe settings in which the Lord meets the author's urgent needs. The first text is ascribed to David as he rejoices in his deliverance from Saul. As was stated in the chapter on Samuel, Psalm 18 appears almost word for word, including the superscription, in 2 Samuel 22, where the poem summarizes Yahweh's work on David's behalf. This text's main point is that God intervened powerfully for David in actual historical circumstances,[35] a fact that justifies the faith expressed. The passage's final verse confesses that the Davidic covenant is a major factor in this deliverance, since covenantal steadfast love is extended to both David and his descendants (18:50).

Psalm 22 follows two royal psalms that state the king's faith in God in the midst of trials (cf. Ps 20—21). This psalm expands the scope and depth of the suffering theme greatly. Here the writer feels God-forsaken (22:1), endures mocking (22:6-8) and suffers physical pain (22:14-18). The statement of faith highlights assurance of deliverance (22:19-24) and confidence that all nations will turn to the God who made them (22:25-31). This believer desires deliverance to result in witness and an ever-expanding kingdom of God. Thus, for this psalmist, suffering becomes redemptive as others marvel at how God cares for the faithful. Lament is transformed into praise born of a specific confession of faith as David's pain is relieved.

Even passages that break the chain of laments and royal psalms reinforce the themes of God's instruction, election and deliverance. They do so by adding other canonical convictions to Psalms' theological framework. For example, Psalm 8 is set between the laments and royal psalms that characterize Psalms 3—7 and 9—18. This psalm praises God for caring for people, an attitude more or less assumed in laments. God's concern for people comes from the fact that the Lord is the Creator (8:1-4) who out of sovereignty and omnipotence has given human beings responsibility over the earth.[36] Psalm 8:5-8 affirms the emphasis in Genesis 1:26-31 on the duties God reveals as unique to the human race.[37] Again the fact that Yahweh is the sole Creator is the reason why the Lord instructs, elects and delivers people. David is given royal status by the same ruler who gives human beings ruler status over creation.

Psalm 19 explains how Yahweh chooses to reveal truths that help believers know how to learn, govern and lament. First, 19:1-6 returns to the creation motif to eliminate any sense that idols are a viable worship option. All of creation declares that it has a maker; it is not self-existent. Not even the sun, a popular object of worship in the ancient world, has deity status. Rather, "the sun . . . is but the work of God's hands, and all worship is to be given to the creator alone."[38] Nature itself reveals its maker. Second, Psalm 19:7-11 extols the accuracy and effectiveness of God's revealed, written word. The written law and its attendant testimonies, precepts, commands, worship regulations and case laws are perfect, certain, right, pure, clean and true respectively. As for their value, these writings change hearts, impart wisdom, give joy, produce insight, provide stability and define fairness. In other words, no part of the written text is errant, frivolous or lacking in importance. Thus the written word of God has unsurpassed worth for every area of life. Third, Psalm 19:12-14 claims that only God's revelation keeps the writer from secret or willful sins. God's word complements nature as a means of teaching monotheism and its meaning within the context of Yahweh's work with Israel. Creation points to the Creator; then the revealed word gives specific substance to the nature of the Creator.[39]

Psalm 41 closes the first section of the book by stressing themes found throughout these chapters. How one may be "blessed" is considered in 41:1-3. God's deliverance from disaster takes precedence in 41:4-12. Praise for the Lord's everlasting care for Israel concludes this Davidic psalm (41:13). God's instruction, deliverance, election and grace all receive attention. Psalm types are echoed as well. The blessing of Yahweh in 41:13 provides an appropriate benediction for this segment.

Canonical Synthesis: The Creator's Written Word
Some canonical observations have already been made about Psalms 1—3 and 18, so the comments here will focus on texts that have not been covered. Psalm 8 and Psalm 19:1-6 fit the canon's enduring focus on the one God who created the heavens and earth. These texts stress how the Lord's creator status leads to divine concern for human beings and to the need to reveal specific principles to them. Yahweh's ruling authority creates care, not oppression. Certainly this Creator merits praise.

Psalm 19:7-11 summarizes what God's written word has meant throughout the canon. When God speaks to Moses, the deuteronomistic historian or the prophets it is not an uncertain, unconvincing or unuseful word. Psalm 119, the longest psalm, reaffirms these points in exacting detail. New Testament texts such as 2 Timothy 3:14-17 and 2 Peter 1:16-21 agree that Scripture comes from God, may be trusted and has great value. Since the words are God's, they are perfect. Since they are Yahweh's, they are authoritative. Since they are so thorough, they are sufficient.

Canonical Synthesis: Psalm 22 and Christ's Suffering
Psalm 22 is best known in Christian circles as the lament used by the Gospels' writers to pattern the description of Jesus' crucifixion. Jesus himself cites Psalm 22:1 as his own lament at feeling God-forsaken (cf. Mt 27:46; Mk 15:34). Given the Old Testament context for laments, Jesus' cry is the beginning of an anguished statement of faith, not an accusation. Matthew 27:39-44, Mark 18:29-32 and Luke 23:35-37 echo Psalm 22:7-8 by noting the mocking Jesus endures. The dividing of garments noted in 22:18 occurs in all four Gospels.[40] In other words, Jesus embraces Psalm 22 as his own lament over suffering, and the Gospels adopt it as a means of telling readers that Jesus is the sufferer/lamenter of all sufferers and lamenters. Thus Psalm 22 is "a hermeneutical guide" for understanding Jesus' suffering.[41] It helps readers of the Gospels know that Jesus suffered unjustly, in faith and with sure hope for deliverance.

The God Who Establishes and Protects: Psalms 42—72
Part two highlights the Lord's ongoing protection of David that allows for the

establishment of the Davidic covenant and its positive results. The super-scriptions list four sources for these texts: the sons of Korah, who were temple musicians (Ps 42—49; cf. 1 Chron 6:22); Asaph, one of David's appointed choirmasters (Ps 50; 73—83; cf. 1 Chron 6:39; 15:17; 2 Chron 5:12); David (Ps 51—65, 68—70); and Solomon (Ps 72). Psalms 66, 67 and 71 are anonymous.[42] The passages ascribed to Korah and Asaph stress the estab-lishment of worship, while those ascribed to David and Solomon focus on divine protection and the continuity of the Davidic covenant. The three anonymous texts emphasize the work of God in Israel's history from creation to David's time.

As a group, Psalms 42—50 are characterized by the community's desire to know and serve God. Psalms 42—43 are a unified lament in which the psalmist is downcast over seeking the Lord and seemingly having no success. Psalm 44 mourns national defeat despite the people's faithfulness. Where is God? Psalm 45 answers in part by stating that the Lord is still with the king, providing queen and throne for him. Psalms 46—49 are statements of faith that God remains Israel's help, and Psalm 50 contains God's own promise to save those who honor him. The God who seems hidden during stressful times responds to seeking, penitent, remnant worshipers.

David's psalms in Psalms 51—65 have a similar seeking tone to them. Psalm 51 begins this process by systematically asking for forgiveness. Ascribed to David's adultery with Bathsheba, this text stresses the fact that sin is the chief way God will be absent from the believer. In this way it agrees with Psalms 6 and 32. The wicked are boasters (52:1) and fools (53:1), but the penitent sinner discovers forgiveness, renewed desire for worship and a fresh start with Yahweh (51:13-19). Psalms 54—64 reflect crisis situations in David's life. Whether set in his early or later years, these passages sound an urgent plea for God's help. Without the Lord's protecting mercy, David's wicked enemies will triumph over him. Psalm 65 acts as a companion passage to Psalm 50, for like its predecessor this psalm praises God for rescuing when sought. The variety of settings and pleas in Psalms 42—65 indicate that the Lord is able to save in any situation.

Psalms 66—68 are particularly important because they initiate the process of summarizing Israelite history that is taken up in Psalms 78, 89 and 104—106. Psalms 66 and 67 establish Israel's history on the twin notions that Yahweh rules all nations and merits their worship (66:1-4; 67:1-7). Yahweh turned the sea into dry land to effect the exodus (66:5-7), tested Israel in the desert (66:8-12a), brought them to the land (66:12b), gave them a worship center and the joy of worship (66:13-15) and protected them in the land (68:7-29). All these truths fuel worship as they produce prayer, praise and faith in the king and the people (66:13-15; 68:24-29). The temple is the focal point of this realization that Yahweh deserves praise for establishing Israel and Israel's worship in the midst of real historical events.

Psalm 72 ends part two with an intercessory prayer that a new king may serve the Lord by ruling God's people justly. The superscription links the text to Solomon, yet 72:20 states that the poem concludes David's prayers. Few scholars believe either man wrote the text, but most experts do conclude that the passage designates a transition in the book. Perhaps 72:20 marks the end of an earlier version of the collected psalms,[43] and there can be no question that a coronation psalm marks a new monarch's rise to power. A text devoted to transition is placed at a seam in the book's structure. Change within the context of continuity is the main theme.

Canonical Synthesis: The Davidic and Abrahamic Covenants
Several canonical ideas merge in Psalm 72. These notions also summarize the heart of the canonical contributions of the whole section. First, God keeps the Davidic covenant by placing David's own son on the throne (2 Sam 7:12). Second, the petitions for enduring rule (72:5) and worldwide dominion (72:8-11) anticipate the fulfillment of promises made to David's family in 2 Samuel 7:16 and Psalm 2:1-11. Third, the standards for royal righteousness (72:1-4) are in keeping with Moses' rules for kings in Deuteronomy 17:14-20. Fourth, the blessing bestowed on Yahweh in 72:18-19 mirrors those in Psalms 41:13, 89:52 and 106:48. These doxologies clearly mark the book's main sections. Fifth, this particular doxology highlights the fact that Yahweh, the One who has done marvelous things on Israel's behalf, is truly the King of the whole earth.[44] Israel will rest secure as long as they worship Yahweh as the only God, their Savior, their heavenly sovereign.

Sixth, the Abrahamic covenant is also mentioned here, since 72:17 asks that all nations bless themselves through this person. Kraus says that "the blessing of Abraham (Genesis 12) is applied to the king. He is the universal bearer of God's blessing."[45] Weiser adds that the king's fame will be a witness to the fact that God's promises to the patriarchs reside with this individual.[46] Therefore this text brings together the Davidic, Mosaic and Abrahamic covenants. The whole of Old Testament theology merges in the succession of the Davidic lineage. This text may not contain specific predictions about the one who fulfills the Davidic promise, but it does divulge how much divine activity rests on that person's life and work.

The God Who Rebukes and Rejects: Psalms 73—89
Subtle shifts in tone, superscriptions and content leading up to historical summaries in Psalms 78 and 89 indicate that part three reflects Israel's decline into sin and exile. This national demise occurs in about 930-587 B.C. and has

been described previously in 1 Kings 11—2 Kings 25 as well as in Isaiah, Jeremiah and the Twelve. The view of history found here matches that in the Prophets: Israel's covenant breaking led God to rebuke, and then reject, the chosen people and to expel them from the promised land. These psalms portray this rebuke and rejection against a background of the remnant's faith struggles and the Lord's patience.

Psalms 73—83 are ascribed to Asaph, who instituted "one of the three chief guilds of Levite temple musicians, the 'sons of Asaph' (I Chron xxv 1-2, 6-9)."[47] Like the Korah psalms in part two, these passages focus attention on Israel as a whole more than on David or the royal family, though the Davidic covenant is not neglected altogether. Even the individualistic Asaph psalms (e.g., Ps 73) deal with matters that affect all the believing remnant, such as why one should serve Yahweh when the wicked seem to prosper. These Asaph psalms give way to texts ascribed to Korah (Ps 84—85), David (Ps 86), Korah again (Ps 87; with Heman, Ps 88), and finally Ethan (Ps 89). Ethan's psalm is a historical summary that demonstrates that the prayers of Asaph, Korah and David did not stave off Jerusalem's capture. Changes in super-scriptions indicate that Yahweh's calls for sin were heard and obeyed by some Israelites but were largely ignored in the end. Not even stalwart members of the remnant could save the people from themselves.

Tonal shifts also reflect Israel's decline. For instance, Psalms 73—76 lead to historical summaries in Psalms 77—78, much as Psalms 43—65 lead to Psalms 66—68. In part two, there is a seeking of God based on community innocence (cf. 44:17-19) that leads to a positive response from God in 50:7-15 and in Psalms 51—65, which in turn results in worship in 68:24-29. In Psalms 73—78, however, a solitary psalmist staves off becoming like the wicked (Ps 73); the faithful cry out to their covenant God but with no declarations of national innocence (Ps 74—76). The section concludes with confessions of Yahweh's greatness in spite of Israel's infidelity in Psalms 77—78. Due to sin, Jerusalem is a ruin (Ps 79), and Israel desperately needs deliverance (Ps 80, 83). Israel has shown little faith in God (78:22), so the Lord was moved to anger (78:58) and then to rejection (78:59). Psalms 73—78 portray the current people as revisiting the sinful eras of the wilderness and the judges, and Psalm 79 leaves no doubt about the final results of this twisted revival. The textual tone has shifted from corporate innocence to remnant intercession.

Though content issues affect tonal details in Psalms 73—83, the contents of Psalms 84—89 conclusively demonstrate Israel's decline and fall. Korah's Psalms 84—85 profess love for the temple yet note that Yahweh is angry at Israel. David's prayer, like 78:58, locates the source of God's anger in Israel's idolatry. Psalm 78:58 expresses God's hatred of idol worship, and 86:8-13 confesses that no god is like Yahweh, that all nations will eventually bow down to the Lord and that God saves the faithful. This monotheistic faith characterized David's life and preserved his covenant with Yahweh. Psalm 89, though, laments the fall of David's house (89:38-45), which means David's faith has not been replicated in history. Polytheism has led to disaster.

Canonical Synthesis: Divine Wisdom and History

Psalm 73 clearly fits into the Israelite wisdom tradition. It reflects the desire to live according to God's counsel found in Psalm 1 and the book of Proverbs. More particularly it seeks to deal with the wicked person's prosperity in a manner like that of Psalms 37 and 49, as well as the book of Job.[48] The worshiper finds peace in the presence of God, the realization that there is no other deity to sustain him and in the conviction that the wicked finally perish (73:17-28). Job's experience parallels the psalmist's, for his determined seeking of answers from God results in a divine presence almost too close for comfort (Job 13:13-19; 19:23-29; 38:1—42:6). Both Job and the psalmist find their relief in divine instruction.

Psalm 78 surveys Israelite history in a manner reminiscent of summaries such as Deuteronomy 1:6—4:49, Joshua 24:1-3, Judges 1—2, 1 Samuel 12:6-18, 2 Kings 17, Isaiah 63:7-14, Jeremiah 2:1—3:5, and Ezekiel 16, 20 and 23. It prefigures passages such as Psalms 89 and 104—106, as well as Nehemiah 9:16-31. God released Israel from bondage, yet they sinned in the desert (78:9-51). Yahweh gave Israel Canaan, yet they venerated idols (78:52-66). The Lord gave the Davidic covenant (78:67-72). What will happen? The pattern is ominous. Israel's history has many glorious moments, though that glory is also clouded by the necessity of divinely created discipline.

Canonical Synthesis: Suffering and the Davidic Covenant

Psalm 89 provides a vantage point for one of the canon's most serious issues. God's promise to David in 2 Samuel 7 is an enduring kingdom (89:19-37). If David's line is no longer in power, then what becomes of these pledges (89:38-45)?[49] The writer's dismay is palpable.[50] This shock leads to questions of time (How long?) and space (Where is your former great love?) that reflect human mortality and physical limitations.[51] Both the Abrahamic and Davidic covenants seem in jeopardy, for land and monarchy are gone. Has God forsaken Zion?[52]

Though this text does not provide all the answers to its own questions, it does hint at solutions found more concretely in other canonical passages. By stressing God's power and truthfulness (89:1-37) the psalmist seems to understand that the ultimate answer lies in Yahweh's character. God cannot lie (Num 23:19) and is eternal (Ex 3:14; Deut 33:27), so the promise must be fulfilled in the future based on the Lord's nature. By reflecting on how God's servant is scorned among the nations the psalmist reminds readers of the suffering servant in Isaiah 53.[53] David's heir must suffer and be delivered as David himself was (Zech 13:1-9). Suffering is part of the glory of the Davidic covenant. It seems that the canonical portrait of David's suffering is transferred to the anticipated Davidic heir. Perhaps the twin beliefs of God's unerring character and the pattern of Davidic suffering and victory fuel the doxology that closes this portion of Psalms (89:52).

As a whole this section continues the canon's emphasis on monotheism. Already Psalms 8:1-9 and 19:1-6 have declared the fact that God alone is the Creator. Psalms 46:10, 50:1-6, 65:1-13, 66:1-4, 67:1-7 and 72:18-19 all stress God's rule over the whole earth. Psalm 53 calls atheism foolish. Psalm 72:18 states that no other God does great things. Therefore it is hardly surprising to find Psalm 78:58 laying Israel's troubles at the feet of their idolatrous ways. Nor is it surprising to read Psalm 81:6-16 quoting Yahweh as saying there is no foreign god or to discover the Davidic Psalm 86 confessing, "You alone are God" (86:10). Psalm 89:1-18 claims that the whole earth is Yahweh's. There is no statement such as "Baal is not real." Still, the overwhelming description of Yahweh as Creator, sustainer, deliverer, healer and ruler really eliminates all other deities from consideration.

The God Who Remembers and Sustains: Psalms 90—106

Psalm 89 leaves Israel and the Davidic monarchy chastened, rejected and cast off. The Babylonian invasion is not mentioned specifically, yet that catastrophe certainly completed the fall of David's house. In this desperate condition the faithful are driven to count on Yahweh's past forgiveness as the basis for future renewal and on Yahweh's status as Creator and sustainer for their hope for survival. They confess that the Lord remembers the remnant of Israel, sustaining them until such time as they can be fully restored to the land. Isaiah, Jeremiah, Ezekiel and the Twelve have already considered these matters in some depth.

To demonstrate the need for reliance on past divine forgiveness, part four begins with a psalm ascribed to Moses. The fact that only two other psalms in this section are associated with an individual (Ps 101, 103) and the fact that those are linked to David reinforces the look to the past for strength. Psalm 90 confesses Yahweh "is the Lord of all, the ruler over all the world (Ps 8:1, 24:1)."[54] God has been an enduring help to Israel from the beginning of the world (90:1),[55] yet Yahweh transcends time itself, for Yahweh exists "from everlasting to everlasting" (90:2). Weiser notes that this phrase "implies an unlimited abundance of power and a presence that overcomes the barriers of time."[56] Thus, Kraus observes, Yahweh is the preexistent God, the one who remains forever, the one whose eternity separates him from time-bound human beings, the Lord of life and death and the living one who judges the earth.[57] It is this Creator who rules the earth, who holds it together by "holding it in His hands."[58]

In contrast, human beings are mere dust (90:3). They are at the mercy of a God to whom a thousand years is like a single day (90:4). Therefore, in light of their transitory existence, human beings must "pray for the wisdom of heart/mind that comes from considering the finitude of human existence, its frustration and brevity."[59] Such wisdom can come only from the eternal God and can be grasped only by the remnant (90:11-12). As Calvin observes, "True believers alone, who know the difference between this transitory state and a blessed eternity, for which they were created, know what ought to be the aim of their hope."[60] The proper response to God's wrath is to seek God's wisdom (90:11-12), mercy (90:13-16) and favor (90:17).[61]

When time-bound people seek shelter in the eternal God (92:1-13), the Lord responds favorably. The Lord promises to those who cleave to him in love (91:14):

I will rescue;
I will protect;
I will answer;
I will be with;
I will deliver;
I will honor;
I will satisfy;
I will show salvation. (91:14-16)

In other words, God will remember and sustain those who remember to love the Lord. As the prophets have shown decisively, exile cannot separate the faithful from Yahweh's covenant love.

Psalms 93—100 also apply old truths to the new and difficult situation Psalm 89 announces. First, these texts confess that "the LORD reigns" (93:1; 96:10; 97:1; 99:1). Second, they state that Yahweh is the judge of the whole earth (96:11-13; 98:8-9). Third, they say the reason Yahweh reigns and judges is that Yahweh is the Creator of the earth (93:1-15; 95:1-7; 100:3). Fourth, the implications of these truths is that there is no other god. All gods are mere idols, only images (96:4-5), so whoever boasts in worthless idols will be put to shame (97:6-7). Only Yahweh is exalted over the whole earth (97:9). These texts equate the gods with nonliving things (e.g., images and idols), which leaves only Yahweh as a viable deity.

Given these truths, wise persons will renounce arrogance and accept chastening, for discipline turns the faithful to the Lord (94:4-15). God will not abandon the righteous (94:14-15). They will be remembered and restored for their monotheistic faith and bold confessions.

Part four concludes with Davidic affirmations of human faithfulness (Ps 101) and divine goodness (Ps 103) as preludes to yet another historical summary (Ps 104—106). The historical summary itself is the most theologically comprehensive one so far. Psalm 104 celebrates Yahweh's creation of and care for the earth. A more thorough statement of the scope of God's concern for the created order is hard to imagine. All history begins with the Lord who at a specific time began all events. Praise is the natural response of all who grasp the magnitude of recognizing Yahweh as the only Creator and sustainer (104:31-35).[62] Next, Psalm 105 acknowledges God's covenant with the patriarchs (105:1-15), Israel's deliverance through Joseph (105:16-25) and the exodus (105:26-45). All these blessings occurred because Yahweh "remembers his covenant forever" (105:8). Even the exile cannot change this fact.

Psalm 106 recalls past restorations. Israel rebelled at the Red Sea, but God still delivered them (106:6-12). They sinned in the desert, yet God forgave (106:13-23). Due to their lack of faith they failed to enter Canaan (106:24-33). When God gave them the land they served idols, but Yahweh rescued the people because the Lord remembered the covenant and loved Israel (106:34-46). If Yahweh pardoned all those transgressions, then it is possible that he will renew the nation once more (106:47). Thus the concluding doxology blesses Yahweh for indomitable, sustaining grace (106:48). Israel's history commends the Lord as surely as it condemns the nation's actions. It is possible, then, that the people may be gathered from all the places the exile has taken them (106:47).

Canonical Synthesis: Psalms 90—106 as Canonical Summary

These chapters serve as a veritable canonical catalog of Yahweh's work. Genesis's emphases on creation, the patriarchal covenant and the saving of Israel through Joseph appear here. Exodus's depiction of the exodus, description of the pre-Sinai nation, insistence on monotheism and denunciation of the golden calf incident are all mentioned. Deuteronomy's declaration of there being no other god is repeated. The Former Prophets' view of history is affirmed. It is significant to note, however, that the Zion and Davidic themes are absent. Only repentance born of agreement with the Law and Former Prophets can recapture the hope inherent in the Latter Prophets' view of the future. When that repentance reaches maturity, though, a remnant ready to return to Zion will have emerged. The eternal God will effect this return for the wise and chastened faithful, since God remembers and sustains.

The God Who Renews and Restores: Psalms 107—150

Restoration and renewal have already been prominent in the canon, especially in the Prophets. After all, the promises about the reign of David's heir in Isaiah, Jeremiah and elsewhere point to the ultimate, long-term renewal of people, land and covenant. Also, texts like Isaiah 44:38 and 45:1 promise that exile is not the last word for Israel. Further, Haggai, Zechariah and Malachi long for renewal of temple, city and people. Finally, the very existence of these three postexilic prophecies in the canon indicates the remnant's desire to grasp God's will for Israel's future. Psalms 107—150 affirm these prophetic impulses by emphasizing the significance of Israel's people (Ps 107—109), Davidic expectations (Ps 110), exultant praise (Ps 111—118), God-given law (Ps 119), pilgrim worship (Ps 120—134) and unreserved blessing of Yahweh (Ps 135—150). As the Lord renews and restores the chosen people, they respond gratefully to the divine initiative.

Psalm 107:1-3 begins part five by praising God for answering the prayer for return from exile offered in 106:47. Wherever Israelites wandered (107:4-16), however they languished (107:16-22), whenever they feared (107:23-32), it was Yahweh who sustained them (107:33-43). This psalm could have been written earlier but now is adapted and applied to the postexilic situation.[63] Psalms 108 and 109, both ascribed to David, may also fit this description. Both those texts support Psalm 107's assertion that Yahweh rescues, not rejects (108:11), the faithful. The remnant will indeed return to the promised land.

As has been noted, the Davidic covenant is hardly mentioned in Psalms 90—106. This silence is broken by Psalm 110, which effectively answers Psalms 89's concern that the Davidic covenant has been set aside by the Lord.[64] Ascribed to David, this text reaffirms God's choice of David's lineage. Some scholars believe that David wrote the passage or that it dates from his time,[65] while most commentators at least set it during the monarchy, considering it a coronation poem for an unnamed new ruler.[66] Kraus thinks the text comes from "the earliest period of the kings,"[67] a proper decision that certainly focuses readers' attention on David and his immediate successors. Jesus is quoted in Mark 12:36 as saying David declared 110:1 while inspired by the Spirit. Though it is not without some problems, the position that this psalm comes from David is accurate.

David utilizes prophetic speech forms in Psalm 110. Mays states that

in style and content it is similar to sayings of the prophets. The psalm has two parts, each opened by a formula for introducing oracular sayings by prophets and seers: "The Lord says" in verse 1 and "The LORD has sworn" in verse 4. Each formula is followed by a saying spoken in divine first person style, a style characteristic of prophetic speech.[68]

In this manner the whole text assumes divine authority and future (both immediate and long-term) perspective. Everything promised in Psalm 110 cannot unfold in David's lifetime, so his descendants must be included in some manner.

Psalm 110 proceeds in two parts: 110:1 states a promise whose fulfillment is described in 110:2-3, and 110:4 offers a second pledge whose completion is discussed in 110:5-7.[69] The prophetic statement in 110:1 extends authority over all foes to David, which sounds like the glory offered God's anointed in Psalm 2:7-11. It also makes the Davidic ruler coregent with the Lord, a designation announced in 80:18 and 89:27.[70] As Gerhard von Rad observes, "The throne of Jahweh and of his anointed were inseparable—indeed, in the light of Ps. cx. 1 f., they were really one."[71] Because of this God-ordained authority, victory will extend from Zion against all enemies (110:2-3).

The second promise is more unusual. Looking back to Genesis 14:17-20, the prophecy promises the king will be "a priest forever, in the order of Melchizedek" (110:4). God will not change his mind, so here "the word of Yahweh is unalterable."[72] Other ancient lands' kings were considered priests, and it is true that sometimes Israelite kings exercised priestlike functions without being rebuked by Yahweh (e.g., 2 Sam 6:13-17).[73] Still, Saul (1 Sam 13:8-15) and Uzziah (2 Kings 15; 2 Chron 26:19-21) are punished for doing what only priests were sanctioned to do. To cite the example of Melchizedek means such objections are set aside. As in Zechariah 6:9-14, the priestly and royal roles are merged in a way denied the Davidic lineage as described in Kings and Chronicles. The victories listed in 110:5-7 must therefore relate to a future person.

This passage reaffirms not only the importance of the Davidic covenant but also its eternal nature and partially redefines it at the same time. Babylon's wrecking of Judah has not ended the pledge to David, only created a new context for its fulfillment. A Davidic king will emerge who will rule victoriously as both king and priest, who will defeat all enemies, who will endure forever. Higher privileges could hardly be imagined.

Psalms 111—118 renew Israel's praise along lines already set forth in part four. God's works (Ps 111) and blessing of the righteous and wise (Ps 112) merit praise, as do Yahweh's incomparability (Ps 113) and deliverance of Israel from Egypt (Ps 114). In other words, this God is living, real. Idols, though, are mere images with no ability to see, hear, walk or think. All who worship them are foolish (115:3-7). Those who worship the Lord have a God who knows (115:12), hears (116:1) and loves (117:2). They have a God who, in exodus-imitating fashion, is able to restore them to their homeland (118:10-14). Once again Yahweh's solitary uniqueness makes other gods so nondescript that they are clearly not alive.

If Israel is to overcome its historical and theological amnesia, then God's written word must regain the prominence expressed in Psalms 1 and 19. Thus the longest chapter in the book is devoted to this topic. The passage is a giant acrostic poem consisting of twenty-two eight-line stanzas in which successive letters of the Hebrew alphabet are utilized. Qualitatively speaking, God's word is "firm in the heavens" (119:89), perfect beyond definition (119:96), righteous forever (119:44), fully truthful and enduringly relevant (119:60). Practically speaking, God's word offers instruction, understanding, guidance, motivation and vindication for the righteous (119:33-40). It leads people to seek good companions (119:63) and to fight evil (119:104). It gives hope in crisis (119:105-112). The list could be extended, but the point is clear: God's word is perfect and valuable. Israel's future must be built on its principles for the consequences stated in Leviticus 26 and Deuteronomy 27—28 not to occur again.

Certainly Psalms 111—118 demonstrate that praise may happen wherever God's people may be. It is impossible to forget, however, Zion's prominence in Samuel, Kings, Isaiah, Ezekiel, Zechariah and the earlier psalms. Renewal of the city as Israel's central worship site is established in Psalms 120—134, all of which carry the title "A Song of Ascents." Though experts have debated this title's meaning,[74] the most logical explanation is that most if not all of these texts "were evidently songs used by the pilgrims on their way up to the Temple at Jerusalem for the feasts."[75] Placed in part five of Psalms, they signal the return of worship caused to cease by the debacle portrayed in Psalm 79.

Psalm 132 uses the Davidic house's hardship as a paradigm for all God's people's woes in exile. David longed to build the Lord a temple as much as the people longed to worship in Jerusalem again (132:1-7). This reference to David's wishes opens the way for other details from 2 Samuel 7. At that time God swore an irreversible oath[76] to the king that his heir would reign and build a temple, that Israel would be at rest in the promised land and that David would be the father of an eternal dynasty (2 Sam 7:7-17). Since these promises are as fixed as God's own integrity, the restored people of Yahweh can expect them to materialize. They will worship the Lord in Zion (132:18); they will serve a Davidic king again; they can trust God's word absolutely. This confident faith undergirds the songs of ascent.

Psalms 135—150 conclude the book with texts that are either anonymous or ascribed to David. These passages sound familiar themes, such as God's election of Israel (135:1-4), God's uniqueness (135:5-7, 15-18), God's role as Creator (135:7), God's work in the exodus and conquest (135:8-12), God's love (Ps 136), God's wrath (Ps 137) and God's rule (Ps 138). To this Lord the psalmist brings all requests for help in spiritual and temporal matters (Ps 139—143). This God is called eternally faithful (145:13), and this God receives unreserved praise from the redeemed remnant (Ps 146—150). Adoration caps the book. The pain so evident in Psalms 78, 89 and 104—106 has given way to rejoicing born of a sense of forgiveness, renewal of covenant and restoration of lost privileges.

Canonical Synthesis: God's Restoration of Israel

Part five of Psalms contains vital canonical details about Israel's overall future as viewed through the lens of their past. Deuteronomy 30:1-10 has stated that covenant curses may be overcome when Yahweh's people repent, and Jehoiachin's survival in exile (cf. 2 Kings 25:27-30; Jer 52:31-34) proves that David's lineage will not die in exile. Haggai, Zechariah and Malachi witness to the fact that Israel does return to the land and to the fact that greater days lie ahead. Psalms 107—150 give further evidence of God's faithfulness to covenants made with Abraham, Israel and David. God's people return to Jerusalem for the express purpose of worshiping their Lord, whom they know to be the only God among all gods who lives and acts. David's family continues to possess an eternal promise, yet their leadership is not physically evident at this time. Their eternal glory is a promise whose fulfillment is deferred but which must come to pass. This delay forces the psalms beyond immediate worship concerns to the embracing of long-term, eschatological hope.[77]

Certain psalms in part five make specific contributions to the canonical witness of this hope. For example, Psalm 110 weds the normal promises of a future Davidic king ruling Israel and the earth to a rarer linking of the priestly and royal roles. Virtually all the explicit Davidic promises found in the Prophets and royal psalms claim the coming Savior will be a king greater than David. Perhaps only Zechariah 6:9-14 and Psalm 110:4 claim that this king will also be a priest. This linkage is not extraordinary in the ancient world in general but is quite unusual in Israel.

Canonical Synthesis: Psalm 110 in the New Testament

The New Testament reflects on this and other aspects of Psalm 110 in some detail. Jesus uses 110:1 in a discussion with the Pharisees in Matthew 22:41-46, Mark 12:35-37 and Luke 20:41-44 to point out that the Lord to whom David refers is the coming Savior. As W. L. Lane says, "In the psalm David clearly affirmed that the divine promise concerned not himself, but the Messiah."[78] It is this person whom God exalts. This verse is applied to Jesus himself "in Acts 2:34 f.; 1 Corinthians 15:25; and Hebrews 1:13 to declare that his enemies will be subject to him."[79] In this way the New Testament agrees with the Old Testament that the coming king will be David's heir and also uses this verse to declare the coming one's identity.

Hebrews 5:5-10 and 6:17-7:28 use Psalm 110:4 to argue that Jesus' priestly work in his death and resurrection replaces the Levitical priesthood. Through suffering Jesus proved himself to be the king-priest (5:9-10), and through rising from the dead he provided a better priesthood due to its eternal nature (7:17-25). His holiness is perfect, which also makes him superior to nondivine priests (7:26-28). These texts agree with the priest-king concept of Zechariah 6:9-14 and Psalm 110:4. They identify Jesus as that person. Mays comments, "Hebrews is right on target in its use of verse 4 when it differentiates the priesthood of Aaron from that of Jesus because the priesthood of Jesus is a messianic, a royal priesthood, the priesthood of the Son (Heb. 1:13; 5:6; 7:17, 21)."[80] It is interesting that Hebrews considers Jesus' suffering a necessary part of the actions that fulfill 110:4.

Conclusion

Psalms reaffirms the teachings of the Law and the Prophets in compelling and potent ways. The book agrees that the Lord created the heavens and the earth and states that no other god has power to hear, walk, speak, help, save or love. In other words, these so-called gods exist in the sense that the ancient peoples venerated them yet not in the sense of having real life or being. Psalms confesses that the Law is given by Yahweh to teach the faithful how to live and how to love the Lord they serve. Psalms claims that the Davidic Savior will rule as king and priest at a future time that will vindicate the faithful and punish the wicked. This collection of sacred songs proclaims that Yahweh rules every thing that has ever, presently or will exist.

These confessions of faith are made in worship against a historical backdrop. The faithful make these statements in a nation that turns away from the living God to serve idols (Ps 78, 89 and 104—106). Despite the opposition of wicked persons the remnant worships on, trusting in the God who delivers the oppressed in a sort of daily exodus. Worship here has content and it has courage. It is not simply a series of emotional highs and lows. It is emotional to be sure, but it is worship based on truth that makes emotions meaningful and redemptive. The fact that this worship exists at all is a tribute to the courage of people who withstood the wicked, had faith in their present crisis and believed in the God who rules and transforms history. Worship sometimes emerges only at great cost, a fact that the next canonical book stresses repeatedly.

16

The God
Who Is
Worth Serving

Job

· · · · · · · · · · · · · · · · · · ·

J OB HAS PROBABLY INSPIRED AS MUCH POPULAR AND CRITICAL WRITING AS ANY
Old Testament book.[1] Its artistic brilliance makes it an attractive subject for
literary scholars. Its thematic range invites philosophic discussion. Its unknown origins have led many biblical historians to speculate about its
authorship, date and intended audience.[2] Above all these obvious qualities,
however, stands its probing into the character of God. Without question Job's
greatest contribution is its theological courage, for it asks hard questions
about whether the only God is worth serving. Job asserts that God merits
human service despite the reality of occasional exceptional suffering and
loss. Job argues that God is worth serving despite constant, recurring mental,
physical, emotional and spiritual pain.

Job, Proverbs, Ecclesiastes and Song of Solomon are part of the ancient
Near Eastern Wisdom tradition.[3] As was stated in the comments on 1 Kings
4:29-34, Solomon and other Israelites participated in this intellectual and
literary school of thought. Long before Israel was a nation Egypt, Babylon
and other countries were writing descriptions of the natural world, helpful
proverbs, enigmatic proverbs, statements about how to serve royalty, disputes over the meaning of life's tragedies and comments about seemingly
unfair situations.[4] Just as Moses did not invent covenants or laws, Israelite
Wisdom writers did not invent these literary types. Rather, as in Moses' case,

they were inspired by God to adapt these art forms to the service of the truths they wished to present. They used existing forms of communication to press their claims about what constitutes wise or foolish living.

It is not possible to summarize the essence of ancient wisdom in a paragraph. Any such attempt will by nature oversimplify the issues at hand. Still, if such a drastic reduction must be made, the heart of wisdom literature is the desire to teach readers how to live well, to live successfully.[5] Those who learn to operate effectively in the many circumstances that punctuate human existence are considered wise. Those who have and yet are unable or refuse to learn to act wisely are deemed naive, simple, or fools respectively, depending on their own responsibility for their lack of understanding.[6] Wisdom must be attained over time.[7] It is not the exclusive property of a single nation, race or class of people. Royalty may or may not be wise, so position does not guarantee wisdom. Each new generation must be taught wisdom, for it is not transferred genetically. In other words, wisdom is developmental by nature, democratic in scope and discipline-oriented in application.

Old Testament Wisdom differs from its ancient counterparts in certain key respects. First, Israelite Wisdom in the canonical context unwaveringly integrates faith into life's daily details. In these books the fear of the Lord is the beginning (Prov 1:7) and sum total (Job 28:28) of wisdom regardless of that wisdom's particular arena. When trying to separate early from late Wisdom traditions in Israel, some scholars differentiate between secular and sacred material, with the former type considered the older of the two.[8] The belief that secular Wisdom gradually moved toward religious expressions is an unproved developmental view of this literature's emergence. The canon makes no such distinction.[9] Rather it always makes one's relationship to God the reason one is able to become wise. Everything one does proves or disproves one's relationship with or fear of the Lord. Second, Israel confessed that only one God exists. Thus only one God is able to inspire or impart wisdom.[10] God possessed wisdom before the foundation of the world, which his status as Creator demonstrates (cf. Job 28; Prov 8). The Old Testament's insistence that the one God is the Creator undergirds all Wisdom's theological formulations.[11] As Creator and only deity, the Lord is the only source for wisdom that allows human beings the means to let faith permeate life. Thus Israel's desire for successful living parallels that of other countries, as does its use of particular literary tools for satisfying that desire. But its means of achieving that goal clearly diverges from its neighbors'.

Several parts of the Law, the Prophets and Psalms introduce ideas found in the Wisdom books.[12] For example, in the Law Abraham defends himself the second time he claims Sarah is his sister by saying he thought there was no "fear of God" in Gerar. Presumably because they had no respect for God, they would kill him to possess his wife. He obviously links a person's relationship to God with his or her behavior (cf. Gen 20:11). Further, Joseph advises Pharaoh to appoint a "discerning and wise" man to lead Egypt's food collection (Gen 41:33). Because Joseph is called to lead (Gen 37:1-11) and filled with God's Spirit (Gen 41:38), he proves himself a wise man by his sound decisions in Genesis 42—50. Moses chooses elders who fear God and exhibit high character (cf. Ex 18:13-27; Num 11:11-30; Deut 1:9-18). These passages all indicate that respect for God inspires character that makes leaders capable of doing sound work.

Deuteronomy adds a second benefit closely associated with wisdom.[13] Here the fear of the Lord is the basis for ethical living and covenant keeping. Moses says in 4:10 that the Sinai covenant was given to instill fear of the Lord in Israel's hearts, a straightforward reference to the origins of a solid relationship with God. In 5:20 Moses says God hoped the result of the covenant would be fear of the Lord that motivated ongoing faithfulness. Therefore this fear is presented as a long-term motivation for consistent covenant keeping. Next, Moses cites fear of the Lord as part of learning to love the Lord (6:2-25), as the driving force behind monotheism and obedience (6:13-19) and as the catalyst for God-given prosperity (6:24-25). Finally, Moses uses the term in passages that summarize Israel's covenantal obligations (cf. 10:12, 20). Fearing God will lead to walking in his ways, loving him and serving him (10:20). Deuteronomy 27—28 claims that this lifestyle will lead to blessing, not judgment. Without question, in the Law the fear of the Lord begins a chain reaction that leads to honorable, faithful, righteous conduct. The same is true in the Wisdom books.

The Prophets further the canon's emphasis on wisdom in leadership and basic ethical living. Samuel's farewell speech fastens on fear of the Lord as the means by which Israel and their kings may be pleasing to God (1 Sam 12:14, 24). Solomon prays for a "discerning heart" to be able to lead Israel (cf. Gen 41:33) in 1 Kings 3:9 and demonstrates his ruling wisdom by solving the case of the prostitutes' babies (1 Kings 3:16-28). Solomon participates in the Wisdom tradition's great literary heritage (1 Kings 4:29-34) and considers fear of the Lord Israel's hope for prosperity in the promised land (1 Kings 8:39-43). Wisdom's value for leadership and covenant fidelity remains a clear point of emphasis. God gives leaders wisdom, and kings and subjects display wisdom by their covenant obedience.

Isaiah and Jeremiah expand wisdom's influence. Isaiah 11:2-3 states that the coming Davidic king will be filled with God's Spirit and thus endowed with wisdom and a delight in the fear of the Lord. Wisdom is thereby linked with the Davidic covenant. Jeremiah argues that not fearing the Lord has led

Israel to break the covenant and invite disaster (Jer 5:22-24), so he agrees with Deuteronomy, Samuel and Kings. Jeremiah 18:18 lists wisdom counselors alongside false prophets and poor teachers (scribes) as leaders who fail the people. It may be assumed that by Jeremiah's career (c. 627-587 B.C.) wisdom teachers were part of Israel's leadership structure.[14] Their failure to help instill fear of the Lord in the people hastened the nation's demise.

As was stated in the previous chapter, certain psalms reflect wisdom notions. Both Psalm 34:11 and Psalm 111:10 mention the fear of the Lord, with the latter text agreeing with Proverbs 1:7 and Job 28:28 that the fear of the Lord begins and summarizes wisdom. Further, Psalms 1, 19, 37 and 119 contrast the way of life based on God's word and the way of death chosen by those who do evil. These texts view life as a series of sound decisions in much the same manner as Job and Proverbs do. They consider knowledge of and reverence for the Lord the foundation stones for successful living. Their linkage of the covenantal word of God, the fear of God and righteous living are in keeping with the emphases in the texts already mentioned.

Thus by the time the canon reaches Job several key wisdom concepts are in place. First, fear of the Lord is the primary way to be wise. Second, fearing the Lord leads to righteous living. Third, righteous living allows Israel to keep the Sinai covenant. Fourth, unwise living, defined as covenant breaking, will lead to the people's suffering the consequences outlined in Deuteronomy 27—28. Fifth, the coming Savior will embody wisdom in its best and fullest sense. Sixth, successful life consists in the keeping of these principles. Job, Proverbs, Ecclesiastes and Song of Solomon will add more details, but the canon offers these items as principles that undergird the Wisdom literature.

With these general principles in place it is hopefully easier to approach Job itself. Several outlines of Job could be accurate, but the following four-point scheme offers an overarching frame of reference under which subpoints may fall. First, Job 1—2 presents a God who lets the faithful be tested. These probings are allowed to answer the question, Does (will) Job serve God for nothing (for no apparent gain)? Only through pain and loss can this question of God's worth be answered. Second, Job 3—37 presents God as One whose character may be called into question. Hard issues are raised about God's nature and activity. Again readers are forced to consider what sort of deity the Lord is and whether the only God is worth loving, serving and obeying. Third, Job 38:1—42:6 displays the God who answers the faithful. Here God addresses Job directly, though not necessarily the way Job anticipated. Fourth, Job 42:7-17 portrays God as the One who vindicates the faithful. Job's losses are reversed, except for the loss of human life. His God praises him and corrects the friends. Overall the book argues that the One who allows testing is also the One who hears, reveals, vindicates and heals. This God vindicates the faith of those who serve without enjoying a pain-free life.

The God Who Lets the Faithful Be Tested: Job 1—2

From the outset the author establishes the fact that none of Job's suffering occurs because of any specific sin on his part. Job 1:1-5 portrays him as a man of high character in the fullest sense of the Wisdom tradition.[15] Stated simply, he fears God and thereby lives rightly before God among human beings (1:1). He has reached the maturity the Wisdom literature seeks to instill in its readers. He has ten children, extensive wealth and evident piety (1:2-5). S. R. Driver and George Gray observe, "Two things the writer intends to stand out: the character of Job and his prosperity; the one as constant, the other as passing; the one as essential."[16] By placing Job's character and his relationship to God in the forefront of the account, the author already begins to focus on how subsequent events affect that relationship.

The scene shifts from earth to where God dwells. There God rules as King over the angels and over Satan. The angels are "neither human nor divine in the full sense, but 'sons of God,' their being derivative from his, and their rank superhuman."[17] God created them. They are in no way equal to the Lord, for they report to him (1:6). Satan, whose name means "adversary or opponent,"[18] also must report to God as one who is not equal to the Lord. As in Zechariah 3:1-2, Satan acts as an accuser in this scene. He explains Job's wisdom and righteousness as naked self-interest that will dissolve if his possessions are removed (1:6-11). Satan asks the theological question of the book, "Does Job serve God for nothing?" (1:9). God responds by allowing Satan to test Job, though limits are set. Satan hungers to attack Job, but just as evidently the Lord does not stop the testing of the faithful. God has confidence in Job's commitment. God's confidence is justified when the wise and righteous one continues to worship the Lord. So far Job confesses Yahweh's worthiness (1:13-22).

God's sovereignty is reaffirmed in Job 2. Once again Yahweh is King in charge of angels, Satan, human affairs and ultimately the tests people endure. This time God allows Satan to strike Job's body, and once again Job passes the test. He is willing to accept both trouble and blessing from the God he serves (2:1-10). So far Job has suffered loss of family, property, servants and health, yet he still considers Yahweh worthy of loyalty and worship. When friends arrive they find an appallingly marred figure whose suffering has not led him to forsake God (2:11-13).

Canonical Synthesis: Suffering and the Righteous

Job's attitude about suffering to this point parallels that of Joseph in Genesis

37—50. Like Job, for no fault of his own Joseph was enslaved, imprisoned and shamefully treated. In time he came to understand his unjust suffering as God's will for preserving the family and nation and thus fulfilling the promise made to Abraham (cf. Gen 45:1-7; 50:19-20). God allowed Joseph to endure pain but only to save life, keep faith with Abraham and vindicate the sufferer. Job seems willing to suffer, though he has not yet seen God's higher purpose or received vindication. The connection between the two men is made even stronger by the fact that both of them are described in Wisdom terminology (cf. Gen 41:33-39; Job 1:1, 8; 2:3).

David is another previous canonical character whose life parallels Job's. God chooses David to succeed Saul (1 Sam 16:1-3) and enables him to kill Goliath and defeat the Philistines (1 Sam 17—18). But Saul tries to eliminate David (1 Sam 19—30), David has to fight to rise to power (2 Sam 1:1—5:5), and once he is king, David encounters many foreign and domestic enemies (2 Sam 15—21). David's summary of his own life highlights deliverance from death and suffering (2 Sam 22:1—23:7; cf. Ps 18). He views the Lord as One who delivers from enemies yet also as One who allows the righteous to undergo significant pain and trials (cf. 2 Sam 15:25-26; 16:11-12).

The prophets experience hardship, persecution and severe difficulties. Elijah, Jeremiah, Ezekiel, Hosea and Amos serve Yahweh under harsh conditions. They lose respect, family, property and freedom as they preach and act out God's word. As monotheists they know that the God who rules the heavens and earth has allowed them to fall under the power of the wicked (cf. 1 Kings 19:1-18; 22:1-40; Jer 11—20; 28; 34—45; Ezek 24:15-27; Hos 1—3; Amos 7:10-17). In Zechariah 3:1-2, Satan appears as one who accuses and condemns God's servants and as one completely under Yahweh's control. Satan is real and active yet unable to do more than God allows. Though pain and suffering are regular parts of the prophets' lives, they in no way use this fact as evidence that other gods have usurped Yahweh's authority, that God is no longer in full command of the situation or that the Lord's power has diminished or is somehow lacking. They receive discomfort as part of their calling and ministry.

Besides the general examples of unjust sufferers in the Old Testament, it is also important to note specific instances of God's testing persons. The classic case is found in Genesis 22:1-19, where God tests Abraham's faith by ordering the sacrifice of Isaac. Abraham passes this test by believing and obeying God's word. Moses says that the extraordinary show of divine power at Sinai is given to test Israel's fear of the Lord (Ex 20:20). He also states that the wilderness era was a test of Israel's commitment to the Lord (Deut 8:2). Such trials prove faith and obedience. God's power and grace are never at issue. Tests occur to demonstrate individual or corporate commitment to the

Lord, to the faithful and to readers of the canon.

All these instances of trials and tests happen within a clearly monotheistic context. The throne room scenes in Job 1—2 are no exception to this principle.[19] What this fact means is that Yahweh is totally sovereign over ease and pain, for both divine command and divine permission leave God in charge of human events.[20] It also means that there is no other God to whom sufferers may turn for healing or relief. Job must approach Yahweh for answers concerning his situation. His friends and family must do so as well. Monotheism thereby becomes both solution and difficulty where suffering is concerned. The book's characters and readers are forced to consider the nature of the one God as they attempt to put the suffering of Joseph, Job and others into perspective.

The God Whose Reputation Is at Stake: Job 3—37

This section contains dialogue between Job and his friends. Job begins the discussion with a lament (3:1-26). Subsequently the main character speaks with his three friends, Eliphaz, Bildad and Zophar, in Job 4—31. Elihu, a fourth friend, concludes the segment with a long oration (Job 32—37). Each speech will not be discussed in detail. Rather the main theological argument of each will be noted and its contribution to Job's and the canon's theology stated. The thrust of these speeches is to explore God's nature, for the story's emphasis shifts from proving Job's character to establishing God's. Now the Lord's reputation is at stake, partly because Yahweh is the only God and partly because God tests the faithful.

Job's opening lament provokes his friends to question his theology and his knowledge of wisdom. This statement is a distinct self-lament directed to God.[21] Job curses the day he was born (3:1-10), asks why people must be born at all, or if born why they cannot die before facing suffering (3:11-23), and mourns his total lack of peace (3:24-26). He says that God makes life a prison (3:23). Norman Habel observes that

> the dominant literary feature of the speech is the intricate pattern of reversals: from birth to prebirth death, from order to primordial chaos, from light to darkness, from gloom in life to pleasure in the underworld, from turmoil and confinement on earth to liberation and peace in Sheol.[22]

In other words, Job's lament asks for a reversal of creation, which implies dissatisfaction with the way the one Creator operates the world. Francis Andersen says, "Job is stunned because he cannot deny that it is the Lord who has done all this to him."[23] Clearly, Andersen continues, "he feels trapped."[24] As a monotheist, Job is left to question the work of the only God who has power. In effect he asks, Should the giver of life give life? What is striking is that unlike most (if not all) biblical laments, this one offers no concrete statement of faith. Job's friends are left to ponder this literary-theological breach of the norm.

Eliphaz's first speech sets the tone for all the friends' comments. After rebuking Job for not being able to help himself when he has taught others (4:1-6), Eliphaz summarizes his own theology by declaring that the innocent and upright are never destroyed (4:7). Only the wicked perish (4:8-11). His basis for this belief system is twofold: a personal vision he received (4:12-21) and knowledge of Wisdom teachings (5:1-7). Eliphaz believes Job has been disciplined by God (5:17) and must appeal to the righteous, saving Lord (5:8-16). Without question Eliphaz believes in simple cause-and-effect retribution for sin. He leaves no room in his worldview for an innocent sufferer such as readers know Job to be.[25] At least at this point he does not consider his friend beyond redemption. He simply wants to remind Job that "innocence and suffering are mutually exclusive."[26]

Certain parts of Eliphaz's theology are correct. He claims Yahweh is just, merciful, forgiving and willing to offer revelation. He thinks creation has purpose and meaning for the faithful. The notion of a God who tests and vindicates is beyond him. His view of strict retribution marks him as a benevolent adherent of ancient Wisdom teachings that emphasize straightforward cause and effect in human events.[27] This incomplete theology hampers his defense of God, his friendship with Job and his ability to have and convey wisdom.

By no means is Job convinced by Eliphaz's arguments. Instead he maintains his desire to die (6:1-10), continues to question why he should suffer (6:11-13) and laments the vanity of life (7:1-10). Further, he accuses his friends of forsaking him (6:14-23). Finally, he asks God why he has made him a target (7:11-20). In a stunning reversal of Psalm 8, he wonders why God pays so much negative attention to human beings (7:17).[28] To Job, God's omniscience has become cruel, God's power an excuse for bullying tactics (7:17-20).[29] Now Job has reversed the praise genre, just as in Job 3 he reshapes the lament into a totally negative literary form. So far the Lord's roles as Creator, sustainer, helper and friend have been questioned, as have the goodness of God's power, knowledge and personal interest in people.

Bildad's initial speech furthers Eliphaz's defense of God's justice. He denies that God perverts justice in the manner Job suggests (8:3). To illustrate his opinions Bildad claims that Job's children died as a direct result of their sins (8:4). Job, however, has not been killed, so he still has a chance to repent (8:5-7).[30] The basis for his authority is ancient proverbial wisdom, which teaches him that every effect has a specific cause and that pain always results from sin (8:11-19). God forgives, so Job should repent (8:20-22). This defense of God's justice properly concludes that the Lord forgives and heals yet also takes sin quite seriously. Ironically this denunciation of sin fails to take into account that people often suffer for the sins of others. Abel, Joseph, Jeremiah and others prove this point. Bildad sees no reason for righteous persons to suffer. He neglects any notion that bearing injustice in faith provides glory for Yahweh. Apparently only those enjoying ease embody a lifestyle that honors God.

In his response to Bildad, Job begins to toy with a novel theological idea. He considers litigation against the Lord as a means of discovering why God has afflicted him, and in subsequent speeches he challenges the Lord's case against him (13:13-19), seeks an advocate (cf. 16:18-21; 19:21-29) and offers testimony on his own behalf (cf. Job 29—31).[31] In other words, Job desires to formalize his probing of Yahweh's character and reputation. God's wisdom and power are obstacles to such an endeavor, so Job doubts God will respond to him at all (9:1-20). Frankly he wonders if the Lord is just, fair and open enough to do so (9:21-23). Does God answer humans who question the only God's goodness? If not, is this God worth serving? If not, Job considers death preferable to life (10:18-22).

Zophar concludes the friends' first cycle of speeches in a rather repetitive manner. Most of what he says is derived from comments made by Job or by the other friends,[32] and his referral to wisdom is the least engaging of them all.[33] He wishes God would answer Job, for then Job's self-righteousness could be exposed as misguided (11:1-6). Zophar claims God's ways are beyond human understanding (11:7-12), a point Job made in 9:1-20, and then tells him to repent (11:13-20), a course of action already urged by Eliphaz and Bildad (5:17-27; 8:5-7). At best one can credit Zophar with a correct knowledge of God's sovereignty and wisdom and with a sincere plea for prayer to be offered with pure motives.[34] At worst he makes God more distant and unknowable than do his friends.

Interestingly, Job's desire to prosecute God leads to his walking a pathway of faith that re-anchors him to the God he has served in the past. By probing the Lord's character he demonstrates a dogged faith that eventually results in his vindication. He knows the friends have given him no answers (12:1-6), and he believes wisdom resides in the Creator, the God who rules over the earth (12:7-25). Job pursues this lawsuit because he hopes in God, because he will hope in God even if Yahweh kills him (13:15). He wants relief, a response and a renewed relationship (13:20-27). Job intends to complete the theological portrait of God begun by him and his friends and already glimpsed by readers of the canon.

Though the rest of the first three friends' speeches are hardly mere repetitions of their first comments, they do not alter their theological horizons measurably. Thus it is more useful to examine Job's growing emphasis on legal action and faith. After Eliphaz accuses Job of hindering devotion to God (15:4) and claiming to have seen God create the world through wisdom (15:7-13), Job responds with a second bedrock confession of faith. Though God has torn him, he believes he has an advocate in heaven who will clear his name (16:15-21). Who is this advocate? Perhaps it is some third party who will mediate between God and himself,[35] but Job 1—2 reveals no such person. The more likely answer is that the advocate is God. No one else avenges shed blood or is "on high" in the sense God is in Job.[36] No one else could inspire "a reliance upon God against God."[37] No other person's testimony could negate Yahweh's.[38] Job begins to conclude that no one can clear the Lord's reputation except the Lord.

Job's third statement of faith comes after Bildad's second speech, in which he accuses Job of wanting the world to stop for his sake and in which he repeats his belief that Job has lost offspring due to sin (18:1-21; cf. 8:4). Job asks for pity for his situation (19:1-22). Sensing none from the friends, he again seeks the Lord. He states emphatically that his redeemer lives (19:25), that he will be vindicated after death or sooner (19:26) and that he longs to see this redemption (19:27). Job understands that he needs external help, that he cannot free himself from the pain he experiences.

Who is the "redeemer" Job believes will settle his case? Who will vindicate him? As in the case of the "advocate" of 16:16, scholars have offered two basic options about this person's identity: God or one who defends Job before God. David Clines notes that "redeemers" were near relatives who bought back family property (Lev 25:25-34; Jer 32:6-15), bought back a family member from slavery (Lev 25:47-54), married a widow to create an heir for a deceased kinsman (Ruth 3:12; 4:1-6) or avenged the death of a relative (Num 35:12, 19-27; Deut 19:6, 11-12; Josh 20:2-5, 9).[39] John Hartley observes that this term is applied to Yahweh, particularly in the context of discussing the exodus (cf. Ex 6:6; Is 41:14; 43:1-7; 44:24; 49:7-9, 26; Ps 74:2).[40] This redeemer must prove Job is on God's side, must live until the end of the earth and must make certain a potentially deceased Job sees God (19:25-27).

Clines and Norman Habel think it improbable that Job would call on God given his anger at the Lord, so they opt for a cosmic lawyer who will argue his case before the Lord.[41] Hartley concludes that only Yahweh qualifies as an ever-living redeemer.[42] Walther Eichrodt says that Job knows that no other god exists to give or take life. Job believes, then, that "God in person will come to meet him, and show himself in face of all human offences as witness, surety, and redeemer, who for all his inconceivable power remains bound in a personal relationship with his creature."[43] Driver and Gray comment that Job thinks that at death all confusion will be cleared up as God takes his side.[44] Given Job's previous statements about God's unquestioned knowledge and power and given his description of the redeemer, it seems appropriate to conclude that only God can vindicate him, for only God has the ability to do so. Such is the nature of Job's struggle that it pushes the boundaries of consistent theology as Job has conceived of it so far. As Walther Zimmerli explains:

> What is stated clearly is that Job, the apparent rebel who refuses to understand his suffering as being part of the necessary order of things, here transcends everything that is not understood and confesses the God who will stand up for his rights as his next of kin, seeing that blood vengeance is carried out—in fact, as his "redeemer," to use an interpretative translation. Can we not see here the God known to Israel since the deliverance in the exodus? If so, however, Job is more than a rebel. He is the "poor man" who does not forsake his faith even when he cannot understand his fate.[45]

Besides the sovereign God who has let him suffer so terribly, Job has no other redeemer, no other advocate, no one else worth believing in though they kill him.

Job's friends' final speeches continue to press him to confess his sins and turn to God. Zophar implies that Job, like other wicked persons, has received his just deserts from God (20:29). Eliphaz asserts that God has not reproved Job's piety but his obvious sin (22:1-11). Still, repentance will result in forgiveness. Job needs to agree with God (22:12-30). Bildad simply restates his conviction that human beings cannot be righteous before God, which means Job should accept his punishment as just (25:1-6). Job's response is threefold. First, he disputes their belief system by arguing that the wicked do not always suffer (21:1-34). God lets them prosper. Second, he confesses that he seeks to know why justice seems reversed yet is unable to discover an adequate answer (23:1—24:25). Third, he refuses to confess sins he has not committed (26:1—27:23). God's ways remain on trial; God's character is still under scrutiny. The confessions of faith have not stopped Job's relentless pursuit of a fuller understanding.

In his final monologue Job claims to have applied scrupulously the revealed truths of wisdom. He readily states that wisdom originates with God, who then reveals it to human beings (28:20-28). Wisdom was created and established by the Creator, so its essence must derive from God's character.[46] Thus Job realizes that God is the only source for finding an explanation for his plight. Just as there is no other advocate or redeemer, so there is no other wisdom teacher who can instruct him. What he has heard already he has obeyed, for he shuns evil of all kinds (31:1-40), a lifestyle that once led to acceptance and honor but now to illness and distress (29:1—30:31). Since seeking and obeying wisdom has not automatically led to unceasing blessing, he continues to demand to hear the charges against him (31:35). He has feared God and departed from evil (28:28). What sort of deity does not honor such conduct?

Job and his first three friends have reached an impasse, with neither side able to change the other. Therefore Elihu, a fourth friend, seeks to break the deadlock by explaining God's ways to the four debaters. Many scholars consider these speeches an unnecessary addition to the text.[47] Other experts, however, observe that Elihu summarizes the friends' refutation of Job[48] and acts as one who believes he speaks for God.[49] He does provide a last defense of the Lord that embodies and expands their theological beliefs. Elihu, Hartley says, offers four foundational points.

1. Suffering may be a disciplinary measure aimed at saving Job from a worse fate (33:19-33).

2. Job should not question or blame God (34:5-9).

3. God governs justly (34:10-30).

4. Job should heed God's teaching and meditate on God's ways (36:5—37:24).[50]

Though Elihu does break some new ground by emphasizing the instructional nature of suffering, he hardly sets aside or radically alters the friends' perspective. Like the others, he leaves no place in his theology for a God who allows the righteous, the pure (cf. 1:1-5), to suffer.

At the end of Job 37 readers may be struck by a peculiar dilemma caused by Job's historical setting and position in the canon. Readers have the benefit of the perspective of Job 1—2 and the knowledge about God's vindication of the faithful already unfolded in the canon.[51] In contrast, Job's historical setting is before Moses' time, so none of the great canonical accounts could help him. Readers may know what to expect, but Job does not, and even these readers do not know precisely what God will do. Thus Job represents all Old Testament figures who were caught in history between harsh reality and full revelation of God's ways. He waits for further information.

Incomplete theology has placed the Lord's reputation at risk. Without an appreciation of the fact that Yahweh allows suffering as a means of showing that God is worth serving under all conditions, the friends decide that this seemingly righteous man is actually a terrible sinner. Not fully aware of all the facts himself, Job seriously entertains the notion that God may not be loving and fair. Without this knowledge the friends consider God aloof and mechanical, while Job experiences Yahweh as too close and nearly unbearable. Either way this portrait of God hardly matches the one in the whole context of the Law, the Prophets and the Psalms. Canonical theological continuity must be rescued.

The God Who Answers the Faithful: Job 38:1—42:6

Part of the friends' anger has stemmed from Job's insistence on bringing a lawsuit against God that would force the Lord to justify what has happened. Elihu thinks that he must and should speak for God, since the other friends have failed to refute Job and because the Lord does not speak directly to human beings. The four friends do not believe Job is faithful to Yahweh, nor do they think God would answer him if he were righteous. To them, the Lord is aloof, content to speak to human beings through cryptic visions (cf. 4:12-21), natural disasters or affliction (cf. 33:14-22). Even Job considers the Lord's wisdom to be beyond human reach (cf. 28:1-28). Therefore the Lord's two speeches in this section prove both Job and the friends wrong about God's attitude toward having a personal relationship with people. They misjudge God's willingness to provide useful revelation. God's speeches also vindicate Job and his faith, for they demonstrate that Job may be both innocent and a sufferer. Job's responses to Yahweh's questions declare the value of serving the Lord under the most extreme of conditions.

God's comments utilize a series of questions aimed at exposing Job's ignorance of God's ways and at reestablishing the Lord's trustworthiness. To achieve these goals, Yahweh emphasizes creation theology in his first speech. Key metaphors are used to highlight the Lord's role as only God and sole Creator. God is master builder, the sea's midwife, light's commanding officer and holder of the world's most intimate secrets (38:4-24).[52] God has laid the foundation for everything on earth (38:4-7), both the inanimate (38:25-38) and animate (38:39—39:30) orders of existence. Further, the Creator sustains all that has been made (cf. 38:25-41). Job does not know how such things are made and kept in place, so he confesses his need to be silent before God (40:3-5). The world is not so disorderly as he supposed.

God's power is emphasized in 40:6—41:34. Here the Lord asks if Job can tame the great sea creatures that terrify sailors. Only the Creator and sustainer has the strength to do so. Though God has not responded immediately to Job's cries, this delay has not been due to weakness. God has waited for other reasons that Job must accept without full explanation. The crucial issue is whether Job will trust the Creator, sustainer and powerful One who has spoken to him or whether he will press his lawsuit, continuing to question the motives of this highly personal deity.

God's statements are unsatisfactory to some scholars but not to Job.[53] Some experts have argued that God does not answer Job's questions,[54] which may in part be true. Still, what God has done is identify with and thereby vindicate one who has been condemned by his friends.[55] God's appearance clears Job's guilt, for God does not list the sins the friends suggest Job has done.[56] God ennobles Job by taking him seriously.[57] Job has learned that God is on his side, and this knowledge satisfies his demands.[58] In other words, Job has discovered that the Lord reveals himself and his ways to the faithful. They are not left to pursue endless lawsuits that cease in death. His advocate/ redeemer does live and does communicate with him.

Given these two divine speeches, Job once again places his trust in God (42:1-6). He states that before he had heard of the Lord, but now he has experienced him (42:5). God's personal revelation has left Job without doubts about Yahweh's power, wisdom, honor and love. Thus he concludes that God must have a reason for allowing suffering. It, too, has a place in God's orderly world. Job does not capitulate to a cosmic bully. He places his faith in a God who reveals more than he had known before. As Claus Westermann observes, "Now he knows God, and no longer just one aspect of God's activity."[59]

Canonical Synthesis: God's Response to Sufferers

This portion of Job resonates with several canonical texts in which God hears the cries of the hurting and acts on their behalf. Israel's cries in Exodus 2:23-25 are answered by the exodus. The nation's repeated calls for help in Judges are met with deliverance time after time. David confesses that God has saved him from all the crises of his turbulent life (2 Sam 22; cf. Ps 18). God responds to Elijah's pain (1 Kings 19:1-18), Hezekiah's political crisis (2 Kings 19:1-37) and to Josiah's desire for spiritual clarity (2 Kings 22:14-20). Yahweh spares Jeremiah's and Amos's lives. Psalms 18, 22 and 40 express joy over how God acts directly in history to save the weak. Therefore Job's laments, like those of earlier characters, are heard, not ignored. The whole canonical witness is that the faithful are not left to face life's problems without relevant revelation to meet those challenges. God delivers because God is the Creator. Job is God's creation, and a faithful one at that.

The God Who Vindicates the Faithful: Job 42:7-17

God's appearance could be considered vindication enough for the beleaguered Job, but the Lord does more. First, God rebukes the friends for not speaking correctly about him as Job has done. Thus Job must intercede for them (42:7-9). Second, God gives Job a new family and restores his possessions (42:10-15). Third, God gives Job long life (42:16-17). All except his lost children returns to the sufferer. His friends are forced to admit that they have been wrong in what they have argued. Their renewal of fellowship depends on intercession on their behalf by the one they had accused. His willingness to do so marks Job as an honorable, forgiving man.

Canonical Synthesis: God's Vindication of Faithful Sufferers

In what way has Job spoken correctly about God? Has God simply rewarded

Job for enduring so much? Job's comments were right in that they were firmly fixed,[60] in this case on faith. He spoke the "naked truth,"[61] in the sense that he never gave in to pressure to confess sins he did not commit. He believed that God was personal, revelational and worthy of service. His faith was not flawless, though it remained fixed on the one God who he assumed would ultimately vindicate him (cf. 19:23-27). Such faith is justified before all who take a lesser theological route, even those who feel they protect God by doing so.

Job's vindication is but the latest in a long canonical list of such episodes. Like Bildad, Zophar and Eliphaz, Joseph's brothers learned that God had indeed made them bow down to Joseph. Moses' Pharaoh, Barak, Goliath, Ahab, Jezebel and a host of other enemies of the remnant have discovered that people of faith are honored by the Lord who allows them to suffer for a time. It is also true that the very existence of Job in the canon vindicates this book's hero before each successive generation of readers. His story is one more proof that those who trust in God will not be put to shame. Those who take their laments to the one God who creates, sustains, hears and heals find the Lord worthy of complete commitment. As they discover this fact they discover true respect for God, which in turn means they have found true wisdom (cf. 28:28).

17

The God
Who Reveals
Wisdom

Proverbs

. . . .

Many of the speeches in Job seek to establish that either Job or his friends possess true wisdom. Each man tries to prove himself more sagacious than his counterpart, only to discover that his knowledge is incomplete. In the final analysis, however, only God expresses life-renewing and life-sustaining wisdom, for only the Lord's words satisfy Job's longing for truth. Only Yahweh possesses flawless wisdom, so Job and his friends must embrace God's revelation of wisdom. Without this revelation, Job remains angry, the friends remain inappropriately triumphant, and readers remain unclear about how the Lord deals with innocent sufferers who ask for answers. Job indicates that wise living under extreme conditions is dependent on divine revelation.

Proverbs provides Wisdom teaching that is equally dependent on God's revealing truth to the obedient, faithful remnant. Here the situations covered are less excruciating than those in Job. Normal life settings are addressed with the intent of helping God's people move from immaturity to maturity. Though this type of material may seem mundane or even secular, the fact is that human beings cannot become wise solely through their own volition. Even common daily activities cannot be carried out wisely without God's revealed standards to provide the definition and means of success. In neither terrible nor reasonably normal times can people fail to seek and adopt Yahweh's teaching and hope to pass life's tests.

Like Job, Proverbs is a product of the ancient Near Eastern Wisdom tradition in general and the Israelite Wisdom tradition in particular. As such, this book utilizes proverbial literary types[1] found in the literature of other countries, most notably Egypt,[2] though also in Babylon and elsewhere.[3] These literary types convey themes common in those lands, such as the wise use of money, the need to serve royalty carefully and well, the necessity of avoiding wicked women, the importance of truthfulness, and so forth.[4] Such topics are of interest to all people who strive to live in a decent and law-abiding society. At the same time the distinctive ideas of Old Testament theology are encased in these sayings as well, which transforms the material from common sense to divine guidance.

Chief among these theological emphases is monotheism. C. H. Toy writes that in Proverbs

> monotheism is taken for granted, God is regarded as supreme and absolute in power, wisdom, and goodness, and the only trace of anthropomorphism in the theistic conception is the unsympathetic (hostile and mocking) attitude of God toward the sinner (1:26, 11:20, al.).[5]

No other God is considered a source for wisdom, and the Lord is referred to as the Creator (cf. 3:19; 8:22-31), giver (2:6-8) and judge (3:11-12; 5:21; 6:16-19) of wisdom and how it is used by human beings. Further, the Lord is the Creator of the earth (3:19), the judge of human behavior (3:11-12; 5:21; 6:16-19; 10:3, 29; 11:1, 28; 12:2) and the revealer of all beneficial truth (2:6; 6:23; 8:22-36). God is the worthy object of sincere, serious faith (1:29; 3:5-6; 3:11-12; 12:2; 16:3; 28:25).

Other canonical emphases appear as well. Yahweh is the protector of the poor (14:31; 17:5; 19:17) and the redeemer of the faithful (3:25-26; 10:29; 23:10-11). The Lord is called Holy One (9:10). Yahweh rules the earth and human events (16:1-9) and determines on what grounds people may be deemed righteous (10:30—11:11). Several connections between Proverbs and the Law are apparent.[6] Finally, the fear of the Lord is the beginning of wisdom (1:7), the definition of uprightness (14:2), the wellspring of consistent and satisfactory living (14:27) and the way to divine reward (22:4). Respect for the Lord ignites, supports and defines faithful living.

In other words, while Proverbs deals with matters of daily human living, this book is hardly nontheological in orientation. Indeed, as the preceding paragraph indicates, in its final, canonical form Proverbs agrees with the major theological ideas found in the earlier books. It is true that the great historical acts of Israel's history are not included,[7] but the references to Solomon (1:1; 10:1; 25:1) and Hezekiah (25:1) set these texts at important junctures in Israelite history. It is also true that the theological truths gleaned from God's acts are not the sum total of Old Testament theology, though they are decidedly important. Reflection and instruction are as valid theological impulses as history is. All contribute to the canon's portrayal of the Lord.

Proverbs' structure is somewhat difficult to determine because the proverbs themselves do not always appear to be related from one line to the next. Despite this difficulty, however, certain points are clear. First, Proverbs is definitely a manual for appropriate living under God's leadership.[8] Second, the text has "clearly marked transitions" due to headings at 1:1, 10:1, 22:17, 24:23, 25:1, 30:1 and 31:1.[9] These transitions state when certain material succeeds another, such as in 25:1, where the text moves to Solomonic proverbs collected during Hezekiah's era. Other times, such as in 30:1 and 31:1, the transitions convey information about the author of specific material. In 22:17 and 24:23 the breaks note that what follows are "sayings of the wise," a nonspecified group. Each of these sections contains similar material, yet each also has unique features of its own, as will be noted later. Third, many commentators state correctly that Proverbs 1—9 acts as an introduction to the rest of the book. This fact makes it possible to discern progression in the parts that constitute the whole of Proverbs. Fourth, Old Testament Wisdom literature considers growth in wisdom truths a developmental process that occurs over time. Thus elders should be the most mature and righteous believers in the community of faith (cf. Deut 6:1-9; Ps 1:1-6; 37:1-26). Any attempt at producing a theological outline of the book must incorporate at least these rudimentary principles.

Given these notions, it is possible to chart a tentative theological outline for Proverbs. In Proverbs 1—9 the text introduces the book's main ideas by presenting the God who calls people to embrace the pursuit and acquisition of wisdom. The fear of the Lord is affirmed as the beginning of wisdom (1:7). The section personifies Wisdom as God's creation and as one who calls the simple to pursue maturity (8:22—9:12). Next, Proverbs 10—24 utilizes teachings of Solomon and the wise to describe how "the righteous" act. The persons addressed here have accepted the challenge to pursue wisdom, though they have not yet attained perfection by any means. They are learning how to follow the God who instructs the righteous. Finally, Proverbs 25—31 examines how leaders are to act. Those addressed in these chapters have moved beyond choosing and growing in wisdom. Those who offer these proverbs are kings (cf. 25:1; 31:1) and wise men (30:1). They discuss the God who shapes leaders. Each of these sections highlights the theological emphases already mentioned in this chapter. Each considers the fear of the Lord the driving force behind wisdom.

The God Who Calls the Simple to Maturity: Proverbs 1—9

Proverbs 1:1-7 conveys the essence of the call to wisdom. The initial heading states that what follows until the next superscription are "proverbs of Solomon son of David, king of Israel" (1:1). Several definitions of *proverb* are possible. Derek Kidner suggests the word means "comparison," though "it came to stand for any kind of sage pronouncement, from a maxim or observation . . . to a sermon (e.g., chapter 5), and from a wisecrack (Ezk. 18:2) to a doctrinal revelation."[10] R. B. Y. Scott says, "Its root meaning is 'likeness, pattern, rule,' and often it has the added sense of a profound or mysterious utterance which has in it an effective power (Num xxiii 7; Jer xxiv 9)."[11] He adds that proverbs are used in prophecy (Is 14:4), taunts (Deut 28:37), solemn declarations (Job 27:1), instructive poems (Ps 78:2) and admonitions (Prov 2).[12] James Crenshaw agrees with Scott that the verb means "to be like" or "to rule." He observes, "The former emphasizes the analogy that lies at the heart of every proverb, while the latter stresses its paradigmatic or exemplary character."[13] In other words, proverbs are sayings that may be used in various contexts but always with the intent of giving readers an analogy that will dominate their thinking and mold their behavior.

Readers are to gain certain skills from the book. They are to be informed about how to know wisdom, sound teachings and words that give insight (1:2). They will discover how to make sound decisions and how to be just and right and fair (1:3). Growth will occur in every level of reader, whether young and simple, or old and wise (1:5). Their teachers will be the wise of the past (1:6). These benefits can only accrue, however, when one begins by respecting the Lord, the one God who is the source of wisdom (1:7). Yahweh both defines and provides wisdom for the seeker.

Two instructors dominate the message of 1:8—9:18. The first is the common ancient Wisdom parent who instructs immature youth,[14] and the second is Wisdom herself, who is portrayed as one inviting the simple to learn her ways. Both personas work to move readers beyond the apprentice stage in the learning process. Both focus on God's role in establishing and monitoring the disciples' progress.

Both teachers exhort the inexperienced to pursue wisdom in 1:8-33; then the parent takes charge in Proverbs 2—7, followed by Wisdom in Proverbs 8—9. The parent confirms that the wisdom about to be taught is valuable because it instills the fear of the Lord in hearers and offers them knowledge of God (2:1-5). What follows is an description of what Yahweh expects. The parent credits God with revealing wisdom, knowledge and understanding (2:6). It is Yahweh who makes it possible for people to be upright, filled with integrity, righteous, just and joyous (2:7-10). God protects those who seek wisdom, and Yahweh judges those who do not (2:7-15). By stating that God reveals, teaches, protects and judges, the parent acts as God's messenger. Therefore the parent parallels the prophet's role as a person who conveys

God's will to those in need of revelation.

With Yahweh's primacy set forth clearly in 2:1-15, the parent offers exhortations, promises, warnings and theological foundations in 2:16—7:27. Promises include being saved from destructive sexual relationships (2:16-19), becoming one of the upright (2:20-22), enjoying favor with God (3:1-4), receiving guidance (3:5-6), experiencing healing (3:7-8), gaining financial reward (3:9-10) and embracing joy (3:13-18). The promises are overwhelming; they leave no area of life without blessing.

Exhortations typically precede the promises. The parent encourages the learner to remember and be loyal to these teachings (3:1-4). Ingratitude and negligence must not overcome the student. Next, the parent counsels faith, trust in the Lord and a humble acknowledgment of God's superior plans for the learner (3:5-8). Faith is the human perspective that leads to all other marks of righteousness. Then the parent stresses honoring God with all one possesses (3:9-10). Reverence must permeate life. Further, readers are told to accept reproof from their fatherly God (3:11-12). The Lord loves the faithful, the parent says, which demonstrates that God is ultimately the student's teacher-parent. As the text progresses, the parent shares God's love and concern for the learner (4:1-9). Finally, the parent exhorts students to persevere in the growth process (3:21-22). This path will not be easy to walk, but it will lead to life. These exhortations present God as One who merits loyalty, faith and honor, for Yahweh is the One who guides, loves, corrects, heals, rewards and protects.

Warnings focus on the results of poor decisions made by those who forsake wisdom. Chief among the dangers is consorting with prostitutes or other types of loose women (2:16-19; 5:1-23; 6:23—7:27). One should embrace one's wife, and only one's wife, for God watches over everyone's ways and will judge the adulterer (5:21). Besides, adultery is often punished by jealous spouses and by personal despair. No other sin makes one so thoroughly miserable. Other warnings include prohibitions against the mistreatment of neighbors and the envying of the wicked (3:28-32), the improper use of money (6:1-5), laziness (6:6-11), lying (6:12-15) and general deceit (6:16-19). God hates such things (6:16). Again the parent teaches what is abhorrent to the Lord, not just to the teacher.

Several theological foundations inherent in the promises, exhortations and warnings have already been mentioned. The most important remaining idea occurs in 3:19-20, where God is said to have created the world by utilizing his own wisdom and knowledge. God the Creator created the world in a wisdom context. The world was shaped by careful thought, so it has organizing and unifying principles. Creation reflects God's wisdom. Human beings can know wisdom yet cannot learn it apart from the God who possesses and reveals it. A comparison with the Law is relevant here, for at Sinai a holy God revealed holy laws, whereas in Proverbs a wise God reveals wisdom, and both law and wisdom guide flawed human beings.

Proverbs 8—9 presents Wisdom calling the simple, the inexperienced and immature, to come to her for instruction. She, too, grounds her statements upon the fear of the Lord, which she defines as the hatred of evil (8:13). Like the parent, she promises great benefits for pursuing truth (8:1-21). As in 3:19-20, Wisdom claims to have been used by God to create the world (8:22-31). Wisdom is not equal to the Lord, for she was made by God (9:22-26). Wisdom comes forth from the Lord as a natural result of his character. Once created, Wisdom becomes a living creation with tasks of her own in God's world (8:27-31). She promises to mediate God's favor and to give life (8:32—9:12), and she endeavors to keep the learner from wicked women (9:13-18).

This description of Wisdom calling to the simple reinforces the parent's emphasis on taking initial steps toward wise living. Those addressed have far to go before they can claim to be among the upright. It is evident that wisdom must be attained over time, and it is plausible to assume that the same God who calls people to this journey will also provide the means to complete it.

Canonical Synthesis: The Law, Creation and Wisdom

Several canonical connections are apparent between Proverbs 1—9 and earlier passages. For example, there are clear parallels between Exodus 20:1-17 and the admonitions in Proverbs 1—9. Idolatry is never mentioned, yet the monotheistic tone of the passage prohibits any veneration of other gods, though the nature of Proverbs 8 causes some scholars to question this conclusion (see below). Blasphemy and the sabbath are left without discussion. The last six commands, however, are reflected. Learners are to respect their parents and those parents' teaching (1:8-9), and they are to turn aside from violence and bloodshed (1:10-19). Adultery is condemned repeatedly (2:16-19; 5:1-23; 6:23—7:27). Stealing is despised (6:30-31), and envy is condemned as the path to violence and divine rejection (3:31-32). It is as if the fear of the Lord summarizes the first four commands and inspires the keeping of the last six.

The nature of revelation in Proverbs 1—9 also intersects with the Law and the Prophets. As is well known, the Sinai covenant includes two basic types of laws: commands and case laws. The latter are built on the former. In Proverbs, the fear of the Lord, God's creation of Wisdom and the ideas mentioned in the preceding paragraph amount to foundational principles upon which expanded teachings about specific situations (e.g., 7:1-5, 6-17) are based. The teaching tone found in Proverbs 1—9 also approximates that found in Deuteronomy, where a "distinctive pedagogical consciousness" is obvious.[15] Moses instructs his "children" in Deuteronomy as overtly as the parent does in Proverbs 2—7. Both the Law and wisdom are direct revelations by God to human beings through mediators. The same is true of prophecy. Moses received revelation from Yahweh; the prophets sat in God's supreme council (cf. 1 Kings 22:19-23; Amos 3:7); Wisdom and the parent speak the Lord's wisdom. Revelation remains the means by which immature sinners learn to be reconciled to God.

Though monotheism is a given in Proverbs 1—7, the language of 8:22-31 leads some experts to conclude that Wisdom is portrayed as a heavenly being. Other commentators believe Wisdom is simply personified in that text. Thus the question arises whether this passage fits the canon's overall theology. As is so often the case, the passage's context helps illuminate the matter. Proverbs 3:19-20 sets the stage for the subsequent text. There God's wisdom and understanding guide his creative work. As Gerhard von Rad comments, "Wisdom was a means of which Jahweh availed himself; perhaps we could say a constructive principle by which he allowed himself to be guided in the construction of the world."[16] With these verses in place, 8:22-31 personifies Wisdom as a creation of God in whom the Lord delighted. Kidner points out that in the next chapter Wisdom takes on a new persona, that of a great lady whose personified rival, folly (9:13-18), is no heavenly being.[17] Thus Wisdom is presented here as an ancient and beautiful helper to the simple. In this way, von Rad says, "creation not only exists, it also discharges truth."[18]

It is the confession that God is a wise Creator (3:19-20) and that God created now-to-be embraced Wisdom (8:22-31) that guards against polytheistic worship of Wisdom. Some of the images here may be similar to those in other ancient goddess poems,[19] but even so the differences between this text and such pieces imply that the book asks readers to choose between, not equate, Yahweh and the goddesses.[20] God created Wisdom; she is not his equal, so why worship her? God is wise; why should the faithful not strive to be like their Creator?[21] Again all worship roads lead back to Yahweh, just as they have since Genesis 1—2, for no other god created or assisted in creation. Proverbs' author rejects "mythicization and deification of the first principle of the world" because of "faith in Yahweh as creator."[22]

This section's emphasis on traditional conceptions of God also places Proverbs squarely in the mainstream of Old Testament theology. When a text emphasizes God's role as Creator, revealer, object of worship, guide, guarantor of righteous behavior, worthy of service and holy judge, it is hardly out of step with the canon as a whole. Perhaps it is clearest to say that virtually no major aspect of Yahweh's character is absent here except what God did for Israel in the exodus and the conquest. Those acts are vital to Old Testament theology, but they are not its totality.

The God Who Instructs the Righteous: Proverbs 10—24

The persistent call to a divinely revealed wisdom in Proverbs 1—9 gives way to straightforward instruction in Proverbs 10—24. Now the readers are expected to move beyond choosing wisdom (cf. 1:20) to obeying the parent's and Wisdom's warnings, promises and exhortations. They are to absorb the teachings that will take them beyond their initial status as the simple. Once again the proverbs are very practical in nature. Once again the text attributes its statements to the Lord and asserts that the key to keeping God's commands remains the fear of the Lord.

This section utilizes proverbial contrasts to a great extent to distinguish between those who have opted to pursue wisdom and those who have not. In effect there is no hope for the foolish, for those who reject sound teaching. Therefore the text fastens attention on those who fear the Lord, with the goal being to help make the simple into mature persons of faith. Several terms describe such determined learners: the wise, the righteous, the upright, the man of understanding, the one who trusts the Lord and the one who listens and guards his tongue. Of all these terms, which in many ways are synonymous, "the righteous" is the most common. Those who embrace the instructions offered here are given that title.

The fear of the Lord characterizes the righteous. This irreplaceable respect for God gives them life or at least prolongs their lives (10:27) in that it combats sin, the source of death for human beings (cf. 14:27; 19:23; 22:4).[23] Fear of the Lord causes the upright to renounce devious ways (14:2). The fear of the Lord acts as an antidote to transgression (16:6) and is noted as having particular power to shun envy (23:17). Given its value in turning aside sin, fear of the Lord gives the righteous confidence and offers them refuge from fear (10:29; 14:26). It is therefore more valuable than any earthly possession (15:16). If in Proverbs 1—9 "the fear of the Lord" means a desire to heed warnings and accept promises that lead to seeking wisdom, then in Proverbs 10—24 it means the acceptance of standards that repulse sinful behavior. The first definition must be embraced before the second can be true of an individual, and the second definition applied to life becomes the proof that one has begun the journey to wisdom, life and righteousness.

This survey of the fear of the Lord in Proverbs 10—24 demonstrates that God despises sin, a fact evident in other statements about Yahweh in this section. God hates false balances (11:1; 20:10, 23), men with perverse minds (11:20), lying lips (12:22), oppressors of the poor (14:31; 22:22-23), the proud (14:25), those who pervert justice (17:15) and those who gloat over their enemies' defeats (24:17-18). Placed together, these proverbs indicate that it is a righteous God who reveals the means to becoming righteous people. Yahweh's holy character dictates that revealed wisdom be a means of becoming holy as God is holy (Lev 11:44), of fulfilling the implications of being made in God's image (Gen 1:26-27).

Since God loathes sin, it will be punished. God vindicates the righteous by actively moving or reproving the wicked. God blesses the righteous with food but chastises the wicked (10:3). Yahweh promises that willful sinners will not go unpunished (11:21). It is God alone who is able to weigh human hearts (21:2), so only the Lord is capable of just punishment and reward.

There can be no question that the righteous realize that the One who creates (3:19-20; 8:22-31) and judges is sovereign over the earth and its inhabitants. God's authority is stated in three basic ways. First, the certainty of blessing for the wise and judgment for the wicked demonstrates that the Lord decides the fortunes of every person (cf. 11:21). Second, the fact that God may countermand human plans means that the Creator maintains rule over the created ones (16:1-9). People may make plans, 16:1 says, but "that which actually eventuates is decided by God."[24] Human beings may justify their actions, but Yahweh probes carefully into their real motives, which may be hidden to those who are pure in their own eyes (16:2). God weighs the spirit (16:2). Yahweh has made everything for a specific purpose, and that purpose will be fulfilled (16:4). Human possibilities are limited "by God and God's free action."[25] Those who commit themselves to Yahweh find that the Lord directs their steps (16:3, 5-9). Third, the fact that God asks the righteous to let him judge the wicked rather than take matters into their own hands signifies divine sovereignty and reliability (20:22-24). Human beings, who are unable to find their way in life (20:24), must surely wait for Yahweh's justice to take its course (20:22).[26] They must trust that God has not forgotten them or lost the ability to govern wisely. Such faith cannot be placed in a deity of limited strength, knowledge or vigor.

This righteous God who created the world with perfect wisdom sets standards for how the righteous are to live in society. Crenshaw observes that Proverbs 10—24 contains multiple prescriptions for solid character and descriptions of wickedness. The righteous fear God, obey parents (20:30), subordinate passions like anger (16:32) and sexual desire (18:22; 19:14), maintain truthful speech (12:19, 22) and are kind to the poor (14:31).[27] Conversely, the foolish love harlots (23:27-28), drink excessively (23:29-35), are lazy (24:30-34) and engage in gossip (18:8).[28] Without fear of the Lord, trust in the Lord and acceptance of God's plan for one's life, foolishness becomes an ingrained lifestyle and wisdom becomes impossible. The moral fiber of the righteous is not only admirable but also an astounding achievement made possible only through divine help. Those who choose the path of wisdom do not fail to make progress, for God plans their success in the venture (16:1-9).

Canonical Synthesis: The Relationship Between Righteousness and Blessing

Perhaps the greatest canonical consideration related to Proverbs 10—24 is its view of retribution. Simply stated, Does righteous living guarantee immediate and unshakable blessing according to Proverbs? Commentators too numerous to mention have thought so, and many of these interpreters consider Job and Proverbs competing viewpoints that counterbalance one another. A reexamination of the meaning of *proverb,* a close reading of the issue in Proverbs 10—24 and a canonical survey of blessing and cursing texts may begin to give an answer to this serious question.

It must be remembered that *proverb* does not mean "absolute promise" in every specific context.[29] A proverb is a comparison that teaches principles and expected outcomes in life. Proverbs have tremendous versatility and are used in a variety of Old Testament settings, always with the intent of prescribing behavior. The issue of retribution cannot be solved by a lexical study of *proverb* alone, but it is important to establish that exactly what Proverbs does or does not promise must be determined contextually.

An analysis of selected passages in Proverbs 10—24 demonstrates that the righteous are not promised an endless, boundless, smooth and successful life. This principle is illustrated by certain items God condemns. For instance, the very existence of all the varieties of evil persons mentioned here precludes a totally peaceful life for the righteous. Further, the righteous live in a world where false balances (11:1), bribes (17:8), purposefully unjust court decisions against them (17:15; 18:5) and prosperity of the wicked (24:1) occur. What distinguishes the righteous is not unbroken ease but a God-given ability to rise after each setback (24:15-16). Finally, 14:21, 14:31, 19:17 and 22:9 command respect and aid for the poor. The poor in these texts are not the wicked, for there is no negative judgment made about them in a section that offers negative assessments of all kinds of sinful persons. Their poverty does not apparently come because of sin, yet poverty is no great blessing, so the expectation of the righteous to always be blessed materially is denied at this point. The text claims no constant ease for those who pursue wisdom any more than it envisions the wicked's suffering unstintingly.

Several earlier canonical texts shed light on this matter as well. Joseph's wisdom and righteousness led to glory but hardly to an easy life. Though not specifically attached to a wisdom framework like that in Proverbs, Deuteronomy 27—28 specifies blessing for covenant obedience and consequences for covenant infidelity not unlike what Proverbs provides. Moshe Weinfeld notes that the concept of retribution in Deuteronomy and Proverbs is expressed in strikingly similar phraseology.[30] If so, it is important to state what happens to the righteous in the Deuteronomy 27—28 scenario. Stated simply, maybe too simply, the righteous remnant suffers along with the wicked, a fact Moses, Joshua, Caleb, Jeremiah, Ezekiel and others discover firsthand. Their righteousness does not shield them from adversity. What they all receive is God's presence, approval and eventual vindication. In other words, they embody the resiliency described in Proverbs 24:15-16.

Psalms 1, 37 and 128 are good representatives of wisdom ideas of retribution in the psalms. Psalm 1 distinguishes between the righteous and the wicked, concluding with the fervent belief that the sinner will eventually be swept away in the time of judgment. It also claims that life is a pathway marked by serious decisions (1:1). Prosperity does mark the life of the wise person (1:3), with the most obvious blessing coming when judgment time appears (1:4-6). Psalm 128 promises good work, happiness and a blessed family life to those who fear the Lord. Psalm 37 claims that the righteous must trust in the Lord and take a long view of life (37:3-4). Evildoers are not to be envied, though they prosper now, for they will eventually be destroyed (37:10), leaving the land to be possessed by the faithful (37:11). Proverbs 24:19-20 says the same. The righteous may have only a little now (37:16), yet God will make sure the future belongs to them (37:17-19) and that their wicked counterparts will perish (37:20).

The picture in these psalms is one of modest yet vital short-term blessings and assurance of eventual vindication. God's blessings never leave the righteous, but they sometimes unfold in the midst of stressful and distressing circumstances. On the other side of the situation, the wicked do come to ruin, yet often after a sustained period of seemingly peaceful pursuit of their particular pleasures. Their doom is sure, but the timing and circumstances of their doom are known only to the Lord. Retribution may or may not be an immediate experience. The same is true of blessing.

Job's discussion of these issues is also instructive. Job's friends consider all suffering a direct rebuke of one's sins by God. They claim that at best the wicked prosper for only a season but usually are immediately blasted for their rebellion. Job disagrees, arguing that he suffers unjustly, that the wicked die fat and wealthy and yet also that God will vindicate him in time. In effect he agrees with Psalm 37. That is, one must trust God to judge the wicked, it is possible for the righteous to experience difficult circumstances, and the righteous can have faith that their redeemer will not fail them. The righteous may be rich or poor; they may be fully satisfied with God's plans for them or be tempted to envy the rich; they may wait for God's timing or be frustrated.

Part of their growth in wisdom rests on their reaction to situations that seem to be less than glorious blessing. Job begins and ends in great blessing, though its central core struggles with the reality of the righteous' enduring pain.

Proverbs 1—24 stresses blessing as the central core of its message about wisdom yet at the same time reflects the painful realities that the righteous face. Thus it is more accurate to consider Job, Proverbs and the earlier Wisdom-oriented texts canonical partners, not canonical and theological opposites. Proverbs and Job's friends do not share a common theology, for Proverbs includes variables the friends neglect. Job and Proverbs share a balanced view of retribution, though how each balances that view is definitely unique.

This approach to retribution raises the issue of the motivation for righteousness, as well as the very definition of the term. Here the righteous person is one who does God's will as it is revealed. In Proverbs 10—24 this is not a legalistic keeping of rules but a purposeful keeping of faith in a relationship. As Brevard Childs asserts, "a righteous person was one who measured up to the responsibilities which the relationship had laid upon him."[31] Thus the righteous ones respect, trust and commit themselves to the Lord.[32] Their growth in wisdom depends on this partnership with the God who reveals truth. At the same time the righteous are not told to be uninterested in the issue of rewards. They should at the least desire to avoid the inevitable disgrace that comes to the foolish, a point the text takes great pains to make. Still, as in Job, the righteous must be willing for their relationship with God to suffice when material blessings are not present. They may be poor, oppressed or under personal attack yet be wise and bound for reward all the same.

Is such righteousness due to personal merit here or in the rest of the canon? No, for in Proverbs it is clear that human beings are incapable of becoming wise without divine revelation. People are clearly dependent on Yahweh's initiative. Their faith in acting on God's mercifully given guidance defines their righteousness (cf. 1:7; 2:6-10; 3:5-6). The same was true for Abraham, who believed God's pledge of a son when such a promise was laughable and was considered righteous for his faith (Gen 15:6). Job's dogged faith was based on his belief in God, which was vindicated in the end. His greatest fear was that he had lost that all-important relationship with the Lord.[33] Like these earlier figures, the righteous in Proverbs must hear, believe and obey. Even their ability to obey rests in God's hands (cf. 16:1-9), so they are as dependent on divine grace for their righteousness as is any other Old Testament individual or group.

The God Who Shapes Leaders: Proverbs 25—31

Through Proverbs 24, the superscriptions have linked the material either to

Solomon, who reigned about 970-930 B.C., or to the unknown "wise" mentioned in 22:17 and 24:23. Now 25:1 sets the collection of the material in Proverbs 25—29 during Hezekiah's rule (c. 715-687), a time in which this king sought resolutely to turn the people back to the Lord (cf. 2 Kings 18-20; Is 36—39). Wisdom was especially needed then in the lives of the leaders who had the task of helping the nation choose to serve God over other options. Mature officials and mature people were crucial to reform. These realities are reflected in the choice of material in Proverbs 25—29 as well as in Proverbs 30—31, where two otherwise unknown leaders contribute the proverbs. Here God raises up persons who can keep themselves and their people from disaster.

Proverbs 25—27 focuses on kings, their followers and fools who disrupt the community. Followers are told to be humble in the monarch's presence (25:2-7), to be faithful messengers (25:11-14), to have good relations with neighbors (25:8-10, 17-22) and to offer generally good, sound, sensible and self-controlled service to their leader. God rewards such behavior (25:22). Fools are worthless to a king and a danger to any community, so they are not to be honored under any circumstances (26:1-28). Humility, hard work and self-control are set forth as keys to successful living in Proverbs 27. Seemingly, if the charge that Proverbs is secular in nature can be made at all it should be levied here, for God is mentioned only in 25:22.

A new emphasis on the Lord's revelation of wisdom emerges in Proverbs 28—29, however, which implies that Proverbs 25—27 set a standard that Proverbs 28—29 declare how to reach. As always, God is the central figure in the acquiring of wisdom. Fear of the Lord remains the prerequisite for blessing (28:14). Trust in the Lord continues to be the key to divine-human relationships that result in enrichment (28:25) and safety (29:25). God is still confessed as the Creator of all people, regardless of their status (29:13), so God is the ultimate and primary source of justice for everyone (29:26). Kings must therefore gain understanding of how to administer justice from Yahweh (28:5; cf. 1 Kings 3:1-14). Yahweh remains the guide of the wise. No other resource is fully trustworthy.

God's role in instructing leaders is highlighted even further by this section's rare (for Proverbs) emphasis on the law and prophecy. Knowing and keeping God's law[34] are paramount in the struggle against wickedness. Those who forsake the law in effect choose to praise the sinful and their beliefs (28:4). Those who keep the law achieve wisdom (28:7); their prayers are heard (28:9). Without prophecy, the application of the law to daily life, people have no restraint, but when people obey the law they are blessed (29:18). Both prophecy and law are God-inspired revelations that teach people how to live, and both require a relationship with Yahweh. Thus Wisdom materials, law and prophecy build a body of teaching that makes sound living possible.

God's intent in giving revelation is, again, to create a group of righteous persons who are wise and faithful.[35] These are the people who are bold (28:1), victorious (28:12), joyous (29:6) and patient (29:11). Because of such character traits they make good leaders (29:2) who protect the poor (29:7), turn away wrath (29:8) and avoid fools (29:9). God blesses their faithfulness (28:20). Their character obviously derives from their relationship to the Lord and their commitment to obeying God's clearly revealed standards.

Among this group of righteous persons will be the rulers Israel needs to move toward righteousness as a nation. Wicked kings are a product of unwise, sinful people (28:2). These so-called leaders do not understand justice because they do not have a relationship with Yahweh (28:5), so they tear their people like wild animals (28:15) through their lust for unjust gain (28:16). By such deeds they perpetuate and increase their transgressions (29:16). Conversely, wise rulers grasp God-given principles of justice (28:5) and are able to dispense fair treatment to their constituents (28:21). They bring joy and stability to the land (29:2,4), they ignore gossip (29:12), and they judge the poor equitably (29:16). Most important, they know that Yahweh is the ultimate ruler (29:26). God has made them what they are by explaining to them how to live. Their authority derives from the Lord.

Slowly but inexorably Proverbs has moved from call to wisdom, to growth in wisdom, to instruction in leadership. Fear of the Lord has driven the entire process. At all times pride, the unwillingness to bow to God's instruction and choosing the wrong life partner have been singled out as particularly devastating blows to the pursuit of wisdom. Proverbs 30—31 closes the book with proverbs by Agur and King Lemuel's mother, neither of which is mentioned elsewhere in Scripture. Their themes are humility and a virtuous spouse, and both are seen as vital for developing sound leaders.

Agur's wisdom is considerable in its scope yet is grounded in self-effacing humility.[36] He begins his words by expressing absolute dependence on the Lord.[37] Agur realizes that he is unable to comprehend fully the ways of the One who creates and is holy (30:2-4). Still, he trusts God's written word (30:5-6) and strives to honor the Lord at all times. William McKane observes that 30:5-9 defends revelation, has specific awareness of Psalm 18:31 and views written Scripture as a vital part of Wisdom learning.[38] Canonical Scripture has clearly become an important aspect of Wisdom thought by Agur's time.[39] Based on his mediated knowledge, Agur launches into six sets of comments about four things (30:11-31).[40] Each series exalts humble, hardworking, wise persons or animals. His conclusion is that passion and excessive talk lead to foolishness and loss. The way of God-oriented humility is best. Quite subtly, the wise, seasoned Agur has shown how admitting one's dependence on Yahweh leads to the possession of wisdom far beyond that possessed by more self-reliant individuals.

Proverbs 31 unfolds in two parts, both of which are statements by Lemuel's mother. The fact that Lemuel and his mother are likely not Israelites[41] demonstrates not only the universal nature of the Wisdom movement but also the acceptance of biblical wisdom outside Israel. In 31:1-9, the mother instructs her son to avoid womanizing (31:3) and wine (31:4-7). Excessive use of wine clouds one's thinking and leads to the perversion of justice (31:5). This matter is quite serious, since she believes a king's main job is to protect the rights of the poor and to judge righteously at all times (31:8-9). Her high view of royal ethics certainly fits Moses' description of good kings in Deuteronomy 17:14-20.

The book concludes with an extensive definition of a good wife (31:10). Lemuel's mother includes every characteristic of a righteous woman that could possibly contrast to the traits of the wicked woman described elsewhere in the book (cf. 7:6-27). This wife works unstintingly, effectively and courageously (31:10-24). She speaks wise words and has strength and dignity (31:25-26). Lemuel's mother praises her with the highest accolade this book offers: she fears the Lord (31:27-31). Once again it is a relationship with Yahweh that leads to wise living. This principle is true for men and women, Israelites or Gentiles.

Canonical Synthesis: Wise Women and Just Rulers

In the Masoretic Text of the Hebrew canon, Proverbs 31 is followed by Ruth, then Song of Solomon. Raymond Dillard and Tremper Longman observe, "All three texts present positive feminine characters who are capable without being completely dependent on males."[42] There is a conscious canonical effort to present Ruth and the woman in Song of Solomon in light of the definition of God-fearing wife in Proverbs 31. This strategy allows for reflection on how women know and serve the Lord in a variety of situations and sets the stage for the problems Esther encounters later in the canon.

Two earlier texts are also interesting in light of Proverbs, with both appearing in Samuel and both being linked to Joab. When Joab wants David to bring Absalom home, he employs a "wise woman" to come tell the king a story similar to the David-Absalom impasse. She succeeds in achieving Joab's goal (2 Sam 14:1-24). A second "wise woman" makes sure the people of Abel throw the rebel Sheba's head over the wall, thus saving the city from ruin (2 Sam 20:14-22). Both of these women, like the wife in Proverbs 31, preserve life and community through their actions. All these women receive proper acclaim for their wisdom and counsel.

Kingship as described in Proverbs 25—31 fits the canonical pattern of rulers serving God and the people instead of using their position for selfish gain. An adherence to God's law is as important in Proverbs 28—29 as it is in Deuteronomy 17:14-20. Fairness to the people of the land figures in 31:8-9 as well as in 1 Kings 21 and Jeremiah 21—29. Rulers derive their authority from God in these chapters as surely as Saul and David do in 1 Samuel 8—16. God's standards have not changed, and Proverbs 31 extends them beyond Israel's borders.

Conclusion

There is no doubt that Proverbs does not include the sort of overtly theological dialogue that characterizes Psalms and Job. Perhaps the sheer volume of discussion in those books overshadows that in Proverbs. Still, at the source of every conceivable realm of wise living stands Yahweh, giving revelation and inviting a relationship based on awe-filled respect and trust. The God who rules and tests, who creates and sustains, is also the God who directs the righteous along their path to wisdom and leadership.

This insistence on the one God who reveals wisdom distinguishes Israelite thinking from that of its ancient counterparts. Wisdom is not just tried and proven common sense. Rather it is as much divine revelation as the Law from which it draws so many of its foundational concepts. The forms of the literature are similar to those of other nations, but the most important detail, Yahweh as its only stated source, is not. In this insistence Israel stands alone. Other nations may claim their gods give knowledge,[43] but Israel offers the canonical conviction that only its God can deliver true, life-changing wisdom.

18

The God
Who Extends
Mercy to the Faithful

Ruth

. . . .

RUTH HAS LONG BEEN LAUDED AS A WONDERFUL STORY THAT SHOWS PEOPLE overcoming life's tragedies through devotion and strong character. R. K. Harrison represents many kindred statements when he writes, "This charming tale of human devotion and kindness is one of the most beautiful in the entire Old Testament, constituting a model of the art of storytelling."[1] The book does include all the elements of excellent writing: strong characters, plot development that includes suspense and resolution, interesting use of setting and subtle narrative technique.[2] Read on a literary level, alone Ruth offers stimulating ideas about pain, loyalty, kindness and reversal of fortunes.

It is also true that Ruth yields vital canonical and theological insight. As the book that follows Proverbs,[3] it presents a woman who embodies the description of the virtuous wife set forth in Proverbs 31. Further, it describes the eventual joyous vindication of the faithful, a theme that is decidedly important in Psalms, Job and Proverbs. Those who trust God, serve the community and aid the poor eventually enjoy Yahweh's favor. As part of the Writings, Ruth examines the bitterness of pain in a manner similar to the laments in Psalms and in Job 3. Yet it also describes the joy of restoration, a subject that dominates Job 42:7-17. Because of the Davidic genealogy in Ruth 4:18-22, David's life and the prophecies connected to the Davidic covenant are also brought to mind. The application of statutes found in Leviticus and

Deuteronomy ties Ruth to the Law. All these elements are linked in a way that demonstrates that Yahweh extends mercy to the faithful and offers grace to all who will embrace the faithful's convictions.

Ruth's purpose is best explained in light of the text's theological outline. The book falls into five clear parts. In 1:1-22, Ruth's two major characters and the main plot conflict are introduced. Two women, bereft of husbands and children, cling to Yahweh and one another. As they do so they encounter the God who extends mercy to the bereaved, though Naomi does not think so at first. Next, 2:1-23 introduces the third major character and by doing so begins to solve the plot's dilemma. As Naomi awakens to new possibilities she conveys faith in the God who extends mercy to the bitter. Then, in 3:1-18 Boaz learns of the possibility of marriage to Ruth. Thus, along with the women, he experiences Yahweh as the God who extends mercy to the humble. Consequently, in 4:1-17 Boaz and Ruth marry, have a child and thereby provide plot resolution. The God who extends mercy to the childless meets the needs of all three main characters. Finally, 4:18-22 offers a genealogy that includes David. This material indicates that God extends mercy to the whole nation.

Robert Hubbard is right to contend that Ruth highlights how God blesses one family and by doing so blesses multitudes.[4] Edward Campbell properly emphasizes the giving of mercy by God to the characters and by the characters to one another. The main characters embrace "a style of living which can be blessed by the God who would have it so among his people."[5] Ruth's purpose is to show the glory of God's mercy acted out in the lives of faithful people. Yahweh's faithful ones love their God (Deut 6:4-9) and their neighbor (Lev 19:18), thereby fulfilling the intent of the Law, the Prophets and the Writings (cf. Mk 12:28-34).

The God Who Extends Mercy to the Bereaved: Ruth 1:1-22

This account is familiar to most Bible readers. Naomi, her husband and her two sons migrate from Bethlehem to Moab to avoid a famine during the era of the Judges (1:1-2). While there, the husband and the sons die (1:3-5). Naomi is left with two Moabite daughters-in-law, Ruth and Orpah. Childless, grieving, she hears of better times in Judah, decides to return home and tries to send the other women back to their homes in Moab (1:6-13). Orpah leaves, but Ruth commits herself to Naomi (1:14-18). Naomi and Ruth return, and Naomi expresses bitterness over her situation (1:19-22). The main problem the plot must solve is how these husbandless, childless women will survive in ancient Israel.

Upon closer examination, several theological principles help shape the action. First, 1:1-5 ascribes no action to the Lord, but 1:6 says that Naomi determines to return to Bethlehem because she hears God has visited the people and given them food. This narrator's comment makes sure that readers realize that God is sovereign over all these events. God's visits in the Old Testament may occur for either blessing or punishment. In 1:6 God blesses,[6] but Naomi, Ruth and Orpah have learned that life does not always result in pleasant events.

Second, because she believes God blesses as well as takes away, Naomi asks Yahweh to bless the younger women with new husbands and homes. Thus they will be secure. Willem Prinsloo observes that Naomi bases her blessing on the kindness the women have shown her and the deceased men, an idea that reappears regularly in the story.[7] Naomi's expectation is that the Lord blesses the faithful, and a good bit of Ruth explores whether this belief is well founded.

Third, in committing herself to Naomi, the Moabite woman Ruth also commits to Israel and to Yahweh (1:16-17). She converts to covenantal faith as Rahab (Josh 2:8-14), Naaman (2 Kings 5:1-18) and Jonah's Ninevites have done earlier in the canon. Israel is open to those who forsake other gods, desire to offer sacrifices to Yahweh (cf. Lev 22:25) and wish to pray in the temple (cf. 1 Kings 8:41-43).[8] Though temple worship is not yet available in the era of the judges, the other principles hold true. Monotheistic faith is not the sole property of Israel or any other nation, and Israel must remain open to those who choose to embrace covenantal beliefs. Ruth's seriousness is marked by her swearing by Yahweh's name, an oath 1:17 indicates she considers binding, permanent and dangerous to break.[9]

Fourth, Naomi attributes her dilemma to the Lord in 1:20-21. She tells the Bethlehemite women to call her Mara ("bitter") instead of Naomi ("pleasant") because of how God has dealt with her. Though she does not know it, however, Yahweh has already extended mercy in her bereavement through Ruth's commitment to her. Her help has arrived. The same is true of Ruth, for God's solution to her present and future lies in her clinging to Naomi and to Yahweh. Each woman is a conduit of divine grace to the other, though stating this fact means running ahead of the story. The statement in 1:20-21 is at least as oriented toward God's sovereignty as is 1:6. Naomi certainly believes that Yahweh is Lord over both affliction and deliverance.[10] Whatever happens in the remainder of the account must derive ultimately from the character of God.

Canonical Synthesis: Suffering and the Righteous
Naomi stands in a long line of canonical figures who suffer through no fault of their own. This group includes, to name a few, Joseph, Joshua, Hannah, David, Jeremiah, Ezekiel, many psalmists and Job. They will be joined later

by Esther, Daniel and others. Like Job and the lamenting psalmists, Naomi is not silent in her affliction. She feels abandoned. Still she affirms God's goodness (1:6). Therefore, as Campbell writes, "looked at from this perspective, it [her discussion of God in 1:20-21] is in a very real sense a profound affirmation of faith."[11] Naomi's faith includes expressing pain, knowing that the one God who visits the land in mercy (1:6) may also visit her in mercy. Like the Job of Job 3—37, though, she does not yet know what will come of her beliefs.

The God Who Extends Mercy to the Bitter: Ruth 2:1-23

Ruth 2 is framed by morning (2:2) and evening (2:17-22) conversations between Ruth and Naomi and by the introduction of Boaz in 2:1 and the explanation of how Ruth worked in his fields in 2:23. Between the frames Ruth meets Boaz, is blessed by him and works hard to provide food for herself and Naomi. This part of the account begins to solve the problems the women face, by both explaining how they will be fed and suggesting that a prospective husband may be available for one of them.

As was true in Ruth 1, Ruth 2 is marked by theologically oriented statements that enrich the description of events. Deftly the narrator mentions that Boaz is a relative of Elimelech and that he is wealthy (2:1). It is wonderful that without specifically knowing this information Ruth gleans in his field (2:3). The text says "she happened" (2:3) to work there, a phrase that has sparked some scholarly debate. R. M. Hals writes, "For Ruth and Boaz it was an accident, but not for God. The tenor of the whole story makes it clear that the narrator sees God's hand throughout."[12] J. M. Sasson thinks Hals reads too much into this text, noting that the book's author does not hesitate to mention direct divine activity at other points in the story. He believes this meeting simply saves time.[13] M. D. Gow disagrees with Sasson, for he considers the omission of God's name secondary to the fact that Boaz and Ruth's meeting is much like other providential male-female introductions (cf. Gen 24).[14] All these interpreters agree that the book affirms God's sovereignty over events, so it is not necessary to consider God absent simply because things work out well with no mention of God's directly determining events. God's sovereignty remains in effect, even when the text uses common human expressions to describe events.

The descriptions of Boaz and Ruth in 2:4-7 also carry theological weight. Ruth is depicted as laboring diligently at all times, which is noticed and praised by others. She embodies the work ethic that is so central to Proverbs' description of the righteous. Boaz's willingness to let the poor and the widow glean in his fields reveals that he keeps the Law (cf. Lev 19:9-10; 23:22; Deut 24:19-22).[15] He is the sort of person who places human need above mere financial gain. Both characters are faithful and righteous by any canonical standard.

When they meet, Boaz blesses Ruth in unquestionably covenantal terms. He promises she will be safe as she works, whereupon she humbly asks why he favors her this way (2:8-10). Boaz says he is helping her because of her kindness to Naomi. Mercy is being rewarded with mercy (2:11), just as it was in 1:8-9.[16] Noting her new identification with Israel, he hopes she will find shelter in Yahweh (2:12). Boaz's personal theology may be summarized in this blessing. He believes that God does reward all who take shelter in the Lord. Wilhelm Rudolph and H. W. Hertzberg consider this conviction the main theme of the book and a central theme in the whole Old Testament.[17] To the extent that they imply God's mercy is expressed in 2:12, they are correct. Boaz sincerely desires for Ruth to be blessed as much as any of God's people. His wish for her to be a full covenant partner who receives God's best represents a personal mercy that transcends racial or national barriers.

Certainly the events in 2:1-16 affect Ruth and Boaz. For the moment, though, they have the greatest effect on Naomi. Upon hearing of Boaz's attentiveness she emerges from her bitterness to bless Yahweh for unceasing kindness, or mercy (2:20). Naomi reveals that Boaz is more than a relative or acquaintance (2:1). He is a "near relative," a "kinsman redeemer" (2:20). Thus he is one whom the Law says may marry the widow, redeem the deceased's land, father a child and give the land to the child. This process keeps ancestral lands within a clan and provides an heir to provide for the widow (cf. Gen 38; Deut 25:5-10). It is also possible for the redeemer to father the child without marrying the woman, in which case the benefits to the child and woman remain.[18] Naomi's excitement is justifiable, since such a marriage could solve the women's financial problems. That she attributes this turn of events to God demonstrates her faith. That God works in this way shows that Yahweh intercedes for all hurting faithful ones, even those whose belief in divine sovereignty turns to bitterness.

The connections of Ruth 2 to earlier canonical texts has the effect of highlighting God's consistent mercy and the importance of wise living based on covenantal principles. God has seen to the needs of the suffering in this story as surely as in previous books. Naomi, Ruth and Boaz live in a way that Deuteronomy 27—28 and Proverbs promise will result in blessing, not punishment. The whole tenor of the account so far underscores that the Law and the Writings can be lived out by those who choose (1:16-17), confess (2:11-12) and praise (2:20) the God who acts mercifully.

The God Who Extends Mercy to the Humble: Ruth 3:1-18

If Naomi is the most pleased person at the end of part two, then Boaz must certainly have this standing at the end of part three. Here the women decide to let Boaz know that Ruth will marry him (3:1-8), he rejoices in this possibility (3:9-13), and they agree to attempt to arrange the union (3:14-18). A complication arises in that a closer relative than Boaz exists, but this problem will be met directly (3:18). Events are moving ever more swiftly now, with a resolution to the problems announced in 1:1-15 in view. Boaz acts with the determination of one who has inherent integrity and who believes he is in the process of receiving divine blessing.

Prinsloo observes that 3:1-18 demonstrates that God often answers prayers through human initiative. Ruth's desire for Boaz to spread his garment over her (3:9) fulfills Boaz's wish that she be protected beneath God's wings (2:12). Naomi's hopes for Ruth's blessings in 1:8-9 are partially met by her own plans in 3:1-4 for Ruth to meet Boaz at the threshing floor.[19] Boaz's swearing by Yahweh in 3:13 also shows that his heart for God matches that of Ruth, for her own confession in 1:16-17 includes an oath to Yahweh. Finally, the possibility of marrying Ruth vindicates Boaz's personal theology stated in 2:11-12. A humble man, he had not expected Ruth's affection (3:10). Receiving her proposal means that his personal righteousness, integrity, kindness and humility have brought him blessing under the shelter of God's wings. Ruth becomes an altogether wonderful blessing for this man who has trusted in God.

It is important to mark the fact that Boaz decides to provide for both Ruth and Naomi (3:16-18). Naomi has always spoken of "our redeemer" (2:20), and Boaz's pledge and subsequent gift (3:11-18) express his willingness to do all Ruth wants done for herself and Naomi.[20] Once again all his desire for Ruth is grounded in his convictions about her character.[21] He chooses a "good wife" based on Wisdom standards (Prov 31:10-31) and includes in his generosity the one (Naomi) to whom and for whom Ruth proved her worthiness.

The God Who Extends Mercy to the Childless: Ruth 4:1-17

As Naomi expected in 3:18, Boaz moves quickly in securing the right to become the nearest kinsman redeemer (4:1). To facilitate matters, though at some risk to herself, Naomi includes Elimelech's land as a part of the redemption costs. To gain the land one must redeem it and care for the woman. But which woman? Hubbard theorizes that the man thought he must support Naomi, who could not have children who would share his other children's inheritance. To get good land he had "only" to care for an older wife. Ruth, however, could have "several sons, the first eligible to claim Elimelech's property as his heir, others perhaps to share in the kinsman's own inheritance (v. 6)."[22] Thus he rejects the opportunity, and Boaz announces his intentions (4:1-10).

The last seven verses in this section contain four distinct theological points. First, the women of the town offer their own blessing. They hope Ruth will be like Leah and Rachel, the matriarchs of the twelve tribes of Israel (4:11). They also pray that this clan will be significant in Bethlehem and that it will prosper like that of Tamar, the heroine of Genesis 38 who must trick a near kinsman into fathering her child. These references to Genesis show that Ruth has been accepted as a full member in Israel's covenantal traditions.

Second, 4:13 says that the Lord gave Ruth conception so that she could bear a son. This child is God's gift.[23] Yahweh is said to act directly for only the second time in the book (cf. 1:6), this time as a way of bringing resolution to the plot.[24] Human beings can extend mercy to one another, but only God can give life. Third, Ruth gives this child to Naomi as a restorer of family and a financial protector for her old age (4:14-17). This gift of divinely given life finalizes Ruth's commitment to Naomi and proves one last time her own righteousness and enormous capacity for merciful love.

Fourth, the women of Bethlehem bless God for how Naomi's fortunes have turned. No more are she and Ruth childless. No longer is their future in doubt. Their mercy toward one another and Boaz has resulted in a joyous conclusion. Prinsloo concludes that

> the fourth pericope can be summarized as follows: although human initiative is emphasized and great stress is laid upon man as a collaborator with Yahweh, the focus naturally falls on the fact that there are limits to human initiative. Yahweh is the one who resolves the crisis and to whom praise ought to be given.[25]

Canonical Synthesis: Hope for the Childless

This section echoes earlier canonical accounts of God's opening wombs. The most famous case is that of Sarah, the mother of all Israel (Gen 21:1-7). Yahweh makes sure that the unloved Leah has children in Genesis 29:31 and then opens the beloved Rachel's womb in 30:22. Samson's mother is similarly blessed (Judg 13:1-3), as is Hannah, Samuel's mother (1 Sam 1:1—2:10). In these instances God acts as the Creator of life. Yahweh offers hope to those who desire the joy and security of children yet are not able for a time to experience this blessing. God removes pain and uncertainty and replaces these with honor and praise.

The God Who Extends Mercy to All Israel: Ruth 4:18-22

Ruth concludes with a genealogy of David's family. This ending transforms the book from an account that expresses God's mercy toward certain righteous persons to a statement about how God acts mercifully on Israel's behalf by giving them their greatest monarch. Ruth recounts the fact that God takes pains to keep David's lineage from dying out before it can even begin. The one who brings the family and Bethlehem lasting renown is now in place.[26] By giving birth to David's ancestor, Ruth contributes as much to Israel as did Leah and Rachel. She is as blessed as Tamar.

Canonical Synthesis: The Davidic Promise
The canonical witness is that this birth will eventually extend mercy throughout the world. Second Samuel 7:1-17 promises an eternal kingdom for David's heir, and Isaiah 9:2-7 and 11:1-10 state that this kingdom will reach around the world. Zechariah 9—14 affirms this universal vision too, as does the New Testament in general and Paul's writings in particular. Through the work of the Davidic king God's mercy will be known in all the countries Yahweh has created. This much comes from mercy offered to a pair of righteous widows.

In every conceivable way this small book proves a worthy successor to Proverbs. Ruth confirms Job's belief that God vindicates and Proverbs' contention that the Lord blesses the righteous. The text demonstrates how laws found in Leviticus and Deuteronomy ought to be obeyed and illustrates once again how the women blessed with children in Genesis, Judges and Samuel are not beneficiaries of happy coincidence but are recipients of divine pleasure. Covenants made with Abraham, Moses and David are honored here. It is hard to imagine a book so short doing more to maintain the faith of the whole canon.

19

The God
Who Oversees
Male-Female Sexuality

Song of Solomon

. . . .

T HEOLOGICAL REFLECTION ON THE OLD TESTAMENT CANON IS DEPENDENT ON
what the text confesses and questions about God's character. This task is
facilitated by the abundance of lucid statements in Scripture that reveal
aspects of the Lord's person and work. Painstaking analysis is necessary to
understand many sections, but even these passages are often illuminated by
other texts' clarity. Thus the fact that two books in the canon, Song of
Solomon and Esther, do not explicitly quote or mention the Lord at all
presents certain challenges to Old Testament theologians.

One possibility that may help break (or at least mitigate) the impasse is
to focus on the function of the Song's canonical position and on its historical
role as part of Israelite Wisdom literature. When these factors are considered,
it is possible to consider Song of Solomon a book that affirms that God
oversees human relationships in their physical and emotional expressions.
The word *oversees* is used because God is not mentioned explicitly in the
text. God is retained as sovereign in the book because the canon includes
Song of Solomon in its treatment of wise living exhibited through wise loving.

Some type of historical approach is necessary for grounding Song of
Solomon in the sort of reality evident in the rest of Scripture. Theology is
never divorced from the historical setting of Old Testament authors and
audiences. The historical setting links the individuals in the text, the author,

the original intended audience and subsequent readers of the canon. Historical reality and a desire for applying Scripture are part of what authors of texts and readers of texts share in common. This component of theological reflection must not be sacrificed.

At the same time theological analysis must not be lost in the determination to keep Song of Solomon from being treated as a nonhistorical document. Efforts to equate the book with Egyptian or Canaanite erotica or fertility cults fall in this category, as do attempts to treat the text solely as a description of love between a man and a woman. Literary parallels with other ancient literature do exist, and male-female relations are extremely relevant in Song of Solomon (to say the least), yet these facts do not remove the need to relate the book to the theological convictions found in the rest of the canon. Suggestions that the book is a drama that emphasizes how Solomon learned the value of God-ordained monogamy are hopeful in their outlook yet hardly confirmed by other Scriptures. Other historically generated readings are no more convincing.

Perhaps more than any other Old Testament book, Song of Solomon needs to be interpreted in light of the whole of the Old Testament canon. Its placement, transcanonical thematic emphases and connection to the other Wisdom books all deserve attention. In this way the book's strengthening of other theological concerns becomes more evident, and its unique contribution to that whole likewise grows plainer. Combining these elements provides one way of navigating between nonhistorical and nontheological readings of the text.

Song of Solomon's placement in the Writings continues notions begun in Proverbs. Throughout Proverbs, love for one's wife and avoidance of wicked women are emphasized repeatedly. The book concludes with a long and challenging description of a virtuous wife who fears the Lord and serves family and community flawlessly (Prov 31:10-31). Ruth depicts not one but two virtuous women who love Yahweh, love one another and serve their community. Boaz proves his wisdom by marrying Ruth and caring for Naomi. Song of Solomon completes the cycle begun in Proverbs 31. If Proverbs 31 highlights sound advice on seeking a suitable mate and Ruth demonstrates the way God brings the righteous together for marriage, then Song of Solomon illustrates free and passionate love between a man and a woman. Ecclesiastes, the next book in the canon, states plainly that human love cannot take the place of one's respect and love for one's Creator. Thus Song of Solomon is introduced and qualified within the canonical context.

Song of Solomon's emphasis on sexuality has parallels outside of the Writings. For instance, Genesis 1—2 reflects an ideal male-female relationship in which total oneness is evident. They are naked and not ashamed

(Gen 2:25). No Old Testament text approximates the Genesis situation as closely as do the lovers' statements in Song of Solomon. Their love recaptures Genesis 2:25 as much as is possible in a sinful world characterized by mixed motives and outright deception. Other relevant passages will be noted. To the extent that one can draw analogies[1] between God's love for Israel and the love reflected in Song of Solomon, it is possible to once again marvel at this love's purity. The love depicted here puts the adulterous love Israel shows for Yahweh in, for example, Hosea 1—3 to shame.

Brevard Childs observes that Song of Solomon's inclusion among the Wisdom books means that the text must be read as the effort "to understand through reflection the nature of the world of human experience in relation to divine reality."[2] Therefore the book may not be interpreted simply as a collection of secular love songs but as the type of love God counsels every couple to emulate.[3] The dangers associated with out-of-control passions make it essential that divinely revealed wisdom oversee human love relationships.[4] Childs correctly assesses wisdom's revelatory role and Song of Solomon's status as guide for wise loving. The book offers an ecstatic freedom for which Proverbs provides appropriate boundaries. Theological balance is thereby achieved by the inclusion of both books in the canon.

With these preliminary comments in place, it is now appropriate to suggest an outline for Song of Solomon. This outline attempts to reflect the book's lack of overt statements about the Lord yet also to stress canonical connections that underscore the text's conviction that God oversees wise and positive human sexuality. It also recognizes the dramatic dialogue that characterizes the book as a whole, for, as M. T. Elliott comments, "dialogue is one of the most important unifiers of the poem. Every word that is spoken is directed to a specific audience and elicits a response."[5] Other divisions are possible, but this six-point scheme at least approximates similar six-point suggestions offered by other commentators.[6]

First, the book's depiction of revealed, wise loving begins with the lovers unashamedly declaring their love for one another (1:2—2:7). Intents are clearly stated. Second, the wise lover strongly desires to be with his or her beloved (2:8—3:5). The lovers believe that the past proves the brightness of their future together. Third, the couple commits to one another in marriage (3:6—5:1). This step makes their relationship a permanent one. Fourth, one waits expectantly for the other, unwilling to accept separation patiently (5:2—6:3). Fifth, when together the pair extol one another's virtues (6:4—8:4). Their praises rekindle their passion. Sixth, the book concludes with professions of the permanence of their commitment to each other (8:5-14). What has begun must carry on until death for this marriage to match the high standards set for marital relationships in the rest of the Wisdom literature and the remainder of the canon. Set within the overall scriptural context the Song of Solomon expresses God's will for complete and sustainable love relationships.

The God Who Oversees Declarations of Love: Song of Solomon 1:2—2:7

Unambiguous confessions of devotion and passion characterize the book's first major section. Such straightforward affection neutralizes all fears and insecurities that may arise in either lover's mind (1:5-7). The more praise comes (1:8-11, 15) the more security and confidence grow (2:1). Passion also emerges from this decision to praise (2:3-6). Wise lovers base their bonds together on shared verbal testimony of mutual admiration.

The God Who Oversees Sexual Desire: Song of Solomon 2:8—3:5

Without the desire to be together a love match cannot endure. No lack of affection exists in this pair! Joy attends both the possibility of reunion (2:8-9) and time together (2:10-13). No amount of seeking one another is treated as inconvenient (3:1-4). They believe life is fullest when lived in one another's presence or even when imagining themselves together. The absence of the beloved is the chief barrier to happiness in life, as far as they are concerned.

These first two sections of the book provide a unique service to Old Testament readers, for hardly any other passage addresses passion that precedes marriage. Perhaps Boaz's determination to marry Ruth hints at the same emotion (Ruth 3:1—4:12), yet that account is vastly understated in tone compared to Song of Solomon 1:2—3:5. Praise, adoration, desire, joy and impatience at absence all lead to commitment that will not be easily shaken or broken. Within the Wisdom context, these verses indicate how one can begin to avoid the wicked woman so graphically depicted in Proverbs 5:1-6, 7:6-27 and 9:13-18. Within the canonical context, these passages stand as directions for loving one's beloved revealed by the Lord.

The God Who Oversees Marriage: Song of Solomon 3:6—5:1

This section begins with Solomon coming to marry his beloved (3:6-11),[7] a day characterized as a time of gladness of heart (3:11). Othmar Keel writes that Solomon's gladness "is a superlative kind of joy. It is a gladness that possesses a person completely, extending from the center to engulf every aspect of the human with happiness (cf. Eccl. 5:20 [19]; Isa. 30:29; Jer. 15:16)."[8] The groom's happiness is understandable, given the passion recounted in 1:2—3:5. Very soon his desire will be united with sexual intimacy, but only after a public profession of commitment seals the union with his intended.[9]

Canonical Synthesis: Marriage

Certain earlier passages correspond to the emphasis on marriage found here.

A few of these texts are in Genesis,[10] where God's creation of human beings in his image (Gen 1:26) and yet as male and female at the same time (Gen 1:27) inaugurates the discussion of how men and women relate to one another. Genesis 2:18-25 recounts the unsuitableness of man living without woman and initiates lifelong commitment between a man and a woman to be a separate entity from the parents and homes from which they come. Genesis 2:25 also describes perfect marital harmony as nakedness without shame, which is another way of saying the first couple was physically, sexually, emotionally and spiritually one. Song of Solomon 1:2—5:1 does not duplicate this original oneness, but it comes very close to doing so.

It is interesting to note how much space the choice and marrying of spouses occupies in the patriarchal narratives. Genesis 24:1-67 describes how a strong, gracious, attractive, risk-taking wife (Rebekah) was chosen for Isaac. Her love comforts Isaac after his mother's death (Gen 24:67). His caressing of his wife in a presumably fairly public place (Gen 26:8) reveals their love to outsiders. Jacob's courtship of Rachel is even more complex, for it must include marrying Leah as well (Gen 29:1-30). Still, it is marked by an attraction so strong that seven years of work to gain her seems like only a few days to him (Gen 29:20). Later, Jacob's son Judah's lack of sexual control leads to embarrassment greater than any suffered by his father, who was at least focused on his love for Rachel (cf. Gen 38:1-30).

Other Old Testament characters, such as Isaiah and Ezekiel, seem to have good marriages, but no record of their premarital feelings are revealed in Scripture. It is left largely to Genesis and Song of Solomon to describe the sort of passion that leads to permanent commitment. As Song of Solomon continues, however, more Old Testament texts become relevant to the discussion of love, marriage and marital fidelity.

The God Who Oversees Separation: Song of Solomon 5:2—6:3

Couples, no matter how committed to one another, cannot be together all the time. Separation is as inevitable as it was before the wedding. Therefore the wise lover will make provision for separation. In effect the text indicates that the sort of passion and expectancy that characterized the drive toward marriage should also mark the desire to be together after the wedding. This passion should deepen and mature. In 2:8—3:5 the woman sought her lover tirelessly, and she does so just as purposefully in 5:2—6:3.[11]

Several earlier canonical texts warn about what happens when this type of passion is lost, forgotten or set aside for a time. David's affair with Bathsheba and Gomer's betrayal of Hosea are particularly obvious cases of marital passion lost or misdirected. The teacher's warnings against adultery in Proverbs 1—9 include the exhortation to be intoxicated with a spouse's love (5:15-23). Satisfaction with one's long-term love will negate succumbing to short-term surrender to temptation.

The God Who Oversees Marital Satisfaction: Song of Solomon 6:4—8:4

Part of remaining satisfied within a long-term relationship depends on offering praise to and deserving adulation from one's beloved. The man responds to the woman's desire for him with extravagant compliments.[12] To him, she has no physical flaws or personality quirks (6:4—7:9). In response she promises to more than fulfill his desire for her. She will gladly love and be loved (7:10—8:4). As in the previous section, the point here is that passion and praise must be evident as much, if not more, after marital commitments have been made as before they were made. This type of passion separates true and honorable desire from sheer lust, which, once slaked, may lead to hatred, not love, as the story of Amnon and Tamar proves so sadly (cf. 2 Sam 13:1-14).

The God Who Oversees Permanent Marital Commitments: Song of Solomon 8:5-14

Even the most ardent and cherished spouse can fall prey to jealousy and insecurity. Thus it is important for pledges of permanence to be made between marriage partners.[13] Love must amount to a seal on the heart, be as strong as death, as unquenchable as an everlasting flame and cherished more than wealth (8:6-7). When a man loves a woman this way, her response must be to desire him at her side (8:14). Wisdom demands that love create assurance about the enduring nature of marital relationships. Such assurance comes only through spoken words that complement physical passion.

Canonical Synthesis: The Permanence of Marriage

Permanence is inherent in the canon's statements about marriage. Only death separates Sarah from Abraham (Gen 23:2), Jacob from Rachel (Gen 35:19) or Ezekiel from his wife (Ezek 24:15-18). Even the key divorce text in the Pentateuch, Deuteronomy 24:1-4, treats the dissolution of marriage as a last resort that must be regulated lest the land be defiled. Malachi 2:14-16 states flatly that God hates divorce resulting from treacherous treatment of spouses. Proverbs 5:15-23 at the least implies that the joy one takes in the spouse of one's youth is to last a lifetime, or as long as both lives last.

It is also appropriate to comment that the marital love depicted here and elsewhere in the canon is heterosexual in nature. Leviticus 18:22 and 20:13 show that the Old Testament is well aware of homosexual sexuality. Its denial there and the rest of the canon's emphasis on male-female marital bonds point to the conclusion that heterosexual marriage is the only type sanctioned in the Old Testament. Paul's statements in Romans 1:18-32 also agree with this conclusion. By no means do the Scriptures indicate that all heterosexual relationships are perfect, as has already been noted. As Childs asserts, the Old Testament's vision for male and female relationships

> turns on the divine structuring of human life in the form of male and female with the potential of greatest joy or deepest grief. The Old Testament continually witnesses to the distortion of God's intention for humanity in heterosexual aberrations (Judg. 20; II Sam. 13). Similarly the Old Testament views homosexuality as a distortion of creation which falls into the shadows outside the blessing.[14]

It must be said that this chapter's comments on love, passion, commitment and permanence are not made with the purpose of arguing that Solomon exemplified these principles. Quite the contrary. His marriages were not all conceived in love, nor were they monogamous in nature. He married for political reasons without hesitation (1 Kings 3:1). His unwise unions eventually contributed to his decision to indulge in idolatry (1 Kings 11:1-8). There is no evidence that he cast off wives to whom he made commitments, but there is also no evidence that he felt deeply about them either.

In a strange way Song of Solomon may therefore be an even more important work than if he had been a model husband. The canon offers Solomon at his best in this case, while also balancing this portrayal with the accounts in 1-2 Kings. Song of Solomon extends God-centered wisdom to all who will listen, and the fact that Solomon himself did not always heed its teachings does not mute its value or render it invalid.

Conclusion

One test of a theological approach is how it deals with challenges to its system. Though the canonical scheme followed in this volume is far from flawless, one of its strengths is its potential for incorporating material from books like Song of Solomon and Esther into its theological reflections. Read in isolation, Song of Solomon is artistically and thematically lovely but not particularly theologically enriching. As part of a unified canon, however, as part of an ongoing interactive, authoritative whole, this book confirms earlier teachings about marriage while adding its own unique contribution about pre- and postmarital passions. As part of the canon Song of Solomon testifies to the one God who created men and women for loving, permanent relationships with one another.

20

The God
Who Defines
Meaningful Living

Ecclesiastes

·····················

O LD TESTAMENT WISDOM LITERATURE SEEKS, AMONG OTHER THINGS, TO find order, purpose and meaning in life. Job and Proverbs have already argued, in quite different ways, that God is the One who reveals truths that allow people to live wisely in an orderly yet sometimes turbulent world. They have asserted that respect for God begins the wisdom process (Prov 1:7) and that God's wisdom is found only through diligent search facilitated by divine revelation (Job 28; Prov 8). Both Job and Proverbs conclude that God creates and dispenses knowledge that renders life bearable and even enjoyable (cf. Job 38:1—42:6; Prov 2:1-15; 8:22-36). Neither book claims that the world is always a friendly place for the righteous or the wicked. Rather they observe the power and wisdom inherent in creation and then probe the limits of revelation and experience to explain life's perplexing issues.

It is within this canonical framework that Ecclesiastes must be interpreted, for it is within this literary and historical context that the book comes to the community of faith. Read in isolation, Ecclesiastes can be co-opted by virtually any point of view a reader may wish to assign it. For example, scholars have treated this text as an essentially existentialist tract,[1] a pessimistic assessment of life,[2] the reflections of a skeptical wisdom teacher[3] and the clearest evidence the Old Testament offers that the resurrection is essential for developing meaningful spirituality.[4] Though there are also potential pitfalls associated with a canonical reading of the text, this approach makes possible a balanced rendering of Ecclesiastes' theological contribution within the whole of Scripture.[5] It also supplements ideas offered by writers who seek to place Ecclesiastes within the Old Testament Wisdom context.[6]

Examined as part of the Wisdom material in the Writings, Ecclesiastes shares Job's ability to probe deeply into the nature of human existence. This book's overall tone is dark. The author's mood at times moves from frustration to depression. What causes the writer's discouragement? It is his conviction that the meaning of life cannot be ascertained solely through experience and observation. Job expresses the same dilemma and then finds meaning in God's personal revelation. Job also realizes the value of true wisdom when compared to the false wisdom his friends espouse. Through a long process, the writer of Ecclesiastes leaves the reader with many of the same conclusions as does the writer of Job, though it is not entirely clear the author embraced these ideas. Like Job, the book of Ecclesiastes confirms the notion that the Lord defines meaningful life. Human beings may not be fully satisfied with this fact, yet it remains a fact all the same.

When approaching Ecclesiastes' contents, one is immediately confronted in the opening section (Eccles 1) with the author's declaration that everything is vain, empty, meaningless (1:2).[7] This phrase also ends the Teacher's comments in 12:8. This thesis pushes interpreters to ask why the author thinks so and how he came to this conclusion. It also causes readers to question what the Teacher means by "everything," a seemingly obvious question that is hardly so by the end of the book. The thesis statement is supported by comments that indicate that history (1:2-11) and the search for wisdom are meaningless (1:12-18). Within this section the writer presents a God who has laid a heavy burden on human beings by giving them a complicated life (1:13).

Following this prologue, Ecclesiastes 2—6 presents a series of the Teacher's experiences and observations about life. Approximately half of all the book's statements about God appear here. God is credited as the one who gives people work, wisdom, knowledge, happiness and possessions. At the same time these gifts are not fully satisfactory to the Teacher because they are not meaningful in and of themselves. Next, Ecclesiastes 7—8 presents God as the One who rules history and who gives wisdom to those who seek it. Proverbs and observations similar to earlier Wisdom writings characterize this section. The Teacher decides that not even wisdom is fully satisfying, for the wise cannot comprehend all the Lord does in the world.

Ecclesiastes 9:1-12 depicts God as the One who superintends death. Everyone, whether wise or foolish, dies eventually. Thus the Teacher encourages his students to enjoy God's gifts while they can. Ecclesiastes 9:13—11:6 follows with observations on wisdom akin to those in Ecclesiastes

7—8. God is mentioned only once, in this instance as One whose ways are mysterious. Once again the text stresses the strenuous nature of the search for wisdom. Ecclesiastes 11:7—12:8 revisits the matter of death. God alone brings life to conclusion. When one dies, "the spirit returns to God who gave it" (12:7). God is the Creator of persons, the giver of both youth and old age (12:1), and the One who makes death a reality.

The book ends with a pupil's assessment of the Teacher's life and work. This student asserts that God merits respect and obedience, for the Lord is the final judge of all people (12:9-14). Wariness over the meaningfulness of life characterizes the student's comments as they do the Teacher's. At the same time, the student defends the validity of the Teacher's observations. The student's assertions are valid because of the book's connection to what earlier texts say about God and about wisdom. As will be discussed, the Teacher's frustration stems from the reality of sin's consequence, not from perceived flaws in the Lord's character or in the value of wisdom.

The God Who Makes Life "Burdensome": Ecclesiastes 1

The Teacher's prologue introduces the notion that life does not necessarily have discernible meaning. In fact, if considered from a certain standpoint it can be utterly vain, without apparent purpose. After all, generations come and go, but nothing new occurs (1:2-11). The Teacher thinks that "generations of men rise and pass away with the same monotonous regularity and ceaseless motions visible in the natural world, and with an equal lack of novelty."[8] He seems both bored and frustrated by a lack of newness in human experience.

Having set his mind to seek meaning through the pursuit of wisdom teachings, he decides that life is burdensome. Life is a harsh task human beings must endure (1:13). Learning does not produce comprehensive answers (1:14-17), but it does create the pain of more questions (1:18). No inherent meaning resides in wisdom itself, for wisdom does not produce solutions that will make life's crooked matters straight. There are "limits that restrict human knowledge, stifling the desire to know and confounding attempts to achieve comprehensive knowledge."[9] The Teacher does not complain that there is no attainable knowledge. Rather he argues that what he does learn does not satisfy his thirst to understand life's apparent inequities.

Of course, Job discusses the difficulty of discerning God's activity and goodness when tragedy strikes hard. Job considers death preferable to life in Job 3. He laments the problem of discovering wisdom in Job 28, and in Job 42:1-6 he confesses he spoke of matters too deep for him to fathom. Frustration and anger like that found in Ecclesiastes characterize his comments. It must be noted, however, that the Teacher's pain is a self-induced agony, unlike Job's externally originated afflictions. Others make Job miserable. The Teacher in effect causes his own pain.

Ecclesiastes 1:12-18 laments the inaccessibility of certain types of wisdom. It is interesting to note that in Genesis 3:6 it is the woman's drive to acquire wisdom uniquely God's that partly fuels her decision to sin.[10] She wished to gain the wisdom of opened eyes, of the knowledge of good and evil and of never-ending life. Likewise the Teacher desires wisdom that has not been granted him. Has he overstepped his own creaturely bounds, or does he seek legitimately to know God's truth? Is it possible within a sinful context to learn what he wants to know? If not, does he create his own burdensome world?

It must be noted that despite his belief that life is burdensome, the author never deviates from monotheism. His frustrations are directed at the one God, just as the laments in Psalms and Job are. Whatever relief the Teacher may receive must originate from the giver of the burden of life. No other possibility exists in the author's mind.

The God Who Bestows Gifts: Ecclesiastes 2—6

Not content to allow vanity and burdensomeness to go unchallenged, the Teacher decides to seek meaning in a variety of venues. Pleasure, wisdom, work and reflection are all sought and assessed (2:1-11). The Teacher concludes that the wise and foolish both die, so all remains vanity (2:15). Work is vain because its fruits may be inherited by a fool (2:18) and because it does not give rest to a discontented mind (2:23).

At the same time the Teacher discovers certain benefits in life. For instance, he admits that wisdom far excels foolishness (2:13). Though the wise and foolish both die, he thinks it is better to live in knowledge and appropriate awareness. Further, despite his anger at work's inability to satisfy all his desires for it, he considers work a gift of God to be enjoyed (2:24-25). God gives wisdom and knowledge in some measure, then, but the Teacher finds this gift vain because it is not given to all (2:26). Foolish persons still exist.

Next, the Teacher discusses the nature of time and events. Every event under the sun has been created by God for an appropriate purpose (3:1-11). Each task people attempt is part of a great time-bordered masterpiece produced by the Creator.[11] But the very awareness of time reminds the Teacher that human beings have a thirst for knowledge of eternity that God does not allow to be quenched through mere reflection (3:11). God's works are thereby mysterious, for they belong to eternity (3:11). Merely knowing that God works in eternity does not explain how God works in eternity.[12] Human beings can simply know that they have a place in God's created time continuum.

Since they have this place, people can also grasp what the Lord requires of them.[13] People ought to rejoice, do good and see value in their labor (3:12-13). Most important, they must fear the Lord because the Lord's works, however hard to grasp, endure forever (3:14). This emphasis on fearing the Lord places the book squarely in the Israelite Wisdom tradition. The Teacher goes on to affirm the notion that God judges both the righteous and the wicked (3:15-17), an idea embraced by the Law, the Prophets and earlier books of the Writings. Those who fear the Lord need not fear judgment. The Teacher decides that God tests human beings so that they will know they are not animals, which may refer to their creation in God's image (cf. Gen 1:26-31). However, the Lord allows both animals and people to die (3:18-22), and the Teacher questions whether either goes to be with God (3:18-22). Thus the Teacher affirms that God gives life, gives work, endures forever, inspires reverence, judges and tests. He is just unable to understand all these facts' full meaning. This inability haunts him. It robs him of the joy he grants to others.

Ecclesiastes 4—6 continues the interchanging of positive and negative comments begun in Ecclesiastes 2—3. On the one hand the Teacher denounces oppression (4:1-3), envy (4:4-6) and loneliness (4:7-12). He decries the vacuity of materialism (5:8-17), the futility of not enjoying one's possessions (6:1-2) and the general boredom of living in a world in which nothing new occurs and the future cannot be known (6:10-12). He thinks it better never to have existed than to suffer as many people do (4:3; 6:3-6), a conviction voiced by Job earlier (Job 3:16).

On the other hand the Teacher affirms the necessity of God-honoring activity. God expects fidelity and faithfulness in worship (5:1). Such thoughtful reverence is due the sovereign Lord of the universe (5:2). Vows must be kept (5:4-6). Visions and dreams are fleeting in value, but fearing the Lord leads to consistent worship that pleases God (5:7). God blesses people with gifts that allow them to forget life's difficulties (5:18-20). These facts mitigate the pain and frustration the Teacher feels yet do not remove them. He still does not appreciate the evil that the Lord allows to continue on earth (6:1-2). He remains convinced that vanity best summarizes the life he lives and the world he observes.

Canonical Synthesis: Ecclesiastes and Genesis 1—3

It is evident that the Teacher interacts with positive theological ideas found earlier in Scripture. First, the text readily affirms the belief that God has created the heavens and earth and endowed human beings with a special ability to know that the material world is not all that exists. Human beings are given a sense of eternity (3:1-14), which is one facet of their being made in God's image (Gen 1:26-31). Second, the Teacher agrees that God has given human beings work to do on earth (2:24-26; 3:22). This conviction also stems from Genesis 1:26-31, as does the Teacher's sense that one's work is a possible means of joy, or good, on earth. Third, the book coincides with earlier Wisdom texts in Psalms, Job and Proverbs that exalt wisdom over foolishness (2:13; 4:13-16). The Teacher says that God's works are intended to help people fear the Lord (3:14). No higher goal attends worship (5:7). As Roland Murphy observes, "Folly is never a viable option. . . . Moreover, folly is explicitly condemned."[14] Foolishness has no place in the Teacher's worldview.

At the same time the book struggles to put life's limitations into context. These constrictions derive from Genesis 2—3 and represent perhaps the best canonical reflections on the intellectual frustration of living in a fallen, sinful world. As was stated earlier, the Teacher is frustrated with the limited knowledge human beings are allowed. His desires parallel those that led Eve to sin. Further, he recognizes that work is God's gift yet realizes that work has the thorn of not being eternal. Thus it is not fully satisfactory (2:17-26; 4:18-20). Genesis 3:17-19 has already promised that this frustration would arise. Work remains necessary, even desirable, in a sinful world, but it does not fulfill the worker.

Finally, the Teacher struggles with having eternity in his heart but mortality in his flesh (3:11). Death awaits the Teacher, and he wonders if humans live after death (3:19-21). He deals with the issue again in 9:10 and 12:7 in a more definitive way, which leads Murphy to conclude that this verse (3:21) focuses on the commonality of death, not on the lack of an afterlife.[15] At the same time, Graham Ogden observes, the question of what happens after death is left open.[16] Hope is not totally absent.[17] Death is the penalty reserved for disobedience in Eden (Gen 2:15-17; 3:1-5). The Teacher wrestles with what that reality means, fully aware that death is inevitable. Meaning does not derive from endless life here. Significance must come from the Creator, who allows the creature to search for suitable answers.

Wisdom provides a framework for meaning. Work, family, reflection and wisdom are better than laziness, loneliness, thoughtlessness and foolishness. The Teacher does not believe all worldviews and life patterns are equal. He does not say God reveals nothing, just that what is revealed does not remove vanity. Wisdom alone is not enough to satisfy, as the rest of the book attests.

The God Who Rules History and Gives Wisdom: Ecclesiastes 7—8

This section contains five statements about God surrounded by Wisdom comments akin to those in Job and Proverbs. The first two references appear together (7:13-14, 15-18) and act as a pivot upon which all of 7:1—8:1 moves.

In 7:13-14 the Teacher claims that God rules both good and bad times and does not explain what the future holds, and in 7:15-18 he counsels fear of God as a means of taking a balanced approach to life. The proverbs and observations in 7:1-12 and 7:19—8:1 suggest caution in thought and in relationships. The Teacher's conclusions about the sinfulness of human beings particularly urge caution. God made people upright, but they have all sinned (7:26-29), so one must be careful in all dealings with others.

The other three references to God come after observations about kings and oppression (8:2-10), subjects quite common in Job and Proverbs. Though the Teacher does not claim that the righteous will always prosper, he does state that those who fear God do fare better in life than those who do not (8:11-13). At times injustice is pervasive (8:14), so people must enjoy the life offered by the God who governs history (8:15). Anyone who claims further wisdom than this claims more than is possible (8:16-17). This last statement may target Wisdom adherents who indeed believe they know more.[18] God has given the wisdom the Teacher lists in Ecclesiastes 7—8, but full knowledge still does not emerge. Some truths remain the sole property of the Creator.

Canonical Synthesis: Sin Opposed to Wisdom

The Teacher's statements in this section do not disagree in substance with Wisdom texts in Psalms, Job and Proverbs. Like earlier books, Ecclesiastes 7—8 counsels taking advice (7:5), seeking a good name (7:1), avoiding hypocrisy (7:16), serving the king appropriately (8:2-4) and so forth.[19] Like Proverbs, Ecclesiastes notes that foolishness has no value. Like Job, Ecclesiastes states unequivocally that wisdom does not answer all life's questions and asserts that not all adherents of Wisdom are as brilliant as they think. Ecclesiastes stresses the power of wisdom yet does not equate it with God. This book is more negative in tone than Proverbs, but it never overthrows Proverbs' high view of the fear of God or its emphasis on seeking wisdom instead of foolishness.

What makes Ecclesiastes' tone more somber than Proverbs' is its continual reflection on Genesis 2—3. The Teacher laments that though God made people upright they have sought sin doggedly and effectively (7:29). Men and women alike share in this depravity, with women taking the brunt of his criticism (7:26-29). Kings, no less than the poor, sin as well (8:2-10). Because of this sin, the wise must seek truths that mitigate the effects of foolishness, failure and death. Seeking truth results in valuable God-given insights (8:16-17), even if these insights do not make the seeker's knowledge equal with that of God. Sin and its consequences remain the Teacher's chief frustration. The giver of wisdom remains his chief source of consolation.

The God Who Superintends Death: Ecclesiastes 9:1-12

Death has hung over the book from the beginning. Each act of life within time is said to have a purpose (3:1-8), but the fact is that time as the Teacher knows it will run out (2:18-21; 3:18-21; 4:13-16; 6:3-6). He has confessed that death eventually overcomes all presently living creatures (3:18-21). In this passage the Teacher reaffirms these ideas in order to highlight God's power over life and death and to stress the value of embracing wisdom as long as life lasts. His statements once again raise the issues of the importance of fearing God and of the nature of death itself.

The Teacher never doubts God's sovereignty over all persons or the belief that the righteous become wise only through God's direction (9:1). At the same time, he states that death waits for both the righteous and the evil (9:2-3). Once dead, they can never return to the life the Teacher experiences now. They no longer participate in what happens "under the sun" (9:6).[20] Therefore the Teacher counsels readers to enjoy food, family and work, for they will not be able to do so in the grave (9:7-10). Wisdom, as important as it is, cannot stave off death or predict when it will come (9:11-12). Readiness equals wisdom in this text, for God sends death without declaring its timing.

Two questions present themselves in 9:1-12: How dark is the Teacher's vision of death? Is this his final word on the subject? The answer to both questions lies in reading this passage in the context of the whole book. Otherwise it not only contradicts many other biblical texts but also pits itself against 3:11 and 12:7.[21] In 3:11 the Teacher asserts that God has placed eternity in the human heart yet has not allowed people to grasp the totality of divine works. Since "eternity" does not receive definition in this life, the possibility that a future beyond death is in view must be kept open. In 12:7 the Teacher states that the human spirit, or breath, will return to the Lord who created it (cf. 12:1), and in 12:14 he claims that all actions will be judged by God. Since the book nowhere argues that one gets what one deserves in life, this judgment may include some time after death.

The vision of death is indeed dark, but by no means is 9:5-6 all that the Teacher says about death. The verses claim, ironically, that the major difference between the living and the dead is that the living know they will die.[22] In 9:7-10 he adds that the living are able to enjoy life, so the unknown recesses of death[23] are far less preferable than the troubles of life.[24] These statements emphasize the benefit of living wisely now. They do not simply reflect the author's ignorance of the afterlife, as Delitzsch argues,[25] or the author's belief that death is oblivion, as Leo Perdue says.[26]

Without question this section leaves control over life and death in God's hands. Divine responsibility has not been forfeited, nor God's right to rule abdicated. The one God directs human affairs. As a true monotheist, the

Teacher brings his complaints into his theological framework, just as those who lament in Psalms and Job have already done.

The God Whose Ways Are Mysterious: Ecclesiastes 9:13—11:6

Part of Ecclesiastes' literary and theological power lies in the way the book protests the lack of divine revelation through considerable references derived from previous revelation. In this way the author manages to argue for God's hiddenness by means of God's openness. The Teacher emphasizes such mystery throughout the book, but the device is especially prevalent in this section, where a great list of Wisdom sayings concludes with the assertion that God's works are not able to be known (11:5). Thus one must work and hope for the best (11:6).

Though the Wisdom teachings in this passage are familiar in content to canonical readers, they also carry the Teacher's individual stylistic stamp. He says wisdom is superior to strength yet cautions that sin destroys much good that wisdom accomplishes (9:13-18). Wisdom deserves honor, but fools are often exalted (10:1-7). Work has its place yet is often frustrating. Therefore one must diversify one's interests against the probability of disaster (10:8—11:4). In the end, God's ways are mysterious, so the wise person works hard and shuns idleness (11:5-6).

Perhaps the Teacher protests too much. After all, he understands the value of wisdom and that it originates in respect for God. He believes that God rules history by governing life and death and that God judges the righteous and the wicked. He asserts that work, joy and family are God's gifts. All these things he readily confesses. What continues to plague him is the realization that he does not know the inner workings of God's mind or the specifics of the timing set by divine decree. In other words, he still wrestles with his own finitude. He is a man, not God, and this fact leads to frustration in one so thoughtful.

The God Who Creates and Judges: Ecclesiastes 11:7—12:8

Given all he has said, it is appropriate for the Teacher to conclude his comments with observations about youth, old age and death. God's role in all three is at the core of his statements. In effect he tells young people to enjoy life, for soon they will be older and incapable of doing so. They should do so, however, with the knowledge that the Creator of life (12:1) is also the judge of everyone (11:9; 12:7). Such an awareness should be sobering, to be sure, yet not so sobering that all joy disappears.

The Teacher advises readers to "remember" (12:1) God before the passing of time brings them to the point of death. When death occurs, the body returns to dust, the spirit returns to God, and all final judgments will be made

(12:7; cf. 11:9). All life comes from God, so all life must return to God.[27] This realization is not offered as a comforting comment here, but it does answer the question raised in 3:21 about the direction of the human spirit upon death as opposed to its animal counterpart.[28] Stressing the human spirit's upward direction does place it in contrast to both the animal's breath and the dustbound, now useless, human body. Human spirit is not divine, though, despite its return to God. Rather it remains under the power of the One who created it.[29] In this way death becomes a means by which people come closer to God. Ogden asserts, "Reversing the process of original creation would seem to imply that Qoheleth [the Teacher] reasons that death will not separate us from God; rather, at that moment we return to his presence."[30] Still, given his desire to know more about the meaning of death, the Teacher finishes his words as they began—with a declaration of vanity.

Canonical Synthesis: Life After Death
There can be no question that 12:1-8 refers to Genesis 2—3. Human beings are God's special creation from dust into whom God has breathed the breath of life (Gen 2:7; Eccles 3:21; 12:1, 7). Sin makes judgment necessary, death inevitable, and final reward solely the Creator's decision (Gen 3:1-19; Eccles 11:7-10). No return to Eden is possible; no exceptions can be made for the wise; no amount of reflection changes this truth. One is left with the revealed affirmations found in the canon. Not embracing these limitations can only lead to vanity, and it is this realization that the Teacher impresses on his students. Every human being from Adam and Eve onward must live with these realities.

But is death the absolute end of human existence in the Old Testament? Gerhard von Rad says that life after death was not of great concern to the Old Testament writers.[31] At the same time, he claims, the Old Testament does not neglect the idea altogether. Psalms 49, 72 and 73 confess that not even death can truly separate the faithful from God. Further, Isaiah 26:19 and Daniel 12:1-3 speak of corpses rising and of a resurrection of the righteous and the wicked. These passages coincide with the translation of Enoch (Gen 5:24) and Elijah's chariot ride to heaven (2 Kings 2:7-12).[32] Daniel Block argues correctly that in Ezekiel the dead are portrayed as having knowledge after death, as having personality after death and as being raised to life by the power of God's Spirit (cf. Ezek 32:17-32; 37:1-14). He also notes the significance of Hosea 13:14, which says that God removes the sting of death and the grave.[33] Isaiah 65:17 and 66:22-24 look forward to a new heaven and new earth in which the remnant live with God and the wicked are punished. Job expects to be vindicated and to know so even, if necessary, after death (cf. Job 14:13-17; 19:23-27).

Ecclesiastes echoes these ideas but bases its hints about the afterlife upon creation principles. God has created human beings, orders their lives, gifts them with wisdom (or not), supervises their death and receives their spirit again. God also allows them to live with frustrations related to the presence of evil, the difficulty of maintaining quality relationships and the necessity of toil. At the same time God offers hope that the future will bring the defeat of wickedness. Genesis 1—3 and Ecclesiastes share these ideas. Neither Genesis nor Ecclesiastes exhibits the full vision found in some of the other Old Testament texts mentioned, but neither do they negate these passages' contentions. In an interesting way, then, Ecclesiastes brings creation concepts into the canonical discussion of good living and inevitable death.

The God Who Judges: Ecclesiastes 12:9-14

The book concludes with words from one of the Teacher's pupils. This individual praises his instructor as wise, pedagogically efficient, prolific in his research and writing and accurate in all he affirmed (12:9-10). Besides this lauding of the Teacher, he stresses the value of all Wisdom sayings and warns against wearying oneself by adding to them (12:11-12). Finally, he finishes the book with exhortations to fear the Lord and to expect God to judge every deed, even those that seem hidden (12:13-14). Coming at the end of both the book of Ecclesiastes and the canonical Wisdom writing, these verses reemphasize the importance of wise living in a sinful world.

Canonical Synthesis: Ecclesiastes and Israelite Wisdom Literature

Each major concept unfolded in this section highlights a crucial Wisdom ideal. First, 12:9-10 implies that Wisdom teachers must be dedicated to the pursuit and declaration of the truth. Neither they nor their hearers have adequate knowledge about how to live in a sinful world. Therefore striving after God's ways becomes essential. The search for wisdom is not an easy one, as Job 28 and Ecclesiastes 2—6 have made clear, but discovery is possible, as the books of Job, Proverbs, Song of Solomon and Ecclesiastes all affirm. Teachers must be leaders in the movement from natural human sin and simplicity to wisdom and maturity. They must search for truth as strenuously as the Teacher has done.

Second, 12:11-12 stresses the value and origin of Wisdom books. Wisdom writings are "goads" to the sluggish and "nails" for the drifting.[34] They give direction to all who will accept them. How can they be so valuable? Because these writings come from "one Shepherd" (12:11), a phrase that refers to God, not the Teacher.[35] The Teacher could be meant if only his writings were being discussed, but the author clearly has a larger body of literature in mind. God reveals wisdom. It is God's creation (cf. Prov 8:22-31). If God rules over life, death and all human events, as the Teacher claims, then surely God superintends the discovery of wisdom as well. This fact means that what the teachers learn and teach has tremendous potential to give life meaning.

Third, 12:13-14 bases all Wisdom teaching on fear of the Lord and expectation of judgment. In this way this text reaffirms earlier passages such as Psalm 111:10, Job 28:28 and Proverbs 1:7. Respect for the one God undergirds all attitudes and expressions of faith. Given this passage's context, fear of the Lord includes the knowledge that God judges all actions. Job argues that this assessment may occur in this life or the next. Proverbs focuses on judgment that is evident in everyday human affairs. Ecclesiastes leaves both options open. It neither fastens upon judgment in this life nor eliminates the possibility of assessment after death. Rather it makes sure that no one gets the idea that we live in an ungoverned universe.

The book of Ecclesiastes makes its contribution to Wisdom literature and to the canon by integrating creation and fall principles with Wisdom probings. In a sinful world marked by consequences outlined in Genesis 3:14-19, it is necessary to cling to Wisdom teachings to avoid utterly foolish behavior. At the same time not even Wisdom research can reveal what God chooses to keep secret from human beings. Mysteries such as the reason for specific timing of events and the exact details of life after death remain mysteries. God's gifts are to be enjoyed, and divine boundaries are to be respected. Still, finding these boundaries creates frustration, as does desiring further knowledge. The Genesis 3:14-19 consequences remain in place, even for Wisdom teachers.

Summary of Wisdom Theology

Israelite Wisdom literature is distinctive, to be sure, but it nonetheless has several points in common with the Law, the Prophets and the remainder of the Writings. For example, this literature, like the Pentateuch, stresses that one God has created the earth, human beings and all knowledge helpful to the human race. It also equates sin with foolishness and fear with obedience in a manner similar to the Sinai covenant. Human beings are utterly incapable of knowing God or God's ways without divine assistance in both the Law and the Wisdom literature. God alone is the source for instruction in righteous living.

Wisdom materials share certain concerns found in the Prophets as well. Job, Proverbs and Ecclesiastes all condemn oppression, injustice and other forms of breaking God's standards. They also point out the reality of judgment awaiting persons who sin in these ways. The God who extends wisdom to foolish sinners does not take lightly the rejection of life-sustaining instruction. Nor does God stand by passively when wickedness occurs. Job and

Ecclesiastes question the timing and reasoning behind God's judgment, yet they affirm that it does happen at God's discretion. No mention of worldwide punishment on the day of the Lord appears, but judgment of individuals has a prominent place. Retribution does occur one person at a time.

The Writings as a whole discuss the struggle to serve God in a world marked by pain and disaster. Many psalms lament life's struggles, as do Job and Ecclesiastes. Lamentations, Esther, Daniel, Ezra and Nehemiah are set in times and places that test the spiritual fiber of God's people. Proverbs, Song of Solomon and Chronicles prove that life can be normal, even joyous, so the picture is hardly totally gloomy. Perhaps Ecclesiastes best epitomizes the human struggle to work through disturbing reality to reach joy and fulfillment. In a post-Genesis 3:14-19 world, fear of the Lord, expectation of judgment and enjoyment of God's gifts, which include wisdom, keep the faithful from foolishness. It may be meaningless, pointless, to seek to know all that God knows, but to fail to search for wisdom leaves people without God's gifts, which the Teacher admits is worse. At their best, Wisdom writings prove that sin, death and foolishness are not all human beings can achieve. They show that people can discover ways revealed by God to demonstrate they are made in God's image. The books that follow Ecclesiastes offer examples of individuals who embrace the way wisdom offers the righteous.

Above all, there can be no question that the Wisdom writers affirm the canon's one-God declaration. Job contends with one God. Proverbs cites only one God as Creator of wisdom. Song of Solomon implies that love comes as God's gift, and nowhere does the book deify passion. Ecclesiastes probes the activity of the Creator. These books seek to make the one God's ways plainer to fellow creatures. They utilize earlier revelation to do so, and they consider the implications of that revelation. Whether in pleasure or in pain, these writers are left with the fear of the one Lord as their starting point and their conclusion.[36]

21

The God
Who Is Righteous
& Faithful

Lamentations

· ·

L AMENTATIONS REVISITS ISRAEL'S MOST PAINFUL MEMORY BY DESCRIBING IN great detail the causes and effects of Jerusalem's fall in 587 B.C. By doing so, the book brings to mind the offering of blessings and consequences found in Leviticus 26 and Deuteronomy 27—28. It also reminds canonical readers of the Former Prophets' conviction that Israel fell due to covenant infidelity (cf. 2 Kings 17) but that some hope persists in the midst of disaster (2 Kings 25). Further, it agrees with the Latter Prophets' belief that Israel's fall occurred because of recurring, persistent sin that was fueled by ineffective prophets, priests and rulers. Lamentations especially mirrors the theology of Jeremiah, Ezekiel, Habakkuk and Zephaniah in these matters. Finally, the book continues the Writings' emphasis on a theological assessment of human suffering. By choosing the lament form the book's author links the pain felt here to that in Psalms, Job and Ecclesiastes. By including the cries of righteous sufferers the book connects not only with Job but with Proverbs and Ruth as well. In a variety of crucial ways, Lamentations furthers the Scriptures' conclusions about the context of suffering by gathering significant earlier themes and reinterpreting them for a specific situation.

Two distinct yet related ideas help unify Lamentations. First, though the text clearly laments Jerusalem's condition, God's righteousness is never set aside. The Lord has kept promises concerning punishment (2:17). Second,

God is faithful to Israel (3:22-23), which means that there remains hope for the future. God will not cast off the people forever, a fact Deuteronomy 30, Isaiah 65—66, Jeremiah 30—33, Ezekiel 36—37, and a host of other texts have already proclaimed. God's righteousness demands that sin be punished. God's faithfulness requires that promises to the faithful be kept. These two characteristics are equally relevant to the nature of God, as Lamentations and the whole of the Old Testament canon attest. By affirming a multifaceted definition of the Lord's personality, Lamentations continues the canon's assertion that one God who is personal and actively involved in human affairs rules history.

With these foundational ideas in mind, it is possible to offer a theological outline of Lamentations based on the seven poems it contains. Lamentations 1 describes the grief Jerusalem feels as it considers the God who afflicts and forsakes the chosen city. Lamentations 2 presents the Lord who has become Jerusalem's enemy, a viewpoint that makes God's work even more ominous than Lamentations 1 indicates. With this foundation of defeat and grief in place, Lamentations 3 asserts that God remains faithful to the remnant. Defeat does not have to be the final word of Israelite history. Indeed it will not be the last word. Lamentations 4 returns to the book's earlier negative tone by stressing the God who scatters Israel. Thus the Lord has deserted Israel in order to be their enemy and has succeeded in dispersing them across the ancient world. Lamentations 5, though equally as honest as Lamentations 1, 2 and 4 about Israel's dire circumstances, finds hope in the God who remains forever. This God, the only God, is able to begin again with the people.

The God Who Afflicts and Forsakes Jerusalem: Lamentations 1
Lamentations 1 sets forth the book's format and tone. This powerful acrostic poem declares that Jerusalem is desolate (1:1). Her friends have forsaken her (1:2-3), her roads and gates are desolate (1:4), and enemies have overthrown her government (1:5-6). The city's fall could hardly be more thorough or spectacular (1:9). Why has such devastation befallen the chosen city? Because the Lord has afflicted the people for their sins against his commands (1:5, 8-9, 14, 18-22). Covenant breaking has resulted in the loss of land and sanctuary (1:10). Thus Lamentations 1 is a dirge sung at the city's funeral.

This chapter includes the basic elements found in other communal laments in the canon. The people address the Lord (1:9), express the calamity their enemies have brought upon them (1:10-16), confess that God has brought the disaster (1:12-15), admit their sins (1:18-21) and ask for deliverance (1:22).[1] Their grief is heartfelt because they realize that it need not have happened and because they know they have betrayed their commitments to the Lord. They realize that God has afflicted them. They understand that the God who protected them from harm has forsaken his role as protector due to their disobedience. In other words, their wounds are solely their own fault. God has not afflicted and forsaken for no reason.

Canonical Synthesis: Jerusalem's Destruction and Zion Theology

This passage reopens the matters of just retribution and Zion theology. Norman Gottwald argues that part of Jerusalem's pain stems from the people's dismay that the city could fall so soon after Josiah's reforms in 622 B.C. (2 Kings 22:3—23:25). Israel feels especially deserted by God because they have done what God asked. Therefore the book's main tension is "between Deuteronomic faith and historical adversity."[2] Gottwald's conclusion might be valid had the city been overrun during Josiah's latter years (c. 622-609 B.C.) or even if the book lamented Josiah's untimely death, but such is not the case. The books of Kings, Jeremiah, Ezekiel and the Twelve have already noted Israel's return to prereform behavior. Psalms 89 and 104—106, among others, have also testified to the prevalent covenant breaking in the land. It is inaccurate to view a reform as necessarily lasting over thirty years, especially in light of the textual evidence to the contrary. Despite the overall difficulty of his treatment, Gottwald does raise the issue of righteous sufferers, which deserves further attention. As a whole the nation merits judgment, but selected individuals may not deserve to suffer with the wicked.

By canonical standards, the people have chosen punishment over blessing. Lamentations 1:5, 14 and 18-21 agree with Leviticus 26 and Deuteronomy 27—28. All these texts state that persistent covenant breaking must lead to defeat and loss of land. Lamentations 1 shares the view of history found in 2 Kings 17—25, Jeremiah 34—39 and Ezekiel 33:23-29. Each of these passages considers Jerusalem's demise a divinely caused devastation that could no longer be delayed.

Bertil Albrektson believes that Gottwald's theory of the key to Lamentations' theology misses the mark. He claims that if there is a tension between faith and history it lies in the "theological tradition of the inviolability of Zion which stands in unbearable contrast to the harsh historical reality after the fall of Jerusalem."[3] Albrektson observes several places where the text utilizes phraseology from Deuteronomy 28 to negate Zion imagery from Psalms 46, 48 and 76 and from Isaiah 29.[4] He then concludes that the people found meaning in this terrible loss of supposedly unconquerable Zion only by considering it a divinely appointed defeat.[5] Jerusalem was simply not supposed to fall because it is God's city, so its toppling must have been caused by the Lord.

It is true that the people may have thought their capital impregnable. Jeremiah's temple sermons (Jer 7, 26) could lead one to this conclusion, Ezekiel portrays the nation as generally unconcerned about temple defilement (Ezek 8:1-18), and Zephaniah depicts sinners who think God will do nothing about their activities (Zeph 1:12). If they did think so, they misunderstood the way Jerusalem of Judah was transformed into Zion the inviolate city of God in earlier passages. Zion is where God is present among the holy ones (Ps 48:9-14; 76:7-12). Zion is ruled by God through men like Hezekiah (Is 37:22-35), not by scoundrels like Jehoiakim or moral vacillators like Zedekiah. Ultimately, as Isaiah 65—66 indicates, Zion will be the place where God will rule over a new heaven and earth devoid of all wicked persons. Both in history and beyond history, Zion is where a holy God dwells among a holy people. Lamentations confesses, like Ezekiel 10:1-22, that when God forsakes the city this lack of divine glory means Jerusalem is not Zion. It is just one more place Babylon must destroy to rule the ancient world.

The God Who Becomes Jerusalem's Enemy: Lamentations 2

The second acrostic intensifies God's activity against Israel. Now Yahweh is not portrayed as having deserted Israel. Rather the Lord has become Jerusalem's purposeful enemy (2:4-5). God has withdrawn his protection from the city (2:3), the protection that saved Zion in Hezekiah's and Isaiah's time (2 Kings 18—19), which has resulted in the destruction of Jerusalem's temple, gates and walls (2:6-9). Religious feasts, prophetic visions and teaching of the Law have all ceased (2:6, 9-10). Inconsolable grief has resulted from these setbacks (2:11-13). Confession of sin and supplication of Yahweh are offered in hopes of relief from guilt and misery (2:14-22).

This dirge leaves no doubt about the reason for the calamity. In language reminiscent of Jeremiah's prophecy (Jer 2:8; 5:12-13; 6:13-15; 23:13-20), the text claims that the prophets are partly to blame because they have spoken lies (2:14). Gottwald observes, "All the frightful judgments might have been averted had the trusted leaders been faithful to their calling and had the sinful people heeded their warning."[6] Carl Keil adds that the prophets' failure to preach repentance kept Israel from removing self-induced misery, from renewing their relationship to the Lord and from avoiding exile.[7] Yahweh inserts "His word, which he commanded from days of old" (2:17 NASB) into this prophetic void. From Deuteronomy 27—28 onward God has promised punishment for covenant infidelity. This word of judgment has now come true, for God's word, which directs history as surely as it directed creation, cannot fail. Israel's false prophets preached slackness towards sin, which caused God to promise devastation, and it is God's word that has proven infallible.

As is the case with Lamentations 1, Lamentations 2 agrees with the overall theological perspective found in Deuteronomy, the Former Prophets, Jeremiah, Ezekiel, Nahum, Hababbuk and Zephaniah. It is deuteronomistic in that it argues that Israelite sin led to loss of land (Deut 27—28; 2 Kings 17; Jer 34—39). It also believes that God's word dictates the flow of history, a theme found throughout Kings and Ezekiel. All these books consider the Babylonian victory tragic in proportion to its avoidability.

The God Who Remains Faithful to the Remnant: Lamentations 3

Lamentations 3 consists of three acrostic poems that inject a hopeful note into the book. Mournful admissions of guilt still occur (3:1-18, 40-54), yet the speaker does not believe that Yahweh's anger is final. In the midst of terrible pain Israel's remnant may discover anew the Lord's grace. They may do so, however, only through "an attitude of humble perseverance in suffering, an acknowledgment of one's own sins, and a return to Yahweh."[8] That they may return at all depends on the Lord's faithfulness to forgive and restore those who are penitent. Faith in God is required for healing.

Two texts express this hope quite clearly. After confessing his sin and the sin of the people (3:1-18), the speaker states that the substance of the Lord's character indicates that all is not lost. God is merciful, for the people have not been totally consumed (3:22). It is impossible for the Lord's compassion to fail (3:22). God's faithfulness is self-renewing each day (3:23), and Yahweh has always sustained those who trust in him (3:24). Therefore it is advisable to wait quietly, all the while bearing patiently the consequences of personal and national sin, for God to save (3:25-30). After all, God does not desire to punish but to bless (3:31-36). The writer is certain that the same unerring word that brought death may once again result in life (3:37-39). If God's nature were different, then the author's conclusions would have to change drastically. As it is, the sovereign Lord of history remains the same.[9]

Canonical Synthesis: God's Willingness to Forgive

God's grace and patient faithfulness are as much a part of deuteronomistic theology as God's wrath. Yahweh's willingness to restore and forgive is stated clearly in Deuteronomy 30:1-10. God will bring Israel back from captivity when they return to him (Deut 30:1-3). The book of Judges illustrates repeatedly the Lord's forgiving spirit, as does God's work with David in 1-2 Samuel. Jehoiachin's good fortune demonstrates divine kindness in 2 Kings 25:27-30. Jeremiah 31:31-34 and Ezekiel 36:26-27 speak of a new covenant, a new spirit and a new heart for Israel after judgment has passed. Wrath always has a redemptive, restorative purpose.

Such convictions about God's faithfulness to the remnant also undergird the psalms of lament. These texts refuse to believe that God will allow wickedness to continue unchecked. They praise the Lord because they expect God's inherent righteousness to triumph eventually.[10] They pray honestly about their own sins because they believe no amount of sacrifices can remove a lack of integrity and because they know God is holy.[11] At all times laments assume that Yahweh's desire to forgive, restore and heal never abates. Again the issue is God's character. If God is not faithful, not consistently holy, then the people are lost and doomed to misery and death. Since God is faithful the devastated have hope.

Brevard Childs notes that Lamentations offers renewal to each successive generation of the people of faith. He writes that through this text the community is "summoned to return to faith in God, but at the same time to lift up its devastation and destruction in corporate prayer."[12] As the community does so, confession and hope replace dirge and despair.[13] The presence of this text in the canon gives every successive remnant reader the chance to apply God's faithfulness to a new situation. Israelites in exile particularly needed to know that they could be the new faithful remnant whatever their circumstances because they were never outside the sphere of God's grace.

The God Who Scatters Israel: Lamentations 4

Despite the steadfast hope based on God's character expressed in Lamentations 3, Israel as a whole has yet to return to the faithful Yahweh. Thus the present reality continues to be grim. Every element of Israelite society has been affected by Jerusalem's fall. Infants die (4:4), some of them because their mothers cook and eat them under siege-induced conditions (4:10). Prophets (4:13) and Nazirites (4:7) share the national misery. In short, God's anger has "divided," or "scattered," the people throughout the world (4:16). So thorough is this scattering that its effect on Israel is compared with the destruction of Sodom (4:6).

Canonical evidence of divine scattering has already appeared in Jeremiah's forced journey to Egypt (Jer 42—44) and Ezekiel's ministry in Babylon. It is also obvious in the books that follow Lamentations. Esther resides in Persia, while Daniel lives most of his life in Babylon. Ezra and Nehemiah are employed by the Persian government and must gain permission to spend time in Jerusalem. Israel has indeed been scattered by the Lord, yet these later texts prove that return to the promised land is possible for people whose vision of Zion remains in force.

The God Who Remains Forever: Lamentations 5

Unlike the first four chapters, Lamentations 5 is not an acrostic poem. It does have twenty-two verses but is not in alphabetic form. Moreover, this passage is clearly a community lament, whereas the earlier texts have an individual tone.[14] The people have taken up the cry for help, a practice that makes it possible for God to cease being their enemy and to restore the scattered ones to the promised land. Yahweh can reverse their difficult circumstances and take away their shame (5:1-18).

As in Lamentations 3, renewal hopes here are rooted in God's character. Here the people confess the Lord's never-ending nature (5:19-22). They know that restoration will not occur in a moment, so their opportunity for revival and rebuilding rest in a God who transcends time.[15] Only a God whose kingdom is not dependent on material circumstances and whose nature is not bounded by time can give those who have nothing and are finite any sense of comfort.[16] These worshipers also realize that unless the Lord renews them they will never rise from the ashes (5:21). If God casts them off forever they have no hope. But the presence of this book in the canon and their understanding of God's character indicate that they have been heard. Yahweh cannot judge the penitent, for it is not within his nature to do so. God would not be God if sin were not punished, but neither would God be God if forgiveness were not extended.[17]

Several psalms connect deliverance with Yahweh's enduring nature.[18] Psalm 9:6-10 says the permanent Lord will eventually judge the wicked. Psalm 93:1-5 and Psalm 103:19 stress that God's eternity makes Yahweh the Lord of history, while Psalm 102:12-13 indicates that the enduring God's mercy can never die. At the same time worshipers who point out God's sovereignty and eternity ask the God of history "how long" they must suffer (Ps 13:1), why they are forsaken (Ps 22:1) and when God's anger will abate (Ps 79:5).[19] Thus Yahweh's endurance presents both problems and possibilities for the hurting, but the confession of those who lament is that they pray to the God whose character will not allow their honest pleas to be ignored.

Conclusion

Like Job, the laments in Psalms and other suffering texts, the book of Lamentations offers a pure form of monotheistic faith. If there is ever a time that persons of faith might seek another deity, it would be when life is not as they wish it to be. If other gods could help, surely one would call on them. In all these texts, however, worshipers indicate they have nowhere else to turn. They have no other god to seek; no other god to whom they may pray; no other god with whom they may have a relationship. Their confession in their darkest hours is that Yahweh is God and there is no other. Their anchoring belief is that the eternal God is faithful, and their guiding hope is that the God who punishes is also the God who forgives, restores and redeems.

Lamentations also takes the latter portion of the Writings into exile. Each book that follows either is set in exile or attempts to overcome the exile and forge a new future for God's people. Lamentations states why Jerusalem fell and points the way to a return to Yahweh and a return to the land. How fully this vision of return materializes remains to be seen. The desperate straits of the Jerusalem remnant have now been demonstrated, and the terror experienced by the exiled remnant will soon be depicted in Esther and Daniel.

22

The God
Who Protects
the Exiles

Esther

. . . .

L AMENTATIONS ENDS WITH THE PLEA THAT GOD WILL RESTORE FALLEN ISRAEL, unless the Lord has "utterly rejected" the people (5:22). How God will treat the chosen nation now that it has been scattered to other lands is a vital issue. Will God still redeem, sustain and heal? Does Yahweh have saving power regardless of where the people may be driven? Is the Lord still interested in the people, given the fact that their sins led to the forfeiture of the land in the first place? Esther, Daniel, Ezra—Nehemiah and Chronicles deal with these and other questions related to God's ongoing relationship with Israel. Esther begins the discussion by illustrating that God protects the exiles.

As is well known, Esther and Song of Solomon are the only two books in the canon that never mention God directly.[1] This fact makes theological reflection on these texts harder, to say the least. At the same time, approaching these books from a canonical perspective makes such analysis possible. In Esther's case, its presence in the Writings near Lamentations and Daniel marks it as a text that deals with Israel's experiences after the debacle (587 B.C.) that drove many Israelites from their homeland. Its Persian setting fastens readers' attention on how Jewish exiles fared in that land. Jeremiah has already revealed a bit about exiles in Egypt, Ezekiel has shown something of the exiles' life in Babylon, and Daniel will demonstrate particular threats to Jews in Babylon. Esther and Ezra—Nehemiah focus on the Persian side of the dispersion. They highlight the importance of seeking God's presence in foreign lands and create interest in other details about this era in Israelite history. They also provide a wider theological background against which Esther may, or must, be read.

Esther is an anonymous book whose events take place in about 487-465. No information about its authorship, date and original audience can be recovered with any certainty. Much of the earlier scholarly discussion revolved around its historical accuracy, with a general consensus about the book's basic soundness resulting in recent times.[2] In the past few decades the book's acceptance into the canon has been examined in some detail, partly because of its seemingly secular nature and partly because it is the one accepted Old Testament book that is not attested in the Dead Sea Scrolls. Roger Beckwith notes that although later rabbinic writers questioned Esther's worthiness of inclusion in the canon, a Septuagint translation of the book was made by 114 B.C., Josephus (A.D. 70) lists the book as Scripture, and all major lists of the Old Testament canon include Esther.[3] It seems certain that the text was considered Scripture from ancient times.

Various purposes for Esther have been forwarded. First, most interpreters argue that the book emphasizes the institution of the Purim festival.[4] This new feast underscores the Jewish conviction that God does protect the chosen people from their enemies. Second, Gillis Gerleman states that the book compares these events in Persia to the exodus from Egypt.[5] Again the emphasis is on how God remembers (cf. Ex 2:23-25) the covenant people in extreme situations. Third, T. C. Vriezen and J. Barton Payne suggest that Esther illustrates God's wise and providential care for Israel and God's sovereignty over all nations.[6] Vriezen and Payne admit the understated quality of Esther's theology but find it evident nonetheless. Asa Boyd Luter and Barry C. Davis also consider divine providence Esther's main theological idea, for they define the Lord as "the God behind the seen," an obvious reference to the absence of explicit references to God in the book.[7] Fourth, Robert Gordis exemplifies much of post-World War II Jewish scholarship by concluding that Esther is fundamentally about the preservation of the Jewish people. He writes that "it is fundamental to the Jewish world-outlook that the preservation of the Jewish people is itself a religious obligation of the first magnitude. This is true because Israel has been the bearer of God's word throughout its history, beginning with the Covenant at Sinai."[8] For the Abrahamic, Sinaiatic and Davidic covenants to continue toward fulfillment the chosen people must survive. Fifth, Walter Kaiser thinks Esther contributes to the Old Testament idea that Israel bears the promise of the coming of God's kingdom.[9] Once more the necessity of Israel's survival is the main point. Sixth, Shemaryahu Talmon asserts that Esther is a "historicized wisdom tale" that embodies many of the major ideas found in Wisdom literature. In this way the book offers sage advice much as the Joseph narrative does.[10]

Each of these options at least implies that Esther has positive elements to contribute to Old Testament theology. Some scholars disagree. For example, L. B. Paton writes that Esther's author "gloats over the wealth and the triumph of his heroes and is oblivious to their moral shortcomings. Morally Est. falls far below the general level of the OT., and even of the Apocrypha."[11] Otto Eissfeldt considers the book too nationalistic and not worthy of the canon. In this opinion he agrees with Martin Luther.[12] Such assessments are overly harsh, particularly when Esther's place in the canon is taken into account. The historical situation leaves the Jews very limited choices. They or their enemies will die. Esther's joy over victory is as appropriate as Lamentations' gloom over defeat. Canonical balance is as evident in this case as it is in the matter of conservative and radical Wisdom literature. Both viewpoints are needed to explore the full variety of divine activity and human response.

Five of the six theories about Esther's purpose stress the Lord's protection of Israel. This preservation has similarities with the Joseph narratives, the exodus accounts and the conquest. It maintains God's faithfulness to the historic covenants, and it guarantees the continuation of a Jewish remnant. It also institutes a new festival late in the Old Testament era, a sure sign that the Lord continues to work with and on behalf of Israel. All these observations are dependent, however, on a canonical reading of Esther, without which these implicit ideas can be lost on readers. A canonical approach allows Esther to be interpreted against a background of monotheistic, covenantal principles.

A theological outline of Esther can now be given. Esther 1:1—4:17 suggests that the Lord allows his people to endure danger in exile. Whatever protection that may emerge does not come prior to serious problems. Next, Esther 5:1—9:19 implies that Yahweh protects Israel's exiles by reversing their fortunes. The well-placed Esther is the conduit for deliverance, much as Joseph was in an earlier dilemma that was less pressing yet surely as deadly. Finally, Esther 9:20—10:3 hints that the Lord is the one who institutes Purim. The new festival makes sure that these lessons learned in exile are not lost on future members of the remnant. Deliverance must be appreciated, recalled, recited and reapplied in each new generation. The God who protects the exiles must remain Israel's God, for no other deity exists inside or outside the promised land. The validity of other gods is not even implied.

The God Who Allows Israel to Endure Danger: Esther 1:1—4:17

This section begins Esther's masterful story by introducing the book's major characters, main plot problem and eventual plot solution. There can be no question about the text's literary brilliance.[13] In exquisitely measured scenes the author describes how King Xerxes (c. 487-465 B.C.) deposes his queen, Vashti, for not coming when called. Her disobedience is particularly ill-timed, since it embarrasses the ruler in front of many party guests (1:1-22). Mordecai, a virtuous Jew, and his beautiful niece, Esther, are introduced in 2:1-18. Esther becomes queen by taking advice and pleasing the king, presumably both aesthetically and sexually (2:15-18). Mordecai shows his worthiness by disclosing a conspiracy against the king (2:19-23). Esther's and Mordecai's conduct shows that the Jews are hardly a threat to the Persian government. Indeed they are valuable citizens.

Esther 3 introduces the book's conflict and chief antagonist. Haman, one of the royal officials, hates Mordecai for not bowing down to him (3:1-5). Thus he slanders the Jews and gains permission to pass an irrevocable law allowing the Jews' enemies to annihilate them (3:6-15). It is clear that the exiles will not be allowed to live in peace. God has not protected them from attacks on their character, their way of life, their very existence. Exile is a dangerous place.

Esther 4 brings the account to a critical point. Mordecai recruits Esther to save the Jews (4:1-9). She fears experiencing her predecessor's fate, but Mordecai presents her with a worse fate, death (4:10-17). The queen agrees to attempt to intercede, but the hoped-for deliverance remains very much in doubt. All that is sure is that victory and the absence of trouble are not the same thing.

Certain hints about the people's dependence on God do appear in this section. For instance, in 3:8 Haman accuses the Jews of adhering to laws and customs that differ from those generally accepted by the Persians. Perhaps this passage refers to "matters of speech, diet, dress, calendar,"[14] but it is more likely that it "refers to the barrier of the Law, which the Jews erected in the post-exilic period to save themselves from being absorbed by the heathen world."[15] Another possible reference to their religious life is the occurrence of fasting in times of trouble in 4:1-3 and again at Esther's request in 4:16. Fasting is hardly the typical way secular people approach a political problem. Surely the people are calling upon the Lord.[16] Also, in 4:14 Mordecai says that if Esther does not help the Jews, then aid will come from another source. He also surmises that she may have been strategically placed among royalty "for such a time as this." This phrase, when read in the overall context of the fasting, is more than a passing statement of Esther's good fortune at becoming queen. She is God's agent for deliverance at this juncture in Israelite history. God has allowed the nation to fall into danger, but the Lord has already provided a means of release.

Canonical Synthesis: God's Purpose for Exile
Canonical readers know that originally Israel's descent into exile was

essentially self-imposed. God's nation of priests (Ex 19:5-6) degenerated into a nation of idolaters, which in turn made them a nation of exiles (2 Kings 17). At the same time faithful persons like Jeremiah and Ezekiel suffered alongside their wicked contemporaries, so righteous sufferers existed from the beginning of the exile. By Esther's time the original exiles were long dead. Jews remaining in Persia were therefore not responsible for the debacle in 587 B.C., so there is no way to consider Haman's threat as specific divine punishment. Instead the nation is being unjustly accused and cruelly persecuted.

This situation is similar to that of the Joseph accounts and the early chapters of Exodus. Joseph came to realize that God sent him to Egypt for a purpose, which was to preserve a remnant (Gen 45:7). His brothers intended evil, yet God meant his experiences to result in good (Gen 50:19-20). Exodus 2:23-25 presents Israel crying out to God for deliverance from their Egyptian slave masters. God responds by calling Moses, which eventually results in the answer to the people's prayers. Leaders who emerge from strange places provide the solutions to Israel's problems in Genesis, Exodus and Esther. In each case the provision of such leaders highlights God's kindness, sovereignty and determination to keep the Abrahamic promises. Allowing Israel to suffer is not an indication of divine indifference.

The God Who Protects the Exiles: Esther 5:1—9:19

Israel's fortunes are swiftly reversed through Esther's intercession before Xerxes and through Mordecai's honesty. Esther sagely requests that Haman be invited to a feast she will prepare (5:1-8). Meanwhile, Haman's hatred for Mordecai grows, so he has a gallows built for his Jewish antagonist (5:9-14). Much to Haman's dismay, the king chooses to honor Mordecai (6:1-14), and Esther exposes Haman's treachery against the Jews (7:1-8). Haman is then hanged on the gallows built for Mordecai (7:9-10). Xerxes allows the Jews to defend themselves, so they are able to overcome their enemies (8:1—9:19). Disaster has been averted.

Two texts in this segment parallel 3:8, 4:1-3, 4:14 and 4:16 in their broad hinting at divine activity on Israel's behalf. First, in 6:14 Haman's friends believe he is in trouble because he opposes a Jew. Gordis believes this passage subtly expresses "the author's unshakable faith in the indestructibility of the Jewish people, and, by that token, in the Providence of God, the Guardian of Israel."[17] It is impossible to say for sure why the friends believe what they do, but their instincts are correct in this case. Second, in 8:17 many people join the Jews out of fear when the king's counteredict becomes public knowledge. Though birthed in fear, this faith seems real, since it continues after the Jewish victory (cf. 9:27).[18] That they became Jews must include accepting their religion's beliefs, since the converts join in the Purim celebrations. As with the interpretation of 4:14, the overall context of 8:17—9:27 connects those who convert out of fear and those who continue to identify with Israel when the threat has passed.

Canonical Synthesis: God's Acceptance of Gentiles

Part of God's reversing of Israel's fortunes in the exodus accounts includes dread of the Jews falling upon the Egyptians' hearts and the inclusion of Gentiles in Jewish festivals. By the end of the tenth plague, the Egyptians believed God would kill them all if they did not free the Israelites, and they were willing to pay God's people to leave (Ex 12:33-36). God's deliverance unfolded in part because the Jews' enemies became frightened to stand against them any longer. Some non-Jews affiliated with Israel at this time, for Moses' Passover regulations include allowances for foreigners and sojourners to take part in the observances (Ex 12:43-41). It is also apparent that non-Israelites accompanied the people as they left Egypt (Ex 12:37-39). In this way the reversing of Israelite fortunes benefited Gentiles as well as Jews. Anyone willing to affiliate with the covenant people is accepted in both Exodus and Esther, a fact that echoes God's promise that all nations will be blessed through Abraham (cf. Gen 12:3; 22:18).

Gentile acceptance of Israelite beliefs is hardly a new concept at this point in the canon. Besides the non-Israelites mentioned in Exodus 12, Moses' Ethiopian wife (Num 12:1), Rahab the Canaanite (Josh 2:1-21), Ruth the Moabite, Naaman the Syrian (2 Kings 5) and Jonah's Assyrians are all examples of persons outside Abraham's lineage who accept Israel's ways by embracing Israel's God. Without exception, all these persons conform to the demands of the divine word they receive. They reject other gods and religious practices in favor of the God proclaimed by Israel. The circumstances under which they come to Yahwistic faith differ, to be sure, but the situation in Esther hardly precludes the possibility of true belief.

The God Who Institutes Purim: Esther 9:20—10:3

Israel's victory is memorialized by the institution of Purim. This festival, like Passover, is begun as a way of reminding God's people that deliverance never ends. In each successive generation the Lord's protection of the chosen people remains constant. Every time Purim is celebrated the people confess that Israel will survive even the terrors of exile. Enemies like Moses' Pharaoh and the evil Haman will arise, but they will never obliterate the people of God.

Canonical Synthesis: God's Commitment to Israel

Brevard Childs observes that 9:20-32 "provides the strongest canonical warrant in the whole Old Testament for the religious significance of the Jewish people in an ethnic sense."[19] He believes it does so by giving Purim cultic importance: by making it a binding observance (9:21, 27, 29, 31-32), by giving it a set time to be observed (9:21, 31), by setting the exact manner in which it must be celebrated (9:19, 22) and by fixing all these matters in writing, especially in the writing of Scripture.[20] This last point is particularly telling. The inclusion of Esther in the canon highlights the necessity of Israel's survival. This survival is as certain as it is sacred, for the Lord must keep all promises that require Jewish participants. All nations must still be blessed through Abraham. David must still be given an eternal kingdom. The promised land must receive Israel back, and the new covenant must still be initiated. Therefore, besides the fact that God does not sanction the killing of the innocent, Israel must survive for the whole program of biblical theology to be completed. Purim provides more evidence that the Lord remains in charge of human history.

No doubt this chapter ascribes more activity to the Lord than some commentators would like. After all, in Esther the Lord is not said to do anything, at least not overtly. Esther's theology is subdued and understated in its approach. Still, as part of the canon, the book participates in an ongoing presentation of God's works and teachings in history. Its presence in the canon marks Esther as a part of a theological whole, and this part testifies that God's plans for Israel cannot be thwarted by those who hate the Jews. In fact Esther indicates that God's plans for all persons, regardless of race or covenantal status, cannot be thwarted. God is sovereign over both Jew and Gentile in Esther as much as he is in the rest of the canon.

As the Writings move into their final phase, Esther introduces the conviction that God will help Israel no matter where the people have been scattered. Daniel learns this principle in Babylon. Ezra and Nehemiah discover this truth in Persia and in a devastated Jerusalem. Chronicles calls exiles back to the promised land so that God's universal power may be evident in every land. Lamentations has said why exile occurred yet has also asserted that God is not finished with Israel. Esther demonstrates how well Yahweh protects Israel. The rest of the Writings repeat these themes while looking to an era when the exiles will be home again, safe and secure in the promised land.

23

The God
Who Protects,
Discloses & Rules

Daniel

. . . .

N O OLD TESTAMENT BOOK OF COMPARABLE SIZE HAS GENERATED AS MUCH scholarly discussion as has Daniel. This relatively short work has inspired dozens of commentaries, articles and monographs and has divided experts along historical, theological and exegetical lines. Certainly Daniel deserves close scrutiny. As a literary work it displays a mixture of narrative and visionary prophecy that invites analysis of how a single book combines diverse genres effectively. As a historical document Daniel encourages interpreters to decide when the book itself was written and to ponder the relevance of its view of human history. As a theological work that is part of the Old Testament canon, this text interconnects important ideas in such a way as to render it a formidable force at the end of the Writings. In short, Daniel makes a significant contribution to Old Testament theology and does so in a way that allows its readers little room for indifference.

Daniel continues the emphasis on God's protection of Israel begun in Esther and also collects canonical ideas that trace as far back as the exodus and the law of Moses (cf. 9:11-15). Like Esther, Daniel resides in exile outside the promised land. More specifically, he shares with Ezekiel the challenges of living in Babylon, having gone there in the deportation conducted by Nebuchadnezzar in 605 B.C. (cf. 1:1-5).[1] In Babylon Daniel and fellow deportees discover, as Esther and Mordecai find later in Persia (c. 487-465), how dangerous it can be to be a person of faith in a foreign country. These Babylonian captives learn, though, that God protects the faithful, thus preserving a remnant of Israel in the teeth of persecution. Daniel also receives revelation about the future, a process that provides positive reassurance that the Lord rules and reveals history in the making. Throughout this book Yahweh and Yahweh alone among all the so-called deities of Babylon is the sovereign ruler of heaven and earth, of mighty kings and lowly exiles. Daniel shares these convictions with the rest of the Old Testament.

The book's presentation of its message does not always fit the canon's normal methods of conveying revelation. Daniel 1—6 offers accounts of Daniel and his friends as they struggle to be true covenantal monotheists in exile. Narratives are not unusual in Isaiah, Jeremiah, Ezekiel and the Twelve, but Daniel 2:24-45 contains a specific, sequential outline of future events, a unique inclusion not found in previous texts. Also, Daniel 7—12 presents early apocalyptic literature. Though scholars offer differing lists of basic apocalyptic aspects, the following characteristics are fairly common:

1. the use of highly symbolic language
2. the periodization of future world history
3. an emphasis on God's sovereignty
4. the use of angels and visions to reveal the future
5. the ultimate victory of God and God's people over the forces of evil[2]

Many interpreters add pseudonymity and prophecy *ex eventu* (after the fact) to these elements.[3] So many apocalyptic books were written in the late Old Testament era and early Christian times that virtually no two works are the same. Diversity marks the genre.[4]

Daniel is also written in two languages: Hebrew and Aramaic. No other Old Testament book uses Aramaic to this extent.[5] Hebrew begins the work in 1:1—2:4a; Aramaic, the official language of the Persian Empire, is used from 2:4b to 7:28; then the text reverts to Hebrew in 8:1—12:13. This literary device fastens attention on the accounts of Daniel and his friends' struggles in Babylon and on the future of their captors. It also encourages readers to consider the outlines of history found in 2:24-45 and 7:1-28 as two parts of the same whole.

Daniel's combining of narrative and apocalyptic materials makes it a particularly appropriate book to appear near the canon's conclusion. The narratives' emphasis on miraculous deliverance of the faithful reminds readers of similar accounts in the Law and the Former Prophets. In a similar way the futuristic statements in Daniel 7—12 remind interpreters that Isaiah, Jeremiah, Ezekiel and the Twelve have stressed God's universal rule and knowledge of the future. Daniel makes a unique contribution to Old Testament theology, but it does so partly by synthesizing earlier truths while confronting a new historical reality. This book's blend of older ideas into newer literary forms provides an interesting backdrop for arresting theological ideas.

Anyone attempting to divide Daniel into a theological outline must break the book either at its change in literary format or after virtually every chapter. The text's theological richness includes large overarching ideas as well as several supporting themes. Though this discussion chooses the former option, it attempts to track important subpoints as well. Daniel 1—6 continues Esther's emphasis on the God who protects, yet it also states that God reveals. Daniel 7—12 claims that the Lord discloses the future and at the same time says that God rules human events, a notion hardly foreign to Daniel 1—6. Together the two sections present a God who protects, discloses and rules. This God is able to sustain those who are faithful, to humble monarchs who are arrogant and to resurrect the dead at the end of time. Only this God can be trusted to redeem the exiled Israel's future. Only this Lord deserves praise from Jewish exiles and Gentile kings alike.

The God Who Protects and Discloses: Daniel 1—6

At first this book hardly appears to stress the Lord's protection of the faithful. After all, the text begins with a description of Babylon's looting of the temple and deportation of talented young Israelites in 605 B.C. (1:1-2). This disaster has been detailed already in 2 Kings 24:1-4, as well as in Jeremiah 25:1-14, 27:19-22, 36:1-3 and 45:1-5. Each reference to the invasion indicates that Israel's sin has caused the defeat, and Daniel 1:1-2 says nothing to contradict this conviction.[6] Daniel 9:1-19 reinforces it when Daniel confesses Israel's sins. God uses Babylon to punish the chosen people and to warn them to repent or lose the land (cf. Deut 28:15-68). Therefore readers must wait to see whether the young deportees mentioned in 1:3-7 are innocent victims who, like Jeremiah and Ezekiel, suffer alongside the exile's perpetrators or are part of the wicked majority. Are they members of the remnant or not?

The answer comes in 1:8-21, where the four young exiles adhere to God's law rather than succumb to Babylonian ways and worldviews. Having been taken into training for the king's service, they refuse to eat foods they believe break the ritual laws set forth in the Law.[7] Apparently these men believe even in exile, perhaps particularly in exile, that "the ground of Israel's well-being is loyalty to the traditional commandments, and her greatest danger anything which prevents this loyalty."[8] The text not only divulges that the young men stay as healthy as their counterparts (1:8-16) but also states that God brings Daniel and his friends into the king's favor (1:9) and that God gives them knowledge and skill in literature, wisdom and the interpretation of dreams (1:17). In other words, Yahweh protects them by honoring their commitment to the covenant through the gift of influence and skill. Whatever they are able to achieve will be a direct result of God's work in their lives and their fidelity to the Lord's will.

With the twin themes of human commitment and divine protection in place, the book proceeds to demonstrate how divine disclosure saves the exiles and their associates from certain death. Having had a troubling dream, King Nebuchadnezzar promises to kill all the wise men, including the four Israelites, if they do not tell him his dream and its interpretation (2:1-13). God reveals both to Daniel, thereby causing him to declare that God rules time, history and wisdom (2:14-23). Yahweh is the One who alone possesses wisdom and power, and Yahweh alone reveals secrets to the faithful. Wisdom is no more secular here than is Psalms, Job, Proverbs or Ecclesiastes, for it originates with God.

Much as Joseph does in Genesis 41, though much more thoroughly, Daniel interprets a dream that describes the future. Since the Lord gives the interpretation, it is clear that God knows and governs the future. Daniel's interpretation establishes the superiority of his God and gives witness to the fact that he "does not outshine the Babylonians by his own wisdom but by the power of his God (v. 30)."[9] Daniel's God's ability to reveal the dream unmasks the weakness and nonreality of Babylon's gods (2:27-30).[10] No other deity has such power, a fact the king himself admits in 2:46-49. No other deity is able to deliver in this manner.

Nebuchadnezzar's dream depicts four kingdoms, including Nebuchadnezzar's, that are succeeded by a kingdom that will never be destroyed (2:31-45). Virtually every commentator cites Babylon, Persia and Greece as three of the kingdoms.[11] Disputes about the identity of the fourth exist, but all agree that these kingdoms are mere preludes to the great final kingdom that will stand forever (2:44). God reveals the future well beyond Daniel's time, down to the second century B.C. Yahweh also claims that history will come to an end at a time he determines.[12]

Ultimate victory is certain. God will triumph effortlessly and will bring salvation and deliverance to all who believe.[13] God's power will purge the earth of kings and kingdoms who do not honor the God who rules history and discloses the future.[14] Isaiah 13—27 and 63—66 have already made this point, as have Jeremiah 46—51, Ezekiel 25—32 and 40—48 and Zechariah 12—14, as well as a number of other passages.

Daniel 3 reverts to the harsh reality of the exiles' present. The God who rules history cannot stand above history and be credible as a deity different from idols. God must remain active in the exiles' affairs in order to demonstrate his superiority. To this end, this chapter recounts Nebuchadnezzar's demand that all his subjects bow down before a massive idol or face death in a fiery furnace (3:1-7). Obviously the challenge to Israelite faith is adherence to the first two of the Ten Commandments.[15] Daniel's three fellow Israelites refuse to bow down to the idol. They declare Yahweh able to deliver them from the furnace and worth serving even if no rescue occurs (3:8-18). Their actual deliverance is achieved through the agency of a nonhuman being (3:19-25). It results in the king's confession that no other god can deliver in this manner (3:29), though it does not conclude with Nebuchadnezzar's swearing sole allegiance to Yahweh, the very attitude that the Israelites embody before him. Daniel 1—3 intends to emphasize not only God's protection of the Israelite remnant but the Lord's desire to gain a relationship with the Babylonians as well.

Daniel 4 reiterates Yahweh's sovereignty over history and desire for relationship with non-Israelites. At the same time the passage renounces arrogance that exalts human achievement at the expense of praise for the God who gives the power to achieve in the first place. The text is a statement from Nebuchadnezzar to his subjects that recounts his falling mad for failing to recognize God's gift of the kingdom. As in Daniel 2, the king has a vision that Daniel interprets. Daniel states that Nebuchadnezzar must recognize that God alone gives kings power or he will become as unknowing as a beast (4:19-27). Despite the warning, Nebuchadnezzar takes credit for his kingdom and suffers the consequences (4:28-33). Only when he confesses that God lives forever (4:34), rules forever (4:34) and rules justly (4:37) does he regain his senses.

Nebuchadnezzar's confession indicates that the God who sustains (1:8-21), reveals (2:14-45) and delivers (3:8-29) is also the God who humbles the proud. It further claims that Yahweh rules monarchs as well as exiles, wise men and commoners.[16] Every character in this story lives under the Lord's scrutiny and care. This fact transcends racial, national and financial boundaries. No inhabitant of earth can rebuke or restrain God (4:35). Each human being is totally dependent on the One Nebuchadnezzar calls the Most High (4:2, 17, 24—25, 34), the holy God (4:8, 9, 18) and the king of heaven (4:26, 37). Though it is not possible to discern the disposition of Nebuchadnezzar's heart, it is clear that his appreciation for Yahweh has grown since Daniel 2.[17]

The next scene unfolds much later. Nebuchadnezzar died in 562 B.C., having served since 608 B.C. Six years of relative instability followed before Nabonidus (556-539 B.C.) seized control.[18] Due to other interests, he allowed his son Belshazzar to rule over Babylon.[19] Daniel 5 describes how the Persian Empire takes control of Babylon in 539 B.C., an event ancient historians depict as fairly bloodless.[20] Now in great age, Daniel plays an important role in the transfer of power through his now-familiar ability to interpret dreams and visions. This text underscores the book's insistence that God directs history and rewards the righteous.

So far the book has chosen to highlight the Lord's superiority to other gods without making overt negative statements about Babylon's deities. Now more blatant comments appear. Belshazzar gives a party at which he and his guests drink from the sacred vessels taken from Jerusalem's temple as they praise "the gods of gold and silver, of bronze, iron, wood and stone" (5:1-4). Thus Belshazzar combines sacrilege and profanation in his revelry.[21] He clearly does not understand the power of the Most High, the holy God, the king of heaven. His arrogance is as obvious as Nebuchadnezzar's, so some punishment is sure to follow.

A hand appears and writes cryptic words on the wall, which prompts the rulers to send for the aged Daniel. They recognize that he has the Spirit of God in him (5:11, 14) and that he is therefore filled with knowledge and wisdom for interpreting dreams (5:12, 14, 16). Daniel links this episode to Daniel 4. In language much less polite than that of 2:27-30 and 4:19, Daniel denounces Belshazzar for exalting himself against Yahweh (5:17-22). He declares that Belshazzar has venerated gods that "do not see or hear or understand" (5:23) instead of the Lord who gives him breath and power (5:23). Daniel clearly has no use for such idolatry, nor does Yahweh, for God decides to finish Belshazzar's rule and give the kingdom to Cyrus and his servants (5:24-31). The God who rules history cannot be mocked by those chosen to receive powers.[22]

Without question Daniel 6 is one of the best-known and often-told accounts in Scripture. It relates Daniel's jealous colleagues' attempting to block his rise to power by inducing the king to pass a law forcing everyone to pray to the emperor or die. Significantly, these enemies know that they must attack Daniel in some point of "the law of his God" if they are to snare him (6:5). Just as significantly, Daniel prays to the Lord as before (6:10). As in Daniel 1, he decides to serve Yahweh. By doing so he faces death, just as his friends did in Daniel 3. Once again God's ability to deliver the faithful becomes the main issue (6:16).

God delivers Daniel from certain death in the lion's den (6:18-23). The author states that God rescued him because of his faith (6:23). It is also true that Daniel did nothing to deserve royal displeasure (6:22). Instead he has served the Persians as faithfully as he served the Babylonians. The book indicates that Israel can remain faithful to Yahweh, be useful to their captors and be blessed by both. In this way Daniel agrees with Esther, its canonical predecessor.

Canonical Synthesis: God's Sovereignty over Israel, History and Idols
Though these chapters make their own unique contribution to Old Testament theology, they also connect in various ways with the whole canon. The

book's setting links its contents to the Law, the Prophets, both Former and Latter, and the Writings. Daniel and his fellow exiles live firsthand the threats of Leviticus 26 and Deuteronomy 27—28. They learn by experience the seriousness of covenant breaking as they leave the land of promise. It must be stressed, however, that, like Joseph's, their forced departure from the land is not due to their own sins. Rather they suffer for the sins of others. Their distress has already been described in 2 Kings 23:31—24:7, where decades of sin begin to culminate in Babylonian dominance of Judah.

The Latter Prophets promise that Babylon will conquer Jerusalem. Isaiah 39:1-8 even says Hezekiah's descendants will serve Babylon's kings (39:7). Isaiah also predicts Cyrus's victory over Babylon (44:28; 45:1). Jeremiah explains that the Babylonian exile will last seventy years (25:1-11). In a prior text, though, he offers hope to the very group of exiles to which Daniel belongs when the prophet compares them favorably with the Jews who remain in Jerusalem (24:1-10). They hear that God prefers them to the "rotten figs" left in the land. Ezekiel shares Daniel's Babylonian experience and Daniel's later visionary tendencies.

The Writings echo the dangers inherent in Daniel's situation. Psalm 137 reflects the anguish felt by Jews in Babylon. Loss of land, status and freedom leads to near despair. Though it deals more specifically with the fall of Jerusalem than with the exilic setting, Lamentations expresses the sense of grief the chosen people feel at forfeiting their divinely given inheritance. As Daniel's canonical companion, Esther sets the stage for the latter book's emphasis on peril and deliverance. No matter how careful the faithful may be, they will still suffer for being who they are and believing as they do. This danger forces the faithful to trust God as they wait for final deliverance from the exile that sin has caused.

Daniel's activities and attitude have much in common with the Wisdom books in the Writings. He and his friends are trained as wise men in Babylon's royal courts, an education that highlights Babylonian literature and culture. But these Israelites remain focused on their own Wisdom heritage. God blesses them all with knowledge, skill and special brilliance in all matters of wisdom (1:17-21). They apply biblical principles to complex matters effectively (1:8-16; 3:1-18). Daniel's counsel is sought at strategic moments, particularly when dreams must be interpreted. Nebuchadnezzar credits Daniel's being filled with God's Spirit as the reason for this wisdom (4:8, 18). Thus Daniel acts as wise man as much as he does as prophetic voice of the future. His position among the wise affords him the opportunity to receive and interpret visions. The same God who reveals wisdom to the authors of Job, Proverbs and Ecclesiastes fills Daniel with insight and discernment.

Besides the common ideas related to Daniel's setting, Daniel 2 continues the canon's teachings on the God who knows and discloses the future. In the Law, Moses predicts Israel's desire for a king (Deut 17:14-15), the rise of a prophet like himself (Deut 18:15-22) and Israel's rebellion against the Lord (Deut 31:14-29). Ahijah (1 Kings 11:26-40; 14:1-18), Jehu (1 Kings 16:1-7), Elijah (1 Kings 17:1; 21:17-24), Elisha (2 Kings 13:14-19), Isaiah (2 Kings 19:20-34; 20:1-19) and Huldah (2 Kings 22:14-20) all offer accurate predictive prophecies in the book of Kings. These servants are joined by Isaiah, Jeremiah, Ezekiel and the Twelve. Their confession is that the Lord is the One who discloses the future to them, which is also Daniel's conviction (2:20-23, 28). More will be said on this subject in the comments on Daniel 7—12, but it ought to be said here that the book's intent is to stress that God's sovereignty over history includes an ability to know and rule the future. God is involved with human events that occur in time, yet he is in no way bound by time.

God's ability to deliver, the major point of Daniel 1, 3 and 6, is hardly a new idea. One of the most evident correspondences is the Lord's determination to fulfill purposes for the nation through a chosen servant. Both Joseph and Daniel suffer in order that others may be preserved. God's deliverance also dominates events such as the exodus, the conquest, David's life, Hezekiah's reign and the first Purim.

Finally, the whole canon testifies to the one God's resolute opposition to arrogance leading to idolatry. Daniel 4—5 agrees with Isaiah 10:5-11, 14:12-15 and 47:10 that God must judge kings and nations who exalt themselves as if God had not given them what they possess. Egomaniacs tend toward self-worship, a brand of idolatry particularly evident in Daniel 3. In response to such pride, Daniel stresses that God gives breath, delivers, is holy, is sovereign, is just and lives forever. No idol or emperor has these characteristics, so none deserves worship. The one God still reigns, despite Israel's exile. The exile makes God's universal reign more evident due to the remnant's witness to Gentiles.

The God Who Knows, Discloses and Rules the Future: Daniel 7—12

Daniel 1—6 focuses on events on earth that are affected by divine activity. Daniel 7—12 highlights visions of the future that Daniel receives from the Lord. Thus if the action in the first half of the book operates from earth to heaven, then the second half moves from heaven toward earth. Each chapter presents God as the One who knows, discloses and rules history. Yahweh is the One who will guide history to a just conclusion and the One who rewards and punishes persons after death as well as before death.

Daniel receives the vision depicted in Daniel 7 in the first year Belshazzar receives power from his father, or about 556 B.C. This vision parallels Nebuchadnezzar's interpreted dream in Daniel 2, so its contents remain relevant through many decades. Its appearance when a new ruler emerges suggests that God's plans for the human race continue to be constant in the midst of changing circumstances.

Again four kingdoms arise before a final kingdom ordained by God supplants them all. At first, Daniel sees four quarreling beasts or kings (7:1-8). These individuals appear to rule earth's events, but 7:9-28 proves otherwise. Two scenes, followed by an interpretation, highlight the Lord's mastery of events. First, God, called here "the Ancient of Days" (7:9), assumes his position as enthroned Lord and begins to judge. God takes power from the arrogant beasts and then prepares to give authority to another. This God is timeless, for he is older than days. Daniel's phraseology here connects with the "I am" statement in Exodus 3:14, the psalmists' declarations that "from everlasting to everlasting you are God" (Ps 90:2) and "they [the heavens] will perish, but you remain" (Ps 102:26-27) and even the Bible's opening statement that "in the beginning God created" (Gen 1:1). The text cannot conceive of a time in which this Being did not live or act as king. Further, the imagery of whiteness and fire indicates the Ancient of Days' purity.[23]

Some scholars note possible Canaanite parallels in 7:9-12.[24] Others mention that option and then emphasize similarities with Ezekiel's visions.[25] John Goldingay observes correctly that whatever elements of Near Eastern imagery may exist have receded into the background.[26] Here the Lord of the Scriptures is the One who has ruled and will rule. As Maurice Casey claims:

> At vs. 9 the Ancient of Days appears for the first time. He is clearly God, and the description is that of an old man. He is not likened to an ancient of days, for the beings described as "like" something are all pure symbols; God really exists. Moreover he had existed for a very long time, and this piece of imagery should not be held to imply that he had not existed for ever before.[27]

This ruler endures forever, in contrast to arrogant earthly rulers who believe themselves all-powerful.

Second, with the true ruler presented, Daniel sees God give the final, everlasting kingdom to one "like a son of man" (7:13-14). Yahweh is able to give the kingdom to whomever he wills, since this kingdom is his. The "son of man" is a heavenly being (7:13) who is capable and worthy of receiving the very kingdom of God and governing it forever (7:14). No mention of David appears here, but Gerhard von Rad notes that only a messianic figure could be given the kingdom of God.[28] Walter Kaiser adds that this one "would not only be the true David, but He would also be the true Son of man, combining in His person the high calling of humanity and the position reserved alone for God."[29] This son of man is capable of ruling without the arrogance so typical of the monarchs depicted in Daniel.

When the son of man receives the kingdom, he will share it with "the saints of the Most High" (7:18, 22). This group will suffer persecution before the kingdom is given (7:25) and will triumph only when the Ancient of Days comes (7:22, 26-27), an event that refers to the day of the Lord mentioned so prominently in the Latter Prophets.[30] In other words, the fourth, dreadful kingdom will be superseded by a permanent one led by the son of man and populated by the people of God. The notion that the Davidic king and the remnant will eventually reign over the arrogant offers real hope to Daniel and other exiles.[31]

Though the details differ from those in earlier texts, the vision found in 8:1-27 agrees totally with its predecessors in two key regards. First, this passage asserts that God is able to disclose the future and rule the future. Human events are by no means tenuous or left open to chance. Yahweh knows and governs the future as readily as the past and present. Second, God will overcome all arrogant kings and will establish his standards over the whole earth. Again the ultimate point is that the God who knows and discloses the future will rule the future. These facts comfort Daniel during changing times that appear to offer God's people at best an uncertain future that matches their turbulent present.

Daniel's concern for the chosen people dominates Daniel 9—10. In a prayer that echoes Exodus 32:11-13, Psalms 78, 89 and 104—106, as well as Ezra 9:6-15 and Nehemiah 9:5-38, Daniel confesses Israel's sins and petitions Yahweh to restore the people (9:1-19). He then receives visions about the Messiah (9:20-27), Persia and Greece (10:1-21). Through confession of sin, reassurance about the coming Savior and trust in God's final victory over Israel's oppressors, the faithful Daniel becomes convinced that Yahweh is not finished with Israel.

The confession grows out of Daniel's conviction that Jeremiah's prediction of a seventy-year exile (Jer 25:11-12; 29:10) will come true. His treatment of Jeremiah's book as God's word may indicate his acceptance of this text as Scripture akin to Moses' Law, which he mentions in 9:11-13. Daniel 9:2 calls Jeremiah's words "the word of the LORD," a further indication that the "books" are sacred books.[32] Daniel confesses that Israel has transgressed against the Law, has not heeded the prophets and has refused to repent (9:4-1). Therefore the loss of land threatened in the Law (cf. Lev 26; Deut 27—28) has occurred (9:14-15). God's holy mountain, Zion, has been forfeited, and its sanctuary destroyed (9:16-17). Daniel pleads with the merciful God to forgive Israel's sin and repeal its punishment (9:17-19). In this prayer he agrees with the assessment of Israel's destruction found in 2 Kings 17 and with the pleas for renewal encased in Psalm 89:46-52 and Psalms 104—106. Daniel is a member of the remnant. As such, he works and prays alongside earlier canonical writers for the restoration of God's people, land and spiritual vibrancy.

Once again it is the God who discloses and rules who becomes Daniel's and, by extension, the rest of the remnant's source of hope. Gabriel appears again, this time to tell the visionary that the holy place will be restored and the Savior will come but that another vicious ruler will arise afterward (9:24-27). All these events will transpire in an enigmatic "seventy weeks." This vision's exact details are probably impossible to ascertain with precision. Still, the general outline is clear: Israel will return to the land, the temple will be renewed, the Messiah will come, and opposition will rise again. Daniel's prayers for renewal will be answered, yet this answer will not be the end of woes for God's people. The faithful must remember that the Lord will not allow history to overwhelm the chosen ones. Yahweh will remain Lord of the future even when Persia, Greece and other kingdoms emerge and exalt themselves on earth (10:1-21). God's people will be secure because Yahweh is their God.

This security grows increasingly important as Daniel 11—12 unfolds. Though space does not permit a full description of the events described in 11:1-39, the text predicts historical details that transpire between the Persian period and Antiochus's death.[33] As in previous visions, this passage promises that evil will not triumph. At the same time, victory will not come cheaply. God's people will be challenged to oppose wickedness (11:32-33). Many of their number will fall, yet only to purify them for later times (11:34-35). They will eventually see idolatrous and arrogant rulers justly punished, but, like the psalmists, they may wonder "how long" such pain will last.[34] Their answer lies in the sovereign purposes of the God who governs history, who is the God of gods (11:36).

After Antiochus, however, at least one more rich and blasphemous king will arise (11:40-45). As is true in 8:23-26 and 9:24-27, the last arrogant one in this passage will not prevail. It is apparent that the book's view of history is that though evil will not ever reign supreme, neither will it ever cease altogether until God reigns supreme. The faithful remnant will never be promised an easy life. Their commitment to the Lord will be tested again and again. Still, the answer to "How long, Lord?" is "Not forever." Evil and evildoers will be eradicated.

Daniel's closing chapter reemphasizes this view of the remnant's place in history. At the end of time there will be unprecedented trouble, but even in the midst of such terror the people of God will stand firm, and their God will use all the power of heaven to deliver them (12:1). So severe is this trouble that only the faithful, those written in the Lord's "register of the citizens of the coming kingdom of God,"[35] will survive (12:1). Their deliverance, however, is not necessarily from death. Many will have died, but God will raise them from the dead (12:2). This resurrection will also be shared by the wicked, who will receive shame, in contrast to the faithful, who will garner everlasting life (12:2). There can be no question that 12:2 asserts a fixed belief in resurrection[36] or that "our author can be seen to be thinking of a general resurrection prior to judgment."[37] What is described here transcends what occurs in earthly life.[38] It is true that this text does not "yield a coherent total doctrine of the afterlife,"[39] but no single biblical passage does, for that matter.

What 12:2-3 means is that there is no refuge in death for the wicked nor any ultimate loss for the righteous when their bodies cease to function. The wicked cannot sin at will and escape into annihilation. They will face their Maker, who will determine their status. As for the faithful, shame and suffering are terrible, yet they are temporary. Everlasting life allows an opportunity for the wise, "who lead many to righteousness" (12:3), to endure forever (12:3). Thus they can serve Yahweh confidently in hope.

Despite these positive comments, the book ends with warnings about future struggles. God's elect will be shattered by the enemy (12:7).[40] They will be purified by this struggle with wickedness (12:10), but it will be as severe as the furnace in Daniel 3. Again the hope Daniel can take to his grave is that the grave is not his final home (12:13).[41] Daniel, like the rest of the remnant, can know that the God who rules history governs life, death and life after death. The God who discloses the future's horrors also reveals undimmed hope. The God who protects the remnant is not bound by time or circumstances when producing that protection.

Canonical Synthesis: God's Sovereignty over the Future

Certain crucial canonical emphases merge and culminate in Daniel 7—12. In fact these emphases are attested so often in the Scriptures that they can merely be outlined here. Some details must be omitted. Still, it is nearly impossible to end this chapter without reference to Daniel's approach to the Messiah, the end of time, the Scriptures and the remnant. Each of these concepts is particularly significant for understanding Old Testament theology, and their appearance near the end of the Writings offers an opportunity for readers to reflect on the whole canon.

Daniel's references to the Davidic king (the Messiah) are few, perhaps only two. Both occur in texts that depict the rise and fall of wicked rulers. Daniel 7:13-14 has inspired a large body of literature and a variety of interpretations.[42] It must be read in light of the rest of Scripture to be understood adequately. These verses appear in the context of judgment and the triumph of the remnant.[43] The one like the son of man is given the never-ending kingdom of God, all nations serve him, and he rules over an endless dominion (7:14). He receives these glorious items directly from God, the only one who can rightly give them. Daniel 9:25-26 presents the Messiah as one "cut off" and left with nothing, while evildoers have power for a time. Afterward God and the righteous will triumph (9:24). Sin will be eradicated, and righteousness will prevail (9:24).

In earlier texts, the Davidic heir is the one who achieves these results. In 2 Samuel 7:16 the Lord's initial promise to David includes an eternal kingdom. Isaiah 9:6-7 and 11:1-10 claim that the Davidic king will rule endlessly over a dominion that is free from strife. Isaiah 53:1-12 presents one who dies to redeem the people. Jeremiah 23:1-8 says that righteousness will be restored when a Davidic descendant whose name is "the LORD Our Righteousness" leads the faithful. Ezekiel 37:1-28 envisions the coming Davidic ruler governing the people after the Spirit of God has raised them from the dead. Psalm 2 and Psalm 110 foresee the Lord giving the kingdom to the chosen one. Numerous other psalms speak of God's choice of David. Canonical readers may justifiably think that the son of man's description in 7:13-14 must of necessity apply to the same person referred to in previous passages. No one else is ever given the kingdom of God. The same is true of 9:24-27. No other figure is cut off and still able to redeem the people from sin. No one else is said to transform, judge and inspire all at the same time. By this point in the canon, it is almost as if it is understood that the Davidic Messiah is meant in 7:13-14 and 9:24-27.

The New Testament uses the phrase "son of man" repeatedly in its discussions of Jesus' identity. Jesus refers to himself as the son of man quite often. He utilizes this title when speaking of his power to judge or of his reception of the kingdom in Matthew 10:23, 24:27, 24:37, 25:31; Mark 13:26, 14:62; Luke 17:22, 17:30, 18:8, 21:36; and John 1:51.[44] Each usage of this term links Jesus to the figure in Daniel 7:13-14. Jesus views himself as the one to whom God will give the right to judge human beings and the kingdom itself.[45] He also believes himself to be the suffering and betrayed son of man, noting that "it is written" that the son of man must suffer (Mt 26:24; cf. Mk 9:12; 14:21; Lk 22:22). Apparently Jesus and those who recorded his words connected the coming king, the suffering and reigning son of man, to Christ's ministry on earth. The thematic connections are evident, and Jesus was correct to conclude that the promised Davidic heir must match Daniel's and the rest of the Old Testament's description to be authentic.

As with the concept of the Messiah, Daniel's accounts of the end of time must be read against the backdrop of the canon. Daniel conceives of history governed by Yahweh, yet this governance does not guarantee comfort for the righteous. Terrible kings and unholy nations will dominate the earth, the Davidic ruler will come, more sin will follow, God will judge the living and the dead through the son of man, and the righteous will then inherit the kingdom of the Lord. There is no question that the Law, the Prophets and the Writings agree with Daniel that the Lord alone rules human history through the agency of his word and the power of his person. The Prophets also stress the rise and fall of powers great and small that arrogantly oppose Yahweh. Even a brief perusal of Isaiah 13—23, Jeremiah 46—51, Ezekiel 25—32, Amos 1:2—2:7 and Zephaniah 2:4—3:5 proves this point. The preceding section has stated how the Prophets stress the Davidic covenant.

Judgment in the Prophets is often stated in terms of "the day of the Lord." Though this phrase does not appear in Daniel, the effect of judgment is much the same. God's appointed "day" in Isaiah 2:5—4:6 removes the wicked from the earth and results in the Lord's residing with the remnant in Zion, ideas that are formulated differently in Daniel yet are hardly foreign to the later book. Isaiah and Daniel particularly agree that the day of judgment will punish the proud, a notion also found in Ezekiel 7:10-13 as well as in Amos 4:1-3 and 6:1-7. Judgment in all these texts is horrible, thorough and absolutely final. God's waiting for repentance will end, and God's wrath at sins against God and human beings will be unleashed. The fact that the righteous will survive and be rewarded is stated clearly in texts like Isaiah 65—66, Zephaniah 3:8-20 and Zechariah 14:1-21. Therefore Daniel shares the overall Old Testament confidence that the Lord who created the earth and human beings will judge wickedness, reward righteousness and provide a permanent dwelling place for the faithful.

Daniel's approach to Scripture is significant for understanding the growth of the canon and how previous writings were perceived by later Old Testament figures. Three details are especially significant. First, Daniel 9:1-19 indicates Daniel's great reverence for the law of Moses. His confessional prayer discloses that Daniel understands that Israel's failure to obey Moses' words was the same as not obeying God's word. Moses' voice was God's voice (9:10), and Moses' law was God's law (9:11). Second, Daniel shares the Former Prophets' view of history and reveres the prophets' statements. He mirrors 2 Kings 17 when describing how and why Israel went into exile (9:1-19). He conceived of Jerusalem as God's chosen city, the mountain of the Lord (9:16-17), one of Isaiah and Zechariah's main points. Daniel also heeded the book of Jeremiah's prophecies (9:1-2), believing that they must be God's words. Third, he intercedes and laments in a manner similar to the exilic psalms in Psalms 90—106. Daniel understands his role as an exile as that of a penitent, consistent and faithful servant of God. Like the other expatriots, he must wait on the Lord for the expiration of the seventy years of exile. Such is God's word, so he must obey.

Seen this way, Daniel's view of earlier Scripture parallels that of another sixth-century B.C. figure. Zechariah 7:8-14 records the prophet's agreement with the Former Prophets' interpretation of Israelite history. This passage also stresses God's standards (7:8-10) and grieves over the nation's unwilling-ness to heed the "prophets," whom he considers inspired and sent by

God's Spirit (7:12). Having refused God's merciful word, the people condemned themselves to hearing Yahweh's judging word (7:12-14). Both Daniel and Zechariah consider the Law and the earlier prophecies God's word. They conclude that this word is inevitably true and that it defines history.

Daniel's view of the remnant is shaped by historical circumstances and futuristic visions. The book affirms that God's faithful refuse to defile themselves by breaking the law (Dan 1). They give God the glory for their achievements (2:28), prefer to die rather than commit idolatry (3:18), share harsh divine decisions (Dan 4—5) and do not change their devotional habits under pressure (Dan 6). In other words, the remnant must be God's people as surely as the Law is God's word. The faithful must belong unreservedly to Yahweh no matter what human events may bring. Daniel's visions assert that the remnant will triumph because their God rules the future. It is not possible for God's people to be defeated, for their God, the only God, is sovereign.

Perhaps no greater proof of the remnant's victory through Yahweh's power exists than the fact that God raises the dead (12:1-3, 13). Hints of this conviction have already appeared in the canon.[46] God's people will live in a new heaven and new earth, according to Isaiah 66:22-24. Ezekiel 37:1-14 envisions a time when God's Spirit will raise the dead. Hosea 13:14 chronicles Yahweh's joy in defeating death on behalf of the faithful (cf. 1 Cor 15:55). In the Writings, Psalm 16:10 says that God will not desert the psalmist even after death. Job says that he will be vindicated after death if necessary (Job 19:23-27). Though several of these texts do not speak of a bodily resurrection, they all contribute to a theme that Daniel 12 consummates by declaring the resurrection. All these texts confess that death does not conclude God's relationship with the remnant either individually or collectively.[47] Yahweh's plans for the elect are not hampered by any circumstance, not even death. God does not just rule the future in a general way. God rules each person's and each nation's future in a personal way.

Conclusion

Daniel's conception of God begins with a firm belief in the Lord's uniqueness and branches into a multifaceted portrait. By the book's end, most of the canon's major confessions about Yahweh have surfaced. God is the One who creates, reveals, saves, judges and rules. The Lord is depicted as One who alone controls all nations, whether ascendant Babylon or defeated Israel. This God is supremely worthy of the sort of dedicated service the remnant must give their Lord. As the remnant acts like the people of God, they make it possible for Jeremiah's seventy years to pass and the promise of return (Deut 30) to materialize.[48] It is to the matter of return to the promised land that the canon now turns.

24

The God
Who Restores
the Remnant to
the Land

Ezra—Nehemiah

. . . .

DANIEL LEAVES INTERPRETERS WITH THE EXPECTATION THAT ISRAEL'S LONG-term fortunes will improve because their God rules history. The remnant can expect to return to the land, renew temple worship, restore the Law's prominence and once again enjoy the full favor of the God who created the heavens and the earth. God's people can also anticipate extreme persecution, but they may take heart in any situation, for the God who rules history will give them an eternal kingdom. What Daniel does not say is exactly how these benefits will be bestowed or even how the exiles will come back to the promised land. Ezra—Nehemiah describes the restoration process (already introduced in Haggai, Zechariah and Malachi) that fulfills the short-term blessings Daniel promises. It does so by emphasizing that it is God who effects Israel's return, God who makes the temple's rebuilding possible, God who turns the people back to the Sinai covenant, God who creates the opportunity for Jerusalem to rise from the ashes of destruction.

The Hebrew canon always considered Ezra—Nehemiah one book. It was not until the Christian era that the two were ever separated, and no Jewish version divided the books until five hundred years ago. Several factors make this connection reasonable. First, the two main characters work together in

Nehemiah 8:1-18. Though the text is fairly clear that the men did not come to Jerusalem at the same time, it is just as plain that their ministries complemented one another at a strategic moment when the people renewed their covenant with Yahweh. Second, both books deal with roughly the same period of time. Ezra and Nehemiah both serve Artaxerxes I, the king of Persia (c. 464-424 B.C.).[1] Their work occurs when the land of Israel has been taken over by non-Jews committed to keeping the chosen people from ruling their homeland. Third, both books stress similar themes. Ezra emphasizes the renewal of Israelite religion more than the rebuilding of the city, while Nehemiah's interests are precisely the opposite, but both men desire to see the spiritual, physical and covenantal revival of their people and their ancestral land. Each man thinks that the land was forfeited through covenant infidelity (Ezra 9:5-15; Neh 1:4-11), each believes strongly in prayer (Ezra 9:5-15; Neh 1:4-11; 4:4-6; 5:19), and each thinks the Lord is sovereign over all earthy events, though they concurrently hold human beings responsible for their actions (Ezra 1:1; 5:5; Neh 2:20; 4:15; 5:1-13). The list could be lengthened, but the point has been made. The two books are quite compatible as one book. Their message is strongest when it is presented as a unity.

An outline of Ezra—Nehemiah reveals a straightforward theological summary of the book's purpose. First, Ezra 1—6 summarizes the history of Israel from the decree of Cyrus (539 B.C.) to Ezra's time (c. 458 B.C.). This section highlights the problems the Jews faced in coming back to the land from exile, yet in doing so it succeeds in stressing the notion that it is the Lord who restores the remnant to the place of promise. Second, Ezra 7—10 emphasizes the God who demands purity. Israel has failed to live up to the covenant's stipulations, and this trend must cease if the exile is to end. Third, Nehemiah 1—7 confesses that it is the Lord who rebuilds Jerusalem. The remnant must work, but they have no chance to succeed unless God calls a leader, removes opposition and gives the people the heart to work. In other words, nothing along these lines has changed since the exodus, the conquest or the monarchy. Fourth, Nehemiah 8—13 presents the God who inspires covenant renewal. Now the Jews respond appropriately to the Lord because their hearts have been altered.[2] They are truly God's people because they are willing to act like the people of God. Their hearts dictate a new attitude toward the One who has brought them back to the land promised to Abraham, Isaac and Jacob, and this attitude has been shaped by the written word of God found in the Law.

When the book ends the renewal is hardly complete. The vision offered by Isaiah, Jeremiah, Ezekiel, Haggai, Zechariah and Malachi has not yet come to fruition. Much must still be done for the Jews to be a holy nation and a kingdom of priests (cf. Ex 19:5-6). Jerusalem is hardly Zion at this juncture of their history. But hope has begun to turn to reality. Progress has been made, and the long-term promises Daniel has offered have not been revoked. The God who sent Israel out of the land has brought them back, just as Deuteronomy 27, 28 and 30 predict. God has been faithful, so what stands in the way of full restoration is the fidelity of the elect nation.

Despite the provisional nature of the renewal, one long-standing problem seems largely to have evaporated. No longer do the faithful bearers of God's message feel compelled to combat idolatry incessantly. The Jews do not seem to be as enamored with foreign deities as in the past, though they do form alliances with those who do not worship Yahweh. They have apparently begun to embrace the notion that there is no other God but Yahweh. Monotheism has become not only a conviction held by the writers of Scripture but a primary element in the whole nation's theological perspective as well. The issue now is how well the people will commit themselves to the covenant.

The God Who Restores the Remnant to the Land: Ezra 1—6

Ezra 1—6 offers a sweeping account of the various victories and setbacks the Jews encounter while attempting to come back to what had been Israel. Starting with the decree of Cyrus (538 B.C.), the text notes how the new Persian ruler extended the Jews the right to return to their ancestral territory and rebuild their temple, and how the decree even provided funds for the venture (1:1-8). The temple was indeed rebuilt in 520-516 B.C. (3:7-13), as the books of Haggai and Zechariah have already mentioned. From that time until Ezra's, though, persistent opposition kept the people from completing the task of restoring consistent worship rites and reconstructing the holy city (4:1—7:7). Thus Ezra and Nehemiah's era is seen as a time when that which has been delayed will be delayed no longer.

This section makes repeated reference to the fact that it is the Lord who oversees this entire episode in Israelite history. In the opening verse, the author states that the Lord places it in Cyrus's heart to allow the people to return and that the decree was issued to fulfill Jeremiah's prediction that the exile would end after seventy years (Jer 25:11-12; 29:10-14). It must also be noted that Isaiah 44:28 and 45:1 mention Cyrus by name as the one God chose to release the nation from Babylonian bondage. God's word continues to rule history, just as it has done since the Lord spoke the world into existence. In Ezra and Nehemiah's day it will be a return to God's written word that sparks covenant renewal (Neh 8:1—9:3). Similarly in 1:5 the Lord stirs the heart of those who decide to return, in 5:5 it is the Lord who protects the people while they build, and in 6:22 it is God who fills the remnant's hearts with joy as they celebrate the Passover. The remnant's fortunes are in the hands of the Lord, who desires at this point in history to honor the pledges made decades earlier through faithful and long-suffering prophets.

It is just as evident that the lives of the Gentile kings are also firmly in Yahweh's grasp.[3] Such was the case with the Syrians in Elijah and Michaiah's day (1 Kings 22:1-53), the Assyrians in Isaiah's time (Is 8:1-10) and the Babylonians during Jeremiah's ministry (Jer 50—51). Rulers are not autonomous. They answer to the God who allowed them to rise to prominence.

The identity of the remnant includes certain specific characteristics here. The remnant consists of those who hear the call to go back to the covenant land. Remnant persons have the faith to attempt to do God's will against what seem to be impossible odds. God's remnant bases their lives on the standards revealed in the Law and the hope and rebuke offered in the Prophets. This new body of believers sees themselves in continuity with the past faithful ones and in dire need of personal and societal purification (cf. 2:61-63).[4] In short, they view themselves as persons who need to avoid the mistakes made by earlier unfaithful generations and who must achieve God-given tasks unique to their own day. God moves them to work, but they willingly choose to obey.[5]

Canonical Synthesis: God's Written Word, Sovereignty and the Remnant
These three great themes, God's word, God's sovereignty and God's remnant, are attested throughout the canon. In the Law it is the Lord's spoken word that calls the world into existence in the first place. It is Yahweh's written word that binds Israel to their God in covenant relationship (cf. Ex 24:4; Deut 31:9-13; 32:47). In the Prophets, it is the law of Moses that encourages and chastens Israel as they conquer the promised land and then stumble their way through the era of the judges (cf. Josh 1:1-9; Judg 2:10-23). Israel's neglect of God's written law and spoken prophetic word leads to the Assyrian and Babylonian conquests, according to 2 Kings 17:7-23. Ezra himself is depicted in Ezra 7:6-10 as a man committed to the Law and in 9:1-15 as one who understands that disobedience of the revealed word of God is a recipe for national disgrace and disaster.

God's sovereignty over history has likewise been stated repeatedly throughout the Old Testament. Egypt's losses in the exodus accounts, Israel's inability to capture Canaan in their own strength, the conquest of Canaan in Joshua's time, David's victories, Israel's crushing defeat and rise from national death, to name just a few instances, are seen as divinely superintended events. God's ability to predict the future is offered as proof that the Lord rules time and history and human beings in Isaiah 40—55 and in Daniel 7—12. The Isaiah texts claim that Yahweh's unique ability to reveal the future marks the

Lord as the only God. Besides him there is no other deity who saves or who knows the future (Is 43:11; 44:6, 8; 45:5-6). Psalms such as 78, 89 and 104—106 that emphasize Israel's history are unanimous in claiming that Yahweh is the supreme ruler of all that takes place on earth. It is hardly suprising, given the canon's overall attitude, that Ezra 1—6 views these postexilic events as works fashioned by Yahweh.

God's faithful remnant has stood apart from unbelievers and covenant breakers from the outset of history. Abel shows himself more righteous than Cain. Abraham and Melchizedek prove committed to Yahweh when others in their era do not. Moses, Aaron, Joshua and Caleb separate themselves from the rest of the people by their conviction that Israel can and should enter the promised land. The prophets, Daniel, Zerubbabel, Ezra and Nehemiah complete the biblical circle of major remnant figures. But many obscure characters stand with these more famous members of the remnant, and like their better-known counterparts they have faith in God, base their lives on the revealed word of God and devote themselves to helping Israel become the kingdom of priests that Yahweh intended from the first installment of the Sinai covenant (Ex 19:5-6). These remnant persons do not often enjoy an easy life, but they do enjoy the favor of God.

The God Who Purifies the Remnant: Ezra 7—10

Haggai and Malachi have already divulged how difficult it is for the returnees to act like the people of God. By comparison, building the temple was simple. A structure can remain in place virtually unmoved for years by the forces of time, but a group of people constantly changes through birth, death, turnover in leadership, historical circumstances and other factors. The remnant must be continually renewed. Purity can be lost in a single generation, and, once lost, it can be regained only through difficult reformation. Such reformation can be achieved only through divine action mediated through the lives of dedicated remnant leaders and followers. With the possible exceptions of Malachi and Nehemiah 13:4-31, probably no biblical passage makes these points any clearer than does Ezra 7—10.

Ezra 7:6-10 identifies Ezra as a priest committed to knowing and teaching the Mosaic law. He is chosen by the Persian ruler to lead a group of exiles to Jerusalem (7:12-26). Ezra assumes responsibility for leading the faithful back to the land (7:11-8:36), establishing funding and functionaries for the temple (8:1-36) and enacting necessary reforms based on the Law (9:1—10:44). Each of these duties underscores his commitment to reestablishing the purity of God's chosen ones.

Ezra's group's return to the land highlights the remnant's need to set themselves apart to fulfill the Abrahamic land promise (cf. Gen 12:1-9) and to actualize the pledges related to repentance and restoration God makes in Deuteronomy 30:1-10. Though there must be human effort for this journey to occur, it is the Lord's direct help that makes it possible. Echoing earlier texts, Ezra 7:6 and 7:27-28 confess that God moves the king's heart and paves the way for Ezra's success. According to 8:21-23, in response to their prayers God protects the travelers as they proceed along the way. Yahweh both initiates and supports the entire effort.

Ezra's concern for a beautified temple and for placing the Levites in service reveals his commitment to purity in worship. He obviously thinks that only the tribe of Levi should take the leadership in temple ceremonies and in the care of the temple itself and that the people must support the Lord's work financially. These convictions echo Exodus 25—Leviticus 27, where the Law focuses attention on these matters. At this point Ezra seems idealistic about how well these practices are currently being carried out and about how widespread adherence to the Law may be.

Ezra's leadership in societal reform is the most evident way that he stresses the purity of the people themselves. In 9:1-4, Ezra discovers extensive intermarriage between Jewish men and women of the surrounding popula-tion.[6] Thus he prays to the Lord, confesses the Jews' sins and states that such activities are the reason the chosen ones have fared so poorly in the past two centuries (9:5-15). To remedy this situation, he takes the decisive step of ordering the non-Jewish wives divorced (10:1-44).

The issue is not racism but the danger of marrying women who worship other gods and turn their husbands toward pagan deities. Moses warns against such marriages in Exodus 34:10-17 and Deuteronomy 7:1-11, and Solomon falls prey to this very sin (1 Kings 11:1-13). The presence of Ruth in the canon proves that marriages between Jews and Gentiles who served the Lord were acceptable. Ezra understands that purity cannot exist where men are more concerned with the youth and beauty of their wives than with the content of their children's faith. No doubt this solution was painful indeed.[7] Such pain would have been unnecessary had the people forged their commitments through adherence to the Law rather than through the worldviews of those around them.

Canonical Synthesis: God's Holy Remnant

When Ezra conceives of a pure remnant, he envisions a group that defines itself by God's word. Israel has lost statehood but has not lost the word of God. It is now this word that determines who is a member of the true Israel, of the remnant, and who is not.[8] A canonical worldview is being developed that interprets life through a scriptural lens. Therefore Ezra measures Israel's worship and societal actions by the Law and the Prophets. When he prays, he prays like the psalmists (cf. 9:5-15). His view of history is informed by the

Prophets, and his plans for reform are based on texts found in the Law. Sacred texts have become the means by which all of life and faith are integrated.

Needless to say, Ezra's ideas about purity coincide with the rest of the canon. A holy people in a holy land has been the goal since Sinai, even since Genesis 12:1-9. Pure worship led by consecrated priests has been the standard since Exodus 20—Leviticus 27 was revealed, and the loss of land has been the main threat since Leviticus 26 and Deuteronomy 27—28 appeared. The need to return to Jerusalem has existed since the proclamation of Isaiah 13—35 and 40—66. God's willingness to cancel exile has been known since Moses declared the words in Deuteronomy 30:1-10. The fact that God would make sure these details unfolded in due time was assured through the words of Jeremiah 25:11-12, Jeremiah 29:10 and Daniel 9:1-19. What is unique about Ezra is that he and his fellow returnees understand what the authors of Scripture have been saying for centuries. People in the text now agree with the writers of the text.

The God Who Rebuilds Jerusalem: Nehemiah 1—7

Nehemiah's ministry begins in the same general period as Ezra's. In the twentieth year of Artaxerxes I (c. 445 B.C.), or about thirteen years after Ezra's first journey to Jerusalem (Ezra 7:7),[9] he becomes burdened for the status of the remnant and the decline of Jerusalem (1:1-3). The remnant suffers distress and reproach, and the city lies defenseless before any potential foe (1:2-3). Nehemiah's ministry is devoted to alleviating these two problems. As he attempts his work, Nehemiah depends on God's character and covenant for the strength and peace he needs to persevere. Like Ezra, he is a theologically motivated man, though his theology leads him to more tasks commonly considered secular than does Ezra's. Nehemiah's life underscores the point made in Proverbs that no aspect of work is secular or sacred. Remnant persons know that life, work, family, nation and theology must always be fully integrated, never separated as if the Lord were not sovereign over some specific thing that occurs in God's creation.

Nehemiah's main priority quickly becomes the rebuilding of the holy city, a concern that also especially marks the books of Ezekiel and Zechariah. Upon learning of the city's plight, he offers a prayer that reveals his personal agreement with the theology of the Law and the Prophets (1:4-11). He confesses that the Lord is the God of heaven, a great and awesome God, a merciful and covenant-keeping God and a God who hears and answers prayer (1:4-6). This statement of faith agrees totally with similar canonical confessions about God's nature, such as those set forth in Exodus 34:6-7 and Psalm 90. Next, Nehemiah states that Israel's exile has occurred because the nation has sinned against the covenant (1:6-7). Finally, he claims that Yahweh has extended through Moses the possibility that repentance and covenant fidelity may lead to national renewal, and on this basis he asks the Lord to move the king to allow him to go and help his people (1:8-11). These last two segments of his prayer most likely refer to the contents of Leviticus 26:27-45 and Deuteronomy 27—28 and 30:1-10. Whatever Nehemiah may achieve in Jerusalem will grow out of his belief in the living God of the Scriptures.

As he had hoped, the king does grant Nehemiah permission to go to Jerusalem. This initial answer to prayer (cf. 1:4-11; 2:4) begins a consistent emphasis on God's sovereignty akin to Ezra's. In the early stages of Nehemiah's ministry, God answers his prayer (2:4-9), puts in his heart plans for Jerusalem (2:12) and encourages prospective workers (2:18-20). Nehemiah sets out to rebuild the city walls, and when the sort of opposition described in Ezra 4:1—6:12 arises to thwart Nehemiah's work, he again prays (4:4-9), exhorts in God's name (4:14, 20) and sees the Lord deliver the people (4:15). Internal struggles are handled the same way (5:1-19), as are conspiracies against him (6:1-14). Thus, when the wall is completed in a mere fifty-two days, even his enemies are aware that the Lord has been behind the entire operation (6:15). The final divine impulse he receives in this section is to number the people with the intention to repopulate Jerusalem (7:5). Every activity Nehemiah attempts is motivated by his theology, inspired by his God and made successful by his God.

Canonical Synthesis: Jerusalem's Renewal
There can be no doubt that Nehemiah 1—7's perspective is that God has effected the rebuilding and repopulating of Jerusalem. Years of delay and defeat have ended. A remnant leader has arisen that settles remnant followers into the process of reclaiming the holy land, the holy city and the holy covenant. This development begins to fulfill what that has been promised in Isaiah 35:1-10, Jeremiah 32—33, Ezekiel 36:16-38, Zephaniah 3:8-20, Zechariah 14:1-21 and Daniel 9:1-27. Still, all that is mentioned in those texts has hardly transpired. The people have made a start, yet the whole of Jerusalem is not holy to the Lord (Zech 14:20), the Davidic ruler is not in place (Jer 33:14-18), the people's hearts are not wholly changed (Ezek 36:26-27), and evildoers are not yet eradicated (Dan 9:24-27). Short-term promises are being kept now, but long-term, permanent solutions to Israel's problems await completion. The canon indicates that more will be done by the God who governs human events.

The God Who Renews the Covenant: Nehemiah 8—13
Just as Haggai, Zechariah and Malachi stress that a rebuilt temple and restored

Jerusalem are irrelevant unless the people are reformed, so Nehemiah 8—13 insists upon a return to covenant obedience as the most significant aspect of national revival. This spiritual reformation must be grounded in and guided by God's revealed word. Yahweh's Law must serve as the basis for confession, repentance, praise and subsequent work. In this phase of his ministry Nehemiah receives Ezra's aid. The result of the application of the Law to the people's setting is heartening, though not even the deep-seated repentance that unfolds in this section guarantees that no slide into old, destructive patterns will ever take place.

The remnant gathers around the Law in 8:1-12. It is important to note that at their own initiative, not under compulsion,[10] the people ask Ezra to teach them from the book of the Law (8:1). This request demonstrates that they have chosen to be the remnant and that they are reformed internally, not just externally.[11] By "the book of the Law" the text most likely means the whole Pentateuch, though Ezra does not read from the entire book at this time.[12] It may also mean that Ezra's teaching through the years has borne solid fruit.[13] The fact that Ezra receives help from the Levites in reading and explaining the word to the crowd indicates that the Levites have also undergone significant reform. They have returned to the knowledge that teaching the Law, preaching God's word and leading Israel in praise is the essence of their calling.[14]

With the revealed standards placed before them, the worshipers proceed to confession and repentance, the logical responses to what they have been taught. At first they express profound sorrow over what they have heard, presumably because they recognize the distance between the standards that are explained and their actual conduct. The Levites comfort them with the knowledge that the Law is to bring joy, not sorrow (8:8-12), a fact that drives earlier texts such as Psalm 19:7-14 and Psalm 119.[15] Their obedience to what they have been taught is apparent in 8:13-18, where they observe the Feast of Tabernacles (Booths). Sorrow leads to covenant keeping and thus to fulfilling its highest purpose.

Confession, repentance, petition and praise merge in 9:1-38. There the people offer a magnificent community psalm that confesses the Lord's greatness, their ancestors' sins and their own transgressions. The statements about Yahweh's holiness and mercy amount to praise, and their plea for deliverance from the extremity of their circumstances constitutes earnest petition of the only God who can answer. Like Psalms 78, 105—106 and 135—136, these verses structure their statements around historical events in Israel's past and interpret those events through the lens of covenantal theology. Yahweh is lauded as Creator (9:6), the One who chose and made covenant with Abraham (9:7-8), Israel's deliverer from Egypt (9:9-11), the nation's sustainer in the wilderness (9:12-21) and Israel's helper and judge after the conquest (9:22-31).[16] God is also the One who is able to aid the Jews in their present distress (9:32-37) and the One with whom the people wish to renew covenant (9:38). The remnant understands the necessity of viewing their past, present and future as the result of their relationship with the God of Abraham, Joshua and Moses.

This prayer also emphasizes the sin that has kept Israel from enjoying the full blessings of the Lord. The worshipers recognize that their ancestors did not keep faith with the Lord (9:16-18, 26, 28) and that they themselves have not been sinless (9:32-35). They differ from their predecessors, however, in that they grasp the essential pattern of history that has led to their predicament. They have adopted the viewpoint of the Law, the Former Prophets, the Prophets, Psalms and Daniel that current conditions are a result of past infidelities but that current conditions are not terminal. Hope lingers because of God's mercy (9:9-10, 19-21, 32). Yahweh's character has become Israel's hope for reforming their behavior.

Israel's commitments are both internal and external. Faith in the Lord and acceptance of responsibility for iniquity are supplemented by specific societal reforms. As evidence that they have indeed embraced the Law of Moses, which is the Lord's commandments and statutes (10:29), the people agree to refuse to give their daughters in marriage to men outside the faith (10:30). They swear to keep the sabbath holy (10:31) and promise to support the Lord's temple financially (10:32-39). Some of the Jews determine to live in Jerusalem (11:1-24). Thus, by the time the newly finished walls are dedicated (12:27-43), the chosen people have established several means by which their forms of worship may be protected and continued.

Reforms are not automatically permanent. They must be maintained vigilantly. Nehemiah leaves Jerusalem for a time, only to discover a good bit of spiritual decline upon his return (13:4-31). He deals decisively with the offenses, but the problems will most likely arise when he is gone again. There is no guarantee that short of the emergence of the long-term blessings outlined in the Prophets and Daniel, any enduring covenant keeping will ensue. In other words, all lasting change must be a work done by the Lord. Human initiative alone will never bring the blessings set forth in Leviticus 26 and Deuteronomy 27—28.

Canonical Synthesis: Renewing the Divine Covenant
The most evident canonical connection in Nehemiah 8—13 is the covenant renewal ceremony's likeness to earlier equivalent events. In Joshua 8:30-35, Joshua leads Israel to renew their covenant vows by reminding them of Moses' teachings. This ceremony occurs at Mt. Gerizim and Mt. Ebal in

obedience to Deuteronomy 27—28. No part of this scene escapes the pervasive word of God. The same is true of Josiah's covenant renewal in 2 Kings 23:1-25. There, the reforming ruler calls his subjects back to covenant obedience based on the Book of the Law found in the temple (cf. 2 Kings 22:3-13). As proof of his seriousness, Josiah eradicates all external forms of idolatrous worship he discovers. Internal and external reforms are both evident, and each type of reform stems from a knowledge of and commitment to God's revealed word. Thus Nehemiah and Ezra's ceremony fits the canonical pattern of repentance, reflection, renewal and response.

This section also connects Ezra—Nehemiah to the whole of the canon. As has been stated repeatedly, in every segment of the book the Law of Moses is considered God's own word for the people, and the view of history found in the Prophets is considered normative. Nehemiah 8—13 continues this conceptual framework. It also highlights the type of material found in the psalms. Nehemiah 9:5-38 mirrors the emphases found in texts such as Psalms 78, 89, 105—106 and 136, for it sets the covenant renewal ceremony in the context of national lament and national petition. This connection with Psalms demonstrates the normative nature of forms of worship found in the psalms in the postexilic era. Community standards are based on the Law, community history and future are based on the Prophets, and community worship is based on the psalms. There can be no question that a canonical awareness defines the author's viewpoint, and when the remnant is truly the remnant their worldview is similarly informed.

Conclusion

This penultimate book of the Old Testament leaves interpreters with both hope and frustration. God has restored Israel to the promised land, to the chosen site of worship, to a secure defensive position, to a set priesthood, to societal purity and to doctrinal normativeness. Yahweh's sovereignty, mercy, compassion and faithfulness have all once again been proven in real historical circumstances. The people have responded well to these divine attributes and the works that necessarily attend them. A serious remnant serves Yahweh now. Still, long-term promises await fulfillment. It is clear, though, that the source of further blessing is the God of Scripture, who inspires the remnant's adherence to their relationship to Yahweh and Yahweh's word.

25

The God
Who Elects,
Chastens & Restores

1-2 Chronicles

· ·

F EW OLD TESTAMENT BOOKS ARE AS EASY TO UNDERESTIMATE AS IS
1-2 Chronicles. Many readers dismiss it as a needless repetition or mere
supplement to Samuel and Kings. Others are nonplussed by its extensive
opening genealogies, by its length or by its supposedly simplistic view of
Israelite history. Even theologians are prone to dismiss the book too lightly.
For example, Gerhard von Rad says, "One cannot avoid the impression of a
certain mental exhaustion—at least in the way the material is presented. And
in theological clarity too, in consistency and inner unity, the Chronicler is
not nearly the equal of the Deuteronomistic work."[1] Such comments do not
do justice to the breadth and vision that the book exhibits. Rather than being
a repetitious, unimaginative work, this history provides an excellent conclusion to the canon by drawing together its major themes and presenting them
in an effective, creative and historically accurate manner. The book has a
canonical awareness that makes it important for grasping the whole message
of Old Testament theology.

The Chronicler writes a history that begins with Adam and ends in the
Persian period. To achieve this task, he uses several sources. The author
claims to have had access to genealogies of various clans and kings (1 Chron
4:33; 5:17), documents such as letters from foreign rulers (2 Chron 32:17-20),
songs of praise and lament (2 Chron 29:30; 35:25), eleven different prophetic

writings (1 Chron 29:29; 2 Chron 9:29; 12:15; 13:22; 20:34; 26:22; 32:32; 33:19; 36:22) and other historical works such as "the book of the kings of Israel and Judah" (e.g., 2 Chron 27:7; 35:27).[2] Besides these resources, it is clear that the Chronicler quotes from a variety of biblical books, including Genesis, Numbers, Joshua, Samuel, Kings, Jeremiah and Psalms.[3] From these materials the author gains historical and theological insight that gives the work credibility and canonical continuity. These references to sources indicate that the author has tried to present an honest and accurate account while describing Israel's past from a specific point of view.

The audience to whom the Chronicler wrote shared much in common with the intended recipients of Malachi and Ezra—Nehemiah. Despite the building of a new, albeit small, temple in 520-516 B.C., Israel's attitude toward worship was distasteful to Malachi (cf. Mal 2:1-9), Ezra (Ezra 9—10) and Nehemiah (Neh 13). Part of Israel's spiritual lethargy stemmed from their difficult financial situation and their problems with neighboring groups.[4] Malachi, Ezra and Nehemiah consider it their job to raise the people's enthusiasm for serving the Lord, and the Chronicler also writes with this goal in mind. Though some of the same themes found in Ezra—Nehemiah and Malachi resurface in Chronicles, the Chronicler attempts to motivate readers through a much more positive outlook than those in earlier canonical books.

Theological reflection provides the means by which the Chronicler interprets history and encourages the remnant. The people's situation cries out for explanation. Why have the Jews suffered so greatly, and how much longer will the pain last? When and how will God bless their willingness to return to the promised land? What constitutes the remnant? What sort of worship pleases God? Does Israel have a political future? What has become of the Davidic promise? Such questions are answered in Chronicles by a historian who understands who rules history. This author claims that Israel's future is determined by a God who elects, chastens and restores.

Though there are many ways to divide the text into a theological outline that illustrates these themes, perhaps it is best to divide the work by marking its largest segments. First, a lengthy genealogy begins the work to demonstrate that the Lord is the God who has chosen Israel from the very creation of the human race (1 Chron 1:1—9:34). Selected narrative comments tie the genealogies to narrative material in the Law and the Former Prophets. Second, the book focuses on the God who makes an eternal covenant with David (1 Chron 9:35—29:30). David is the book's main character, and the Davidic covenant the text's defining moment. Third, the Chronicler stresses the God who chooses Solomon to follow David and build the temple (2 Chron 1—9). Out of love for David the Lord places his son on the throne, and out of love for God Solomon fulfills his father's dream of a temple for Yahweh. Fourth, the writer emphasizes the God who chastens and restores the chosen people (2 Chron 10—36). This final section is especially adamant in its assertion that God has been fair to Israel, that Israel has broken the Sinai covenant and that Israel must seek the Lord to be successful and blessed in the land.

At all times the book demonstrates a canonical awareness and insists upon the monotheistic ideal. The Chronicler stands by the theology of the Law, the Prophets and the Writings and does so while citing many of the earlier books. This book unhesitatingly says that Israel has stood or fallen depending on their fidelity to the Lord, who alone is God (cf. 2 Chron 32:19; 33:13). The author depends on God's written word to support this conclusion. In doing so, the Chronicler proves a worthy person to write the canon's final chapter. As M. J. Selman observes, "Chronicles stands apart in its attempt to interpret the Old Testament from beginning to end. It is also appropriately placed at the end of the canon in the Hebrew Bible, as that book of the Old Testament which sums up the rest."[5] Without question this book must not be underestimated, or a vital part of the canonical whole will be lost.

The God Who Chooses Israel from Creation: 1 Chronicles 1:1—9:34

In the postexilic period it was no doubt easy for the Jews to wonder if they had any significance in the family of nations. After all, they were a subjected people, wholly subservient to the powerful Persian Empire. The Chronicler addresses this issue by stressing that God has been working toward and through the Israelites from the creation of the human race.[6] Two basic genealogies are offered to make this point. The first spans 1:1—2:2 and covers the era from Adam to Jacob (Israel), while the second describes the birth of the tribes of Israel down to the return from exile (2:3—9:34). Through the connecting of creation, the patriarchs, the conquest and the loss of the land, the author mirrors the basic narrative outline found in the Law and the Prophets. This scheme also allows the Chronicler to assert that God had Israel in mind from the beginning of time and to do so through a literary device that telescopes history into a few pages.

It is obvious that the Chronicler utilizes the genealogical material from Genesis in 1:1—2:2. Elements of Genesis 5:1-32, 10:1-32, 11:10-26, 25:12-18, 35:23-26 and 36:1-43 appear.[7] This awareness of Genesis indicates that the Chronicler had access to that book and desired to shape his account in a similar way. Further, it suggests that the Chronicler shares the belief that the Lord created the heavens, the earth and all the nations of the world. Finally, it shows that the Chronicler considers the lives of Abraham, Isaac and Jacob the capstone of early human history. All that precedes their times is a prelude to the important work God does in and through their lives. Many scholars maintain that the genealogical material was a late addition to Chronicles. Sara

Japhet disagrees, noting that the style and thematic emphases in this section correspond to the rest of the book. Therefore, she concludes,

> the integrity of the genealogical material, reworking and summarizing the sources in Genesis, yet all the while maintaining the original data and order, is itself the purpose of this chapter. Its aim is to delineate human history as the stage for the enacting of the history of Israel. It also expresses a unique concept of the election of Israel . . . as beginning with Adam.[8]

This historical and theological perspective encourages postexilic Jews to remember that their heritage is as important as history itself and reminds them that even the mighty Persians are under God's control. Their significance derives from the Creator who chose them from the beginning of time.

Israel's prominence does not diminish in 2:2—9:34, but this second genealogy starts the book's emphasis on the people's responsibilities toward their Creator. Comments on faithfulness and disobedience begin to appear. The Chronicler does not believe that Israel's chosen status allows the people to be less accountable to the Lord. Indeed the author claims the opposite. God's chosen ones have a greater obligation to the Lord and to one another than does any nation on earth.

For instance, the genealogy of Jacob's family begins with Judah, not Reuben, who is the oldest son. According to 5:1-2, the reason for this reordering is that Reuben sinned against his father by sleeping with one of Jacob's concubines, an episode depicted in Genesis 35:22 and denounced by the dying Jacob in Genesis 49:3-4. Even though Judah receives priority in 1 Chronicles 2:3-8, the Chronicler does not fail to point out the sins of Judah and his sons by noting the story about Tamar from Genesis 38:2-7 (1 Chron 2:3-8). Similarly, the tribes that settled beyond the Jordan (cf. Num 32:1-42) are described as idolaters, which led to their destruction by the Assyrians (5:23-26). Judah's fall to the Babylonians is said to have happened because of unfaithfulness to the Lord (9:1). In other words, the Chronicler fundamentally agrees with the perspective of the Law and the Prophets that Israel's miseries have come as a result of covenant infidelity.

David's prominence is felt even in this wide-ranging genealogy. He is the most important member of Judah's family (cf. 3:1-9) and is cited as the one God chose to lead the nation (5:2). The Chronicler also highlights David's decision to make Jerusalem the nation's capital (3:4), which brings that city to the forefront of all other places in the promised land. These references set the stage for 1 Chronicles 10—29, where David's career will be reported in great detail.

Aaron's and Levi's families also receive special treatment. The Chronicler takes time to note that only Aaron's descendants were to be priests (6:49) and that the Levites were to assist the priests in temple functions (6:48). These comments render illegitimate all others who take on worship leadership roles such as offering sacrifices, serving as permanent temple musicians or making atonement for Israel's sins. To be specific, anything akin to Jeroboam's religion, which employed a variety of persons for these tasks (cf. 1 Kings 12:25-33), is denounced. The priestly and levitical roles are considered God-given, since they are described in Moses' law (6:49). As the book proceeds, the worship leaders will grow in significance alongside Moses, David and the prophets.

This section's constant references to previous canonical material marks its agreement with prominent themes found in those texts. Genesis' belief that the Lord is Creator of the heavens, earth, human race and Israel is assumed. Yahweh's deliverance and gift of the land as depicted in Exodus—Joshua are inherent in the genealogies. God's choice of David to receive an eternal kingdom, which is described in 2 Samuel 7:1-17, is repeated. The reasoning behind Israel's demise is the same in 1 Chronicles 5:23-26 as in 2 Kings 17. Ezra—Nehemiah, Haggai, Zechariah and Malachi are echoed in the information about the returning exiles in 9:2-34, a fact that signals the Chronicler's agreement with restoration theology embedded in Deuteronomy 30 and a number of texts in the Prophets.

Deftly, through the use of genealogy as a telescoping device, the author has demonstrated agreement with the canon's conviction that the Lord is Creator, sustainer, covenant maker, judge, giver of land and restorer of the chosen people. Above all, the Lord must rule human history for all these ideas to be correct. No other god is considered part of this rule. No other god is identified as a living entity.

The God Who Chooses David: 1 Chronicles 9:35—29:30

This section continues Chronicles' interaction with other Old Testament books.[9] Primarily it does so by relating information already found in Samuel and Kings, for it focuses on the work of David and Solomon. It also achieves this task by highlighting central characters such as Moses, specific groups such as the Levites, special places such as Jerusalem and the temple, and fundamental theological concepts attributed to Yahweh throughout the Scriptures. All these notions revolve around the person of David, since he is the one to whom the only God chooses to give an eternal covenant.

Two events in David's life are particularly important for grasping the Chronicler's theological purpose in the Davidic accounts. First, the offer of an eternal kingdom demonstrates the Lord's desire to bless David and benefit Israel. Saul's unfaithfulness leads to his dismissal and the termination of his dynasty (9:35—10:14). In contrast, David's heart for Yahweh and desire to build a temple lead the Lord to promise David a never-ending dynasty. This pledge corresponds to 2 Samuel 7:1-17 and inspires prophetic expectations of a Davidic king who will reign in peace (Is 11:1-9), righteousness (Jer 23:1-8), glory (Ezek 34:11-31) and humility (Zech 9:9-10). This promise is also echoed in Davidic psalms such as Psalm 2 and Psalm 110, as well as in the son of man passage in Daniel 7:13-14. Without question the Chronicler views the Davidic covenant as the key not only to Israel's past but to their future as well. There is no way to overestimate the significance of this episode.

Second, David's role in establishing worship and in preparing for the building of the temple reveals the Chronicler's emphasis on proper worship in the place God has chosen.[10] Not only does David collect the materials for the temple (22:2-19; 29:1-9), but he also sets the duties of the Levites (23:1-32), the priests (24:1-31), the musicians (25:1-31) and the gatekeepers (26:1-19). In every possible way, David undergirds the work of worship, thereby proving himself the sort of ideal king described in Moses' initial standards for kings (Deut 17:14-20). His work also establishes the primacy of Jerusalem as the place where sacrifices must be made and the Day of Atonement ceremonies associated with the ark of the covenant observed. Thus the Chronicler agrees with 1 Kings 1—12 that Jerusalem is the one place that God has chosen as a central sanctuary. Jerusalem's sacredeness is intended to ward off idolatry and to fulfill Moses' intentions stated in Deuteronomy 12:1-7.

Though David is the main character who links Chronicles to Samuel, Kings and the Prophets, he is not the only person who does so. In 16:39-40 and 22:11-13 the text mentions the law of the Lord and the law of Moses, both of which refer to the same material.[11] The first passage states that the priests were to teach the law, while the second is part of David's advice to Solomon concerning how to be a faithful leader. Moses is mentioned later in Chronicles (cf. 2 Chron 34:14), so his significance does not cease after this segment. David's adherence to the God-inspired, Mosaic law connects the Chronicler's theology of worship, priesthood and kingship to Exodus, Leviticus and Deuteronomy. Only Mosaic worship is legitimate in God's eyes and in the eyes of the Chronicler.

Canonical views of the Lord permeate these chapters. For instance, after 1 Chronicles 11—15 repeatedly states that God gives David his throne and many victories, in 16:8-36 the Chronicler adapts Psalms 96 and 105—106 in a hymn to God's glory as exhibited through Israel.[12] This psalm confesses that the Lord fulfills covenant promises (16:8-22) and that the Lord is King over the whole earth (16:23-33).[13] It states that Yahweh gave the promised land to Israel to keep faith with Abraham, Isaac and Jacob (16:16-18). Further, it claims that because the Lord is the Creator there is no other god and that the gods of the nations are mere idols (16:26). Yahweh is said to be the judge of all persons, and a righteous judge at that, as well as the only one who can save (16:31-35). Significantly the text calls all nations, not just Israel, to recognize the Lord's greatness and to worship the Creator, who alone is God. Here the Chronicler shows solidarity with the theology of the canonical psalmic tradition by echoing beliefs from passages that are themselves excellent summaries of convictions held by the whole of the Psalter.

David's final exhortations to Solomon summarize this section's theology. He stresses that God has chosen him to lead Israel, Solomon to succeed him and Solomon to build the temple (28:1-10). In language reminiscent of Joshua 1:1-9 he tells Solomon to keep God's commands, for the Lord will never forsake him (28:8, 20). His last prayer for his people is that they recognize God's goodness and sovereignty and that they never cease to seek the Lord (29:10-20). Canonical interpreters know that the nation will indeed stop seeking the Lord, which will in turn lead to their demise. In fact 5:23-26 has already announced this eventuality. The Chronicler realizes, as the Former and Latter Prophets before him do, that Israel's defeats are unnecessary. Their setbacks are the product of theological amnesia, not divine infidelity or incapability, and their restoration depends on the God who has punished them.

The God Who Chooses Solomon to Succeed David and Build the Temple: 2 Chronicles 1—9

According to David's farewell speech, Solomon's rise to power is part of the Lord's election of David (1 Chron 29:5), so Solomon's reign is an extension of the promises made in 1 Chronicles 17. His authority is derived from the promise itself. The work he is given to do is based upon his election, upon the Lord's decision to allow a temple to be built and upon the Lord's ability to gift him for leadership. Thus, due to Yahweh's choice of Solomon, the nation, the dynasty and the king himself will benefit. God's sovereign choice here is saturated in mercy and faithfulness.

God's empowering of Solomon for the ruling of Israel is apparent in 1:1-17. This text, which is a parallel passage to 1 Kings 3:1-15, recounts Solomon's asking the Lord to give him wisdom to govern the people (1:7-10). God is pleased with the request and therefore gives Solomon wisdom, wealth and renown (1:12). Only the Lord can bestow these gifts, for Chronicles and the rest of the canon have already testified that Yahweh rules human events, giving kingdoms to rulers according to his will. The Wisdom literature in the Writings has stated that the Lord alone gives wisdom to those who seek it (cf. Prov 1—9). God's blessing of Solomon in this manner demonstrates Yahweh's ongoing faithfulness to David and the Davidic covenant and to the Israelites, who need strong, God-honoring leadership.

Solomon's most important task is to build the temple, a job the Lord chose him specifically to do (1 Chron 28:10). Details about the temple's construction, dedication and divine blessing take up the bulk of this part of Chronicles (2 Chron 2—7). Once the building is completed, the people bring the ark of the covenant to the house of worship, a ceremony that concludes with the Lord's glory, or presence, filling the temple (5:13-14). God chooses to dwell in this place, a sign that divine approval attends the whole process. Besides giving a physical context for God's presence, the temple bears witness to the nation's high regard for the Lord, serves as the focal point for worship, facilitates obedient worship and stands as a visible symbol of Yahweh's covenant with Israel.[14]

Much of the temple's permanent theological importance is stated in Solomon's dedicatory prayer and the Lord's response to that prayer. Solomon confesses that God is unique among the other so-called gods in the giving of mercy, the keeping of covenant fidelity and the showing of love (6:14-17). He understands that Yahweh must choose to dwell in the temple, since God cannot be contained in any amount of space (6:18-21). Most of all, the king admits that the people will sin, so he asks the Lord to forgive as the nation returns to the worship that the temple represents (6:22-39). He bases his prayer on the Davidic covenant and God's choice of this resting place for divine glory and earnest worship (6:40-42). Solomon counts on the fact that the Lord is powerful, transcendent, immanent, forgiving, all-seeing and willing to answer prayer. God's character is the basis upon which the long-term significance of the temple must rest.

Yahweh's response to the monarch's intercession provides both an interpretative key to the rest of Chronicles and a link to the rest of the canon. Solomon's prayer assumes the relevance of the covenant blessings outlined in Leviticus 26 and Deuteronomy 27—28 and the requirements for covenant renewal explained in Deuteronomy 30:1-10. It takes for granted the fact that Israel's sin will necessitate a redemptive response from God. Yahweh affirms these assumptions in 7:11-14. Israel will be disciplined for unconfessed sin, and God will restore the chosen people if they repent wholeheartedly. In 7:14 God pledges to hear from heaven and heal Israel whenever Israel turns from sin and seeks the Lord. The desire to humble oneself, to pray, to seek the Lord and to repent after falling into sin permeates much of the rest of Chronicles,[15] just as Leviticus 26, Deuteronomy 27—28 and Deuteronomy 30 influence the whole of the Old Testament.

What does it mean for Israel to "seek God"? Walther Eichrodt thinks it means a faith in God that leads the remnant to abase themselves, trust in God's sovereignty and thereby experience the Lord's deliverance in history.[16] Rex Mason adds that seeking God in this way takes special courage.[17] R. L.

Braun suggests that interior seeking must fuel external obedience for true seeking to occur.[18] All these observations are in keeping with the overall flow of Chronicles. Each one stresses that those who please the Lord exhibit an interior change of attitude that results in changed behavior. Israel's future is clearly dependent on this sort of seeking.

The Chronicler ends the description of Solomon's career by noting that his wealth, wisdom and administrative skills brought the king great fame (2 Chron 8—9). Canonical readers may wonder how the account could possibly omit Solomon's idolatry, which is such a large concern in 1 Kings 11. In fact the earlier passage blames the division of the kingdom on this sin. At this point the Chronicler's treatment of Solomon seems even kinder than that of David, since David's shedding of blood and numbering of the Israelites are at least mentioned.

Therefore it is vital to note 10:15, where the text says that the kingdom was divided according to the word of Ahijah the prophet, an oracle canonical interpreters know was uttered against Solomon's sin (cf. 1 Kings 11:1-39). In other words, the author expects that readers know the material in Kings and trusts that the connection between Solomon's sin and the demise of the united kingdom has been made. The Chronicler apparently thinks that the reader will be as canonically literate as he is and will thus be able to connect relevant ideas.

This section has clearly continued several prominent canonical concerns. First, the passage stresses the Davidic covenant, for Solomon's ministry is presented as an extension of his father's reign. God is keeping faith with David. Second, God is also keeping promises made to Abraham, Isaac, Jacob and Moses, since the people are firmly in control of the promised land and have even been able to establish the central sanctuary mentioned in Deuteronomy 12:1-7. Third, God remains as sovereign over history as in the Former Prophets. What Solomon achieves comes as a direct work of the Lord. Fourth, the temple's prominence is in keeping with emphases found in Kings, Ezekiel, Haggai, Zechariah, Malachi and Ezra—Nehemiah. How Israel relates to their God determines how they will fare in history. Fifth, the section reinforces the canon's assertion that a proper response to God begins with an interior faith that creates external obedience. Mere cultic compliance has no more saving value here than it has in the earlier books.

The God Who Chastens and Restores the Chosen People: 2 Chronicles 10—36

Much of the history has been fairly placid to this point. David and Solomon have governed a united Israel that has flourished in the land God has given the chosen people. Election has entailed responsibilities, but the nation and its leaders have been able to respond appropriately to the Lord. All this tranquillity is shattered in the book's final major section, for Israel divides, slides into ever greater sin and finally experiences the consequences that so concern Solomon in his dedicatory prayer. Just as he hoped, though, the Lord's kindness and willingness to forgive are not exhausted by the nation's transgressions. Those who seek the Lord do find forgiveness, personal renewal and the opportunity to lead national restoration. Such individuals are the true remnant of Israel; most of them live in Judah, not Samaria; and it is these persons who receive the most attention in this segment.

Israel's political disintegration and its immediate aftermath are shaped by prophetic words spoken by God-sent messengers. Ahijah states that God will divide the kingdom between Rehoboam, Solomon's son, and Jeroboam, the man who creates a rival state and an alternative religious system (10:15). Shemaiah declares that Yahweh will desert Rehoboam, thus allowing Egypt to defeat him, because the king has deserted the Lord (12:1-5). Though not a prophet, King Abijah uses prophetic language to blast Jeroboam for turning the people to images of pseudogods instead of helping them to trust in the living God (13:1-9). God punishes Jeroboam for this infidelity (13:20-22).

Godly monarchs, inspired prophets and committed priests provide leadership the Chronicler admires in 2 Chronicles 14—20. Two kings, Asa and Jehoshaphat, are the most prominent characters. Both lead reform movements based on the Law and its application to the current situation. Neither man is perfect by any means, but both are spiritual giants compared to their counterparts in northern Israel.

Jehoshaphat's and Asa's careers act as examples of how the kings and the people may please the Lord. As long as idols are rejected, the Law is taught and obeyed, the nation trusts solely in Yahweh, the prophetic word is believed and the priests are faithful in the execution of their God-given duties, the country will flourish as a direct gift from the Lord. This conduct demonstrates real seeking of Yahweh. Negative examples, such as those offered by Jehoram, Ahaziah and Athaliah (21:1—23:11), make this definition of seeking God even plainer, as do the mixed examples of Joash, Amaziah, Uzziah and Jotham (23:12—27:9).

Comparison and contrast continue to mark the Chronicler's account in 2 Chronicles 28—33. Three monarchs, Ahaz, Hezekiah and Manasseh, appear here, with Ahaz acting as a wicked ruler, Hezekiah operating as an almost totally righteous leader and Manasseh demonstrating how wicked kings can repent. Ahaz's wickedness stems from his devotion to idols that he believes will make him powerful, his unwillingness to heed the prophets and his closing of the temple (28:1-27). In other words, he fits the Chronicler's definition of unfaithfulness perfectly. He has no redeeming values and causes the nation to suffer at the hands of the Assyrians, who are depicted as agents of God's wrath (28:19-20). Rather than seek the Lord, he turns to other gods when faced with a crisis. God's chastening is all he can experience.

Hezekiah's reign stands in stark contrast to that of his father, Ahaz. He reopens the temple, reestablishes temple worship, leads the nation in Passover and restores the Levites to their lawful place in worship leadership (29:1—31:19). As a result God makes him successful (31:20-21). It is important to note, however, that this success does not insulate Hezekiah from difficult circumstances, for the Assyrians invade the land, capturing virtually all of Judah except Jerusalem (32:1). Like Asa and Jehoshaphat, Hezekiah must prove his faithfulness in the midst of trying times.

The Assyrian invasion sets the stage for a clear conflict between the canonical worldview and that of other ancient peoples. Assyria believes that the power of a nation's god is proven by the influence and military might of that god's adherents. Thus they declare that other gods have not delivered their enemies from their devastating assaults, so the Lord cannot deliver Israel either (32:9-17). As the Chronicler says, the Assyrians treat the Lord as if the living God were just another idol made by human hands (32:18-19). Hezekiah and the prophet Isaiah pray for the nation, and Yahweh redeems Israel from destruction and then kills the Assyrian ruler who questioned the Lord's power (32:20-23). This episode underscores the Chronicler's conviction that the Lord rules history, reveals the future, warns the faithful about the present, punishes the wicked and blesses the righteous. It also highlights the model of seeking the Lord the author has favored since 2 Chronicles 7:14. Hezekiah, Isaiah and the faithful remnant survive, while Sennacherib pays for his blasphemy with his life.

Unlike Hezekiah, Manasseh comes to serve the Lord only after much idolatry and ignoring of God's prophets (33:1-10). His divinely ordained punishment is administered in brutal fashion by the Assyrians (33:11). Japhet notes that distress may turn someone against the Lord, as in Ahaz's case, or turn a person toward Yahweh. Manasseh's decision to serve God provides readers with a perfect example of how they themselves may restore their own relationship with the Lord.[19] H. G. M. Williamson concurs, noting that Manasseh's repentance is the most extraordinary of its kind in Chronicles and that the theological language employed here indicates that this episode is meant to be an example for others.[20] The Chronicler states that Manasseh seeks God, prays, humbles himself and repents, the very formula for renewal set forth in 7:14.[21] Repentance affects his theology as well, for he finally believes that "the LORD is God" (33:13). Seeking the Lord obviously means seeking only the Lord, for only the Lord is God.

One final notable ruler emerges before a string of forgettable and regrettable monarchs preside over and facilitate the nation's demise. Josiah seeks the Lord while he is still a young man (34:3), which causes him to remove all the images he can discover in his dominion (34:4-7) and motivates him to renovate the temple (34:8-13). In these ways he acts much like Asa, Jehoshaphat and Hezekiah before him. What pushes his reforms even further is the discovery in the temple of the Book of the Law of the Lord given through Moses (34:14-15). Josiah grasps the nation's failure to keep the covenant, a realization that is confirmed by the prophet Huldah (34:16-28). All future activities connected to the reforms, including covenant renewal and the observing of Passover (34:29—35:19), are grounded in both the written and prophetically revealed will of God.

Those who succeed Josiah on the throne neither follow the Lord from early age nor seek God when punished. They reject the prophets' warnings and neglect Moses's law (36:11-16). Like the author of 2 Kings 17, the Chronicler believes that these sins bring the consequences outlined in Leviticus 26 and Deuteronomy 27—28 that Solomon fears in 6:14-42. Babylon destroys Jerusalem, and the nation is exiled for seventy years, just as Jeremiah predicted (35:17-21; cf. Jer 25:9-11; 29:10). Perhaps the most hopeful thing that can be said at this point is that some renewal may occur after the seventy years have ended.

Unlike the book of Kings, Chronicles ends with the exile in Israel's past. Cyrus allows the Jews to return to their homeland after 539 B.C. (36:22-23). So Chronicles concludes where Ezra—Nehemiah begins, but the Chronicler has explained how the nation came to be exiled. Having begun with Adam, the first man, the author concludes with a new beginning for the people of God. The implication is that if Manasseh could seek the Lord, then surely the exiles can do so as well. The covenant has not been revoked. It has just moved through its most drastic means of effecting redemption and creating a remnant. The same God who forgave individuals who had been chastened will also pardon the whole nation if the people will humble themselves, pray, seek the Lord and turn from their sins.

Canonical Synthesis: The Chronicler's Canonical Consciousness

This final section is lengthy and theologically dense and covers nearly four centuries of Israelite history. Thus it has many connections to earlier books, six of which particularly deserve mention. First, this material exhibits a clear canonical consciousness that indicates the Chronicler's awareness of using authoritative works. Of course, 1 Chronicles 1:1—2 Chronicles 9:31 demonstrates the author's familiarity with the Law, the Former Prophets and Ezra—Nehemiah. These chapters underscore the Chronicler's special respect for the book of Kings, for Jeremiah's prophecy and for the Psalms. The

Chronicler shapes the theological emphases in those books to the needs of his history yet remains in agreement with them. Chronicles thereby affirms the authority of the whole of the Old Testament while making its own contribution to that tradition.

Second, the Chronicler's historical theory reveals a clear general agreement with that of the Former and Latter Prophets. Both the Chronicler and the author of Joshua—Kings think the nation's demise resulted from covenant breaking, the worship of other gods and a refusal to heed the prophets, who were agents of mercy sent by God to help the people avoid punishment (2 Kings 17; 2 Chron 36:14-17). Both historians have high regard for the prophetic word, for both cite prophetic oracles as turning points in Israel's past. These convictions are shared by the prophets, especially Isaiah and Jeremiah, both of whom include material that appears in 2 Kings (cf. 2 Kings 18:1—20:19 and Is 36:1—39:8; 2 Kings 24:18—25:30 and Jer 52:1-34). This same perspective is reflected in the historical psalms, such as Psalms 105—106, texts that the Chronicler uses in 1 Chronicles 16:8-36.

Third, the Chronicler's hopes for the future are based on the same notions as those found in Deuteronomy 30:1-10, Daniel 7—12 and 2 Samuel 7:1-17. The book's constant references to seeking the Lord demonstrate faith in Yahweh's desire to forgive and restore the chosen people. Like Daniel, the Chronicler finds assurance in the knowledge that Jeremiah has said the exile will last seventy years and then end. Israel's opportunity to return to Jerusalem after Cyrus's decree proves that the prophetic word has been accurate again and that the faithful may reclaim the promised land. Just as God's covenant with Abraham, Isaac and Jacob has not been revoked, so the eternal covenant with David must continue. The kingdom of the Lord and the kingdom of David cannot be separated (cf. 2 Chron 13:8).[22]

Fourth, the Chronicler's emphasis on retribution for sin is in keeping with the rest of the Old Testament. Since Julius Wellhausen's time,[23] scholars have noted, discussed and many times criticized the Chronicler for supposedly adopting a stereotypical view of history. The Chronicler does believe in divine retribution. Saul (1 Chron 10:13), Hezekiah (2 Chron 32:26), Manasseh (2 Chron 33:10-13) and others suffer for their sins. Jerusalem falls because of idolatry and rejection of the prophets.[24] Still, not every difficulty Israel faces comes as a direct result of sin. Hezekiah's Assyrian crisis proves this point. Raymond Dillard and Japhet correctly conclude that the Lord always offers mercy before sending punishment and that punishment is delayed as long as possible. God intervenes in Israel's history to spare them first but then intervenes with judgment as a last resort. God's punishment is always fair. Even harsh intervention has a redemptive purpose. Thus it is an overstatement to consider the Chronicler's view of retribution rigid and automatic.[25]

Manasseh's story shows that grace is always God's preferred option.

This attitude toward retribution fits the perspective found in the Former Prophets and historical psalms, to be sure. It also coincides with the theory of retribution found in Proverbs and wisdom-oriented psalms such as Psalms 1 and 37. As in Chronicles, the key to assessing the harshness of retribution in these texts must lie in the Lord's revelation of an opportunity to avoid disaster and the Lord's patience with sinners. The very existence of the Wisdom literature provides a warning to the foolish to turn from their stupidity. God has tried to teach the wicked how to change and be blessed. Time has been given for repentance and renewal. None of these books eschews grace for a mechanistic judgment scheme. What punishment that does come is fair. Unjust suffering is another matter that should not be associated with retribution.

Fifth, the Chronicler's opinions on what constitutes the true people of God match much of the rest of the canon. From the beginning, Yahweh has expected obedience that grows out of faith in the Lord's word and the Lord's character. It is faith that causes God to accept Abram in Genesis 15:6 and faith that motivates Abraham to serve Yahweh in Genesis 15:12-21 and 22:1-19. Moses states that love for God and neighbor form the core of acceptable lawkeeping (Lev 19:18; Deut 6:4-9). The writer of 2 Kings 17:13-14 claims that failing to believe the Lord and thus follow the Law led to Israel's destruction. Jeremiah 31:31-34 and Ezekiel 36:16-32 state that the future remnant will have new hearts, while Hosea 4:1 and Micah 6:8 consider knowledge of the Lord and love of mercy keys to obedient covenant behavior. Psalms deals extensively with the interior attitudes necessary to please the Lord, and Job, Proverbs and Ecclesiastes discuss in detail the worldview that results in correct behavior in daily life. All these ideas are certainly akin to the Chronicler's notion of seeking the Lord. Until one seeks the Lord, it is unlikely that one will obey the Lord.

The people of God also display specific commitments to the Lord's plans in history. The remnant stands by God's directions, whether they are to possess the promised land (Num 13—14; Josh 1:1-9), oppose Baalism (1 Kings 17—18), rebuke rulers (Is 7:1-25), preach against corrupt worship (Jer 7:1-15), endure exile by looking to the future (Ezek 33—48) or return to the devastated land of promise (Ezra—Neh; Hag 1—2). Remnant persons embrace God's view of the past, the present and the future. They actualize Yahweh's goals for teaching the world that there is no other god but the Lord. The Chronicler envisions the people of God as individuals from every tribe of Israel who are willing to do God's bidding. Their desire to seek God leads them to obey God. He believes that such persons have existed throughout the history of Israel, even during the era of the divided kingdom.[26]

The Chronicler argues that the remnant keeps worship at the center of their existence. For this goal to be achieved, the priests, Levites, kings and people must adhere to the Law. They must respect the temple and heed the word of the prophets. Keeping worship central entails a communitywide commitment. These principles are supported by previous texts that favor a central sanctuary, demand purity of worship and call for ethical integrity. Leviticus, Deuteronomy, Kings, Isaiah, Jeremiah, Ezekiel, Psalms and Ezra—Nehemiah agree wholeheartedly with these emphases.

Sixth, the Chronicler believes as strongly as any Old Testament author that the Lord is God and there is no other (2 Chron 33:13). All other gods are idols, the works of human hands (2 Chron 32:19). No deity besides Yahweh has any creating or sustaining capability in Chronicles. At the heart of the Chronicler's beliefs on this matter is the notion that Yahweh is the Creator, which means that all other supposed gods are merely idols (1 Chron 16:26). Israel's covenant with God, uniqueness among the nations and future blessing all depend on insisting that this monotheistic principle is true and nonnegotiable.

Conclusion

Chronicles supplies an appropriate conclusion for the Writings and the rest of the canon through its historical awareness, canonical consciousness, sensitivity toward the importance of worship and emphasis on divine retribution. The breadth of the Chronicler's vision, spanning as it does from Adam to the exile, enhances its suitability as a summary book. Its placement at the end of the Writings makes this most diverse of all Old Testament histories a fitting end to the most diverse segment of the Law, the Prophets and the Writings.

The book's historical awareness allows it to encompass viewpoints that range from Genesis to Ezra—Nehemiah. Historical concerns are as evident in portions of the Writings as in the Law and the Prophets, for the historically oriented psalms, Ruth, Esther, Daniel and Ezra—Nehemiah all offer theologies of history that fit earlier parts of the canon. All these texts claim that the Lord rules history. They believe that the flow of history bears out this conviction. They claim that prophetic messages have warned the people of coming events and that these warnings have been proven by subsequent events. These are theological readings of history, but they are not readings oblivious to facts or reality. The authors are convinced that their worldview and theory of history best explain what has and will occur in space and time better than do the notions forwarded by other theorists.

Chronicles' constant citing of earlier texts gives the canon the status of authoritative Scripture. When the Chronicler cites material from the Law, the

Prophets and the Writings, he shows a willingness to accept these passages as true and binding. These citations come from a wide range of genres. Genealogies, narratives, prophecies and psalms are all noted, which at the least implies that by the Chronicler's time no single type of literature was isolated as the only kind of holy writing. Law is obviously the most important part of the canon for the writer, but it is certainly not his sole source of authority.

Sensitivity toward worship pervades every section of Chronicles. The priests, Levites and their vital ministries are highlighted as indispensable keys to national renewal. Through this emphasis, the Chronicler displays solidarity with Leviticus, Deuteronomy, Samuel, Kings, Isaiah, Jeremiah, Ezekiel, Psalms and Ezra—Nehemiah. Worship is considered the main way in which the chosen people maintain their relationship with Yahweh. The Writings are especially important for a canonical understanding of worship because Psalms appears there, but the Writings hardly have a monopoly on this concern.

Divine blessing and retribution have been important in the canon since Genesis 3. With sin came the need for redemptive punishment that removes the guilt of sin without making sin acceptable to the human race. Texts such as Leviticus 26, Numbers 13—14, Deuteronomy 27—28, Judges 1—2, 2 Kings 17, Isaiah 36—39, Jeremiah 34—45 and Ezekiel 1—32 provide perspective for Wisdom books like Job, Proverbs and Ecclesiastes, as well as the Wisdom psalms and narratives such as Ruth and Esther that deal with just and unjust suffering. God has revealed that there are direct causes and effects that undergird human existence. Yahweh has also revealed that obeying the law, heeding prophecies and prophetic histories, applying Wisdom principles and seeking the Lord in worship negate the threats associated with those causes and effects. Yahweh has not hidden the painful reality of unjust suffering in any segment of the canon. Chronicles deals with such pain, though not to the extent that Jeremiah, Job or Ecclesiastes does. Still, the appearance of the full range of ideas connected to retribution links Chronicles to those works that find life's miseries nearly unbearable.

26

The God
of the
Old Testament

A Summary

....

THIS VOLUME BEGAN WITH CERTAIN METHODOLOGICAL ASSERTIONS. IT claimed that the proper starting place for Old Testament theology is the canon, for the text of Scripture itself has been confessed and obeyed by communities of faith from the time of Moses to the present. The text of Scripture claims to be the written word of God and provides the theological positions of its writers. Any other beginning point not only admits the existence of other vital concerns, such as particular theological systems or historical matters, but also certifies the primacy of those concerns.

Further, it was claimed that monotheism provides an appropriate centering theme for examining Old Testament theology, since that notion is fundamental to all other major canonical statements about the Lord. This conviction is accompanied by the belief that God must be the primary focus of theological reflection. Finally, it was argued that biblical theology requires a reading of the Old Testament that allows its discrete witness to emerge so that a proper grasp of its treatment in the New Testament might be gained. The Old Testament has a great deal to contribute to biblical and systematic theology, but that contribution must be collected in proper sequence.

This chapter seeks to summarize the volume's findings and to reassert the validity of these methodological foundations. It does so to build bridges to New Testament and biblical theology and to offer a definition of God's character, a description of God's actions and a sketch of God's people. These elements reveal that the God of the Old Testament is the God of the New Testament as well and that the New Testament writers were correct in stressing themes they derived from their understanding of what they called the Scriptures (2 Tim 3:16-17; 2 Pet 1:21).

The Primacy of the Canon

Several passages demonstrate the validity of beginning theological reflection by stressing the value of the canon as the written word of God. There can be no question that the Law leaves the impression that all that appears there has come through divine revelation. After all, Genesis purports to know what God thinks, how characters feel and what future history holds. Further, Exodus 20—Leviticus 27 constantly claims to have come as a result of what God told Moses, and the text quotes the Lord directly in a straightforward manner. Numbers displays the same omniscient narrative traits as does Genesis, and Deuteronomy divulges its divine origins in ways similar to those in Exodus 20—Leviticus 27. Deuteronomy 32:47 states that the written words of the covenant placed near the ark of the covenant are Israel's life.

Whether one examines the references to Moses' law in the Prophets or notes the indirect assumptions about covenant keeping that pervades those books, it is evident that the Law is considered a normative written, not just oral, record of what the Old Testament writers consider divine revelation. Isaiah 8:19-22 asks the people to look to the Law and testimonies for God's word. Zechariah cites the words of the prophets alongside the Law as coming from God (Zech 7:12). Kings makes consistent reference to the law of Moses (1 Kings 2:1-3; 2 Kings 14:6) and in 2 Kings 17:13 considers both the Law and the words of the prophets God's commands. Jeremiah calls Israel to covenant keeping in Jeremiah 1—10, and Ezekiel cites passages from the Law and earlier prophets in numerous places.

It is just as evident that the prophets believed that they spoke God's words on God's behalf. Their constant claims to quote Yahweh ("thus says the LORD") and their references to divinely induced visions are but two instances of this conscious commitment to saying only what God has told them to say. The writer of the Former Prophets respects the works of the prophets in a manner similar to, if not exactly like, the attitude displayed about the Law.

The Writings confirm the notion that the Law and the Prophets are authoritative writing worthy of acceptance by the remnant. Psalms 19 and 119 are particularly important passages in this regard. Both testify to the purity, perfection, value and binding nature of the Law. Daniel and Ezra—Nehemiah agree but also identify Jeremiah's prophecy of a seventy-year exile as God's will (Dan 9:1; Ezra 1:1). The Chronicler caps the Writings by citing passages from virtually every previous segment of the canon. A decided canonical awareness lends credibility and authority to Chronicles' historical perspective. When the Writings end, a strong sense of what Scripture is has been gained. Not all issues related to the closing of the canon are answered by the text itself, but it is fair to say that the community of faith that existed after the Chronicler had a large and time-tested body of what they considered God's written word.

It is this body of writing that Jesus refers to in Luke 24:44, that Paul mentions in 2 Timothy 3:16-17, that Peter discusses in 1 Peter 1:21 and that John quotes in Revelation. Though allusions to apocryphal books do appear in the New Testament (e.g., Jude 9), there is no indisputable reference to the Apocrypha in which an author claims it has scriptural authority. Thus when the New Testament writers drew exegetical and theological conclusions it was from material in the Law, the Prophets and the Writings and indeed from the Old Testament conceived in that sequence (e.g., Lk 24:44). All evangelism, discipleship and church planting were ordered by what they considered the teachings of God's Word.

The Lord's Character and Actions

From the first verse of Genesis, the canon defines the Lord by character traits and by deeds accomplished. In the Law, the Lord is depicted initially as unaided Creator of the heavens and earth and all they contain (Gen 1—2). God is responsible for human beings, animals and the plants of the ground. Thus it is important to stress that in Genesis 3—50 Yahweh sustains all that has been created. God creates, makes promises to, sets standards for, judges, forgives and protects such diverse individuals as Adam, Eve, Cain, Abraham, Sarah, Lot, Ishmael, Isaac, Jacob, Esau, Leah, Rachel and Joseph. All these activities flow from the Lord's role as Creator. After Genesis 12:1-9 the primary focus of the Law is the nation God has created.

Exodus—Deuteronomy highlights the only God's role as redeemer, covenant maker, Holy One, judge and giver of the gift of land to the Israelites. Most of these functions are prefigured in Genesis. Still, the text develops the many ways in which the Lord works in history. The text also begins to make definitive judgments about Yahweh's character, such as that the Lord is merciful, gracious, patient, rich in goodness and truth, and fair in judgment (Ex 34:6-7). God is called holy (Lev 11:44) and the only living God (Deut 32:39). The canon clearly attempts to unite presentation of action and definitional statements, not pit them against one another.

Joshua—Malachi portrays Yahweh as the Lord of history, whether that history is past, present or future. God is the One who gives Israel the land, the One who sets up and topples kingdoms, the One who states what the future holds. As Lord of history, Yahweh decides how people must treat one another and how they must worship their Creator. When Israel breaks covenant with the Creator, they are punished, and the same happens when the nations, who are as much Yahweh's creation as is Israel, abuse one another and ignore their Creator (cf. Is 13—23; Jer 46—51; Ezek 1—32; Amos 1—2). At the same time Yahweh stands ready to forgive all who repent. Judgment is intended to purify the remnant, who will inherit the kingdom of God (cf. Is 11:1-10; 65—66; Jer 31—32; Ezek 33—48; Zeph 3:8-20), not to leave the human race with no hope or to unleash indiscriminate divine wrath. God is never angry unfairly or for no reason, and Yahweh is just as much healer as judge.

In these books, the fact that the Lord alone is God means that the coming Savior is one sent from God (2 Sam 7:1-17; Is 7:14; 11:1-10; 42:1-4; 49:1-6; 52:13—53:12; Jer 23:1-8), even one who is said to be God (Is 9:6-7). It also means that Israel and the nations must turn to the Lord alone for salvation (Is 40—48). Idolatry and the supposed existence of other gods are not only disputed but also lampooned as sheer folly, betraying an inability to think cogently (Is 44:9-20; Jer 10:1-25). Monotheism means that Yahweh alone will spare or judge all creation (Ezek 33—48), for no one else has the right to do so.

The Writings refine and reinforce the primary definitional notions found in the Law and the Prophets. Israelite worship celebrates God's position as creator, redeemer, judge and healer. Wisdom literature bases its conclusions on the revealed wisdom offered by a wise God. Narratives confess that Yahweh aids women like Esther and Ruth as well as men like Daniel, Ezra and Nehemiah. Crucial texts, most notably Psalm 90, continue to assert that Yahweh is timeless, powerful, wrathful, willing to hear prayers and glad to forgive. The promises made to Abraham and David remain valid, and Israel's future is still dependent on the fulfillment of those pledges.

By the end of the canon God's character and activities have been established over two millennia of datable human existence and over an even longer period of unchartable time that stretches back to creation. They have been depicted in narrative, poetry, prophecy and apocalyptic materials. Along the way, God's personality grows more understandable yet more unfathomable at the same time. Each new revelation leads to the knowledge that human thought cannot exhaust the revealed nature of the Creator, sustainer, redeemer, covenant maker, ruler, judge and healer. Still, an understandable consistency undergirds the whole canonical description of Yahweh: the Lord is God, and there is no other. From this foundational concept all other meaningful statements proceed.

New Testament writers never question the validity of the thesis of one God, though they, like their Old Testament counterparts, often minister to persons who hold a polytheistic worldview. Jesus is able to assume a monotheistic consensus in his ministry, though Paul does not have this theological luxury (cf. Acts 14:8-18). The Gospels, Paul's epistles and Hebrews link Jesus to the creation, thus making him one with the only God (Jn 1:1-18; Col 1:9-18; Heb 1:8-12). Jesus himself claims to be the "I AM" of Exodus 3:14, which equates him with the God of the exodus and the Sinai covenant who allows no rivals (Jn 8:48-59). Matthew and Luke declare Jesus to be the son of David through a selective use of genealogies akin to that of the Chronicler, and Mark designates Jesus as the son of man, phraseology that could only remind readers of Daniel 7:13-14. In this way the New Testament confesses Jesus to be the Son of God, in fulfillment of Psalm 2, and God, in fulfillment of Isaiah 9:6-7. All these designations are dependent on the notions that there is one God who has promised a Savior, that Jesus is that Savior and that Jesus is God.

The People of God

Every one of the preceding ideas affects the Old Testament's definition of God's people. For instance, God's revealed, written word is compiled by God's people. There would be no sacred text unless the Lord chose to convey understandable ideas in human language through persons who believe in the one God. Also, the people of God are the recipients of much, though not all, of the divine activity depicted in the sacred writings. Further, the people of God, the remnant, are the persons through whom Yahweh has decided to mediate truth to the entire created world. Thus a definition of God's people is a crucial theological element and one that obviously interested the New Testament writers a great deal.

The definition of God's people gradually shifts in the Law, though certain principles guide the process throughout. In Genesis 1—11, the people of God are first of all the initial human beings, who have a faith relationship with the Lord that leads them to obey divine prohibitions (Gen 2:1-25). After Genesis 3, however, the human population quickly divides into two groups, those who serve the Lord and those who do not. The account of Cain's and Abel's sacrifices starts this schism, and by Genesis 6:5 God's faithful ones have shrunk to one family, which is a small remnant indeed. Abraham's election and ministry, as well as the lives of his sons and grandsons, demonstrate how the Lord works through a remnant that believes covenantal promises and worships only the God who made those pledges. Individuals like Melchizedek (Gen 14:18-20) prove that membership in the people of God does not depend on genetic linkage to Abraham. Rather the God who has created all persons relates to a multinational remnant.

Though arrangements are made for non-Israelites to be part of God's people in Exodus—Deuteronomy, the text's focus is squarely on how Israel may become God's holy nation (Ex 19:5-6). Abraham's descendants are considered Yahweh's people as they trust the Lord, love him with all their hearts and are thereby able to keep the covenant first offered at Sinai and then renewed on the east side of the Jordan River. As the Lord's people, they are promised land, relationship and blessing as they remain faithful to God (Lev 26; Deut 27—28). Their existence is one way in which the Lord's promise to bless all nations through Abraham will be fulfilled (Gen 12:1-9).

Israel's failure to live up to the faith, love and obedience principles are chronicled in painful detail in the Prophets. This failure leads the Lord to present a new plan for the future. This blueprint is based on the covenantal promises already in place yet branches out into new areas. God has not cast off Israel. God decides to offer David an eternal covenant (2 Sam 7:1-17), which means that God's people must always be ruled by a Davidic heir. The prophets uniformly depict this ruler as one whose kingdom is flawless and ongoing (Is 9:1-7; Jer 23:1-8), one whose character is pure and one whose rule is God-given (Ps 2; Dan 7:13-14).

This Davidic king will govern a new sort of people of God. Jeremiah 31:31-34 states that this people will enter into a new covenant with Yahweh and will all know the Lord. In effect there will be no remnant within the covenant group, as is the case in Jeremiah's era, for those considered covenant bearers will all be persons of faith. Ezekiel adds that the Lord will create this new group by a direct invasion of God's Spirit in the hearts of the people (Ezek 36:22-32) that will produce within them a new heart. Taken together, Jeremiah's and Ezekiel's comments portray the future people of God as being faithful individuals created and empowered by the Spirit of God. Both prophets believe the new covenant people will enjoy the strong leadership of the Davidic ruler (Jer 33:14-18; Ezek 36:22-32). Zephaniah 3:8-20 indicates that this new people will come from a variety of nations. What emerges is a portrait of a people serving the Lord under the authority of the Davidic ruler, believing in the Lord, being empowered by the Lord and consisting of individuals from all the nations created by the Lord. In this way all promises made to Abraham, Israel and David are kept, and God's love for the whole creation is manifested.

It must be noted that certain elements concerning the people of God in the Writings could be and were misunderstood. Esther's joy in the defeat of Gentile opponents, Ezra's dismissal of foreign wives and Chronicles' emphasis on ritual purity are just three examples of such texts. Still, it must also be noted that Ruth is accepted into the people of God, that the psalms confess the universal rule of the coming Davidic king and that Daniel's God is at least taken seriously in Babylonian circles. By Jesus' time many Jews believed that to be the people of God Abraham's ancestors needed to remain separate not just in matters of faith but in all cultural matters as well. This exclusivistic tendency has been discussed in great length other places and will not be repeated here. It is sufficient here to state that Ezra, Esther and Chronicles do not criticize the inclusion of persons who believe in the one God, embrace Mosaic principles and long for the renewal that will come through the Davidic heir. Those books call for the exclusion of idolaters and the defeat of genocidal maniacs. The inclusion of foreigners in several texts in the Writings indicates that the problem is not with the fact that some persons are Gentiles but with what those Gentiles believe and practice.

These tensions and possibilities also mark the New Testament passages that deal with the definition of the people of God. To highlight the Davidic and Abrahamic covenants and to stress Jesus' role as Savior of all nations, Matthew and Luke include genealogies traced back to Abraham and Adam respectively (Mt 1:1-17; Lk 3:23-38). Matthew then proceeds to portray Jesus as the one promised to Israel in the Old Testament, while Luke—Acts describes the expansion of Christianity from its inception through its spread to both Jews and Gentiles throughout the Roman Empire. Paul's life and epistles are in large part driven by the conviction that God's people cannot be defined by race, gender, economic status or nationality (cf. Rom 2:28). Indeed Paul claims that all who have faith in Jesus Christ are God's people, Abraham's true children (Gal 3:26-29). At the same time Paul thinks the Jews continue to have a special place in God's plans and asserts that Gentiles could not have known about Christ without the ministry of faithful Jews (Rom 9—11).

Paul's theology of the people of God is driven by his beliefs about the Spirit and the persons with whom God makes a new covenant. Second Corinthians 3:1-6 is an especially important passage for discerning Paul's approach to these issues. In 3:3 he refers to Ezekiel 11:19 when he states that Christ has been written on the Corinthians' hearts through the agency of the Holy Spirit. Further, in 3:6 Paul asserts that he is a minister of the new covenant, a clear reference to Jeremiah 31:31-34, and that this ministry of the Spirit gives the Corinthians life. To seek salvation from any other source than Christ's implantation upon the heart through the work of the Holy Spirit is futile. For Paul, the law was glorious and remains glorious as it convinces people of their sin, but to hope for salvation through keeping its standards is the way to death (3:7-11). Paul argues in Romans 9:31-32 that faith has always been the means by which one kept the law, not that keeping the law engendered faith.

Paul's vision of a multinational, multiracial, biblically grounded people of God is shared by John, especially in Revelation. In his apocalypse, John addresses churches that had Gentile members (Rev 1—3) and envisions a great multitude of believers from all races and lands standing before God's throne (7:9-17). At the end of Revelation, Christ is declared King of kings and Lord of lords (19:11-16) and is described as the One to whom the kingdom of God has been given (20:1-5). Reigning with him are the people of God, who have sung the victory song of Moses (15:1-4; cf. Ex 15:1-18) and who have confessed that God is the Creator and that Jesus is the Lamb of God. The fact that they will reign with the One to whom the kingdom has been given coincides with the promises made to the remnant in Daniel 7:18-27. There can be no question that John thinks that the future people of God depicted in the Old Testament are the Christians of his day and all subsequent eras.

John, Luke and Paul agree, then, on certain key theological elements, all of which they derive from the Scriptures. They think the "coming days" mentioned by the prophets will bring a new covenant accompanied by the emergence of the Davidic king predicted in numerous passages. They are convinced that the Spirit of God must act on the hearts of human beings in order to create the new people of God. Each believes that Jews will be part of the people of God but that the new remnant will consist of persons from the whole of God's created world. Based on this reading of the Old Testament, they conclude that Jesus is the promised one, that the Spirit has convinced Christians of this fact and that persons from many nations have become part of the people of God. They believe that Christ's work has begun the "coming days" the prophets expected and that final judgment will some day conclude human history. Their reading of the Old Testament data brings them to these assertions, and their reading is so careful that if their convictions about Jesus were wrong, one would at least have to say that their expectations were correct.

Conclusion

These comments in no way exhaust the linkages between the Old Testament theology charted in this volume and the New Testament. Nor by any means have all major implications of Old and New Testament theology been mentioned. Many doctrinal and ethical matters have hardly been broached. Still, the connections that have been made indicate that a true biblical theology exists and needs to be pursued in more detail along canonical, monotheistic, faith-oriented and integrative lines. Certainly the apostles thought they had done so. Thus current theologians need to discern why they came to this conclusion and state anew the scriptural elements of belief in the Lord, who alone is God.

If biblical theologians are to be successful in this task they must pay special attention to the Old Testament canon. Just as it is quite difficult to build a complete doctrine of the Trinity or of the Son of God on the Old Testament alone, so it is exceedingly hard to construct an adequate doctrine of God founded solely on New Testament passages. Without question the New Testament confesses monotheism, the fact that the Lord is the Creator, the notion that God is creating a holy people and that the Lord is sovereign and timeless. Many of the reasons for these confessions, however, are assumed from the Old Testament, not proven by extensive analysis. Those who do not know the Old Testament canon are therefore more vulnerable to unbiblical definitions of God than are those who do. Only serious attention to the Old Testament's theoretical, historical and experientially based statements about the Lord can render a full and certain theology. Anything less rests on a foundation weaker than the one the New Testament writers themselves considered safe.

Appendix

Old Testament Theology
Since 1993

. . . .

As the preface to this volume indicated, the primary research for this work stops at 1993. This fact is especially true for single or multivolume projects devoted specifically to the whole of Old Testament theology. One reason for this choice is that academic publishing continues unabated while one writes a scholarly book, which means that without some stopping place a work like this one could scarcely ever be finished. Another reason is that volumes that appear after one has written the bulk of a manuscript cannot be fairly integrated into the body of an argument without appearing forced. Subsequent statements are needed to be fair to their influence.

At the same time, several significant works have been published since 1993. Some of these will undoubtedly be influential for years to come. Therefore this appendix is offered as a means of noting and assessing briefly certain volumes that could have helped this book's discussion. Some would have acted as dialogue partners. Others would have provided evidence for the main currents of my argument, while others would have argued against my ideas. Each work either continues time-honored ways of approaching Old Testament theology, adapts those means in some way or offers radically new ways of analyzing the topic. Other works no doubt deserve mention but will not be covered. Only studies devoted to the whole of Old Testament theology or to theories for examining Old Testament theology will be noted. Theologically oriented commentaries and articles, for example, will not be discussed.

Single-theme approaches to Old Testament theology have played a huge role in the discipline since Walther Eichrodt's epoch-making study of covenant. Horst Dietrich Preuss's *Old Testament Theology* (two volumes) continues this tradition by using election as the Old Testament's central theme.[1] Preuss's magnum opus appeared in Germany in 1991-1992, so these volumes should have been included from the start. Their appearance in English in the prestigious Old Testament Library series in 1995-1996 marked the study as an important contribution to both German-speaking and English-speaking audiences.

Preuss is very clear about his aims, purposes and methodology. Having surveyed the history of the discipline, he sets forth five underlying presuppositions. First, he does not intend to write a history of Israelite religion, "but rather a systematically oriented and structured theology of the Old Testament."[2] Second, a theology of the Old Testament "ought to clarify the place of the Old Testament within a comprehensive theology."[3] It should help solve current hermeneutical and ethical questions. Third, Old Testament theology ought to be systematic "because the Old Testament in the final analysis probably does have a center."[4] Fourth, an Old Testament theology ought to focus upon what the text says about God. At this point he agrees wholeheartedly with Walther Zimmerli.[5] Fifth, the systematic approach must set forth the material in as comprehensive a fashion as possible.[6]

Arguing that the Old Testament witnesses more to God's activity than to God's nature, Preuss selects the Lord's activity in election as the central theme that best accomplishes the goals of his presuppositions.[7] From this base, in the first volume he proceeds to chart the Old Testament's accounts of divine election, the obligations of those God elects, the names the Old Testament reveals for the God who elects and the world of worship. The second volume undertakes a study of election in the Old Testament canon and then moves to pertinent issues such as ethics, worship, eschatology and the relationship of Israel to the nations. In every chapter Preuss refers extensively to the major works in the field.

Preuss's effort may prove to be the last of the great single-theme theologies to come from Germany. As he notes in his introductory chapter, many scholars wonder aloud these days if it is possible to write a comprehensive Old Testament theology, and few dare to make the effort to do so.[8] It is also true that scholarship is moving away from arguing for a specific single theme that unites the Old Testament. Some authors are questioning the advisability of claiming that the Old Testament is a unity. Therefore it seems unlikely that such magisterial volumes will appear in the next generation.

This reality is sad on three counts. First, as I argued in the first chapter, Old Testament theology needs centering themes to keep the discipline from descending into unnecessary fragmentation. Second, single-theme approaches allow authors to discuss issues related to the central theme in a coherent manner. Third, single-theme approaches challenge the author to attempt to account for the whole of Old Testament theology, a task that best allows the opportunity for the writing of biblical theology to emerge.

Preuss's work demonstrates the strengths and weaknesses of the single-theme method. The basic strengths are noted in the preceding paragraph. It must be stated that Preuss's chosen theme is a vital, centering theme in the text and is one that allows him to stress the character of God as the major point of Old Testament theology. Exposure to his conclusions could have bolstered my statements on election and might have aided a clearer explication of how the one God operates within history. Without question Preuss is an able proponent of the single-theme methodology.

The greatest weakness is that Preuss locates revelation outside the text and in a manner that undermines his arguments for unity. He writes that

> we certainly do not have before us in the Old Testament God's revelation as such; rather, we have testimonies to this revelation and the various responses to them. . . . Even so, this testimony continues to be altered and to allow for new interpretations grounded in the experiences of later witnesses that evoke once more a response.[9]

This approach to revelation does not do justice to the text's claims about being the very words of God, which in turn undermines the text's authority in the ethical and theological areas Preuss rightly highlights. His allusions to later witnesses that differ from earlier witnesses on the one hand simply states how passages are used and reused in the canonical process. On the other hand, without some strong emphasis on the normative nature of revelation his comments can be used to support the conclusion that there are numerous competing voices in the Old Testament, a subject to which I will return.

Three works devoted primarily to methodology underscore the theoretical ferment Preuss mentions. In *The Collapse of History: Reconstructing Old Testament Theology* (1994), Leo G. Perdue argues that the time has come for a new paradigm for Old Testament theology. At the outset of his book Perdue claims that history can no longer be the organizing principle for the discipline, since theological, cultural and philosophical currents now dispute its centrality.[10] After analyzing the history and present condition of the field, Perdue comments correctly that there is room for new approaches to the subject. He then suggests four stages for Old Testament theology. First, the meaning of the text must be extracted. This stage particularly requires literary sensitivity.[11] Second, the text's multiple themes and ideas must be unpacked so that the Old Testament's "multiple theologies" may become known.[12] It is important to recognize that at this point Perdue parts with those who hold to the necessity of determining the Old Testament's unity. Rather he seeks to uncover the canon's inherent multiplicity. Third, it is valuable to examine how texts have been interpreted throughout the centuries. Fourth, past interpretations need to be correlated with current ethical, theological and cultural concerns.

Some elements of Perdue's methodology are consistent with those of several earlier writers. For example, he believes that the text must be explicated in a way that makes it relevant to the contemporary world, and he claims that examining the text itself is the chief means of discovering Old Testament theology. He also demonstrates a healthy respect for the discipline's great past interpreters. Just as clearly Perdue calls for a new day in Old Testament theology. It is time, he believes, for scholars to admit that multiple, possibly conflicting, theologies exist in the text. Therefore it is best to describe these differing theologies without necessarily feeling the need to unite them into a whole.

Perdue is representative of other scholars presently at work in the field, for he models the growing emphasis on pluralism in biblical studies as a whole. Postmodernists and postliberals are pressing the notion that there are many competing voices in the Bible and that it is impossible to consider one more appropriate or divinely revealed than another. While this volume has sought to assert the unity of the Old Testament text, I have not hidden the diversity within that unity. It is not true that Moses, Jeremiah and the Chronicler all say the same thing. Still, their shared emphasis on monotheism indicates that they believe they are describing the many character traits of the one God who truly exists, which more than implies that as the canon develops its authors consciously work toward a multifaceted presentation of the same deity. Similarly the canon uniformly considers Israel the elect people and deals with subjects related to Israel based on this premise. Again, the biblical authors do not all say the same things about Israel, but this fact hardly sanctions the conclusion that competing theologies are evidenced in the text.

The second methodological work is John Sailhamer's *Introduction to Old Testament Theology: A Canonical Approach* (1995). Sailhamer's work is the first evangelical proposal for utilizing a canonical approach to Old Testament theology. In fact, despite Brevard Childs's extensive writings, it is the first comprehensive theoretical statement of its kind by any expert. Of all the works published since 1993, this one would have helped sharpen and shape my own methodology more than any other.

Based on his understanding of the history of the discipline, Sailhamer concludes that four basic issues need to be addressed in order to establish a hermeneutical base for Old Testament theology. First, one must determine whether Old Testament theology ought to focus on text or event. In choosing the former option, Sailhamer places himself firmly in the evangelical tradition of considering the written text the word of God and of attempting to recapture the author's intention through painstaking exegesis. In doing so he distinguishes between the text's prehistory, its interpretation and experiences based upon it.[13] He argues, "It is the written text as we have it in its final form that is inspired and useful for instruction. It is the message of this text that is the locus of revelation."[14] This affirmation places Old Testament theology in the position of examining the text that exists rather than attempting to reconstruct events behind the text.

Second, Sailhamer asserts that theologians must decide between traditional critical approaches such as source and form criticism and some form of canonical criticism. Again the distinction Sailhamer pinpoints is between a theological methodology that stresses the received text and one that emphasizes details reconstructed from theoretical data behind the text.[15] As could be expected from his discussion of text/event, he opts for a canonical approach.[16]

Third, Sailhamer states that Old Testament theology must be either descriptive or confessional. After a careful analysis of the benefits and dangers of each category, he concludes that "an OT theology for the Christian is necessarily confessional."[17] This stance differs from what Sailhamer considers a standard, sheerly descriptive historical-critical position, which purports to "maintain the same objectivity that would be expected in writing about other religious documents. There should be no attempt to evaluate the truthfulness of the contents of OT theology."[18] Truth is not the issue in this viewpoint: "objectivity" that refuses to make decisions about truth and error is paramount.

Numerous historical-critical scholars have stated that the Old Testament is authoritative and true, though their definitions of *true* have varied. John Bright, Childs, Eichrodt, T. C. Vriezen and Zimmerli believe that a totally descriptive approach to Old Testament theology is inadequate, a point Sailhamer concedes.[19] Still, Sailhamer is correct to assert that the Old Testament itself claims to be more than an optional means of understanding and serving God. Its emphasis on monotheism makes that conclusion impossible, as does its emphasis on God's revelation of the Scriptures as the only such written revelation that carries the Lord's approval. The text itself calls on its readers to adopt its view of God, history and the future.

Fourth, Sailhamer addresses the much-discussed matter of whether Old Testament theology ought to follow a diachronic or synchronic format. He concludes that each type of analysis could be used to good effect. The issue is not which is the only way to analyze Old Testament theology but how well either type fits the system the theologian uses.[20] Still, for his own purposes, he chooses the diachronic approach so that the Old Testament can be read "in terms of each of its parts rather than attempting to view it as a whole."[21] This choice is in keeping with his other three main points, each of which focuses upon the structural wholeness of the Old Testament canon without losing sight of its historical integrity.

In his proposal for a canonical theology, Sailhamer states that Old Testament theology ought to be text-based, canon-oriented, confessional and diachronic. For these goals to be reached the exegete must utilize historical data and intertextual and contextual connections between passages. The canonical theologian must grasp the compositional strategies inherent in the canonical books and should seek the original author's intended meaning for each passage.[22] Sailhamer offers some samples of what such a theology might look like, but the real test of his methodology will come when he publishes his projected volume on Old Testament theology proper.

Sailhamer's work is thorough, detailed, even painstaking. It sets a high standard for methodological works in the field, whether those works are penned by an evangelical or nonevangelical scholar. This volume parallels my own in its insistence on the necessity of analyzing the canonical text, of stressing the unity of Scripture, of linking history and canonical sequence and of affirming the authoritative nature of the biblical text. Had it existed when the bulk of my writing was done it would have shored up several gaps in my methodological statements. Sailhamer conceives of the actual writing of theology differently than I do, but specific instances of these disagreements have been worked out only in personal discussions so far. I eagerly await his Old Testament theology.

Another volume dedicated primarily to method published in 1995 was Rolf Knierim's *The Task of Old Testament Theology: Substance, Method and Cases*.[23] This innovative work appeared near the end of Knierim's distinguished career, during which he influenced many significant Old Testament thinkers.[24] One of the interesting factors in Knierim's volume is its inclusion of responses to his work by Walter Harrelson, W. Sibley Towner and Roland Murphy. This format gives the book the feel of a seminar or section of the Society of Biblical Literature, which allows readers to gain instant access to what selected experts think of Knierim's claims. Knierim proposes a methodology for Old Testament theology and then attempts to provide case studies to illustrate how the theory may be applied to the text. Thus Knierim does not attempt a complete Old Testament theology, but he does give a good sense of how that theology might operate.

Knierim's methodology is based on two premises and unfolds in eleven parts, none of which can be developed in detail here. Having begun his book by asserting that the Old Testament "contains a plurality of theologies,"[25] Knierim offers two basic principles: there is a need to "discern kinds and degrees of quantitative and qualitative relationships among the Old Testament's theologies," and there is a need to discern the Old Testament's fundamental aspect, a decision that "amounts to the discernment of a canon in and for the canon."[26] In other words, he believes the goal of his methodology is to find an appropriate way to link the various theologies inherent in the Old Testament. This interest in unity separates him from authors who argue that there is no way to unite the canon's disparate theologies without a biased preference for one theology against another.

In seeking this unity, Knierim primarily states what a methodology should not be. In doing so he disagrees with several earlier scholars. For instance, he writes that Old Testament theology should not seek a unifying principle that excludes all others, be based on "methodological antinomies" such as concept versus story, use traditional systematic theology categories to frame its arguments or be descriptive or confessional.[27] Instead it ought to be systematic in the sense that categories drawn from the Old Testament itself that are especially useful for uniting the canon's various parts ought to be highlighted.[28] Further, Old Testament theology should not choose one segment of the canon's historical development over another as the key era for grasping its theological claims. Neither should this methodology ignore the social setting of the Old Testament, consider the Old Testament's ongoing usage as a vantage point from which to begin analysis, lean upon charismatic elements in interpretation, think that this methodology could not also be applied to other ancient religions, fail to attempt to link the Old and New Testaments or suppose that comprehensive volumes on Old Testament theology are the only sort of books that are helpful to the discipline.[29] He concludes that each of these details must contribute to a pluralistic presentation that revolves around the Lord's universal dominion.[30] This dominion is predicated on the Old Testament's insistence that Yahweh is the Creator, the one and only God,[31] and underscores the fact that the Lord rules this dominion in righteousness and justice.

Knierim believes that the day is gone when scholarly consensus can be built. Rather the day has come when a variety of methodological initiatives are needed. At the same time Knierim settles upon a foundational theme that offers linkage to commonly discussed notions such as revelation, hope, land, justice, the nations, and others. Thus it is not the themes he chooses that separate him from other writers. Instead his straightforward call for methodological pluralism sets him apart.

Knierim's volume would have helped my analysis in three specific ways. First, his insistence on creation as a primary principle in Old Testament theology would have added new horizons to my discussions of history, world order and justice. Second, his emphasis on monotheism as the underlying principle for God's dominion over and care for the earth could have challenged me to include canonical data on issues related to human stewardship over creation. Third, taking his insistence on justice and right-eousness as key components of Yahweh's nature more seriously would probably have improved my statements on the canon's demands for social renewal. Knierim's whole project challenges interpreters to stress the Bible's claims upon contemporary life. Old Testament theology can and should be considered carefully when theologically motivated ethics are discussed.

Though Knierim's book has much to commend it, at the same time it shares many of the problems of earlier works. Knierim takes the Old Testament seriously as Scripture, to be sure, yet does not specifically locate divine authority in the text. He believes the final form of the canon is the focal point of Old Testament theology, but his belief in the existence of competing theologies that must be united by some external hermeneutical principle does not allow the canon to be normative. One is left with the impression that he may have chosen a compelling theme to unite theological analysis at the expense of other compelling notions without sufficient reason.

Walter Brueggemann's *Theology of the Old Testament: Testimony, Dispute, Advocacy* (1997) illustrates the difficulties in Knierim's methodology. Brueg-gemann argues that the current situation is that we are in an era of tremendous epistemological change.[32] Earlier generations sought methodological certi-tude, but such certitude is not possible, especially in a postmodern age. Not even canonical, Jewish, feminist or other nontraditional means of reading the text provide sufficient diversity for the theological task, however well formulated they may be.[33] Brueggemann writes,

> A rendering of the text that is faithful to its polyphonic character is what is now required, centered enough for its first reading community, which trusts its coherent grammar and its reliable cadences; open enough to be compelling for its second listening community, which may be drawn to its truthfulness but is fearful of any authoritarian closure or reductionism.[34]

Like Knierim, Brueggemann cites the need for pluralism in interpretation. Unlike Knierim, Brueggemann refuses to settle upon specific principles under which all other themes must be placed. To do so would be reductionism or authoritarian closure. With no fixed locus of authority, Brueggemann's position may make as much sense as Knierim's, whether one likes it or not.

Brueggemann's concern is to avoid theology that is specifically church-based or Christian, enveloped in certitude or reductionism, devoted to the New Testament's supersession of the Old Testament or based upon power politics in interpretation. He thinks that too often Old Testament theology has been anti-Semitic or nearly so in the past and that it has too often settled upon interpretations that close off other possibilities. The cure for this situation is to focus upon the text in a way that allows its many theological perspectives to coexist peacefully even though they do not agree in many respects. It is interesting that Brueggemann's open approach has no place for evangelical writings, perhaps because they are too committed to certitude to be acceptable.

Brueggemann's analysis of the Old Testament is consistent with his methodological presuppositions. He carefully details Israel's basic testimony of God's greatness and stability.[35] Next, he explains "Israel's countertestimony," which focuses upon God's hiddenness and the ambiguity in the Lord's character.[36] Then he turns to Israel's testimony about their relationship to the Lord and finally to Israel's testimony about how they have and have not lived according to the requirements of that relationship.[37] As is true of his other books, Brueggemann's analysis of the text's claims are often brilliantly stated. His comments upon the text's propositional statements are extraordinary. Many of his comments would have served as support for my own, and others would have forced me to expand my comments.

As could be expected, where I differ markedly from Brueggemann is in methodological presuppositions, especially those that relate to the normativeness of the biblical text. It is striking that in every segment of the text, in every testimony Brueggemann mentions, the text itself stresses the normative nature of Scripture. Within the biblical narrative stands one living God who speaks and reveals to human beings. In the narrative these words are offered as divine authority, not as ideas that may be passed over if they make the reader "fearful of any authoritarian closure or reductionism."[38] Many clear statements in the text are at least as closure-oriented as any interpretation of those passages. It is as prejudicial to excuse the text's ubiquitous claims for authority as it is to assert the relevance of those claims. If these passages that stress closure and certitude are excluded, then the text has been read in a manner foreign to its original community's understanding and in a way that leaves its second community with themselves as final authorities over its claims.

I also differ with Brueggemann's assessment of the canon's portrayal of God. Given the fact that the Old Testament never claims to describe any God but Yahweh, it seems appropriate to argue that the text explains various elements of the one God's personality. Therefore these different descriptions should not be interpreted as competing voices or theologies but as complementary statements about the same character. It is important to note that many of the same supposedly differing components of God's character appear nearly side by side in the same passage, which further indicates that a diverse presentation of the same God is offered, not a conflicting portrayal of God.

There can be no doubt that Brueggemann's volume will be much discussed and influential. It will serve as a model for those committed to postmodern and postliberal pluralistic readings of the Old Testament. For this very reason it will also be opposed by those who consider the canonical text the unified, coherent and authoritative word of God. Those who disagree with Brueggemann may be guilty of using the text for their own ends, but Brueggemann may beware lest his exclusion of those he considers authoritarian and reductionistic becomes merely a means to accomplish his own ends.

Christopher Seitz's arguments for the authority and coherence of the final canonical form of the Old Testament text in *Word Without End: The Old Testament as Abiding Theological Witness* (1998) differ with Brueggemann's conclusions.[39] Though it is not a complete Old Testament theology, this volume may well serve as a programmatic volume for canonical critics. In many ways Seitz is closer to Sailhamer's theories than to Brueggemann's, though he does not share Sailhamer's convictions about the inspiration of Scripture. A former colleague of Childs, Seitz is committed to a canonical approach to the text that treats the Old Testament as an abiding witness, as a bridge to biblical theology and as a significant source for preaching and teaching in the church.

Seitz divides his essays into three distinct sections. First, he establishes his approach to biblical theology.[40] Second, he presents exegetical studies that model the connection between interpretation and theology.[41] Third, he addresses practical matters to demonstrate that exegesis and theology can make an important contribution to the work of the church.[42] He contends that the church will be impoverished if they are neglected. This full-orbed presentation is an appropriate methodology for explaining Old Testament theology to the church.

Perhaps the first section is the most significant of the three at this point in the history of Old Testament theology. In these chapters Seitz sets forth his conviction that Old Testament theology for the church must necessarily entail attempts to link the Testaments. Beginning his specific comments on biblical theology with an analysis of Gerhard von Rad's work, Seitz argues that von Rad's search for theology's existential dimension can be successful only if Christ's claims are taken seriously.[43] Further, Seitz claims that the alienation between Jew and Gentile evident in the New Testament can be overcome only through reference to the Old Testament Scriptures and careful correlation of those Scriptures to the claims of Christ.[44] Christians cannot sit in judgment of the Old Testament, then, for it is only on the basis of the whole of Scripture that believers may be reconciled to God and to other persons.[45]

Next, Seitz opposes the idea that the Holy Spirit still gives Scripture-level revelation[46] and states that calling the Old Testament the Hebrew Bible removes the christological center of Christian biblical theology.[47] Each of these convictions places Seitz squarely in the Childs mode of writing Old Testament theology in the service of biblical theology in the Christian context. At the same time he makes his own unique contribution to the discipline.

To these assertions Seitz adds vital comments about current Old Testament studies and the nature of biblical authority. In the former essay Seitz sets forth his concerns about the limitations of both traditional historical criticism and more recent reader-oriented approaches to interpretation.[48] In the latter chapter, Seitz comments that historical criticism plays a preparatory role in interpretation, not a final one. That is, historical criticism may help readers know how the Old Testament differs from other books and prepare them to be close, careful exegetes.[49] But it is the task of canonical analysis to aid the quest to "find larger unitary purpose and theological synthesis in a book on whose proper interpretation the life of the church depends."[50] Only through such unitary readings can the legitimate theological emphases of fundamentalists and higher critics alike be appreciated.[51] Biblical authority must not be lost, or the church will have lost its right to speak to the world.

Seitz largely succeeds in his attempt to model his methodology in his exegetical studies. It is impossible to critique all his essays here, so suffice it to say that each one seeks to unify biblical books such as Isaiah, sections of Scripture such as Isaiah and Psalms or theological notions such as the use of the divine name in the Pentateuch. At every point he stresses the primacy of the text of the Old Testament canon for Old Testament theology. At no time does he concede Brueggemann's contention that those who engage in specifically Christian biblical theology are "massively reductionist" in their approach.[52] At no time does he strike even a faintly anti-Jewish chord.

There are many ways having access to Seitz's volume would have helped the writing of my own, but two stand out in my mind. First, his rationale for Old Testament theology being studied as part of biblical theology is stronger than my own. His contention that true Christian unity is dependent upon acceptance of the whole Bible is telling. Second, his years of experience with the canonical method help his description of the canon's theology outstrip mine. In other words, Seitz's volume, like Sailhamer's, would have enriched and in some ways corrected my methodological statements.

Still, I do not agree with Seitz on certain key issues. Most of these disagreements are the same as my reservations with Childs's work. First, though I am grateful for Seitz's emphasis on the canon as the locus of theology, I do not share his reluctance to equate the Bible with God's Word. Second, because of this reluctance, I believe Seitz undermines his statements about the text's authority and coherence. The Bible's authority rests on the extent to which it is God's revealed, written Word. Third, though I appreciate Seitz's careful attempts to describe the unity of Isaiah, I do not share his opinions on the book's original author. Again, the authority of a text is in question wherever it makes truth claims (such as authorship) that are not true. As I have stated repeatedly in this volume, I believe the best canonical approach weds canonical theology and evangelical views of history. Despite these disagreements, I am thankful for Seitz's courageous and careful scholarship. He and Childs have argued for the coherence of biblical theology in an era when this viewpoint has come under increasing attack.

At the present time Old Testament theology stands at yet another crossroads. Old and new methodologies vie for supremacy. Preuss's volumes demonstrate that the single theme approach may not be dead yet. A projected work by the veteran evangelical scholar Bruce Waltke on the kingdom of God as a governing Old Testament theme also makes this point. At the same time canonical theologians such as Seitz and Sailhamer continue to write, and Rolf Rendtorff will soon publish an Old Testament theology volume based on canonical theology and intertextuality. All these experts believe that the search for unifying elements is an important facet of Old Testament theology.

Other scholars are not as absorbed with canonical, thematic and unitary concerns. Knierim, Perdue and Brueggemann believe that Old Testament theology is a series of competing theologies that are defined in large part by their sociopolitical settings. Brueggemann goes further in his emphasis on pluralism than do Knierim and Perdue, however, for he does not believe that unity is a necessary goal of Old Testament theology. He argues for open readings of the text, though he apparently does reject approaches he does not deem open enough. He champions pluralistic interpretation.

The future relevance of Old Testament theology depends upon the extent to which the discipline attaches significance to the unity of the canonical text as evidenced in its intertextual connections. It is the canonical text alone that reveals the unity of the character of God, whose personal coherence and perfection guarantee the coherence and perfection of the revealed, written Scripture.[53] The Old Testament's connection to the New Testament must also be highlighted, or the biblical illiteracy so evident in most churches will render the Old Testament irrelevant and unread before too many more years pass. If this scenario unfolds, then a worldwide preference for polytheism may make Christianity a much smaller remnant than it is today. Even so, we have it on the highest authority that the gates of hell will not prevail against the multinational remnant that serves the living God of the Scriptures.

Notes

Chapter 1: History & Methodology

[1]See the detailed efforts of Gerhard F. Hasel to chart the trends in Old Testament theology in *Old Testament Theology: Basic Issues in the Current Debate,* 4th ed. (Grand Rapids, Mich.: Eerdmans, 1991).

[2]Note the lists of such passages in Michael A. Fishbane, *Biblical Interpretation in Ancient Israel* (Oxford: Clarendon, 1985), p. 106. This work is an excellent analysis of intertextuality, or how Scriptures allude to, quote and interpret other Scriptures.

[3]Cf. Brevard S. Childs, *Biblical Theology of the Old and New Testaments: Theological Reflection on the Christian Bible* (Minneapolis: Fortress, 1992), pp. 30-51.

[4]See Calvin's and Luther's commentaries and sermons on the Old Testament.

[5]Cf. John Haralson Hayes and Frederick C. Prussner, *Old Testament Theology: Its History and Development* (Atlanta: John Knox, 1985).

[6]For this concern consult Rolf Rendtorff, *Canon and Theology: Overtures to an Old Testament Theology,* ed. and trans. Margaret Kohl, Overtures to Biblical Theology (Minneapolis: Fortress, 1993), pp. 31-45.

[7]For the latter concern note Jon Douglas Levenson, "Theological Consensus or Historicist Evasion? Jews and Christians in Biblical Studies," in *Hebrew Bible or Old Testament: Studying the Bible in Judaism and Christianity,* ed. Roger Brooks and John Joseph Collins (Notre Dame, Ind.: University of Notre Dame Press, 1990), pp. 109-45.

[8]Douglas K. Stuart and Gordon D. Fee, *How to Read the Bible for All Its Worth* (Grand Rapids, Mich.: Zondervan, 1981), p. 27.

[9]Note particularly the discussion of the developments between 1878 and 1920.

[10]For example, in *A Theology of the Old Testament* (Garden City, N.Y.: Doubleday, 1974), John L. McKenzie says that he attempts to write as if the New Testament did not exist (p. 319) because "the Old Testament is not a Christian book" (p. 320).

[11]Johann P. Gabler, "An Oration on the Proper Distinction Between Biblical and Dogmatic Theology and the Specific Objectives of Each," in *The Flowering of Old Testament Theology: A Reader in Twentieth-Century Old Testament Theology, 1930-1990,* ed. Ben Charles Ollenburger, Elmer A. Martens and Gerhard F. Hasel (Winona Lake, Ind.: Eisenbrauns, 1992), pp. 495-96.

[12]Cf. Ralph L. Smith, *Old Testament Theology: Its History, Method and Message* (Nashville, Tenn.: Broadman, 1993), pp. 21-22.

[13]Gabler, "An Oration," p. 497.

[14]Ibid., p. 499.

[15]Ibid., p. 500.

[16]Ibid.

[17]Ibid.

[18]Ibid.

[19]Ibid.

[20]Ibid., pp. 500-501.

[21]Ibid., p. 501.

[22]Ibid.

[23]Cf. Georg Lorenz Bauer, *The Theology of the Old Testament, or A Biblical Sketch of the Religious Opinions of the Ancient Hebrews from the Earliest Times to the Commencement of the Christian Era* (London: Charles Fox, 1838), pp. 1-6. This English translation is an abridged version of

Theologie des Alten Testaments oder Abriss der religiösen Begriffe der alten Hebräer von den ältesten Zeiten bis auf den Anfang der christlichen Epoche (Leipzig: In der Weygandschen Buchhandlung, 1796).

[24]Robert C. Dentan, *Preface to Old Testament Theology*, rev. ed. (New York: Seabury, 1963), p. 27.

[25]Georg Lorenz Bauer, *Hebräische Mythologie des alten und neuen Testaments, mit Parallelen aus der Mythologie anderer Völker, vornemlich der Griechen und Römer* (Leipzig: In der Weygandschen Buchhandlung, 1802).

[26]In the introduction to his *Theology*, after noting that a person's relationship to God is of utmost importance, Bauer writes, "It is intended in the following pages to examine what were the opinions entertained concerning these relations of God to man, and of man to his Maker, by the ancient Hebrews. We shall endeavor to place before the reader an impartial investigation of their ideas of God, and their notions of his Providence: to trace the history of their religion, as it is to be collected from the Books of the sacred writers, through each successive stage of its development. . . . The importance of such an examination is obvious. Christianity is the offspring of Judaism, and an accurate knowledge of the theology of the New Testament can be attained by those only who are acquainted with the theology of the Old Testament" (p. vii).

[27]Gabler, "An Oration," p. 501.

[28]Dentan, *Preface to Old Testament Theology*, p. 28.

[29]Wilhelm Martin Lebrecht de Wette, *Lehrbuch der christlichen Dogmatik in ihrer historischen Entwickelung dargestellt*, 3rd ed., 2 vols. (Berlin: G. Reimer, 1831), 1:vi-x.

[30]For an excellent description of Fries's influence on de Wette, see John W. Rogerson, *W. M. L. de Wette, Founder of Modern Biblical Criticism: An Intellectual Biography*, Journal for the Study of the Old Testament Supplement Series (referred to hereafter as JSOTSup) 126 (Sheffield, U.K.: Sheffield Academic Press, 1992), pp. 22-110.

[31]Cf. ibid., pp. 106-7.

[32]Cf. Dentan, *Preface to Old Testament Theology*, p. 30.

[33]De Wette, *Lehrbuch der christlichen Dogmatik*, 1:64.

[34]Ibid., 1:30.

[35]Smith, *Old Testament Theology*, p. 35.

[36]Vatke claimed that it was necessary to incorporate and juxtapose both the objective (historical) and subjective (religious ideas and beliefs) aspects of Scripture in a discussion of Old Testament religion. See Wilhelm Vatke, *Biblische Theologie, wissenschaftlich dargestellt, Die Religion des Alten Testaments* (Berlin: G. Bethge, 1835), pp. 13-14.

[37]Ibid., pp. 184ff.

[38]Ibid., p. 185. Cf. Wilhelm Martin Lebrecht de Wette, *Beiträge zur Einleitung in das Alte Testament* (Halle, Germany: Schimmelpfennig, 1806-1807).

[39]Ibid., pp. 177-84.

[40]R. K. Harrison, *Introduction to the Old Testament: With a Comprehensive Review of Old Testament Studies and a Special Supplement on the Apocrypha* (Grand Rapids, Mich.: Eerdmans, 1969), p. 423.

[41]Ernst Wilhelm Hengstenberg, *Christologie des Alten Testaments und Commentar über die Messianischen Weissagungen* (Berlin: L. Oehmigke, 1829-1835).

[42]Dentan, *Preface to Old Testament Theology*, p. 40.

[43]Ernst Wilhelm Hengstenberg, *History of the Kingdom of God in the Old Testament* (Edinburgh: T & T Clark, 1871), pp. 21-89.

[44]Cf. Brevard S. Childs, *Introduction to the Old Testament as Scripture* (Philadelphia: Fortress, 1980), p. 37.

[45]Heinrich Andreas Christoph Havernick, *Vorlesungen über die Theologie des Alten Testaments*, ed. Hermann Schultz and Heinrich August Hahn (Erlangen, Germany: C. Heyder, 1848).

[46]Cf. Dentan, *Preface to Old Testament Theology*, p. 43.

[47]J. Christian K. von Hofmann, *Weissagung und Erfüllung im alten und im Neuen Testamente*

(Nordlingen, Germany: C. H. Beck, 1841-1844).

[48]Ben Charles Ollenburger, "From Timeless Ideas to the Essence of Religion: Method in Old Testament Theology before 1930," in *The Flowering of Old Testament Theology: A Reader in Twentieth-Century Old Testament Theology, 1930-1990,* ed. Ben Charles Ollenburger, Elmer A. Martens and Gerhard F. Hasel (Winona Lake, Ind.: Eisenbrauns, 1992), p. 12.

[49]Gustav Friedrich Oehler, *Theology of the Old Testament,* trans. Ellen D. Smith (vol. 1) and Sophia Taylor (vol. 2), 2 vols. (Edinburgh: T & T Clark, 1882-1883), 1:65.

[50]Ibid., 1:65-66.

[51]Ibid., 2:439ff.

[52]Julius Wellhausen, *Prolegomena to the History of Ancient Israel* (Gloucester, Mass.: Peter Smith, 1983); originally published as *Prolegomena zur Geschichte Israels* (Berlin: G. Reimer, 1878).

[53]Dentan, *Preface to Old Testament Theology,* p. 50.

[54]Toy's firing caused great grief to the seminary's president, James Petigru Boyce. John Broadus reports that upon parting from Toy at the train station, Boyce placed his arm around Toy and said, "Oh, Toy, I would freely give that arm to be cut off if you could be where you were five years ago, and stay there." See John Albert Broadus, *Memoir of James Petigru Boyce* (New York: Armstrong, 1893), p. 264.

[55]Walther Eichrodt, *Theology of the Old Testament,* trans. J. A. Baker, 2 vols., Old Testament Library (Philadelphia: Westminster Press, 1961-1967), 1:30-31.

[56]A. B. Davidson, *The Theology of the Old Testament,* ed. S. D. F. Salmond, International Theological Library (Edinburgh: T & T Clark, 1904).

[57]Bernhard Stade, *Biblische Theologie des Alten Testaments,* Grundriss der theologischen Wissenschaften (Tübingen, Germany: Mohr/Siebeck, 1905).

[58]E. Kautzsch, *Biblische Theologie des Alten Testaments* (Tübingen, Germany: Mohr/Siebeck, 1911).

[59]William Lindsay Alexander, *A System of Biblical Theology,* ed. and trans. James Ross (Edinburgh: T & T Clark, 1888).

[60]Hermann Schultz, *Old Testament Theology: The Religion of Revelation in Its Pre-Christian Stage of Development,* trans. J. A. Paterson, 4th ed., 2 vols. (Edinburgh: T & T Clark, 1892), 1:11.

[61]Ibid., 1:56. Schultz here says, "Hence the history of this religion is the history of the kingdom of God, of redemption and reconciliation. Even sacred legend has no other centre. In this religion, wisdom is knowledge of the way of life, in which the divine law is found, in other words, knowledge of the laws of the kingdom of God."

[62]Ibid., 1:59.

[63]Ibid., 1:11-12.

[64]Ibid., 1:ix-x.

[65]Dentan, *Preface to Old Testament Theology,* p. 53.

[66]August Dillmann, *Handbuch der Alttestamentlichen Theologie,* ed. Rudolf Kittel (Leipzig: S. Hirzel, 1895), pp. 52-61.

[67]For example, James Orr, *The Problem of the Old Testament* (New York: Scribner's, 1906).

[68]For instance, Hermann Gunkel's approach to form criticism posited an oral stage for the Pentateuch that crossed source lines. See Hermann Gunkel, *Die Sagen der Genesis* (Göttingen, Germany: Vandenhoeck und Ruprecht, 1901).

[69]Cf. Karl Barth, *The Epistle to the Romans,* trans. Edwyn Clement Hoskyns, 6th ed. (London: Oxford University Press, 1933).

[70]Karl Barth, *Church Dogmatics* (Edinburgh: T & T Clark, 1936-1977).

[71]Dentan, *Preface to Old Testament Theology,* p. 61.

[72]Eduard König, *Theologie des Alten Testaments, kritisch und vergleichend dargestellt* (Stuttgart, Germany: C. Belser, 1922).

[73]Eichrodt, *Theology of the Old Testament,* 1:31.

[74]Otto Eissfeldt, "The History of Israelite-Jewish Religion and Old Testament Theology," in *The*

*Flowering of Old Testament Theology: A Reader in Twentieth-Century Old Testament Theology,
1930-1990,* ed. Ben Charles Ollenburger, Elmer A. Martens and Gerhard F. Hasel (Winona
Lake, Ind.: Eisenbrauns, 1992), pp. 20-21.

[75]Walther Eichrodt, "Does Old Testament Theology Still Have Independent Significance Within
Old Testament Scholarship?" in *The Flowering of Old Testament Theology: A Reader in
Twentieth-Century Old Testament Theology, 1930-1990,* ed. Ben Charles Ollenburger, Elmer
A. Martens and Gerhard F. Hasel (Winona Lake, Ind.: Eisenbrauns, 1992), p. 33.

[76]Ibid.

[77]Ibid., p. 34.

[78]Ibid., p. 33.

[79]Ibid., pp. 38-39.

[80]Cf. Eichrodt, *Theology of the Old Testament,* vol. 1.

[81]Eichrodt, "Old Testament Theology," p. 33.

[82]Eichrodt, *Theology of the Old Testament,* 1:36-37.

[83]Ibid., 1:26.

[84]Ibid.

[85]Ibid., 1:27.

[86]Ludwig Köhler, *Old Testament Theology,* trans. A. S. Todd (Philadelphia: Westminster Press,
1957), p. 30.

[87]Cf. ibid, pp. 192ff.

[88]Paul Heinisch, *Theologie des Alten Testaments* (Bonn: Peter Hanstein, 1940).

[89]H. H. Rowley, *The Relevance of the Bible* (London: J. Clarke, 1942).

[90]Norman Henry Snaith, *The Distinctive Ideas of the Old Testament* (London: Epworth, 1944).

[91]George Ernest Wright, *The Challenge of Israel's Faith* (Chicago: University of Chicago Press,
1944).

[92]Theodorus Christiaan Vriezen, *An Outline of Old Testament Theology,* trans. S. Neuijen (Oxford:
Basil Blackwell, 1962), pp. 128-47.

[93]Ibid., p. 99.

[94]Otto Justice Baab, *The Theology of the Old Testament* (New York: Abingdon-Cokesbury, 1949).

[95]Dentan, *Preface to Old Testament Theology,* p. 73.

[96]Otto Procksch, *Theologie des Alten Testaments* (Gütersloh, Germany: Bertelsmann, 1950), pp.
44ff.

[97]Eichrodt, *Theology of the Old Testament,* 1:33 n. 1.

[98]George Ernest Wright, *The Old Testament Against Its Environment,* Studies in Biblical Theology
2 (London: SCM, 1950), p. 12.

[99]Ibid., p. 13.

[100]Ibid., p. 15.

[101]Ibid.

[102]Ibid., pp. 20-41.

[103]George Ernest Wright, *God Who Acts: Biblical Theology as Recital,* Studies in Biblical Theology
8 (London: SCM, 1952), p. 38.

[104]Ibid., pp. 43-44.

[105]Ibid., pp. 45-46.

[106]Ibid., pp. 116-17.

[107]Ibid., p. 126.

[108]Ibid., p. 127.

[109]Edmond Jacob, *Theology of the Old Testament,* trans. Arthur Weston Heathcote and Philip J.
Allcock (New York: Harper & Row, 1958), p. 32.

[110]For example, George Angus Fulton Knight, *A Christian Theology of the Old Testament*
(Richmond, Va.: John Knox, 1959).

[111]Gerhard von Rad, *Old Testament Theology,* trans. David Muir Gibson Stalker, 2 vols. (New
York: Harper & Row, 1962-1965), 1:3-4.

[112]Ibid., 1:106-7.

[113]Ibid., 1:122.

[114]Ibid., 1:123ff.

[115]Edward J. Young, *The Study of Old Testament Theology Today* (London: James Clark, 1958).

[116]J. Barton Payne, *The Theology of the Older Testament* (Grand Rapids, Mich.: Zondervan, 1962), p. 3.

[117]Ibid.

[118]Ibid., pp. 3-4. Note also Payne's approval of Hofmann and Hengstenberg, ibid., pp. 27, 31.

[119]Werner H. Schmidt, *The Faith of the Old Testament: A History,* trans. John Sturdy (Philadelphia: Westminster Press, 1983), pp. 1-4.

[120]George Ernest Wright, *The Old Testament and Theology* (New York: Harper & Row, 1969), p. 9.

[121]See ibid., pp. 97-122.

[122]Brevard S. Childs, *Biblical Theology in Crisis* (Philadelphia: Westminster Press, 1970).

[123]Ibid., pp. 139-47.

[124]Harrison, *Introduction to the Old Testament.* This massive work spans 1215 pages.

[125]Walther Zimmerli, *Old Testament Theology in Outline,* trans. David Eliot Green (Atlanta: John Knox, 1978), p. 10.

[126]Ibid., p. 116.

[127]Georg Fohrer, *Theologische Grundstrukturen des Alten Testaments* (Berlin: Walter de Gruyter, 1972), pp. 113-32.

[128]Elmer A. Martens, "The Multicolored Landscape of Old Testament Theology," in *The Flowering of Old Testament Theology: A Reader in Twentieth-Century Old Testament Theology, 1930-1990,* ed. Ben Charles Ollenburger, Elmer A. Martens and Gerhard F. Hasel (Winona Lake, Ind.: Eisenbrauns, 1992), p. 47.

[129]McKenzie, *A Theology of the Old Testament,* p. 319.

[130]Ibid., p. 320.

[131]Ibid., p. 319.

[132]Walter C. Kaiser Jr., *Toward an Old Testament Theology* (Grand Rapids, Mich.: Zondervan, 1978), p. 4.

[133]Ibid.

[134]Ibid., p. 7.

[135]Ibid., pp. 35-40.

[136]Ibid., pp. 22-25.

[137]Ibid., pp. 25-32.

[138]Ibid., pp. 263-69.

[139]Samuel L. Terrien, *The Elusive Presence: Toward a New Biblical Theology* (San Francisco: Harper and Row, 1978), p. xviii.

[140]Ibid., p. 43.

[141]Ibid.

[142]Ibid., pp. 50-389.

[143]Cf. Smith's critique of Terrien's omission of an extended discussion of sin in Smith, *Old Testament Theology,* p. 57.

[144]Cf. James A. Sanders, *Torah and Canon* (Philadelphia: Fortress, 1972).

[145]Ronald E. Clements, *Old Testament Theology: A Fresh Approach* (London: Marshall, Morgan & Scott, 1978), p. 15.

[146]Ibid., p. 16. For an extended defense of this position, consult Roger T. Beckwith, *The Old Testament Canon of the New Testament Church and Its Background in Early Judaism* (London: SPCK, 1985).

[147]He partly fulfills this task later in Ronald E. Clements, *Wisdom in Theology* (Grand Rapids, Mich.: Eerdmans, 1992).

[148]Clements, *Old Testament Theology,* pp. 24-25.

[149]Ibid., p. 118.

[150]Ibid., pp. 120-44.

[151]Ibid., pp. 121-22.
[152]Ibid., pp. 149-54.
[153]Claus Westermann, *Elements of Old Testament Theology*, trans. Douglas W. Stott (Atlanta: John Knox, 1982), p. 9.
[154]Ibid.
[155]Ibid., p. 11.
[156]Childs, *Introduction to the Old Testament*, pp. 74-75.
[157]Elmer A. Martens, *God's Design: A Focus on Old Testament Theology* (Grand Rapids, Mich.: Baker, 1981), p. 3.
[158]Ibid.
[159]Ibid., pp. 11-24.
[160]Ibid., p. 3.
[161]Hartmut Gese, "Tradition and Biblical Theology," in *Tradition and Theology in the Old Testament*, ed. Douglas A. Knight (London: SPCK, 1977), p. 325.
[162]Ibid., p. 322. For a fuller discussion of this unity, see Hartmut Gese, *Zur biblischen Theologie*, 2nd ed. (Tübingen, Germany: Mohr/Siebeck, 1983), pp. 9-30.
[163]Gese, "Tradition and Biblical Theology," p. 325.
[164]Gese, *Zur biblischen Theologie*, p. 11.
[165]Ibid., p. 13.
[166]Gese, "Tradition and Biblical Theology," p. 310.
[167]Note especially his work on the Messiah and John's prologue in Gese, *Zur biblischen Theologie*, pp. 128-51, 152-201.
[168]Jesper Högenhaven, *Problems and Prospects of Old Testament Theology*, Biblical Seminar 6 (Sheffield, U.K.: JSOT Press, 1988), p. 50.
[169]Brevard S. Childs, *The New Testament as Canon: An Introduction* (Philadelphia: Fortress, 1984).
[170]Brevard S. Childs, *Old Testament Theology in a Canonical Context* (Philadelphia: Fortress, 1985), p. 6.
[171]Ibid.
[172]Ibid.
[173]Ibid., p. 7.
[174]Ibid., p. 9.
[175]Ibid., p. 6.
[176]Ibid., p. 15.
[177]Ibid., p. 16.
[178]Ibid.
[179]Ibid., p. 17.
[180]Ibid.
[181]Ibid., p. 25.
[182]Ibid., p. 26.
[183]Paul D. Hanson, *The People Called: The Growth of Community in the Bible* (San Francisco: Harper & Row, 1986).
[184]Ibid., pp. 10-29.
[185]Ibid., pp. 172-76.
[186]Ibid., p. 2.
[187]Ibid., pp. 499-518.
[188]Note the critique of Hanson's work in Childs, *Biblical Theology of the Old and New Testaments*, p. 18.
[189]Christoph Barth, *God with Us: A Theological Introduction to the Old Testament*, ed. and trans. G. W. Bromiley (Grand Rapids, Mich.: Eerdmans, 1991).
[190]Walter A. Brueggemann, *Old Testament Theology: Essays on Structure, Theme and Text*, ed. Patrick Dwight Miller Jr. (Minneapolis: Fortress, 1992), p. 2.
[191]Ibid., p. 4.

[192]Cf. ibid., pp. 5-10, 42-43, 109-10, etc.

[193]Ibid., pp. 20-21.

[194]Ibid., p. 25.

[195]Ibid., p. 26.

[196]Ibid., p. 42.

[197]Childs, *Biblical Theology of the Old and New Testaments,* pp. 91-92.

[198]Ibid., p. 93.

[199]Ibid., pp. 140-41.

[200]Rolf Rendtorff, *The Problem of the Process of Transmission in the Pentateuch,* trans. John J. Scullion, JSOTSup 89 (Sheffield, U.K.: Sheffield Academic Press, 1990), p. 101.

[201]Ibid., p. 118.

[202]Ibid., p. 136.

[203]Ibid., p. 156.

[204]Ibid., pp. 177-206.

[205]Rendtorff, *Canon and Theology,* p. 13.

[206]Ibid., p. 27.

[207]Ibid., p. 29.

[208]Smith, *Old Testament Theology,* pp. 21-93.

[209]Ibid., p. 15.

[210]Zimmerli, *Old Testament Theology in Outline,* p. 12.

[211]This conclusion lies at the heart of Childs's *Biblical Theology.*

[212]Hasel, *Old Testament Theology,* pp. 28-114.

[213]On this point I agree with Clements, *Old Testament Theology,* p. 16; and Childs, *Biblical Theology,* pp. 91-92. I have set forth my own conclusions about the propriety of using the Palestinian canon in "Canon of the Old Testament," in *Foundations for Biblical Interpretation: A Complete Library of Tools and Resources,* ed. David S. Dockery, Kenneth A. Matthews and Robert B. Sloan (Nashville, Tenn.: Broadman, 1994), pp. 134-55.

[214]Cf. Hasel, *Old Testament Theology,* p. 112.

[215]I have outlined the Old Testament's broad thematic coherence in *Old Testament Survey* (Nashville, Tenn.: Broadman, 1992). This volume addresses specific intertextual matters as well.

[216]Note the comments on Exodus 20:1-17 for this volume's clearest statement on the text's approach to monotheism.

Chapter 2: Genesis

[1]David J. A. Clines, *The Theme of the Pentateuch,* JSOTSup 10 (Sheffield, U.K.: JSOT Press, 1978), p. 26.

[2]George Smith, *The Chaldean Account of Genesis* (London: S. Low, Marston, Searle, and Rivington, 1876).

[3]Hermann Gunkel, "The Influence of Babylonian Mythology upon the Biblical Creation Story," in *Creation in the Old Testament,* ed. Bernhard Ward Anderson (London: SPCK, 1984), pp. 25-52; Gunkel's article was first published as *Schopfung und Chaos in Urzeit und Endzeit* (Göttingen, Germany: Vandenhoeck und Ruprecht, 1895).

[4]For example, John D. Davis, *Genesis and Semitic Tradition* (1894; reprint, Grand Rapids, Mich.: Baker, 1980).

[5]Cf. Gordon J. Wenham, *Genesis,* Word Biblical Commentary 1-2 (Waco, Tex.: Word, 1987-1994); and Claus Westermann, *Genesis,* trans. John J. Scullion, 3 vols. (Minneapolis: Augsburg, 1984-1986).

[6]Wenham, *Genesis,* 1:31-32.

[7]Claus Westermann, *Creation,* trans. John J. Scullion (Philadelphia: Fortress, 1974), p. 57.

[8]Hermann Gunkel, *Genesis,* 3rd ed., Handkommentar zum Alten Testament 1/1 (Göttingen, Germany: Vandenhoeck und Ruprecht, 1964), p. 111.

[9]Gerhard von Rad, *Genesis,* trans. John Henry Marks, rev. ed., Old Testament Library (Philadelphia: Westminster Press, 1971), pp. 57-58.

[10]For a list of possible interpretations consult Victor Paul Hamilton, *The Book of Genesis: Chapters 1—17,* New International Commentary on the New Testament (Grand Rapids, Mich.: Eerdmans, 1990), pp. 132-34.

[11]Cf. Wenham, *Genesis,* 1:28.

[12]Cf. Westermann, *Genesis,* 1:237-38.

[13]Martin Luther, "Lectures on Genesis 1—5," in *Luther's Works,* ed. Jaroslav Jan Pelikan and Helmut T. Lehman, 55 vols. (St. Louis, Mo.: Concordia, 1955-1976), 1:203.

[14]G. C. Aalders, *Genesis,* trans. William Heynen, 2 vols., Bible Student's Commentary (Grand Rapids, Mich.: Zondervan, 1981), 1:108-9.

[15]Hamilton, *The Book of Genesis,* p. 202.

[16]Westermann, *Genesis,* 1:263.

[17]Cf. Hamilton, *The Book of Genesis,* p. 224.

[18]Walter A. Brueggemann, *Genesis,* Interpretation: A Bible Commentary for Teaching and Preaching (Atlanta: John Knox, 1982), pp. 71-72.

[19]J. Barton Payne, *The Theology of the Older Testament* (Grand Rapids, Mich.: Zondervan, 1962), p. 205.

[20]Brevard S. Childs, *Biblical Theology of the Old and New Testaments: Theological Reflection on the Christian Bible* (Minneapolis: Fortress, 1992), p. 121.

[21]Cf. Wenham, *Genesis,* 1:144.

[22]Cf. Davis, *Genesis and Semitic Tradition,* pp. 110-34.

[23]Ibid., pp. 111-13.

[24]William J. Dumbrell, *Covenant and Creation: A Theology of Old Testament Covenants* (Nashville, Tenn.: Thomas Nelson, 1984), p. 43.

[25]Noah's covenant is conditional in the sense that it entails accountability.

[26]Westermann, *Genesis,* 1:492.

[27]Hamilton, *The Book of Genesis,* p. 325.

[28]Brueggemann, *Genesis,* p. 89.

[29]Wenham, *Genesis,* 1:202.

[30]Thomas Wingate Mann, *The Book of the Torah: The Narrative Integrity of the Pentateuch* (Atlanta: John Knox, 1988), p. 26.

[31]Note the arguments in John Van Seters, *In Search of History: Historiography in the Ancient World and the Origins of Biblical History* (New Haven, Conn.: Yale University Press, 1983); and Van Seters, *Prologue to History: The Yahwist as Historian in Genesis* (New Haven, Conn.: Yale University Press, 1992).

[32]Cf. John Bright, *A History of Israel,* 2nd ed. (Philadelphia: Westminster Press, 1972), pp. 67-102.

[33]Clines, *The Theme of the Pentateuch.*

[34]Hamilton, *The Book of Genesis,* p. 423.

[35]Brueggemann, *Genesis,* p. 145.

[36]Walther Zimmerli, *Old Testament Theology in Outline,* trans. David Eliot Green (Atlanta: John Knox, 1978), p. 147.

[37]On the relational nature of the faith/righteousness link see Brevard S. Childs, *Old Testament Theology in a Canonical Context* (Philadelphia: Fortress, 1985), pp. 219-20.

[38]Westermann, *Genesis,* 2:109.

[39]Zimmerli, *Old Testament Theology,* p. 147.

[40]Walter C. Kaiser Jr., *Toward an Old Testament Theology* (Grand Rapids, Mich.: Zondervan, 1978), p. 92.

[41]Gerhard von Rad, *Old Testament Theology,* trans. David Muir Gibson Stalker, 2 vols. (New York: Harper & Row, 1962-1965), 1:171.

[42]E. J. Carnell, *The Case for Orthodox Theology* (Philadelphia: Westminster Press, 1959), p. 18.

[43]Cf. Romans 9:10-18.

[44]Note Victor Paul Hamilton's excellent treatment of Jacob's growth in faith in *Handbook on the Pentateuch* (Grand Rapids, Mich.: Baker, 1982), pp. 117-28.

[45]Von Rad, *Old Testament Theology,* 1:172.

[46]Wenham, *Genesis,* 2:238.

[47]The verb here is not in the intensive stem.

[48]Westermann, *Genesis,* 2:409.

[49]Ibid. Cf. John Skinner, *A Critical and Exegetical Commentary on Genesis,* International Critical Commentary (New York: Scribner's, 1910), pp. 405-12.

[50]Derek Kidner, *Genesis: An Introduction and a Commentary,* Tyndale Old Testament Commentaries (Downers Grove, Ill.: InterVarsity Press, 1967), p. 174.

[51]Yehezkel Kaufmann, *The Religion of Israel: From Its Beginnings to the Babylonian Exile,* trans. and abridged by Moshe Greenberg (Chicago: University of Chicago Press, 1960), p. 145.

[52]Elmer A. Martens, *God's Design: A Focus on Old Testament Theology* (Grand Rapids, Mich.: Baker, 1981), p. 87.

[53]Skinner, *Genesis,* p. 458.

[54]Kidner, *Genesis,* p. 193.

[55]Westermann, *Genesis,* 3:79.

[56]Claus Westermann, *Elements of Old Testament Theology,* trans. Douglas W. Stott (Atlanta: John Knox, 1982), p. 122.

[57]Zimmerli, *Old Testament Theology,* p. 146.

[58]Brueggemann, *Genesis,* p. 379.

[59]Martens, *God's Design,* p. 34.

[60]Note the description of these details in Gerald Lewis Bray, *The Doctrine of God* (Downers Grove, Ill.: InterVarsity Press, 1993), pp. 53-110.

Chapter 3: Exodus

[1]Cf. David J. A. Clines, *The Theme of the Pentateuch,* JSOTSup 10 (Sheffield, U.K.: JSOT, 1978).

[2]John Durham concludes that God's presence is the book's main theme. See John Durham, *Exodus,* Word Biblical Commentary 3 (Waco, Tex.: Word, 1987), p. xxx.

[3]Walther Eichrodt makes covenant the centering theme. See Walther Eichrodt, *Theology of the Old Testament,* trans. J. A. Baker, 2 vols., Old Testament Library (Philadelphia: Westminster Press, 1961-1967), vol. 1.

[4]Though Israel is not yet a nation in the sense that they possess land and have a government, they are a people with enough ethnic, religious and economic identity for both terms to apply to them. See Ronald E. Clements's discussion of these issues in *Old Testament Theology: A Fresh Approach* (London: Marshall, Morgan & Scott, 1978), pp. 82-87.

[5]Cf. Elmer A. Martens, *God's Design: A Focus on Old Testament Theology* (Grand Rapids, Mich.: Baker, 1981), p. 17; and Walter C. Kaiser Jr., *Toward an Old Testament Theology* (Grand Rapids, Mich.: Zondervan, 1978), p. 100.

[6]Cf. John Bright, *A History of Israel,* 2nd ed. (Philadelphia: Westminster Press, 1972), pp. 105-14; and Michael Grant, *The History of Ancient Israel* (New York: Scribner's, 1984), p. 36.

[7]Scholars rarely doubt the historical accuracy of Exodus 1:11-14. Cf. Walther Zimmerli, *Old Testament Theology in Outline,* trans. David Eliot Green (Edinburgh: T & T Clark, 1978), p. 22; and Ernest W. Nicholson, *Exodus and Sinai in History and Tradition* (Atlanta: John Knox, 1978), pp. 53-54.

[8]Donald E. Gowan focuses on God's "absence" in Exodus 1:1—2:22 and reemergence in Exodus 2:23-25 in *Theology in Exodus: Biblical Theology in the Form of a Commentary* (Louisville, Ky.: Westminster/John Knox, 1994), pp. 1-24. Though Gowan does not take Genesis 15:13-16 into account adequately, he effectively links Exodus 1—2 to the suffering Joseph encounters in Genesis 37—50.

[9]For a discussion of the possible identity of Moses' parents consult Walter C. Kaiser Jr., "Exodus," in *Expositor's Bible Commentary,* ed. Frank E. Gaebelein (Grand Rapids, Mich.: Zondervan, 1976-1992), 2:308.

[10]Brevard S. Childs, *The Book of Exodus,* Old Testament Library (Philadelphia: Westminster Press, 1974), p. 18.

[11]Durham argues the opposite. He states that Moses feels at home in Midian because he has a wife, safety and the opportunity to worship God with these people. Thus Durham reads Egypt as the strange land (*Exodus*, p. 24). Childs accepts the traditional interpretation that Moses did not feel at home (*Exodus*, p. 32), as does Kaiser ("Exodus," p. 313). Later texts contradict Durham's thesis, since Moses seems unfamiliar with God in Exodus 3:1-6 and has not circumcised his son by Exodus 4:24-26.

[12]Gowan, *Theology in Exodus*, p. 28.

[13]Durham, *Exodus*, p. 33.

[14]Martens, *God's Design*, p. 16.

[15]Edmond Jacob, *Theology of the Old Testament*, trans. Arthur Weston Heathcote and Philip J. Allcock (New York: Harper & Row, 1958), p. 51.

[16]Ibid., p. 52.

[17]Zimmerli, *Old Testament Theology*, p. 152.

[18]William Foxwell Albright, *From the Stone Age to Christianity: Monotheism and the Historical Process*, 2nd ed. (Garden City, N.Y.: Doubleday, 1957), p. 261. See also David Noel Freedman, "The Name of the God of Moses," *Journal of Biblical Literature* 79 (1960): 151-56.

[19]Gowan, *Theology in Exodus*, p. 83.

[20]Durham, *Exodus*, p. 39.

[21]Gustav Friedrich Oehler, *Theology of the Old Testament*, trans. Ellen D. Smith (vol. 1) and Sophia Taylor (vol. 2), 2 vols. (Edinburgh: T & T Clark, 1882-1883), 1:95.

[22]Eichrodt, *Theology of the Old Testament*, 1:190.

[23]Kaiser, *Toward an Old Testament Theology*, p. 107.

[24]Carl F. H. Henry, *God, Revelation and Authority*, vol. 2, *God Who Speaks and Shows, Fifteen Theses, Part One* (Waco, Tex.: Word, 1976), p. 220.

[25]This opinion differs with Samuel L. Terrien's conviction that here God "is known as unknown." See Samuel L. Terrien, *The Elusive Presence: Toward a New Biblical Theology* (San Francisco: Harper & Row, 1978), p. 119. Though God cannot be manipulated because of this revelation, as has been stated, the purpose of this revelation is to make God known as the same God who has blessed Israel for over four centuries and the human race since "in the beginning" (Gen 1:1).

[26]Kaiser, "Exodus," p. 331.

[27]Jacob, *Theology of the Old Testament*, p. 285 n. 1.

[28]Kaiser, "Exodus," pp. 331-32.

[29]Cf. Jacob, *Theology of the Old Testament*, p. 202.

[30]Kaiser, "Exodus," pp. 331.

[31]Norman Charles Habel, "The Form and Significance of the Call Narratives," *Zeitschrift für die alttestamentliche Wissenschaft* 77 (1965): 303-5.

[32]Ernst Kutsch, "Gideons Berufung und Altarbau, Jdg 6, 11-24," *Theologische Literaturzeitung* 81 (1956): 75-84.

[33]Clements, *Old Testament Theology*, p. 76.

[34]Claus Westermann, *Isaiah 40—66*, trans. David Muir Gibson Stalker, Old Testament Library (Philadelphia: Westminster Press, 1969), p. 124.

[35]D. A. Carson, *The Gospel According to John* (Grand Rapids, Mich.: Eerdmans, 1991), p. 343.

[36]Raymond E. Brown, *The Gospel According to John, I—XII: A New Translation with Introduction, Notes and Commentary*, Anchor Bible 29 (Garden City, N.Y.: Doubleday, 1982), p. 536.

[37]F. F. Bruce, *The Gospel of John* (Grand Rapids, Mich.: Eerdmans, 1983), pp. 205-6.

[38]Brown, *The Gospel According to John, I—XII*, p. 537.

[39]Ewell Ray Clendenen, "Religious Background of the Old Testament," in *Foundations for Biblical Interpretation: A Complete Library of Tools and Resources*, ed. David S. Dockery, Kenneth A. Mathews and Robert Bryan Sloan (Nashville, Tenn.: Broadman, 1994), p. 284.

[40]Durham, *Exodus*, p. 76.

[41]Ibid., p. 77.

[42]John Herbert Sailhamer, *The Pentateuch as Narrative: A Biblical-Theological Commentary* (Grand Rapids, Mich.: Zondervan, 1992), p. 251.

[43]Childs, *Exodus,* p. 115.

[44]Oswald T. Allis, *God Spake by Moses: An Exposition of the Pentateuch* (London: Marshall, Morgan & Scott, 1951), p. 65.

[45]Durham, *Exodus,* pp. 86-87.

[46]Robert Alan Cole, *Exodus: An Introduction and Commentary,* Tyndale Old Testament Commentaries (Downers Grove, Ill.: InterVarsity Press, 1973), p. 89.

[47]For an excellent survey of the relevant texts consult Victor Paul Hamilton, *Handbook on the Pentateuch* (Grand Rapids, Mich.: Baker, 1982), pp. 163-66.

[48]Cf. Richard Swinburne, *The Concept of Miracle* (London: Macmillan, 1970), for a sophisticated defense of miracles. Also consult Richard L. Purtill, "Miracles: What If They Happen?" in *Thinking About Religion: A Philosophical Introduction to Religion* (Englewood Cliffs, N.J.: Prentice-Hall, 1978); Norman L. Geisler, *Miracles and Modern Thought* (Grand Rapids, Mich.: Zondervan, 1982); and Colin Brown, *Miracles and the Critical Mind* (Grand Rapids, Mich.: Eerdmans, 1984).

[49]Cf. James Maxwell Miller, *The Old Testament and the Historian* (Philadelphia: Fortress, 1976), p. 19.

[50]Edwin M. Yamauchi, "The Current State of Old Testament Historiography," in *Faith, Tradition and History: Old Testament Historiography in Its Near Eastern Context,* ed. A. R. Millard, James Karl Hoffmeier and David W. Baker (Winona Lake, Ind.: Eisenbrauns, 1994), p. 28.

[51]Modern historians are currently discussing how all these issues impact the writing of history. Few if any historians still claim to be totally objective or uninfluenced by their cultural or educational background. For analyses of these topics, see James T. Kloppenberg, "Objectivity and Historicism: A Century of American Historical Writing," *American Historical Review,* October 1989, pp. 1011-30; Frank Stricker, "Why History? Thinking About the Uses of the Past," *The History Teacher* 25/3 (May 1992): 293-312; John Higham, "Beyond Consensus: The Historian as Moral Critic," in Higham, *Writing American History: Essays on Modern Scholarship* (Bloomington: Indiana University Press, 1970).

[52]Frank Moore Cross, *Canaanite Myth and Hebrew Epic: Essays in the History of the Religion of Israel* (Cambridge, Mass.: Harvard University Press, 1973), pp. 121-23.

[53]Martens, *God's Design,* p. 40.

[54]David Noel Freedman, "Strophe and Meter in Exodus 15," in *Pottery, Poetry and Prophecy: Studies in Early Hebrew Poetry* (Winona Lake, Ind.: Eisenbrauns, 1980), p. 216.

[55]Ibid.

[56]Martens, *God's Design,* p. 43.

[57]Gerhard von Rad, *Old Testament Theology,* trans. David Muir Gibson Stalker, 2 vols. (New York: Harper & Row, 1962-1965), 1:175-176.

[58]Martens, *God's Design,* pp. 11-24.

[59]Ibid., pp. 119-23, 193-96.

[60]Ibid., pp. 167-75.

[61]Brevard S. Childs, *Biblical Theology of the Old and New Testaments: Theological Reflection on the Christian Bible* (Minneapolis: Fortress, 1992), p. 131.

[62]Childs, *Exodus,* p. 119.

[63]Leon Morris, *New Testament Theology* (Grand Rapids, Mich.: Zondervan, 1986), p. 31.

[64]Donald G. Bloesch, *Essentials of Evangelical Theology,* vol. 1, *God, Authority and Salvation* (San Francisco: Harper & Row, 1982), p. 182.

[65]C. E. B. Cranfield, *A Critical and Exegetical Commentary on the Epistle to the Romans,* 2 vols., International Critical Commentary (Edinburgh: T & T Clark, 1979), 2:487.

[66]Ibid., 2:488.

[67]Kaiser, *Toward an Old Testament Theology,* p. 106.

[68]Martin Noth, *Exodus,* trans. John Stephen Bowden, Old Testament Library (Philadelphia: Westminster Press, 1962), p. 132.

[69]Ibid.

[70]Ibid., p. 149; and Durham, *Exodus,* p. 241.

[71]William J. Dumbrell, *Covenant and Creation: A Theology of Old Testament Covenants*

(Nashville, Tenn.: Thomas Nelson, 1984), p. 80.

[72]This progression of ideas is taken from Henry, *God, Revelation and Authority.*

[73]Dumbrell, *Covenant and Creation,* p. 88.

[74]The Hebrew implies a causal force.

[75]Kaiser, "Exodus," p. 416.

[76]See Albrecht Alt's seminal essays on these laws in his *Essays in Old Testament History and Religion* (Oxford: Oxford University Press, 1966), pp. 81-132.

[77]Theodorus Christiaan Vriezen, *An Outline of Old Testament Theology,* trans. S. Neuijen (Oxford: Basil Blackwell, 1962), p. 318.

[78]Von Rad, *Old Testament Theology,* 1:210.

[79]Zimmerli, *Old Testament Theology,* pp. 116-17.

[80]Bright, *A History of Israel,* p. 154. See chapter one of this volume for a lengthier discussion of this matter.

[81]Dale Patrick, *Old Testament Law* (Atlanta: John Knox, 1985), p. 43.

[82]Zimmerli, *Old Testament Theology,* p. 120.

[83]Kaiser, "Exodus," p. 423.

[84]Zimmerli, *Old Testament Theology,* p. 124.

[85]Brevard S. Childs, *Old Testament Theology in a Canonical Context* (Philadelphia: Fortress, 1985), p. 69.

[86]Patrick, *Old Testament Law,* p. 51.

[87]Childs, *Old Testament Theology,* p. 74.

[88]Kaiser, "Exodus," p. 425.

[89]For example, Noth, *Exodus,* p. 173.

[90]Patrick, *Old Testament Law,* pp. 66-67.

[91]George E. Mendenhall, "Covenant Forms in Israelite Traditions," *Biblical Archaeologist* 17 (1954): 58.

[92]Martens, *God's Design,* p. 93.

[93]Von Rad, *Old Testament Theology,* 2:237.

[94]Roy Lee Honeycutt Jr., "Exodus," in *Broadman Bible Commentary,* ed. Clifton J. Allen, rev. ed. (Nashville, Tenn.: Broadman, 1973), 1:418.

[95]The depositing of stones inscribed with basic covenant obligations in a sanctuary was a common way to seal covenants in ancient times. See Moshe Weinfeld, *"berith"* (covenant), in *Theological Dictionary of the Old Testament,* ed. G. Johannes Botterweck and Helmer Ringgren, 12 vols. (Grand Rapids, Mich.: Eerdmans, 1975), 2:265.

[96]It is not extremely important to separate polytheism, idolatry and blasphemy here. Distinguishing between the finer points of covenant breaking does not concern Moses at this point. Even if the people intend "to represent the God of the covenant with a physical image" (Sailhamer, *The Pentateuch as Narrative,* p. 311), their making of an idol is treated as a repudiation of the whole covenant by God (Ex 32:7-10) and by Moses (Ex 32:19).

[97]Carl Friedrich Keil, "Exodus," in Carl Friedrich Keil and Franz Julius Delitzsch, *Commentary on the Old Testament,* 10 vols. (Grand Rapids, Mich.: Eerdmans, 1980), 1:225 (original ed. *Biblischer Commentar über das Alte Testament,* Leipzig: Dorffling und Franke, 1862-1872).

[98]Eichrodt, *Theology of the Old Testament,* 1:69.

[99]Dumbrell, *Covenant and Creation,* p. 107.

[100]Note the excellent discussion of Paul's defense of his ministry in 2 Corinthians in Scott Hafemann, *Suffering and Ministry in the Spirit: Paul's Defense of His Ministry in II Corinthians 2:14—3:3* (Grand Rapids, Mich.: Eerdmans, 1990).

[101]Cf. Kaiser, "Exodus," p. 487.

[102]Geerhardus Vos, *Biblical Theology: Old and New Testaments* (Grand Rapids, Mich.: Eerdmans, 1948), p. 153.

[103]For a survey of relevant texts consult Gwynne Henton Davies, "Tabernacle," in *Interpreter's Dictionary of the Bible,* ed. George Arthur Buttrick, 4 vols. (Nashville, Tenn.: Abingdon, 1962), 4:498-506.

Chapter 4: Leviticus

[1]Jacob Milgrom, *Leviticus 1-16: A New Translation with Introduction, Notes and Commentary,* Anchor Bible 3 (Garden City, N.Y.: Doubleday, 1991), p. 42.

[2]Cf. Theodorus Christiaan Vriezen, *An Outline of Old Testament Theology,* trans. S. Neuijen (Oxford: Basil Blackwell, 1962), p. 280; and Gerhard von Rad, *Old Testament Theology,* trans. David Muir Gibson Stalker, 2 vols. (New York: Harper & Row, 1962-1965), 1:242.

[3]Gordon J. Wenham, *The Book of Leviticus,* New International Commentary on the Old Testament (Grand Rapids, Mich.: Eerdmans, 1979), pp. 16-25.

[4]Brevard S. Childs, *Biblical Theology of the Old and New Testaments: Theological Reflection on the Christian Bible* (Minneapolis: Fortress, 1992), p. 90.

[5]Cf. Ronald E. Clements, "Leviticus," in *Broadman Bible Commentary,* vol. 2, ed. Clifton J. Allen (Nashville, Tenn.: Broadman, 1969-1972), p. 6.

[6]John G. Gammie, *Holiness in Israel,* Overtures to Biblical Theology (Minneapolis: Fortress, 1989), p. 4.

[7]Cf. George Ernest Wright, *The Old Testament Against Its Environment,* Studies in Biblical Theology 2 (London: SCM, 1950), pp. 78-93.

[8]Milgrom, *Leviticus 1-16,* p. 43.

[9]Cf. Yehezkel Kaufmann, *The Religion of Israel: From Its Beginnings to the Babylonian Exile,* trans. and abridged by Moshe Greenberg (Chicago: University of Chicago Press, 1960), pp. 53-58; and Wright, *The Old Testament Against Its Environment,* pp. 78-93.

[10]Milgrom, *Leviticus 1-16,* p. 134.

[11]Ibid., pp. 174-76.

[12]Clements, "Leviticus," p. 11.

[13]Milgrom, *Leviticus 1-16,* p. 52-53.

[14]Walther Eichrodt, *Theology of the Old Testament,* trans. J. A. Baker, 2 vols., Old Testament Library (Philadelphia: Westminster Press, 1961-1967), 1:404.

[15]Elmer A. Martens, *God's Design: A Focus on Old Testament Theology* (Grand Rapids, Mich.: Baker, 1981), p. 56.

[16]Wenham, *Leviticus,* p. 77.

[17]Thomas Wingate Mann, *The Book of the Torah: The Narrative Integrity of the Pentateuch* (Atlanta: John Knox, 1988), pp. 117-19.

[18]Von Rad, *Old Testament Theology,* 1:260.

[19]Cf. Bernhard Duhm, *Das Buch Jesaia* (Göttingen, Germany: Vandenhoek und Ruprecht, 1892), pp. 7-22.

[20]Diether Kellerman, "asham," in *Theological Dictionary of the Old Testament,* ed. G. Johannes Botterweck and Helmer Ringgren, rev. ed., 12 vols. (Grand Rapids, Mich.: Eerdmans, 1977), 1:435.

[21]R. N. Whybray, *Isaiah 40—66,* New Century Bible (Grand Rapids, Mich.: Eerdmans, 1981), p. 179.

[22]Wenham, *Leviticus,* p. 111.

[23]Charles Augustus Briggs, *Messianic Prophecy: The Prediction of the Fulfillment of Redemption Through the Messiah* (1886; reprint, Peabody, Mass.: Hendrickson, 1988).

[24]The causative stem is used here.

[25]Milgrom, *Leviticus 1-16,* p. 495.

[26]Ibid.

[27]John E. Hartley, *Leviticus,* Word Biblical Commentary 4 (Waco, Tex.: Word, 1992).

[28]Baruch A. Levine, *Leviticus,* Jewish Publication Society Torah Commentary (Philadelphia: Jewish Publication Society, 1989), pp. 58-59.

[29]Walter C. Kaiser Jr., "Leviticus," in *New Interpreter's Bible,* vol. 1 (Nashville, Tenn.: Abingdon, 1994), p. 1070.

[30]Cf. Brevard S. Childs, *Old Testament Theology in a Canonical Context* (Philadelphia: Fortress, 1985), pp. 149-50; and von Rad, *Old Testament Theology,* 1:245.

[31]Note the categories in Levine, *Leviticus,* pp. 63-98.

[32]Hartley, *Leviticus,* pp. 142-43.

[33]R. K. Harrison, *Leviticus: An Introduction and Commentary,* Tyndale Old Testament Commentary (Downers Grove, Ill.: InterVarsity Press, 1980), pp. 121-26.

[34]Childs, *Old Testament Theology,* p. 85.

[35]Milgrom, *Leviticus 1-16,* pp. 704-13.

[36]See Kaufmann's discussion in *The Religion of Israel,* pp. 106-15.

[37]Mary Douglas, *Purity and Danger: An Analysis of the Concepts of Pollution and Taboo* (London: Routledge and Kegan Paul, 1966).

[38]Hartley, *Leviticus,* p. 144.

[39]Cf. Levine, *Leviticus,* p. 250.

[40]Kaiser, "Leviticus," p. 1109.

[41]George Angus Fulton Knight, *Leviticus,* Daily Study Bible (Philadelphia: Westminster Press, 1981), p. 89.

[42]Hartley, *Leviticus,* p. 240.

[43]Cf. Carl Friedrich Keil, "Leviticus," in Carl Friedrich Keil and Franz Julius Delitzsch, *Commentary on the Old Testament,* 10 vols. (Grand Rapids, Mich.: Eerdmans, 1980), 1:395 (original ed. *Biblischer Commentar über das Alte Testament,* Leipzig: Dorffling und Franke, 1862-1872).

[44]Cf. Wenham, *Leviticus,* pp. 154-55.

[45]Cf. Childs's survey in *Old Testament Theology,* p. 89.

[46]Ibid., pp. 89-90.

[47]See Wenham's excellent treatment of these issues in *Leviticus,* pp. 161-225.

[48]Childs, *Old Testament Theology,* p. 90.

[49]Harrison, *Leviticus,* p. 175.

[50]Keil, "Leviticus," 1:406.

[51]Clements, "Leviticus," p. 47.

[52]Levine, *Leviticus,* p. 111.

[53]Hartley, *Leviticus,* p. 278.

[54]Levine, *Leviticus,* pp. 117-24.

[55]Cf. Hartley's superb treatment of these matters in *Leviticus,* pp. 298-301.

[56]Keil, "Leviticus," 1:416.

[57]Marvin H. Pope, "Homosexuality," in *Interpreter's Dictionary of the Bible: Supplemental Volume,* ed. Keith R. Crim (Nashville, Tenn.: Abingdon, 1976), p. 415.

[58]Hartley, *Leviticus,* p. 297.

[59]Wenham, *Leviticus,* p. 252.

[60]Carl F. H. Henry, *God, Revelation and Authority,* vol. 6, *God Who Stands and Stays* (Waco, Tex.: Word, 1983), p. 326.

[61]Gammie, *Holiness in Israel,* p. 34.

[62]Wenham, *Leviticus,* p. 272.

[63]Henry, *God, Revelation and Authority,* 6:330.

[64]Clements, "Leviticus," p. 59.

[65]Martin Noth, *Leviticus,* trans. J. E. Anderson, rev. ed. (Philadelphia: Westminster, 1965), p. 162.

[66]Harrison, *Leviticus,* p. 213.

[67]Vriezen, *An Outline of Old Testament Theology,* p. 281.

[68]Eichrodt, *Theology of the Old Testament,* 1:129.

[69]Though I disagree with von Rad's reconstruction of the origins of Israel's religious life, his analysis of the problems Israel faced in this regard is accurate. See von Rad, *Old Testament Theology,* 1:19ff.

[70]Claus Westermann, *Elements of Old Testament Theology,* trans. Douglas W. Stott (Atlanta: John Knox, 1982), pp. 195-96.

[71]Cf. Paul D. Hanson, *The People Called: The Growth of Community in the Bible* (San Francisco: Harper & Row, 1986), p. 51.

[72]Christopher J. H. Wright, *An Eye for an Eye: The Place of Old Testament Ethics Today* (Downers Grove, Ill.: InterVarsity Press, 1983), p. 61.

[73]Hartley, *Leviticus,* p. 429.

[74]Harrison, *Leviticus,* p. 230.

[75]Cf. Levine, *Leviticus,* p. 275; Hartley, *Leviticus,* p. 459; and Wenham, *Leviticus,* p. 327.

[76]Dale Patrick, *Old Testament Law* (Atlanta: John Knox, 1985), pp. 238-39.

[77]R. Laird Harris, "Leviticus," in *Expositor's Bible Commentary,* vol. 2, ed. Frank E. Gaebelein (Grand Rapids, Mich.: Zondervan, 1976-1992), p. 598.

[78]Frank Thielman, *Paul and the Law: A Contextual Approach* (Downers Grove, Ill.: InterVarsity Press, 1994), p. 129.

[79]Henry, *God, Revelation and Authority,* 6:324.

[80]Ralph L. Smith, *Old Testament Theology: Its History, Method and Message* (Nashville, Tenn.: Broadman, 1993), p. 191.

[81]Christoph Barth, *God with Us: A Theological Introduction to the Old Testament,* ed. and trans. G. W. Bromiley (Grand Rapids, Mich.: Eerdmans, 1991), p. 100.

[82]Walther Zimmerli, *Old Testament Theology in Outline,* trans. David Eliot Green (Atlanta: John Knox, 1978), p. 190.

[83]Cf. Hans Walter Wolff, *Joel and Amos: A Commentary on the Books of the Prophets Joel and Amos,* ed. S. Dean McBride Jr., trans. S. Dean McBride Jr. et al., Hermeneia (Philadelphia: Fortress, 1977), p. 159.

Chapter 5: Numbers

[1]Martin Noth, *Numbers,* trans. James D. Martin, Old Testament Library (Philadelphia: Westminster Press, 1968), p. 11.

[2]John Herbert Sailhamer, *The Pentateuch as Narrative: A Biblical-Theological Commentary* (Grand Rapids, Mich.: Zondervan, 1992), p. 381.

[3]Gordon J. Wenham, *Numbers: An Introduction and Commentary,* Tyndale Old Testament Commentaries (Downers Grove, Ill.: InterVarsity Press, 1981), p. 127.

[4]Eugene H. Merrill, "A Theology of the Pentateuch," in *A Biblical Theology of the Old Testament,* ed. Roy B. Zuck et al. (Chicago: Moody Press, 1991), p. 61.

[5]Wenham, *Numbers,* pp. 39-49.

[6]See George Buchanan Gray, *A Critical and Exegetical Commentary on Numbers,* International Critical Commentary (New York: Scribner's, 1903), pp. xlviii-lii; Philip J. Budd, *Numbers,* Word Biblical Commentary 5 (Waco, Tex.: Word, 1984), pp. xxxi-xxxii; and R. K. Harrison, *Numbers,* Wycliffe Exegetical Commentary (Chicago: Moody Press, 1990), pp. 25-28.

[7]Ronald Barclay Allen, "Numbers," in *Expositor's Bible Commentary,* ed. Frank E. Gaebelein (Grand Rapids, Mich.: Zondervan, 1976-1992), 2:753.

[8]Harrison, *Numbers,* p. 160.

[9]Allen, "Numbers," 2:773.

[10]Cf. Harrison, *Numbers,* p. 162, for a summary of these ideas.

[11]John Joseph Owens, "Numbers," in *Broadman Bible Commentary,* ed. Clifton J. Allen (Nashville, Tenn.: Broadman, 1969-1972), 2:110.

[12]Budd, *Numbers,* p. 103.

[13]Cf. the survey of these texts in Gerhard von Rad, *Old Testament Theology,* trans. David Muir Gibson Stalker, 2 vols. (New York: Harper & Row, 1962-1965), 1:280-89.

[14]Brevard S. Childs, *Biblical Theology of the Old and New Testaments: Theological Reflection on the Christian Bible* (Minneapolis: Fortress, 1992), p. 422.

[15]Elmer A. Martens, *God's Design: A Focus on Old Testament Theology* (Grand Rapids, Mich.: Baker, 1981), p. 79.

[16]Sailhamer, *The Pentateuch as Narrative,* p. 388.

[17]Wenham, *Numbers,* p. 127.

[18]Jacob Milgrom, *Numbers,* Jewish Publication Society Torah Commentary (Philadelphia: Jewish Publication Society, 1989), p. 454.

[19]Cf. Harrison, *Numbers,* p. 267.

[20]For a survey of opinions consult Milgrom, *Numbers,* pp. 448-56.

[21]Sailhamer, *The Pentateuch as Narrative,* p. 397.

22Von Rad, *Old Testament Theology,* 1:281.

23Timothy R. Ashley, *The Book of Numbers,* New International Commentary on the Old Testament (Grand Rapids, Mich.: Eerdmans, 1993), p. 393.

24Wenham, *Numbers,* p. 154.

25Ibid., p. 174.

26Milgrom, *Numbers,* p. 199.

27Allen, "Numbers," 2:900.

28See Milgrom's discussion in *Numbers,* pp. 476-80.

29Harrison, *Numbers,* p. 335.

30Ibid., p. 336.

31Ashley, *Numbers,* p. 520.

32Cf. Childs, *Biblical Theology,* p. 416.

33Wenham, *Numbers,* pp. 189-91.

34Owens, "Numbers," p. 152.

35Allen, "Numbers," 2:947.

36Milgrom, *Numbers,* p. 237.

37Gray, *Numbers,* p. 403.

38Wenham, *Numbers,* p. 197.

39Ibid., p. 167.

40Allen, "Numbers," 2:888.

41Wenham, *Numbers,* p. 168.

42Milgrom, *Numbers,* p. 480.

Chapter 6: Deuteronomy

1Ernest W. Nicholson, *God and His People: Covenant and Theology in the Old Testament* (Oxford: Clarendon, 1986).

2A. D. H. Mayes, *Deuteronomy,* New Century Bible (Grand Rapids, Mich.: Eerdmans, 1981), pp. 29-55.

3George E. Mendenhall, "Covenant Forms in Israelite Tradition," *Biblical Archaeologist* 17 (1954): 50-76; George E. Mendenhall, "The Suzerainty Treaty Structure: Thirty Years Later," in *Religion and Law: Biblical-Judaic and Islamic Perspectives,* ed. Edwin Brown Firmage, Bernard G. Weiss and John W. Welch (Winona Lake, Ind.: Eisenbrauns, 1990), pp. 85-100; Dennis J. McCarthy, *Old Testament Covenant: A Survey of Current Opinions* (Oxford: Basil Blackwell, 1972); Dennis J. McCarthy, *Treaty and Covenant: A Study in Form in the Ancient Oriental Documents and the Old Testament,* rev. ed., Analecta Biblica 21A (Rome: Pontifical Biblical Institute, 1978); and Moshe Weinfeld, "Deuteronomy: The Present State of Inquiry," *Journal of Biblical Literature* 86 (1967): 249-62.

4Meredith G. Kline, *Treaty of the Great King: The Covenant Structure of Deuteronomy* (Grand Rapids, Mich.: Eerdmans, 1963); P. C. Craigie, *The Book of Deuteronomy,* New International Commentary on the Old Testament (Grand Rapids, Mich.: Eerdmans, 1976); Earl S. Kalland, "Deuteronomy," in *Expositor's Bible Commentary,* vol. 3, ed. Frank E. Gaebelein (Grand Rapids, Mich.: Zondervan, 1976-1992); and Eugene H. Merrill, *Deuteronomy,* New American Commentary 4 (Nashville, Tenn.: Broadman, 1994).

5Martin Noth, *The Deuteronomistic History,* trans. David Orton, JSOTSup 15 (Sheffield, U.K.: Sheffield Academic Press, 1981).

6Kline, *Treaty of the Great King;* Craigie, *Book of Deuteronomy;* Kalland, "Deuteronomy"; and Merrill, *Deuteronomy.*

7George Ernest Wright, "Deuteronomy," in *Interpreter's Dictionary of the Bible,* ed. George A. Buttrick, 4 vols. (Nashville, Tenn.: Abingdon, 1962), 2:326.

8John Herbert Sailhamer, *The Pentateuch as Narrative: A Biblical-Theological Commentary* (Grand Rapids, Mich.: Zondervan, 1992), pp. 423-24.

9Craigie, *Book of Deuteronomy,* p. 90.

10Walther Eichrodt, *Theology of the Old Testament,* trans. J. A. Baker, 2 vols., Old Testament

Library (Philadelphia: Westminster Press, 1961-1967), 1:44.

[11]Christoph Barth, *God with Us: A Theological Introduction to the Old Testament,* ed. and trans. G. W. Bromiley (Grand Rapids, Mich.: Eerdmans, 1991), pp. 144-47.

[12]Walter C. Kaiser Jr., *Toward an Old Testament Theology* (Grand Rapids, Mich.: Zondervan, 1978), p. 125.

[13]Christopher J. H. Wright, *God's People in God's Land: Family, Land and Property in the Old Testament* (Grand Rapids, Mich.: Eerdmans, 1990), p. 9.

[14]Kaiser, *Toward an Old Testament Theology,* p. 124.

[15]Ewell Ray Clendenen, "Life in God's Land: An Outline of the Theology of Deuteronomy," in *The Church at the Dawn of the Twenty-first Century,* ed. Paige Patterson et al. (Dallas: Criswell Publications, 1989), p. 160. Cf. Elmer A. Martens, *God's Design: A Focus on Old Testament Theology* (Grand Rapids, Mich.: Baker, 1981), p. 104.

[16]John D. W. Watts, "Deuteronomy," in *Broadman Bible Commentary,* ed. Clifton J. Allen (Nashville, Tenn.: Broadman, 1969-1972), 2:192.

[17]Craigie, *Deuteronomy,* p. 144.

[18]Merrill, *Deuteronomy,* pp. 133-34.

[19]John Alexander Thompson, *Deuteronomy: An Introduction and Commentary,* Tyndale Old Testament Commentaries (Downers Grove, Ill.: InterVarsity Press, 1974), p. 112.

[20]Eichrodt, *Theology of the Old Testament,* 1:53.

[21]Watts, "Deuteronomy," p. 207.

[22]Kline, *Treaty of the Great King,* p. 63.

[23]Moshe Weinfeld, *Deuteronomy 1—11: A New Translation with Introduction, Notes and Commentary,* Anchor Bible 5 (Garden City, N.Y.: Doubleday, 1991), p. 288.

[24]Craigie, *Book of Deuteronomy,* p. 157.

[25]Dale Patrick, *Old Testament Law* (Atlanta: John Knox, 1985), p. 254.

[26]Raymond Edward Brown, *The Message of Deuteronomy: Not by Bread Alone* (Downers Grove, Ill.: InterVarsity Press, 1993).

[27]Watts, "Deuteronomy," p. 214.

[28]Craigie, *Book of Deuteronomy,* p. 169.

[29]Watts, "Deuteronomy," p. 214.

[30]Brown, *The Message of Deuteronomy,* p. 96.

[31]Weinfeld, *Deuteronomy 1-11,* p. 338.

[32]Merrill, *Deuteronomy,* p. 164.

[33]S. R. Driver, *A Critical and Exegetical Commentary on Deuteronomy,* International Critical Commentary (New York: Scribner's, 1895), p. 92.

[34]Kline, *Treaty of the Great King,* p. 67.

[35]Thompson, *Deuteronomy,* p. 129.

[36]Kline, *Treaty of the Great King,* p. 68.

[37]Brown, *The Message of Deuteronomy,* pp. 114-15.

[38]Craigie, *Book of Deuteronomy,* p. 189.

[39]Weinfeld, *Deuteronomy 1—11,* pp. 435-36.

[40]Claus Westermann, *Elements of Old Testament Theology,* trans. Douglas W. Stott (Atlanta: John Knox, 1982), pp. 32-33.

[41]Barth, *God with Us,* p. 264.

[42]Brevard S. Childs, *Biblical Theology of the Old and New Testaments: Theological Reflection on the Christian Bible* (Minneapolis: Fortress, 1992), p. 372.

[43]Ibid., pp. 372-73.

[44]Christopher J. H. Wright, *An Eye for an Eye: The Place of Old Testament Ethics Today* (Downers Grove, Ill.: InterVarsity Press, 1983), p. 28.

[45]Cf. Weinfeld, *Deuteronomy 1—11,* pp. 62-65.

[46]Kline, *Treaty of the Great King,* p. 79.

[47]Craigie, *Book of Deuteronomy,* pp. 215-16.

[48]Thompson, *Deuteronomy,* p. 36.

[49]Ibid. See also J. Gordon McConville, *Law and Theology in Deuteronomy,* JSOTSup 33 (Sheffield, U.K.: JSOT Press, 1984), pp. 25-26; and Gerhard von Rad, *Deuteronomy,* trans. Dorothea M. Barton, Old Testament Library (Philadelphia: Westminster Press, 1966), p. 94.

[50]George Ernest Wright, *The Old Testament Against Its Environment,* Studies in Biblical Theology 2 (London: SCM, 1950), p. 63.

[51]Brown, *The Message of Deuteronomy,* pp. 178-79.

[52]Craigie, *Book of Deuteronomy,* p. 257.

[53]Eichrodt, *Theology of the Old Testament,* 1:436-37.

[54]Calum M. Carmichael, *The Laws of Deuteronomy* (Ithaca, N.Y.: Cornell University Press, 1974), p. 216.

[55]Patrick, *Old Testament Law,* p. 123.

[56]Carmichael, *The Laws of Deuteronomy,* p. 113.

[57]Thompson, *Deuteronomy,* p. 218.

[58]Brown, *The Message of Deuteronomy,* p. 196.

[59]Kline, *Treaty of the Great King,* p. 106.

[60]Carmichael, *The Laws of Deuteronomy,* pp. 141-42.

[61]Cf. Craigie, *Book of Deuteronomy,* pp. 288-91; and Carmichael, *The Laws of Deuteronomy,* p. 147.

[62]Brown, *The Message of Deuteronomy,* p. 219.

[63]Note the discussion of the relationship of the Ten Commandments and Deuteronomy in Georg Peter Braulik, "The Sequence of the Laws in Deuteronomy 12—26 and in the Decalogue," in *A Song of Power and the Power of Song: Essays on the Book of Deuteronomy,* Sources for Biblical and Theological Study 3, ed. Duane L. Christensen (Winona Lake, Ind.: Eisenbrauns, 1993), pp. 321-22.

[64]Gerhard von Rad, *Old Testament Theology,* trans. David Muir Gibson Stalker, 2 vols. (New York: Harper & Row, 1962-1965), 1:121-22.

[65]Cf. Mayes, *Deuteronomy,* pp. 332-33.

[66]Cf. von Rad, *Deuteronomy,* p. 159.

[67]Von Rad, *Old Testament Theology,* 1:122.

[68]For a comprehensive discussion of these issues consult William A. Heth and Gordon J. Wenham, *Jesus and Divorce: The Problem with the Evangelical Consensus* (Nashville, Tenn.: Thomas Nelson, 1984).

[69]Kline, *Treaty of the Great King,* p. 121.

[70]Sailhamer, *The Pentateuch as Narrative,* p. 470. Cf. Driver, *Deuteronomy,* p. 296.

[71]Craigie, *Book of Deuteronomy,* p. 24.

[72]Eichrodt, *Theology of the Old Testament,* 1:53-54.

[73]Westermann, *Elements of Old Testament Theology,* p. 31.

[74]Edmond Jacob, *Theology of the Old Testament,* trans. Arthur Weston Heathcote and Philip J. Allcock (New York: Harper & Row, 1958), p. 116.

[75]Von Rad, *Old Testament Theology,* 1:230.

[76]Barth, *God with Us,* p. 178. Cf. Walther Zimmerli, *Old Testament Theology in Outline,* trans. David Eliot Green (Atlanta: John Knox, 1978), pp. 112-13.

[77]For a sound summary of the importance of placing the law book with the ark of the covenant consult Merrill, *Deuteronomy,* pp. 398-99.

Chapter 7: Joshua

[1]For a fuller discussion of these five details, consult Paul R. House, *1, 2 Kings,* New American Commentary 8 (Nashville, Tenn.: Broadman, 1995), pp. 54-58.

[2]For two thorough analyses of the role of the motif of land in the Pentateuch, see David J. A. Clines, *The Theme of the Pentateuch,* JSOTSup 10 (Sheffield, U.K.: JSOT, 1978); and, especially, John Herbert Sailhamer, *The Pentateuch as Narrative: A Biblical-Theological Commentary* (Grand Rapids, Mich.: Zondervan, 1992).

[3]For solid analyses of God's portrayal as warrior in the Old Testament consult Robert G. Boling and George Ernest Wright, *Joshua: A New Translation with Introduction, Notes and Commen-*

tary, Anchor Bible 6 (Garden City, N.Y.: Doubleday, 1982), pp. 27-37.

[4]E. John Hamlin, *Inheriting the Land: A Commentary on the Book of Joshua,* International Theological Commentary (Grand Rapids, Mich.: Eerdmans, 1983), p. 4.

[5]Walter C. Kaiser Jr., *Toward an Old Testament Theology* (Grand Rapids, Mich.: Zondervan, 1978), pp. 124-27.

[6]Trent C. Butler, *Joshua,* Word Biblical Commentary 7 (Waco, Tex.: Word, 1983), p. 22.

[7]Ibid.

[8]John Gray, *Joshua, Judges, Ruth,* New Century Bible (Grand Rapids, Mich.: Eerdmans, 1986), p. 68.

[9]J. Alberto Soggin, *Joshua,* trans. R. A. Wilson, Old Testament Library (Philadelphia: Westminster Press, 1972), p. 61.

[10]Boling, *Joshua,* p. 188.

[11]Butler, *Joshua,* p. 103.

[12]Marten H. Woudstra, *The Book of Joshua,* New International Commentary on the Old Testament (Grand Rapids, Mich.: Eerdmans, 1981), p. 103.

[13]Donald Harold Madvig, "Joshua," in *Expositor's Bible Commentary,* ed. Frank E. Gaebelein (Grand Rapids, Mich.: Zondervan, 1976-1992), 3:277-78.

[14]Hamlin, *Inheriting the Land,* pp. 57-62.

[15]Gray, *Joshua, Judges, Ruth,* p. 91.

[16]Butler, *Joshua,* p. 130.

[17]Christoph Barth, *God with Us: A Theological Introduction to the Old Testament,* ed. and trans. G. W. Bromiley (Grand Rapids, Mich.: Eerdmans, 1991), pp. 178-79.

[18]Elmer A. Martens, *God's Design: A Focus on Old Testament Theology* (Grand Rapids, Mich.: Baker, 1981), pp. 104-5.

[19]For an analysis of how the whole canon views the law as a gift, consult Elmer A. Martens, "Embracing the Law: A Biblical Theological Perspective," *Bulletin for Biblical Research* 2 (1992): 1-28.

[20]Cf. Boling, *Joshua,* pp. 13-27.

[21]Martens, *God's Design,* pp. 107-8.

[22]Brevard S. Childs, *Biblical Theology of the Old and New Testaments: Theological Reflection on the Christian Bible* (Minneapolis: Fortress, 1992), p. 147.

[23]Gray, *Joshua, Judges, Ruth,* p. 123.

[24]Madvig, "Joshua," p. 316.

[25]Gerhard von Rad, *Old Testament Theology,* trans. David Muir Gibson Stalker, 2 vols. (New York: Harper & Row, 1962-1965), 1:303.

[26]Paul D. Hanson, *The People Called: The Growth of Community in the Bible* (San Francisco: Harper & Row, 1986), p. 64.

[27]Hamlin, *Inheriting the Land,* p. 110.

[28]Martens, *God's Design,* p. 115.

[29]T. S. Eliot, *The Complete Poems and Plays, 1909-1950* (New York: Harcourt Brace & World, 1971), p. 107.

[30]Hanson, *The People Called,* p. 65.

[31]Ibid.

[32]Von Rad, *Old Testament Theology,* 1:22.

[33]Ibid., 1:26.

[34]Barth, *God with Us,* p. 182.

Chapter 8: Judges

[1]For an excellent description of the historical factors that impacted Israel during these years, consult John Bright, *A History of Israel,* 2nd ed. (Philadelphia: Westminster Press, 1972), pp. 166-75.

[2]For a detailed analysis of how irony appears throughout the book, consult Lillian R. Klein, *The Triumph of Irony in the Book of Judges,* Bible and Literature Series 14 (Sheffield, U.K.: Almond, 1989).

[3]Note that Joshua 1:1 begins with a notice of Moses' death. Thus both books begin with a formulaic statement about the previous book's main character.

[4]Cf. John Gray, *Joshua, Judges, Ruth,* New Century Bible (Grand Rapids, Mich.: Eerdmans, 1986), pp. 188-89; Robert G. Boling, *Judges: A New Translation with Introduction, Notes and Commentary,* Anchor Bible 6A (Garden City, N.Y.: Doubleday, 1975), pp. 63-67; and George Foot Moore, *A Critical and Exegetical Commentary on Judges,* International Critical Commentary (New York: Scribner's, 1895), pp. 3-10.

[5]K. Lawson Younger Jr., "Judges 1 in Its Near Eastern Literary Context," in *Faith, Tradition and History: Old Testament Historiography in Its Near Eastern Context,* ed. A. R. Millard, James K. Hoffmeier and David W. Baker (Winona Lake, Ind.: Eisenbrauns, 1994), pp. 208-12.

[6]Ibid., pp. 225-27.

[7]Brevard S. Childs, *Introduction to the Old Testament as Scripture* (Philadelphia: Fortress, 1980), p. 259.

[8]For descriptions of Canaanite religion, see Gerhard von Rad, *Old Testament Theology,* trans. David Muir Gibson Stalker, 2 vols. (New York: Harper & Row, 1962-1965), 1:15-35; and William Foxwell Albright, *Yahweh and the Gods of Canaan: A Historical Analysis of Two Contrasting Faiths* (Garden City, N.Y.: Doubleday, 1969), pp. 110-52.

[9]Moore, *Judges,* p. xi.

[10]J. Alberto Soggin, *Judges,* trans. John Stephen Bowden, Old Testament Library (Philadelphia: Westminster Press, 1981), pp. 1-4.

[11]Edward R. Dalglish, "Judges," in *Broadman Bible Commentary,* ed. Clifton J. Allen (Nashville, Tenn.: Broadman, 1969-1972), 2:399.

[12]Klein, *The Triumph of Irony,* pp. 19-20.

[13]Dan Block argues that Deborah's primary role was as prophet and that the people who came to her "were not asking her to solve their legal disputes but to give them the divine answer to their cries." He correctly assesses her main function, but there is no real reason to deny her the same sort of role that Samuel exercises in 1 Samuel 1—12. He both decided cases and gave prophetic words, and the same seems to be true of Deborah. See Daniel Isaac Block, "Deborah Among the Judges," in *Faith, Tradition and History: Old Testament Historiography in Its Near Eastern Context,* ed. A. R. Millard, James K. Hoffmeier and David W. Baker (Winona Lake, Ind.: Eisenbrauns, 1994), pp. 229-53.

[14]For a comparison of the two call stories, consult Norman Charles Habel, "The Form and Significance of the Call Narratives," *Zeitschrift für die alttestamentliche Wissenschaft* 77 (1965): 297-305.

[15]E. John Hamlin, *At Risk in the Promised Land: A Commentary on the Book of Judges,* International Theological Commentary (Grand Rapids, Mich.: Eerdmans, 1990), p. 102.

[16]Arthur Ernest Cundall, "Judges," in Arthur Ernest Cundall and Leon Morris, *Judges and Ruth: An Introduction and Commentary,* Tyndale Old Testament Commentaries (Downers Grove, Ill.: InterVarsity Press, 1968), p. 130.

[17]Herbert M. Wolf, "Judges," in *Expositor's Bible Commentary,* vol. 3, ed. Frank E. Gaebelein (Grand Rapids, Mich.: Zondervan, 1976-1992), p. 448.

[18]Given the standards already articulated in the Law, it is hardly possible that this text is a favorable comment on Jephthah's character. For an opposing viewpoint see Boling, *Judges,* p. 205.

[19]Cf. the discussion of ancient architecture and how animals were kept in one-room homes in Kenneth E. Bailey, "The Manger and the Inn: What the Bible Really Says About Jesus' Birth," *The Catholic Digest,* January 1989, p. 86.

[20]For an excellent, thoughtful analysis of this account consult Klein, *The Triumph of Irony,* pp. 87-99.

[21]For a succinct statement on the implications of being a Nazirite, consult James D. Martin, *The Book of Judges,* Cambridge Bible Commentary (London: Cambridge University Press, 1975), pp. 156-58.

[22]Boling, *Judges,* p. 229.

[23]On Dagon's lineage and place in the Canaanite pantheon, see Charles Fox Burney, *The Book*

of Judges, with Introduction and Notes, Library of Biblical Studies (1918; reprint, New York: KTAV, 1970), pp. 384-87.

[24]This conclusion comes from the fact that prophets from other countries in Abraham's era were often portrayed as having special intercessory skill, an attribute he seems to possess in Genesis 20:7.

[25]See the discussion of the relationship between these texts in Brevard S. Childs, *Biblical Theology of the Old and New Testaments: Theological Reflection on the Christian Bible* (Minneapolis: Fortress, 1992), p. 150.

[26]J. Barton Payne, *The Theology of the Older Testament* (Grand Rapids, Mich.: Zondervan, 1962), pp. 335-36.

[27]Klein, *The Triumph of Irony,* pp. 162-63.

[28]Cf. Michael Wilcock, *The Message of Judges: Grace Abounding,* Bible Speaks Today (Downers Grove, Ill.: InterVarsity Press, 1992), p. 169.

[29]Ibid., p. 175.

[30]Burney, *The Book of Judges,* p. 444.

[31]Klein, *The Triumph of Irony,* p. 167.

Chapter 9: Samuel

[1]Samuel has always been considered one volume in the Hebrew canon. The book was split in Greek and Hebrew translations, perhaps due to its length or subject matter. Samuel and Kings 1—4 are called Kingdoms by the Septuagint, which obviously reflects the books' emphasis on the monarchy. See P. Kyle McCarter Jr., *I Samuel: A New Translation with Introduction, Notes and Commentary,* Anchor Bible 8 (Garden City, N.Y.: Doubleday, 1980), pp. 3-4. For convenience, references to specific texts will be cited as coming from 1-2 Samuel.

[2]For succinct surveys of these important matters consult Joyce G. Baldwin, *1 and 2 Samuel,* Tyndale Old Testament Commentaries (Downers Grove, Ill.: InterVarsity Press, 1988), pp. 17-32; R. P. Gordon, *I and II Samuel* (Grand Rapids, Mich.: Zondervan, 1986), pp. 19-66; and McCarter, *I Samuel,* pp. 12-30.

[3]Cf. Robert M. Polzin, *Samuel and the Deuteronomist: A Literary Study of the Deuteronomistic History, Part Two, 1 Samuel* (San Francisco: Harper & Row, 1989); Robert M. Polzin, *David and the Deuteronomist: A Literary Study of the Deuteronomic History, Part Three, 2 Samuel* (Bloomington: Indiana University Press, 1993); J. P. Fokkelman, *Narrative Art and Poetry in the Books of Samuel: A Full Interpretation Based on Stylistics and Structural Analyses* (vol. 1, *King David, II Sam 9—20 and I Kings 1—2),* Studia Semitica Neerlandica 20, 2 vols. (Assen, Netherlands: Van Gorcum, 1981); and Peter D. Miscall, *1 Samuel: A Literary Reading* (Bloomington: Indiana University Press, 1986).

[4]For example, Ralph W. Klein, *1 Samuel,* Word Biblical Commentary 10 (Waco, Tex.: Word, 1983); A. A. Anderson, *2 Samuel,* Word Biblical Commentary 11 (Waco, Tex.: Word, 1989); McCarter, *I Samuel,* and P. Kyle McCarter Jr., *II Samuel: A New Translation with Introduction, Notes and Commentary,* Anchor Bible 9 (Garden City, N.Y.: Doubleday, 1984).

[5]Walter A. Brueggemann states Samuel's perspective accurately when he writes that the book claims "the monarchy did not appear in Israel either because of the initiative of dazzling personalities or because of large concentrations of socioeconomic, military power, but because of the inscrutable, inexplicable initiative of Yahweh" (see Brueggemann's *Old Testament Theology: Essays on Structure, Theme and Text,* ed. Patrick Dwight Miller Jr. [Minneapolis: Fortress, 1992], p. 219).

[6]Cf. Christoph Barth, *God with Us: A Theological Introduction to the Old Testament,* ed. and trans. G. W. Bromiley (Grand Rapids, Mich.: Eerdmans, 1991), pp. 190-91.

[7]See Polzin, *Samuel and the Deuteronomist,* pp. 30-36, for an analysis of the parallels between 1 Samuel 2:1-10 and 2 Samuel 23:1-7. For an opposing viewpoint consult Miscall, *1 Samuel,* p. 15-16.

[8]Cf. Brevard S. Childs, *Introduction to the Old Testament as Scripture* (Philadelphia: Fortress, 1980), p. 273.

[9]Gordon, *I and II Samuel,* p. 84.

[10]Klein, *1 Samuel,* p. 34.

[11]Cf. David F. Payne, *I and II Samuel,* Daily Study Bible (Philadelphia: Westminster Press, 1982), pp. 25-26.

[12]Baldwin, *1 and 2 Samuel,* p. 69.

[13]McCarter notes that the word usually translated "departed" means "exiled," which heightens the sense of defeat, banishment and divine departure (see *I Samuel,* p. 16).

[14]Payne, *I and II Samuel,* p. 31.

[15]Gordon, *I and II Samuel,* p. 98.

[16]Walter C. Kaiser Jr., *Toward an Old Testament Theology* (Grand Rapids, Mich.: Zondervan, 1978), pp. 141-42.

[17]Cf. Gordon's comments on Isaiah 40—46 in *I and II Samuel,* pp. 25-26.

[18]Payne, *I and II Samuel,* p. 31.

[19]William J. Dumbrell, *Covenant and Creation: A Theology of Old Testament Covenants* (Nashville, Tenn.: Thomas Nelson, 1984), p. 134.

[20]For a survey of opinions consult Klein, *1 Samuel,* p. 79; McCarter, *I Samuel,* pp. 26-30; and Gordon, *I and II Samuel,* pp. 26-30.

[21]McCarter, *I Samuel,* p. 161.

[22]Cf. Kaiser, *Toward an Old Testament Theology,* p. 145; and Dumbrell, *Covenant and Creation,* pp. 134-35.

[23]Baldwin, *1 and 2 Samuel,* p. 102.

[24]Barth, *God with Us,* p. 193.

[25]Walther Eichrodt argues that a sense of theocracy undergirds the whole sense of law in Deuteronomy. See Eichrodt, *Theology of the Old Testament,* trans. J. A. Baker, 2 vols., Old Testament Library (Philadelphia: Westminster Press, 1961-1967), 1:55ff., 1:90ff., 2:243.

[26]Barth, *God with Us,* p. 199.

[27]Miscall, *I Samuel,* p. 86.

[28]Polzin, *Samuel and the Deuteronomist,* p. 130.

[29]McCarter, *I Samuel,* p. 230.

[30]Gordon, *I and II Samuel,* pp. 133-34.

[31]Cf. Gerhard von Rad, *Old Testament Theology,* trans. David Muir Gibson Stalker, 2 vols. (New York: Harper & Row, 1962-1965), 1:325.

[32]Baldwin, *1 and 2 Samuel,* p. 109.

[33]Payne, *I and II Samuel,* p. 71.

[34]Kenneth L. Barker, ed., *New International Version Study Bible* (Grand Rapids, Mich.: Zondervan, 1978), p. 394.

[35]On Saul as a tragic figure see von Rad, *Old Testament Theology,* 1:324-27; and David M. Gunn, *The Fate of King Saul,* JSOTSup 14 (Sheffield, U.K.: Sheffield Academic Press, 1980).

[36]Eichrodt, *Theology of the Old Testament,* 1:443.

[37]John Calvin, *Institutes of the Christian Religion,* ed. John Thomas McNeill, trans. Ford Lewis Battles, 2 vols., Library of Christian Classics 20 (Philadelphia: Westminster Press, 1960), 1:176.

[38]Dumbrell, *Covenant and Creation,* p. 138.

[39]Baldwin, *1 and 2 Samuel,* p. 151.

[40]Payne, *I and II Samuel,* p. 155.

[41]Gordon, *I and II Samuel,* p. 223.

[42]McCarter, *II Samuel,* pp. 133-34.

[43]For other possible meanings for "Yahweh of hosts" see Anderson, *2 Samuel,* p. 86; and von Rad, *Old Testament Theology,* 1:18-19.

[44]William Lee Holladay, *The Psalms Through Three Thousand Years: Prayerbook of a Cloud of Witnesses* (Minneapolis: Fortress, 1993), p. 24.

[45]For example, Claus Westermann sees little value in the titles (see Claus Westermann, *The Living Psalms,* trans. J. R. Porter [Grand Rapids, Mich.: Eerdmans, 1989], pp. 19-20); but Brevard S. Childs argues that the titles are at least developed by exegetical means and important for

analyzing canonical theology. See Brevard S. Childs, "Psalm Titles and Midrashic Exegesis," *Journal of Semitic Studies* 16/2 (1971): 137-50; and Childs, *Introduction to the Old Testament,* pp. 520-22. Derek Kidner says, "What matters is their truth, which there is no reason to doubt, and which finds incidental confirmation in the light which they throw on the psalms they introduce" (see Derek Kidner, *Psalms: An Introduction and a Commentary,* 2 vols., Tyndale Old Testament Commentaries [Downers Grove, Ill.: InterVarsity Press, 1973-1975], 1:246). This volume accepts Kidner's cautiously optimistic opinion.

[46]See the chapter on Psalms for other implications of this interaction.

[47]For an excellent summary of the diversity of historical, textual and editorial opinions on 2 Samuel 7:1-17, consult McCarter, *II Samuel,* pp. 209-31.

[48]Peter R. Ackroyd, *The Second Book of Samuel,* Cambridge Bible Commentary (London: Cambridge University Press, 1977), p. 76.

[49]Dumbrell, *Covenant and Creation,* p. 147.

[50]Gordon, *I and II Samuel,* p. 238.

[51]Barth, *God with Us,* p. 198.

[52]Dumbrell, *Covenant and Creation,* p. 150.

[53]Elmer A. Martens, *God's Design: A Focus on Old Testament Theology* (Grand Rapids, Mich.: Baker, 1981), p. 141.

[54]Kaiser, *Toward an Old Testament Theology,* pp. 152-55; and Dumbrell, *Covenant and Creation,* p. 152.

[55]Barth, *God with Us,* p. 198.

[56]Cf. Kaiser's survey of texts about the son in *Toward an Old Testament Theology,* pp. 159-64.

[57]Barth, *God with Us,* p. 198.

[58]Cf. Carl Friedrich Keil, "The Book of Samuel," in Carl Friedrich Keil and Franz Julius Delitzsch, *Commentary on the Old Testament,* 10 vols. (Grand Rapids, Mich.: Eerdmans, 1980), 2:347 (original ed. *Biblischer Commentar über das Alte Testament,* Leipzig: Dorffling und Franke, 1862-1872).

[59]Hans Wilhelm Hertzberg, *I and II Samuel,* trans. John Stephen Bowden, Old Testament Library (Philadelphia: Westminster Press, 1964), p. 289.

[60]Ibid.

[61]Cf. Leonhard Rost, *The Succession to the Throne of David,* trans. Michael D. Rutter and David M. Gunn (Sheffield, U.K.: Almond, 1982; original ed. *Die Uberlieferung von der Thronnachfolge Davids, Beiträge zur Wissenschaft von Alten und Neuen Testament,* Stuttgart, Germany: Kohlhammer, 1926); R. N. Whybray, *The Succession Narrative: A Study of II Samuel 9-20 and I Kings 1 and 2,* Studies in Biblical Theology 2/9 (Naperville, Ill.: Allenson, 1968); and Fokkelman, *Narrative Art and Poetry in the Books of Samuel.*

[62]For a summary of such conclusions consult McCarter, *II Samuel,* pp. 9-16.

[63]Rolf August Carlson, *David, the Chosen King: A Traditiohistorical Approach to the Second Book of Samuel,* trans. Eric J. Sharpe and Stanley Rudman (Uppsala, Sweden: Almqvist and Wiksell, 1964).

[64]Brueggemann, *Old Testament Theology,* pp. 235-51.

[65]Ibid., pp. 250-51.

[66]Cf. Childs, *Introduction to the Old Testament,* pp. 273-75; and Polzin, *Samuel and the Deuteronomist,* pp. 30-36.

[67]Polzin, *David and the Deuteronomist,* p. 202.

[68]Hertzberg, *I and II Samuel,* p. 385. Cf. Childs, *Introduction to the Old Testament,* p. 274.

[69]Gordon, *I and II Samuel,* p. 307.

[70]Von Rad, *Old Testament Theology,* 1:322.

[71]Walther Zimmerli, *Old Testament Theology in Outline,* trans. David Eliot Green (Edinburgh: T & T Clark, 1978), p. 57.

[72]Barth, *God with Us,* p. 214.

Chapter 10: 1-2 Kings

[1]Brevard S. Childs, *Introduction to the Old Testament as Scripture* (Philadelphia: Fortress, 1980),

p. 289.

[2]Gwilym H. Jones, *1 and 2 Kings,* 2 vols., New Century Bible (Grand Rapids, Mich.: Eerdmans, 1984), 1:106.

[3]For example, John Gray, *I and II Kings,* Old Testament Library (Philadelphia: Westminster Press, 1963), p. 95; Martin Noth, *Könige, Part 1,* Biblischer Kommentar: Altes Testament 9 (Neukirchen-Vluyn, Germany: Neukirchener, 1968), p. 30; and Simon John DeVries, *1 Kings,* Word Biblical Commentary 12 (Waco, Tex.: Word, 1985), p. 30.

[4]John Skinner, *I and II Kings,* Century Bible (Edinburgh: T. C. and E. C. Jack, 1904), p. 63.

[5]Solomon ruled Israel about 970-930 B.C.

[6]For a selection of wisdom writings from other countries, see James B. Pritchard, ed., *Ancient Near Eastern Texts Relating to the Old Testament,* 2nd ed. (Princeton, N.J.: Princeton University Press, 1955), pp. 405-40. For surveys of ancient wisdom literature, see R. B. Y. Scott, *The Way of Wisdom in the Old Testament* (New York: Macmillan, 1971); James L. Crenshaw, *Old Testament Wisdom: An Introduction* (Atlanta: John Knox, 1981), pp. 212-35; and John H. Walton, *Ancient Israelite Literature in Its Cultural Context: A Survey of Parallels Between Biblical and Ancient Near Eastern Texts* (Grand Rapids, Mich.: Zondervan, 1989), pp. 169-200.

[7]As Duane A. Garrett points out, while the title (Song 1:1) of the Song of Songs "seems to indicate Solomonic authorship," other interpretations are plausible. See Garrett, *Proverbs, Ecclesiastes, Song of Songs,* New American Commentary 14 (Nashville, Tenn.: Broadman, 1993), pp. 348-52.

[8]Scott, *The Way of Wisdom,* p. 36.

[9]Cf. Crenshaw, *Old Testament Wisdom,* pp. 42-54.

[10]Brian Peckham, "Israel and Phoenicia," in *Magnalia Dei, the Mighty Acts of God: Essays on the Bible and Archaeology in Memory of G. Ernest Wright, Part 2,* ed. Frank Moore Cross, Werner Erich Lemke and Patrick Dwight Miller Jr. (Garden City, N.Y.: Doubleday, 1976), pp. 231-32.

[11]Walther Zimmerli, *Old Testament Theology in Outline,* trans. David Eliot Green (Edinburgh: T & T Clark, 1978), pp. 178-79.

[12]Walther Eichrodt, *Theology of the Old Testament,* trans. J. A. Baker, 2 vols., Old Testament Library (Philadelphia: Westminster Press, 1961-1967), 1:449.

[13]Herbert Donner, "The Separate States of Israel and Judah," in *Israelite and Judaean History,* ed. John Haralson Hayes and James Maxwell Miller, Old Testament Library (Philadelphia: Westminster Press, 1977), p. 387.

[14]Martin Noth, *The History of Israel,* trans. Peter R. Ackroyd, 2nd ed. (New York: Harper & Row, 1960), p. 232. Noth considers the accounts about Jeroboam as evidence that the author of Kings writes a subjective history (*The History of Israel,* pp. 232-34).

[15]John Bright, *A History of Israel,* 2nd ed. (Philadelphia: Westminster Press, 1972), p. 238.

[16]Ibid.

[17]DeVries, *1 Kings,* 12:162.

[18]Ronald E. Clements, *Old Testament Theology: A Fresh Approach* (London: Marshall, Morgan & Scott, 1978), p. 166.

[19]The years covered in 1 Kings 12—16 span 930-869 B.C. Cf. Paul R. House, *1, 2 Kings,* New American Commentary 8 (Nashville, Tenn.; Broadman, 1995), pp. 43-44.

[20]Brevard S. Childs, *Old Testament Theology in a Canonical Context* (Philadelphia: Fortress, 1985), p. 143.

[21]F. Charles Fensham, "A Few Observations on the Polarisation Between Yahweh and Baal in 1 Kings 17-19," *Zeitschrift für die alttestamentliche Wissenschaft* 92 (1980): 234.

[22]Leila Leah Bronner, *The Stories of Elijah and Elisha as Polemics Against Baal Worship,* Pretoria Oriental Series 6 (Leiden: E. J. Brill, 1968), p. 25. Bronner rejects Wellhausen's, Childs's and Gunkel's claims that Elijah was a henotheist.

[23]For a survey of relevant opinions see Wolfgang Roth, "The Story of the Prophet Micaiah (1 Kings 22) in Historical-Critical Interpretation 1876-1976," in *The Biblical Mosaic: Changing Perspectives,* ed. Robert M. Polzin and Eugene Rothman, Semeia Studies (Philadelphia:

Fortress, 1982), pp. 106-31; Robert Goldenberg, "The Problem of False Prophecy: Talmudic Interpretations of Jeremiah 28 and 1 Kings 22," in *The Biblical Mosaic: Changing Perspectives,* ed. Robert M. Polzin and Eugene Rothman, Semeia Studies (Philadelphia: Fortress, 1982); and Simon John DeVries, *Prophet Against Prophet: The Role of the Micaiah Narrative (1 Kings 22) in the Development of Early Prophetic Tradition* (Grand Rapids, Mich.: Eerdmans, 1978).

[24]For a thorough analysis of this phrase, see Martinus Adrianus Beek, "The Meaning of the Expression 'The Chariots and Horsemen of Israel,'" *Oudtestamentische Studiën* 17 (1972): 1-10.

[25]Mordechai Cogan and Hayim Tadmor, *II Kings: A New Translation with Introduction, Notes and Commentary,* Anchor Bible 11 (Garden City, N.Y.: Doubleday, 1988), pp. 33-34.

[26]Cf. Zimmerli, *Old Testament Theology in Outline,* pp. 101-2.

[27]See the discussion of the messenger motif in Gerhard von Rad, *Old Testament Theology,* trans. David Muir Gibson Stalker, 2 vols. (New York: Harper & Row, 1962-1965), 2:36-39.

[28]The verb is in the causative stem.

[29]John Haralson Hayes, *Amos, the Eighth-Century Prophet: His Times and His Preaching* (Nashville, Tenn.: Abingdon, 1988), p. 21.

[30]Noth, *The History of Israel,* p. 250.

[31]Cf. Theodor Oestreicher, *Das Deuteronomische Grundgesetz,* Beiträge zur Förderung christ-licher Theologie 27/4 (Gütersloh, Germany: Bertelsmann, 1923), p. 38.

[32]Cf. Mordechai Cogan, *Imperialism and Religion: Assyria, Judah and Israel in the Eighth and Seventh Centuries B.C.E.,* Society of Biblical Literature Monograph Series 19 (Missoula, Mont.: Scholars Press, 1974), pp. 1-7; and John William McKay, *Religion in Judah Under the Assyrians, 732-609 B.C.,* Studies in Biblical Theology 2/26 (Naperville, Ill.: Allenson, 1973), pp. 67-73.

[33]Cogan, *Imperialism and Religion,* pp. 9-21.

[34]John N. Oswalt, *The Book of Isaiah: Chapters 1—39,* New International Commentary on the Old Testament (Grand Rapids, Mich.: Eerdmans, 1986), p. 659.

[35]J. A. Motyer, *The Prophecy of Isaiah: An Introduction and Commentary* (Downers Grove, Ill.: InterVarsity Press, 1993), p. 282.

[36]See the survey of opinions in House, *1, 2 Kings,* pp. 371-72.

[37]This comment reflects the belief that the law book contains Mosaic materials. Cf. R. K. Harrison, *Introduction to the Old Testament: With a Comprehensive Review of Old Testament Studies and a Special Supplement on the Apocrypha* (Grand Rapids, Mich.: Eerdmans, 1969), p. 732; Eugene H. Merrill, *Deuteronomy,* New American Commentary 4 (Nashville, Tenn.: Broadman, 1994), pp. 27-37. For a survey of other opinions consult Moshe Weinfeld, *Deuteronomy 1—11: A New Translation with Introduction, Notes and Commentary,* Anchor Bible 5 (Garden City, N.Y.: Doubleday, 1991), pp. 37-84.

[38]Noth, *The History of Israel,* p. 281.

[39]Gerhard von Rad, *Studies in Deuteronomy,* trans. David Muir Gibson Stalker, Studies in Biblical Theology 9 (London: SCM, 1963), p. 90.

[40]Von Rad, *Old Testament Theology,* 1:343.

[41]Martin Noth, *The Deuteronomistic History,* trans. David Orton, JSOTSup 15 (Sheffield, U.K.: Sheffield Academic Press, 1981), p. 97.

[42]Cf. Clements, *Old Testament Theology,* pp. 100-102.

Chapter 11: Isaiah

[1]Bunyan Davie Napier, "Prophet," in *Interpreter's Dictionary of the Bible,* ed. George Arthur Buttrick, 4 vols. (Nashville, Tenn.: Abingdon, 1962), 3:896-919.

[2]Cf. Edgar W. Conrad, *Reading Isaiah,* Overtures to Biblical Theology (Minneapolis: Fortress, 1991).

[3]Cf. Christopher R. Seitz, *Isaiah 1—39,* Interpretation: A Bible Commentary for Teaching and Preaching (Louisville, Ky.: John Knox, 1993); and Christopher R. Seitz, ed., *Reading and Preaching the Book of Isaiah* (Philadelphia: Fortress, 1988).

[4]Cf. Rolf Rendtorff, *Canon and Theology: Overtures to an Old Testament Theology,* ed. and

trans. Margaret Kohl, Overtures to Biblical Theology (Minneapolis: Fortress, 1993), pp. 146-89.

[5]Cf. Brevard S. Childs, *Introduction to the Old Testament as Scripture* (Philadelphia: Fortress, 1980), pp. 311-38; and Ronald E. Clements, "The Unity of the Book of Isaiah," *Interpretation* 36/2 (April 1982): 17-129. It may be more accurate to say that Clements's approach leans toward canonical tendencies while maintaining a keen interest in redaction analysis.

[6]Childs, *Introduction to the Old Testament,* pp. 325-38.

[7]J. A. Motyer, *The Prophecy of Isaiah: An Introduction and Commentary* (Downers Grove, Ill.: InterVarsity Press, 1993), pp. 9-34.

[8]For an excellent analysis of the centrality of God's holiness in Isaiah, consult John G. Gammie, *Holiness in Israel,* Overtures to Biblical Theology (Minneapolis: Fortress, 1989), pp. 71-101. Cf. J. J. M. Roberts, "Isaiah in Old Testament Theology," *Interpretation* 36/2 (April 1982): 130-43. Roberts observes, "If there is any one concept central to the whole Book of Isaiah, it is the vision of Yahweh as the Holy One of Israel" (p. 131).

[9]John N. Oswalt, *The Book of Isaiah: Chapters 1—39,* New International Commentary on the Old Testament (Grand Rapids, Mich.: Eerdmans, 1986), p. 34.

[10]Christopher R. North, *The Second Isaiah* (Oxford: Clarendon, 1964), p. 16.

[11]John Skinner, *The Book of the Prophet Isaiah,* 2 vols., Cambridge Bible Commentary (1917; reprint, Cambridge: Cambridge University Press, 1963), 2:xlviii.

[12]John D. W. Watts, *Isaiah 1—33,* Word Biblical Commentary 24 (Waco, Tex.: Word, 1985), p. lv.

[13]Cf. North, *The Second Isaiah,* pp. 12-13, 17-18.

[14]Cf. R. N. Whybray, *Isaiah 40—66,* New Century Bible (Grand Rapids, Mich.: Eerdmans, 1981), p. 30.

[15]Watts, *Isaiah 1—33,* p. lv.

[16]The most obvious example of this interest is found in Acts 8:26-39, where Philip tells the Ethiopian eunuch that Isaiah 53 refers to Jesus.

[17]Seitz, *Isaiah 1—39,* p. 125.

[18]Hans Wildberger, *Isaiah 1—12,* trans. Thomas H. Trapp, Continental Commentaries (Minneapolis: Fortress, 1991), p. 21.

[19]See the excellent bibliography of works related to Isaiah 7:1-17 in ibid., pp. 279-82.

[20]Even an author as conservative as Walter C. Kaiser Jr. accepts this interpretation. See Walter C. Kaiser Jr., *The Messiah in the Old Testament,* Studies in Old Testament Biblical Theology (Grand Rapids, Mich.: Zondervan, 1995), pp. 158-62.

[21]Motyer, *The Prophecy of Isaiah,* p. 86.

[22]Otto Kaiser, *Isaiah 1—12,* trans. R. A. Wilson, Old Testament Library (Philadelphia: Westminster Press, 1972), p. 105.

[23]Cf. Joseph A. Alexander, *Commentary on the Prophecies of Isaiah* (1846; reprint, Grand Rapids, Mich.: Zondervan, 1953); and Joseph A. Alexander, *Commentary on the Later Prophecies of Isaiah,* ed. John Edie (New York: Wiley and Putnam, 1847), pp. 190-91; and Ronald E. Clements, *Isaiah 1—39,* New Century Bible (Grand Rapids, Mich.: Eerdmans, 1980), pp. 98-100.

[24]Cf. Edward J. Young, *The Book of Isaiah,* 2nd ed., 3 vols., New International Commentary on the Old Testament (Grand Rapids, Mich.: Eerdmans, 1972), 1:174.

[25]Cf. Motyer, *The Prophecy of Isaiah,* p. 102; and contra Wildberger, *Isaiah 1—12,* p. 404.

[26]John F. A. Sawyer, *Isaiah,* 2 vols., Daily Study Bible (Philadelphia: Westminster Press, 1984), 1:125-27.

[27]Seitz, *Isaiah 1—39,* p. 115.

[28]Cf. Oswalt, *Isaiah 1—39,* pp. 300-301. For a description of events during this era, consult John Bright, *A History of Israel,* 2nd ed. (Philadelphia: Westminster Press, 1972), pp. 278-83.

[29]The event mentioned probably occurred about 712 B.C. Cf. Bright, *A History of Israel,* p. 280; and John Haralson Hayes and Stuart A. Irvine, *Isaiah, the Eighth-Century Prophet: His Times and His Preaching* (Nashville, Tenn.: Abingdon, 1987), pp. 268-69.

[30]Gerhard von Rad, *Old Testament Theology,* trans. David Muir Gibson Stalker, 2 vols. (New York: Harper & Row, 1962-1965), 2:120.

[31]Clements, *Isaiah 1—39,* p. 146.

[32]For a discussion of the various meanings of "stranger," consult Sawyer, *Isaiah,* 1:142; and Otto Kaiser, *Isaiah 13—39,* trans. R. A. Wilson, Old Testament Library (Philadelphia: Westminster Press, 1974), p. 25.

[33]Cf. Young, *Isaiah,* 1:463-64; and Motyer, *The Prophecy of Isaiah,* p. 152.

[34]Walter C. Kaiser Jr., *Toward an Old Testament Theology* (Grand Rapids, Mich.: Zondervan, 1978), p. 211.

[35]For an excellent survey of opinions consult Clements, *Isaiah 1—39,* pp. 196-200.

[36]H. H. Rowley, *The Relevance of Apocalyptic: A Study of Jewish and Christian Apocalypses from Daniel to the Revelation,* 3rd ed. (1944; reprint, Greenwood, S.C.: Attic, 1980), pp. 16-17. See also Paul D. Hanson, *The Dawn of Apocalyptic: The Historical and Sociological Roots of Jewish Apocalyptic Eschatology,* rev. ed. (Philadelphia: Fortress, 1986), p. 11.

[37]Sawyer, *Isaiah,* 1:204.

[38]Clements, *Isaiah 1—39,* pp. 196-97.

[39]Oswalt, *Isaiah 1—39,* p. 504.

[40]Richard Schultz, "The King in the Book of Isaiah," in *The Lord's Anointed: Interpretation of Old Testament Messianic Texts,* ed. Philip E. Satterthwaite, Richard S. Hess and Gordon J. Wenham, Tyndale House Studies (Grand Rapids, Mich.: Baker, 1995), pp. 150-54.

[41]Ibid., p. 150.

[42]Motyer, *The Prophecy of Isaiah,* p. 257.

[43]Paul D. Hanson, *Isaiah 40—66,* Interpretation: A Bible Commentary for Teaching and Preaching (Louisville, Ky.: John Knox, 1995), p. 29. Hanson correctly views Isaiah 40:18-20 as the beginning of monotheism as a strategic theme in Isaiah 40—55.

[44]Skinner, *The Book of the Prophet Isaiah,* 2:11.

[45]Cf. Bernhard Duhm, *Das Buch Jesaia* (Göttingen, Germany: Vandenhoeck und Ruprecht, 1892), p. 311.

[46]James Muilenburg, "The Book of Isaiah, Chapters 40—66," in *Interpreter's Bible,* vol. 5 (New York: Abingdon, 1951-1957). Muilenburg considers all Israel the servant. Johannes Lindblom thinks the servant is an allegorical image of Israel; see his *The Servant Songs in Deutero-Isaiah: A New Attempt to Solve an Old Problem* (Lund, Sweden: Gleerup, 1951). Several mediating positions along these lines have also been offered. For a thorough introduction to these issues, consult Christopher R. North, *The Suffering Servant in Deutero-Isaiah: A Historical and Critical Study,* 2nd ed. (London: Oxford University Press, 1956), pp. 6-116.

[47]For example, Whybray, *Isaiah 40—66,* pp. 70-73.

[48]For example, Young, *Isaiah,* vol. 3; and Geoffrey W. Grogan, "Isaiah," in *Expositor's Bible Commentary,* vol. 6, ed. Frank E. Gaebelein (Grand Rapids, Mich.: Zondervan, 1976-1992).

[49]For instance, John D. W. Watts suggests in *Isaiah 34—66,* Word Biblical Commentary 25 (Waco, Tex.: Word, 1987), pp. 119, 187, 201 and 229, that Cyrus, Darius and Zerubbabel may be the servant(s).

[50]Cf. von Rad, *Old Testament Theology,* 2:250-62; George W. Coats, *The Moses Tradition,* JSOTSup 161 (Sheffield, U.K.: Sheffield Academic Press, 1993), pp. 133-41, 182-89; Scott J. Hafemann, *Paul, Moses, and the History of Israel: The Letter/Spirit Contrast and the Argument from Scripture in 2 Corinthians 3* (Tübingen, Germany: Mohr/Siebeck, 1995), pp. 101-19; and Gordon Paul Hugenberger, "The Servant of the Lord in the 'Servant Songs' of Isaiah," in *The Lord's Anointed: Interpretation of Old Testament Messianic Texts,* ed. Philip E. Satterthwaite, Richard S. Hess and Gordon J. Wenham, Tyndale House Studies (Grand Rapids, Mich.: Baker, 1995), pp. 105-40. Hugenberger's article offers a thorough introduction to the scholarly dialogue on the servant songs and makes a compelling case for the second Moses option.

[51]H. Wheeler Robinson, "The Hebrew Conception of Corporate Personality," in *Werden und Wesen des Alten Testaments,* ed. Paul Volz, Beihefte zur Zeitschrift für die Altestamentliche Wissenschaft 66 (Berlin: Töpelmann, 1936), pp. 49-62.

[52]Hanson, *Isaiah 40—66,* p. 41.

[53]Cf. H. G. M. Williamson, *The Book Called Isaiah: Deutero-Isaiah's Role in Composition and*

Redaction (Oxford: Oxford University Press, 1994), p. 2.

[54]This interpretation is based on accepting the "Israel" of Isaiah 49:3 as part of the text instead of as a later gloss. For an analysis of the issues at stake, see John L. McKenzie, *Second Isaiah: A New Translation with Introduction, Notes and Commentary,* Anchor Bible 20 (Garden City, N.Y.: Doubleday, 1968), pp. 105; and North, *The Second Isaiah,* pp. 187-88.

[55]Cf. Hanson, *Isaiah 40—66,* pp. 140-41.

[56]Cf. Motyer, *The Prophecy of Isaiah,* p. 401.

[57]Claus Westermann, *Prophetic Oracles of Salvation in the Old Testament,* trans. Keith R. Crim (Louisville, Ky.: Westminster/John Knox, 1991), pp. 42-43.

[58]Cf. Motyer, *The Prophecy of Isaiah,* p. 408.

[59]Clements considers the phrase "a light to the nations" one of the major themes that demonstrates Isaiah's unity. See Ronald E. Clements, "A Light to the Nations: A Central Theme of the Book of Isaiah," in *Forming Prophetic Literature: Essays on Isaiah and the Twelve in Honor of John D. W. Watts,* ed. James W. Watts and Paul R. House, JSOTSup 235 (Sheffield, U.K.: Sheffield Academic Press, 1996).

[60]McKenzie, *Second Isaiah,* p. 133.

[61]Von Rad, *Old Testament Theology,* 2:257.

[62]Walther Zimmerli, *Old Testament Theology in Outline,* trans. David Eliot Green (Edinburgh: T & T Clark, 1978), pp. 223-24.

[63]Von Rad, *Old Testament Theology,* 2:257 n. 31.

[64]North, *The Suffering Servant in Deutero-Isaiah,* pp. 147-48.

[65]Claus Westermann, *Isaiah 40—66,* trans. David Muir Gibson Stalker, Old Testament Library (Philadelphia: Westminster Press, 1969), p. 267.

[66]Motyer, *The Prophecy of Isaiah,* p. 440.

[67]James D. Smart, *History and Theology in Second Isaiah: A Commentary on Isaiah 35, 40—66* (London: Epworth, 1967), p. 195.

[68]Motyer, *The Prophecy of Isaiah,* pp. 443-44. For an analysis of Isaiah 54—55 as a "call to decision" and its connection to earlier chapters, consult Ulrich E. Simon, *A Theology of Salvation: A Commentary on Isaiah 40—55* (London: SPCK, 1953), pp. 222-41.

[69]North suggests Isaiah 55:3-5 reflects on Psalm 18:43-45 and says it places emphasis on spiritual, rather than political, leadership. See North, *The Second Isaiah,* pp. 258-59.

[70]Smart, *History and Theology in Second Isaiah,* p. 224. It must be noted, however, that Smart identifies the servant with Israel, so he does not take the same approach as does this volume.

[71]Motyer, *The Prophecy of Isaiah,* pp. 454-55.

[72]For further analysis of the servant and the church's interpretation of the servant songs, consult John Goldingay, *God's Prophet, God's Servant: A Study in Jeremiah and Isaiah 40—55,* Bible Classics Library (Carlisle, U.K.: Paternoster, 1994).

[73]Roberts, "Isaiah in Old Testament Theology," pp. 133-34; and North, *The Second Isaiah,* pp. 13-16.

[74]McKenzie, *Second Isaiah,* pp. lviii-lxi; and Skinner, *The Book of the Prophet Isaiah,* 2:xlvi-li. Cf. Westermann, *Prophetic Oracles of Salvation,* p. 39.

[75]Cf. Roberts, "Isaiah in Old Testament Theology," p. 134; McKenzie, *Second Isaiah,* p. lxvii; and Motyer, *The Prophecy of Isaiah,* p. 22.

[76]H. H. Rowley, *The Faith of Israel: Aspects of Old Testament Thought* (London: SCM, 1956), p. 185.

[77]Motyer, *The Prophecy of Isaiah,* p. 461.

[78]Cf. Rendtorff, *Canon and Theology,* pp. 181-89.

[79]Von Rad, *Old Testament Theology,* 2:280.

[80]Cf. Rendtorff, *Canon and Theology,* pp. 155-60.

[81]For a treatment of how Isaiah 59—60 fits into the book's motif of light and darkness, see Hanson, *Isaiah 40—66,* pp. 219-20; and Clements, "A Light to the Nations."

[82]Westermann says "the similarity is unmistakable" (*Prophetic Oracles of Salvation,* p. 85).

[83]Cf. von Rad, *Old Testament Theology,* 2:280-82.

[84]Cf. McKenzie, *Second Isaiah,* p. 181, for a description of the parallels between Isaiah 61:1

and Isaiah 42:1-4.

[85]Hanson, *Isaiah 40—66,* p. 224. Note the humility of this individual and that of the servant in Isaiah 42:1-4.

[86]On Jerusalem's elect status see Ronald E. Clements, *Old Testament Theology: A Fresh Approach* (London: Marshall, Morgan & Scott, 1978), p. 91.

[87]Just as there are two Israels, one servant/remnant and one unbelieving, so there are the same two Gentile groups. Gentiles who serve Zion in Isaiah 60:10-11 bring gifts willingly to an open city, but rebellious and oppressing Gentiles are punished (Is 60:12-14).

[88]Motyer, *The Prophecy of Isaiah,* pp. 540-41.

[89]Zimmerli, *Old Testament Theology in Outline,* p. 226.

Chapter 12: Jeremiah

[1]The order of Jeremiah 46—51 is also somewhat different. Certain verses found in the Hebrew text are not found in the Septuagint, so the latter version is also somewhat shorter than the former.

[2]For example, Ernest W. Nicholson, *Preaching to the Exiles: A Study of the Prose Tradition in the Book of Jeremiah* (Oxford, U.K.: Basil Blackwell, 1970).

[3]For example, R. K. Harrison, *Jeremiah and Lamentations: An Introduction and Commentary,* Tyndale Old Testament Commentaries (Downers Grove, Ill.: InterVarsity Press, 1973).

[4]Moshe Weinfeld, *Deuteronomy and the Deuteronomic School* (1972; reprint, Winona Lake, Ind.: Eisenbrauns, 1992), p. 1.

[5]William Lee Holladay, *Jeremiah,* 2 vols., ed. Paul D. Hanson, Hermeneia (Philadelphia: Fortress, 1986-1989), 2:78-80.

[6]Ibid., 2:35-70.

[7]Brevard S. Childs, *Introduction to the Old Testament as Scripture* (Philadelphia: Fortress, 1980), p. 353.

[8]Ibid.

[9]Brevard S. Childs, *Old Testament Theology in a Canonical Context* (Philadelphia: Fortress, 1985), pp. 135-44.

[10]Nicholson, *Preaching to the Exiles.*

[11]Norman Charles Habel, "The Form and Significance of the Call Narratives," *Zeitschrift für die alttestamentliche Wissenschaft* 77 (1965): 297-323.

[12]Most scholars believe Jeremiah 1:2 refers to when Jeremiah begins his career, but Holladay thinks it marks his birth (*Jeremiah,* 1:17).

[13]Ibid., 1:30.

[14]J. A. Thompson, *The Book of Jeremiah,* New International Commentary on the Old Testament (Grand Rapids, Mich.: Eerdmans, 1980), pp. 148-50.

[15]Cf. Ronald E. Clements, "Patterns in the Prophetic Canon," in *Canon and Authority: Essays in Old Testament Religion and Theology,* ed. George W. Coats and Burke O'Connor Long (Philadelphia: Fortress, 1977), pp. 42-55.

[16]Peter R. Ackroyd, *Studies in the Religious Tradition of the Old Testament* (London: SCM, 1987), pp. 79-104.

[17]Clements comments that Jeremiah 2:1-3 covers all Israel's territory, social institutions and history. See Ronald E. Clements, *Jeremiah,* Interpretation: A Bible Commentary for Teaching and Preaching (Atlanta: John Knox, 1988), p. 23.

[18]Walther Eichrodt, *Theology of the Old Testament,* trans. J. A. Baker, 2 vols., Old Testament Library (Philadelphia: Westminster Press, 1961-1967), 2:294.

[19]Robert P. Carroll, *Jeremiah,* Old Testament Library (London: SCM, 1986), p. 145.

[20]The Hebrew word means "to turn around." James Leo Green says the word occurs 1,059 times in the Old Testament, with 111 of the usages appearing in Jeremiah. See James Leo Green, "Jeremiah," in *Broadman Bible Commentary,* ed. Clifton J. Allen (Nashville, Tenn.: Broadman, 1969-1972), 6:11.

[21]Many scholars have suggested that Jeremiah fears a Scythian invasion. Note this possibility in

Henri Cazelles, "Jeremiah and Deuteronomy," in *A Prophet to the Nations: Essays in Jeremiah Studies*, ed. Leo G. Perdue and Brian Watson Kovacs (Winona Lake, Ind.: Eisenbrauns, 1984), pp. 129-49.

[22]Cf. Brevard S. Childs, "The Enemy from the North and the Chaos Tradition," *Journal of Biblical Literature* 78 (1959): 187-98; and Walter A. Brueggemann, *To Pluck Up, to Tear Down: A Commentary on the Book of Jeremiah 1—25*, International Theological Commentary (Grand Rapids, Mich.: Eerdmans, 1988), p. 50.

[23]Cf. Holladay, *Jeremiah*, 1:154-55.

[24]P. C. Craigie, Page H. Kelley and Joel F. Drinkard Jr., *Jeremiah 1—25*, Word Biblical Commentary 26 (Dallas: Word, 1991), p. 74. As Gerhard von Rad observes, "Jeremiah was still far from regarding Jahweh's relationship to Jerusalem and Judah as broken for good and all"; see von Rad, *Old Testament Theology*, trans. David Muir Gibson Stalker, 2 vols. (New York: Harper & Row, 1962-1965), 2:196.

[25]John Bright, *Jeremiah: A New Translation with Introduction, Notes and Commentary*, Anchor Bible 21 (Garden City, N.Y.: Doubleday, 1965), p. 49.

[26]The question about adultery, divorce and remarriage is probably based on Deuteronomy 24:1-4.

[27]Holladay, *Jeremiah*, 2:45.

[28]William McKane, *A Critical and Exegetical Commentary on Jeremiah*, ed. John Adney Emerton and C. E. B. Cranfield, 2 vols., International Critical Commentary (Downers Grove, Ill.: InterVarsity Press, 1973), 1:161.

[29]Cf. Carroll, *Jeremiah*, pp. 214-18, for interpretive options.

[30]Else Kragelund Holt, "Jeremiah's Temple Sermon and the Deuteronomists: An Investigation of the Redactional Relationship Between Jeremiah 7 and 26," *Journal for the Study of the Old Testament* 36 (1986): 77.

[31]Clements, *Jeremiah*, p. 44.

[32]Stanley Romaine Hopper, "Exposition of Jeremiah," in *Interpreter's Bible* (Nashville, Tenn.: Abingdon, 1951-1957), 5:872.

[33]For an apt and lucid description of these offices in Israelite history, consult Joseph Blenkinsopp, *Sage, Priest, Prophet: Religious and Intellectual Leadership in Ancient Israel* (Louisville, Ky.: Westminster/John Knox, 1995).

[34]Brueggemann, *To Pluck Up, to Tear Down*, p. 90.

[35]John Goldingay, *God's Prophet, God's Servant: A Study in Jeremiah and Isaiah 40—55*, Bible Classics Library (Carlisle, U.K.: Paternoster, 1994), p. 16.

[36]Weinfeld, *Deuteronomy and the Deuteronomic School*, p. 1. Cf. the first section of this chapter.

[37]Kathleen M. O'Connor, *The Confessions of Jeremiah: Their Interpretation and Role in Chapters 1—25*, Society of Biblical Literature Dissertation Series 94 (Atlanta: Scholars Press, 1988), p. 25.

[38]Bright, *Jeremiah*, p. 87.

[39]Holladay, *Jeremiah*, 1:461.

[40]Gerhard von Rad, "The Confessions of Jeremiah," in *Theodicy in the Old Testament*, ed. James L. Crenshaw, Issues in Religion and Theology 4 (Philadelphia: Fortress, 1983), p. 90.

[41]Carroll, *Jeremiah*, pp. 333-34.

[42]Von Rad, *Old Testament Theology*, 2:202.

[43]Eichrodt, *Theology of the Old Testament*, 2:398.

[44]A. R. Diamond, *The Confessions of Jeremiah in Context: Scenes of Prophetic Drama*, JSOTSup 45 (Sheffield, U.K.: Sheffield Academic Press, 1987), p. 144.

[45]Samuel E. Balentine, "Jeremiah, Prophet of Prayer," *Review and Expositor* 78/3 (summer 1981): 33.

[46]Von Rad, *Old Testament Theology*, 2:104-5.

[47]Cf. Carroll, *Jeremiah*, p. 406.

[48]Bright, *Jeremiah*, p. 215.

[49]Edmond Jacob, *Theology of the Old Testament*, trans. Arthur Weston Heathcote and Philip J.

Allcock (New York: Harper & Row, 1958), p. 337.

[50]Walther Zimmerli, *Old Testament Theology in Outline,* trans. David Eliot Green (Edinburgh: T & T Clark, 1978), p. 92.

[51]Childs, *Old Testament Theology,* p. 119.

[52]Cf. Nicholson, *Preaching to the Exiles,* p. 195. For a fuller discussion of true and false prophecy in this volume, consult the comments on Jeremiah 27—29.

[53]The Septuagint places Jeremiah 46—51 after 25:13 and presents the condemned countries in a different order. Theologically this move reinforces and explains why God will judge them. The Hebrew order focuses on the elect nation's punishment as primary before condemning the others. It also offers less satisfaction to unrepentant readers who console themselves by comparing their piety favorably to the sins of the Gentiles.

[54]For example, Thompson, *Jeremiah,* p. 524; and Holt, "Jeremiah's Temple Sermon," p. 77.

[55]Robert P. Carroll, *From Chaos to Covenant: Uses of Prophecy in the Book of Jeremiah* (London: SCM, 1981), pp. 192-97.

[56]James A. Sanders, "Hermeneutics in True and False Prophecy," in *Canon and Authority: Essays in Old Testament Religion and Theology,* ed. George W. Coats and Burke O'Connor Long (Philadelphia: Fortress, 1977), pp. 21-41.

[57]Von Rad, *Old Testament Theology,* 2:209-10.

[58]Thomas W. Overholt, *The Threat of Falsehood: A Study in the Theology of the Book of Jeremiah,* Studies in Biblical Theology 2/16 (London: SCM, 1970), p. 1.

[59]Ibid., pp. 11-23.

[60]Ibid., p. 103.

[61]Nicholson, *Preaching to the Exiles,* pp. 96-97.

[62]Childs, *Old Testament Theology,* p. 139.

[63]Mark E. Biddle, "The Literary Frame Surrounding Jeremiah 30:1—33:26," *Zeitschrift für die alttestamentliche Wissenschaft* 100/3 (1988): 409-13.

[64]Cf. Nicholson, *Preaching to the Exiles,* pp. 83-84. Several scholars focus on the interior nature of the new covenant as the main difference between it and the old covenant(s). As has been stated, however, interiorization of the law was expected, according to Deuteronomy. The means by which the law becomes internalized may differ, but the external-versus-internal dichotomy is not the primary change. For excellent discussions of the internal nature of the new covenant consult John Skinner, *Prophecy and Religion: Studies in the Life of Jeremiah* (Cambridge: Cambridge University Press, 1922), pp. 320-34; Carroll, *From Chaos to Covenant,* pp. 215-25; Thompson, *Book of Jeremiah,* pp. 579-81; and Holladay, *Jeremiah,* 2:198.

[65]Jacob, *Theology of the Old Testament,* p. 216.

[66]Nicholson, *Preaching to the Exiles,* pp. 83-84.

[67]Ronald E. Clements, *Old Testament Theology: A Fresh Approach* (London: Marshall, Morgan & Scott, 1978), p. 103.

[68]Von Rad, *Old Testament Theology,* 2:213-14.

[69]Cf. H. D. Potter, "The New Covenant in Jeremiah 31:31-34," *Vetus Testamentum* 33/3 (1983): 347-55. Potter says, "The Israelite could not circumcise the foreskin of his own heart, nor the Nubian change his skin: God alone could operate on his corrupted creature" (p. 352).

[70]For an analysis of the close relationship between these messages and earlier ones in the Former Prophets and Jeremiah, consult Nicholson, *Preaching to the Exiles,* pp. 108-13; and Weinfeld, *Deuteronomy and the Deuteronomic School,* pp. 27-32.

[71]Holladay, *Jeremiah,* 2:304.

[72]Thompson, *Book of Jeremiah,* p. 680.

[73]Charles Lee Feinberg, "Jeremiah," in *Expositor's Bible Commentary,* ed. Frank E. Gaebelein (Grand Rapids, Mich.: Zondervan, 1976-1992), p. 6:646.

[74]Cf. Nicholson, *Preaching to the Exiles,* pp. 109-11.

[75]Clements, *Old Testament Theology,* p. 77.

[76]Cf. Isaiah 13—23; Ezekiel 25—32; Amos 1:2—2:16.

[77]Note the discussion of these matters in Holladay, *Jeremiah*, 2:312-14.

[78]Ibid., 2:431.

[79]Thompson, *Book of Jeremiah*, p. 731.

[80]Bright, *Jeremiah*, p. 353.

Chapter 13: Ezekiel

[1]For a more detailed defense of a canonical approach to Ezekiel, see Brevard S. Childs, *Introduction to the Old Testament as Scripture* (Philadelphia: Fortress, 1979), pp. 369-72.

[2]Ibid., p. 361.

[3]Walther Eichrodt, *Ezekiel*, trans. Cosslett Quin, Old Testament Library (London: SCM, 1970), p. 59.

[4]John Battersby Harford, *Studies in the Book of Ezekiel* (Cambridge: Cambridge University Press, 1935), p. 3.

[5]Moshe Greenberg, *Ezekiel 1—20: A New Translation with Introduction, Notes and Commentary*, Anchor Bible 22 (Garden City, N.Y.: Doubleday, 1983), p. 61.

[6]Eichrodt, *Ezekiel*, p. 61.

[7]Edmond Jacob, *Theology of the Old Testament*, trans. Arthur Weston Heathcote and Philip J. Allcock (New York: Harper & Row, 1958), p. 126.

[8]Walther Zimmerli, *Old Testament Theology in Outline*, trans. David Eliot Green (Edinburgh: T & T Clark, 1978), p. 103.

[9]Cf. John William Wevers, *Ezekiel*, New Century Bible (London: Nelson, 1969), pp. 50-51.

[10]Cf. Childs, *Introduction to the Old Testament*, p. 361.

[11]Douglas K. Stuart, *Ezekiel*, Communicator's Commentary 18 (Dallas: Word, 1989), p. 47.

[12]Leslie C. Allen, *Ezekiel 20—48*, Word Biblical Commentary 29 (Dallas: Word, 1994), p. 61.

[13]Ibid., p. 121.

[14]Eichrodt, *Ezekiel*, p. 104.

[15]Harford, *Studies in the Book of Ezekiel*, p. 4.

[16]Brevard S. Childs, *Old Testament Theology in a Canonical Context* (Philadelphia: Fortress, 1985), p. 39.

[17]The first date listed in Ezekiel 1:2 sets the call accounts in the fifth year of Jehoiachin's exile, or about 593 B.C. This passage occurs after 390 days of ministry (cf. Ezek 4:5) and may be dated in 592 B.C. See Wevers, *Ezekiel*, pp. 43, 78.

[18]For an analysis of the possible cults that are functioning, see Greenberg, *Ezekiel*, pp. 168-73.

[19]For a discussion of the Old Testament's emphasis on God's dwelling among a worshipful people, consult Joseph Blenkinsopp, *Ezekiel*, Interpretation: A Bible Commentary for Teaching and Preaching (Louisville, Ky.: John Knox, 1990), pp. 59-60.

[20]Ralph Holland Alexander, "Ezekiel," in *Expositor's Bible Commentary*, ed. Frank E. Gaebelein (Grand Rapids, Mich.: Zondervan, 1976-1992), 6:793.

[21]Note Eichrodt's use of this term for the remnant in *Ezekiel*, pp. 142-46.

[22]Allen, *Ezekiel 20—48*, p. 165.

[23]Cf. Walther Zimmerli, *Ezekiel*, vol. 1, ed. Frank Moore Cross and Klaus Baltzer, trans. Ronald E. Clements; vol. 2, ed. Paul D. Hanson and Leonard Jay Greenspoon, trans. James D. Martin; 2 vols., Hermeneia (Philadelphia: Fortress, 1979-1983), 1:262.

[24]The exact rites practiced have not yet been fully explained. It is safe to say, however, that the prophets depicted resorted to magical arts for their basis of authority instead of to the covenant. See ibid., 1:297-98.

[25]Cf. John Bernard Taylor, *Ezekiel: An Introduction and Commentary*, Tyndale Old Testament Commentaries (London: Tyndale, 1969), p. 127.

[26]Eichrodt, *Ezekiel*, p. 183.

[27]Allen, *Ezekiel 20—48*, p. 208.

[28]Blenkinsopp, *Ezekiel*, pp. 76, 86-89.

[29]Zimmerli, *Ezekiel*, 1:238.

[30]Ronald E. Clements, *Old Testament Theology: A Fresh Approach* (London: Marshall, Morgan

& Scott, 1978), p. 59.

[31]Jacob, *Theology of the Old Testament,* pp. 320-21.

[32]For a discussion of Ezekiel's view of divine election of Israel in this text see Eichrodt, *Ezekiel,* pp. 218-19.

[33]Cf. Zimmerli, *Ezekiel,* 1:363.

[34]Stuart, *Ezekiel,* p. 148.

[35]Ronald M. Hals, *Ezekiel,* Forms of the Old Testament Literature 19 (Grand Rapids, Mich.: Eerdmans, 1989), p. 117.

[36]Lawrence Boadt, *Reading the Old Testament: An Introduction* (New York: Paulist, 1984), p. 391.

[37]Eichrodt, *Ezekiel,* p. 234.

[38]Michael A. Fishbane, "Sin and Judgment in the Prophecies of Ezekiel," *Interpretation* 38/2 (April 1984): 142.

[39]Ibid.

[40]An excellent discussion of Jeremiah 31:29-30 and Ezekiel 18 along these lines occurs in Joel S. Kaminsky, *Corporate Responsibility in the Hebrew Bible,* JSOTSup 196 (Sheffield, U.K.: Sheffield Academic Press, 1995), pp. 139-78.

[41]Greenberg, *Ezekiel,* p. 369. Cf. Alexander, "Ezekiel," p. 836.

[42]Childs, *Old Testament Theology,* p. 57.

[43]Eichrodt, *Ezekiel,* pp. 270-72. Cf. Exodus 22:28 and 34:19-28. For a similar viewpoint see Zimmerli, *Ezekiel,* 1:411.

[44]Fishbane, "Sin and Judgment," pp. 142-44.

[45]Wevers, *Ezekiel,* p. 178.

[46]Boadt, *Reading the Old Testament,* p. 389.

[47]Jacob, *Theology of the Old Testament,* pp. 121-27.

[48]Blenkinsopp, *Ezekiel,* p. 122.

[49]Carol A. Newsom, "A Maker of Metaphors: Ezekiel's Oracles Against Tyre," *Interpretation* 38/2 (1984): 163.

[50]Daniel Isaac Block observes, "Not a word is said about the righteous. Would they also have been in Sheol? If so, where would their beds have been located? On the other hand, we note that all his depictions of the netherworld occur in oracles against foreign nations (Is 14:9-20). But where is Israel in all of this?" See Daniel Isaac Block, "Beyond the Grave: Ezekiel's Vision of Death and Afterlife," *Bulletin for Biblical Research* 2 (1992): 128.

[51]For a list of other options consult Lamar Eugene Cooper Sr., *Ezekiel,* New American Commentary 17 (Nashville, Tenn.: Broadman, 1994), pp. 241-45.

[52]P. C. Craigie, *Ezekiel,* Daily Study Bible (Philadelphia: Westminster Press, 1983), pp. 236-38.

[53]Blenkinsopp, *Ezekiel,* pp. 152-53.

[54]Elmer A. Martens, *God's Design: A Focus on Old Testament Theology* (Grand Rapids, Mich.: Baker, 1981), pp. 193-96.

[55]Daniel Isaac Block, "The Prophet of the Spirit: The Use of RWH in the Book of Ezekiel," *Journal of the Evangelical Theological Society* 32/1 (March 1989): 41.

[56]Ibid., p. 39.

[57]J. Barton Payne, *The Theology of the Older Testament* (Grand Rapids, Mich.: Zondervan, 1962), p. 479.

[58]Cf. Walter C. Kaiser Jr., *The Messiah in the Old Testament,* Studies in Old Testament Biblical Theology (Grand Rapids, Mich.: Zondervan, 1995), p. 196; and Stuart, *Ezekiel,* p. 349.

[59]Cf. Blenkinsopp, *Ezekiel,* p. 177.

[60]Christoph Barth, *God with Us: A Theological Introduction to the Old Testament,* ed. and trans. G. W. Bromiley (Grand Rapids, Mich.: Eerdmans, 1991), p. 339.

[61]Blenkinsopp, *Ezekiel,* pp. 193-94.

[62]Stuart, *Ezekiel,* p. 390.

[63]Cf. Martens, *God's Design,* pp. 226-27.

[64]Zimmerli, *Ezekiel,* 2:547.

[65]Cf. Zimmerli, *Old Testament Theology in Outline,* pp. 229-30, for other parallels between Ezekiel's and Zechariah's eschatalogical visions.

[66]Cf. Zimmerli, *Ezekiel,* 2:547.

[67]Eichrodt, *Ezekiel,* pp. 593-94.

[68]Cf. Kaiser, *The Messiah in the Old Testament,* pp. 193-99.

[69]Cf. Charles Augustus Briggs, *Messianic Prophecy: The Prediction of the Fulfillment of Redemption Through the Messiah* (1886; reprint, Peabody, Mass.: Hendrickson, 1988), p. 497.

Chapter 14: The Book of the Twelve

[1]Cf. James Nogalski, *Literary Precursors to the Book of the Twelve,* Beihefte Zeitschrift für die alttestamentliche Wissenschaft 217 (Berlin: Walter de Gruyter, 1993); and James Nogalski, *Redactional Processes in the Book of the Twelve,* Beihefte Zeitschrift für die alttestamentliche Wissenschaft 218 (Berlin: Walter de Gruyter, 1993).

[2]Cf. Barry Alan Jones, *The Formation of the Book of the Twelve: A Study in Text and Canon,* Society of Biblical Literature Dissertation Series 149 (Atlanta: Scholars Press, 1995).

[3]For analyses of the Twelve from redactional, literary and historical perspectives, read the essays in James W. Watts and Paul R. House, eds., *Forming Prophetic Literature: Essays on Isaiah and the Twelve in Honor of John D. W. Watts,* JSOTSup 235 (Sheffield, U.K.: Sheffield Academic Press, 1996).

[4]For an extensive analysis of the literary connections in the Twelve, consult Paul R. House, *The Unity of the Twelve,* JSOTSup 97/Bible and Literature Series 27 (Sheffield, U.K.: Almond, 1990). If I were to write this book again, the most fundamental change I would make is to change the title to *Literary Unity in the Twelve* to reflect the fact that literary unity is but one type of coherence the Twelve exhibits. The book's epilogue reflects this belief (cf. pp. 243-45), but the title does not.

[5]For a study of the canonical linkage between the various books of the Twelve see Andrew Yueking Lee, "The Canonical Unity of the Scroll of the Minor Prophets" (Ph.D. diss., Baylor University, 1985).

[6]For a discussion of the historical circumstances of this era consult the concise comments in C. Hassell Bullock, *An Introduction to the Old Testament Prophetic Books* (Chicago: Moody Press, 1986), pp. 85-87; and James D. Newsome Jr., *The Hebrew Prophets* (Atlanta: John Knox, 1984), pp. 30-32.

[7]Several good summaries of these issues have been written, though a comprehensive study of research on Hosea has not yet appeared. Two sound and readable examples are H. H. Rowley, *Men of God: Studies in Old Testament History and Prophecy* (London: Nelson, 1963), pp. 66-97; Francis I. Andersen and David Noel Freedman, *Hosea: A New Translation with Introduction, Notes and Commentary,* Anchor Bible 24 (Garden City, N.Y.: Doubleday, 1980), pp. 40-76.

[8]Cf. Andersen and Freedman, *Hosea,* pp. 157-59.

[9]Cf. Douglas K. Stuart, *Hosea—Jonah,* Word Biblical Commentary 31 (Waco, Tex.: Word, 1987), pp. 26-27.

[10]Cf. Hans Walter Wolff, *Hosea: A Commentary on the Book of the Prophet Hosea,* trans. Gary Stansell, Hermeneia (Philadelphia: Fortress, 1974), pp. 12-16; and James Luther Mays, *Hosea,* Old Testament Library (Philadelphia: Westminster Press, 1969), pp. 25-26.

[11]Cf. Georg Fohrer, *Introduction to the Old Testament,* trans. David Eliot Green (Nashville, Tenn.: Abingdon, 1968), p. 421; and Crawford Howell Toy, "Note on Hosea 1—3," *Journal of Biblical Literature* 32 (1913): 75-79.

[12]See the excellent explanation of this viewpoint in Thomas Edward McComiskey, "Hosea," in *The Minor Prophets: An Exegetical and Expository Commentary,* ed. Thomas Edward McComiskey, 2 vols. (Grand Rapids, Mich.: Baker, 1992-1993), 1:10-17.

[13]Cf. Andersen and Freedman, *Hosea,* pp. 68-76. One of the strengths of this commentary is the authors' ability to demonstrate these linguistic linkages throughout the latter parts of the prophecy.

[14]Mays, *Hosea,* p. 61.

[15]Claus Westermann, *Basic Forms of Prophetic Speech,* trans. Hugh Clayton White (Philadelphia: Westminster Press, 1967), pp. 199-200.

[16]William Rainey Harper, *A Critical and Exegetical Commentary on Amos and Hosea,* International Critical Commentary (New York: Scribner's, 1905), p. 250.

[17]Walther Zimmerli, *Old Testament Theology in Outline,* trans. David Eliot Green (Edinburgh: T & T Clark, 1978), p. 188.

[18]James Limburg, *Hosea—Micah,* Interpretation: A Bible Commentary for Teaching and Preaching (Atlanta: John Knox, 1988), p. 26.

[19]Cf. Elmer A. Martens, *God's Design: A Focus on Old Testament Theology* (Grand Rapids, Mich.: Baker, 1981), p. 172.

[20]Wolff, *Hosea,* p. 213.

[21]Norman Henry Snaith, *Mercy and Sacrifice: A Study of the Book of Hosea* (London: SCM, 1953), p. 45.

[22]Cf. Bunyan Davie Napier, *Song of the Vineyard: A Guide Through the Old Testament,* rev. ed. (Philadelphia: Fortress, 1981), pp. 250-52.

[23]Cf. Bullock, *An Introduction to the Old Testament Prophetic Books.*

[24]Leslie C. Allen, *The Books of Joel, Obadiah, Jonah and Micah,* New International Commentary on the Old Testament (Grand Rapids, Mich.: Eerdmans, 1976), p. 30.

[25]For a comparison of parallels see S. R. Driver, *The Books of Joel and Amos, with Introduction and Notes,* Cambridge Bible Commentary 25 (Cambridge: Cambridge University Press, 1901), p. 19; and Hans Walter Wolff, *Joel and Amos: A Commentary on the Books of the Prophets Joel and Amos,* ed. S. Dean McBride Jr., trans. S. Dean McBride Jr. et al., Hermeneia (Philadelphia: Fortress, 1977), p. 10.

[26]Cf. Stuart, *Hosea—Jonah,* p. 228.

[27]Raymond Bryan Dillard, "Joel," in *The Minor Prophets: An Exegetical and Expository Commentary,* ed. Thomas Edward McComiskey, 2 vols. (Grand Rapids, Mich.: Baker, 1992-1993), 1:280.

[28]The list includes Isaiah 2:1; 13:6; 13:9; 22:5; 34:8; Jeremiah 46:10; Ezekiel 7:10; 13:5; 30:3; Joel 1:15; 2:1; 2:11; 2:31; 3:14; Amos 5:18-20; Obadiah 15; Zephaniah 1:7-8, 14-18; Zechariah 14:1. Cf. Gerhard von Rad, *Old Testament Theology,* trans. David Muir Gibson Stalker, 2 vols. (New York: Harper & Row, 1962-1965), 2:99-125.

[29]Zimmerli, *Old Testament Theology in Outline,* p. 105.

[30]Thomas Edward McComiskey, *The Covenants of Promise: A Theology of the Old Testament Covenants* (Grand Rapids, Mich.: Baker, 1985), p. 87.

[31]Scott J. Hafemann, *Paul, Moses and the History of Israel: The Letter/Spirit Contrast and the Argument from Scripture in 2 Corinthians 3,* Wissenschaftliche Untersuchungen zum Neuen Testament (Tübingen, Germany: Mohr/Siebeck, 1995), p. 182. Hafemann's painstaking analysis of Paul's use of "the letter and the spirit" demonstrates that the New Testament interprets Joel 2:28-29 contextually and canonically.

[32]Ronald E. Clements, *Old Testament Theology: A Fresh Approach* (London: Marshall, Morgan & Scott, 1978), pp. 144-46. Clements claims that four themes characterize restoration passages: return from exile, renewal of the Davidic lineage, the rebuilding of Zion and Zion's role as protective home of the remnant.

[33]Cf. Brevard S. Childs, *Old Testament Theology in a Canonical Context* (Philadelphia: Fortress, 1985), pp. 106, 230.

[34]Walter C. Kaiser Jr., *Toward an Old Testament Theology* (Grand Rapids, Mich.: Zondervan, 1978), pp. 188-90.

[35]Cf. Newsome, *The Hebrew Prophets,* p. 16.

[36]Cf. David Noel Freedman and Francis I. Andersen, *Amos: A New Translation with Introduction, Notes and Commentary,* Anchor Bible 24A (New York: Doubleday, 1989), pp. 237.

[37]J. A. Motyer, *The Day of the Lion: The Message of Amos,* Bible Speaks Today (Downers Grove, Ill.: InterVarsity Press, 1974), pp. 39-40.

[38]Peter C. Craigie, *Twelve Prophets*, 2 vols., Daily Study Bible (Philadelphia: Westminster Press, 1984/1985), 1:131.

[39]Driver, *Joel and Amos; p. 139.*

[40]Cf. Hans Walter Wolff, *Joel and Amos: A Commentary on the Books of the Prophets Joel and Amos*, ed. S. Dean McBride Jr., trans. S. Dean McBride Jr. et al., Hermeneia (Philadelphia: Fortress, 1977), p. 175.

[41]Motyer, *The Day of the Lion*, pp. 66-68.

[42]Billy K. Smith and Frank S. Page, *Amos, Obadiah, Jonah*, New American Commentary 19B (Nashville, Tenn.: Broadman, 1995), pp. 93-94.

[43]Wolff, *Joel and Amos*, p. 264.

[44]For a comparison of concepts, see Thomas J. Finley, *Joel, Amos, Obadiah*, Wycliffe Exegetical Commentary (Chicago: Moody Press, 1990), p. 246-48.

[45]Zimmerli, *Old Testament Theology in Outline*, p. 185.

[46]This punishment will be administered personally by Yahweh. Cf. Childs, *Old Testament Theology*, pp. 164-65; and von Rad, *Old Testament Theology*, 2:137-38.

[47]H. G. M. Williamson thinks that this connection between prophecy and the plumbline may also explain why Amos 7:10-17 is placed after Amos 7:7-9. See H. G. M. Williamson, "The Prophet and the Plumb-Line: A Redaction-Critical Study of Amos 7," in *The Place Is Too Small for Us: The Israelite Prophets in Recent Scholarship*, ed. R. P. Gordon, Sources for Biblical and Theological Study 5 (Winona Lake, Ind.: Eisenbrauns, 1995), p. 471.

[48]Cf. James Luther Mays, *Amos*, Old Testament Library (Philadelphia: Westminster Press, 1969), p. 125.

[49]For a discussion of prophetic visions consult Johannes Lindblom, *Prophecy in Ancient Israel* (Philadelphia: Fortress, 1963), pp. 122-37.

[50]Cf. Driver, *Joel and Amos*, p. 221; and Harper, *Amos and Hosea*, p. 198.

[51]Cf. Driver, *Joel and Amos*, p. 223.

[52]Cf. John B. Polhill, *Acts*, New American Commentary 26 (Nashville, Tenn.: Broadman, 1992), pp. 329-30.

[53]Wolff, *Joel and Amos*, p. 355; and Stuart, *Hosea—Jonah*, p. 400.

[54]F. F. Bruce, *New Testament Development of Old Testament Themes* (Grand Rapids, Mich.: Eerdmans, 1968), p. 79.

[55]Finley, *Joel, Amos, Obadiah*, pp. 327-28.

[56]Cf. Bullock's summary in Bullock, *An Introduction to the Old Testament Prophetic Books*, pp. 255-56.

[57]Note Stuart's list of all oracles against foreign nations in *Hosea—Jonah*, pp. 405-6.

[58]J. M. Powis Smith, William Hayes Ward and Julius August Bewer, *A Critical and Exegetical Commentary on Micah, Zephaniah, Nahum, Habakkuk, Obadiah and Joel*, International Critical Commentary (New York: Scribner's, 1911), pp. 21-22.

[59]Raymond Bryan Dillard and Tremper Longman III, *An Introduction to the Old Testament* (Grand Rapids, Mich.: Zondervan, 1994), pp. 389-90.

[60]See the survey of relevant opinions in Brevard S. Childs, *Introduction to the Old Testament as Scripture* (Philadelphia: Fortress, 1980), pp. 417-21; and R. K. Harrison, *Introduction to the Old Testament: With a Comprehensive Review of Old Testament Studies and a Special Supplement on the Apocrypha* (Grand Rapids, Mich.: Eerdmans, 1969), pp. 904-14.

[61]Cf. Stuart, *Hosea—Jonah*, pp. 440-42; and Bullock, *An Introduction to the Old Testament Prophetic Books*, pp. 44-48.

[62]Cf. Stuart, *Hosea—Jonah*, pp. 435-37; and Smith and Page, *Amos, Obadiah, Jonah*, pp. 210-22.

[63]Note how Childs raises these issues in *Introduction to the Old Testament*, p. 425; and *Old Testament Theology*, pp. 106, 128.

[64]For a discussion of irony in Jonah, consult Edwin M. Good, *Irony in the Old Testament*, Bible and Literature Series 3, 2nd ed. (Sheffield, U.K.: Almond, 1981), pp. 39-55; and Mona West, "Irony in the Book of Jonah: Audience Identification with the Hero," *Perspectives in Religious Studies* 11 (1984): 232-42.

[65]Craigie, *Twelve Prophets*, 1:214.

[66]Allen, *The Books of Joel, Obadiah, Jonah and Micah*, p. 213.

[67]Limburg, *Hosea—Micah*, p. 154.

[68]For a thorough discussion of this topic consult David Gerald Hagstrom, *The Coherence of the Book of Micah: A Literary Analysis*, Society of Biblical Literature Dissertation Series 89 (Atlanta: Scholars Press, 1988). The different approaches to Micah's structure reflect the fact that there are divergent opinions about Micah's authorship and composition.

[69]For example, John T. Willis, "The Structure of Micah 3—5 and the Function of Micah 5:9-14 in the Book," *Zeitschrift für die alttestamentliche Wissenschaft* 81 (1969): 191-97; and Allen, *The Books of Joel, Obadiah, Jonah and Micah*, pp. 257-61.

[70]For example, Smith, Ward and Bewer, *Micah, Zephaniah, Nahum, Habakkuk, Obadiah and Joel*, pp. 8-12; and Carl Friedrich Keil, "Micah," in Carl Friedrich Keil and Franz Julius Delitzsch, *Commentary on the Old Testament*, 10 vols. (Grand Rapids: Eerdmans, 1980), 10:442 (original ed. *Biblischer Commentar über das Alte Testament*, Leipzig: Dorffling und Franke, 1862-1872.)

[71]For example, James Luther Mays, *Micah*, Old Testament Library (Philadelphia: Westminster Press, 1976), pp. 2-12; and Hagstrom, *The Coherence of the Book of Micah*, pp. 21-22.

[72]The list of cities and their punishments in Micah 1:10-16 is one play on words after another. For an excellent translation of this section, consult Hans Walter Wolff, *Micah the Prophet*, trans. Ralph David Gehrke (Philadelphia: Fortress, 1981), pp. 14-16.

[73]Cf. Mays, *Micah*, pp. 62-63.

[74]Claus Westermann, *Elements of Old Testament Theology*, trans. Douglas W. Stott (Atlanta: John Knox, 1982), p. 144.

[75]Ralph L. Smith, *Micah—Malachi*, Word Biblical Commentary 32 (Waco, Tex.: Word, 1984), p. 44.

[76]Thomas Edward McComiskey, "Micah," in *Expositor's Bible Commentary*, ed. Frank E. Gaebelein (Grand Rapids, Mich.: Zondervan, 1976-1992), 7:427.

[77]Wolff, *Micah the Prophet*, p. 93.

[78]Delbert R. Hillers, *Micah*, ed. Paul D. Hanson, Hermeneia (Philadelphia: Fortress, 1984), pp. 6-7.

[79]J. M. P. Smith, "Micah," in J. M. Powis Smith, William Hayes Ward and Julius August Bewer, *A Critical and Exegetical Commentary on Micah, Zephaniah, Nahum, Habakkuk, Obadiah and Joel*, International Critical Commentary (New York: Scribner's, 1911), p. 150.

[80]Allen, *The Books of Joel, Obadiah, Jonah and Micah*, p. 397.

[81]McComiskey, "Micah," p. 444.

[82]Carl Edwin Armerding, "Nahum," in *Expositor's Bible Commentary*, ed. Frank E. Gaebelein (Grand Rapids, Mich.: Zondervan, 1976-1992), 7:457.

[83]Childs, *Introduction to the Old Testament*, p. 445.

[84]J. M. P. Smith, "Nahum," in Smith, Ward and Bewer, *Critical and Exegetical Commentary on Micah, Zephaniah, Nahum, Habakkuk, Obadiah and Joel*, p. 281. Gerhard von Rad observes that the lack of references to Israelite sin may be due to the fact that Nahum may write after Josiah's reform. See von Rad, *Old Testament Theology*, 2:189.

[85]George A. Smith, *The Book of the Twelve Prophets, Commonly Called the Minor Prophets*, 2 vols., rev. ed., Expositor's Bible (New York: Harper & Brothers, 1928), 2:89-90.

[86]Elizabeth Rice Achtemeier, *Nahum—Malachi*, Interpretation: A Bible Commentary for Teaching and Preaching (Atlanta: John Knox, 1986), p. 14.

[87]Armerding, "Nahum," pp. 453-54.

[88]J. J. M. Roberts, *Nahum, Habakkuk and Zephaniah*, Old Testament Library (Louisville, Ky.: Westminster/John Knox, 1991), p. 67.

[89]John D. W. Watts, *The Books of Joel, Obadiah, Jonah, Nahum, Habakkuk and Zephaniah*, Cambridge Bible Commentary (Cambridge: Cambridge University Press, 1975), p. 120.

[90]Bullock, *An Introduction to the Old Testament Prophetic Books*, p. 224.

[91]Harrison, *Introduction to the Old Testament*, p. 930.

[92]Cf. Roberts, *Nahum, Habakkuk and Zephaniah*, pp. 82-84, for a discussion of options. Roberts argues that the threat stated in the book predates 604 B.C. He also thinks some later reworking of material occurred. Carl Edwin Armerding says that the book may reflect "Habakkuk's

spiritual struggles over a long period of time, possibly beginning as early as 626 and continuing as late as 590 or after." See Carl Edwin Armerding, "Habakkuk," in *Expositor's Bible Commentary,* ed. Frank E. Gaebelein (Grand Rapids, Mich.: Zondervan, 1976-1992), 7:493. Regardless, Habakkuk's work, like Jeremiah's, takes place during troubling political and theological times.

[93]Childs, *Introduction to the Old Testament,* p. 453.

[94]Carl Friedrich Keil, "Habakkuk," in Carl Friedrich Keil and Franz Julius Delitzsch, *Commentary on the Old Testament,* 10 vols. (Grand Rapids, Mich.: Eerdmans, 1980), 10:64-67 (original ed. *Biblischer Commentar über das Alte Testament,* Leipzig: Dorffling und Franke, 1862-1872).

[95]Maria Eszenyei Széles, *Wrath and Mercy: A Commentary on the Books of Habakkuk and Zephaniah,* trans. George Angus Fulton Knight, International Theological Commentary (Grand Rapids, Mich.: Eerdmans, 1987), p. 31.

[96]Craigie, *Twelve Prophets,* 2:93.

[97]Keil, "Habakkuk," 10:74.

[98]Achtemeier, *Nahum—Malachi,* p. 55.

[99]See the surveys of opinion in Adele Berlin, *Zephaniah: A New Translation with Introduction, Notes and Commentary,* Anchor Bible 25A (Garden City, N.Y.: Doubleday, 1994), pp. 31-47; Roberts, *Nahum, Habakkuk and Zephaniah,* pp. 161-64; and Paul R. House, *Zephaniah—A Prophetic Drama,* JSOTSup 69/Bible and Literature Series 16 (Sheffield, U.K.: Almond, 1988), pp. 9-14.

[100]Roberts, *Nahum, Habakkuk and Zephaniah,* p. 163. Probably the best treatment of Zephaniah that argues for a later date is Ehud Ben Zvi, *A Historical-Critical Study of the Book of Zephaniah,* Beihefte Zeitschrift für die Altestamentliche Wissenschaft 198 (Berlin: Walter de Gruyter, 1991). Ben Zvi dates the final form of the book after 587 B.C.

[101]Cf. Berlin, *Zephaniah,* pp. 17-20, and House, *The Unity of the Twelve,* p. 94.

[102]For an analysis of how the imagery here amounts to a reversal of creation, read Michael De Roche, "Zephaniah 1:2-3: The 'Sweeping of Creation,'" *Vetus Testamentum* 30 (1980): 104-9. For a comparison of flood imagery and this text see Watts, *The Books of Joel, Obadiah, Jonah, Nahum, Habakkuk and Zephaniah,* p. 156.

[103]Achtemeier, *Nahum—Malachi,* p. 70.

[104]Berlin, *Zephaniah,* p. 90.

[105]O. Palmer Robertson, *The Books of Nahum, Habakkuk and Zephaniah,* New International Commentary on the Old Testament (Grand Rapids, Mich.: Eerdmans, 1990), pp. 254-55.

[106]Berlin, *Zephaniah,* pp. 15-16.

[107]Craigie, *Twelve Prophets,* 2:119.

[108]Watts, *The Books of Joel, Obadiah, Jonah, Nahum, Habakkuk and Zephaniah,* p. 164.

[109]Berlin, *Zephaniah,* pp. 16-17.

[110]Cf. Craigie, *Twelve Prophets,* 2:128; Szeles, *Wrath and Mercy,* p. 107; Berlin, *Zephaniah,* p. 133.

[111]Cf. House, *Zephaniah,* p. 132.

[112]Peter R. Ackroyd, *Exile and Restoration: A Study of Hebrew Thought of the Sixth Century B.C.,* Old Testament Library (Philadelphia: Westminster Press, 1968), pp. 153-55.

[113]David L. Petersen, *Haggai and Zechariah 1—8,* Old Testament Library (Philadelphia: Westminster Press, 1984), p. 20.

[114]Cf. Carol L. Meyers and Eric M. Meyers, *Haggai, Zechariah 1—8: A New Translation with Introduction, Notes and Commentary,* Anchor Bible 25B (Garden City, N.Y.: Doubleday, 1987), pp. xxix-xl.

[115]Bullock, *An Introduction to the Old Testament Prophetic Books,* p. 306.

[116]Zimmerli, *Old Testament Theology in Outline,* p. 69.

[117]John Bright, *The Kingdom of God: The Biblical Concept and Its Meaning for the Church* (Nashville, Tenn.: Abingdon-Cokesbury, 1953), p. 159.

[118]Joyce G. Baldwin, *Haggai, Zechariah, Malachi: An Introduction and Commentary,* Tyndale Old Testament Commentaries (Downers Grove, Ill.: InterVarsity Press, 1972), p. 39.

[119]Edmond Jacob, *Theology of the Old Testament*, trans. Arthur Weston Heathcote and Philip J. Allcock (New York: Harper & Row, 1958), p. 162.

[120]Cf. chapter one of this volume.

[121]Paul L. Redditt, *Haggai, Zechariah, Malachi*, New Century Bible (Grand Rapids, Mich.: Eerdmans, 1995), p. 20.

[122]Von Rad, *Old Testament Theology*, 2:282.

[123]The phrase "the covenant which I made with you when I brought you up from Egypt" does not appear in the Septuagint. Thus Baldwin (*Haggai, Zechariah, Malachi*, p. 47) thinks it may be a scribal notation that was added to the text. Meyers and Meyers think it is not unlikely that the phrase is original to the text (Meyers and Meyers, *Haggai, Zechariah 1—8*, p. 51).

[124]Cf. Pieter A. Verhoef, *The Books of Haggai and Malachi*, New International Commentary on the Old Testament (Grand Rapids, Mich.: Eerdmans, 1987), pp. 100-101.

[125]Carl Friedrich Keil, "Haggai," in Carl Friedrich Keil and Franz Julius Delitzsch, *Commentary on the Old Testament*, 10 vols. (Grand Rapids, Mich.: Eerdmans, 1980), 10:212 (original ed. *Biblischer Commentar über das Alte Testament*, Leipzig: Dorffling und Franke, 1862-1872).

[126]Walter C. Kaiser Jr., *The Messiah in the Old Testament*, Studies in Old Testament Biblical Theology (Grand Rapids, Mich.: Zondervan, 1995), pp. 209-11.

[127]Cf. Baldwin, *Haggai, Zechariah, Malachi*, p. 59.

[128]John D. W. Watts, "Zechariah," in *Broadman Bible Commentary*, ed. Clifton J. Allen (Nashville, Tenn.: Broadman, 1969-1972), 7:311.

[129]Note the excellent survey of opinions in Redditt, *Haggai, Zechariah, Malachi*, pp. 94-102.

[130]For example, Childs, *Introduction to the Old Testament*, pp. 485-86; and Bullock, *An Introduction to the Old Testament Prophetic Books*, pp. 314-16.

[131]Meyers and Meyers, *Haggai, Zechariah 1—8*, p. 101.

[132]Petersen, *Haggai and Zechariah 1—8*, p. 133.

[133]Baldwin, *Haggai, Zechariah, Malachi*, p. 90.

[134]Childs, *Introduction to the Old Testament*, p. 476.

[135]Carl Friedrich Keil, "Zechariah," in Carl Friedrich Keil and Franz Julius Delitzsch, *Commentary on the Old Testament*, 10 vols. (Grand Rapids, Mich.: Eerdmans, 1980), 10:237 (original ed. *Biblischer Commentar über das Alte Testament*, Leipzig, Germany: Dorffling und Franke, 1862-1872)

[136]Meyers and Meyers, *Haggai, Zechariah 1—8*, p. 243.

[137]Kaiser, *The Messiah in the Old Testament*, pp. 209-11.

[138]Redditt, *Haggai, Zechariah, Malachi*, p. 66.

[139]Meyers and Meyers, *Haggai, Zechariah 1—8*, pp. 355-56.

[140]Cf. Keil, "Zechariah," 10:300; Baldwin, *Haggai, Zechariah, Malachi*, pp. 136-37; Kaiser, *The Messiah in the Old Testament*, pp. 214-15; and Charles Augustus Briggs, *Messianic Prophecy: The Prediction of the Fulfillment of Redemption Through the Messiah* (1886; reprint, Peabody, Mass.: Hendrickson, 1988), pp. 448, 491.

[141]Cf. Meyers and Meyers, *Haggai, Zechariah 1—8*, pp. 360-62; Petersen, *Haggai and Zechariah 1—8*, pp. 277-78; and Ackroyd, *Exile and Restoration*, pp. 198-99. Zimmerli, in *Old Testament Theology in Outline*, p. 25, observes that this text may have helped lead the Essenes of Qumran to look for two future leaders, one priestly, the other royal.

[142]The Hebrew phrase is better translated "and there shall be a priest upon his throne" than "beside his throne." In this case "priest" and "his throne," the branch's throne, are inextricably linked.

[143]Cf. Ronald Webster Pierce, "Literary Connectors and a Haggai/Zechariah/Malachi Corpus," *Journal of the Evangelical Theological Society* 27/3 (1984): 277-89; and Ronald Webster Pierce, "A Thematic Development of the Haggai/Zechariah/Malachi Corpus," *Journal of the Evangelical Theological Society* 27/4 (1984): 401-11.

[144]Note the earlier discussion in this chapter.

[145]David L. Petersen, *Zechariah 9—14 and Malachi*, Old Testament Library (Louisville, Ky.: Westminster/John Knox, 1995), p. 41.

[146]Baldwin, *Haggai, Zechariah, Malachi,* p. 162.

[147]Walther Eichrodt, *Theology of the Old Testament,* trans. J. A. Baker, 2 vols., Old Testament Library (Philadelphia: Westminster Press, 1961-1967), 1:493.

[148]Cf. Kaiser, *The Messiah in the Old Testament,* pp. 216-17.

[149]Jacob, *Theology of the Old Testament,* p. 101.

[150]Zimmerli, *Old Testament Theology in Outline,* p. 240.

[151]Cf. Redditt, *Haggai, Zechariah, Malachi,* p. 133.

[152]For example, Petersen, *Zechariah 9—14 and Malachi,* p. 121.

[153]Cf. Redditt, *Haggai, Zechariah, Malachi,* p. 133.

[154]Achtemeier, *Nahum—Malachi,* p. 162.

[155]Baldwin, *Haggai, Zechariah, Malachi,* p. 195.

[156]Petersen, *Zechariah 9—14 and Malachi,* p. 125.

[157]Kaiser, *The Messiah in the Old Testament,* pp. 226-27.

[158]Bullock, *An Introduction to the Old Testament Prophetic Books,* p. 322.

[159]Iain M. Duguid, "Messianic Themes in Zechariah 9—14," in *The Lord's Anointed: Interpretation of Old Testament Messianic Texts,* ed. Philip E. Satterwaithe, Richard S. Hess and Gordon J. Wenham, Tyndale House Studies (Grand Rapids, Mich.: Baker, 1995), p. 280.

[160]Bruce, *New Testament Development of Old Testament Themes,* p. 112.

[161]Cf. the description of the historical situation in Petersen, *Zechariah 9—14 and Malachi,* pp. 9-23; and Verhoef, *The Books of Haggai and Malachi,* pp. 25-32.

[162]Baldwin, *Haggai, Zechariah, Malachi,* pp. 215-16.

[163]J. M. Powis Smith, Hinckley Gilbert Mitchell and Julius August Bewer, *A Critical and Exegetical Commentary on Haggai, Zechariah, Malachi and Jonah,* International Critical Commentary 24 (New York: Scribner's, 1912) p. 11.

[164]Verhoef, *The Books of Haggai and Malachi,* pp. 238-39.

[165]Petersen, *Zechariah 9—14 and Malachi,* p. 193.

[166]Craigie, *Twelve Prophets,* 2:237.

[167]Verhoef, *The Books of Haggai and Malachi,* p. 285.

[168]Baldwin, *Haggai, Zechariah, Malachi,* p. 242.

[169]Cf. Verhoef, *The Books of Haggai and Malachi,* pp. 287-88.

[170]For instance, Exodus 20:14 condemns adultery, Exodus 20:16 and 19:16-21 denounce liars, Deuteronomy 24:14-15 opposes oppressing workers, and Exodus 22:22-24 and Deuteronomy 24:17-18 command the protection of the weak. See Achtemeier, *Nahum—Malachi,* pp. 185-86.

Chapter 15: Psalms

[1]See chapter one for a discussion of the process by which the threefold canon was developed.

[2]Martin Luther, "First Lectures on the Psalms," ed. Hilton C. Oswald, trans. Herbert J. A. Bouman, in *Luther's Works,* vols. 10-11, gen. ed. Jaroslav Jan Pelikan and Helmut T. Lehman, 55 vols. (St. Louis, Mo.: Concordia, 1955-1976); John Calvin, *Commentary on the Book of Psalms,* vol. 4 in *Calvin's Commentaries,* trans. James Anderson, 45 vols. (Grand Rapids, Mich.: Baker, 1996); this work is a reprint of *Calvin's Commentaries,* 45 vols. (Edinburgh: Calvin Translation Society, 1844-1856). The original Psalms material is from Jean Calvin, *In Librum Psalmorum Iohannes Calvini Commentarius* (Geneva: Oliva Roberti Stephani, 1557).

[3]For a survey of works from this era, consult Franz Julius Delitzsch, "Psalms," in Carl Friedrich Keil and Franz Julius Delitzsch, *Commentary on the Old Testament,* 10 vols. (Grand Rapids, Mich.: Eerdmans, 1980), 5:47-57 (original ed. *Biblischer Commentar über das Alte Testament,* Leipzig: Dorffling und Franke, 1862-1872); and Charles Augustus Briggs and Emily Grace Briggs, *A Critical and Exegetical Commentary on the Book of Psalms,* 2 vols., International Critical Commentary (New York: Scribner's, 1906-1907), 1:cii-cvi.

[4]Calvin, *Commentary on the Book of Psalms,* pp. 102-5.

[5]Robert Lowth, *Lectures on the Sacred Poetry of the Hebrews,* trans. George Gregory (Andover, Mass.: Crocker and Brewster, 1829); original ed. *De Sacra Poesi Hebraeorum: Praelectiones Acadamiae Oxonii Habitae,* 2 vols. (Oxonii, Italy: Typographeo Clarendoniano, 1753).

[6]Wilhelm Martin Lebrecht de Wette, *Commentar über die Psalmen* (Heidelberg, Germany: Mohr und Zimmer, 1811).

[7]Cf. Delitzsch, "Psalms," 5:3-78.

[8]C. H. Spurgeon, *The Treasury of David,* 7 vols. (New York: Funk, 1882-1886).

[9]Briggs and Briggs, *Psalms,* 1:liv-cx.

[10]Hermann Gunkel, *The Psalms: A Form-Critical Introduction, with an Introduction by James Muilenburg,* trans. Thomas Marland Horner (Philadelphia: Fortress, 1967), p. vi. This is a reprint of vol. 1 of *Die Religion in Geschichte und Gegenwart: Handworten Buch in gemeinverstandlicher Darstellung,* 2nd ed., 5 vols. (Tübingen, Germany: Mohr, 1927-1931).

[11]Cf. Hermann Gunkel, *Ausgewählte Psalmen,* 4th ed. (Göttingen, Germany: Vandenhoeck und Ruprecht, 1917); Hermann Gunkel, *Die Psalmen übersetzt und erklärt,* Handkommentar zum Alten Testament 2/2, 4th ed. (Göttingen, Germany: Vandenhoeck und Ruprecht, 1926); and Hermann Gunkel and Joachim Begrich, *Einleitung in die Psalmen: Die Gattungen der religiösen Lyrik Israels* (Göttingen, Germany: Vandenhoeck und Ruprecht, 1933).

[12]Gunkel, *The Psalms,* pp. 10-39.

[13]Hans-Joachim Kraus, *Psalms,* trans. Hilton C. Oswald, 2 vols. (Minneapolis: Fortress, 1993).

[14]Ibid., 1:32, 64.

[15]Hans-Joachim Kraus, *Theology of the Psalms,* trans. Keith R. Crim (Minneapolis: Augsburg, 1986).

[16]Brevard S. Childs, *Introduction to the Old Testament as Scripture* (Philadelphia: Fortress, 1980), pp. 191-94.

[17]James Luther Mays, *Psalms,* Interpretation: A Bible Commentary for Teaching and Preaching (Louisville, Ky.: John Knox, 1994).

[18]The Hebrew texts breaks Psalms into the following segments: 1—41, 42—72, 73—89, 90—106 and 107—150.

[19]Cf. Gerald Henry Wilson, *The Editing of the Hebrew Psalter,* Society of Biblical Literature Dissertation Series 76 (Chico, Calif.: Scholars Press, 1985).

[20]John H. Walton, "Psalms: A Cantata About the Davidic Covenant," *Journal of the Evangelical Theological Society* 34/1 (March 1991): 21-31.

[21]See chapter nine of this volume, note 45.

[22]Mays, *Psalms,* p. 34.

[23]Kraus, *Theology of the Psalms,* p. 22.

[24]Ibid., p. 23.

[25]Ludwig Köhler, *Old Testament Theology,* trans. A. S. Todd (Philadelphia: Westminster Press, 1957), p. 30.

[26]Calvin, *Commentary on the Book of Psalms,* p. 1.

[27]Artur Weiser, *The Psalms,* trans. Herbert Hartwell, Old Testament Library (Philadelphia: Westminster Press, 1962), p. 102.

[28]Cf. P. C. Craigie, *Psalms 1—50,* Word Biblical Commentary 19 (Waco, Tex.: Word, 1983), pp. 296-300.

[29]Cf. Patrick Dwight Miller Jr., *Interpreting the Psalms* (Philadelphia: Fortress, 1986), pp. 87-88.

[30]A. A. Anderson, *The Book of Psalms,* 2 vols., New Century Bible (London: Oliphants, 1972), 1:63.

[31]Claus Westermann, *The Psalms: Structure, Content and Message,* trans. Ralph David Gehrke (Minneapolis: Augsburg, 1980), p. 105.

[32]Sigmund Olaf Plytt Mowinckel, *The Psalms in Israel's Worship,* trans. D. R. Ap-Thomas, 2 vols. (Nashville, Tenn.: Abingdon, 1962), 1:47-48; Weiser, *The Psalms,* p. 109; William Lee Holladay, *The Psalms Through Three Thousand Years: Prayerbook of a Cloud of Witnesses* (Minneapolis: Fortress, 1993), p. 23; and Derek Kidner, *Psalms: An Introduction and a Commentary,* 2 vols., Tyndale Old Testament Commentaries (Downers Grove, Ill.: InterVarsity Press, 1973-1975), 1:50.

[33]Claus Westermann, *The Living Psalms,* trans. J. R. Porter (Grand Rapids, Mich.: Eerdmans,

1989), p. 65.

[34]Willem A. VanGemeren, "Psalms," in *Expositor's Bible Commentary,* ed. Frank E. Gaebelein (Grand Rapids, Mich.: Zondervan, 1976-1992), 5:77.

[35]Kraus, *Psalms,* 1:265-66.

[36]Walther Eichrodt, *Theology of the Old Testament,* trans. J. A. Baker, 2 vols., Old Testament Library (Philadelphia: Westminster Press, 1961-1967), 2:120.

[37]Kraus, *Theology of the Psalms,* p. 148.

[38]Anderson, *The Book of Psalms,* 1:169.

[39]Kraus, *Theology of the Psalms,* p. 38.

[40]Cf. Matthew 27:35, Mark 15:24, Luke 23:34 and John 19:23-24.

[41]Miller, *Interpreting the Psalms,* p. 109.

[42]Kidner, *Psalms,* 1:165.

[43]Cf. Anderson, *The Book of Psalms,* 1:527; Kidner, *Psalms,* 1:5; and Mays, *Psalms,* p. 239.

[44]VanGemeren, "Psalms," p. 475.

[45]Kraus, *Psalms,* 2:80.

[46]Weiser, *The Psalms,* p. 504.

[47]Mitchell J. Dahood, *Psalms,* 3 vols., Anchor Bible 16-17A (Garden City, N.Y.: Doubleday, 1966-1970), 2:188.

[48]Cf. John I. Durham, "Psalms," in *Broadman Bible Commentary,* ed. Clifton J. Allen (Nashville, Tenn.: Broadman, 1969-1972), 4:318; Weiser, *The Psalms,* p. 507; and Dahood, *Psalms,* 2:187.

[49]For an excellent summary of this problem, see VanGemeren, "Psalms," pp. 583-84.

[50]Claus Westermann, *Elements of Old Testament Theology,* trans. Douglas W. Stott (Atlanta: John Knox, 1982), p. 66.

[51]Mays, *Psalms,* p. 287.

[52]Cf. Christoph Barth, *God with Us: A Theological Introduction to the Old Testament,* ed. and trans. G. W. Bromiley (Grand Rapids, Mich.: Eerdmans, 1991), pp. 292-95.

[53]Kraus, *Psalms,* 2:210.

[54]Ibid., 2:215.

[55]Marvin Embry Tate, *Psalms 51—100,* Word Biblical Commentary 20 (Dallas: Word, 1990), p. 440.

[56]Weiser, *The Psalms,* p. 597.

[57]Kraus, *Psalms,* 2:218.

[58]Westermann, *The Living Psalms,* p. 159.

[59]Mays, *Psalms,* p. 293.

[60]Calvin, *Commentary on the Book of Psalms,* 5:473.

[61]Cf. VanGemeren, "Psalms," pp. 595-98.

[62]Elmer A. Martens, *God's Design: A Focus on Old Testament Theology* (Grand Rapids, Mich.: Baker, 1981), p. 163.

[63]Kraus, *Psalms,* 2:331.

[64]Mays, *Psalms,* p. 353.

[65]For example, Holladay, *The Psalms Through Three Thousand Years,* p. 23; and Kidner, *Psalms,* 2:391-92.

[66]For example, Weiser, *The Psalms,* p. 693; and Durham, "Psalms," p. 396.

[67]Kraus, *Psalms,* 2:347.

[68]Mays, *Psalms,* p. 350.

[69]VanGemeren, "Psalms," p. 697.

[70]Kraus, *Theology of the Psalms,* p. 100.

[71]Gerhard von Rad, *Old Testament Theology,* trans. David Muir Gibson Stalker, 2 vols. (New York: Harper & Row, 1962-1965), 1:46.

[72]Anderson, *The Book of Psalms,* 2:771.

[73]Kraus, *Psalms,* 2:351.

[74]For various options consult Mowinckel, *The Psalms in Israel's Worship,* 1:3; VanGemeren,

"Psalms," pp. 768-69; and Walter C. Kaiser Jr., *The Journey Isn't Over: The Pilgrim Psalms for Life's Challenges and Joys* (Grand Rapids, Mich.: Baker, 1993), pp. 13-18.

[75]Kidner, *Psalms,* 2:429.

[76]Anderson, *The Book of Psalms,* 2:883.

[77]Cf. Brevard S. Childs, *Biblical Theology of the Old and New Testaments: Theological Reflection on the Christian Bible* (Minneapolis: Fortress, 1992), p. 193.

[78]William L. Lane, *The Gospel of Mark,* New International Commentary on the New Testament (Grand Rapids. Mich.: Eerdmans, 1974), p. 436.

[79]Eduard Schweizer, *The Good News According to Mark,* trans. Donald Harold Madvig (Atlanta: John Knox, 1970), p. 256.

[80]Mays, *Psalms,* p. 354.

Chapter 16: Job

[1]This point is amply illustrated by the comprehensive bibliography of works on Job found in David J. A. Clines, *Job 1—20,* Word Biblical Commentary 17 (Dallas: Word, 1989), pp. lxiii-cxv.

[2]See the discussion of these matters later in this chapter.

[3]These are the Wisdom books in the canon itself. The Apocrypha includes Sirach and the Wisdom of Solomon, both of which fit this tradition. For a discussion of Sirach and the Wisdom of Solomon, consult James L. Crenshaw, *Old Testament Wisdom: An Introduction* (Atlanta: John Knox, 1981), pp. 149-80.

[4]For selections of this ancient literature read James B. Pritchard, ed., *Ancient Near Eastern Texts Relating to the Old Testament,* 3rd ed. (Princeton, N.J.: Princeton University Press, 1969).

[5]Cf. R. B. Y. Scott, *The Way of Wisdom in the Old Testament* (New York: Macmillan, 1971), p. 5; Roland Edmund Murphy, *Wisdom Literature and Psalms,* ed. Lloyd R. Bailey Sr. and Victor Paul Furnish, Interpreting Biblical Texts (Nashville, Tenn.: Abingdon, 1983), pp. 29-31; Gerhard von Rad, *Wisdom in Israel,* trans. James Davidson Martin (Nashville, Tenn.: Abingdon, 1972), pp. 113-37; and Crenshaw, *Old Testament Wisdom,* pp. 31-36, 239.

[6]Crenshaw, *Old Testament Wisdom,* p. 81.

[7]Cf. Paul R. House, *Old Testament Survey* (Nashville, Tenn.: Broadman, 1992), pp. 222-32.

[8]Gerhard von Rad, *Old Testament Theology,* trans. David Muir Gibson Stalker, 2 vols. (New York: Harper & Row, 1962-1965), 1:418-59; and William McKane, *Prophets and Wise Men,* Studies in Biblical Theology 1/44 (Naperville, Ill.: Allenson, 1965), pp. 48-54.

[9]Cf. Brevard S. Childs, *Introduction to the Old Testament as Scripture* (Philadelphia: Fortress, 1979), pp. 526-44.

[10]Cf. von Rad, *Wisdom in Israel,* pp. 177-85.

[11]This is the compelling conclusion Leo G. Perdue draws in *Wisdom and Creation: The Theology of Wisdom Literature* (Nashville, Tenn.: Abingdon, 1994).

[12]Cf. Lindsay Wilson, "The Book of Job and the Fear of God," *Tyndale Bulletin* 46/1 (May 1995): 59-61.

[13]Cf. Moshe Weinfeld, *Deuteronomy and the Deuteronomic School* (1972; reprint, Winona Lake, Ind.: Eisenbrauns, 1992), pp. 244-81.

[14]Cf. Joseph Blenkinsopp, *Sage, Priest, Prophet: Religious and Intellectual Leadership in Ancient Israel* (Louisville, Ky.: Westminster/John Knox, 1995), pp. 37-41.

[15]Perdue, *Wisdom and Creation,* p. 129.

[16]S. R. Driver and George Buchanan Gray, *A Critical and Exegetical Commentary on the Book of Job,* International Critical Commentary (Edinburgh: T & T Clark, 1950), p. 1.

[17]Clines, *Job 1—20,* p. 8.

[18]Franz Julius Delitzsch, "Job," in Carl Friedrich Keil and Franz Julius Delitzsch, *Commentary on the Old Testament,* 10 vols. (Grand Rapids, Mich.: Eerdmans, 1980), 4:53 (original ed. *Biblischer Commentar über das Alte Testament,* Leipzig: Dorffling und Franke, 1862-1872).

[19]John C. L. Gibson, *Job,* Daily Study Bible (Philadelphia: Westminster Press, 1985), pp. 10-11.

[20]Delitzsch, "Job," 4:59.

[21]Claus Westermann, *The Structure of the Book of Job: A Form-Critical Analysis,* trans. Charles Albert Muenchow (Philadelphia: Fortress, 1981), pp. 37-38.

[22]Norman Charles Habel, *The Book of Job,* Old Testament Library (Philadelphia: Westminster Press, 1985), p. 105.

[23]Francis I. Andersen, *Job,* Tyndale Old Testament Commentaries (Downers Grove, Ill.: InterVarsity Press, 1976), p. 99.

[24]Ibid., p. 109.

[25]Clines, *Job 1—20,* p. 154.

[26]John D. W. Watts, John Joseph Owens and Marvin Embry Tate, "Job," in *Broadman Bible Commentary,* ed. Clifton J. Allen (Nashville, Tenn.: Broadman, 1969-1972), 4:47.

[27]This volume does not believe the canon favors one type over the other. Rather a deliberate balance has been struck that adheres by emphasizing monotheism and fear of the Lord. See this chapter and the next chapter on Proverbs.

[28]John E. Hartley, *The Book of Job,* New International Commentary on the Old Testament (Grand Rapids, Mich.: Eerdmans, 1988), p. 151.

[29]Driver and Gray, *Job,* p. 74.

[30]Clines, *Job 1—20,* p. 201.

[31]Habel, *The Book of Job,* p. 54. This tracing of Job's "legal metaphor" may be Habel's most distinctive contribution to studies on Job.

[32]Ibid., pp. 204-6.

[33]Andersen, *Job,* pp. 156-57.

[34]Edouard Dhorme, *A Commentary on the Book of Job,* trans. Harold Knight (London: Nelson, 1967), pp. cxxv, 163-65.

[35]Habel, *The Book of Job,* p. 275.

[36]Andersen, *Job,* p. 183.

[37]Westermann, *The Structure of the Book of Job,* p. 102.

[38]Hartley, *The Book of Job,* p. 264.

[39]Clines, *Job 1—20,* p. 459.

[40]Hartley, *The Book of Job,* p. 292.

[41]Cf. Clines, *Job 1—20,* p. 459; and Habel, *The Book of Job,* p. 305.

[42]Hartley, *The Book of Job,* pp. 293-94.

[43]Walther Eichrodt, *Theology of the Old Testament,* trans. J. A. Baker, 2 vols., Old Testament Library (Philadelphia: Westminster Press, 1961-1967), 2:519.

[44]Driver and Gray, *Job,* p. 172.

[45]Walther Zimmerli, *Old Testament Theology in Outline,* trans. David Eliot Green (Edinburgh: T & T Clark, 1978), p. 164.

[46]Perdue, *Wisdom and Creation,* p. 186.

[47]For example, Driver and Gray, *Job,* pp. xl-xli; and Marvin H. Pope, *Job: A New Translation with Introduction, Notes and Commentary,* Anchor Bible 15 (Garden City, N.Y.: Doubleday, 1965), p. xxvi.

[48]Cf. Westermann, *The Structure of the Book of Job,* pp. 145-46; and Andersen, *Job,* p. 51.

[49]Cf. Habel, *The Book of Job,* pp. 443-47.

[50]Hartley, *The Book of Job,* pp. 485-86.

[51]See the introductory portion of this chapter for examples of this principle.

[52]Cf. Hartley, *The Book of Job,* pp. 493-97.

[53]Cf. von Rad, *Wisdom in Israel,* p. 225.

[54]For example, Watts, Owens and Tate, "Job," p. 150.

[55]Samuel L. Terrien, *The Elusive Presence: Toward a New Biblical Theology* (San Francisco: Harper & Row, 1978), p. 371.

[56]Habel, *The Book of Job,* p. 578.

[57]Robert L. Alden, *Job,* New American Commentary 11 (Nashville, Tenn.: Broadman, 1993), p. 368.

[58]Pope, *Job,* p. 289.

[59]Westermann, *The Structure of the Book of Job*, p. 128.

[60]Watts, Owens and Tate, "Job," p. 150.

[61]Habel, *The Book of Job*, p. 584.

Chapter 17: Proverbs

[1]For a thorough yet succinct description of these types, consult Duane A. Garrett, *Proverbs, Ecclesiastes, Song of Songs,* New American Commentary 14 (Nashville, Tenn.: Broadman, 1993), pp. 28-39. Cf. William McKane, *Proverbs: A New Approach,* Old Testament Library (Philadelphia: Westminster Press, 1970), pp. 10-22.

[2]Cf. R. B. Y. Scott, *Proverbs, Ecclesiastes: A New Translation with Introduction, Notes and Commentary,* Anchor Bible 18 (Garden City, N.Y.: Doubleday, 1965), pp. xl-lii; James L. Crenshaw, *Old Testament Wisdom: An Introduction* (Atlanta: John Knox, 1981), pp. 212-35; and James Bennett Pritchard, ed., *Ancient Near Eastern Texts Relating to the Old Testament,* 3rd ed. (Princeton, N.J.: Princeton University Press, 1969), pp. 412ff.

[3]Cf. W. G. Lambert, *Babylonian Wisdom Literature* (Oxford: Clarendon, 1960).

[4]Crenshaw, *Old Testament Wisdom,* pp. 212-35. Cf. Roland Edmund Murphy, *Introduction to the Wisdom Literature of the Old Testament,* Old Testament Reading Guide (Collegeville, Minn.: Liturgical Press, 1965).

[5]Crawford Howell Toy, *A Critical and Exegetical Commentary on the Book of Proverbs,* International Critical Commentaries (New York: Scribner's, 1904), p. xv. Note also von Rad's conviction that Israel's anti-image convictions "definitely separated herself from the cults of the surrounding nations and showed herself more and more incapable of doing justice to these cults" (Gerhard von Rad, *Wisdom in Israel,* trans. James Davidson Martin [Nashville, Tenn.: Abingdon, 1972], p. 185).

[6]Cf. Moshe Weinfeld, *Deuteronomy and the Deuteronomic School* (1972; reprint, Winona Lake, Ind.: Eisenbrauns, 1992), pp. 260-74; and Gerhard von Rad, *Old Testament Theology,* trans. David Muir Gibson Stalker, 2 vols. (New York: Harper & Row, 1962-1965), 1:437-38.

[7]Walther Eichrodt, *Theology of the Old Testament,* trans. J. A. Baker, 2 vols., Old Testament Library (Philadelphia: Westminster Press, 1961-1967), 2:81-82; Raymond Bryan Dillard and Tremper Longman III, *An Introduction to the Old Testament* (Grand Rapids, Mich.: Zondervan, 1994), p. 235; and von Rad, *Old Testament Theology,* 1:435.

[8]Toy, *Proverbs,* pp. x-xvi.

[9]Scott, *Proverbs,* p. xv.

[10]Derek Kidner, *The Proverbs: An Introduction and Commentary,* Tyndale Old Testament Commentaries (Downers Grove, Ill.: InterVarsity Press, 1964), p. 58.

[11]Scott, *Proverbs,* p. 36.

[12]Ibid.

[13]Crenshaw, *Old Testament Wisdom,* p. 67.

[14]Readers are addressed as "my son" in Israelite, Egyptian, Babylonian and Assyrian wisdom literature. Cf. Scott, *Proverbs,* p. 37-38.

[15]Weinfeld, *Deuteronomy and the Deuteronomic School,* p. 301; cf. pp. 299-306.

[16]Von Rad, *Old Testament Theology,* 1:447.

[17]Kidner, *Proverbs,* pp. 78-79.

[18]Von Rad, *Wisdom in Israel,* p. 165.

[19]Note McKane, *Proverbs,* pp. 352-54; and Scott, *Proverbs,* p. 70, for a discussion of proposed linguistic parallels.

[20]Dillard and Longman, *An Introduction to the Old Testament,* p. 243.

[21]Kidner, *Proverbs,* p. 79.

[22]Von Rad, *Wisdom in Israel,* p. 156.

[23]Eichrodt, *Theology of the Old Testament,* 2:401.

[24]Scott, *Proverbs,* p. 106.

[25]Von Rad, *Old Testament Theology,* 1:438.

[26]McKane, *Proverbs,* pp. 546, 548. See also von Rad, *Wisdom in Israel,* pp. 195-206, for a

discussion of how Israelite wisdom literature assesses suffering.

[27]Crenshaw, *Old Testament Wisdom,* pp. 82-86.

[28]Ibid., pp. 86-91.

[29]Note the comments on the definition of "proverb" in the section on Proverbs 1—9 in this chapter.

[30]Weinfeld, *Deuteronomy and the Deuteronomic School,* pp. 307-13.

[31]Brevard S. Childs, *Old Testament Theology in a Canonical Context* (Philadelphia: Fortress, 1985), p. 208.

[32]Note the discussion of these and related concepts in Eichrodt, *Theology of the Old Testament,* 2:268-315.

[33]Von Rad, *Old Testament Theology,* 1:414.

[34]The reference here goes beyond the realm of conventional morality. It is indeed God's revealed Torah that is mentioned. Cf. McKane, *Proverbs,* p. 624; Scott, *Proverbs,* p. 166; Garrett, *Proverbs,* p. 223; and Weinfeld, *Deuteronomy and the Deuteronomic School,* pp. 336, 362.

[35]The terms "the righteous," "the wise"and "the faithful" are virtually synonymous in Proverbs 28—29.

[36]This interpretation differs from that of scholars who consider the words akin to the despair passages in Ecclesiastes. For this point of view consult McKane, *Proverbs,* p. 647; Scott, *Proverbs,* p. 22; and Toy, *Proverbs,* p. xvii.

[37]Cf. Garrett, *Proverbs,* p. 236.

[38]McKane, *Proverbs,* pp. 647-48.

[39]Brevard S. Childs, *Introduction to the Old Testament as Scripture* (Philadelphia: Fortress, 1980), pp. 556-57.

[40]Toy, *Proverbs,* pp. 517ff.

[41]Kidner, *Proverbs,* p. 24; McKane, *Proverbs,* p. 407; and Scott, *Proverbs,* pp. 22, 184.

[42]Dillard and Longman, *An Introduction to the Old Testament,* p. 242.

[43]See McKane's discussion of this issue in certain types of Egyptian literature in *Proverbs,* pp. 51-65.

Chapter 18: Ruth

[1]R. K. Harrison, *Introduction to the Old Testament: With a Comprehensive Review of Old Testament Studies and a Special Supplement on the Apocrypha* (Grand Rapids, Mich.: Eerdmans, 1969), p. 1059.

[2]Note the excellent treatments of these details in Adele Berlin, *Poetics and Interpretation of Biblical Narrative,* Bible and Literature Series 9 (Sheffield, U.K.: Almond, 1983), pp. 83-110; and Barbara Green, "The Plot of the Biblical Story of Ruth," *Journal for the Study of the Old Testament* 23 (1982): 55-68.

[3]Ruth is placed in different sections of the canon in different Hebrew traditions. For a discussion of these matters read Edward Fay Campbell Jr., *Ruth: A New Translation with Introduction, Notes and Commentary,* Anchor Bible 7 (Garden City, N.Y.: Doubleday, 1975), pp. 32-36; Brevard S. Childs, *Introduction to the Old Testament as Scripture* (Philadelphia: Fortress, 1980), p. 564; and Robert L. Hubbard Jr., *The Book of Ruth,* New International Commentary on the Old Testament (Grand Rapids, Mich.: Eerdmans, 1988), pp. 4-7. This volume holds that the canonical order of the Masoretic Text deserves priority. At the least Campbell is correct in saying, "Modern commentators agree that, whatever the internal order, the tradition which places Ruth among the Writings rather than after Judges must be original" (*Ruth,* p. 34).

[4]Hubbard, *The Book of Ruth,* pp. 39-42.

[5]Campbell, *Ruth,* p. 30.

[6]Leon Morris, "Ruth," in Arthur Ernest Cundall and Leon Morris, *Judges and Ruth: An Introduction and Commentary,* Tyndale Old Testament Commentaries (Downers Grove, Ill.: InterVarsity Press, 1968), p. 252.

[7]Willem S. Prinsloo, "The Theology of the Book of Ruth," *Vetus Testamentum* 30 (1980): 332. This excellent article provides a foundation for much of this chapter.

[8]Yehezkel Kaufmann, *The Religion of Israel: From Its Beginnings to the Babylonian Exile,* trans.

and abridg. Moshe Greenberg (Chicago: University of Chicago Press, 1960), pp. 130-31, 301.
[9]Hubbard, *The Book of Ruth,* pp. 118-20. For a discussion of how Ruth's commitment to Naomi led to a commitment to Yahweh, see Danna Nolan Fewell and David M. Gunn, *Compromising Redemption: Relating Characters in the Book of Ruth,* Literary Currents in Biblical Interpretation (Louisville, Ky.: Westminster/John Knox, 1990), pp. 94-96.
[10]Cf. Prinsloo, "The Theology of the Book of Ruth," p. 333.
[11]Campbell, *Ruth,* p. 32.
[12]Ronald M. Hals, *The Theology of the Book of Ruth,* Facet Books Biblical Series 23 (Philadelphia: Fortress, 1969), p. 12.
[13]Jack Murad Sasson, *Ruth: A New Translation with a Philological Commentary and a Formalist-Folklorist Interpretation,* 2nd ed., Johns Hopkins Near Eastern Studies (Sheffield, U.K.: JSOT Press, 1989), p. 45.
[14]Murray D. Gow, *The Book of Ruth: Its Structure, Theme and Purpose* (Leicester, England: Apollos, 1992), pp. 48-50.
[15]Morris, "Ruth," p. 270.
[16]Prinsloo, "The Theology of the Book of Ruth," p. 335.
[17]Cf. Wilhelm Rudolph, *Die Bücher Ruth, Hohelied und Klagelieder: Übersetzt und Erklärt,* 2nd ed., Kommentar zum Alten Testament 17 (Gütersloh, Germany: Gerd Mohn, 1962), pp. 32-33; and Hans Wilhelm Hertzberg, *Die Bücher Josua, Richter und Ruth,* Das Alte Testament Deutsch: Neues Göttinger Bibelwerk 9 (Göttingen, Germany: Vandenhoeck und Ruprecht, 1953), p. 257.
[18]For a discussion of this custom in Ruth, consult H. H. Rowley, *The Servant of the Lord and Other Essays on the Old Testament* (London: Lutterworth, 1952), pp. 163-86.
[19]Prinsloo, "The Theology of the Book of Ruth," p. 337.
[20]Cf. Sasson, *Ruth,* pp. 91-92.
[21]Prinsloo, "The Theology of the Book of Ruth," p. 338.
[22]Hubbard, *The Book of Ruth,* p. 61.
[23]Morris, "Ruth," p. 312.
[24]Cf. Hubbard, *The Book of Ruth,* p. 267.
[25]Prinsloo, "The Theology of the Book of Ruth," p. 339.
[26]Oswald Loretz, "The Theme of the Ruth Story," *Catholic Biblical Quarterly* 22 (1960): 392.

Chapter 19: Song of Solomon

[1]A good example of a responsible effort to do so is Paige Patterson, *Song of Solomon,* Bible Study Helps/Everyman's Bible Commentaries (Chicago: Moody Press, 1986).
[2]Brevard S. Childs, *Introduction to the Old Testament as Scripture* (Philadelphia: Fortress, 1980), p. 574.
[3]Ibid., pp. 575-78.
[4]Brevard S. Childs, *Old Testament Theology in a Canonical Context* (Philadelphia: Fortress, 1985), p. 193.
[5]M. Timothy Elliott, *The Literary Unity of the Canticle,* Europaische Hochschulschriften (Frankfurt: Peter Lang, 1989), p. 240.
[6]In fact the division itself is the same as those found in Tom Gledhill, *The Message of the Song of Songs: The Lyrics of Love,* Bible Speaks Today (Downers Grove, Ill.: InterVarsity Press, 1994), pp. 9-11, and Elliott, *The Literary Unity of the Canticle,* pp. x-xi.
[7]Not every interpreter believes this text depicts Solomon's nuptials. It seems appropriate to interpret Solomon as the groom here given the verse's linking of the woman's desire for her beloved in 3:1-5, Solomon's arrival in 3:6-11 and the comment about the king's wedding day and gladness of heart in 3:11. For a discussion of the role of 3:6-11 in the book, see John G. Snaith, *Song of Songs,* New Century Bible (Grand Rapids, Mich.: Eerdmans, 1993), pp. 49-57; G. Lloyd Carr, *The Song of Solomon: An Introduction and Commentary,* Tyndale Old Testament Commentaries (Downers Grove, Ill.: InterVarsity Press, 1984), pp. 106-13; and Duane A. Garrett, *Proverbs, Ecclesiastes, Song of Songs,* New American Commentary 14 (Nashville, Tenn.:

Broadman, 1993), p. 401.

[8]Othmar Keel, *The Song of Songs,* Continental Commentaries (Minneapolis: Fortress, 1994), p. 137.

[9]Gledhill, *The Message of the Song of Songs,* p. 152.

[10]Cf. Carr, *The Song of Solomon,* p. 56.

[11]Note the discussion of the effect of absence in Roland Edmund Murphy, *The Song of Songs,* ed. S. Dean McBride Jr., Hermeneia (Minneapolis: Augsburg Fortress, 1990), p. 168.

[12]Cf. Franz Julius Delitzsch, "Song of Solomon," in Carl Friedrich Keil and Franz Julius Delizsch, *Commentary on the Old Testament,* 10 vols. (Grand Rapids, Mich.: Eerdmans, 1980), 6:109 (original ed. *Biblischer Commentar über das Alte Testament,* Leipzig: Dorffling und Franke, 1862-1872).

[13]Cf. Garrett, *Proverbs, Ecclesiastes, Song of Songs,* pp. 426-27.

[14]Childs, *Old Testament Theology,* p. 194.

Chapter 20: Ecclesiastes

[1]Such treatments tend to focus on what they perceive as the book's belief in the absurdity of life. Cf. James L. Crenshaw, *Ecclesiastes,* Old Testament Library (Philadelphia: Westminster Press, 1987), pp. 23-54; and Michael Vass Fox, *Qohelet and His Contradictions,* JSOTSup 71/Bible and Literature Series 18 (Sheffield, U.K.: Almond, 1989), pp. 13-16, where Fox compares Ecclesiastes to Albert Camus's writings.

[2]Cf. R. B. Y. Scott, *Proverbs, Ecclesiastes: A New Translation with Introduction, Notes and Commentary,* Anchor Bible 18 (Garden City, N.Y.: Doubleday, 1965), pp. 201-4; and R. B. Y. Scott, *The Way of Wisdom in the Old Testament* (New York: Macmillan, 1971), pp. 170-84.

[3]Cf. Robert Gordis, *Koheleth—The Man and His World: A Study in Ecclesiastes,* 3rd ed. (New York: Schocken, 1968), pp. 122-32; and Donald Kent Berry, *An Introduction to Wisdom and Poetry of the Old Testament* (Nashville, Tenn.: Broadman, 1995), pp. 161-64.

[4]Cf. Franz Julius Delitzsch, "The Book of Ecclesiastes," in Carl Friedrich Keil and Franz Julius Delitzsch, *Commentary on the Old Testament,* 10 vols. (Grand Rapids, Mich.: Eerdmans, 1980), 6:179-217 (original ed. *Biblischer Commentar über das Alte Testament,* Leipzig: Dorffling und Franke, 1862-1872).

[5]Cf. Brevard S. Childs, *Introduction to the Old Testament as Scripture* (Philadelphia: Fortress, 1979), pp. 580-89; and Duane A. Garrett, *Proverbs, Ecclesiastes, Song of Songs,* New American Commentary 14 (Nashville, Tenn.: Broadman, 1993), pp. 277-79.

[6]Cf. Gerhard von Rad, *Wisdom in Israel,* trans. James Davidson Martin (Nashville, Tenn.: Abingdon, 1972), pp. 226-37; Walther Zimmerli, *Old Testament Theology in Outline,* trans. David Eliot Green (Edinburgh: T & T Clark, 1978), pp. 161-63; and Roland Edmund Murphy, *Ecclesiastes,* Word Biblical Commentary 23A (Waco, Tex.: Word, 1992), pp. lxi-lxix.

[7]For options concerning the meaning of this key term see Michael Vass Fox, "The Meaning of HEBEL for Qohelet," *Journal of Biblical Literature* 105/3 (1986): 409-27. Fox considers "absurd" the best rendering of the term.

[8]Scott, *Proverbs, Ecclesiastes,* p. 211.

[9]Crenshaw, *Ecclesiastes,* p. 76.

[10]Cf. Charles Conrad Forman, "Koheleth's Use of Genesis," *Journal of Semitic Studies* 5 (1960): 258-59; R. N. Whybray, *Ecclesiastes,* Old Testament Guides (Sheffield, U.K.: Sheffield Academic Press, 1989), pp. 60-61; and Garrett, *Proverbs, Ecclesiastes, Song of Songs,* pp. 278-79.

[11]Derek Kidner, *A Time to Mourn and a Time to Dance: Ecclesiastes and the Way of the World,* Bible Speaks Today (Downers Grove, Ill.: InterVarsity Press, 1976), p. 39.

[12]Graham S. Ogden, *Qoheleth, Readings: A New Biblical Form* (Sheffield, U.K.: Sheffield Academic Press, 1987), p. 55.

[13]Fox, *Qohelet and His Contradictions,* pp. 191-92.

[14]Murphy, *Ecclesiastes,* p. lxii.

[15]Ibid., p. lxxiii.

[16]Ogden, *Qoheleth,* p. 62.

[17]Several commentators disagree with this conclusion. They generally think, like Whybray, that Ecclesiastes asserts that "there is, as far as can be known, no real life after death (3:21)" (Whybray, *Ecclesiastes,* p. 59). Leo G. Perdue thinks the passage means life "ends in a final nonexistence." See Perdue, *Wisdom and Creation: The Theology of Wisdom Literature* (Nashville, Tenn.: Abingdon, 1994), p. 299. Such conclusions do not take the whole of Ecclesiastes sufficiently into account.

[18]Gerhard von Rad, *Old Testament Theology,* trans. David Muir Gibson Stalker, 2 vols. (New York: Harper & Row, 1962-1965), 1:457.

[19]J. Barton Payne, *The Theology of the Older Testament* (Grand Rapids, Mich.: Zondervan, 1962), p. 345.

[20]Walter C. Kaiser Jr., *Ecclesiastes: Total Life* (Chicago: Moody Press, 1980), p. 97.

[21]Kidner, *A Time to Mourn,* pp. 82-83 n. 4.

[22]For readings of Ecclesiastes 9:5-6 as ironic, see Ogden, *Qoheleth,* p. 149; and Crenshaw, *Ecclesiastes,* p. 161.

[23]Cf. Gordis, *Koheleth,* p. 307.

[24]Cf. Fox, *Qohelet and His Contradictions,* p. 258.

[25]Delitzsch, "The Book of Ecclesiastes," 6:361-62.

[26]Perdue, *Wisdom and Creation,* p. 219.

[27]Garrett, *Proverbs, Ecclesiastes, Song of Songs,* p. 343.

[28]Gordis, *Koheleth,* p. 349.

[29]Theodorus Christiaan Vriezen, *An Outline of Old Testament Theology,* trans. S. Neuijen (Oxford: Basil Blackwell, 1962), pp. 191, 202.

[30]Ogden, *Qoheleth,* p. 207.

[31]Von Rad, *Old Testament Theology,* 2:350.

[32]Von Rad, *Old Testament Theology,* 1:406-7.

[33]Daniel Isaac Block, "Beyond the Grave: Ezekiel's Vision of Death and Afterlife," *Bulletin for Biblical Research* 2 (1992): 113-41.

[34]Kaiser, *Ecclesiastes,* p. 124.

[35]Cf. Murphy, *Ecclesiastes,* p. 125; Delitzsch, "The Book of Ecclesiastes," 6:435; and Garrett, *Proverbs, Ecclesiastes, Song of Songs,* p. 344.

[36]Elmer A. Martens, *God's Design: A Focus on Old Testament Theology* (Grand Rapids, Mich.: Baker, 1981), p. 180.

Chapter 21: Lamentations

[1]Paul Wayne Ferris Jr., *The Genre of Communal Lament in the Bible and the Ancient Near East,* Society of Biblical Literature Dissertation Series 127 (Atlanta: Scholars Press, 1992), pp. 136-44.

[2]Norman K. Gottwald, *Studies in the Book of Lamentations,* Studies in Biblical Theology 14 (London: SCM, 1954), p. 53. Note the fuller context of his conclusion on pp. 47-62.

[3]Bertil Albrektson, *Studies in the Text and Theology of the Book of Lamentations with a Critical Edition of the Peshitta Text,* Studia Theologica Lundensia 21 (Lund, Sweden: Gleerup, 1963), p. 223.

[4]Ibid., pp. 223-37.

[5]Ibid., p. 239.

[6]Gottwald, *Studies in the Book of Lamentations,* p. 67.

[7]Carl Friedrich Keil, "The Lamentations of Jeremiah," in Carl Friedrich Keil and Franz Julius Delitzsch, *Commentary on the Old Testament,* 10 vols. (Grand Rapids, Mich.: Eerdmans, 1980), 8:394 (original ed. *Biblischer Commentar über das Alte Testament,* Leipzig; Dorffling und Franke, 1862-1872).

[8]Claus Westermann, *Lamentations: Issues and Interpretation,* trans. Charles Albert Muenchow (Minneapolis: Fortress, 1994), p. 193.

[9]Cf. Iain W. Provan, *Lamentations,* New Century Bible (Grand Rapids, Mich.: Eerdmans, 1991), p. 83.

[10]Cf. Ferris, *The Genre of Communal Lament,* p. 100.

[11]Christoph Barth, *God with Us: A Theological Introduction to the Old Testament,* ed. and trans. G. W. Bromiley (Grand Rapids, Mich.: Eerdmans, 1991), p. 274.

[12]Brevard S. Childs, *Introduction to the Old Testament as Scripture* (Philadelphia: Fortress, 1980), p. 595.

[13]Brevard S. Childs, *Old Testament Theology in a Canonical Context* (Philadelphia: Fortress, 1985), p. 103.

[14]Delbert R. Hillers, *Lamentations: A New Translation with Introduction, Notes and Commentary,* Anchor Bible 7A (New York: Doubleday, 1992), p. 161.

[15]Walter C. Kaiser Jr., *A Biblical Approach to Personal Suffering* (Chicago: Moody Press, 1982), p. 118.

[16]S. Paul Re'Mi, "Lamentations," in *God's People in Crisis: A Commentary on the Books of Amos and Lamentations,* ed. Robert Martin-Achard and S. Paul Re'Mi, International Theological Commentary (Grand Rapids, Mich.: Eerdmans, 1984).

[17]Westermann, *Lamentations,* pp. 223-24.

[18]Hans-Joachim Kraus, *Klagelieder (Threni),* 3rd ed., Biblischer Kommentar Altes Testament 20 (Neukirchen-Vluyn, Germany: Neukirchener Verlag, 1968), p. 91.

[19]Ibid.

Chapter 22: Esther

[1]Note the related discussion in chapter nineteen. Some Greek versions of Esther include prayers and notations that contain God's name. As chapter one states, this volume focuses on the received Hebrew text. For a survey of these additions, see Carey A. Moore, *Esther,* Anchor Bible 7B (Garden City, N.Y.: Doubleday, 1971), pp. lxi-lxiv; and David J. A. Clines, *The Esther Scroll: The Story of the Story,* JSOTSup 30 (Sheffield, U.K.: JSOT Press, 1984), pp. 69-72, 215-48.

[2]Note the discussions of historical matters in F. B. Huey Jr., "Esther," in *Expositor's Bible Commentary,* ed. Frank E. Gaebelein (Grand Rapids, Mich.: Zondervan, 1976-1992), 4:784-93; Moore, *Esther,* pp. xxxiv-xlix; Brevard S. Childs, *Introduction to the Old Testament as Scripture* (Philadelphia: Fortress, 1980), pp. 599-602.

[3]Roger T. Beckwith, *The Old Testament Canon of the New Testament Church and Its Background in Early Judaism* (Grand Rapids, Mich.: Eerdmans, 1985), pp. 312-17, 322-23.

[4]Cf. Walther Zimmerli, *Old Testament Theology in Outline,* trans. David Eliot Green (Edinburgh: T & T Clark, 1978), pp. 129-30; Childs, *Introduction,* pp. 603-5; and Moore, *Esther,* pp. liii-liv.

[5]Gillis Gerleman, *Esther,* Biblischer Kommentar Altes Testament 21 (Neukirchen-Vluyn, Germany: Neukirchener Verlag, 1973).

[6]Theodorus Christiaan Vriezen, *An Outline of Old Testament Theology,* trans. S. Neuijen (Oxford: Basil Blackwell, 1962), p. 73; and J. Barton Payne, *The Theology of the Older Testament* (Grand Rapids, Mich.: Zondervan, 1962), p. 437.

[7]Asa Boyd Luter and Barry C. Davis, *God Behind the Seen: Expositions of the Books of Ruth and Esther,* Expositor's Guide to the Historical Books (Grand Rapids, Mich.: Baker, 1995).

[8]Robert Gordis, *Megillat Esther: The Masoretic Text with Introduction, New Translation and Commentary* (New York: KTAV, 1974), p. 13.

[9]Walter C. Kaiser Jr., *Toward an Old Testament Theology* (Grand Rapids, Mich.: Zondervan, 1978), pp. 258-61.

[10]Shemaryahu Talmon, " 'Wisdom' in the Book of Esther," *Vetus Testamentum* 13 (1960): 419-55.

[11]Lewis Bayles Paton, *A Critical and Exegetical Commentary on the Book of Esther,* International Critical Commentary (1908; reprint, Edinburgh: T & T Clark, 1976), p. 96.

[12]Otto Eissfeldt, *The Old Testament: An Introduction Including the Apocrypha and Pseudopigrapha, and Also Similar Types from Qumran—The History of the Formation of the Old Testament,* trans. Peter R. Ackroyd, 3rd ed. (New York: Harper & Row, 1965), pp. 511-12.

[13]See the analyses of Esther's literary qualities in Clines, *The Esther Scroll;* Michael Vass Fox, *Character and Ideology in the Book of Esther,* Studies on Personalities of the Old Testament (Columbia: University of South Carolina Press, 1991); and Linda Day, *Three Faces of a Queen: Characterization in the Book of Esther,* JSOTSup 186 (Sheffield, U.K.: Sheffield Academic Press,

1995).

[14]Moore, *Esther,* p. 39.

[15]Paton, *Critical and Exegetical Commentary on the Book of Esther,* p. 203.

[16]Fox, *Character and Ideology,* p. 240.

[17]Gordis, *Megillat Esther,* p. 48.

[18]Fox, *Character and Ideology,* pp. 121-22. Moore (*Esther,* p. 82) considers this verse an "enhancement" of the story, not a literal event, an opinion shared by Paton (*Critical and Exegetical Commentary on the Book of Esther,* p. 281). Gordis indicates that the Gentiles were not necessarily sincere in their conversion (*Megillat Esther,* p. 57).

[19]Childs, *Introduction to the Old Testament,* p. 606. Cf. Gordis, *Megillat Esther,* p. 13.

[20]Childs, *Introduction to the Old Testament,* pp. 603-4.

Chapter 23: Daniel

[1]Ezekiel was exiled in the second Babylonian deportation, which occurred in 597 B.C. His ministry spanned 593-571.

[2]For a survey of apocalyptic works and their characteristics consult H. H. Rowley, *The Relevance of Apocalyptic,* 2nd ed. (London: Lutterworth, 1950), pp. 11-149; Paul D. Hanson, *The Dawn of Apocalyptic: The Historical and Sociological Roots of Jewish Apocalyptic Eschatology,* rev. ed. (Philadelphia: Fortress, 1986), pp. 1-31; and J. J. Collins, *Daniel: With an Introduction to Apocalyptic Literature,* Forms of Old Testament Literature 20 (Grand Rapids, Mich.: Eerdmans, 1984), pp. 2-39.

[3]Cf. L. F. Hartman and A. A. Di Lella, *The Book of Daniel,* Anchor Bible 23 (Garden City, N.Y.: Doubleday, 1977), pp. 67-71.

[4]Cf. Collins, *Daniel,* pp. 6-19.

[5]Ezra 4:8—6:18 and Ezra 7:12-26 are also written in Aramaic.

[6]Walther Zimmerli, *Old Testament Theology in Outline,* trans. David Eliot Green (Edinburgh: T & T Clark, 1978), p. 234.

[7]For the options about why they may have interpreted eating these foods as making them unclean, see John E. Goldingay, *Daniel,* Word Biblical Commentary 30 (Dallas: Word, 1989), pp. 18-19.

[8]Gerhard von Rad, *Old Testament Theology,* trans. David Muir Gibson Stalker, 2 vols. (New York: Harper & Row, 1962-1965), 2:309.

[9]Collins, *Daniel,* p. 53.

[10]Edward J. Young, *The Prophecy of Daniel: A Commentary* (Grand Rapids, Mich.: Eerdmans, 1949), p. 70.

[11]N. W. Porteous, *Daniel,* Old Testament Library (Philadelphia: Westminster Press, 1965), p. 47; Young, *Prophecy of Daniel,* p. 76; Collins, *Daniel,* p. 52.

[12]Von Rad, *Old Testament Theology,* 2:311.

[13]Elmer A. Martens, *God's Design: A Focus on Old Testament Theology* (Grand Rapids, Mich.: Baker, 1981), p. 202.

[14]William S. Towner, *Daniel,* Interpretation: A Bible Commentary for Teaching and Preaching (Atlanta: John Knox, 1984), p. 39.

[15]Brevard S. Childs, *Old Testament Theology in a Canonical Context* (Philadelphia: Fortress, 1985), p. 67.

[16]Cf. Towner, *Daniel,* pp. 67-68.

[17]Young, *Prophecy of Daniel,* p. 114.

[18]Joyce G. Baldwin, *Daniel,* Tyndale Old Testament Commentaries (Downers Grove, Ill.: InterVarsity Press, 1978), p. 73.

[19]Porteous, *Daniel,* p. 76.

[20]Collins, *Daniel,* pp. 68-69.

[21]Hartman and Di Lella, *The Book of Daniel,* p. 187.

[22]Von Rad, *Old Testament Theology,* 2:310.

[23]Baldwin, *Daniel,* p. 141.

[24]See Collins's summary in *Daniel*, pp. 77-78.

[25]E.g., Zimmerli, *Old Testament Theology in Outline*, p. 231.

[26]Goldingay, *Daniel*, p. 165.

[27]Maurice Casey, *Son of Man: The Interpretation and Influence of Daniel 7* (London: SPCK, 1979), p. 23.

[28]Von Rad, *Old Testament Theology*, 2:312.

[29]Walter C. Kaiser Jr., *Toward an Old Testament Theology* (Grand Rapids: Zondervan, 1978), p. 246.

[30]Casey, *Son of Man*, p. 22.

[31]Christoph Barth, *God with Us: A Theological Introduction to the Old Testament*, ed. and trans. G. W. Bromiley (Grand Rapids, Mich.: Eerdmans, 1991), p. 357.

[32]Cf. R. H. Charles, *A Critical and Exegetical Commentary on the Book of Daniel* (Oxford: Clarendon, 1929), p. 225; Baldwin, *Daniel*, pp. 164-65; and Young, *Prophecy of Daniel*, p. 183. It must be noted that Charles's late dating of Daniel influences his emphasis on the collection of Scripture. None of these writers believed the canon was closed when Daniel 9 was written.

[33]Cf. Baldwin, *Daniel*, pp. 182-201; J. A. Montgomery, *A Critical and Exegetical Commentary on the Book of Daniel*, International Critical Commentary (Edinburgh: T & T Clark, 1927), pp. 468-70; and Hartman and Di Lella, *The Book of Daniel*, pp. 286-305.

[34]Childs, *Old Testament Theology*, p. 231.

[35]Charles, *Critical and Exegetical Commentary on the Book of Daniel*, p. 326.

[36]Walther Eichrodt, *Theology of the Old Testament*, trans. J. A. Baker, 2 vols., Old Testament Library (Philadelphia: Westminster Press, 1961-1967), 2:512.

[37]Baldwin, *Daniel*, p. 204.

[38]Zimmerli, *Old Testament Theology in Outline*, p. 233.

[39]Goldingay, *Daniel*, p. 308.

[40]Young, *Prophecy of Daniel*, p. 260.

[41]John Joseph Owens, "Daniel," in *Broadman Bible Commentary*, ed. Clifton J. Allen (Nashville, Tenn.: Broadman, 1960-1973), 6:460.

[42]Note the extensive bibliography in Casey, *Son of Man*, pp. 241-59.

[43]Baldwin, *Daniel*, p. 148.

[44]For an excellent analysis of these passages and others related to the "son of man" concept in the New Testament, consult Otto Michel, "The Son of Man," in *The New International Dictionary of New Testament Theology*, ed. Colin Brown, 3 vols. (Grand Rapids, Mich.: Zondervan, 1975-1978), 3:13-34; and Carsten Colpe, "ὁ υἱὸς τοῦ ἀνθρώπου" in *Theological Dictionary of the New Testament*, trans. G. W. Bromiley, 10 vols. (Grand Rapids, Mich.: Eerdmans, 1964-1976), 8:400-477.

[45]The book of Revelation focuses on the judging aspect of the son of man when it relates Daniel 7:13-14 to Jesus' future work. See Casey, *Son of Man*, pp. 142-50.

[46]Cf. J. Barton Payne, *The Theology of the Older Testament* (Grand Rapids, Mich.: Zondervan, 1962), pp. 443-63.

[47]Cf. R. A. Anderson, *Signs and Wonders: A Commentary on the Book of Daniel*, International Theological Commentary (Grand Rapids: Eerdmans, 1984), p. 148.

[48]Cf. A. VanGemeren, *The Progress of Redemption: The Story of Salvation from Creation to the New Jerusalem* (Grand Rapids, Mich.: Baker, 1988), pp. 295-97.

Chapter 24: Ezra—Nehemiah

[1]Cf. Ezra 7:1 and Nehemiah 2:1.

[2]Cf. Brevard S. Childs, *Introduction to the Old Testament as Scripture* (Philadelphia: Fortress, 1980), p. 636.

[3]Cf. M. A. Throntveit, *Ezra—Nehemiah*, Interpretation: A Bible Commentary for Teaching and Preaching (Louisville, Ky.: John Knox, 1992), pp. 13-15.

[4]Derek Kidner, *Ezra and Nehemiah: An Introduction and Commentary*, Tyndale Old Testament

Commentaries (Downers Grove, Ill.: InterVarsity Press, 1979), pp. 21-22.

[5]Christoph Barth, *God with Us: A Theological Introduction to the Old Testament,* ed. and trans. G. W. Bromiley (Grand Rapids, Mich.: Eerdmans, 1991), p. 259.

[6]As L. W. Batten observes, the problem seems to lie with men marrying non-Jewish women, not with Jewish women marrying Gentiles. See L. W. Batten, *A Critical and Exegetical Commentary on the Books of Ezra and Nehemiah,* International Critical Commentary (New York: Scribner's, 1913), pp. 351-52.

[7]Kidner, *Ezra and Nehemiah,* p. 72.

[8]Gerhard von Rad, *Old Testament Theology),* trans. David Muir Gibson Stalker, 2 vols. (New York: Harper & Row, 1962-1965), 1:89-91.

[9]The exact chronology of Ezra's and Nehemiah's ministries has occupied scholars for decades, if not centuries. Note the explanations offered in Kidner, *Ezra and Nehemiah,* pp. 146-58; H. G. M. Williamson, *Ezra, Nehemiah,* Word Biblical Commentary 16 (Waco, Tex.: Word, 1985), pp. xxxix-lviv; David J. A. Clines, *Ezra, Nehemiah, Esther,* New Century Bible (Grand Rapids, Mich.: Eerdmans, 1984), pp. 14-24; and F. Charles Fensham, *The Book of Ezra, Nehemiah,* New International Commentary on the Old Testament (Grand Rapids, Mich.: Eerdmans, 1982), pp. 5-9.

[10]Williamson, *Ezra, Nehemiah,* p. 287.

[11]Cf. Childs, *Introduction to the Old Testament,* pp. 636-37.

[12]Clines, *Ezra, Nehemiah, Esther,* p. 182; and Fensham, *The Book of Ezra, Nehemiah,* p. 216. Joseph Blenkinsopp thinks that this law consisted of Deuteronomic law supplemented by priestly materials; see Joseph Blenkinsopp, *Ezra—Nehemiah: A Commentary,* Old Testament Library (Philadelphia: Westminster Press, 1987), pp. 152-57.

[13]Cf. Childs, *Introduction to the Old Testament,* p. 636.

[14]Barth, *God with Us,* p. 157.

[15]Cf. Childs, *Introduction to the Old Testament,* p. 636.

[16]This outline is given in Throntveit, *Ezra—Nehemiah,* p. 103.

Chapter 25: 1-2 Chronicles

[1]Gerhard von Rad, *Old Testament Theology,* trans. David Muir Gibson Stalker, 2 vols. (New York: Harper & Row, 1962-1965), 1:348.

[2]Note the discussion of the Chronicler's sources in E. L. Curtis, *A Critical and Exegetical Commentary on the Books of Chronicles,* International Critical Commentary (New York: Scribner's, 1910), pp. 17-26; J. M. Myers, *1 Chronicles,* Anchor Bible 12 (Garden City, N.Y.: Doubleday, 1965), pp. xlv-lxiii; J. Barton Payne, "1, 2 Chronicles," in *Expositor's Bible Commentary,* ed. Frank E. Gaebelein (Grand Rapids, Mich.: Eerdmans, 1979-1981), 4:309-11; and Sara Japhet, *I and II Chronicles,* Old Testament Library (Louisville, Ky.: Westminster/John Knox, 1993), pp. 14-23.

[3]For a fuller list, see M. J. Selman, *1 Chronicles: An Introduction and Commentary,* Tyndale Old Testament Commentaries (Downers Grove, Ill.: InterVarsity Press, 1994), pp. 25-26; and Myers, *1 Chronicles,* pp. xlix-lxiii.

[4]Cf. John Bright, *A History of Israel,* 2nd ed. (Philadelphia: Westminster Press, 1972), pp. 364-92. See also P. R. Ackroyd, *The Chronicler in His Age,* JSOTSup 101 (Sheffield, U.K.: Sheffield Academic Press, 1991).

[5]Selman, *1 Chronicles,* p. 42.

[6]Michael Wilcock, *The Message of Chronicles: One Church, One Faith, One Lord,* Bible Speaks Today (Downers Grove, Ill.: InterVarsity Press, 1987), pp. 19-31; and J. A. Thompson, *1, 2 Chronicles,* New American Commentary 9 (Nashville, Tenn.: Broadman, 1994), p. 49.

[7]Cf. Myers, *1 Chronicles,* p. l; and Japhet, *I and II Chronicles,* pp. 52-56.

[8]Japhet, *I and II Chronicles,* p. 56.

[9]The canonical connections are so evident here that there will be no separate section of canonical comment in this portion of the chapter.

[10]For an extensive discussion of David's role in the worship traditions see William Riley, *King and Cultus in Chronicles: Worship and the Reinterpretation of History,* JSOTSup 160 (Sheffield,

U.K.: Sheffield Academic Press, 1993), pp. 53-76.

[11]Cf. J. R. Shaver, *Torah and the Chronicler's History Work: An Inquiry into the Chronicler's References to Laws, Festivals and Cultic Institutions in Relationship to Pentateuchal Legislation,* Society for Biblical Literature Dissertation Series 196 (Atlanta: Scholars Press, 1989), p. 76.

[12]Simon J. DeVries, *1 and 2 Chronicles,* Forms of Old Testament Literature 11 (Grand Rapids, Mich.: Eerdmans, 1989), pp. 150-51.

[13]Selman, *1 Chronicles,* pp. 169-70.

[14]Elmer A. Martens, *God's Design: A Focus on Old Testament Theology* (Grand Rapids, Mich.: Baker, 1981), pp. 226-28.

[15]Cf. Roddy L. Braun, *Understanding the Basic Themes of 1, 2 Chronicles* (Dallas: Word, 1991), pp. 81-83; and H. G. M. Williamson, *1 and 2 Chronicles,* New Century Bible (Grand Rapids, Mich.: Eerdmans, 1982), p. 32.

[16]Walther Eichrodt, *Theology of the Old Testament,* trans. J. A. Baker, 2 vols., Old Testament Library (Philadelphia: Westminster Press, 1961-1967), 2:308.

[17]Rex Mason, *Preaching the Tradition: Homily and Hermeneutics After the Exile* (Cambridge: Cambridge University Press, 1990), pp. 48, 61, 128, 138.

[18]Braun, *Understanding the Basic Themes of 1, 2 Chronicles,* p. 82.

[19]Japhet, *I and II Chronicles,* pp. 1009-10.

[20]Williamson, *1 and 2 Chronicles,* p. 389.

[21]Thompson, *1, 2 Chronicles,* p. 370.

[22]Walter C. Kaiser Jr., *Toward an Old Testament Theology* (Grand Rapids, Mich.: Zondervan, 1978), p. 261.

[23]Julius Wellhausen, *Prolegomena to the History of Ancient Israel* (1878; reprint, Gloucester, Mass.: Peter Smith, 1983), pp. 203-10.

[24]Note the discussion of these themes in Robert North, "Theology of the Chronicler," *Journal of Biblical Literature* 82/4 (December 1963): 369-81.

[25]Cf Japhet, *I and II Chronicles,* pp. 43-47; and Raymond Bryan Dillard, "Reward and Punishment in Chronicles: The Theology of Immediate Retribution," *Westminster Journal of Theology* 46 (1984): 164-72.

[26]H. G. M. Williamson, *Israel in the Book of Chronicles* (London: Cambridge University Press, 1977), p. 140.

Appendix

[1]Horst Dietrich Preuss, *Old Testament Theology,* trans. Leo G. Perdue, 2 vols., Old Testament Library Series (Louisville, Ky.: Westminster/John Knox, 1995-1996).

[2]Ibid., 1:19.

[3]Ibid., 1:20.

[4]Ibid.

[5]Ibid.

[6]Ibid.

[7]Ibid., 1:25.

[8]Ibid., 1:15.

[9]Ibid., 1:23.

[10]Leo. G. Perdue, *The Collapse of History: Reconstructing Old Testament Theology* (Minneapolis: Augsburg Fortress, 1994), pp. 7-11.

[11]Ibid., p. 306.

[12]Ibid.

[13]John H. Sailhamer, *Introduction to Old Testament Theology: A Canonical Approach* (Grand Rapids, Mich.: Eerdmans, 1995), p. 84.

[14]Ibid.

[15]Ibid., pp. 86-112.

[16]Ibid., pp. 112-13.

[17]Ibid., p. 183.

[18]Ibid., p. 182.

[19]Ibid., pp. 172-74.

[20]Ibid., p. 193.

[21]Ibid., p. 199.

[22]Ibid., pp. 191-255.

[23]Rolf P. Knierim, *The Task of Old Testament Theology: Substance, Method and Cases* (Grand Rapids, Mich.: Eerdmans, 1995).

[24]Note his influence on the writers in Henry T. C. Sun et al., *Problems in Biblical Theology: Essays in Honor of Rolf Knierim* (Grand Rapids, Mich.: Eerdmans, 1997).

[25]Knierim, *The Task of Old Testament Theology,* p. 1.

[26]Ibid., p. 17.

[27]Ibid., pp. 17-18.

[28]Ibid., p. 18.

[29]Ibid., pp. 18-20.

[30]Ibid., p. 20.

[31]Ibid., p. 14.

[32]Walter Brueggemann, *Theology of the Old Testament: Testimony, Dispute, Advocacy* (Minneapolis: Fortress, 1997), p. 49.

[33]Ibid., pp. 89-114.

[34]Ibid., p. 89.

[35]Ibid., pp. 117-313.

[36]Ibid., pp. 317-403.

[37]Ibid., pp. 407-704.

[38]Ibid., p. 89.

[39]Christopher R. Seitz, *Word Without End: The Old Testament as Abiding Theological Witness* (Grand Rapids, Mich.: Eerdmans, 1998).

[40]Ibid., pp. 3-109.

[41]Ibid., pp. 113-247.

[42]Ibid., pp. 251-344.

[43]Ibid., p. 40.

[44]Ibid., p. 44.

[45]Ibid., pp. 46-49.

[46]Ibid., p. 60.

[47]Ibid., pp. 61-74.

[48]Ibid., pp. 75-82.

[49]Ibid., p. 99.

[50]Ibid., p. 101.

[51]Ibid., p. 100.

[52]This is Brueggemann's assessment of Childs's project and would surely apply to Seitz's work as well. See Brueggemann, *Theology of the Old Testament,* p. 92.

[53]On this point, see Carl F. H. Henry, *God, Revelation and Authority,* 6 vols. (Waco, Tex.: Word, 1976-1983), 2:69-76.

Bibliography

Aalders, G. Charles. *Genesis*. Translated by William Heyned. 2 vols. Bible Student's Commentary. Grand Rapids, Mich.: Zondervan, 1981.

Achtemeier, Elizabeth Rice. *Nahum-Malachi*. Interpretation. Atlanta: John Knox Press, 1986.

Ackroyd, Peter R. *The Chronicler in His Age*. JSOTS 101. Sheffield, U.K.: Sheffield Academic Press, 1991.

———. *Exile and Restoration: A Study of Hebrew Thought of the Sixth Century B.C.* Old Testament Library. Philadelphia: Westminster Press, 1968.

———. *The Second Book of Samuel*. Cambridge Bible Commentary. London: Cambridge University Press, 1977.

———. *Studies in the Religious Tradition of the Old Testament*. London: SCM Press, 1987.

Albrektson, B. *Studies in the Text and Theology of the Book of Lamentations with a Critical Edition of the Peshitta Text*. Studia Theologica Lundensia 21. Lund, Sweden: Gleerup, 1963.

Albright, William Foxwell. *From the Stone Age to Christianity: Monotheism and the Historical Process*. 2nd ed. Garden City, N.Y.: Doubleday, 1957.

———. *Yahweh and the Gods of Canaan: A Historical Analysis of Two Contrasting Faiths*. Garden City, N.Y.: Doubleday, 1969.

Alden, Robert L. *Job*. New American Commentary. Nashville: Broadman, 1993.

Alexander, Joseph A. *Commentary on the Prophecies of Isaiah*. 1846. Reprint, Grand Rapids, Mich.: Zondervan, 1953.

Alexander, Ralph Holland. "Ezekiel." In *Expositor's Bible Commentary*. Vol. 6. Edited by Frank E. Gaebelein. Grand Rapids, Mich.: Zondervan, 1986.

Alexander, William Lindsay. *A System of Biblical Theology*. Edited and translated by James Ross. Edinburgh: T & T Clark, 1888.

Allen, Leslie C. *The Books of Joel, Obadiah, Jonah and Micah*. New International Commentary on the Old Testament. Grand Rapids, Mich.: Eerdmans, 1976.

———. *Ezekiel 20-48*. Word Biblical Commentary 29. Dallas: Word, 1994.

Allen, Ronald Barclay. "Numbers." In *Expositor's Bible Commentary*. Vol. 2. Edited by Frank E. Gaebelein. Grand Rapids, Mich.: Zondervan, 1990.

Allis, Oswald T. *God Spake by Moses: An Exposition of the Pentateuch*. London: Marshall, Morgan & Scott, 1951.

Alt Albrecht. *Essays in Old Testament History and Religion*. Oxford: Oxford University Press, 1966.

Andersen, Frances I., *Job*. Tyndale Old Testament Commentary. Downers Grove, Ill.: InterVarsity Press, 1976.

Andersen, Francis I., and David Noel Freedman. *Hosea: A New Translation with Introduction, Notes, and Commentary*. Anchor Bible 24. New York: Doubleday, 1980.

Anderson, A. A. *The Book of Psalms*. 2 vols. New Century Bible. London: Oliphants, 1972.

———. *2 Samuel*. Word Biblical Commentary 11. Waco, Tex.: Word, 1989.

Anderson, R. A. *Signs and Wonders: A Commentary on the Book of Daniel*. International Theological Commentary. Grand Rapids, Mich.: Eerdmans, 1984.

Armerding, Carl Edwin. "Nahum." In *Expositor's Bible Commentary*. Vol. 7. Edited by Frank E. Gaebelein. Grand Rapids, Mich.: Zondervan, 1985.

Ashley, Timothy R. *The Book of Numbers*. New International Commentary on the Old Testament. Grand Rapids, Mich.: Eerdmans, 1993.

Baab, Otto Justice. *The Theology of the Old Testament*. New York: Abingdon-Cokesbury, 1949.

Bailey, Kenneth E. "The Manger and the Inn: What the Bible Really Says About Jesus' Birth." *The Catholic Digest*, January 1989, p. 86.

Baldwin, Joyce G. *Daniel*. Tyndale Old Testament Commentary. Downers Grove, Ill.: InterVarsity Press, 1978.

———. *Haggai, Zecharaiah, Malachi: An Introduction and Commentary*. Tyndale Old Testament Commentary. Downers Grove, Ill: InterVarsity Press, 1972.

———. *1 & 2 Samuel*. Tyndale Old Testament Commentary. Downers Grove, Ill.: InterVarsity Press, 1988.

Balentine, Samuel E. "Jeremiah, Prophet of Prayer." *Review and Expositor* 78/3 (Summer 1981): 33.

Barker, Kenneth L., ed. *New International Version Study Bible*. Grand Rapids, Mich.: Zondervan, 1978.

Barth, Christoph. *God With Us: A Theological Introduction to the Old Testament*. Edited and translated by Geoffrey W. Bromiley. Grand Rapids, Mich.: Eerdmans, 1991.

Barth, Karl. *Church Dogmatics*. 16 vols. Edinburgh: T & T Clark, 1936-1977.

———. *The Epistle to the Romans*. 6th ed. Translated by Edwyn Clement Hoskyns. London: Oxford University Press, 1933.

Batten, L. W. *A Critical and Exegetical Commentary on the Books of Ezra and Nehemiah*. International Critical Commentary. New York: Scribner's, 1913.

Bauer, Georg Lorenz. *Hebräische Mythologie des alten und neuen Testaments, mit Parallelen aus der Mythologie anderer Völker, vornemlich der Griechen und Römer*. Leipzig: In der Weygandschen Buchhandlung, 1802.

———. *The Theology of the Old Testament, or A Biblical Sketch of the Religious Opinions of the Ancient Hebrews from the Earliest Times to the Commencement of the Christian Era*. London: Charles Fox, 1838.

Beckwith, Roger T. *The Old Testament Canon of the New Testament Church and Its Background in Early Judaism*. London: SPCK, 1985.

Beek, Martinus Adrianus. "The Meaning of the Expression 'The Chariots and Horsemen of Israel.' " *Oudtestamentische Studiën* 17 (1972): 1-10.

Berlin, Adele. *Poetics and Interpretation of Biblical Narrative*. Bible and Literature Series 9. Sheffield, U.K.: Almond, 1983.

———. *Zephaniah: A New Translation with Introduction, Notes, and Commentary*. Anchor Bible 25A. New York: Doubleday, 1994.

Berry, Donald Kent. *An Introduction to Wisdom and Poetry of the Old Testament*. Nashville: Broadman, 1995.

Biddle, Mark E. "The Literary Frame Surrounding Jeremiah 30:1-33:26." *Zeitschrift für die alttestamentliche Wissenschaft* 100/3 (1988): 409-13.

Blenkinsopp, Joseph. *Ezekiel*. Interpretation. Louisville, Ky.: John Knox Press, 1990.

———. *Ezra-Nehemiah: A Commentary*. Old Testament Library. Philadelphia: Westminster Press, 1987.

———. *Sage, Priest, Prophet: Religious and Intellectual Leadership in Ancient Israel*. Louisville, Ky.: Westminster John Knox, 1995.

Block, Daniel I. "Deborah Among the Judges." In *Faith, Tradition and History: Old Testament Historiography in Its Near Eastern Context*. Edited by A. R. Millard, James Karl Hoffmeier and David W. Baker. Winona Lake, Ind.: Eisenbrauns, 1994.

———. "Ezekiel's Vision of Death and Afterlife." *Bulletin for Biblical Research* 2 (1992): 128.

Bloesch, Donald G. *Essentials of Evangelical Theology*. Vol. 1, *God, Authority and Salvation*. San Francisco: Harper & Row, 1982.

Boadt, Lawrence. *Reading the Old Testament: An Introduction*. New York: Paulist, 1984.

Boling, Robert G. *Judges: A New Translation with Introduction, Notes and Commentary*. Anchor Bible 6A. Garden City, N.Y.: Doubleday, 1975.

Boling, Robert G., and George Ernest Wright. *Joshua: A New Translation with Introduction, Notes and Commentary*. Anchor Bible 6. Garden City, N.Y.: Doubleday, 1982.

Braulik, Georg Peter. "The Sequence of the Laws in Deuteronomy 12-26 and in the Decalogue." In *A Song of Power and the Power of Song: Essays on the Book of Deuteronomy*. Sources for Biblical and Theological Study 3. Edited by Duane L. Christensen. Winona Lake, Ind.: Eisenbrauns, 1993.

Braun, R. L. *Understanding the Basic Themes of 1, 2 Chronicles*. Dallas: Word, 1991.

Bray, Gerald Lewis. *The Doctrine of God*. Downers Grove, Ill.: InterVarsity Press, 1993.

Briggs, Charles Augustus. *Messianic Prophecy: The Prediction of the Fulfillment of Redemption Through the Messiah*. 1886. Reprint, Peabody, Mass.: Hendrickson, 1988.

Briggs, Charles Augustus, and Emily Grace Briggs. *A Critical and Exegetical Commentary on the Book of Psalms*. 2 vols. International Critical Commentary. New York: Scribner's, 1906-1907.

Bright, John. *A History of Israel*. 2nd ed. Philadelphia: Westminster Press, 1972.

————. *Jeremiah: A New Translation with Introduction, Notes and Commentary*. Anchor Bible 21. Garden City, N.Y.: Doubleday, 1965.

————. *The Kingdom of God: The Biblical Concept and Its Meaning for the Church*. Nashville: Abingdon-Cokesbury, 1953.

Broadus, John Albert. *Memoir of James Petigru Boyce*. New York: Armstrong, 1893.

Bronner, Leila Leah. *The Stories of Elijah and Elisha as Polemics Against Baal Worship*. Pretoria Oriental Series 6. Leiden: E. J. Brill, 1968.

Brown, Colin. *Miracles and the Critical Mind*. Grand Rapids, Mich.: Eerdmans, 1984.

Brown, Raymond Edward. *The Gospel According to John, I-XII: A New Translation with Introduction, Notes and Commentary*. Anchor Bible 29. Garden City, N.Y.: Doubleday, 1982.

————. *The Message of Deuteronomy: Not by Bread Alone*. Downers Grove, Ill.: InterVarsity Press, 1993.

Bruce, F. F. *The Gospel of John*. Grand Rapids, Mich.: Eerdmans, 1983.

————. *New Testament Development of Old Testament Themes*. Grand Rapids, Mich: Eerdmans, 1968.

Brueggeman, Walter A. *Genesis*. Interpretation. Atlanta: John Knox Press, 1982.

————. *Old Testament Theology: Essays on Structure, Theme and Text*. Edited by Patrick Dwight Miller Jr. Philadelphia: Fortress, 1992.

————. *Theology of the Old Testament: Testimony, Dispute, Advocacy*. Minneapolis: Fortress, 1997.

————. *To Pluck Up, to Tear Down: A Commentary on the Book of Jeremiah 1—25*. International Theological Commentary. Grand Rapids, Mich.: Eerdmans, 1988.

Budd, Philip J. *Numbers*. Word Biblical Commentary 5. Waco, Tex.: Word, 1984.

Bullock, C. Hassell. *An Introduction to the Old Testament Prophetic Books*. Chicago: Moody Press, 1986.

Burney, Charles Fox. *The Book of Judges, with Introduction and Notes*. Library of Biblical Studies. 1918. Reprint, Grand Rapids, Mich.: Zondervan, 1953.

Butler, Trent C. *Joshua*. Word Biblical Commentary 7. Waco, Tex.: Word, 1983.

Calvin, John. *Commentary on the Book of Psalms*. In *Calvin's Commentaries*. Vol. 4. Translated by James Anderson. Edinburgh: Calvin Translation Society, 1844-1856. Reprint, Grand Rapids, Mich.: Baker, 1996.

————. *Institutes of the Christian Religion*. Edited by John Thomas McNeill and translated by Ford Lewis Battles. 2 vols. Library of Christian Classics 20. Philadelphia: Westminster Press, 1960.

Campbell, Edward Fay, Jr. *Ruth: A New Translation with Introduction, Notes and Commentary*. Anchor Bible 7. Garden City, N.Y.: Doubleday, 1975.

Carlson, Rolf August. *David, the Chosen King: A Traditiohistorical Approach to the Second Book of Samuel*. Translated by Eric J. Sharpe and Stanley Rudman. Uppsala, Sweden: Almqvist and Wiksell, 1964.

Carmichael, Calum M. *The Laws of Deuteronomy*. Ithaca, N.Y.: Cornell University Press, 1974.

Carnell, Edward John. *The Case for Orthodox Theology*. Philadelphia: Westminster Press, 1959.

Carr, G. Lloyd. *The Song of Solomon: An Introduction and Commentary*. Tyndale Old Testament

Commentary. Downers Grove, Ill.: InterVarsity Press, 1984.

Carroll, Robert P. *From Chaos to Covenant: Uses of Prophecy in the Book of Jeremiah*. London: SCM Press, 1981.

――――. *Jeremiah*. Old Testament Library. London: SCM Press, 1986.

Carson, Donald A. *The Gospel According to John*. Grand Rapids, Mich.: Eerdmans, 1991.

Casey, Maurice. *Son of Man: The Interpretation and Influence of Daniel 7*. London: SPCK, 1979.

Cazelles, Henri. "Jeremiah and Deuteronomy." In *A Prophet to the Nations: Essays in Jeremiah Studies*. Edited by Leo G. Perdue and Brian Watson Kovacs. Winona Lake, Ind.: Eisenbrauns, 1984.

Charles, R. H. *A Critical and Exegetical Commentary on the Book of Daniel*. Oxford: Clarendon, 1929.

Childs, Brevard S. *Biblical Theology in Crisis*. Philadelphia: Westminster Press, 1970.

――――. *Biblical Theology of the Old and New Testaments: Theological Reflection on the Christian Bible*. Minneapolis: Fortress, 1992.

――――. *The Book of Exodus*. Old Testament Library. Philadelphia: Westminster Press, 1974.

――――. "The Enemy from the North and the Chaos Tradition." *Journal of Biblical Literature* 78 (1959): 187-98.

――――. *Introduction to the Old Testament as Scripture*. Philadelphia: Fortress, 1979.

――――. *The New Testament as Canon: An Introduction*. Philadelphia: Fortress, 1984.

――――. *Old Testament Theology in a Canonical Context*. Philadelphia: Fortress, 1986.

――――. "Psalm Titles and Midrashic Exegesis." *Journal of Semitic Studies* 16/2 (1971): 137-50.

Clements, Ronald E. *Isaiah 1—39*. New Century Bible. Grand Rapids, Mich.: Eerdmans, 1980.

――――. *Jeremiah*. Interpretation. Atlanta: John Knox Press, 1988.

――――. "Leviticus." In *Broadman Bible Commentary*. Vol. 2. Edited by Clifton J. Allen. Nashville: Broadman, 1969.

――――. "A Light to the Nations: A Central Theme of the Book of Isaiah." In *Forming Prophetic Literature: Essays on Isaiah and the Twelve in Honor of John D. W. Watts*. Edited by James W. Watts and Paul R. House. JSOTSup 235. Sheffield, U.K.: Sheffield Academic Press, 1996.

――――. *Old Testament Theology: A Fresh Approach*. London: Marshall, Morgan & Scott, 1978.

――――. "Patterns in the Prophetic Canon." In *Canon and Authority: Essays in Old Testament Religion and Theology*. Edited by George W. Coats and Burke O'Connor Long. Philadelphia: Fortress, 1977.

――――. "The Unity of the Book of Isaiah." *Interpretation* 36/2 (April 1982): 17-29.

――――. *Wisdom in Theology*. Grand Rapids, Mich.: Eerdmans, 1992.

Clendenen, Ewell Ray. "Life in God's Land: An Outline of the Theology of Deuteronomy." In *The Church at the Dawn of the 21st Century*. Edited by Paige Patterson et al. Dallas: Criswell Publications, 1989.

――――. "Religious Background of the Old Testament." In *Foundations for Biblical Interpretation: A Complete Library of Tools and Resources*. Edited by David S. Dockery, Kenneth A. Matthews and Robert Bryan Sloan. Nashville: Broadman, 1994.

Clines, David J. A. *The Esther Scroll: The Story of the Story*. JSOTSup 30. Sheffield, U.K.: JSOT Press, 1984.

――――. *Ezra, Nehemiah, Esther*. New Century Bible. Grand Rapids, Mich.: Eerdmans, 1984.

――――. *Job 1—20*. Word Biblical Commentary 17. Dallas: Word, 1989.

――――. *The Theme of the Pentateuch*. JSOTSup 10. Sheffield, U.K.: JSOT Press, 1986.

Cogan, Mordechai. *Imperialism and Religion: Assyria, Judah and Israel in the Eighth and Seventh Centuries B.C.E.* Society of Biblical Literature Monograph Series 19. Missoula, Mont.: Scholars Press, 1974.

Cogan, Mordechai, and Hayim Tadmor. *II Kings: A New Translation with Introduction, Notes and Commentary*. Anchor Bible 11. Garden City, N.Y.: Doubleday, 1988.

Cole, Robert Alan. *Exodus: An Introduction and Commentary*. Tyndale Old Testament Commentaries. Downers Grove, Ill.: InterVarsity Press, 1973.

Collins, J. J. *Daniel: With an Introduction to Apocalyptic Literature*. Forms of Old Testament

Literature 20. Grand Rapids, Mich.: Eerdmans, 1984.

Colpe, Carsten. *Theological Dictionary of the New Testament*. Vol. 8. Translated by Geoffrey W. Bromiley. Grand Rapids, Mich.: Eerdmans, 1972.

Conrad, Edgar W. *Reading Isaiah*. Overtures to Biblical Theology 27. Minneapolis: Fortress, 1991.

Cooper, Lamar Eugene, Sr. *Ezekiel*. New American Commentary 17. Nashville: Broadman, 1994.

Craigie, Peter C. *The Book of Deuteronomy*. New International Commentary on the Old Testament. Grand Rapids, Mich.: Eerdmans, 1976.

———. *Ezekiel*. Daily Study Bible. Philadelphia: Westminster Press, 1983.

———. *Psalms 1—50*. Word Biblical Commentary 19. Waco, Tex.: Word, 1983.

———. *Twelve Prophets*. 2 vols. Daily Study Bible. Philadelphia: Westminster Press, 1984-1985.

Craigie, Peter C., Paige H. Kelley and Joel F. Drinkard Jr. *Jeremiah 1—25*. Word Biblical Commentary 26. Dallas: Word, 1991.

Cranfield, C. E. B. *A Critical and Exegetical Commentary on the Epistle to the Romans*. 2 vols. International Critical Commentary. Edinburgh: T & T Clark, 1979.

Crenshaw, James L. *Ecclesiastes*. Old Testament Library. Philadelphia: Westminster Press, 1987.

———. *Old Testament Wisdom: An Introduction*. Atlanta: John Knox Press, 1981.

Cross, Frank Moore. *Canaanite Myth and Hebrew Epic: Essays in the History of the Religion of Israel*. Cambridge, Mass.: Harvard University Press, 1973.

Cundall, Arthur E. "Judges." In Arthur Ernest Cundall and Leon Morris, *Judges and Ruth: An Introduction and Commentary*. Tyndale Old Testament Commentaries. Downers Grove, Ill.: InterVarsity Press, 1968.

Curtis, E. L. *A Critical and Exegetical Commentary on the Books of Chronicles*. International Critical Commentary. New York: Scribner's, 1910.

Dahood, Mitchell J. *Psalms*. 3 vols. Anchor Bible 16-17A. Garden City, N.Y.: Doubleday, 1966-1970.

Dalglish, Edward R. "Judges." In *Broadman Bible Commentary*. Vol 2. Edited by Clifton J. Allen. Nashville: Broadman, 1969.

Davidson, A. B. *The Theology of the Old Testament*. Edited by S. D. F. Salmond. International Theological Library. Edinburgh: T & T Clark, 1904.

Davies, Gwynne Henton. "Tabernacle." In *Interpreter's Dictionary of the Bible*. Edited by George Arthur Buttrick. 4 vols. Nashville: Abingdon, 1962.

Davis, John D. *Genesis and Semitic Tradition*. 1894. Reprint, Grand Rapids, Mich.: Baker, 1980.

Day, Linda. *Three Faces of a Queen: Characterization in the Book of Esther*. JSOTSup 186. Sheffield, U.K.: Sheffield Academic Press, 1995.

———. *1 Kings*. Word Biblical Commentary 12. Waco, Tex.: Word, 1985.

———. *Prophet Against Prophet: The Role of the Micaiah Narrative (1 Kings 22) in the Development of Early Prophetic Tradition*. Grand Rapids, Mich.: Eerdmans, 1978.

Delitzsch, Franz Julius. "The Book of Ecclesiastes." In Carl Friedrich Keil and Franz Julius Delitzsch, *Commentary on the Old Testament*. 10 vols. Grand Rapids, Mich.: Eerdmans, 1980.

———. "Job." In Carl Friedrich Keil and Franz Julius Delitzsch, *Commentary on the Old Testament*. 10 vols. Grand Rapids, Mich.: Eerdmans, 1980.

———. "Psalms." In Carl Friedrich Keil and Franz Julius Delitzsch, *Commentary on the Old Testament*. 10 vols. Grand Rapids, Mich.: Eerdmans, 1980.

———. "Song of Solomon." In Carl Friedrich Keil and Franz Julius Delitzsch, *Commentary on the Old Testament*. 10 vols. Grand Rapids, Mich.: Eerdmans, 1980.

Dentan, Robert C. *Preface to Old Testament Theology*. Rev. ed. New York: Seabury, 1963.

DeRoche, Michael. "Zephaniah 1:2-3: The 'Sweeping of Creation.'" *Vetus Testamentum* 30 (1980): 104-9.

DeVries, Simon J. *1 and 2 Chronicles*. Forms of Old Testament Literature 11. Grand Rapids, Mich.: Eerdmans, 1989.

de Wette, Wilhelm Martin Lebrecht. *Beiträge zur Einleitung in das Alte Testament*. Halle, Germany: Schimmelpfennig, 1806-1807.

———. *Commentar über die Psalmen*. Heidelberg, Germany: Mohr und Zimmer, 1811.

————. *Lehrbuch der christlichen Dogmatik in ihrer historischen Entwickelung dargestellt.* 2 vols. 3rd ed. Berlin: G. Reimer, 1831.

Dhorme, Edouard. *A Commentary on the Book of Job.* Translated by Harold Knight. London: Nelson, 1967.

Diamond, A. R. *The Confessions of Jeremiah in Context: Scenes of Prophetic Drama.* JSOTSup 45. Sheffield, U.K.: Sheffield Academic Press, 1987.

Dillard, Raymond B. "Joel." In *The Minor Prophets: An Exegetical and Expository Commentary.* Vol. 1, *Hosea, Joel, Amos.* Edited by Thomas Edward McComiskey. Grand Rapids, Mich.: Baker, 1992.

————. "Reward and Punishment in Chronicles: The Theology of Immediate Retribution." *Westminster Theological Journal* 46 (1984): 164-72.

Dillard, Raymond B., and Tremper Longman III. *An Introduction to the Old Testament.* Grand Rapids, Mich.: Zondervan, 1994.

Dillmann, August. *Handbuch der alttestamentlichen Theologie.* Edited by Rudolf Kittel. Leipzig, Germany: S. Hirzel, 1895.

Donner, Herbert. "The Separate States of Israel and Judah." In *Israelite and Judaean History.* Edited by John Haralson Hayes and James Maxwell Miller. Old Testament Library. Philadelphia: Westminster Press, 1977.

Douglas, Mary. *Purity and Danger: An Analysis of the Concepts of Pollution and Taboo.* London: Routledge and Kegan Paul, 1966.

Driver, S. R. *The Books of Joel and Amos, with Introduction and Notes.* Cambridge Bible Commentary. Cambridge: Cambridge University Press, 1901.

————. *A Critical and Exegetical Commentary on Deuteronomy.* International Critical Commentary. New York: Scribner's, 1895.

Driver, S. R., and George Buchanan Gray. *A Critical and Exegetical Commentary on the Book of Job.* International Critical Commentary. Edinburgh: T & T Clark, 1950.

Duguid, Iaian M. "Messianic Themes in Zechariah 9-14." In *The Lord's Anointed: Interpretation of Old Testament Messianic Texts.* Edited by Philip E. Satterthwaite, Richard S. Hess and Gordon J. Wenham. Tyndale House Studies. Grand Rapids, Mich.: Baker, 1995.

Duhm, Bernhard. *Das Buch Jeaia.* Göttingen, Germany: Vandenhoeck und Ruprecht, 1892.

Dumbrell, William J. *Covenant and Creation: A Theology of Old Testament Covenants.* Nashville: Thomas Nelson, 1984.

Durham, John. *Exodus.* Word Biblical Commentary 3. Waco Tex.: Word, 1987.

————. "Psalms." In *Broadman Bible Commentary.* Vol. 4. Edited by Clifton J. Allen. Nashville: Broadman, 1971.

Eichrodt, Walther. "Does Old Testament Theology Still Have Independent Significance Within Old Testament Scholarship?" In *The Flowering of Old Testament Theology: A Reader in Twentieth-Century Old Testament Theology, 1930-1990.* Edited by Ben Charles Ollenburger, Elmer A. Martens and Gerhard F. Hasel. Winona Lake, Ind.: Eisenbrauns, 1992.

————. *Ezekiel.* Translated by Cosslett Quin. Old Testament Library. London: SCM Press, 1970.

————. *Theology of the Old Testament.* Translated by J. A. Baker. 2 vols. Old Testament Library. Philadelphia: Westminster Press, 1961-1967.

Eissfeldt, Otto. "The History of Israelite-Jewish Religion and Old Testament Theology." In *The Flowering of Old Testament Theology: A Reader in Twentieth-Century Old Testament Theology, 1930-1990.* Edited by Ben Charles Ollenburger, Elmer A. Martens and Gerhard F. Hasel. Winona Lake, Ind.: Eisenbrauns, 1992.

————. *The Old Testament: An Introduction Including the Apocrypha and Pseudopigrapha, and Also Similar Types from Qumran: The History of the Formation of the Old Testament.* 3rd ed. Translated by Peter R. Ackroyd. New York: Harper & Row, 1965.

Eliot, T. S. *The Complete Poems and Plays, 1909-1950.* New York: Harcourt, Brace & World, 1971.

Elliott, M. Timothy. *The Literary Unity of the Canticle.* Europaische Hochschulschriften. Frankfurt, Germany: Peter Lang, 1989.

Feinberg, Charles Lee. "Jeremiah." In *Expositor's Bible Commentary.* 12 vols. Grand Rapids, Mich:

Zondervan, 1976-1992.

Fensham, F. C. *The Books of Ezra, Nehemiah*. New International Commentary on the Old Testament. Grand Rapids, Mich.: Eerdmans, 1982.

———. "A Few Observations on the Polarisation Between Yahweh and Baal in 1 Kings 17-19." *Zeitschrift für die alttestamentliche Wissenschaft* 92 (1980): 234.

Ferris, Paul Wayne, Jr. *The Genre of Communal Lament in the Bible and the Ancient Near East*. Society of Biblical Literature Dissertation Series 127. Atlanta: Scholars Press, 1992.

Fewell, Danna Nolan, and David M. Gunn. *Compromising Redemption: Relating Characters in the Book of Ruth*. Literary Currents in Biblical Interpretation. Louisville, Ky.: Westminster John Knox, 1990.

Finley, Thomas J. *Joel, Amos, Obadiah*. Wycliffe Exegetical Commentary. Chicago: Moody Press, 1990.

Fishbane, Michael A. *Biblical Interpretation in Ancient Israel*. Oxford: Clarendon, 1985.

———. "Sin and Judgment in the Prophecies of Ezekiel." *Interpretation* 38/2 (April 1984): 142.

Fohrer, Georg. *Introduction to the Old Testament*. Translated by David Eliot Green. Nashville: Abingdon, 1968.

———. *Theologische Grundstrukturen des Alten Testaments*. Berlin: Walter de Gruyter, 1972.

Fokkelman, J. P. *Narrative Art and Poetry in the Books of Samuel: A Full Interpretation Based on Stylistics and Structural Analyses*. Vol. 1, *King David, II Sam 9-20 and I Kings 1-2*. Studia Semitica Neerlanica 20. Assen, Netherlands: Van Gorcum, 1981.

Forman, Charles Conrad. "Koheleth's Use of Genesis." *Journal of Semitic Studies* 5 (1960): 258-59.

Fox, Michael Vass. *Character and Ideology in the Book of Esther*. Studies on Personalities of the Old Testament. Columbia: University of South Carolina Press, 1991.

———. "The Meaning of HEBEL for Qohelet." *Journal of Biblical Literature* 105/3 (1986): 409-27.

———. *Qohelet and His Contradictions*. JSOTSup 71. Bible and Literature Series 18. Sheffield, U.K.: Almond, 1989.

Freedman, David Noel. "The Name of the God of Moses." *Journal of Biblical Literature* 79 (1960): 151-56.

———. "Strophe and Meter in Exodus 15." In *Pottery, Poetry and Prophecy: Studies in Early Hebrew Poetry*. Winona Lake, Ind.: Eisenbrauns, 1980.

Freedman, David Noel, and Francis I. Andersen. *Amos: A New Translation with Introduction, Notes and Commentary*. Anchor Bible 24. Garden City, N.Y.: Doubleday, 1989.

Gabler, Johann P. "An Oration on the Proper Distinction Between Biblical and Dogmatic Theology and the Specific Objectives of Each." In *The Flowering of Old Testament Theology: A Reader in Twentieth-Century Old Testament Theology, 1930-1990*. Edited by Ben Charles Ollenburger, Elmer A. Martens and Gerhard F. Hasel. Winona Lake, Ind.: Eisenbrauns, 1992.

Gammie, John G. *Holiness in Israel*. Overtures to Biblical Theology. Minneapolis: Fortress, 1989.

Garrett, Duane A. *Proverbs, Ecclesiastes, Song of Songs*. New American Commentary. Nashville: Broadman, 1993.

Geisler, Norman L. *Miracles and Modern Thought*. Grand Rapids, Mich.: Zondervan, 1982.

Gerleman, Gillis. *Esther*. Biblischer Kommentar Altes Testament 21. Neukirchen-Vluyn, Germany: Neukirchener Verlag, 1973.

Gese, Harmut. "Tradition and Biblical Theology." In *Tradition and Theology in the Old Testament*. Edited by Douglas A. Knight. London: SPCK, 1977.

———. *Zur biblischen Theologie*. 2nd ed. Tübingen, Germany: Mohr/Siebeck, 1983.

Gibson, John C. L. *Job*. Daily Study Bible. Philadelphia: Westminster Press, 1985.

Gledhill, Tom. *The Message of the Song of Songs: The Lyrics of Love*. The Bible Speaks Today. Downers Grove, Ill.: InterVarsity Press, 1994.

Goldenberg, Robert. "The Problem of False Prophecy: Talmudic Interpretations of Jeremiah 28 and 1 Kings 22." In *The Biblical Mosaic: Changing Perspectives*. Edited by Tobert M. Polzin and Eugene Rothman. Semeia Studies. Philadelphia: Fortress, 1982.

Goldingay, John E. *Daniel*. Word Biblical Commentary 30. Dallas: Word, 1989.

———. *God's Prophet, God's Servant: A Study in Jeremiah and Isaiah 40—55*. Carlisle, U.K.:

Paternoster, 1994.

Good, Edwin M. *Irony in the Old Testament*. Bible and Literature Series 3. 2nd ed. Sheffield, U.K.: Almond, 1981.

Gordis, Robert. *Koheleth—The Man and His World: A Study in Ecclesiastes*. 3rd ed. New York: Schocken, 1968.

———. *Megillat Esther: The Masoretic Text with Introduction, New Translation and Commentary*. New York: KTAV, 1974.

Gordon, R. P. *I and II Samuel*. Grand Rapids, Mich.: Zondervan, 1986.

Gottwald, Norman K. *Studies in the Book of Lamentations*. Studies in Biblical Theology 14. London: SCM Press, 1954.

Gow, Murray D. *The Book of Ruth: Its Structure, Theme and Purpose*. Leicester, England: Apollos, 1992.

Gowan, Donald E. *Theology in Exodus: Biblical Theology in the Form of a Commentary*. Louisville, Ky.: Westminster John Knox, 1994.

Grant, Michael. *The History of Ancient Israel*. New York: Scribner's, 1984.

Gray, George Buchanan. *A Critical and Exegetical Commentary on Numbers*. International Critical Commentary. New York: Scribner's, 1903.

Gray, John. *Joshua, Judges, Ruth*. New Century Bible. Grand Rapids, Mich.: Eerdmans, 1986.

———. *I and II Kings*. Old Testament Library. Philadelphia: Westminster Press, 1963.

Green, Barbara. "The Plot of the Biblical Story of Ruth." *Journal for the Study of the Old Testament* 23 (1982): 55-68.

Green, James Leo. "Jeremiah." In *Broadman Bible Commentary*. Vol. 6. Edited by Clifton J. Allen. Nashville: Broadman, 1978.

Greenberg, Moshe. *Ezekiel 1—20: A New Translation with Introduction, Notes and Commentary*. Anchor Bible 22. Garden City, N.Y.: Doubleday, 1983.

Grogan, Geoffrey W. "Isaiah." In *Expositor's Bible Commentary*. Vol 6. Grand Rapids, Mich.: Zondervan, 1976-1992.

Gunkel, Hermann. *Ausgewählte Psalmen*. 4th ed. Göttingen, Germany: Vandenhoeck und Ruprecht, 1917.

———. *Genesis*. 3rd ed. Handkommentar zum Alten Testament 1/1. Göttingen, Germany: Vandenhoeck und Ruprecht, 1964.

———. "The Influence of Babylonian Mythology upon the Biblical Creation Story." In *Creation in the Old Testament*. Edited by Bernhard Ward Anderson. London: SPCK, 1984.

———. *Die Psalmen übersetzt und erklärt*. Handkommentar zum Alten Testament 2/2. 4th ed. Göttingen, Germany: Vandenhoeck und Ruprecht, 1926.

———. *The Psalms: A Form-Critical Introduction with an Introduction by James Muilenburg*. Translated by Thomas Marland Horner. Reprint, Philadelphia: Fortress, 1967.

———. *Die Sagen der Genesis*. Göttingen, Germany: Vandenhoeck und Ruprecht, 1901.

Gunkel, Hermann, and Joachim Begrich. *Einleitung in die Psalmen: Die Gattungen der religiösen Lyrik Israels*. Handkommentar zum Alten Testament 2. 4th ed. Göttingen, Germany: Vandenhoeck und Ruprecht, 1933.

Gunn, David M. *The Fate of King Saul*. JSOTSup 14. Sheffield, U.K.: Sheffield Academic Press, 1980.

Habel, Norman Charles. *The Book of Job*. Old Testament Library. Philadelphia: Westminster Press, 1985.

———. "The Form and Significance of the Call Narratives." *Zeitschrift für die alttestamentliche Wissenschaft* 77 (1965): 303-5.

Hafemann, Scott J. *Paul, Moses and the History of Israel: The Letter/Spirit Contrast and the Argument from Scripture in 2 Corinthians 3*. Tübingen, Germany: Mohr/Siebeck, 1995.

———. *Suffering and Ministry in the Spirit: Paul's Defense of His Ministry in II Corinthians 2:14-3:3*. Grand Rapids, Mich.: Eerdmans, 1990.

Hagstrom, David Gerald. *The Coherence of the Book of Micah: A Literary Analysis*. Society of Biblical Literature Dissertation Series 89. Atlanta: Scholars Press, 1988.

Hals, Ronald M. *Ezekiel.* Forms of the Old Testament Literature 19. Grand Rapids, Mich.: Eerdmans, 1989.

————. *The Theology of the Book of Ruth.* Facet Books Biblical Series 23. Philadelphia: Fortress, 1969.

Hamilton, Victor Paul. *The Book of Genesis: Chapters 1—17.* New International Commentary on the Old Testament. Grand Rapids, Mich.: Eerdmans, 1990.

————. *Handbook on the Pentateuch.* Grand Rapids, Mich.: Baker, 1982.

Hamlin, E. John. *At Risk in the Promised Land: A Commentary on the Book of Judges.* International Theological Commentary. Grand Rapids, Mich.: Eerdmans, 1990.

————. *Inheriting the Land: A Commentary on the Book of Joshua.* International Theological Commentary. Grand Rapids, Mich.: Eerdmans, 1983.

Hanson, Paul D. *The Dawn of Apocalyptic: The Historical and Sociological Roots of Jewish Apocalyptic Eschatology.* Rev. ed. Philadelphia: Fortress, 1983.

————. *Isaiah 40—66.* Interpretation. Louisville, Ky.: John Knox Press, 1995.

————. *The People Called: The Growth of Community in the Bible.* San Francisco: Harper & Row, 1987.

Harford, John Battersby. *Studies in the Book of Ezekiel.* Cambridge: Cambridge University Press, 1935.

Harper, William Rainey. *A Critical and Exegetical Commentary on Amos and Hosea.* International Critical Commentary. New York: Scribner's, 1905.

Harris, R. Laird. "Leviticus." In *Expositor's Bible Commentary.* Vol. 2. Grand Rapids, Mich.: Zondervan, 1976-1992.

Harrison, R. K. *Introduction to the Old Testament: With a Comprehensive Review of Old Testament Studies and a Special Supplement on the Apocrypha.* Grand Rapids, Mich.: Eerdmans, 1969.

————. *Jeremiah and Lamentations: An Introduction and Commentary.* Tyndale Old Testament Commentary. Downers Grove, Ill.: InterVarsity Press, 1973.

————. *Leviticus: An Introduction and Commentary.* Tyndale Old Testament Commentary. Downers Grove, Ill.: InterVarsity Press, 1980.

————. *Numbers.* Wycliffe Exegetical Commentary. Chicago: Moody Press, 1990.

Hartley, John E. *The Book of Job.* New International Commentary on the Old Testament. Grand Rapids, Mich.: Eerdmans, 1988.

————. *Leviticus.* Word Biblical Commentary 4. Waco, Tex.: Word, 1992.

Hartman, L. F., and A. A. Diella. *The Book of Daniel.* Anchor Bible 23. Garden City, N.Y.: Doubleday, 1977.

Hasel, Gerhard F. *Old Testament Theology: Basic Issues in the Current Debate.* 4th ed. Grand Rapids, Mich.: Eerdmans, 1991.

Havernick, Heinrich Andreas Christoph. *Vorlesungen über die Theologie des Alten Testaments.* Edited by Hermann Schultz and Heinrich August Hahn. Erlangen, Germany: C. Heyder, 1848.

Hayes, John Haralson. *Amos, the Eighth-Century Prophet: His Times and His Preaching.* Nashville: Abingdon, 1988.

Hayes, John Haralson, and Stuart A. Irvine. *Isaiah, the Eighth-Century Prophet: His Times and His Preaching.* Nashville: Abingdon, 1987.

Hayes, John Haralson, and Frederick C. Prussner. *Old Testament Theology: Its History and Development.* Atlanta: John Knox Press, 1985.

Heinisch, Paul. *Theologie des Alten Testamentes.* Bonn: Peter Hanstein, 1940.

Hengstenberg, Ernst Wilhelm. *Christologie des Alten Testaments und Commentar über die Messianischen Weissagungen.* Berlin: L. Oehmigke, 1829-1835.

————. *History of the Kingdom of God in the Old Testament.* Edinburgh: T & T Clark, 1871.

Henry, Carl F. H. *God, Revelation and Authority.* Vol. 4, *God Who Speaks and Shows (Fifteen Theses, Part Three).* Waco Tex.: Word, 1979.

————. *God, Revelation and Authority.* Vol. 6, *God Who Stands and Stays (Part Two).* Waco, Tex.: Word, 1983.

Hertzberg, Hans Wilhelm. *Die Bücher Joshua, Richter und Ruth.* Das Alte Testament Deutsch:

Neues Göttinger Bibelwerk 9. Göttingen, Germany: Vandenhoeck und Ruprecht, 1953.

———. *I and II Samuel*. Translated by John Stephen Bowden. Old Testament Library. Philadelphia: Westminster Press, 1964.

Heth, William A., and Gordon J. Wenham. *Jesus and Divorce: The Problem with the Evangelical Consensus*. Nashville: Thomas Nelson, 1984.

Higham, John. "Beyond Consensus: The Historian as Moral Critic." In *Writing American History: Essays on Modern Scholarship*. Bloomington: Indiana University Press, 1970.

Hillers, Delbert R. *Lamentations: A New Translation with Introduction, Notes and Commentary*. Anchor Bible 7A. Garden City, N.Y.: Doubleday, 1992.

———. *Micah*. Edited by Paul D. Hanson. Hermeneia. Philadelphia: Fortress, 1984.

Hofmann, J. Christian K. von. *Weissagung und Erfüllung im Alten und im Neuen Testamente*. Nordlingen, Germany: C. H. Beck, 1841.

Hogenhaven, Jesper. *Problems and Prospects of Old Testament Theology*. Biblical Seminar 6. Sheffield, U.K.: JSOT Press, 1988.

Holladay, William Lee. *Jeremiah*. 2 vols. Edited by Paul D. Hanson. Hermeneia. Philadelphia: Fortress, 1986-1989.

———. *The Psalms Through Three Thousand Years: Prayerbook of a Cloud of Witnesses*. Minneapolis: Fortress, 1993.

Holt, Else Kragelund. "Jeremiah's Temple Sermon and the Deuteronomists: An Investigation of the Redactional Relationship Between Jeremiah 7 and 26." *Journal for the Study of the Old Testament* 36 (1986): 77.

Honeycutt, Roy Lee, Jr. "Exodus." In *Broadman Bible Commentary*. Vol. 1. Edited by Clifton J. Allen. Rev. ed. Nashville: Broadman, 1973.

Hopper, Stanley Romaine. "Exposition of Jeremiah." In *Interpreter's Bible*. 12 vols. Nashville: Abingdon, 1951-1957.

House, Paul R. "Canon of the Old Testament." In *Foundations for Biblical Interpretation: A Complete Library of Tools and Resources*. Edited by David S. Dockery, Kenneth A. Matthews and Robert B. Sloan. Nashville: Broadman, 1994.

———. *1, 2 Kings*. New American Commentary 8. Nashville: Broadman, 1995.

———. *Old Testament Survey*. Nashville: Broadman, 1992.

———. *The Unity of the Twelve*. JSOTSup 97/Bible and Literature Series 27. Sheffield, U.K.: Almond, 1990.

———. *Zephaniah—A Prophetic Drama*. JSOTSup 69/Bible and Literature Series 16. Sheffield, U.K.: Almond, 1988.

Hubbard, Robert L., Jr. *The Book of Ruth*. New International Commentary on the Old Testament. Grand Rapids, Mich.: Eerdmans, 1988.

Huey, F. B., Jr. "Esther." In *Expositor's Bible Commentary*. 12 vols. Grand Rapids, Mich.: Zondervan, 1976-1992.

Hugenberger, Gordon Paul. "The Servant of the Lord in the 'Servant Songs' of Isaiah." In *The Lord's Anointed: Interpretation of Old Testament Messianic Texts*. Edited by Philip E. Satterthwaite, Richard S. Hess and Gordon J. Wenham. Grand Rapids, Mich.: Baker, 1995.

Jacob, Edmond. *Theology of the Old Testament*. Translated by Arthur Weston Heathcote and Philip J. Allcock. New York: Harper & Row, 1958.

Japhet, Sara. *I and II Chronicles*. Old Testament Library. Louisville, Ky.: Westminster John Knox, 1993.

Jones, Barry Alan. *The Formation of the Book of the Twelve: A Study in Text and Canon*. Society of Biblical Literature Dissertation Series 149. Atlanta: Scholars Press, 1995.

Jones, Gwilym H. *1 and 2 Kings*. 2 vols. New Century Bible. Grand Rapids, Mich.: Eerdmans, 1984.

Kaiser, Otto. *Isaiah 1—12*. Translated by R. A. Wilson. Old Testament Library. Philadelphia: Westminster Press, 1972.

Kaiser, Walter C., Jr. *A Biblical Approach to Personal Suffering*. Chicago: Moody Press, 1982.

———. *Ecclesiastes: Total Life*. Chicago: Moody Press, 1980.

————. "Exodus." In *Expositor's Bible Commentary*. 12 vols. Grand Rapids, Mich.: Zondervan, 1976-1992.

————. *The Journey Isn't Over: The Pilgrim Psalms for Life's Challenges and Joys*. Grand Rapids, Mich.: Baker, 1993.

————. "Leviticus." In *New Interpreter's Bible Commentary*. 12 vols. Nashville: Abingdon, 1994.

————. *The Messiah in the Old Testament*. Studies in Old Testament Biblical Theology. Grand Rapids, Mich.: Zondervan, 1995.

————. *Toward an Old Testament Theology*. Grand Rapids, Mich.: Zondervan, 1978.

Kalland, Earl S. "Deuteronomy." In *Expositor's Bible Commentary*. Vol. 3. Grand Rapids, Mich.: Zondervan, 1976-1992.

Kaminsky, Joel S. *Corporate Responsibility in the Hebrew Bible*. JSOTSup 196. Sheffield, U.K.: Sheffield Academic Press, 1995.

Kaufmann, Yehezkel. *The Religion of Israel: From Its Beginnings to the Babylonian Exile*. Translated and abridged by Moshe Greenberg. Chicago: University of Chicago Press, 1960.

Kautzsch, E. *Biblische Theologie des Alten Testaments*. Tübingen, Germany: Mohr/Siebeck, 1911.

Keel, Othmar. *The Song of Songs*. Continental Commentaries. Minneapolis: Fortress, 1994.

Keil, Carl Friedrich. "The Book of Samuel." In Carl Friedrich Keil and Franz Julius Delitzsch, *Commentary on the Old Testament*. 10 vols. Grand Rapids, Mich.: Eerdmans, 1980.

————. "Exodus." In Carl Friedrich Keil and Franz Julius Delitzsch, *Commentary on the Old Testament*. 10 vols. Grand Rapids, Mich.: Eerdmans, 1980.

————. "Habakkuk." In Carl Friedrich Keil and Franz Julius Delitzsch, *Commentary on the Old Testament*. 10 vols. Grand Rapids, Mich.: Eerdmans, 1980.

————. "Haggai." In Carl Friedrich Keil and Franz Julius Delitzsch, *Commentary on the Old Testament*. 10 vols. Grand Rapids, Mich.: Eerdmans, 1980.

————. "The Lamentations of Jeremiah." In Carl Friedrich Keil and Franz Julius Delitzsch, *Commentary on the Old Testament*. 10 vols. Grand Rapids, Mich.: Eerdmans, 1980.

————. "Leviticus." In Carl Friedrich Keil and Franz Julius Delitzsch, *Commentary on the Old Testament*. 10 vols. Grand Rapids, Mich.: Eerdmans, 1980.

————. "Micah." In Carl Friedrich Keil and Franz Julius Delitzsch, *Commentary on the Old Testament*. 10 vols. Grand Rapids, Mich.: Eerdmans, 1980.

————. "Zechariah." In Carl Friedrich Keil and Franz Julius Delitzsch, *Commentary on the Old Testament*. 10 vols. Grand Rapids, Mich.: Eerdmans, 1980.

Kellerman, Diether. "Asham." In *Theological Dictionary of the Old Testament*. Vol. 1. Edited by G. Johannes Botterweck and Helmer Ringgren. Rev. ed. Grand Rapids, Mich.: Eerdmans, 1981.

Kidner, Derek. *Genesis: An Introduction and a Commentary*. Tyndale Old Testament Commentary. Downers Grove, Ill.: InterVarsity Press, 1967.

————. *Ezra and Nehemiah: An Introduction and Commentary*. Tyndale Old Testament Commentary. Downers Grove, Ill.: InterVarsity Press, 1979.

————. *The Proverbs: An Introduction and Commentary*. Tyndale Old Testament Commentary. Downers Grove, Ill.: InterVarsity Press, 1964.

————. *Psalms: An Introduction and a Commentary*. 2 vols. Tyndale Old Testament Commentary. Downers Grove, Ill.: InterVarsity Press, 1973-1975.

————. *A Time to Mourn and a Time to Dance: Ecclesiastes and the Way of the World*. The Bible Speaks Today. Downers Grove, Ill.: InterVarsity Press, 1976.

Klein, Lillian R. *The Triumph of Irony in the Book of Judges*. Bible and Literature Series 14. Sheffield: Almond, 1989.

Klein, Ralph W. *1 Samuel*. Word Biblical Commentary 10. Waco, Tex.: Word, 1983.

Kline, Meredith G. *Treaty of the Great King: The Covenant Structure of Deuteronomy*. Grand Rapids, Mich.: Eerdmans, 1963.

Kloppenberg, James T. "Objectivity and Historicism: A Century of American Historical Writing." *American Historical Review* (October 1989): 1011-30.

Knierim, Rolf P. *The Task of Old Testament Theology: Substance, Method and Cases*. Grand Rapids, Mich.: Eerdmans, 1995.

Knight, George Angus Fulton. *A Christian Theology of the Old Testament.* Richmond, Va.: John Knox Press, 1959.

———. *Leviticus.* Daily Study Bible. Philadelphia: Westminster Press, 1981.

Köhler, Ludwig. *Old Testament Theology.* Translated by A. S. Todd. Philadelphia: Westminster Press, 1957.

König, Eduard. *Theologie des Alten Testaments, Kritisch und vergleichend dargestellt.* Stuttgart, Germany: C. Belser, 1922.

Kraus, Hans-Joachim. *Klagelieder (Threni).* 3rd ed. Biblischer Kommentar: Altes Testament 20. Neukirchen-Vluyn, Germany: Neukirchener Verlag, 1968.

———. *Psalms.* Translated by Hilton C. Oswald. 2 vols. Minneapolis: Fortress, 1993.

———. *Theology of the Psalms.* Translated by Keith R. Crim. Minneapolis: Augsburg, 1986.

Kutsch, Ernst. "Gideons Berufung und Altarbau, Jdg 6, 11-24." *Theologische Literaturzeitung* 81 (1956): 75-84.

Lambert, W. G. *Babylonian Wisdom Literature.* Oxford: Clarendon, 1960.

Lane, William L. *The Gospel of Mark.* New International Commentary on the New Testament. Grand Rapids, Mich.: Eerdmans, 1974.

Lee, Andrew Yueking. "The Canonical Unity of the Scroll of the Minor Prophets." Ph.D. dissertation, Baylor University, 1985.

Levenson, Jon Douglas. "Theological Consensus or Historicist Evasion? Jews and Christians in Biblical Studies." In *Hebrew Bible or Old Testament: Studying the Bible in Judaism and Christianity.* Edited by Roger Brooks and John Joseph Collins. Notre Dame, Ind.: University of Notre Dame Press, 1990.

Limburg, James. *Hosea-Micah.* Interpretation. Atlanta: John Knox Press, 1988.

Lindblom, Johannes. *Prophecy in Ancient Israel.* Philadelphia: Fortress, 1963.

Loretz, Oswald. "The Theme of the Ruth Story." *Catholic Biblical Quarterly* 22 (1960): 392.

Lowth, Robert. *Lectures on the Sacred Poetry of the Hebrews.* Translated by George Gregory. Andover, Mass.: Crocker and Brewster, 1829.

Luter, Asa Boyd, and Barry C. Davis. *God Behind the Seen: Expositions of the Book of Ruth and Esther.* Expositor's Guide to the Historical Books. Grand Rapids, Mich.: Baker, 1995.

Luther, Martin. "First Lectures on the Psalms." Edited by Hilton C. Oswald. Translated by Herbert J. A. Bouman. In *Luther's Works.* Vols. 10-11. Edited by Jaroslav Jan Pelikan and Helmut T. Lechman. 55 vols. St. Louis: Concordia, 1955-1976.

———. "Lectures on Genesis 1-5." In *Luther's Works.* Vol. 1. Edited by Jaroslav Jan Pelikan and Helmut T. Lechman. 55 vols. St. Louis: Concordia, 1955-1976.

Madvig, Donald Harold. "Joshua." In *Expositor's Bible Commentary.* 12 vols. Grand Rapids, Mich.: Zondervan, 1976-1992.

Mann, Thomas Wingate. *The Book of the Torah: The Narrative Integrity of the Pentateuch.* Atlanta: John Knox Press, 1988.

Martens, Elmer A. "Embracing the Law: A Biblical Theological Perspective." *Bulletin for Biblical Research* 2 (1992): 1-28.

———. *God's Design: A Focus on Old Testament Theology.* Grand Rapids, Mich.: Baker, 1981.

———. "The Multicolored Landscape of Old Testament Theology." In *The Flowering of Old Testament Theology: A Reader in Twentieth-Century Old Testament Theology, 1930-1990.* Edited by Ben Charles Ollenburger, Elmer A. Martens and Gerhard F. Hasel. Winona Lake, Ind.: Eisenbrauns, 1992.

Martin, James D. *The Book of Judges.* Cambridge Bible Commentary. London: Cambridge University Press, 1975.

Mason, Rex. *Preaching the Tradition: Homily and Hermeneutics After the Exile.* Cambridge: Cambridge University Press, 1990.

Mayes, A. D. H. *Deuteronomy.* New Century Bible. Grand Rapids, Mich.: Eerdmans, 1981.

Mays, James Luther. *Amos.* Old Testament Library. Philadelphia: Westminster Press, 1969.

———. *Hosea.* Old Testament Library. Philadelphia: Westminster Press, 1969.

———. *Micah.* Old Testament Library. Philadelphia: Westminster Press, 1976.

————. *Psalms*. Interpretation. Louisville, Ky.: John Knox Press, 1994.

McCarter, P. Kyle, Jr. *I Samuel: A New Translation with Introduction, Notes and Commentary*. Anchor Bible 8. Garden City, N.Y.: Doubleday, 1980.

————. *II Samuel: A New Translation with Introduction, Notes and Commentary*. Anchor Bible 9. Garden City, N.Y.: Doubleday, 1984.

McCarthy, Dennis J. *Old Testament Covenant: A Survey of Current Opinions*. Oxford: Basil Blackwell, 1972.

————. *Treaty and Covenant: A Study in Form in the Ancient Oriental Documents and the Old Testament*. Rev. ed. Analecta Biblica 21A. Rome: Pontifical Biblical Institute, 1978.

McComiskey, Thomas Edward. *The Covenants of Promise: A Theology of the Old Testament Covenants*. Grand Rapids, Mich.: Baker, 1985.

————. "Hosea." In *The Minor Prophets: An Exegetical and Expository Commentary*. Vol. 1, *Hosea, Joel, Amos*. Edited by Thomas Edward McComiskey. Grand Rapids, Mich.: Baker, 1992.

————. "Micah." In *Expositor's Bible Commentary*. 12 vols. Grand Rapids, Mich.: Zondervan, 1976-1992.

McConville, Gordon. *Law and Theology in Deuteronomy*. JSOTSup 33. Sheffield, U.K.: JSOT Press, 1984.

McKane, William. *A Critical and Exegetical Commentary on Jeremiah*. Vol. 1. Edited by John Adney Emerton and C. E. B. Cranfield. International Critical Commentary. Edinburgh: T & T Clark, 1986.

————. *Prophets and Wise Men*. Studies in Biblical Theology 1/44. Naperville, Ill.: Allenson, 1965.

————. *Proverbs: A New Approach*. Old Testament Library. Philadelphia: Westminster Press, 1970.

McKay, John William. *Religion in Judah Under the Assyrians, 732-609 B.C.* Studies in Biblical Theology 2/26. Naperville, Ill.: Allenson, 1973.

McKenzie, John L. *Second Isaiah: A New Translation with Introduction, Notes and Commentary*. Anchor Bible 20. Garden City, N.Y.: Doubleday, 1968.

————. *A Theology of the Old Testament*. Garden City, N.Y.: Doubleday, 1974.

Mendenhall, George E. "Covenant Forms in Israelite Traditions." *Biblical Archaeologist* 17 (1954): 58.

————. "The Suzerainty Treaty Structure: Thirty Years Later." In *Religion and Law: Biblical-Judaic and Islamic Perspectives*. Edited by Edwin Brown Firmage, Bernard G. Weiss and John W. Welch. Winona Lake, Ind.: Eisenbrauns, 1990.

Merrill, Eugene H. *Deuteronomy*. New American Commentary 4. Nashville: Broadman, 1994.

————. "A Theology of the Pentateuch." In *A Biblical Theology of the Old Testament*. Edited by Roy B. Zuck et al. Chicago: Moody Press, 1991.

Meyers, Carol L., and Eric M. Meyers. *Haggai, Zechariah 1—8: A New Translation with Introduction, Notes and Commentary*. Anchor Bible 25B. Garden City, N.Y.: Doubleday, 1987.

Michel, Otto. "The Son of Man." In *The New International Dictionary of New Testament Theology*. Vol 3. Edited by Colin Brown. Grand Rapids, Mich.: Zondervan, 1978.

Milgrom, Jacob. *Leviticus 1—16: A New Translation with Introduction, Notes and Commentary*. Anchor Bible 3-3A. Garden City, N.Y.: Doubleday, 1991.

————. *Numbers*. Jewish Publication Society Torah Commentary. Philadelphia: Jewish Publication Society, 1989.

Miller, James Maxwell. *The Old Testament and the Historian*. Philadelphia: Fortress, 1976.

Miller, Patrick Dwight, Jr. *Interpreting the Psalms*. Philadelphia: Fortress, 1986.

Miscall, Peter D. *1 Samuel: A Literary Reading*. Bloomington: Indiana University Press, 1986.

Montgomery, J. A. *A Critical and Exegetical Commentary on the Book of Daniel*. International Critical Commentary. Edinburgh: T & T Clark, 1927.

Moore, Carey A. *Esther*. Anchor Bible 7B. Garden City, N.Y.: Doubleday, 1971.

Moore, George Foot. *A Critical and Exegetical Commentary on Judges*. International Critical Commentary. New York: Scribner's, 1895.

Morris, Leon. *New Testament Theology*. Grand Rapids, Mich.: Zondervan, 1986.

———. "Ruth." In Arthur Ernest Cundall and Leon Morris, *Judges and Ruth: An Introduction and Commentary*. Tyndale Old Testament Commentary. Downers Grove, Ill.: InterVarsity Press, 1968.

Motyer, J. A. *The Day of the Lion: The Message of Amos*. The Bible Speaks Today. Downers Grove, Ill.: InterVarsity Press, 1974.

———. *The Prophecy of Isaiah*. Downers Grove, Ill.: InterVarsity Press, 1993.

Mowinckel, Sigmund Olaf Plytt. *The Psalms in Israel's Worship*. Translated by D. R. Ap-Thomas. 2 vols. Nashville: Abingdon, 1962.

Muilenberg, James. "The Book of Isaiah, Chapters 40—66." In *Interpreter's Bible*. Vol. 5. New York: Abingdon, 1956.

———. *The Servant Songs in Deutero-Isaiah: A New Attempt to Solve an Old Problem*. Lund, Sweden: C. W. K. Gleerup, 1951.

Murphy, Roland Edmund. *Ecclesiastes*. Word Biblical Commentary 23A. Waco, Tex.: Word, 1992.

———. *Introduction to the Wisdom Literature of the Old Testament*. Old Testament Reading Guide. Collegeville, Minn.: Liturgical Press, 1965.

———. *The Song of Songs*. Edited by S. Dean McBride Jr. Hermeneia. Minneapolis: Augsburg Fortress, 1990.

———. *Wisdom Literature and Psalms*. Edited by Lloyd R. Bailey Sr. and Victor Paul Furnish. Interpreting Biblical Texts. Nashville: Abingdon, 1993.

Myers, J. M. *I Chronicles*. Anchor Bible 12. Garden City, N.Y.: Doubleday, 1965.

Napier, Bunyan Davie. "Prophet." In *Interpreter's Dictionary of the Bible*. Edited by George Arthur Buttrick. 4 vols. Nashville: Abingdon, 1962.

———. *Song of the Vineyard: A Guide Through the Old Testament*. Rev. ed. Philadelphia: Fortress, 1981.

Newsom, Carol A. "A Maker of Metaphors: Ezekiel's Oracles Against Tyre." *Interpretation* 38 (1984): 163.

Newsome, James D., Jr. *The Hebrew Prophets*. Atlanta: John Knox Press, 1984.

Nicholson, Ernest W. *Exodus and Sinai in History and Tradition*. Atlanta: John Knox Press, 1978.

———. *God and His People: Covenant and Theology in the Old Testament*. Oxford: Clarendon, 1986.

———. *Preaching to the Exiles: A Study of the Prose Tradition in the Book of Jeremiah*. Oxford: Basil Blackwell, 1970.

Nogalski, James. *Literary Precursors to the Book of the Twelve*. Beihefte Zeitschrift für alttestamentliche Wissenschaft 217. Berlin: Walter de Gruyter, 1993.

———. *Redactional Processes in the Book of the Twelve*. Beihefte Zeitschrift für alttestamentliche Wissenschaft 218. Berlin: Walter de Gruyter, 1993.

North, Christopher R. *The Second Isaiah*. Oxford: Clarendon, 1964.

———. *The Suffering Servant in Deutero-Isaiah: An Historical and Critical Study*. 2nd ed. London: Oxford University Press, 1956.

North, Robert. "Theology of the Chronicles." *Journal of Biblical Literature* 82/4 (December 1963): 369-81.

Noth, Martin. *The Deuteronomistic History*. Translated by David Orton. JSOTSup 15. Sheffield, U.K.: Sheffield Academic Press, 1981.

———. *Exodus*. Translated by John Stephen Bowden. Old Testament Library. Philadelphia: Westminster Press, 1962.

———. *The History of Israel*. Translated by Peter R. Ackroyd. 2nd ed. New York: Harper & Row, 1960.

———. *Könige, Part 1*. Biblischer Kommentar: Altes Testament 9. Neukirchen-Vluyn, Germany: Neukirchener, 1968.

———. *Leviticus*. Translated by J. E. Anderson. Rev. ed. Old Testament Library. Philadelphia: Westminster Press, 1977.

———. *Numbers*. Translated by James D. Martin. Old Testament Library. Philadelphia: Westminster Press, 1968.

O'Connor, Kathleen M. *The Confessions of Jeremiah: Their Interpretation and Role in Chapters 1—25*. Society of Biblical Literature Dissertations Series 94. Atlanta: Scholars Press, 1988.

Oehler, Gustav Friedrich. *Theology of the Old Testament*. Translated by Ellen D. Smith (vol. 1) and Sophia Taylor (vol. 2). Edinburgh: T & T Clark, 1882-1883.

Oestreicher, Theodor. *Das Deuteronomische Grundgesetz*. Beiträge zur Förderung christlicher Theologie 27/4. Gütersloh, Germany: Bertelsmann, 1923.

Ogden, Graham S. *Qoheleth Readings: A New Biblical Form*. Sheffield, U.K.: Sheffield Academic Press, 1987.

Ollenburger, Ben Charles. "From Timeless Ideas to the Essence of Religion: Method in Old Testament Theology Before 1930." In *The Flowering of Old Testament Theology: A Reader in Twentieth-Century Old Testament Theology, 1930-1990*. Edited by Ben Charles Ollenburger, Elmer A. Martens and Gerhard F. Hasel. Winona Lake, Ind.: Eisenbrauns, 1992.

Orr, James. *The Problem of the Old Testament*. New York: Scribner's, 1906.

Oswalt, John N. *The Book of Isaiah: Chapters 1—39*. New International Commentary on the Old Testament. Grand Rapids, Mich.: Eerdmans, 1986.

Overhold, Thomas W. *The Threat of Falsehood: A Study in the Theology of the Book of Jeremiah*. Studies in Biblical Theology 2/16. London: SCM Press, 1970.

Owens, John Joseph. "Daniel." In *Broadman Bible Commentary*. Vol. 6. Nashville: Broadman, 1978.

———. "Numbers." In *Broadman Bible Commentary*. Vol. 2. Edited by Clifton J. Allen. Nashville: Broadman, 1969.

Paton, Lewis Bayles. *A Critical and Exegetical Commentary on the Book of Esther*. International Critical Commentary. Reprint, Edinburgh: T & T Clark, 1976.

Patrick, Dale. *Old Testament Law*. Atlanta: John Knox Press, 1985.

Patterson, Paige. *Song of Solomon*. Bible Study Helps/Everyman's Bible Commentaries. Chicago: Moody Press, 1986.

Payne, David F. *I and II Samuel*. Daily Study Bible. Philadelphia: Westminster Press, 1982.

Payne, J. Barton. "1, 2 Chronicles." In *Expositor's Bible Commentary*. Vol 4. Grand Rapids, Mich.: Eerdmans, 1988.

———. *The Theology of the Older Testament*. Grand Rapids, Mich.: Zondervan, 1962.

Peckham, Brian. "Israel and Phoenicia." In *Magnalia Dei, the Mighty Acts of God: Essays on the Bible and Archaeology in Memory of G. Ernest Wright, Part 2*. Edited by Frank Moore Cross, Werner Erich Lemke and Patrick Dwight Miller Jr. Garden City, N.Y.: Doubleday, 1976.

Perdue, Leo G. *The Collapse of History: Reconstructing Old Testament Theology*. Minneapolis: Augsburg Fortress, 1994.

———. *Wisdom and Creation: The Theology of Wisdom Literature*. Nashville: Abingdon, 1994.

Petersen, David L. *Haggai and Zechariah 1—8*. Old Testament Library. Philadelphia: Westminster Press, 1984.

———. *Zechariah 9—14 and Malachi*. Old Testament Library. Louisville, Ky.: Westminster John Knox, 1995.

Pierce, Ronald Webster. "Literary Connectors and Haggai/Zechariah/Malachi Corpus." *Journal of the Evangelical Theological Society* 27/3 (1984): 277-89.

———. "A Thematic Development of the Haggai/Zechariah/Malachi Corpus." *Journal of the Evangelical Theological Society* 27/4 (1984): 401-11.

Polhill, John B. *Acts*. New American Commentary. Nashville: Broadman, 1992.

Polzin, Robert M. *David and the Deuteronomist: A Literary Study of the Deuteronomic History*. Part 3, *2 Samuel*. Bloomington: Indiana University Press, 1993.

———. *Samuel and the Deuteronomist: A Literary Study of the Deuteronomistic History*. Part 2, *1 Samuel*. San Francisco: Harper & Row, 1989.

Pope, Marvin H. "Homosexuality." In *Interpreter's Dictionary of the Bible: Supplemental Volume*. Edited by Keith R. Crim. Nashville: Abingdon, 1976.

———. *Job: A New Translation with Introduction, Notes and Commentary*. Anchor Bible. Garden

City, N.Y.: Doubleday, 1965.

Porteous, N. W. *Daniel.* Old Testament Library. Philadelphia: Westminster Press, 1965.

Potter, H. D. "The New Covenant in Jeremiah 31:31-34." *Vetus Testamentum* 33/3 (1983): 347-55.

Preuss, Horst Dietrich. *Old Testament Theology.* Translated by Leo G. Perdue. 2 vols. Louisville, Ky.: Westminster John Knox, 1995.

Prinsloo, Willem S. "The Theology of the Book of Ruth." *Vetus Testamentum* 30 (1980): 332.

Pritchard, James Bennett, ed. *Ancient New Eastern Texts Relating to the Old Testament.* 2nd ed. Princeton, N.J.: Princeton University Press, 1955.

———. *Ancient Near Eastern Texts Relating to the Old Testament.* 3rd ed. Princeton, N.J.: Princeton University Press, 1969.

Procksch, Otto. *Theologie des Alten Testaments.* Gütersloh, Germany: Bertelsmann, 1950.

Provan, Iaim W. *Lamentations.* New Century Bible. Grand Rapids, Mich.: Eerdmans, 1991.

Purtill, Richard L. "Miracles: What If They Happen?" In *Thinking About Religion: A Philosophical Introduction to Religion.* Englewood Cliffs, N.J.: Prentice-Hall, 1978.

Redditt, Paul L. *Haggai, Zechariah, Malachi.* New Century Bible. Grand Rapids, Mich.: Eerdmans, 1995.

Re'Mi, S. Paul. "Lamentations." In Robert Martin-Achard and S. Paul Re'mi, *God's People in Crisis: A Commentary on the Books of Amos and Lamentations.* International Theological Commentary. Grand Rapids, Mich.: Eerdmans, 1984.

Rendtorff, Rolf. *Canon and Theology: Overtures to an Old Testament Theology.* Edited and translated by Margaret Kohl. Overtures to Biblical Theology. Minneapolis: Fortress, 1993.

———. *The Problem of the Process of Transmission in the Pentateuch.* Translated by John J. Scullion. JSOTSup 89. Sheffield, U.K.: Sheffield Academic Press, 1990.

Riley, William. *King and Cultus in Chronicles: Worship and the Reinterpretations of History.* JSOTSup 160. Sheffield, U.K.: Sheffield Academic Press, 1993.

Roberts, J. J. M. "Isaiah in Old Testament Theology." *Interpretation* 36/2 (April 1982): 130-43.

———. *Nahum, Habakkuk and Zephaniah.* Old Testament Library. Louisville, Ky.: Westminster John Knox, 1991.

Robertson, O. Palmer. *The Books of Nahum, Habakkuk and Zephaniah.* New International Commentary on the Old Testament. Grand Rapids, Mich.: Eerdmans, 1990.

Robinson, H. Wheeler. "The Hebrew Conception of Corporate Personality." In *Weden und Wesen des Alten Testaments.* Edited by Paul Volz. Beihefte zur Zeitschrift für die alttestamentliche Wissenschaft 66. Berlin: Töpelmann, 1936.

Rogerson, John W. *W. M. L. de Wette, Founder of Modern Biblical Criticism: An Intellectual Biography.* JSOTSup 126. Sheffield, U.K.: Sheffield Academic Press, 1992.

Rost, Leonhard. *The Succession to the Throne of David.* Translated by Michael D. Rutter and David M. Gunn. Reprint, Sheffield, U.K.: Almond, 1982.

Roth, Wolfgang. "The Story of the Prophet Michaiah (1 Kings 22) in Historical-Critical Interpretation 1876-1976." In *The Biblical Mosaic: Changing Perspectives.* Edited by Robert M. Polzin and Eugene Rothman. Semeia Studies. Philadelphia: Fortress, 1982.

Rowley, Harold Henry. *The Faith of Israel: Aspects of Old Testament Thought.* Philadelphia: Westminster Press, 1956.

———. *Men of God: Studies in Old Testament History and Prophecy.* London: Nelson, 1963.

———. *The Relevance of Apocalyptic: A Study of Jewish and Christian Apocalypses from Daniel to the Revelation.* 3rd ed. Reprint, Greenwood, S.C.: Attic, 1980.

———. *The Servant of the Lord and Other Essays on the Old Testament.* London: Lutterworth, 1952.

Rudolph, Wilhelm. *Die Bücher Ruth, Hohelied und Klagelieder: Übersetzt und Erklärt.* 2nd ed. Kommentar zum Alten Testament 17. Gütersloh, Germany: Gerd Mohn, 1962.

Sailhamer, John Herbert. *Introduction to Old Testament Theology: A Canonical Approach.* Grand Rapids, Mich.: Eerdmans, 1995.

———. *The Pentateuch as Narrative: A Biblical-Theological Commentary.* Grand Rapids, Mich.:

Zondervan, 1992.

Sanders, James A. "Hermeneutics in True and False Prophecy." In *Canon and Authority: Essays in Old Testament Religion and Theology*. Edited by George W. Coats and Burke O'Connor Long. Philadelphia: Fortress, 1977.

———. *Torah and Canon*. Philadelphia: Fortress, 1972.

Sasson, Jack Murad. *Ruth: A New Translation with a Philological Commentary and a Formalist-Folklorist Interpretation*. 2nd ed. Johns Hopkins Near Eastern Studies. Sheffield, U.K.: JSOT Press, 1989.

Sawyer, John F. A. *Isaiah*. 2 vols. Daily Study Bible. Philadelphia: Westminster Press, 1984.

Schmidt, Werner H. *The Faith of the Old Testament*. Translated by John Sturdy. Philadelphia: Westminster Press, 1983.

Schultz, Hermann. *Old Testament Theology: The Religion of Revelation in its Pre-Christian Stage of Development*. Translated by J. A. Paterson. 2 vols. 4th ed. Edinburgh: T & T Clark, 1892.

Schultz, Richard. "The King in the Book of Isaiah." In *The Lord's Anointed: Interpretation of Old Testament Messianic Texts*. Edited by Philip E. Satterthwaite, Richard S. Hess and Gordon J. Wenham. Tyndale House Studies. Grand Rapids, Mich.: Baker, 1995.

Schweizer, Eduard. *The Good News According to Mark*. Translated by Donald Harold Madvig. Atlanta: John Knox Press, 1970.

Scott, R. B. Y. *Proverbs, Ecclesiastes: A New Translation with Introduction, Notes and Commentary*. Anchor Bible. Garden City, N.Y.: Doubleday, 1965.

———. *The Way of Wisdom in the Old Testament*. New York: Macmillan, 1971.

Seitz, Christopher R. *Isaiah 1—39*. Interpretation. Louisville, Ky.: John Knox Press, 1993.

———. *Word Without End: The Old Testament as Abiding Theological Witness*. Grand Rapids, Mich.: Eerdmans, 1998.

———, ed. *Reading and Preaching the Book of Isaiah*. Philadelphia: Fortress, 1988.

Selman, M. J. *1 Chronicles: An Introduction and Commentary*. Tyndale Old Testament Commentary. Downers Grove, Ill.: InterVarsity Press, 1994.

Shaver, J. R. *Torah and the Chronicler's History Work: An Inquiry into the Chronicler's References to Laws, Festivals and Cultic Institutions in Relationship to Pentateuchal Legislation*. Society of Biblical Literature Dissertation Series 196. Atlanta: Scholars Press, 1989.

Simon, Ulrich E. *A Theology of Salvation: A Commentary on Isaiah 40—55*. London: SPCK, 1953.

Skinner, John. *The Book of the Prophet Isaiah*. 2 vols. Cambridge Bible Commentary. Reprint, Cambridge: Cambridge University Press, 1963.

———. *A Critical and Exegetical Commentary on Genesis*. International Critical Commentary. New York: Scribner's, 1910.

———. *I and II Kings*. Century Bible. Edinburgh: T. C. and E. C. Jack, 1904.

———. *Prophecy and Religion: Studies in the Life of Jeremiah*. Cambridge: Cambridge University Press, 1922.

Smart, James D. *History and Theology in Second Isaiah: A Commentary on Isaiah 35, 40—66*. London: Epworth, 1967.

Smith, Billy K., and Frank S. Page. *Amos, Obadiah, Jonah*. New American Commentary. Nashville: Broadman, 1995.

Smith, George. *The Chaldean Account of Genesis*. London: S. Low, Marston, Searle and Rivington, 1876.

Smith, George Adam. *The Book of the Twelve Prophets, Commonly Called the Minor Prophets*. 2 vols. Rev. ed. Expositor's Bible. New York: Harper & Brothers, 1928.

Smith, J. M. Powis. "Micah." In J. M. Powis Smith, William Hayes Ward and Julius August Bewer, *A Critical and Exegetical Commentary on Micah, Zephaniah, Nahum, Habakkuk, Obadiah and Joel*. International Critical Commentary. New York: Scribner's, 1911.

———. "Nahum." In J. M. Powis Smith, William Hayes Ward and Julius August Bewer, *A Critical and Exegetical Commentary on Micah, Zephaniah, Nahum, Habakkuk, Obadiah and Joel*. International Critical Commentary. New York: Scribner's, 1911.

Smith, J. M. Powis, Hinckley Gilbert Mitchell and Julius August Bewer. *A Critical and Exegetical*

Commentary on Haggai, Zechariah, Malachi and Jonah. International Critical Commentary 24. New York: Scribner's, 1912.

Smith, J. M. Powis, William Hayes Ward and Julius August Bewer. *A Critical and Exegetical Commentary on Micah, Zephaniah, Nahum, Habakkuk, Obadiah and Joel*. International Critical Commentary 24. New York: Scribner's, 1911.

Smith, Ralph L. *Micah-Malachi*. Word Biblical Commentary 32. Waco, Tex.: Word, 1984.

———. *Old Testament Theology: Its History, Method and Message*. Nashville: Broadman, 1993.

Snaith, John G. *Song of Songs*. New Century Bible. Grand Rapids, Mich.: Eerdmans, 1993.

Snaith, Norman Henry. *The Distinctive Ideas of the Old Testament*. London: Epworth, 1944.

———. *Mercy and Sacrifice: A Study of the Book of Hosea*. London: SCM Press, 1953.

Soggin, J. Alberto. *Joshua*. Translated by R. A. Wilson. Old Testament Library. Philadelphia: Westminster Press, 1972.

———. *Judges*. Translated by John S. Bowden. Old Testament Library. Philadelphia: Westminster Press, 1981.

Spurgeon, C. H. *The Treasury of David*. 7 vols. New York: Funk, 1882-1886.

Stade, Bernhard. *Biblische Theologie des Alten Testaments*. Grundriss der theologischen Wissenschaften. Tübingen, Germany: Mohr/Siebeck, 1905.

Stricker, Frank. "Why History? Thinking About the Uses of the Past." *The History Teacher* 25/3 (May 1992): 293-312.

Stuart, Douglas K. *Ezekiel*. Communicator's Commentary 18. Dallas: Word, 1989.

———. *Hosea-Jonah*. Word Biblical Commentary. Waco, Tex.: Word, 1987.

Stuart, Douglas K., and Gordon D. Fee. *How to Read the Bible for All Its Worth*. Grand Rapids, Mich.: Zondervan, 1981.

Sun, Henry T. C., et al. *Problems in Biblical Theology: Essays in Honor of Rolf Knierim*. Grand Rapids, Mich.: Eerdmans, 1997.

Swinburne, Richard. *The Concept of Miracle*. London: Macmillan, 1970.

Széles, Maria Eszenyei. *Wrath and Mercy: A Commentary on the Books of Habakkuk and Zephaniah*. Translated by George Angus Fulton Knight. International Theological Commentary. Grand Rapids, Mich.: Eerdmans, 1987.

Talmon, Shemaryahu. "'Wisdom' in the Book of Esther." *Vetus Testamentum* 13 (1960): 419-55.

Tate, Marvin Embry. *Psalms 51-100*. Word Biblical Commentary 20. Dallas: Word, 1990.

Taylor, John Bernard. *Ezekiel: An Introduction and Commentary*. Tyndale Old Testament Commentary. London: Tyndale, 1969.

Terrien, Samuel L. *The Elusive Presence: Toward a New Biblical Theology*. San Francisco: Harper & Row, 1978.

Thielman, Frank. *Paul and the Law: A Contextual Approach*. Downers Grove, Ill.: InterVarsity Press, 1994.

Thompson, John Alexander. *The Book of Jeremiah*. New International Commentary on the Old Testament. Grand Rapids, Mich.: Eerdmans, 1980.

———. *Deuteronomy: An Introduction and Commentary*. Tyndale Old Testament Commentary. Downers Grove, Ill.: InterVarsity Press, 1974.

———. *1, 2 Chronicles*. New American Commentary 9. Nashville: Broadman, 1994.

Throntveit, M. A. *Ezra-Nehemiah*. Interpretation. Louisville, Ky.: John Knox Press, 1992.

Towner, W. S. *Daniel*. Interpretation. Atlanta: John Knox Press, 1992.

Toy, Crawford Howell. *A Critical and Exegetical Commentary on the Book of Proverbs*. International Critical Commentaries. New York: Scribner's, 1904.

———. "Note on Hosea 1-3." *Journal of Biblical Literature* 32 (1913): 75-79.

VanGemeren, Willem A. *The Progress of Redemption: The Story of Salvation from Creation to the New Jerusalem*. Grand Rapids, Mich.: Baker, 1988.

———. "Psalms." In *Expositor's Bible Commentary*. Vol. 5. Grand Rapids, Mich.: Zondervan, 1976-1992.

Van Seters, John. *In Search of History: Historiography in the Ancient World and the Origins of Biblical History*. New Haven, Conn.: Yale Univeristy Press, 1983.

Vatke, Wilhelm. *Biblische Theologie, wissenschaftlich dargestellt: Die Religion des Alten Testaments*. Berlin: G. Bethge, 1835.

———. *Prologue to History: The Yahwist as Historian in Genesis*. New Haven, Conn.: Yale University Press, 1992.

Verhoef, Pieter A. *The Books of Haggai and Malachi*. New International Commentary on the Old Testament. Grand Rapids, Mich.: Eerdmans, 1987.

von Rad, Gerhard. "The Confessions of Jeremiah." In *Theodicy in the Old Testament*. Edited by James L. Crenshaw. Issues in Religion and Theology 4. Philadelphia: Fortress, 1983.

———. *Deuteronomy*. Translated by Dorothea M. Barton. Old Testament Library. Philadelphia: Westminster Press, 1966.

———. *Genesis*. Translated by John Henry Marks. Rev. ed. Old Testament Library. Philadelphia: Westminster Press, 1971.

———. *Old Testament Theology*. Vol. 1, *The Theology of Israel's Historical Traditions*. Translated by David Muir Gibson Stalker. New York: Harper & Row, 1962.

———. *Old Testament Theology*. Vol. 2, *The Theology of Israel's Prophetic Traditions*. Translated by David Muir Gibson Stalker. New York: Harper & Row, 1965.

———. *Studies in Deuteronomy*. Translated by David Muir Gibson Stalker. Studies in Biblical Theology 9. London: SCM Press, 1963.

———. *Wisdom in Israel*. Translated by Davidson Martin. Nashville: Abingdon, 1972.

Vos, Geerhardus. *Biblical Theology: Old and New Testaments*. Grand Rapids, Mich.: Eerdmans, 1948.

Vriezen, Theodorus Christian. *An Outline of Old Testament Theology*. Translated by S. Neuijen. 2nd ed. Oxford: Basil Blackwell, 1970.

Walton, John H. *Ancient Israelite Literature in Its Cultural Context: A Survey of Parallels Between Biblical and Ancient Near Eastern Texts*. Grand Rapids, Mich.: Zondervan, 1989.

———. "Psalms: A Cantata About the Davidic Covenant." *Journal of the Evangelical Theological Society* 34/1 (March 1991): 21-31.

Watts, James W., and Paul R. House, eds. *Forming Prophetic Literature: Essays on Isaiah and the Twelve in Honor of John D. W. Watts*. JSOTSup 235. Sheffield, U.K.: Sheffield Academic Press, 1996.

Watts, John D. W. *The Books of Joel, Obadiah, Jonah, Nahum, Habakkuk and Zephaniah*. Cambridge Bible Commentary. Cambridge: Cambridge University Press, 1975.

———. "Deuteronomy." In *Broadman Bible Commentary*. Vol. 2. Edited by Clifton J. Allen. Nashville: Broadman, 1969.

———. *Isaiah 1—33*. Word Biblical Commentary 24-25. Waco, Tex.: Word, 1985-1987.

———. "Zechariah." In *Broadman Bible Commentary*. Vol. 7. Edited by Clifton J. Allen. Nashville: Broadman, 1969.

Watts, John D. W., John Joseph Owens and Marvin Embry Tate. "Job." In *Broadman Bible Commentary*. Vol. 4. Edited by Clifton J. Allen. Nashville: Broadman, 1971.

Weinfeld, Moshe. *"Berith"* (Covenant). In *Theological Dictionary of the Old Testament*. Vol. 2. Edited by G. Johannes Botterweck and Helmer Ringgren. Grand Rapids, Mich.: Eerdmans, 1975.

———. *Deuteronomy: A New Translation with Introduction, Notes and Commentary*. Anchor Bible 5-5A. Garden City, N.Y.: Doubleday, 1991.

———. "Deuteronomy: The Present State of Inquiry." *Journal of Biblical Literature* 86 (1967): 249-62.

———. *Deuteronomy and the Deuteronomic School*. Reprint, Winona Lake, Ind.: Eisenbrauns, 1992.

Weiser, Artur. *The Psalms*. Translated by Herbert Hartwell. Old Testament Library. Philadelphia: Westminster Press, 1962.

Wellhausen, Julius. *Prolegomena to the History of Ancient Israel*. Gloucester, Mass.: Peter Smith, 1983. (*Prolegomena zur Geschichte Israels*. Berlin: G. Reimer, 1878.)

Wenham, Gordon. *The Book of Leviticus*. New International Commentary on the Old Testament. Grand Rapids, Mich.: Eerdmans, 1979.

———. *Genesis*. Word Biblical Commentary 1-2. Waco, Tex.: Word, 1987-1994.

———. *Numbers: An Introduction and Commentary*. Tyndale Old Testament Commentary. Downers Grove, Ill.: InterVarsity Press, 1981.

West, Mona. "Irony in the Book of Jonah: Audience Identification with the Hero." *Perspectives in Religious Studies* 11 (1984): 232-42.

Westermann, Claus. *Basic Forms of Prophetic Speech*. Translated by Hugh Clayton White. Philadelphia: Westminster Press, 1967.

———. *Elements of Old Testament Theology*. Translated by Douglas W. Stott. Atlanta: John Knox Press, 1982.

———. *Genesis*. Translated by John J. Scullion. 3 vols. Minneapolis: Augsburg, 1984-1986.

———. *Isaiah 40—66*. Translated by David Muir Gibson Stalker. Old Testament Library. Philadelphia: Westminster Press, 1969.

———. *Lamentations: Issues and Interpretation*. Translated by Charles Albert Muenchow. Minneapolis: Fortress, 1994.

———. *The Living Psalms*. Translated by J. R. Porter. Grand Rapids, Mich.: Eerdmans, 1989.

———. *Prophetic Oracles of Salvation in the Old Testament*. Translated by Keith R. Crim. Louisville, Ky.: Westminster John Knox, 1991.

———. *The Psalms: Structure, Content and Message*. Translated by Ralph David Gehrlee. Minneapolis: Fortress, 1980.

———. *The Structure of the Book of Job: A Form-Critical Analysis*. Translated by Charles Albert Muenchow. Philadelphia: Fortress, 1981.

Wevers, John William. *Ezekiel*. New Century Bible. London: Nelson, 1969.

Whybray, R. N. *Ecclesiastes*. Old Testament Guides. Sheffield, U.K.: Sheffield Academic Press, 1989.

———. *Isaiah 40—66*. New Century Bible. Grand Rapids, Mich.: Eerdmans, 1981.

———. *The Succession Narrative: A Study of II Sam. 9—20 and I Kings 1 and 2*. Studies in Biblical Theology 2/9. Naperville, Ill.: Allenson, 1968.

Wilcock, Michael. *The Message of Chronicles: One Church, One Faith, One Lord*. The Bible Speaks Today. Downers Grove, Ill.: InterVarsity Press, 1987.

———. *The Message of Judges: Grace Abounding*. The Bible Speaks Today. Downers Grove, Ill.: InterVarsity Press, 1992.

Wildberger, Hans. *Isaiah 1—12*. Translated by Thomas H. Trapp. Continental Commentaries. Minneapolis: Fortress, 1991.

Williamson, H. G. M. *The Book Called Isaiah: Deutero-Isaiah's Role in Composition and Redaction*. Oxford: Oxford University Press, 1994.

———. *1 and 2 Chronicles*. New Century Bible. Grand Rapids, Mich.: Eerdmans, 1982.

———. *Ezra, Nehemiah*. Word Biblical Commentary 16. Waco, Tex.: Word, 1985.

———. *Israel in the Book of Chronicles*. London: Cambridge University Press, 1977.

———. "The Prophet and the Plumb-Line: A Redaction-Critical Study of Amos 7." In *The Place Is Too Small for Us: The Israelite Prophets in Recent Scholarship*. Edited by R. P. Gordon. Sources for Biblical and Theological Study 5. Winona Lake, Ind.: Eisenbrauns, 1995.

Willis, John T. "The Structure of Micah 3—5 and the Function of Micah 5:9-14 in the Book." *Zeitschrift für die alttestamentliche Wissenschaft* 81 (1969): 91-197.

Wilson, Gerald Henry. *the Editing of the Hebrew Psalter*. Society of Biblical Literature Dissertation Series 76. Chico, Calif.: Scholars Press, 1985.

Wilson, Lindsay. "The Book of Job and the Fear of God." *Tyndale Bulletin* 46/1 (May 1995): 59-61.

Wolf, Herbert M. "Judges." In *Expositor's Bible Commentary*. 12 vols. Grand Rapids, Mich.: Zondervan, 1976-1992.

Wolff, Hans Walter. *Hosea: A Commentary on the Book of the Prophet Hosea*. Translated by Gary Stansell. Hermeneia. Philadelphia: Fortress, 1974.

———. *Joel and Amos: A Commentary on the Books of the Prophets Joel and Amos*. Edited by S. Dean McBride Jr. Translated by S. Dean McBride Jr. et al. Hermeneia. Philadelphia: Fortress,

1977.
———. *Micah the Prophet*. Translated by Ralph David Gehrke. Philadelphia: Fortress, 1981.

Woudstra, Marten H. *The Book of Joshua*. New International Commentary on the Old Testament. Grand Rapids, Mich.: Eerdmans, 1981.

Wright, Christopher J. H. *An Eye for an Eye: The Place of Old Testament Ethics Today*. Downers Grove, Ill.: InterVarsity Press, 1983.

———. *God's People in God's Land: Family, Land and Property in the Old Testament*. Grand Rapids, Mich.: Eerdmans, 1990.

Wright, George Ernest. *The Challenge of Israel's Faith*. Chicago: University of Chicago Press, 1944.

———. "Deuteronomy." In *Interpreter's Dictionary of the Bible*. Edited by George Arthur Buttrick. 4 vols. Nashville: Abingdon, 1962.

———. *God Who Acts: Biblical Theology as Recital*. Studies in Biblical Theology 8. London: SCM Press, 1952.

———. *The Old Testament Against Its Environment*. Studies in Biblical Theology 2. London: SCM Press, 1950.

———. *The Old Testament and Theology*. New York: Harper & Row, 1969.

Yamauchi, Edwin M. "The Current State of Old Testament Historiography." In *Faith, Tradition and History: Old Testament Historiography in Its Near Eastern Context*. Edited by A. R. Millard, James Karl Hoffmeier and David W. Baker. Winona Lake, Ind.: Eisenbrauns, 1994.

Young, Edward J. *The Book of Isaiah*. 3 vols. 2nd ed. New International Commentary on the Old Testament. Grand Rapids, Mich.: Eerdmans, 1972.

———. *The Prophecy of Daniel: A Commentary*. Grand Rapids, Mich.: Eerdmans, 1949.

———. *The Study of Old Testament Theology Today*. London: James Clark, 1958.

Younger, K. Lawson, Jr. "Judges 1 in Its Near Eastern Literary Context." In *Faith, Tradition and History: Old Testament Historiography in Its Near Eastern Context*. Edited by A. R. Millard, James Karl Hoffmeier and David W. Baker. Winona Lake, Ind.: Eisenbrauns, 1994.

Zimmerli, Walther. *Ezekiel*. Vol. 1. Translated by Ronald E. Clements. Edited by Frank Moore Cross and Klaus Baltzer. Vol 2. Translated by James D. Martin. Edited by Paul D. Hanson and Leonard Jay Greenspoon. Hermeneia. Philadelphia: Fortress, 1979-1983.

———. *Old Testament Theology in Outline*. Translated by Eliot Green. Atlanta: John Knox Press, 1978.

Zvi, Ehud Ben. *A Historical-Critical Study of the Book of Zephaniah*. Beihefte Zeitschrift für die alttestamentliche Wissenschaft 198. Berlin: Walter de Gruyter, 1991.

Subject Index

Author Index

Scripture Index